London Lives

MW01038175

London Lives is a fascinating new study that exposes the lesser-known experiences of eighteenth-century thieves, paupers, prostitutes and highwaymen. It charts the experiences of hundreds of thousands of Londoners who found themselves submerged in poverty or prosecuted for crime, and surveys their responses, to illustrate the extent to which plebeian Londoners influenced the pace and direction of change in social policy. Calling upon a new body of digital evidence, the book illuminates the lives of prison escapees, expert manipulators of the poor relief system, celebrity highwaymen, lone mothers and vagrants; revealing how they each played the system to the best of their ability in order to survive in their various circumstances of misfortune. In these acts of desperation, the poor and the criminal exercised a profound and effective form of agency that changed the system itself, and shaped the evolution of the modern state.

TIM HITCHCOCK is Professor of Digital History at the University of Sussex.

ROBERT SHOEMAKER is Professor of Eighteenth-Century British History at the University of Sheffield.

London Lives

*Poverty, Crime and the Making of
a Modern City, 1690–1800*

Tim Hitchcock and Robert Shoemaker

CAMBRIDGE
UNIVERSITY PRESS

CAMBRIDGE
UNIVERSITY PRESS

University Printing House, Cambridge CB2 8BS, United Kingdom

Cambridge University Press is part of the University of Cambridge.

It furthers the University's mission by disseminating knowledge in the pursuit of education, learning and research at the highest international levels of excellence.

www.cambridge.org
Information on this title: www.cambridge.org/9781107639942

© Tim Hitchcock & Robert Shoemaker 2015

First published 2015
Reprinted 2016

Printed in the United Kingdom by Clays, St Ives plc

A catalogue record for this publication is available from the British Library

Library of Congress Cataloguing in Publication data
Hitchcock, Tim, 1957–
London lives : poverty, crime and the making of a modern city, 1690–1800 /
Tim Hitchcock and Robert Shoemaker.
  pages cm
Includes bibliographical references.
ISBN 978-1-107-63994-2 (Paperback) – ISBN 978-1-107-02527-1 (Hardback)
1. Crime–England–London–History–18th century.   2. Poor–England–
London–Social conditions–18th century.   3. Criminals–England–London–
Social conditions–18th century.   4. Criminal justice, Administration of–
England–London–History–18th century.   5. Public welfare–England–London–
History–18th century.   6.   London (England)–Social conditions–18th century.
I. Shoemaker, Robert Brink. II. Title.
HV6950.L7H57 2014
364.109421'09033–dc23   2014017598

ISBN 978-1-107-63994-2 Paperback
ISBN 978-1-107-02527-1 Hardback

This book is dedicated to everyone who helped create the *Old Bailey Online* and *London Lives*

Contents

Figures

Preface

This book is one facet of a larger project: 'Plebeian Lives and the Making of Modern London, 1690–1800'. Originally funded by the ESRC (RES-000-23-1217), this project digitised and made searchable some 240,000 pages of manuscript materials reflecting on criminal justice and poor relief in eighteenth-century London. The website, *London Lives 1690–1800: Crime, Poverty and Social Policy in the Metropolis*, provides access to these materials in combination with fifteen modern data sets created by previous projects. In total *London Lives* gives direct access to 3.35 million name instances, and allows users to link together records relating to the same individual. In doing so, it makes it possible to trace individual life histories and to assess the role plebeian Londoners played in shaping the development of modern social policy. This book is constructed as a product of that website and largely reflects the results of our research in it.

Since the vast majority of the sources consulted are freely available on the *London Lives* website, this book is best read online, allowing you to click through directly from the primary sources cited and quoted in the text to transcriptions and images of the original documents. Where possible, we have also linked to modern secondary literature and to printed primary sources, including Google Books and the *English Short Title Catalogue* for printed primary literature, and to the British Library's *Ethos* system for unpublished doctoral theses. With Google Books we have linked to volumes available through 'Snippet' or 'Preview' functions, but not to those which provide only bibliographical data. With one exception we have restricted links to freely available materials. Where a pay wall makes the materials inaccessible for many or most readers, we have noted our use of the sites, including URLs and a date, but have not provided direct links. The exception to this rule of thumb is journal articles where a secure link could be identified, even when the relevant source was not freely available to all users.

We hope that these links will facilitate a new approach to reading monographs in which readers switch back and forth between the original sources, the contextual secondary interpretation, and the monograph itself - gaining a deeper understanding of the period and argument. The book is also designed to be read offline and in hard copy; and we have used a standard footnote referencing system so that readers can locate and follow up our sources, both online and in print, however they choose to read the book. For readers of the hard copy who wish to follow up references to the *London Lives* website ('*LL*'), document reference numbers should simply be typed in the appropriate box on the search page. For references to 'sets', see below, p. 24, n. 67. For 'lives', go to www.londonlives.org/static/Lives.jsp.

Whether online or offline, or in some combination of the two, we hope you will find this book both accessible and rewarding.

Acknowledgements

First of all, we would like to thank the funders who made this book and the underlying electronic resources possible: the ESRC, funders of the 'Plebeian Lives' project; and the AHRC and Big Lottery Fund, who underwrote the *Old Bailey Online*, which in turn laid the foundations for 'Plebeian Lives'.

This book may have two names on the cover, but it is the product of the work of many more; all of whom deserve more credit than can be given in a simple acknowledgement. Most importantly, Dr Sharon Howard managed the digitisation projects that underpin this book (both *London Lives* and, from 2005, the *Old Bailey Online*), and she also managed the online PMwiki environment in which the book was drafted as a collaborative text. Every page reflects her technical skill, her commitment to the project and her willingness to devise a solution to each new problem. Neither this book, nor the *London Lives* website would exist without her.

The 'Plebeian Lives' project was implemented by the Higher Education Digitisation Service at the University of Hertfordshire and the Humanities Research Institute at the University of Sheffield. At Hertfordshire, Ian Brearey, Asif Mohammed Farook and Geoff Laycock managed the initial rekeying process that underpins the site. At Sheffield we are particularly indebted to Jamie McLaughlin, Digital Humanities Developer at the HRI, who designed the underlying data infrastructure and made the website work. Katherine Rogers and Ed MacKenzie developed the automated text markup, and David Shepherd, former Director of the HRI, and Michael Pidd, Manager of HRI Digital, oversaw all the technical work, ensuring that the project came to a successful conclusion. Mary Clayton and Louise Falcini served as untiring research assistants in the archives of London, ensuring that the right materials were digitised to the best standard we could afford. And a team of 'data developers', under the leadership of Dr Philippa Hardman, embedded and checked the XML mark-up that makes it possible to search the digitised text effectively. We are grateful to Anna Bayman, Eilidh

Garrett, Carol Lewis-Roylance, Susan Parkinson, Anna Simmons, Gwen Smithson, Nicola Wilcox and Catherine Wright for their hard work. Ed Duncan and Viki Philpott contributed to the project as postgraduate interns, researching and writing several biographies ('*lives*'). The list could go on. A website such as *London Lives* is not a book, it does not have an author (or even two). It is the product of many hands, and we would like to give credit to the wider collaboration involved. The same could be said about the original *Old Bailey Online* project.

We were beneficiaries of many contributions on the journey from website to book. Our undergraduate students, at both Sheffield and Hertfordshire, helped us to understand the material and suffered as we tried out one idea after another. Several Sheffield students are among the authors of the *lives*. Our postgraduate students, current and former, contributed through both reading sections of the text and acting as sounding boards for our ideas as they evolved. In this capacity we are grateful to Louise Falcini, Des Newell, Dianne Payne, Janice Turner, Richard Ward and Matthew White. We have also benefited hugely from the advice and criticism of many academic friends who took the time to read the manuscript. Their generosity was unstinting and exemplifies the best traditions of the scholarly community. Most importantly, Jeremy Boulton went through the text with a fine-toothed comb, saving us from real error and embarrassing misinterpretations. He and Leonard Schwarz also very generously allowed us access to their work on the St Martin in the Fields workhouse registers and settlement examinations. Joanna Innes also read the full manuscript, and her comments gave us pause for thought, again saving us from significant errors. John Levin, Katrina Navickas, Heather Shore, Brodie Waddell, Tim Wales, Richard Ward and Phil Withington all read and commented insightfully on sections of the text.

Our home departments and institutions, at the Universities of Sheffield and Hertfordshire, and more recently Sussex, have also been hugely supportive. When combined with colleagues in the wider academy, we have been fortunate to work in a stimulating community of historians. We would particularly like to thank John Beattie, Simon Devereaux, Drew Gray, Peter King, Andrea McKenzie and Deirdre Palk. Robert Shoemaker is also indebted to Elizabeth Foyster, David Garrioch, David Lemmings, Randall McGowen, Nick Tosney and Phil Withington; while Tim Hitchcock has benefited from working with Adam Crymble, Simon DeDeo, Seth Denbo, Richard Deswarte, Jo Guldi, Sara Klingenstein, William Turkel, Peter Webster, Susan Whyman and Jane Winters.

The ideas presented in this book evolved over two decades and more; and did so in dialogue with a powerfully supportive historical community. Much of this community was forged at the Long Eighteenth-Century Seminar at the Institute of Historical Research, and we would like to acknowledge our debt to the convenors, past and present: Arthur Burns, Pene Corfield, Adam Crymble, Amanda Goodrich, Leonie Hannan, Sally Holloway, Julian Hoppitt and Sarah Lloyd. The valued friends and colleagues who have attended the seminar over the decades are too numerous to name, but each has made history writing more fun. Sections of the text and argument have also been presented at other seminars and conferences, and we would like to thank the organisers and audiences of BSECS (Oxford, 2009), Anglo-American Conference (London, 2009), NACBS (Louisville, 2009), British Crime Historians (Sheffield, 2010), MLA (Los Angeles, 2011), UC Berkeley (2011), Oxford Brookes (2011), Centre for the Historical Record and Public History (Kingston, 2011), David Nichols Smith Conference (Melbourne, 2011), Cambridge Graduate Seminar in Modern British History (2012), Oxford e-Research Centre (2012), Gerald Aylmer Seminar, RHS (2012), Centre for English Local History, University of Leicester (2013), Free University of Brussels (2013), University of British Columbia, Victoria (2013) and the Open University (Milton Keynes, 2013).

This is also a better book for the contributions of the anonymous readers who ploughed through the sample chapters and final manuscript. We tried hard to heed their warnings against hyperbole and breathlessness, and while we may not have succeeded completely, we know the text is better for their warnings. We would also like to thank Richard Fisher, who encouraged the project of the e-monograph from its inception, and Elizabeth Friend-Smith, commissioning editor. Charlotte Thomas acted as production editor, Dr Jacqueline French copy-edited the manuscript and the index was compiled by Dr Richard Ward. We are grateful to all three for their great care and hard work.

On a personal level we would like to thank our partners and sons, Sonia and Nick Hitchcock, and Wendy Bracewell and Roland Shoemaker. This book took a decade from conception to publication and debts beyond repayment were incurred on every day of that decade.

Our errors and failures are our own, but this book is the product of friends and family, collaborators and critics, and we thank them all.

Abbreviations

BL	British Library
LL	*London Lives 1690 to 1800: Crime, Poverty and Social Policy in the Metropolis* (www.londonlives.org)
LMA	London Metropolitan Archives
ODNB	*Oxford Dictionary of National Biography* (www.oxforddnb.com)
PP	*Parliamentary Papers* (parlipapers.chadwyck.co.uk)
WAC	Westminster Archives Centre

1 Introduction

Thomas Limpus

Thomas Limpus was born into modest circumstances on 23 July 1760, to parents who frequently relied on the parish to make ends meet. He shared his fourteenth Christmas with a rag-tag collection of twenty-five boys and men from eight years old to eighty in a mixed men's ward at St Martin in the Fields workhouse.[1] For those few weeks he was a member of the 'workhouse family' and celebrated the most important ritual of the year with its members. But this was only the first of the many temporary and artificial communities he was obliged to join as a result of his encounters with the institutions of poor relief and justice over the next twenty-five years. In 1777, at seventeen years old, he stole a handkerchief and was sentenced to three years hard labour on the hulks; he was also forced to share his food, labour and life with a newly formed group of long-term prisoners.

Within months of his release, now aged twenty, he was once again caught stealing a handkerchief and was held for three months in Tothill Fields Bridewell with a constantly changing population of disorderly vagrants and prostitutes noted for spending their days gambling and retailing dirty jokes. And following an appearance before the Westminster sessions charged with 'Petit Larceny', he spent most of the next year in New Prison.[2] In each institution he was forced to engage with a new group of people and new figures of authority, and to develop along with his fellow prisoners strategies for survival in that temporary home. At the

---

[1] He was in ward 14, which was run by four older female inmates and housed both long-stay older men (most of whom were probably disabled in some way) and younger boys and men who stayed for only a few weeks, and like Limpus were soon 'discharged'. *LL*, St Martin in the Fields Workhouse Registers, 25 November 1774 – 19 January 1775 (smdswhr_505_50557). See *International Genealogical Index (IGI)* (familysearch.org, 31 Dec. 2013) for his christening on 6 August 1760, in St Martin in the Fields. His parents were Henry and Mary Limpus. See also *LL*, set, 'Thomas Limpus'. We are grateful to Jeremy Boulton for providing us with the results of his unpublished research on Limpus.
[2] *LL*, Middlesex Sessions: Sessions Papers, October 1781 (LMSMPS507450053).

same time, and along with his many contemporaries, his recidivism and later direct challenges to the working of those institutions helped to illustrate the failure of the prisons and hulks to eradicate the problems of crime and disorder.[3]

By early September of 1782, Limpus was once again at liberty on the streets of Westminster and was once more caught stealing a handkerchief. This time, however, his sentence was transportation. Since exile to America was no longer possible following the American Revolution, he was sent to 'Africa, for the term of seven years'. He was shipped to Gorée on the west coast, only to be told by the captain of the garrison when he arrived that as his own troops were starving, Limpus and his fellow prisoners could not remain.[4] They were told they were 'free men', and would have to 'do the best [they] ... could'.[5] Limpus managed to return to London within a few months, a breathing demonstration of the failure of the policy of transporting criminals to Africa. Tried for 'returning from transportation', he was sentenced to hang, along with fifty-seven other men and women – the largest number ever sentenced to death at the Old Bailey in a single session. Having delivered this terrible sentence, the judge berated Limpus and his contemporaries standing at the bar for having 'lost their terror' of the court and its punishments, and having become bold 'in defiance of the laws'.[6] The judge was right.

Having pronounced these death sentences, the judge had to turn to a group of eighteen convicts who had, like Limpus, 'returned from transportation' and, despite the fact this was a capital offence, offer them the same punishment a second time. At a time of social crisis, it would not have been politic to add to the increasing toll of executions. So a group of criminal mutineers captured following a convict uprising on a transport ship, the *Swift*, condemned for their 'violent combination of numbers', were pardoned and given their lives.[7] Just three months later, with Limpus's own death sentence commuted to transportation for life, he himself mutinied in company with many of those same eighteen men. Together they took over the *Mercury* and temporarily brought Britain's

[3] Limpus was not, at least initially, a violent or difficult prisoner. In 1782 he served on the jury of a coroner's inquest that dutifully and conveniently found that a fellow prisoner, William Cadman, had died following a 'Visitation of God in a natural way'. *LL*, Middlesex Coroners' Inquests, 1 May 1781 – 31 December 1799 (LMCOIC651010028).
[4] Emma Christopher, *A Merciless Place: The Fate of Britain's Convicts after the American Revolution* (Oxford University Press, 2011), p. 224.
[5] *LL*, Old Bailey Proceedings, 10 September 1783 (t17830910-41).
[6] *LL*, Old Bailey Proceedings, 10 September 1783 (s17830910-1).
[7] *LL*, Old Bailey Proceedings, 10 September 1783 (t17830910-28).

Figure 1.1 Samuel Scott, *A Crowd*, n.d. *c.* 1760. T08478. © Trustees of
the Tate Gallery.

century-long policy of sending its criminals to indentured servitude to
an end.

Following almost three years in a convict hulk and a foiled escape
attempt on Guy Fawkes Day in 1784, in 1787 the criminal justice system
finally won its unequal battle with Thomas Limpus by sending him to the
far side of the world to a new-style penal colony.[8] But this was not before
he and his fellow convicts, through their persistent acts of resistance,
both individual and collective, had helped to transform the penal system.
Thomas Limpus was one of the at least 283 men and women from
London (over a third of the total) shipped to distant exile in Australia
on the First Fleet.[9]

---

[8] After a period of penal servitude on Norfolk Island, he earned a conditional pardon and
appears to have lived the rest of his life there: Christopher, *A Merciless Place*, pp. 263,
334, 357.

[9] Emma Christopher, 'Steal a handkerchief, see the world: the trans-oceanic voyaging of
Thomas Limpus', in Ann Curthoys and Marilyn Lake, eds., *Connected Worlds: History in
Trans-national Perspective* (Canberra: ANU E Press, 2006), p. 79 (epress.anu.edu.au, 30
Dec. 2013); Mollie Gillen, *The Founders of Australia: A Biographical Dictionary of the First
Fleet* (Sydney: Library of Australian History, 1989), p. 221. See also Christopher,
A Merciless Place.

Plebeian London

This book is about Thomas Limpus and Mary Cut-and-Come-Again.[10] It is about Mary Dyson, Sarah Cowden and Paul Patrick Kearney; Mary Whistle and Henry Bates – all paupers or criminals, or both.[11] It is about the hundreds of thousands of Londoners who, although they were obliged to negotiate from positions of weakness with overseers and constables, magistrates and judges, helped shape social policy over the course of the eighteenth century. It is about how working Londoners, acting often autonomously but sometimes in alliance with those in power, contributed to the evolution of criminal justice and social welfare by playing the system and frequently confounding it. Both through the subtle pressure of supplicants, inmates and prisoners (whose very survival depended on collaborating with the institutions of the state), and through direct challenges in court or prison, in parishes, on shipboard and on the streets, Thomas Limpus and his fellow accused criminals and paupers, acting both together and alone, determined which policies and institutions would survive (and in what form) and which would collapse in chaos.

The men and women who form the subjects of this book, *plebeian Londoners*, were a complex group, but they shared a common *relationship to authority*. These Londoners were at the sharp end of the administration of criminal justice and poor relief – they were the men and women tried at the Old Bailey, committed to houses of correction and punished as vagrants. And they were the most vulnerable of Londoners, forced by their poverty to apply for parish relief. Their common characteristic was that they were confronted by the need to negotiate from a position of relative weakness.

Despite this shared relationship to authority, plebeian Londoners cannot be reduced to a set of identifiable socioeconomic characteristics. We are hampered in our analysis of this issue by the fact that the language of social description in the eighteenth century was imprecise, while the characteristics of wealth and status that marked social divisions were themselves fluid. As a result we have no convenient shorthand for describing those at the lower end of the social scale. This was not a class society in a Marxist or nineteenth-century sense, and despite significant inequalities of wealth, status and power, there are few clear lines to be

---

[10] *LL*, set, 'Thomas Limpus'; and *LL*, set, 'Mary Cut and Come-again'.
[11] *LL*, set, 'Mary Dyson'; *LL*, set, 'Sarah Cowden'; *LL*, set, 'Paul Patrick Kearney'; for Mary Whistle see the section 'Workhouses and the poor' in Chapter 3; and *LL*, set, 'Henry Bates'.

drawn between social groups. Thus, to use convenient shorthand terms such as 'lower class' or 'middle class', which eighteenth-century historians (including ourselves) often do, effectively imposes crude categorisations on a much more complex reality. Even 'the poor' is a notoriously elastic concept which can be defined narrowly to include only those in receipt of relief or charity (paupers), or much more broadly as all those whose economic circumstances were sufficiently precarious that they were in real danger of being forced to rely on relief, owing to old age or misfortune, at some point during their lives. Even relatively prosperous working Londoners could fall into poverty, just as they might at any time be accused of a crime. For the purpose of this book, we have equated 'the poor' not only with those in receipt of poor relief (historians put this figure at over 10 per cent of the national population at any one time in the second half of the century), but also the up to 60 per cent who experienced significant poverty at some point during their lives, a figure which is broadly comparable to Leonard Schwarz's estimate that half of the adult male population in London at the end of the century worked in unskilled or semi-skilled trades.[12] These are the men and women who were likely to possess that relationship to authority which we have characterised as 'plebeian'.

But even taking into account this unifying characteristic, plebeian Londoners were a very mixed group. We can see this first and foremost in many of the lives discussed in this book. While some, like Thomas Limpus, inherited relative social insecurity from their parents, others, like Paul Patrick Kearney or Mary Whistle, were formerly successful businessmen and respectable householders who encountered adversity and were reduced to begging or reliance on a workhouse. Consequently, if we attempt a sociological analysis of plebeian London, the results are complicated. Owing to the limitations of the surviving sources, we can discern very little about the status, occupations and levels of income and property ownership of those who were charged with crimes, or even of those in receipt of poor relief. The type of information most often provided is occupation, yet even this is rare. The most detailed source

---

[12] Lynn Hollen Lees, *The Solidarities of Strangers: The English Poor Laws and the People, 1700–1948* (Cambridge University Press, 2006), p. 45; Joanna Innes, 'The "mixed economy of welfare" in early modern England: assessments of the options from Hale to Malthus (c. 1683–1803)', in Martin Daunton, ed., *Charity, Self-Interest and Welfare in the English Past* (London: UCL Press, 1996), p. 165; Leonard Schwarz, 'Income distribution and social structure in London in the late eighteenth century', *Economic History Review*, 32:2 (1979), 258. Dependency rates in London were marginally lower than the national average, with higher numbers of casual poor: David Green, *Pauper Capital: London and the Poor Law, 1790–1870* (Farnham, Surrey: Ashgate, 2010), pp. 28–34.

analysed in this book, the *Old Bailey Proceedings*, provides occupational labels for only 10.4 per cent of the defendants brought to trial between 1690 and 1800.[13] As with most occupational evidence, we lack sufficient information to fully assess the meanings of the terms used – whether, for example, someone labelled a 'carpenter' was a master, journeyman or apprentice. Nevertheless, judging by what we know of the status and income of the occupations most frequently listed, those charged with crime were predominantly at the bottom of the social scale, although this was not invariably the case. Among the 7,064 defendants accorded an occupation in the *Proceedings*, over a thousand different occupational labels can be found. However, the four most common were servants (32.3 per cent of defendants labelled), labourers (4.3 per cent), porters (3.8 per cent) and soldiers (3.4 per cent). An additional 6.9 per cent were labelled as apprentices and journeymen, in a variety of mostly artisanal trades such as carpenter, tailor, shoemaker and weaver. In so far as it is possible to generalise from this disparate evidence, the vast majority of Old Bailey defendants came from what historians might call the lower, or lower-middle, classes. In contrast, only a small minority of defendants came from more elite backgrounds: 2.7 per cent of defendants were labelled as gentlemen, 'esquire' or 'Mr', 0.3 per cent as captain and 0.2 per cent as merchants. Although these elite defendants are not our central focus (they were more likely to be accused of murder than theft) and they maintained their distance from their fellow defendants, even in Newgate Prison (where they paid for separate apartments), for the most part all those tried at the Old Bailey shared similar experiences of arrest, prison and trial – of being at the sharp end of a relationship with judicial authority. This helps explain why Lord George Gordon made common cause with his fellow prisoners when he was incarcerated in Newgate in the 1780s, by providing some with financial support.[14]

---

[13] The original parchment indictments in the gaol delivery rolls do systematically contain occupation or status labels, since they were legally required, but the information provided is unhelpful owing to the common use of the vague terms 'yeoman' and 'labourer' to refer to individuals who possessed a wide range of specific occupations; although a status label was required, it did not have to be accurate. See J. S. Cockburn, 'Early-modern Assize records as historical evidence', *Journal of the Society of Archivists*, 5:4 (1975), 222–5.

[14] We have been unable to remove the small number of elite defendants from the statistics from the *Proceedings* provided in this book, but the numbers are too small to make a material difference. For Gordon's support of his fellow prisoners, see Douglas Hay, 'The laws of God and the laws of man: Lord George Gordon and the death penalty', in J. Rule and R. Malcolmson, eds., *Protest and Survival: The Historical Experience* (London: The Merlin Press, 1993), pp. 60–111.

While we lack equivalent evidence of occupational background for those who were in receipt of poor relief, such people were, at the time of asking for support, manifestly at the bottom end of the social scale, sharing that characteristic with a significant proportion, but not all, of those tried at the Old Bailey. We do not know how much overlap there was between the individuals who committed (or were simply charged with) crimes and those who were in receipt of poor relief. A systematic analysis comparing lists of names of accused criminals and paupers has not yet been completed, but preliminary analysis (using the automated matching facility on the *London Lives* website) reveals few direct matches; most concern individuals who had been tried at the Old Bailey and either had recently been, or were subsequently, subjected to a settlement examination, reflecting the precarious position of individuals with these experiences. There is probably a specific reason why more matches were not found: those in receipt of financial support had much less impetus to resort to crime. However, there is also a more important explanation: while there is much we do not know about the relationship between poverty and crime, it has become increasingly clear that only a fraction of those in economic need actually resorted to theft to support them-selves, and that poverty was only one of many possible motivations for committing crime.[15] For reasons of both opportunity and temperament, Londoners responded to poverty in different ways. At the same time, there is significant evidence that accused criminals and the poor were often part of the same communities, and even the same families. The automated matching facility has revealed several married couples in which the wife was in receipt of parochial relief while the husband was tried for criminal activity. For example, when John Askew's wife was giving birth in a workhouse in 1782 and she sent him a message that she needed for support 'a few shillings more than the workhouse would allow her', he went out and stole a pair of linen sheets worth seven shillings. Given that both the poor and accused criminals came from a wide range of generally deprived economic circumstances, it is likely that there was considerable overlap in terms of their social composition and even family backgrounds.[16]

[15] This conclusion is supported by the most recent examination of the statistical correlations between numbers of prosecutions and levels of economic deprivation, as measured by the price of grain and periods of war and peace. See Peter King, *Crime, Justice and Discretion in England, 1740–1820* (Cambridge University Press, 2000), pp. 145 61.

[16] The relationship between poverty and crime is a subject Robert Shoemaker intends to explore in a forthcoming article.

If plebeian Londoners shared a complex social identity, their methods of engaging with authority were similarly multifaceted, depending on shifting alliances among those directly challenging authority or, when possible, with those able to exercise some institutional power. A grocer or weaver, or even a butcher, might join the gangs of young men, such as the 'butcher boys', who made up a distinctive part of the mob. A widow and decayed householder, standing on her legal settlement and respectable demeanour when seeking relief from the overseer, might present herself as a repentant prostitute to the Magdalen Hospital. Each role, from lowly labourer to censorious good wife, brought with it a script and cultural baggage that Londoners took up and put off as the situation demanded; each identity implying different communities of interest, both with men and women in similar circumstances, and in temporary alliances with parish and judicial officials. In the process, relationships could appear inconsistent and contradictory: ratepayers combined with respectable paupers in opposition to the vestry when their expectations of a parish pension in old age were threatened, while simultaneously supporting the reformation of manners societies when confronted by the ungodly and the disorderly. The poor shared an interest with trading justices in seeing justice done often and cheaply, putting them in opposition to the bench (the collectivity of justices) and parish officers, but they could equally find themselves in a justice's parlour accused of crime. Each new challenge brought into being a new alliance created in defence or pursuit of shared interests.

Plebeian Londoners were not averse to using the law; 10.3 per cent of the prosecutors at the Old Bailey for whom we have information were in low-status occupations, and the poor also used summary justice.[17] Indeed, their prosecutions were often malicious, taking advantage of the possibility of using the law as an aggressive weapon.[18] Some plebeian Londoners even more actively collaborated with the system by participating in the administration of justice and poor relief on the ground – either by acting as informers and thief-takers, or by taking up official positions including constables and night watchmen, prison turnkeys, and

---

[17] These victim occupations include labourers, journeymen, servants, porters, carpenters, shoemakers, soldiers, weavers and even laundresses and washerwomen. For summary justice, see Peter King, 'The summary courts and social relations in eighteenth-century England', *Past and Present*, 183 (2004), 140–7; Drew Gray, *Crime, Prosecution and Social Relations: The Summary Courts of the City of London in the Late Eighteenth Century* (Houndmills: Palgrave, 2009), pp. 29–31, 168–9.

[18] Douglas Hay, 'Prosecution and power: malicious prosecution in the English courts, 1750–1850', in Douglas Hay and Francis Snyder, eds., *Policing and Prosecution in Britain 1750–1850* (Oxford: Clarendon Press, 1989), pp. 343–96.

masters and mistresses of workhouses. The subjects of this book thus did not engage in a single clear dialogue or dialectic with the rich and powerful (who were in any case a similarly complex and diverse collection of groups). Instead, they entered a series of sometimes confusing and contradictory alliances in pursuit of their interests. Nonetheless, the sum total of their actions repeatedly forced the authorities to rethink their social policies and respond to these pressures from below.

The problem

The very existence of the growing metropolis of London, with its multiple roles as a political, imperial, industrial, cultural and economic capital, has often been used as part of a wider explanation of the course of British social and economic history.[19] However, most historians have shied away from exploring the forces that shaped London itself. By focusing on two interrelated aspects of the history of what would soon be Western Europe's first million-person city – crime and poverty, and their institutional *doppelgängers* of criminal justice and poor relief – this book attempts to explain how the demands and actions of plebeian Londoners helped create the most complex and expensive system of police and justice, relief and charity Britain had ever seen.

In a little over a hundred years, between the 1690s and the 1790s, a centuries-old system of discretionary justice characterised by citizen arrests and householder policing, by exemplary hangings and pardoned convicts, was transformed. It was replaced by one in which policing and prosecution were reshaped as an increasingly bureaucratic and rules-based system, administered by a cadre of salaried officers and professional lawyers and justices. The process of arrest and prosecution first evolved from a system dependent on public participation and unpaid parish officers serving by rotation into one peppered with substitute paid officers working alongside freelance thief-takers in search of rewards; it then gradually became a more bureaucratic system of regular officers working directly under judicial control.[20] During the same period, the adversarial trial and an increasingly rigorous notion of procedure came to

---

[19] For the classic statement of this perspective, see E. A. Wrigley, 'A simple model of London's importance in changing English society and economy, 1650–1750', *Past & Present*, 37 (1967), 44–70.

[20] Most authoritatively, see John Beattie, *Crime and the Courts in England, 1660–1800* (Princeton University Press, 1986); and John Beattie, *Policing and Punishment in London, 1660–1750: Urban Crime and the Limits of Terror* (Oxford University Press, 2001).

characterise criminal justice.[21] Prosecution and defence counsel, the right to silence and an assumption of innocence each took root in judicial soil. Concurrently, punishments for the most serious crimes were transformed from the simple and inexpensive expedient of hanging a proportion of those convicted to include heavy reliance on transportation and imprisonment.[22] And yet these were not necessarily the outcomes favoured by the elites. Many in parliament simply wanted to hang more people rather than spend scarce resources on policing and punishment. Few besides victims of crime and secretaries of state welcomed the thief-takers, while the newly regularised night watch and Bow Street Runners were created out of the fear of crime and concern that criminal justice was losing its on-going battle with a rising tide of disorder.[23]

In the same years poor relief was also transformed. By the beginning of the nineteenth century Londoners were spending over half a million pounds a year on parochial poor relief, or approximately nine shillings, seven pence per head of the population. A hundred years earlier they had spent less than one shilling, six pence per head.[24] Even accounting for a century of inflation, costs more than tripled.[25] The same period also witnessed the evolution of a new parish-based bureaucracy of belonging and removal, extensive institutional care for most paupers in workhouses and an increasingly integrated system of medical provision.[26] Moreover, a plethora of new associational charities spread a carpet of alternative

---

[21] John H. Langbein, *The Origins of Adversary Criminal Trial* (Oxford University Press, 2003); John Beattie, 'Scales of justice: defense counsel and the English criminal trial in the eighteenth and nineteenth centuries', *Law and History Review*, 9:2 (1991), 221–67.

[22] For London's pivotal role in this transition, see John Beattie, 'London crime and the making of the "Bloody Code", 1689–1718', in Lee Davison *et al.*, eds., *Stilling the Grumbling Hive: The Response to Social and Economic Problems in England 1689–1750* (Stroud: Alan Sutton, 1992), pp. 49–76.

[23] John Beattie, *The First English Detectives: The Bow Street Runners and the Policing of London, 1750–1840* (Oxford University Press, 2012); Elaine A. Reynolds, *Before the Bobbies: The Night Watch and Police Reform in Metropolitan London, 1720–1830* (Basingstoke: Macmillan, 1998).

[24] Based on the 1803 returns for London and Middlesex: £525,261, against a population of 1,096,784 recorded in the 1801 census; and national returns from the Board of Trade for 1696 of £400,000 per annum, with a national population of 5.2 million. The national figure has been adopted for the 1700 comparator. Paul Slack, *The English Poor Law, 1531–1782* (Basingstoke: Macmillan, 1990), p. 30, Table 1.

[25] Using the Retail Price Index, the 1s. 7d. expenditure in 1700 was worth 2s. 11d in 1800; in relation to average earnings, this figure was 3s. 0d. See 'Purchasing power of British pounds from 1245 to present' (www.measuringworth.com/ppoweruk, 20 Jan. 2014).

[26] See David Green, *Pauper Capital: London and the Poor Law, 1790–1870* (Farnham, Surrey: Ashgate, 2010); Steve Hindle, *On the Parish?: The Micro-Politics of Poor Relief in Rural England c. 1550–1750* (Oxford University Press, 2004); Lees, *Solidarities of Strangers*; Paul Slack, *From Reformation to Improvement: Public Welfare in Early Modern England* (Oxford: Clarendon Press, 1999).

forms of relief and succour across the landscape, creating a uniquely rich and complex poor relief environment.[27] And yet, even more than with the reconfiguration of criminal justice, no one sought this particular outcome. There were no calls to increase the local poor rates or to provide more extensive provision for the less well off. Many argued about how the system might be changed, or ideally eliminated, and new charitable provisions used the plight of narrowly defined groups of the poor (such as foundlings and young girls) to justify their activities. But most eighteenth-century commentators believed the system of parish relief and charities was already overgenerous and that the general run of the poor were essentially and irredeemably feckless and 'undeserving'.

To read the newspapers and pamphlets, the preambles of innumerable acts of parliament, and vestry minutes, one would expect punishment to have become more brutal and poor relief expenditure and care to have become ever less comprehensive. Even those among the elite who wished to reform social policies from humanitarian or religious motives did so in response to perceptions that crime and the cost of poor relief were rising, and they sought to place significant constraints on the support they hoped to make available. Of course, like Thomas Limpus and his plebeian contemporaries, elite commentators and projectors did not form a single coherent class, nor did they adopt a single identity and perspective. While each new scheme and act, the brainchild of an elite projector, sought to redefine the relationship between authority and disorder, it also privileged one part of elite society over another. While the watch acts of Westminster empowered select vestries and justices to impose a new order on the streets, they also sidelined Westminster's traditional governors sitting in the Court of Burgesses. And although the rise of defence counsel was authorised by judges, and driven forward by the actions of defendants, it ended up marginalising the role of jurors and those same judges. Nevertheless, the evolution of these newly regularised systems of policing and justice, and this uniquely expensive and complex system of charity and relief, occurred despite the powerfully expressed, if occasionally contradictory, opinions of the elite. While elites were the actors who ultimately implemented change, they did so within constraints shaped by forces beyond their control.

This book seeks to explain why and how elite expectations were so often confounded. It does so by re-examining changes in social policy in light of the behaviour of the criminal and the pauper – from the

[27] Donna T. Andrew, *Philanthropy and Police: London Charity in the Eighteenth Century* (Princeton University Press, 1989); Sarah Lloyd, *Charity and Poverty in England, c. 1680–1820: Wild and Visionary Schemes* (Manchester University Press, 2009).

perspective of plebeian Londoners. It argues that the changing character of policing, justice and poor relief was in large measure the result of the collective behaviour of the individual men and women who had most invested in the system – the defendants and supplicants whose lives depended upon their ability to use these systems effectively. Of course, plebeian Londoners did not define the ideal form of a workhouse or articulate the supposed benefits of the reformed prison; however, they helped force the pace of change and define the limits of the possible, continually seeking new ways to turn frequently oppressive policies to their advantage.

This is not the conventional way these topics have been presented. In recent decades historians have written extensively on crime and poverty, but have focused their attention primarily on elite responses to perceived social problems. With few exceptions, they have also tended to write about poor relief and criminal justice in isolation, building complex histories but not relating one to the other, despite the fact that poverty and crime were clearly interrelated social phenomena. Writing within the whig tradition, an older generation of historians gave the credit for reforming criminal justice to men such as Henry Fielding and John Howard, and writers such as Cesare Beccaria and Jonas Hanway, abetted by an increasingly active parliament.[28] Although in the 1960s and 1970s a sociological and Marxist-inspired 'history from below' pursued quantitative analyses of patterns of crime and compiled a richly detailed history of popular protest and other 'social crimes', by the 1980s most historians had switched their attention back to criminal justice.[29] They came to the conclusion that the 'dark figure' of unrecorded crime made it impossible to study crime rates per se, while disillusionment with Marxism led to the virtual abandonment of studies of crime as a form of social protest.[30]

[28] For example, see Leon Radzinowicz and Roger G. Hood, *A History of English Criminal Law and its Administration from 1750*, Vol. IV (London: Stevens & Sons, 1968); and Sidney Webb and Beatrice Webb, *English Prisons under Local Government* (London: Longmans, Green and Co., 1922; repr. 1963).

[29] Beattie, *Crime and the Courts*; J. S. Cockburn, *A History of English Assizes, 1558–1714* (Cambridge University Press, 1972); Douglas Hay et al., *Albion's Fatal Tree: Crime and Society in Eighteenth-Century England* (London: Allen Lane, 1975); Peter Linebaugh, *The London Hanged: Crime and Civil Society in the Eighteenth Century* (London: Allen Lane, 1991); George Rudé, *Paris and London in the Eighteenth Century: Studies in Popular Protest* (New York and London: Viking Press, 1971); E. P. Thompson, *Whigs and Hunters: The Origin of the Black Act* (London: Allen Lane, 1975). Much of this literature on 'social crime' focused on rural society and fell into relative decline following the revival of urban history in the 1990s. See Andrew Charlesworth, 'An agenda for historical studies of rural protest in Britain, 1750–1850', *Rural History*, 2 (1991), 231–40.

[30] There has been a recent revival in work in this area. See, for example, Katrina Navickas, *Loyalism and Radicalism in Lancashire, 1798–1815* (Oxford University Press, 1999).

Research came to focus on the roles of the politicians, judges, justices of the peace and jurors who were seen as shaping judicial, policing and penal policies (though as the work of Douglas Hay suggests, this was a topic where a Marxist perspective was still productive).[31]

Leading this new engagement with criminal justice, in work published over the last thirty years, John Beattie focused our attention on the influence of City merchants and tradesmen on the development of both local and national policy (including the transformation of the night watch and the passage of the 1718 Transportation Act) and most recently on the role of the magistrates Henry Fielding and John Fielding in spearheading reforms such as the introduction of the Bow Street Runners. While Beattie and the generation of scholars (notably Simon Devereaux) who have followed in his footsteps have consistently argued that the fear of crime motivated changes in criminal justice, they do not accord the men and women identified as the criminals any substantive role.[32] Similarly, legal historians, particularly John Langbein, have sought an explanation for the rise of counsel and the development of the adversarial trial almost exclusively in the decisions of judges and the histrionics of lawyers such as William Garrow, to the exclusion of any consideration of the defendants whose trials and legal fees justified and paid for the presence of lawyers.[33] Recent attempts to widen these explanations to include broader cultural developments – increasing intolerance of violence and new ideas about privacy and morality – have similarly located the origins of change with the middling sort and elites rather than in the behaviour of criminals. David Lemmings has recently argued that 'increasing middling consciousness of respectability and sensitivity to the perceived failings of the common people' resulted in a pattern of declining popular participation and agency within 'cultures of governance' over the course of the century.[34]

---

[31] See, for instance, Peter King, *Crime and Law in England, 1750–1840: Remaking Justice from the Margins* (Cambridge University Press, 2006); and Douglas Hay and Paul Craven, eds., *Masters, Servants and Magistrates in Britain and the Empire, 1562–1955* (Chapel Hill: University of North Carolina Press, 2004).

[32] Beattie, *Crime and the Courts*; Beattie, *Policing and Punishment*; Beattie, *The First English Detectives*; Simon Devereaux, 'Recasting the theatre of execution: the abolition of the Tyburn ritual', *Past & Present*, 202 (2009), 127–74.

[33] Langbein, *Origins of Adversary Criminal Trial*; Beattie, 'Scales of justice'; John Hostettler and Richard Braby, *Sir William Garrow: His Life, Times, and Fight for Justice* (Hook, Hampshire: Waterside Press, 2010).

[34] It should be noted that this argument is based on national evidence, with limited attention paid to London: David Lemmings, *Law and Government in England during the Long Eighteenth Century: From Consent to Command* (Houndmills: Palgrave Macmillan, 2011), p. 180. See also Randall McGowen, 'The Bank of England and the policing of forgery 1797–1821', *Past &Present*, 186 (2005), 81–116; Greg T. Smith, 'Violent crime and the

The beginning of an alternative approach can be found in the work of Peter King. In *Remaking Justice from the Margins*, he describes a system shaped primarily by relatively minor functionaries – jurors, clerks, lawyers and justices of the peace – taking advantage of the discretionary nature of criminal justice to invent important new policies, such as the differential treatment of young and female offenders and the increasing use of magistrates' courts.[35] But even here, the marginal figures given pride of place are from a secure middling sort and exclude the men and women labelled as criminals and forced to play the lead in the theatre of justice.

More promisingly, Heather Shore and Mary Clayton have documented the remarkably successful legal tactics of two thieves and prostitutes, Mary Harvey and Charlotte Walker; and Andrea McKenzie has studied the popular culture that surrounded the 'game' highwayman.[36] With respect to punishment, accounts of the experiences of poor men and women imprisoned for debt, or hanged by the state, can be found in the work of Joanna Innes and Vic Gatrell.[37] However, in general, historians of crime and criminal justice have claimed their own 'right to silence' in respect of the role and agency of the hundreds of thousands of men and women who were forced to negotiate their futures with magistrates and the courts.

The history of poverty and poor relief in the long eighteenth century has been much less fully studied than crime and criminal justice, but it, too, has only partially engaged with the experience of the people most directly affected or explored their roles in the evolution of policy. An older historiography grounded in a Fabian tradition, and exemplified by the work of Sidney and Beatrice Webb, explored poor relief as part of a wider story of the evolution of state administration and was designed to frame contemporary (early twentieth-century) debate around social welfare and public administration.[38] More recently, in the work of Paul

---

public weal in England, 1700–1900', in R. McMahon, ed., *Crime, Law and Popular Culture in Europe 1500–1900* (Abingdon: Willan Publishing, 2008); Faramerz Dabhoiwala, *The Origins of Sex: A History of the First Sexual Revolution* (London: Allen Lane, 2012).

[35] King, *Crime and Law*.

[36] Mary Clayton, 'The life and crimes of Charlotte Walker, prostitute and pickpocket', *London Journal*, 33:1 (2008), 3–19; Andrea McKenzie, 'From true confessions to true reporting? The decline and fall of the Ordinary's *Account*', *London Journal*, 30:1 (2005), 55–70; Heather Shore, '"The reckoning": disorderly women, informing constables and the Westminster justices, 1727–33', *Social History*, 34:4 (2009), 409–27.

[37] Joanna Innes, *Inferior Politics: Social Problems and Social Policies in Eighteenth-Century Britain* (Oxford University Press, 2009); V. A. C. Gatrell, *The Hanging Tree: Execution and the English People, 1770–1868* (Oxford University Press, 1994).

[38] Most importantly, see Sidney Webb and Beatrice Webb, *English Poor Law History, Part I: The Old Poor Law*, *English Local Government* (London: Longmans, Green and Co., 1927, repr. 1963).

Slack, Steve Hindle, Mary Fissell and Joanna Innes, this strand of historical analysis has come to focus on the micro politics of the institutions of redistribution (parishes, hospitals and charities) and to use the evidence produced by them to model social, gender and class relations more generally.[39] The institutional focus of this work has, however, tended to exclude any substantial perspective from below.

In parallel, economic historians and demographers have used many of the sources of the history of poor relief (patterns of expenditure, evidence of hardship) as central components in a wider understanding of the evolution of social and economic relations. This work has formed part of the project of modelling the demographic and economic changes that characterised the 'first industrial nation'. Most importantly, the Cambridge Group for the History of Population and Social Structure has created a substantial statistical model of both demographic and economic change that has in turn been used to create a social science of family formation, and by extension of poverty as a life-cycle condition. This literature grinds the evidence of human experience down to its smallest compass in order to construct a compelling model of lives characterised by life-cycle rituals and the most basic of life's experiences: birth, marriage, death, illness and deprivation. In the work of E. A. Wrigley and Roger Schofield, and more broadly in that of a generation of Cambridge-trained social historians, a statistical framework for a material history of poverty has been created.[40] Most recently, in the work of Leonard Schwarz, Jeremy Boulton, Alysa Levene and Alannah Tomkins, this focus on the material and life-cycle components of poor relief and poverty has taken centre stage.[41] As a result we are possessed of an increasingly sophisticated overview of the statistics of poverty and the administrative characteristics of the system. Nevertheless, in this

---

[39] Hindle, *On the Parish?*; Slack, *From Reformation to Improvement*; Mary Fissell, *Patients, Power, and the Poor in Eighteenth-Century Bristol* (Cambridge University Press, 1991); Innes, *Inferior Politics*.

[40] E. A. Wrigley and R. S. Schofield, *The Population History of England, 1541–1871: A Reconstruction* (London: Edward Arnold, 1981); E. A. Wrigley, *Poverty, Progress, and Population* (Cambridge University Press, 2004); Martin Daunton, *Progress and Poverty: An Economic and Social History of Britain, 1700–1850* (Oxford University Press, 1995).

[41] Jeremy Boulton and John Black, 'Paupers and their experience of a Georgian workhouse: St. Martin in the Fields, Westminster, 1725–1830', in J. Hamlett, L. Hoskins and R. Preston, eds., *Residential Institutions in Britain, 1725–1950: Inmates and Environments* (London: Pickering & Chatto, 2013); Leonard Schwarz, *London in the Age of Industrialisation: Entrepreneurs, Labour Force and Living Conditions, 1700–1850* (Cambridge University Press, 1992); Alysa Levene, *The Childhood of the Poor: Welfare in Eighteenth-Century London* (London: Palgrave Macmillan, 2012); Alannah Tomkins, *The Experience of Urban Poverty, 1723–82: Parish, Charity and Credit* (Manchester University Press, 2006).

literature paupers themselves remain largely passive objects of policy, rather than active participants in its creation.

There are, however, substantial recent attempts to give the poor a voice. To a large extent this has taken the form of work on the 'narratives' of the poor. James Stephen Taylor, Pamela Sharpe, Thomas Sokoll, Peter King, Alysa Levene and Steven King have each sought to give new meaning to the pauper letters, petitions, working-class autobiographies and neglected life writing that, by the nineteenth century, make up a significant component of the archive.[42] These historians have focused on the social exchange represented by the provision of support by parishes and charities, variously described as the result of pauper 'strategies', 'negotiations' and 'makeshifts', and on the ways in which these apparently less powerful actors were able to move within the system.[43] This work, however, has largely limited itself to either describing behaviour and negotiation within a shared, if changing, culture of obligation, or else charting the effectiveness of the actions of paupers in gaining more relief.[44] At its most ambitious, in the work of historians such as Peter Jones, Samantha Shave and David Green for the early nineteenth century, these pauper scripts are seen to reflect a wider moral economy, or to evidence substantive pauper resistance.[45] Yet even where they are tied to a clear political culture, little or no attempt has been made to explain how the actions of the poor contributed to the evolution of the wider system.

While not seeking to conflate the often distinct roles of criminals and paupers, this study goes beyond these literatures to posit a new model of pauper and criminal agency, and to emphasise its distinctive effect in shaping the evolution of policy. In many respects it builds on the work of Kevin Siena, who has explored how the demands of the sick poor

---

[42] James Stephen Taylor, *Poverty, Migration, and Settlement in the Industrial Revolution: Sojourners' Narratives* (Palo Alto, Calif.: Society for the Promotion of Science and Scholarship, 1989); Thomas Sokoll, ed., *Essex Pauper Letters, 1731–1837* (Oxford University Press, 2001); Pamela Sharpe, '"The bowels of compation": a labouring family and the law, c.1790–1834', in Tim Hitchcock, Peter King and Pamela Sharpe, eds., *Chronicling Poverty: The Voices and Strategies of the English Poor, 1640–1840* (Houndsditch: Macmillan, 1997); Alysa Levene (general ed.), *Narratives of the Poor in Eighteenth-Century Britain*, 4 vols. (London: Pickering & Chatto, 2006).

[43] Steven King and Alannah Tomkins, eds., *The Poor in England, 1700–1850: An Economy of Makeshifts* (Manchester University Press, 2003); Hindle, *On the Parish?*

[44] Hindle, *On the Parish?*, ch. 7.

[45] Green, *Pauper Capital*; Peter D. Jones, '"I cannot keep my place without being deascent": pauper letters, parish clothing and pragmatism in the south of England, 1750–1830', *Rural History*, 20:1 (2009), 31–49; S. A. Shave, 'The dependent poor? (Re)constructing the lives of individuals "on the parish" in rural Dorset, 1800–1832', *Rural History*, 20:1 (2009), 67–97.

contributed to the evolution of workhouse medicine, and Peter Linebaugh, whose study of the workplace struggles of the London hanged focused attention on the actions of some of the most important players in this drama.[46] It is also substantially influenced by the work of Catharina Lis and Hugo Soly, Arlette Farge and Seth Rockman in their studies of other times and places.[47] Unlike previous work, our approach focuses directly on the roles of the poor and the criminal in helping to shape the changing character of the institutions and policies with which they were forced to engage.

Agency

The case for the influence of plebeian Londoners is predicated on the belief that they possessed real and effective agency; that their behaviour was capable not just of stimulating a response but of contributing more directly to the evolution of both institutions and policies. In recent decades the role of agency in the lives of the poor has grown increasingly significant for our understandings of the history of early modern and nineteenth-century Britain.[48] While the label of 'pauper agency' has been used by several historians, no one has identified the causal line of influence that links intentions to historical change. By evidencing a more substantial role for pauper and criminal agency in determining the evolving structures of eighteenth-century society, this volume seeks to outline such a causal link.

'Agency' is a slippery and uncertain term, and the form of agency identified in this book is in many ways limited. We do not claim any real self-consciousness on the part of the poor and the criminal beyond a gnawing need to achieve a particular outcome in a narrowly confined negotiation with power. In many respects the 'agency' identified here takes the form of a veto on innovation. Some policies – such as prescriptions against begging – were rendered simply unenforceable. But there is also a substantive creative energy of directed demand at play. Setting one

---

[46] Kevin P. Siena, *Venereal Disease, Hospitals, and the Urban Poor: London's 'Foul Wards', 1600–1800* (University of Rochester Press, 2004); Linebaugh, *The London Hanged.*

[47] Catharina Lis and Hugo Soly, *Disordered Lives: Eighteenth-Century Families and Their Unruly Relatives* (Cambridge: Polity Press, 1996); Arlette Farge and Jacques Revel, *The Vanishing Children of Paris: Rumor and Politics before the French Revolution* (Cambridge, Mass.: Harvard University Press, 1993); Arlette Farge, *Fragile Lives: Violence, Power and Solidarity in Eighteenth-Century Paris* (Cambridge: Polity Press, 1993); Seth Rockman, *Scraping By: Wage Labor, Slavery, and Survival in Early Baltimore* (Baltimore: Johns Hopkins University Press, 2009).

[48] See for example, Henry French and Jonathan Barry, eds., *Identity and Agency in England, 1500–1800* (New York: Palgrave Macmillan, 2004); Lynn MacKay, *Respectability and the London Poor, 1780–1870: The Value of Virtue* (London: Pickering & Chatto, 2013).

parish against another in relation to pauper settlement, appearing ill and about to give birth at a workhouse door, using lawyers to counteract informers, hiring defence counsel in Old Bailey trials; all forced open narrow cracks in apparently working hegemonic systems and stimulated change. The accusations directed at the Bow Street Runners of acting as self-interested 'thief-takers' forced them to justify their roles in new ways and become more professional; while the powerful demands of the sick and elderly obliged parish overseers to abandon their optimistic expectations of recouping the cost of relief from the labour of the poor, and to rebuild their workhouses with extensive medical provision. Endless pamphlet writers, projectors and parliamentarians proposed reforms to criminal justice and poor relief, creating a landscape of ideas and exercising their own form of agency, but it was the poor and the criminal who primarily determined which reforms appeared feasible, and more importantly which initiatives took root and survived.

It is also important to recognise that the engagement of paupers and criminals with the systems of relief and justice necessarily took on a character determined by the motivations that underpinned them. The prospect of almost immediate death, or the pang and pains of serious hunger and illness, can both encourage profound conservatism and drive desperate risk taking. The objectives of the poor tended to be short term in character. In the words of a modern account of poverty: 'when the present is at stake, the future can be sacrificed'.[49] As a result the tactics of the poor and criminal were necessarily focused on incremental changes in pursuit of short-term advantage, and on the conservative maintenance of well-understood relationships and rights. However, in many ways this incremental character made the agency of plebeian Londoners more effective, since it is easier for an overseer or a judge to make an exception in one instance than it is to respond to a wider challenge to the system's legitimacy.

Finally, the metropolitan character of the subjects of this book – their co-location in a complex administrative environment – is central to the particular flavour of agency suggested here. Peter King has described the relationships of power that underpinned the exercise of justice in rural Britain as a set of triangular negotiations between the poor, landed society and the middling sort; by allying with one group against the other, the poor acquired a degree of power.[50] In London, because of the many overlapping and confused jurisdictional boundaries, the poor and the criminal were able to exercise still greater authority. The capital was

---

[49] Quoted as universal and proverbial wisdom in Deepa Narayan and Patti Petesch, *Voices of the Poor from Many Lands: A Compilation* (Oxford University Press, 2002), p. 184.
[50] King, *Crime and Law*.

replete with poorly policed neighbourhoods that straddled the boundary between the old City and the surrounding county of Middlesex. Moorfields, Rag Fair and Lincoln's Inn Fields all sat on this boundary, creating spaces of refuge in which to hide from authority. As importantly, the sheer number of magistrates – the trading justices of contemporary ridicule – gave the poor some choice over whose justice they wanted enforced. The patchwork of courts, rotation offices and magistrates' parlours ensured that the law never acted with one mind. When frustrated by the behaviour of an officer or magistrate, the poor and the criminal were often able to secure support from one of their colleagues. Paupers could appeal to the Lord Mayor or county justices for redress against their parish of settlement, forcing many overseers to abandon any attempt to enforce the poor law due to its cost in favour of informal and negotiated arrangements involving the paupers concerned and the officers of other parishes.[51]

This complexity grew as the century progressed. The rise of associational charities gave the more settled poor alternatives to an appeal to the overseer; and the growing role of legal settlement after 1692 created a new currency of belonging to the parish. Increasing literacy rates and the wide dissemination of print allowed some plebeian Londoners, notably highwaymen, the chance to sell their stories to a broad audience.[52] Appeals by politicians to 'public opinion', even if these were not meant to reach below the middle class, provided the 'mob' with occasions to voice their own grievances, as they did dramatically in 1768 and 1780.[53]

One way of characterising this particular flavour of 'agency' is to set it within Michel de Certeau's distinction between 'tactics' and 'strategies';

---

[51] Jeremy Boulton, 'Double deterrence: settlement and practice in London's West End, 1725–1824', in Anne Winter and Stephen King, eds., *Migration, Settlement and Belonging in Europe, 1500–1930s: Comparative Perspectives* (New York: Berghahn, 2013), pp. 54–80.

[52] Although historians have disagreed about how to measure literacy, nationally and by mid-century approximately 60 per cent of men and 40 per cent of women could sign their names. These figures were substantially higher in London, where even the poor were largely literate. Of 200 men and women examined following an application for relief to St Clement Danes, 1752–4, almost half, sixty-seven men and thirty women could sign their names: *LL*, St Clement Danes Parish: Pauper Settlement, Vagrancy and Bastardy Exams, 25 March 1752 – 27 December 1753 (WCCDEP35811). See also John Brewer, *The Pleasures of the Imagination: English Culture in the Eighteenth Century* (London: HarperCollins, 1997), pp. 167–8; Jerry White, *London in the Eighteenth Century: A Great and Monstrous Thing* (London: Bodley Head, 2012), p. 253. On highwaymen, see Robert Shoemaker, 'The street robber and the gentleman highwayman: changing representations and perceptions of robbery in London, 1690–1800', *Cultural and Social History*, 3:4 (2006), 381 405.

[53] Nicholas Rogers, *Crowds, Culture, and Politics in Georgian Britain* (Oxford: Clarendon Press, 1998).

between the everyday behaviour that everyone uses to make the world bend to their desires (tactics); and the systems and institutions that define the context in which an individual practises everyday life (strategies).[54] 'Tactics' are what every member of society necessarily uses to engage with social structures – whether walking the street or paying taxes. However, because the poor and the criminal are at the sharp end of explicit and well-articulated strategies, the impact of their tactics is heightened. Just as the strategic imposition of a new tax on a particular industry makes the 'tactics' of that industry's producers and consumers – their willingness to pay it – instrumental in determining the tax's success, so social policy is successful only if the poor and the criminal engage with it in the ways intended. As a result, the very poverty and apparent powerlessness of the poor and the criminal – their identification as 'problems' – both ensure that they become the object of 'strategies' and in turn give greater significance to their 'tactics'. Additionally, the highly pressured circumstances they confront – hunger and possible execution – make them doubly motivated to develop a profound knowledge of the narrow social systems with which they were forced to engage. Our approach is not intended to deny the importance of decisions made by policy-makers, or the roles of economic and ecological forces that frame individual lives in unexpected ways, but to draw attention to the complex relationship that existed between plebian tactics and elite strategies.

De Certeau's formulation of the structural relationship between tactics and strategies remains largely descriptive in character. This volume seeks to go one step further by arguing that the agency of the poor and the criminal lies in their ability to change the character of the systems they are forced to work within. Essentially, we argue that the tactics of the criminal and the poor are in direct, imaginative and constructive dialogue with the institutions and individuals which administer criminal justice and poor relief and, moreover, that the origins of many changes in these structures can be usefully located in the everyday actions of those same groups. In other words, a motive force for reform and change is the imaginative exploitation of the systems of 'police'. The poor and the criminal use tactics to deflect and modify the strategies created by their social superiors, and, in order to make these systems work effectively, the managers of criminal justice and poor relief necessarily respond by reformulating both how the systems work on a day-to-day basis, and eventually by changing statutes and regulations. Needless to say, the

[54] Michel de Certeau, *The Practice of Everyday Life* (Berkeley: University of California Press, 1988). One could almost as easily start from Anthony Giddens's concept of 'structuration', sociological 'choice theory', or Gramsci's notion of 'cultural hegemony'.

shape of these changes, whether they take the form of a workhouse or a punishment like transportation, are shaped by ideologies and political and economic forces beyond collective or individual plebeian control, but through their tactics the poor and the criminal both constrain the choices available and influence how new practices are implemented – how 'strategies' evolve. Thus while the poor, for example, did not determine the shape of the modern prison, as spelled out in the 1779 Penitentiary Act, the Act was in part a direct response to repeated plebeian escapes from gaols and the hulks.[55]

It is important to be clear about how this formulation of pauper and criminal agency adds to or disrupts other approaches. It is in many ways different to Michel Foucault's conception of the roles of both 'micro-technologies' and discourses in shaping change.[56] By locating a force for change in the imaginative engagement of the pauper and criminal, this work is intended to reinsert the individual as an actor capable of writing his or her own lines. We believe that Foucault's emphasis on the over-arching role of (elite) languages not only underestimates the importance of the semi-autonomous culture of the poor but also underplays the ability of individuals, driven by need and personal fear, to move beyond the confines of a dominant culture. At the same time, we explicitly sidestep the project of locating historical change in the development of self-conscious collective political action. In contrast to Edward Thompson and the British Marxist tradition, this volume attempts to re-emphasise the on-going importance of everyday need and desperation, and the roles of men and women of all ages and multiple backgrounds, acting independently of any systematic politics. The cultures of the poor, their 'tactics', are in our analysis not seen as inevitable precursors of political consciousness. The forms of resistance and subversion documented here undoubtedly form a constituent element of Thompson's 'class struggle without class', and they prefigure the rise of a new popular politics from the late eighteenth century, but they are distinct phenomena.[57] The contingent, temporary and overlapping alliances navigated by someone such as Thomas Limpus create a uniquely eighteenth-century context in which opposition was expressed to an evolving system of governance. While aspects of this structural dynamic of change are more or less present in all societies, they are more effective in generating

---

[55] Simon Devereaux, 'The making of the Penitentiary Act, 1775–1779', *Historical Journal*, 42:2 (1999), 405–33.

[56] Particularly relevant here is Michel Foucault, *Discipline and Punish: The Birth of the Prison* (Harmondsworth: Penguin Books, 1979).

[57] E. P. Thompson, 'Eighteenth-century English society: class struggle without class?', *Social History*, 3:2 (1978), 133–65.

change in complex, generally urban, environments of the sort exemplified by eighteenth-century London.[58]

This emphasis on effective agency located in direct relations between plebeians and the administration of criminal justice and poor relief also distances our analysis from the approach taken by James C. Scott and his identification of the 'weapons of the weak' and 'hidden transcripts'.[59] While agreeing with Scott about the powerfully disruptive character of subaltern behaviour and cultures, and the ability of subaltern groups to creatively frustrate systems of authority, we seek to go further. In pauper letters, or the refusals of the royal pardon in the 1780s, we identify a creative and imaginative agency of shared intent, composed of individual actions motivated by individual circumstances, but exercised collectively, and often publicly, as a result of common experiences and shared understandings. That London provides a complex landscape of competing authorities in which agency can be exercised also sets this work apart from that focused on rural and peasant communities.[60]

To define this particular form of 'agency' as simply as possible: we suggest that basic human need and fear, whether in the form of hunger, disease or the prospect of death on the scaffold, motivate the poor and the accused criminal to explore, within their cultural context, the structures of society as thoroughly as possible (more thoroughly than any other group).[61] In Peter Mandler's words, 'for the poor' rich social knowledge is 'essential to survival'.[62] While a single person, often in alliance with more powerful actors such as overseers or lawyers, may take the imaginative leap that identifies the tensions within a system and discerns the best way to manipulate that system for short term gain, our claim is that this knowledge rapidly spreads, creating shared and copied

---

[58] Of the wider British Marxist school of historical writing, this work is most indebted to Raphael Samuel and his powerful empathetic engagement with individual economic and social strategies. See, for instance, Raphael Samuel, 'Comers and goers', in H. J. Dyos and Michael Wolff, eds., *The Victorian City: Images and Reality*, Vol. I (London: Routledge & Kegan Paul, 1973), pp. 123–60.

[59] James C. Scott, *Weapons of the Weak: Everyday Forms of Peasant Resistance* (New Haven: Yale University Press, 1985); James C. Scott, *Domination and the Arts of Resistance: Hidden Transcripts* (New Haven, Conn.: Yale University Press, 2008).

[60] Scott has been particularly influential in relation to works on rural social relations. See K. D. M. Snell, *Parish and Belonging: Community, Identity and Welfare in England and Wales, 1700–1950* (Cambridge University Press, 2009); Barry Reay, *Microhistories: Demography, Society, and Culture in Rural England, 1800–1930* (Cambridge University Press, 2002).

[61] For a related argument, see John Bohstedt, *The Politics of Provisions: Food Riots, Moral Economy, and Market Transition in England, c. 1550–1850* (Farnham, Surrey: Ashgate, 2010).

[62] Peter Mandler, ed., *The Uses of Charity: The Poor on Relief in the Nineteenth-Century Metropolis* (Philadelphia: University of Pennsylvania Press, 1990), p. 1.

tactics that exert collective pressure on the system. If a hundred people are put on trial and have before them the example of a successful device by which to secure a favourable outcome, their use of that device is both consistent and self-reinforcing. It is the shared character of these tactics, despite the frequent absence of an explicit collective voice, that turns individual actions (the negotiations and makeshifts of the historical literature) into a collective, at times even strategic, engagement with the social system. While plebeian Londoners, with their long traditions of taking to the streets to celebrate and protest, were experienced at acting in groups to secure their aims, most of the behaviour we document took the form of individual lobbying and acts of resistance.[63] From this perspective changes in social policy are a response to a many-headed and querulous demand for resources or change which, in aggregate, amounts to a significant form of collective action.

Methodology

Capturing the individual and collective behaviour of people whose lives are recorded almost exclusively in some of the most intractable of bureaucratic sources compiled by those in power – in account books, removal orders, gaol delivery lists and trial accounts – is difficult.[64] Confronted with an eighteenth-century archive of a parish or a court, it is almost impossible to read the text it contains without subtly privileging the perspective of the clerk and the elite men whose explicit purposes the archive served. Parish records are generally about controlling expenditure, rather than about revealing the experience of poverty.[65] And the archives of criminal justice are necessarily focused on an individual violation of the law, the process of evidencing that event and managing a bureaucracy of prosecution and punishment, rather than on revealing the life of the criminal, or indeed the victim.[66] The shared plebeian experience of negotiating these systems was not directly recorded, and

---

[63] Rudé, *Paris and London*; Robert Shoemaker, *The London Mob: Violence and Disorder in Eighteenth-Century England* (London: Hambledon and London, 2004).

[64] Eric Ketelaar, 'Archival temples, archival prisons: modes of power and protection', *Archival Science*, 2 (2002), 221–38.

[65] Tim Hitchcock, 'Digital searching and the re-formulation of historical knowledge', in M. Greengrass and L. Hughes, eds., *The Virtual Representation of the Past* (Farnham, Surrey: Ashgate, 2008), pp. 81–90.

[66] One major exception to this statement is the Ordinary's *Accounts*, which purport to tell the lives of the convicts who were executed at Tyburn. These biographies, however, were significantly shaped by the agendas of the Ordinaries (chaplains of Newgate prison) who wrote them. See Andrea McKenzie, *Tyburn's Martyrs: Execution in England, 1675–1775* (London: Hambledon Continuum, 2007) and Linebaugh, *London Hanged*.

not the point. And while evidence of long lives lived in the shadow of the parish and magistrate has survived, it is spread almost randomly across hundreds of thousands of pages.

To construct a history from below, the first and most necessary task is therefore to dismember the archives themselves, and reconstruct them with plebeian lives in mind. For this book this dismemberment was achieved through the large-scale digitisation of the records of London crime and poverty. By transcribing in full the printed *Proceedings of the Old Bailey* (which document the vast majority of felony trials held in London) and a large selection of manuscript materials from the archives of parishes, quarter sessions and the Old Bailey, and combining these in an online resource, *London Lives*, new possibilities for documenting individual lives and the collective experience of groups of plebeian men and women were created. In order for evidence pertaining to individual lives to be assembled, the *London Lives* website includes a feature which allows all relevant documents for single individuals to be identified and brought together in 'sets'. The resulting collection of documented lives, or more accurately (since comprehensive demographic and other data is not available) fragments of lives, approaching 3,000 at the time of writing, provides a key resource for this book.[67] Overlaying these 'lives' are collections of individual instances of 'roles' defined by particular events, such as having received parish relief, having been incarcerated in Bridewell or having hired William Garrow as defence counsel. As a result new collective patterns of behaviour, examples of recidivism and links between different bodies of records have been identified.[68]

We have also worked with archives in more conventional ways, since the digitised records, while substantial, are not complete. They do not include those of any voluntary societies (with the exception of a sample of the records of the Marine Society) and contain only a small proportion of the parochial records, although the three detailed parish archives we have digitised were chosen as representative of contrasting social environments and different parts of London. While St Botolph Aldgate, straddling the eastern border of the City, was a large and relatively poor parish inhabited by artisans and labourers, St Clement Danes in the west end contained a mixture of social classes. In contrast to both, St Dionis Backchurch, located in the heart of the City of London, was a small and wealthy parish with less than a thousand inhabitants. The records of

---

[67] Sets have been created by a wide range of users, but all the sets referred to in this book were either created by the authors or checked by them for accuracy. To search for sets, simply choose 'set search' on the left-hand menu of the keyword search page.

[68] For more information about *London Lives*, see the site's 'About this project' page.

these parishes have been supplemented with the workhouse and settlement records of one of London's largest parishes, St Martin's in the Fields – digitised as a part of Leonard Schwarz and Jeremy Boulton's 'Pauper Lives' project.[69] Another important gap in the existing digitised archives is in the records of quarter sessions. While we have digitised all surviving manuscript sessions papers for Middlesex, Westminster and the City, the actual records of prosecutions of petty crime – the indictments, recognizances and commitments to houses of correction contained in the sessions rolls – are outside the scope of this project (though the records of the City house of correction – Bridewell – are included).[70] Finally, the records of the governors of the City of London – the Repertories of the Court of Aldermen, Journals of the Court of Common Council and the notebooks kept by the Lord Mayor when acting as a justice of the peace – remain undigitised.[71]

While the vast extent of the surviving archives of London's complex web of governance means that no one can look at everything, we have not omitted consulting key documents from these and other undigitised archives, particularly in the London Metropolitan Archives, National Archives and British Library. We have also made extensive use of newly searchable digital resources created by others, including eighteenth-century printed books, newspapers and the *Parliamentary Papers*. By combining these resources with the results of the new methodologies made possible through the digitisation undertaken for this book, we have been able to construct a richly, if not comprehensively, evidenced interpretation of eighteenth-century London. While evidence of plebeian agency often remains difficult to identify (it must often be carefully discerned from between the lines of records created by their social superiors), we believe we have effectively privileged a plebeian perspective.

As well as using the innovative methodology of dismembering and reordering the archive, this book is also intended as an experiment in presenting historical evidence to the reader in a new form. As explained in the preface, it was conceived and written in the hope that it would be read online and onscreen with the archive of lives and documents that underpins its conclusions directly (and freely) available to the reader.

---

[69] See http://research.ncl.ac.uk/pauperlives/. We are grateful to the project directors for making their data available for our research.

[70] In addition, the Middlesex and Westminster sessions papers contain some calendars of the inmates in houses of correction.

[71] A substantial subsection of the notebooks are available as Greg T. Smith, ed., *Summary Justice in the City: A Selection of Cases Heard at the Guildhall Justice Room, 1753–1781* (London Record Society, 48, 2013).

This is intended to make real the traditional purpose of a footnote – to allow the relevance of a specific piece of evidence to be confirmed, and the research journey of the authors to be made explicit. At its most ambitious, this book and its associated web resources represents an attempt to create a vertically integrated research project and publication that allows the sources of social history to be ordered around individual criminals and paupers, and then presented in a form that can be instantly accessed and evaluated. It is an attempt to escape the intellectual dominance of the archives and published book, the very structures of which imply a single (elite) reading, and to replace it with a history that both focuses on plebeian Londoners and at the same time decentres the *authority* of the authors as the only arbiters of the evidence. It is our strong hope that, having clicked through from the text of this book to the underlying electronic resources, readers will be encouraged to conduct their own research. With such further investigation, and the on-going march of digitisation and technological innovation, we are more conscious than most that our conclusions can only be provisional and suggestive.

2 Beggarman, thief: 1690–1713

Introduction

In the spring of 1704 the governors of the London Workhouse were confronted by one of the uncomfortable realities generated by a rapidly growing city. Two brothers, Thomas and John Brinnish, had been taken up from the streets and brought before them, where they informed the governors that the churchwarden of their home parish in Bristol had given the brothers three shillings and directed them to the charity of Londoners. Thirty years earlier they would almost certainly have simply been whipped and sent on their way. However, in an increasingly bureaucratic system, the governors first wrote to the keeper of the workhouse at Bristol for more information.[1] In the process, the Brinnish brothers were inducted into a system of vagrant and pauper removal, itself part of an evolving bureaucracy of poor relief and criminal justice that was changing in response to legislation, civic innovation and the actions of the reformation of manners societies. These in turn had been prompted in part by the 1688 Revolution, which led to more frequent meetings of parliament and the growth of voluntary societies seeking reform.

Whether the Brinnish brothers were aware of and consciously took advantage of the new opportunities these innovations accorded the poor is unknown, but by their actions plebeian Londoners both forced the pace of change and took advantage of the new opportunities that arose. Driven by economic hardship, the poor and the criminal brought substantial pressures to bear on the institutions of relief and justice in the 1690s. Both the amount spent relieving poverty and the number of crimes prosecuted rose in the decade after 1688. In the small City parish of St Dionis Backchurch, expenditure peaked in 1694 at £582, a figure that would not be reached again for over four decades, and in the ten

---

[1] LMA, 'Minutes of the Court of the President and Governors for the Poor of London, 1702–1705', CLA/075/01/007, 17 May 1704, f. 127.

years after 1690 expenses averaged £414 per annum.[2] Rising rates of criminal prosecutions reveal a crisis of gender, prompted by the imbalance in migration which saw a large number of young, unmarried women in the metropolis, whose independent status rendered them quickly suspected of theft and sexual immorality. Driven in part by the recruitment of men into the armed forces, prosecutions of women reached historically unprecedented levels. In 1695 women accounted for an all-time high of 53.2 per cent of all defendants at the Old Bailey, when 257 women were tried, compared to only 223 men. Over the next seven years close to half (48.2 per cent) of all those accused of non-violent theft at the Old Bailey were women.[3]

Following the disruptions to trade during William III's wars in the first half of the 1690s, the second half saw social problems exacerbated by the triple catastrophes of recoinage, harvest failure and demobilisation. A series of crises began with the 'Great Recoinage' of 1696, when long-standing problems resulting from the frequent clipping and counterfeiting of coins in London and across the country were finally addressed by the complete replacement of the coinage. This, in turn, led to significant economic disruption and inflation, compounded by harvest failures in 1697 and 1698 that further raised the cost of living, with bread prices in London peaking in 1697 at about 60 per cent above the long-term average. Real wages declined, reaching a level in 1697–9 which was 15 per cent lower than in 1694–5. Rising poverty was exacerbated by the increase in unemployment that followed the demobilisation of soldiers in 1697 at the end of the Nine Years War.[4]

What emerged in response to these pressures were two interrelated developments that together changed the relationship between the state in all its local and national forms and the inhabitants of London, creating a distinct landscape of power and authority, mapped in new documents and practices. Justices of the peace, Lord Mayors, constables and parish officers all had to adapt. But most importantly, with the most to lose, criminals and paupers needed to learn how to make a new system work for them.

---

[2] Online data set: St Dionis Backchurch Poor Law Expenditure 1688–1803.

[3] *Old Bailey Online*, Statistics: Defendant gender, 1695, and Defendant gender: Thefts, 1696–1702. Note that the 1695 figure has been pro-rated to account for the fact that the January edition of the *Proceedings* has not survived. Similarly, the figure for 1696 to 1702 is calculated on the basis of surviving editions of the *Proceedings* only.

[4] D. W. Jones, *War and Economy in the Age of William III and Marlborough* (London: Basil Blackwell, 1988); Christopher Edgar Challis, *A New History of the Royal Mint* (Cambridge University Press, 1992); W. G. Hoskins, 'Harvest fluctuations and English economic history, 1620–1759', *Agricultural History Review*, 16:1 (1968), 19; E. A. Wrigley and R. S. Schofield, *The Population History of England, 1541–1871: A Reconstruction* (London: Edward Arnold, 1981), p. 643.

First, a top-down process of reforming the system of poor relief that had begun in the 1660s with the definition of pauper 'settlement' was honed and refined in the 1690s through the introduction of pauper badges and settlement certificates to regulate pauper migration. This was accompanied by a justice-controlled system of centralised pauper discipline. For paupers a bureaucracy of belonging and exclusion came into being, bringing with it both constraints and opportunities.[5] And finally, with the re-establishment of the London Workhouse in 1698, and the Vagrant Costs Act of 1699, the policing of unacceptable migration moved increasingly from the parish to the justices in their collective capacity as the county bench and, in the City, the Court of Aldermen.

Second, the criminal justice system was forced to adapt to new pressures and to accommodate new personnel. In response to concerns about rising crime and vice, the state and voluntary societies resorted to civic activism to discipline the disorderly communities of the capital, injecting a mercenary element into criminal justice. In response to statutory rewards and moral suasion, an army of thief-takers and informers, some with criminal backgrounds themselves, effectively moved the oversight of deviance, of policing that ragged boundary between a settled community and its miscreants, from the jurisdiction of private victims and religious authority to self-appointed policemen.

This chapter will examine the evolution of poor relief and criminal justice in the two decades following the 'Glorious Revolution' and assess plebeian responses to these new policies and practices. By the end of the first decade of the eighteenth century, it will argue, many of the systems of policing crime, poverty and belonging that would characterise the next century were in place. In the process, it will suggest that the creation of a new landscape of authority, worked out in a distinct ecology of documentation and overseen by justices of the peace, created a system through which the poor were increasingly separated from the parish community, and more clearly identified as social problems, and yet, along with some criminals, unintentionally accorded a new kind of agency.

Growth and disorder

In the second half of the seventeenth century, London was transformed both geographically and socially by substantial population growth. From around 400,000 at mid-century, over the next fifty years the city grew by

---

[5] For a recent discussion of the notion of a 'right to relief' that contradicts this point, see Steve Hindle, *On the Parish?: The Micro-Politics of Poor Relief in Rural England, c.1550–1750* (Oxford University Press, 2004), ch. 6.

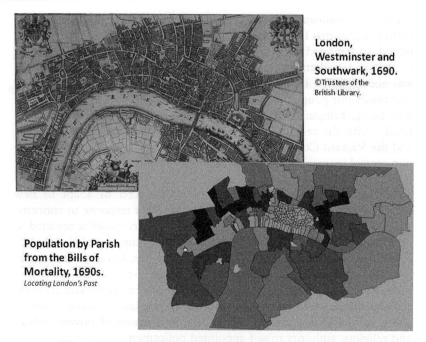

Figure 2.1 London, Westminster and Southwark, *c.* 1690 © Trustees of
the British Library; and population estimates, *Locating London's Past,*
'Broken down by Parish: 1690s'.

almost half to close to 600,000.[6] By the turn of the century, the population was spread ever more unevenly between the small wealthy parishes
of the City, which housed only about 20 per cent of the population of the
metropolis as a whole, and the large, rambling and in some cases poor
and poorly policed parishes of the suburbs.[7]

It was in many of these extramural parishes that a constant stream of
much needed but frequently unwelcome migrants made their homes;
drawn to the capital in search of employment. Like all inhabitants of large
early-modern cities, Londoners suffered a cripplingly high mortality. In
the entirely typical year of 1700, London's demographic seismometer,

[6] There is some dispute about the precise numbers, but see E. A. Wrigley, 'A simple model of
London's importance in changing English society and economy, 1650–1750', *Past &
Present*, 37 (1967), 44. Vanessa Harding suggests that population growth in the late
seventeenth century was stronger than previously recognised: 'The population of London,
1550–1700: a review of the published evidence', *London Journal*, 15:2 (1990), 123.
[7] Craig Spence, *London in the 1690s: A Social Atlas* (London: Centre for Metropolitan
History, 2000), p. 63.

the *Bills of Mortality*, recorded 19,443 burials compared to only 14,639 christenings.[8] It was migrants to the extramural parishes of the capital who filled the shoes of the dead.

The hands and minds needed to fuel London's growth came in the form of young unmarried people in their late teens and early twenties. A majority were women seeking employment in domestic service. Craft apprenticeships and the boom in the building trades following the Great Fire employed many young men, though apprenticeship was no longer the driving force of urban growth that it had once been.[9] The result was what historians of social policy characterise as a remarkably low *dependency ratio*, meaning that very young children and the elderly formed a relatively small proportion of the population as a whole.[10] In decades witnessing a steady rise in the amount of poor relief distributed by parishes, the proportion of the population in London who conformed to the stereotype of the 'deserving' poor was at a historic low, allowing parish pensions to rise.[11] At the same time, their very mobility led many of the new migrants to London to be marked out as 'undeserving'. They were also, in many cases, identifiably different. Patricia Fumerton has argued that the later seventeenth century witnessed the rise of a distinctive unsettled plebeian culture which encouraged migration.[12] London's migrants came not only from all parts of the British Isles, but increasingly from the whole of Western Europe, bringing new accents and new ways.[13]

In effect the settled communities of London found themselves under increasing pressures; all the more so in the large and socially mixed suburbs that ringed the City where already weak parish government was confronted with increasing levels of migration in an unfamiliar guise.[14] But even in the small and wealthy parishes of the City (not

[8] *A Collection of the Yearly Bills of Mortality, from 1657 to 1758 Inclusive. Together with several other bills of an earlier date* (1759), p. 122. In the ten years between 1695 and 1704, the Bills recorded an average annual surplus of 4,917 deaths over christenings.

[9] Peter Earle, *A City Full of People: Men and Women of London, 1650–1750* (London: Methuen, 1994), pp. 39–46.

[10] Nationally, the latter half of the century witnessed the lowest 'dependency ratio' in pre-modern English history. See Wrigley and Schofield, *Population History of England*, pp. 443–5. In-migration would have made the equivalent figures for London even more pronounced.

[11] On levels of expenditure per hundred thousand of the population, see Paul Slack, *Poverty and Policy in Tudor and Stuart England* (London: Longman, 1988), pp. 181–2.

[12] Patricia Fumerton, *Unsettled: The Culture of Mobility and the Working Poor in Early Modern England* (University of Chicago Press, 2006).

[13] Earle, *City Full of People*, pp. 46–9.

[14] See Roger Finlay and Beatrice Shearer, 'Population growth and suburban expansion', in A. L. Beier and Roger Finlay, eds., *London 1500–1700: The Making of the Metropolis* (London: Longman, 1986), pp. 37–59.

directly affected by growing population), settled elites must have felt surrounded by strangers. In January 1694, against a backdrop of historically high bread prices, the City grand jury complained:

That greate numbers of loose idle & ill disposed persons from all partes of this kingdome doe resorte unto this City & partes adiacent. And doe here shelter themselves not following any lawfull callings or employments. And haveing noe visible estates or honest way to mainteyne themselves doe turne Robbers on the highway Burglarers Pickpockets and Gamesters that follow other unlawfull wayes to supporte themselves.[15]

Crime rates and the cost of meeting the demands of the poor rose accordingly.[16] In 1695 the Board of Trade estimated that poor relief in the capital as a whole had reached over £40,000 per year, amounting to fully 10 per cent of all money raised nationally, with an overall expenditure of approximately £69 per thousand inhabitants per year.[17] The City of London was regularly forced to raise extra cash to subsidise poor relief expenditure in poorer parishes. In January 1694, at least ten petitions were submitted by its suburban parishes (those lying outside the medieval walls of the City but within its jurisdiction), complaining vehemently about the growing cost of relieving the poor. In the words of the parish officers of St Bride's, St Bride's was 'scituate in the Suburbs of this City ... their Poore dailey increaseing upon them'.[18] In response, the City distributed £1,712 – 95 per cent of which went to these extramural parishes.[19]

Not only was this growing expenditure a subject of complaint from parish officers and ratepayers, and in an expanding literature of political economy, but the publicity of poverty raised serious concerns about disorder.[20] Aggressive begging and vagrancy became an increasingly

---

[15] *LL*, City of London Sessions: Sessions Papers, 6 December 1693 – 23 December 1694 (LMSLPS150050021). Anxiety about migration to the City had a long history even in 1694, and the language used here is mirrored in several sixteenth- and seventeenth-century presentments.

[16] Nationally, Paul Slack identifies this period as witnessing a marked rise in poor relief, with urban parishes in the vanguard: Slack, *Poverty and Policy*, p. 182.

[17] The Board of Trade estimate for London for 1695 was £40,847. See Stephen Macfarlane, 'Social policy and the poor in the later seventeenth century', in Beier and Finlay, eds., *London 1500–1700*, p. 255. See also, Spence, *London in the 1690s*, p. 109; compared to national Board of Trade figures at £400,000, in Slack, *Poverty and Policy*, pp. 170–1.

[18] *LL*, City of London Sessions: Sessions Papers, 6 December 1693 – 23 December 1694 (LMSLPS150050187).

[19] Spence, *London in the 1690s*, p. 109.

[20] For an overview of this literature, see Joyce Oldham Appleby, *Economic Thought and Ideology in Seventeenth-Century England* (Princeton University Press, 1978; repr. 2004), and Julian Hoppit, *A Land of Liberty? England 1689–1727* (Oxford: Clarendon Press, 2000), pp. 190–4.

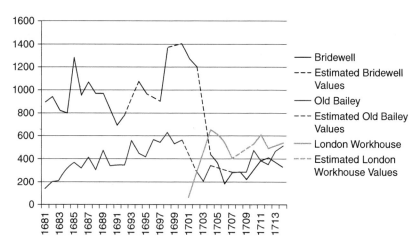

Figure 2.2 Prosecutions and commitments, 1681–1714: The Old Bailey, Bridewell and London Workhouse. Online data set: Crime Prosecutions.xlsx.

common subject for the Lord Mayor's proclamations and grand jury presentments. And despite their efforts, things seemed to be getting worse. In July 1693 the grand jury complained of the 'neglect of the poor, & their being suffered to beg in great numbers up & down the streets of this City, to be a dishonour to the City, & an injury to the Inhabitants'.[21] Poverty, and particularly the related practices of begging and vagrancy, was strongly associated in the public mind with crime, and criminal prosecutions increased accordingly. In the 1680s the number of felonies tried at the Old Bailey had more than doubled, to an annual average of 337 in the latter half of the decade, and this number increased still further to 495 per year in the 1690s. In 1698 the number of offences tried reached its highest level since publication of the *Proceedings* began in 1674.[22] Similarly, in 1698 and 1700–2 (figures for 1699 are missing) the number of commitments to Bridewell reached the highest levels recorded since the early seventeenth century, which would not be exceeded until 1772.

Theft, as always, was the most common category of crime, but the character of prosecutions at the Old Bailey changed with an increase in

---

[21] *LL*, City of London Sessions: Sessions Papers, 8 December 1692 – 28 November 1693 (LMSLPS150040128).

[22] These figures have been adjusted to account for up to three missing sessions in each year (out of eight). For similar data for the City of London only, see John Beattie, *Policing and Punishment in London, 1660–1750: Urban Crime and the Limits of Terror* (Oxford University Press, 2001), p. 41.

prosecutions of clipping and counterfeiting coins. These tripled to 13.2 per cent of prosecutions in 1690–6, reflecting both harsh economic conditions and the government's struggle to regain control of the currency, before it was finally forced to implement a complete recoinage.

The 1688 Revolution and the reformation of manners

Perceptions of substantial increases in poverty and crime form an important context for the moral and social reform initiatives which followed directly on from the Revolution of 1688.[23] At least momentarily, between 1690 and 1693 it seemed possible that Britain could lead Europe to a new Protestant dispensation with William III at its head.[24] But if this 'reformation' was to succeed, religious conviction needed to be accompanied by social discipline. The ambition to create a 'godly monarchy' demanded a programme of moral and social reform. Religious revival prompted by the providential belief that the country had been blessed by God in having been delivered from a Catholic monarchy implied that Britain, and pre-eminently London, needed to reform itself.

For a brief moment the politics of religion and foreign affairs worked together with that of poverty and crime to move policy. With continuing periods of economic dislocation and the perception of growing crime, social problems rose to the forefront of many minds. As a result the 1690s witnessed an accelerating programme of activity and innovation in addressing social problems, which both had significant (and often unintended) consequences for the poor and prompted forceful and effective opposition from many quarters.

The first and longest lasting initiative was the reformation of manners campaign launched with royal support in 1689.[25] Prompted by a letter of

---

[23] Tony Claydon, *William III and the Godly Revolution* (Cambridge University Press, 1996); Steve Pincus, *1688: The First Modern Revolution* (New Haven, Conn.: Yale University Press, 2009).

[24] W. R. Ward, 'The relation of enlightenment and religious revival in central Europe and in the English-speaking world', in Derek Baker, ed., *Reform and Reformation: England and the Continent c. 1500–1700* (Oxford: Blackwell, 1979), pp. 281–305; W. R. Ward, 'Power and piety: the origins of religious revival in the early eighteenth century', *Bulletin of the John Rylands Library of Manchester*, 63:1 (1980); and Claydon, *William III*.

[25] The standard, but now outdated, work on this subject remains Dudley W. R. Bahlman, *The Moral Revolution of 1688* (New Haven, Conn.: Yale University Press, 1957; repr. Archon Books, 1968). The most recent comprehensive studies are in the form of unpublished PhD dissertations: A. G. Craig, 'The movement for the reformation of manners, 1688–1715' (Edinburgh University, 1980); and Tina Beth Isaacs, 'Moral crime, moral reform, and the state in early eighteenth-century England: a study of piety and politics' (University of Rochester, 1979). See also Faramerz Dabhoiwala, *The Origins of Sex: A History of the First Sexual Revolution* (London: Allen Lane, 2012),

encouragement from King William addressed to the Bishop of London and the two archbishops in February, the reformers sought 'a General Reformation of the Lives and Manners of all our subjects'.[26] Despite this broad ambition, the primacy of concerns about poverty and crime in driving reform can be seen in the justifications for the first sustained efforts to prosecute vice in London. In August 1689, apparently prompted by the future Archbishop of Canterbury and current rector of the parish, Thomas Tenison, the churchwardens and overseers of the poor of the large Westminster parish of St Martin in the Fields observed:[27]

a dayly increase of poor in the said parish and that the encouragers thereof are people of evill fame who keep reputed bawdy houses in severall by alleys and places in the said parish whereby severall great disorders and misdeamenors [sic] are dayly committed against the peace ...

They went on to ask the Westminster justices to suppress the brothels in order to ease 'the great burden which at present lyes upon them'.[28] In response, groups of justices meeting at the St Martin's vestry committed over 200 prostitutes and other 'loose [or lewd], idle and disorderly persons' to the Westminster house of correction over a six-month period.[29] In the City of London, the new Lord Mayor issued a proclamation in November against vice, leading to a similar increase in commitments to Bridewell.[30]

The first *society* devoted to the prosecution of vice, however, was launched in the autumn of 1690 in Tower Hamlets on the other side of London. In response to a royal proclamation against highway robbers issued on 30 October, a group of 'churchwardens, constables, and several other officers and inhabitants of the Tower Hamblets [sic]', claiming that brothels were 'the common receptacles, or rather, dens of notorious thieves, robbers, traytors and other criminals', resolved that the

---

ch. 2; Faramerz Dabhoiwala, 'Sex and societies for moral reform, 1688–1800', *Journal of British Studies*, 46:2 (2007), 290–319; Robert Shoemaker, *Prosecution and Punishment: Petty Crime and the Law in London and Rural Middlesex, c. 1660–1725* (Cambridge University Press, 1991), ch. 9; and Robert Shoemaker, 'Reforming the city: the reformation of manners campaign in London, 1690–1738', in L. Davison *et al.*, eds., *Stilling the Grumbling Hive: The Response to Social and Economic Problems in England, 1689–1750* (Stroud: Alan Sutton, 1992), pp. 99–120.
[26] *His Majesties Letter to the Lord Bishop of London* (London, 1689), p. 4.
[27] Dabhoiwala, 'Sex and societies', 298.
[28] LMA, Middlesex Sessions: 'Sessions papers', MJ/SP/1689/08/010.
[29] Shoemaker, *Prosecution and Punishment*, pp. 238–9.
[30] Dabhoiwala, 'Sex and societies', 298 and n. 47; LL, Bridewell Royal Hospital: Minutes of the Court of Governors, 6 January 1689 – 8 August 1695, see 16 December 1689 (BBBRMG202010034) and following pages.

suppression of bawdy houses was 'a necessary expedient' if highway robbery was to be stopped. The proliferation of 'impudent harlots', they argued, led 'our sons and servants to debauchery, and consequently to embezzle and steal from us ... thereby families are begger'd and parishes much impoverished'.[31] The suppression of prostitution would help parish officials cope with recent increases in both crime *and* poverty.

The following year, 1691, saw the foundation of the first society explicitly devoted to a *reformation of manners*, in the Strand. Further royal encouragement prompted orders from both the Middlesex sessions and the City's Court of Aldermen requiring local officials to ensure the laws were properly enforced.[32] Additional societies were formed, and the following years and decades witnessed waves of prosecutions of vice offences – the campaign did not finally end until 1738. Reformers, often motivated as much by concerns to maintain social order as by religious zeal, initiated tens of thousands of prosecutions in the metropolis alone.[33] These societies constituted, at least temporarily, an important new form of non-governmental policing. Eschewing entirely the church courts and largely bypassing parish officials (except when they themselves were supporters of the campaign), the reformers, a coalition of artisans, tradesmen, gentry and noblemen, used the law aggressively to discipline the disorderly poor.

They were quick to claim initial success. In 1694 the Tower Hamlets society reported that 'in the space of two or three years' it had punished 'seven or eight hundred criminals'. In the year ending January 1694 alone, they claimed to have prosecuted 157 men and women for being 'night-walkers and plyers in bawdy-houses' and 155 keepers of disorderly houses and brothels.[34] Confirmation of the early impact of the reformers can also be seen in the records of the various criminal jurisdictions of the City and Middlesex. Largely the result of the activities of the St Martin's justices, commitments to the Westminster house of correction peaked as early as 1690, with 768 commitments, of which 62.5 per cent were for prostitution or loose, idle and disorderly conduct.[35] According to the Lord Mayor's 'waiting' and 'charge' books (which record the cases

---

[31] *Antimoixeia: or, the Honest and Joynt Design of the Tower-Hamblets for the General Suppression of Bawdy Houses, As Incouraged by the Publick Magistrates* (1691).

[32] Bahlman, *Moral Revolution*, pp. 17–18, 33–4.

[33] Shoemaker, 'Reforming the city', p. 105, Table 6.1.

[34] *Proposals for a National Reformation of Manners* (1694), pp. 24, 34–5; Online data set: SRM Prosecutions, 1693–1738.

[35] LMA, Middlesex Sessions: 'Session rolls', MJ/SR/1751–1764 (Westminster sessions only); total figure has been adjusted to account for the one unavailable calendar for that year. The percentage is based on the January and April Sessions: MJ/SR/1751 (January 1690); MJ/SR/1754 (April 1690).

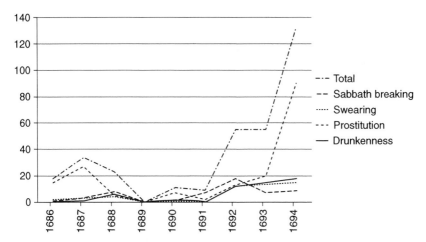

Figure 2.3 Vice offences recorded in Lord Mayor's waiting and charge books, 1686–1694. Online data set: LM Waiting and Charge Books 1686–1733.xlsx.

brought before the Lord Mayor in his capacity as the leading justice of the peace in the City of London), there was a significant increase in vice cases brought before him in 1692–4, when prosecutions for prostitution, drunkenness, swearing and Sabbath abuse averaged over eighty per year, compared to just sixteen per year in the previous six years.[36] Some of these offenders were committed to Bridewell, the City of London's house of correction. The commitment and punishments of ninety-three vice offenders were recorded in the minute books of the Court of Governors between July and December 1693.[37]

The characteristics of the reformers' prosecutions demonstrate the extent to which their notion of *vice* was concerned with a wide-ranging notion of disorder, rather than restricted to specific 'crimes'. This was one of the reasons their activities prompted so much opposition. Many accusations were based on loosely substantiated *suspicion* and an assessment of the general character of the accused, rather than specific evidence of delinquent behaviour. On 22 September 1693, for example, Eleanor Rawlinson and Elizabeth Thorne appeared before the Bridewell

[36] Online data set: LM Waiting and Charge Books 1686–1733.xlsx
[37] *LL*, Bridewell Royal Hospital: Minutes of the Court of Governors, 7 July 1693 (BBBRMG202010284) *et seq.* This figure includes only those prisoners who were present in Bridewell at the time the court sat. It is likely that even more people accused of these offences had been committed, but discharged before the governors met.

governors charged by James Jenkins and Bodenham Rewse with 'being idle Lewd persons and Suspected to be comon Pickpockett(s)'.[38] Jenkins and Rewse had been employees of the original Tower Hamlets reformation of manners society and were some of the campaign's most active informers. According to the Lord Mayor's charge book, these men often arrested people on the basis of precisely this kind of limited evidence. They both lived outside the City in the Strand (Jenkins was a jeweller or a clockmaker and Rewse an embroiderer), and in the summer and autumn of 1693 regularly brought women before the Lord Mayor. In October six women were charged by them with being common nightwalkers, 'having been several times in Bridewell known to be persons of lewd life and conversation'.[39] That same month, evidence provided by Jenkins was used to justify committing two women to Newgate prison, charged with being common nightwalkers and 'suspected to be housebreakers'.[40] In most instances, these prosecutions were directed at what might be called the 'usual suspects'.

The reformers were frequently accused of targeting the poor, whose delinquencies were publicly visible, while ignoring the sins committed in private by the rich. This was a charge which the reformers essentially admitted, justifying their approach by noting the difficulties of finding evidence against private crimes and of prosecuting the rich, and arguing that in any case the very publicity of sins committed on the streets was a greater affront to God and therefore a higher priority.[41]

As this criticism implies, the reformers' aggressive use of the law to target large numbers of poor offenders, often on the basis of reputation and prejudice alone, attracted substantial opposition from several quarters, and this opposition ultimately forced the reformers to change their tactics and reduce their ambitions. Justices of the peace complained that the reformers frequently failed to follow the correct legal procedures and undermined their powers of discretion. Constables were alienated by the pressure reformers put on them to carry out their duties more systematically, including attempts to supervise their activities and report delinquent officers to sessions.[42] More audaciously, there was also substantial and effective opposition from plebeian Londoners, both on the streets and in the courts.

---

[38] *LL*, Bridewell Royal Hospital: Minutes of the Court of Governors, 22 September 1693 (BBBRMG202010313). See also *LL*, set, 'James Jenkins', and set, 'Bodenham Rewse'.

[39] LMA, City of London: 'Mansion House charge book', CLC/286/MS00487/002, 16 November 1693.

[40] LMA, City of London: Sessions, 'City sessions rolls', CLA/047/LJ/02, Newgate Prison Calendar, October 1693.

[41] Isaacs, 'Moral crime, moral reform', p. 348.

[42] Shoemaker, *Prosecution and Punishment*, pp. 241–4, 252–72.

In a system in which the prosecution of crime was generally the responsibility of the victim, prosecuting vice required a different approach. Because vice offences were essentially victimless, they had to be prosecuted by volunteers or paid agents. Londoners quickly branded these men with the opprobrious label of 'informer', a name made more hateful as a result of the role informers had played in the prosecution of dissenters in the 1670s. As a group of reformers from Southwark complained in 1695, 'we are abused, reproached and detained and the people in the streets stirred up against us to the hazard and danger of our lives'.[43] These men were not exaggerating. In 1693–4 Jenkins was assaulted twice, as well as threatened and called by 'the name of informer'.[44] James Cooper, 'the most active City constable in the 1690s', who often worked with Jenkins and Rewse in arresting prostitutes and coiners, was also the target of threats, rescues and attacks.[45] On 29 July 1693 Robert Lowth, a servant to a coffeeman, was bound over 'for calling James Jenkins and James Cooper by the name of informers and threatening them'.[46]

Opponents of the reformers also used the law to fight back. Complaints against the Middlesex justice Ralph Hartley, responsible for convicting over 500 alehouse keepers and tradesmen for Sabbath breaking in the autumn of 1691, resulted in a judicial investigation leading to his expulsion from the Middlesex commission of the peace.[47] Many of Hartley's opponents were his fellow justices, but popular opposition was also important, with the justices concerned that his actions generated hostility to the bench. An investigating committee of magistrates claimed Hartley's method was 'a great oppression upon the people, and tends to the ruin of most victuallers and alehouse keepers, and makes the present government uneasy to them, as appears to us by their frequent and daily complaints'.[48]

Informers and other supporters of the campaign were also subjected to numerous lawsuits, which they claimed were vexatious. Jonathan Easden, for instance, a member of the original Tower Hamlets society and a carpenter, was subjected to a series of prosecutions in 1692–4 for assault,

---

[43] Edinburgh University Library (EUL), Laing Mss., III, 394, f. 503.

[44] LMA, City of London: Sessions, 'City sessions rolls', CLA/047/LJ/03, October 1693, recognizance 20 and unnumbered indictment of Thomas Dias; 'Mansion House charge book', 25 November 1693 and 29 July 1694.

[45] Beattie, *Policing and Punishment*, p. 246. See also *LL*, set, 'James Cooper'.

[46] LMA, City of London: 'Mansion House charge book', 29 July 1693. See also 8 July 1693, and LMA, City of London: 'Lord Mayor's waiting book', vol.xv, CLA/004/01/01/ 015, 15 July 1694.

[47] Shoemaker, *Prosecution and Punishment*, pp. 253–60.

[48] EUL, Laing Mss., III, 394, ff. 221–6.

blackmailing keepers of brothels and their clients, and being a 'barreter', or common troublemaker.[49] In April 1694 he was indicted for the murder of Ann Roberts's unborn child, following her miscarriage during an attempt to arrest her. Roberts and her mistress, a Mrs Young, had abused Easden by calling him 'Perjured Rogue' after he accused Young of being 'an ill Woman, and a Bawd'. At his trial, it appeared that the prosecution was malicious: Roberts had not been hurt in the incident, but 'a great deal of malice appeared to be betwixt them, and no positive proof was [presented] against him as to the matter of Fact'.[50] Although Easden was acquitted, evidence of his extortionate treatment of bawds and prostitutes was presented to the House of Commons in the following year.[51]

Even when prosecutions against informers were unsuccessful, defending them was costly. In 1692 parish officers from St Leonard Shoreditch spent £24 defending a lawsuit brought in the Court of Common Pleas by Frances Hinton alias West, 'a person of very lewd life and conversation' accused of running a brothel. Although Hinton lost the case, the officers could not secure their expenses as Hinton was 'a very poore woman'.[52] They were still trying to recover their costs four years later. Arguably the threat of such costly prosecutions contributed to the reformers' tactical shift in 1694 towards prosecuting prostitutes rather than brothel keepers. Not only was prosecution by commitment to a house of correction cheaper, but prostitutes were less likely to be able to afford vexatious counter prosecutions.[53]

Informers were also forced to shift their tactics. To prevent them from being subjected to physical harm, counter prosecutions or loss of business, the reformers advised informers not to act in their own neighbourhoods, and the justices who supported them agreed to protect their anonymity wherever possible.[54] As Dabhoiwala has argued, by transforming neighbourhood policing into a mercenary and impersonal activity, these practices 'helped accelerate the professionalization of policing'.[55] They also reduced the number of informers willing to act and further distanced them from their communities. An important aspect of this transformation was the participation of some of the most active

[49] LL, set, 'Jonathan Easden'.
[50] LL, Old Bailey Proceedings, 18 April 1694 (t16940418-27).
[51] Dabhoiwala, 'Sex and societies', 305–6.
[52] LL, Middlesex Sessions: 'Sessions papers', December 1696 (LMSMPS500460185).
[53] LMA, Middlesex Sessions: 'Sessions books', MJ/SBB/500, October 1692, pp. 50–1; Shoemaker, Prosecution and Punishment, p. 246. Some prostitutes, however, successfully challenged their commitments.
[54] EUL, Laing Mss, III, 394, ff. 329–58, 415–20; [Edward] Fowler, A Vindication of a Late Undertaking of Certain Gentlemen (1692), p. 12.
[55] Dabhoiwala, 'Sex and societies', 306–7.

informers in other aspects of policing for a reward, such as apprehending coiners and acting as thief-takers, activities that undoubtedly served to exacerbate popular hostility against them. Jenkins, Rewse and Cooper all added thief-taking to their activities as informers from at least 1693.

These changes in tactics ensured the continuing survival of the reformation of manners campaign beyond the early 1690s; however, by making the reformers appear mercenary and act anonymously, they led to increased popular hostility. Despite claims of success (in 1698 Josiah Woodward wrote that the reformers 'had so far succeeded, that the impudence of lewd women, and the blasphemies of licentious tongues are manifestly abated in our streets'), rates of recidivism were high, particularly for those accused of being 'disorderly persons'.[56] Elizabeth Bird, for instance, was brought before the court of governors at Bridewell six times between June 1693 and December 1694 accused of a range of street-walking offences.[57] (There are several additional charges in these years recorded against women with the same name involving petty theft that may refer to the same woman.) On 24 November 1693, Bird and two other women were committed by the Lord Mayor to Bridewell on the oaths of Jenkins and Rewse for being nightwalkers and pickpockets and 'having been several times in Bridewell and other gaoles [and] known to be such persons', highlighting just how ineffective such prosecutions and punishments were.[58] Jane Glover and Elizabeth Prince had similar records of repeated arrests for prostitution and theft in the early 1690s.[59] When Prince appeared before the Bridewell Court of Governors on 3 November 1693 charged with an 'act of lewdness', Jenkins affirmed that 'Prince was but this very last week bailed out of Bridewell for being a nightwalker and endeavouring to have picked up him the said James Jenkins' – a singularly inadvisable act.[60] The reformers' annual 'blacklists' of offenders published between 1699 and 1707 included the number of offences charged in each year against each name; between 6 and 35 per cent of the offenders on each list had been charged more than once.[61]

[56] Josiah Woodward, *An Account of the Rise and Progress of the Religious Societies in the City of London, etc. and of the Endeavours for Reformation of Manners* (2nd edn, 1698), p. 86.
[57] *LL*, set, 'Elizabeth Bird'.
[58] *LL*, Bridewell Royal Hospital: Minutes of the Court of Governors, 6 January 1689–8 August 1695 (BBBRMG202010333).
[59] *LL*, set, 'Jane Glover'; and set, 'Elizabeth Prince'.
[60] *LL*, Bridewell Royal Hospital: Minutes of the Court of Governors, 6 January 1689–8 August 1695 (BBBRMG202010327).
[61] *A Sixth Black List of Names or Reputed Names of Eight Hundred and Forty Three Leud and Scandalous Persons, who, By the Endeavours of a Society for Promoting a Reformation of Manners in the City of London, and Suburbs thereof, have been Legally Prosecuted and Convicted* (1700).

The social crisis of the late 1690s injected new life into an increasingly unpopular campaign, and drove further developments in the societies' approach to law enforcement. But by then plebeian (and other) opposition to the reformers had achieved marked success in narrowing the range of offences prosecuted and limiting the number of people who were willing to act in the controversial role of an informer.

Reconfiguring poor relief

During these same years, when the reformation of manners campaign became an arena of conflict between 'disorderly' London and a subset of its more settled inhabitants, the nature of parish relief for the 'deserving poor' was also changing. The scope of entitlement to poor relief expanded, while the system for its distribution evolved significantly. War, high food prices, the recoinage and demobilisation all contributed to growing pauper demands on the parishes of London, which in turn helped drive innovation. In part, this evolution took much the same form of individual and magisterial initiatives as had the reformation of manners. In early December 1688, for instance, a group of concerned citizens, including Thomas Firmin and Sir Robert Clayton, organised a voluntary house-to-house collection in aid of the poor, to which William III gave both his support and money – donating initially £2,000 in 1688, and later £1,000 a year throughout the 1690s to what became known as the *King's Letter* fund. Yet because this money was administered by the Lord Mayor and Common Council, and restricted to City parishes, unlike the reformation of manners, it helped to increase the power of the City authorities over relief at the expense of the parishes or ad hoc groups of activists, while doing nothing for the Middlesex parishes.[62]

The most significant innovations in the system of relief followed from national legislation that redefined the notion of 'settlement'. Although inherent in the Old Poor Law and system of vagrant removal, the legal concept of 'settlement' was only clearly laid out in 1692, while the technology of 'certificating' that settlement was not created until 1697. In combination with the new physical marker of a 'badge', this legislation helped secure the settled poor's 'right to relief', or 'entitle[ment]', in the language of the House of Lords, against the authority of parish officers, while explicitly excluding a large body of migrant poor from the limited safety net provided by parochial care.[63] This legislation also changed the

---

[62] Macfarlane, 'Social policy and the poor', p. 259.
[63] PP, *Journals of the House of Lords*, 7 March 1697/8, p. 227 (parlipapers.chadwyck.co.uk, 30 Dec. 2013).

system of oversight, effectively excluding the local minister from much of the administration of poor relief, expanding the role of justices and reinforcing quarter sessions as a court of appeal for both paupers and parish officers. In the City of London, this was in turn furthered by the creation of a City-wide Corporation of the Poor, or London Workhouse in 1698.

The notion that every individual had a settlement, that they had a parish and community that owed them care and to which they owed allegiance, was implicit in the Old Poor Laws passed in the late sixteenth century and codified in 1601, and explicit in the system of vagrancy removal that evolved throughout the sixteenth and seventeenth centuries. But for paupers seeking relief during the seventeenth century, decisions about settlement and support 'ultimately turned on the discretion of parish officers', in the words of Steve Hindle, forcing paupers and migrants to negotiate from a position of weakness.[64] This began to change following the Restoration with the passage, in 1662, of a statute 'for the better Releife of the Poore of this Kingdom', widely, if inaccurately, referred to as the *Act of Settlement*.[65] This Act specified that a settlement could be gained through birth, apprenticeship or service and that in cases of dispute, an appeal could be made to a justice of the peace. In all cases, however, the onus of notifying the parish in writing of one's intention to establish a settlement lay with the individual migrant and carried the risk of immediate removal from the parish should the request be refused. This ensured that only a minority of people would bother to establish a legal settlement under the auspices of the 1662 Act.

The same Act also provided for basic 'certificates', under the hand of a minister, for those seeking work during the harvest. However, judging by the small number of examinations, appeals and certificates that survive in the archives for the three decades after 1662, it was only after 1692, with the passage of a supplementary *Act for the better Explanation and supplying the Defects of the former Laws for the Settlement of the Poor*, that a fully functioning system of poor law settlement and appeal was created.[66] After 1692 the poor were only required to give notification in writing of their intention to settle in a parish if they did not fall into one of the many categories of entitlement. So from this date, settlement on the basis of apprenticeship, service for a year, paying parish taxes or serving as a

---

[64] Hindle, *On the Parish?*, p. 310.
[65] 14 Charles II c. 12 (www.british.history.ac.uk, 30 Dec. 2013).
[66] 3 & 4 William and Mary c. 11 (www.british.history.ac.uk, 30 Dec. 2013). See also James Stephen Taylor, 'The impact of pauper settlement, 1691–1834', *Past & Present*, 73 (1976), 42–74.

parish officer became automatic, requiring no further action on the part of the individual. This effectively ensured that the existence of a legal settlement became the norm, rather than the exception, and inadvertently created the circumstances that would generate large numbers of retrospective 'settlement examinations'. The 1692 Act made universal what had previously been a legal status secured by only a minority of the migratory poor; it also transformed it from something the poor had to actively establish into one which the authorities needed to disprove.

The 1692 Act was a part of the early 1690s reformation of policy that emerged from the Revolution of 1688.[67] Passed in response to the increasing cost of relief, it shifted the balance of power between parish officers, parishioners and justices of the peace in favour of the justices, and more indirectly, the poor. From 1692 overseers and churchwardens were obliged to keep a register of the poor for the scrutiny of both ratepayers and justices, and to review the list of paupers receiving relief at each Easter meeting of the vestry when the parish accounts were normally audited by a justice. The Act also vested sweeping powers of removal by warrant in the hands of any two justices sitting in petty sessions; it furthermore required, on pain of substantial fines, that churchwardens accept the justices' adjudications, providing only that any individual (including paupers) who found themselves 'aggrieved' by the workings of the Act could 'appeal to the next General Quarter Sessions'.[68]

A measure of the Act's impact on the relationship between justices, parish officers and the poor can be found in the growing number of appeals filed with the City of London sessions against orders for relief and removal issued by the justices. Removals, certificates and appeals can be found prior to 1692 but were relatively uncommon. In the City, in the two full years prior to the passage of the Act, there were five appeals seeking to overturn an order for relief or removal (and a further six appeals relating to rating issues). However, in the two full years after the passage of the Act (1693–4), this number rose to over forty appeals against orders for removal and relief, and a further thirteen petitions from suburban parishes for support in relieving the poor.[69]

The tensions created by this legislation are illustrated in the case of Henry Bates, his wife Mary and their two children.[70] In the early 1680s,

---

[67] It was engrossed on 27 January 1691/2. *PP, Journals of the House of Commons*, 26 January 1691/2 (parlipapers.chadwyck.co.uk, 30 Dec. 2013).

[68] 3 & 4 William and Mary c. 11, viii (www.british.history.ac.uk, 30 Dec. 2013).

[69] See *LL*, City of London Sessions: Sessions Papers, 10 January 1690 – 23 December 1694 (LMSLPS150010002 to LMSLPS150050194). The winter of 1693–4 was also marked by historically high bread prices.

[70] *LL*, set, 'Henry Bates'.

Bates had been a successful grocer, renting a shop worth '20£ per annum' in St Botolph Bishopsgate, but by the winter of 1688 he was living in St Mary Woolchurch and seeking a new occupation. He approached the minister for help in securing admission to the 'Society of Porters', as a tacklehouse or ticket porter.[71] In what appears to have been a relatively casual act that he no doubt later regretted, Andrew Crisp, the incumbent, confirmed that Bates 'an Inhabitant of our said p[ar]ish, hath Demeaned himself Honestly & Cively amongst his neighbours ... [and was] Industrious And Willing to worke for his liveing'.[72] Before 1692 a certificate under the hand of the minister was sufficient to establish a settlement, but afterwards the rules became more complex. In the autumn of 1692, Bates, now employed as a ticket porter, was living in St George Botolph Lane with his family when he found himself in need of relief and applied to the parish. However, taking advantage of the change in the law, St George sought to remove him 'according to the late Act of Parliament', claiming that he had settled in the parish without formal written notification to the minister.[73]

The churchwardens approached two justices who examined Bates on oath, issued a warrant removing him to a third parish, St Botolph Billingsgate, where Bates had lived prior to 1682, and ordered that parish to provide for him and his family. Billingsgate, in turn, appealed later the same month against the warrant, suggesting that Bates's true settlement lay in St Botolph Bishopsgate.[74] Two counter appeals were lodged, and Mary, Henry's wife, was examined on oath about the level of taxes the couple had paid in St George Botolph Lane.[75] It was only after five months of toing and froing and the submission of at least nine separate warrants, petitions and appeals that the matter was settled by the Lord Mayor and aldermen sitting in sessions, who firmly laid the responsibility for Henry and Mary Bates and their children on the parish of St Mary Woolchurch on the basis of the 1688 appeal to the Society of Porters. That Bates could produce that written appeal gave him a powerful card to play in a newly bureaucratic system of warrants and complex

[71] Walter M. Stern, *The Porters of London* (London: Longman, 1960), pp. 13–14.
[72] *LL*, City of London Sessions: Sessions Papers, 8 December 1692 – 28 November 1693 (LMSLPS150040208).
[73] *LL*, City of London Sessions: Sessions Papers, 13 March 1691 – 14 December 1692 (LMSLPS150030173).
[74] *LL*, City of London Sessions: Sessions Papers, 13 March 1691 – 14 December 1692 (LMSLPS150030174).
[75] *LL*, City of London Sessions: Sessions Papers, 8 December 1692 – 28 November 1693 (LMSLPS150040205).

settlement rules. The churchwardens of St Mary Woolchurch could only complain that the 'Certificate was obteyned by Surprise'.[76]

We cannot know how Henry and Mary experienced this process, though it is clear that all of this legal activity was generated by their simple and apparently compelling request for relief. However, we do know that Henry at least was certainly not cowed by it. In the early summer of 1693 he was committed to Bridewell for: 'being very Trouble some to the parishioners of the parish where he dwells and being very abusive to the Churchwardens'.[77] The 1692 Poor Law Act was not passed in direct response to pressure from the poor. European examples and the perception that overseers and churchwardens were wasting parish funds, leading to rising levels of parish expenditure, were more powerful motives in framing this legislation. Neverthless, in clipping the wings of parish officers and extending and reinforcing the direct involvement of justices in the oversight of poor relief and the allocation of casual payments, the poor were given a new avenue of complaint and claim. Thirty years later, the Act was explicitly identified as having led to:

many persons ...[applying] to some justices of the peace, without the knowledge of any officers of the parish, [who] thereby, upon untrue suggestions, and sometimes upon false or frivolous pretences, have obtained relief.[78]

It had, therefore, driven up the cost of providing for the poor.

This relationship was in its turn modified by a further Act passed five years later in 1697: 'for Supplying some Defects in the Laws for the Relief of the Poor of this Kingdom'.[79] This Act regularised the form and status of settlement certificates, mandated the badging of the parish poor and further extended the role of justices and quarter sessions in managing the system. Following a formal examination, from 1697 a settlement certificate could be issued under the hands of two parish officers, two credible witnesses and two local justices (but not the minister). The certificates and associated examinations became the central documents of identity for half the English population. In the process this Act created a new documentation of belonging that in the words reproduced on thousands of pre-printed certificates 'owned and acknowledged [the person named] ...to be ... Inhabitants legally settled in the Parish'.

---

[76] *LL*, City of London Sessions: Sessions Papers, 8 December 1692 – 28 November 1693 (LMSLPS150040207).
[77] *LL*, Bridewell Royal Hospital: Minutes of the Court of Governors, 6 January 1689 – 8 August 1695 (BBBRMG202010285).
[78] 9 George I c. 7 (www.workhouses.org.uk, 30 Dec. 2013).
[79] 8 & 9 William III c. 30.

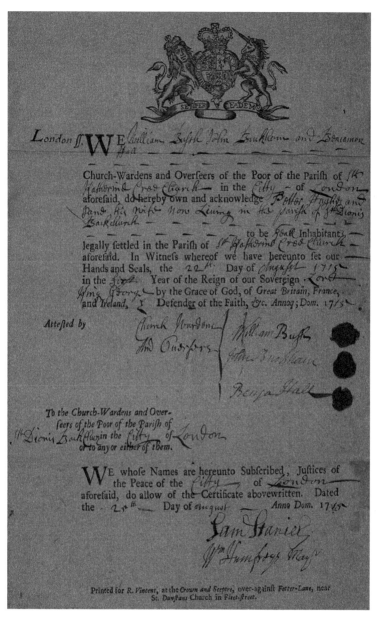

Figure 2.4 Printed settlement certificate filled out on behalf of Petter and Jane Hughes, 22 August 1715. *LL*, St Dionis Backchurch Parish: Churchwardens Vouchers/Receipts, 28 March 1683 – 15 October 1729 (GLDBPP307010160).

Despite the expansion of judicial oversight, the new system had real advantages for the London parishes in which so many immigrants lived. If any migrant whose settlement was confirmed by certificate became ill or unemployed and applied for relief, the cost of maintaining and removing them could now be charged to the parish of settlement. At the same time, it was almost always in the interest of the parish providing the certificate (even at the normal cost of 2s. to 3s. 6d.) to do so in the hope that individuals and their families could either maintain themselves elsewhere without parish support, or establish an alternative settlement through serving in a parish office, or renting a tenement worth £10 per year.[80]

For the poor, the legal and bureaucratic security implied in the certificates was new and helped to shield them from both the overwhelming 'discretion of parish officers' and often the process of removal and appeal experienced by paupers such as Henry Bates.[81] Certificates were explicitly intended as an aid to economic migration. In the words of the Act, they would allow the poor to reside where 'their labour is wanted'. However, in the process of confirming a 'legal settlement', they also gave the migratory poor a new kind of evidence of their status that, short of the certificate itself being proven a forgery or legally defective on a technicality, was beyond challenge by either parish officers or a justice.[82] Consequently, certificates placed a gentle upward pressure on levels of relief. As some alms and expenses could now be charged to a distant parish, there was less incentive for parish officers to stint and cavil at the costs. But most of all certificates gave paupers a newly secure position from which to negotiate with the parish. When Mary Tite petitioned the vestry of St Clement Danes for thirty shillings in order to set herself up as a market trader in 1702, she rested her claim on the fact, 'that she had gained a Certificate of her being an Inhabitant Legally settled'.[83]

This is not to suggest that huge numbers of certificates were actually produced. Normally initiated at the request of the officers of a migrant's new parish, procuring a certificate required the active collaboration of both the poor and the officers of the original parish of settlement. To create a legally binding document, six signatures had to be collected

---

[80] A further 'Act for explaining an Act made the last Session' was passed hurriedly in the spring of 1697–8, making explicit the circumstances in which certificate holders could establish a new settlement. 9 William III c. 11.

[81] Hindle, *On the Parish?*, p. 310.

[82] The issue of whether having a certificate precluded gaining a settlement through other means, and the status of the children and grandchildren of certificate holders, ensured that appeals and legal challenges would continue. For the role of appeals and precedent in the evolution of the law of settlement, see Carolyn Steedman, 'Lord Mansfield's women', *Past & Present*, 176 (2002), 105–43.

[83] LL, St Clement Danes Parish: Minutes of Parish Vestries, 22 January 1700 – 1 May 1709 (WCCDMV362170138).

(costly both in time and in clerk's fees), and the resulting certificate was valid only in relation to a single move to a named parish. If an individual wanted to move again a further certificate and more signatures were required. As a result, certificates were probably reserved primarily for migrants moving to an established employment rather than those simply seeking work. But the legal character of 'certificates' effectively embedded the status of being 'settled' more firmly within the system of parochial poor relief. Within ten years of the passage of the Act, when the parish of St Clement Danes created a register of the certificates they had both issued and received in the four years between 1703 and 1707, they could identify twenty-four documents evidencing the settlement status of eighty-four individuals, including seventeen families.[84] It is impossible to determine precisely what percentage of the parish poor based their claims on the existence of a certificate, but with a population at this date in the region of 11,000, St Clement Danes probably relieved between 300 and 500 individuals on a regular basis, making the certificate poor a relatively rare, but significant (and administratively expensive), part of the system.

The same Act also required that the parish poor display a badge with the initials of the parish and 'a large Roman P', in red or blue cloth, prominently on their outer clothing. Asking the poor to wear a badge was not new in 1697. Examples of the practice can be traced back to medieval precedent, and three years before the Act was passed the Middlesex sessions ordered the 'Poor to Wear Badges'.[85] Individual parishes, such as St Botolph Aldgate, had also pursued a policy of badging since at least 1691.[86] Nevertheless badges became much more common from 1697.[87]

In part, as Steve Hindle has argued, the requirement to wear a badge was a self-conscious attempt to stigmatise the parish poor and to discourage applications for relief. But like certificates, badges also formed an important new claim to belonging that effectively both labelled individuals as 'settled' and licensed them to beg, particularly from door to door. The relevant clause in the Act obliging the poor to display a badge suggests that they would be a means of preventing money being 'misapplied & consumed by the idle, sturdy and disorderly beggars', and

[84] LL, St Clement Danes Parish: Register of Pauper Settlement and Bastardy Examinations, 8 June 1703 – 14 June 1707 (WCCDRD366000201-WCCDRD366000213).
[85] LL, Middlesex Sessions: Sessions Papers, 14 October 1693 (LMSMPS500770013).
[86] LL, St Botolph Aldgate Parish: Churchwardens and Overseers of the Poor Account Books, 1689–1715 (GLBAAC100000103).
[87] In the most comprehensive recent analysis of badging in an English context, Steve Hindle recognises the ambiguity of badges as symbols, and their multivalent meanings for both elite commentators and parish officers, but substantially downplays their strategic value to the poor as a technology of identity: Steve Hindle, 'Dependency, shame and belonging: badging the deserving poor, c. 1550–1750', Cultural & Social History, 1:1 (2004), 6–35.

ensuring that it was given to 'such as are as well impotent as poor'.[88] The implication is that the parish badge would reassure uncertain almsgivers that the pauper before them was a deserving beggar, rather than an idle and disorderly one and, moreover, that any casual observer could readily judge whether parish officers were relieving deserving, settled parishioners or wasting ratepayers' money on the idle and unsettled. Parish officers did not need badges to identify their poor. They had registers and accounts listing pensioners and collectioners; instead, badges were designed for the benefit of a wider public.

One measure of the authority of badges, and their power to confer legitimacy on the begging poor, is the extent to which they rapidly formed objects of counterfeit and fraud. Within months of the passage of the Act, Charles Tompkins was committed to Bridewell charged with 'prtending. to be a Pensionr. in a parish of this Citty wth a False Badge in his pocket'.[89] Two years later, Phenix Wilkinson was charged 'For Cheating the parish of St James Dukes Place' when she applied for a badge for a dead relative.[90] The settlement status implied by a badge was also recognised by parishes and justices. Badges were carefully restricted to the settled poor, and refusal to wear one was frequently used as a pretext for denying relief. At St Dionis Backchurch, badges were limited to 'pentioners', and the parish actively avoided supplying a badge to casual and occasional paupers.[91] In 1708 the vestry resolved that William Adams should be granted a pension of 2 shillings a week, but was 'excused some time from wearing the Badge to try what Application he will make for Reliefe elsewhere'.[92] Justices also recognised the implication of settlement conferred by wearing a parish badge. In 1704 St Clement Danes had little choice but to provide Elizabeth Parke with relief in response to a warrant under the hands of two justices which established her settlement on the grounds that she 'wore the parish badge for many yrs past'.[93]

Of course, the flip side of this new technology of identity was that some people would find themselves labelled in ways that they did not welcome.

[88] 8 & 9 William III c. 30.
[89] LL, Bridewell Royal Hospital: Minutes of the Court of Governors, 23 August 1695 – 2 May 1701 (BBBRMG202020206).
[90] LL, Bridewell Royal Hospital: Minutes of the Court of Governors, 23 August 1695 – 2 May 1701 (BBBRMG202020429).
[91] LL, St Dionis Backchurch Parish: Churchwardens and Overseers of the Poor Account Books, 1689–1720 (GLDBAC300000444).
[92] LL, St Dionis Backchurch Parish: Minutes of Parish Vestries, 7 January 1690 – 19 December 1711 (GLDBMV305000332).
[93] LL, St Clement Danes Parish: Register of Pauper Settlement and Bastardy Examinations, 8 June 1703 – 14 June 1707 (WCCDRD366000086).

Certainly, this must have been how Joanne Palmer felt in 1706, at the age
of 81, when, she appealed against

> the parish of St. Giles fields in wch. parish she has lived fifty years, without being
> the least [cost] or charge to the said parish till age [and in]firmity put her under a
> necessity of ma[king] application thereunto . . .

and asked the justices at Hicks Hall to order 'a pention without a
badge'.[94]

For at least the first two and a half decades after the passage of the
1697 Act, until the creation of parish workhouses throughout London,
with their residential character and distinctive pauper clothing which
made badges largely redundant, most settled paupers appear to have
worn them. A measure of their commonality can be found in the poor
law accounts of St Botolph Aldgate. The parish had a long tradition of
badging the poor even before the passage of the Act, but in July
1699 the accounts record the purchase of '15 dozen Badges' which
lasted until April 1701 when they ordered 'Seven Dozen' more.[95] In
the next twelve years, at least a further 280 badges were purchased,
bringing the total to over 500 for a pauper population of no more
than this.[96]

Together the Poor Law Acts of 1692 and 1697 effectively re-ordered
the relationship between the parish, the poor and the justices, and
worked to bring the vast majority of both the settled and the migratory
poor, including able-bodied adults, more firmly within the system of
parish relief. They reinforced the triangular relationship between overseers, paupers and justices, ensuring that justices were given greater
authority to both oversee the workings of the parishes and act as a court
of appeal against the 'discretion' of parish officers. At the same time, they
empowered the poor, creating a new kind of agency. Certificates allowed
unemployed but able-bodied men and women to establish their 'legal
settlement' as an insurance against old age and infirmity. A group of
economic migrants who through most of the seventeenth century were in
constant danger of being labelled and punished as vagrants were given
the opportunity to prove their *bone fides* with a certificate. In a similar way
badges effectively regulated the role of begging by providing a stamp of

[94] *LL*, Middlesex Sessions: Sessions Papers, July 1706 (LMSMPS506880038).
[95] *LL*, St Botolph Aldgate Parish: Churchwardens and Overseers of the Poor Account
Books, 1689–1715 (GLBAAC100000253 and GLBAAC100000314).
[96] The parish ordered a further 17s. 6d. worth in July 1706; twelve dozen in January 1712
and a further six dozen in June 1713. *LL*, St Botolph Aldgate Parish: Churchwardens
and Overseers of the Poor Account Books, 1689–1715 (GLBAAC100000253,
GLBAAC100000331, GLBAAC100000423 and GLBAAC100000455).

legitimacy to the pleas of established pensioners.[97] From 1697 the charitable and sympathetic could rely on a parish badge to make the distinction between impotent and poor beggars and their 'disorderly' brethren.

For the English, and particularly London, poor, these developments created a comprehensive and flexible system that was theoretically universal in scope. Nevertheless, a vagrant residuum remained that would never fit easily in to a system largely built on the assumption that the poor should stay put. Just as a new ecology of identity evolved, national and city-wide schemes to regulate vagrancy, and punish, employ and educate the disorderly poor were created.

The London Workhouse and the Vagrant Costs Act

The aspiration to create a workhouse and house of correction for the whole City of London was not new in the 1690s. At regular intervals throughout the sixteenth and seventeenth centuries, both the City and the Middlesex bench had attempted to create employment schemes or residential workhouses to supersede parish relief as solutions to the Janus-faced problems of rising poverty and disorder.[98] However, many contemporaries saw the re-establishment of the London Workhouse in 1698 as a facet of the wider reformation of manners, alongside the revitalisation of the reforming societies.[99] If the societies were dedicated to reforming the poor through punishment, the London Workhouse was designed to achieve the same end by 'inuring the poor to labour' and training up their children to a religious and industrious life.

The City of London initially hoped that specific provision for the creation of a Corporation of the Poor covering the whole area within the Bills of Mortality would be included in national legislation.[100]

---

[97] For an analysis of the geography of begging in eighteenth-century London, see Tim Hitchcock, 'Locating beggars on the streets of eighteenth-century London', in Kim Kippen and Lori Woods, eds., *Worth and Repute: Valuing Gender in Late Medieval and Early Modern Europe* (Toronto: Centre for Reformation and Renaissance Studies, 2011), pp. 73–92.

[98] See Paul Slack, 'Hospitals, workhouses and the relief of the poor in early-modern London', in Andrew Cunningham and Ole Peter Grell, eds., *Health Care and Poor Relief in Protestant Europe 1500–1700* (London: Routledge, 1997), pp. 234–51; Paul Slack, *From Reformation to Improvement: Public Welfare in Early Modern England* (Oxford: Clarendon Press, 1999), pp. 90, 101; and Joanna Innes, 'Prisons for the poor: English bridewells, 1555–1800', in F. Snyder and D. Hay, eds., *Labour, Law and Crime: An Historical Perspective* (London: Tavistock, 1987), pp. 42–122.

[99] Josiah Woodward, *The Duty of Compassion to the Souls of Others* (1697), p. xii. See also Woodward, *Sodom's Vices* (1700), pp. 14–15.

[100] This initiative followed the example of the Corporation established at Bristol in 1696. See Mary Fissell, *Patients, Power and the Poor in Eighteenth-Century Bristol* (Cambridge University Press, 1991), ch. 4.

However, when this failed, the Lord Mayor, Sir Humphrey Edwin, simply revived Samuel Hartlib's mid-century workhouse on the authority of a 45-year-old Act. The City initially sought to create a non-residential employment scheme, and in the autumn of 1698 committed over £5,000 to the project. Two 'undertakers' were hired and a six-week course of training in spinning wool was run for parish children. The expectation was that any 'willing industrious & capeable person may earn from two shillings to four shillings per weeke & some five or six shillings per weeke'.[101] Over 400 people, children but also women, were trained to spin wool from home.[102]

Like the 1692 and 1697 parliamentary Acts, this initiative effectively shifted power away from the churchwardens and overseers of the poor to the City authorities. The response from the parishes was immediate: many refused to collect the money due to the new Corporation. More difficult, however, was the attitude of parish officers to the employment itself. They simply continued to pay regular pensions, while refusing to inspect or oversee the work as the Corporation expected.[103] As a result the employment scheme collapsed within months and the City was forced to turn instead to establishing a residential workhouse, leasing a house in Half-Moon Alley off Bishopsgate Street in August 1699.

In part, as Stephen Macfarlane has argued, opposition to the Corporation was founded in politics, with the traditionally tory parishes of the City set against a new whig establishment, but it was also driven by a belief that increasing the powers of the Corporation would, in the words of a petition from a group of parish officers from Farringdon Ward Without, create a 'new magistracy... making them masters of the Liberty of the People'. Yet the workhouse enhanced the agency of the poor. The petitioners complained that by exercising the powers of a justice of the peace, the Corporation would

impower ... the President &c. on complaint (of too small an Allowance) made by any poor Person, to summons the Church-Wardens, Overseers, and Collectors to appear before them, and to administer Oaths, and on Examination to order such weekly Allowance to the Person complaining.

In the eyes of the parish officers, the Corporation was being authorised to put the decision over whom to relieve in the hands of 'Strangers to the Poor', thus empowering the poor, 'those who are always craving and

---

[101] Quoted in Macfarlane, 'Social policy and the poor', p. 262.
[102] Although we do not know the gender and age breakdown of the paupers involved in this scheme, the spinning was specifically chosen as 'such work as women & Children in the Contrey use to do'. Quoted in Macfarlane, 'Social policy and the poor', p. 262.
[103] Macfarlane, 'Social policy and the poor', p. 262.

never satisfied', at the expense of the officers, who were 'the best Judges of the Necessities of their Poor'.[104]

The workhouse opened in 1699 and was divided, like Bridewell, between a 'keeper's side' or house of correction, which could accommodate, set to labour and physically punish about fifty people (both adults and children) at any one time, and a 'steward's side', which functioned as a residential workhouse and industrial school catering for poor children over the age of seven. The steward's side charged 12 pence per week for each pauper to parishes and individual benefactors, effectively establishing a de facto rate for parish pensions in the City. There was no question of taking all the parish poor into the workhouse, and there was no 'workhouse test'. Who would be sent to the house and who would remain at home on a pension was negotiated between the poor and the parish. However, the remarkable aspect of the house is that beside the children of the parish poor, it also made room for the vagrant children of the 'Black Guard' of homeless orphans who pilfered from the quays and slept rough on the streets and in the annealing yards of the glass houses of the east end. Although these children were initially taken up as 'vagrants', most were then transferred to the steward's side, turning the London Workhouse into a refuge for children who had been singularly failed by the parish authorities. In 1703 the annual report claimed that 427 children had been maintained in the preceding year, who, when they reached their early teens, would be either sent back to their parishes to be apprenticed or, if they were from the unsettled 'Black Guard', apprenticed directly from the house, primarily into maritime service, the textile trades or domestic service.[105]

By parish standards the conditions in the workhouse were good, and the system actually seems to have worked, or at least, the grand jury for the City thought so:

Wee do find to our Great Satisfaction, none of those Young Criminals which were formerly used to be brought before Us, and ... Wee are very Sensible, that this is in a great Measure, if not intirely Owing to the Workhouse Erected in this City, which hath received therein, All those poor, and Vagrant Children, which lay up and down in the Streets of this City (Commonly called by the Name of the Black Guard) and there hath Educated Imployed, and fitted for Trades and other Imployments.[106]

[104] *Reasons Humbly Offered to this Honourable House why a Bill Pretended to Give Further Powers to the Corporation for Setting the Poor of the City of London... Should Not Pass* (n.d.,? 1700).
[105] Macfarlane, 'Social policy and the poor', p. 264.
[106] *LL*, City of London Sessions: Sessions Papers, 10 August 1705 – 20 November 1706 (LMSLPS150170027).

The Corporation, however, while apparently popular with the poor, continued to encounter significant opposition from the parishes, partly for reasons of cost, but also owing to the shift of authority inherent in centralising relief. By 1708 several parishes were questioning the legal basis of the Corporation, and in 1712 it was forced to change its by-laws and drastically reduce its workhouse function in relation to the parish poor. It continued to thrive as a house of correction and survived into the nineteenth century, but from 1713 it restricted the number of parish children taken in to the steward's side and concentrated on educating and boarding children sponsored by individual benefactors at a cost of £50 for City children, and £70 for children from elsewhere.[107]

However, for several years the parish officers had once again been sidelined, and the poor were given a new entitlement. The existence of the Corporation, and its emphasis on reclaiming vagrant children, also helped to elide the boundary between criminal vagrancy and settled poverty. In a different way, by expanding the reach of the vagrancy legislation, the Vagrancy Costs Act, 'An Act for the more effectual Punishment of Vagrants and sending them whither by Law they ought to be sent', which followed sharp on the heels of the foundation of the Corporation, muddied this same distinction in Middlesex.[108] This statute, applicable nationally, transferred the financing of the removal of vagrants from constables and the parish rates to the county rates, overseen by the county bench. In the City, with its system of wards and Common Council, the Act had little effect, but in Middlesex it gave new powers to the magistrates.

Until 1700 Middlesex parish constables retained the central role in the policing of vagrancy, arresting pretty much whomever they felt could be countenanced within the long and shaggy list of bear wards, players of interludes and diverse other offences that legally defined 'vagrancy'. For the most part, almost anyone unable to 'give a good account' of themselves to a constable could be considered a vagrant. By law, on arrest vagrants were meant to be taken to the nearest justice who could order that they be 'stripped to the waste and whipt until bloody', prior to being confined at hard labour in the nearest house of correction and then returned to the parish constable to be removed parish by parish, constable by constable, to their place of settlement.

---

[107] Macfarlane, 'Social policy and the poor', pp. 268–9. For evidence of the continuing role of the 'keeper's side' as a house of correction, see Faramerz Dabhoiwala, 'Summary justice in early-modern London', *English Historical Review*, 121:492 (2006), 803–5.
[108] 11 William III c. 18 (www.british.history.ac.uk, 30 Dec. 2013).

In the City the policing of vagrancy fell to the officers of Bridewell and the London Workhouse, with the assistance of constables and beadles, who were ward rather than parish officers. However, in Middlesex the constables were parish officers and their role was central. Until 1700 they were responsible for raising their own rate, or relied on general parish rates, to repay themselves for the expense of punishing and removing vagrants. The Act of 1699 changed all this. By shifting the cost of removal to the county rate, it ensured that constables would henceforth have to both deliver up individual vagrants for examination by a justice (in order to 'certificate' the relevant expenditure) and produce their accounts at the end of the year. Within months of the Act's passage, printed blanks of vagrant removal orders were being issued, and by 1701 the Middlesex bench had begun to actively audit the accounts of constables.[109] While constables benefited financially from this new arrangement, this was achieved at the expense of surrendering their control over who was to be labelled as a vagrant to the justices. The constables' discretionary power over the unsettled and disorderly poor was substantially undermined.

'Vagrancy' is a poorly defined category that defies analysis. Many people taken up as vagrants were long-term residents with established connections to the community, but who offended against one or another sensibility; others were economic migrants unsuccessfully seeking work in the capital; still others lived off crime and immorality. We cannot determine if more vagrants were actually removed after 1699, though the new system naturally created a larger number of documents. But just as the new system of settlement certificates changed the relationship between overseers and the parish poor, the Vagrant Costs Act limited the power of parish constables. Both vagrants and paupers could now more easily appeal over the heads of local officials – making their ability to present a badge, a certificate or a credible story all the more important.

The reformation of manners renewed

Despite the popular opposition to 'informers', the late 1690s and early 1700s witnessed what Dudley Bahlman termed a 'second great wave of enthusiasm for a reformation of manners', prompted partly by the socio-economic crisis caused by recoinage, bad harvests and demobilisation.[110] Initiatives included the formation of the Society for the Promotion of

---

[109] For an early printed order, see *LL*, Middlesex Sessions: Sessions Papers, 17 May 1701 (LMSMPS500790012).

[110] Bahlman, *Moral Revolution*, p. 24.

Christian Knowledge (SPCK) in 1698 and the related Society for the Propagation of the Gospel in Foreign Parts (SPG) in 1701, which used charity schools, the publication of cheap moralising tracts and the establishment of overseas missions to evangelise on behalf of a newly self-confident Anglican establishment.[111] Yet while the SPCK and the SPG targeted their reforming efforts at the settled, the literate and the very distant, the renewed reformation of manners campaign continued to focus on the disorderly poor at home.

Several new societies were formed; Josiah Woodward claimed in 1698 there were 'now near twenty Societies of various Qualities and Functions, formed in a Subordination and Correspondency with one another and engaged in this Christian Design in and about this City and Suburbs'.[112] New legislation against immorality was introduced in parliament in 1698–9, and although no new laws were passed, the associated 'rush of addresses, speeches, and proclamations by the king and commons' drew attention to the campaign.[113] Concurrently, following the example of the SPCK and often using the same printer, the reformers embarked on a publishing campaign, including sermons, an *Account of the Societies for Reformation of Manners, in London and Westminster, and other Parts of the Kingdom* (by Woodward, the Societies' chief propagandist), which went through five editions between 1699 and 1701, and annual *Black Lists* detailing the names of sexual offenders.[114] Judging by the latter, by 1700 the number of prosecutions by the reformers was more than double those in 1694, the year in which they published their first list.[115] As with the early 1690s, women were their principal target, accounting for 92.6 per cent of named offenders in 1700.[116]

This intensification of the reformers' efforts once again met with substantial opposition, both from the political classes (who ensured defeat of the parliamentary bills) and plebeian Londoners. There were

---

[111] The best modern history of the early years of the SPCK remains Leonard W. Cowie, *Henry Newman: An American in London, 1708–1743* (London: SPCK, 1956).

[112] Woodward, *Account of the Rise and Progress*, p. 83.

[113] Dabhoiwala, 'Sex and societies', 294–5; David Hayton, 'Moral reform and country politics in the late seventeenth-century House of Commons', *Past & Present*, 128 (1990), 58–60.

[114] Joseph Downing acted for both the SPCK and the Societies for the Reformation of Manners. See Joseph Downing, *A New Catalogue of Books and Small Tracts Against Vice and Immorality; and for Promoting the Knowledge & Practice of the Christian Religion...* ([1708]); Isaacs, 'Moral crime, moral reform', p. 152.

[115] Although the list published in 1700 was described as the 'sixth' black list, no lists survive for the years 1695–7.

[116] *A Sixth Black List of Names.*

renewed physical attacks on informers, and complaints that justices of the peace did nothing to stop them. In his sermon to the societies preached on 27 June 1698 at St Mary le Bow, Thomas Jekyll complained that while 'the common people rage and rattle against those that endeavour to reclaim them', the magistrates 'do all that in them lies, to make [prosecution of vice] both troublesome and dangerous, and thereby to beat [informers] off from engaging any further therein'. Informers were 'again beaten, and wounded at the very doors of these magistrates, without protection and redress, and meet with nothing upon complaint but scoffs and jears'.[117]

These complaints were justified. The Middlesex magistracy was sharply divided: while some justices were strong supporters of the campaign, others, owing to legal scruples or concerns to maintain their reputations in their neighbourhoods, rejected the reformers' systematic approach to prosecuting vice and refused to cooperate.[118] However, plebeian Londoners were also active opponents. The reformers were once again subjected to considerable physical abuse, culminating in the murder of two prominent constables associated with the societies; the evidence suggests that these incidents represent the tip of an iceberg of violence committed against them. In 1702 a group of constables were making arrests at May Fair when they were attacked by a mob of about '30 soldiers' with brickbats, and John Cooper, a parish constable of St James Westminster, was stabbed to death. A participant in the riot, Thomas Cook, a prizefighter nicknamed 'the butcher of Gloucester', escaped to Ireland, where, commenting on reformation of manners activities in Dublin, 'he wondered at the people of Ireland to Suffer Such Rogues for that in London they used them like Doges'.[119] Brought back to London, Cook was eventually tried and hanged for the murder. While he continued to deny participation in the killing to the point of his own death on the scaffold, he acknowledged he was 'a sworn Enemy to those who were employ'd in the Reformation of Manners'.[120] Popular sympathy for Cook was manifested in a ballad which reasserted his innocence.[121]

One of the men who had unsuccessfully tried to rescue Cooper from the crowd was John Dent, a constable of St Mary le Strand, who had

---

[117] Thomas Jekyll, *A Sermon Preach'd at St Mary-le-Bow, June 27, 1698. Before the Societies for Reformation of Manners* (1698), pp. iii–iv.

[118] Shoemaker, *Prosecution and Punishment*, p. 258.

[119] LL, Middlesex Sessions: Sessions Papers, July 1703 (LMSMPS500900044). See also LL, set, 'John Cooper'; and set,'Thomas Cook'.

[120] LL, Ordinary of Newgate Prison: Ordinary's Accounts, 11 August 1703 (OA170308110308110001).

[121] *An Excellent New Copy of Verses, Being the Sorrowful Lamentation of Mrs Cooke* (1703).

supported the reformation of manners campaign since 1692.[122] Dent was himself eventually murdered, seven years after Cooper, in March 1709, while arresting 'lewd and disorderly persons'.[123] According to a fellow constable, over the years Dent

> had been aiding and assisting to the apprehending and prosecuting of several thousands of lewd and profligate persons, besides a vast number of Sabbath breakers, profane swearers, and drunkards … he has often been much abused, beaten, mobb'd and wounded; and in a very great danger of his life, in detecting, and bringing to justice, the lewd and disorderly persons …[124]

There is evidence to substantiate this claim. In 1701 Dent, along with John Wilkinson, another constable, brought Philip and Charles Conyer before a justice and accused them of assaulting and beating the two constables and 'endeavouring to raise a mob upon them in execution of their office, searching after lewd and disorderly persons'.[125] (In response, the Conyers filed a counter prosecution, a recognizance, 'no. 203', against both Wilkinson and Dent for assaulting them.) It was the arrest of Anne Dickins, 'a common lewd woman of the town', near Drury Lane in March 1709 which led to Dent's death.[126] Three soldiers attempted to rescue Dickins, claiming she had been illegally arrested and calling the constables 'informing dogs'.[127] They drew their swords and Dent was killed in the mêlée that followed. After his death, Dent remained notorious in plebeian memory: six months later, Mary Thomas, a reputed brothel keeper, was accused of 'drinking or permitting to be drank in a profane and dissolute manner a health to the soul of John Dent in hell'.[128]

The reformers were also undermined by legal challenges, particularly to their practice of arresting women like Dickins for 'lewd and disorderly' conduct. Arrests based on mere suspicion and reputation remained commonplace, but were repeatedly and successfully challenged, sometimes by the prostitutes themselves. In 1701 Elizabeth Claxton, a woman committed by Justice John Perry to New Prison after being 'taken in a disorderly house', was able to obtain legal counsel and have her case

---

[122] Dabhoiwala, 'Sex and societies', 305. See also *LL*, set, 'John Dent'.

[123] *LL*, Middlesex Sessions: Sessions Papers, April 1709 (LMSMPS501050014).

[124] Thomas Bray, *The Good Fight of Faith … Exemplified in a Sermon Preached the 24th of March 1708/9* (1709), p. 15. Dent's reformation of manners activities are substantiated in the registers of prosecutions kept by the reformers, which indicate that he brought several people accused of working on the Sabbath before justices of the peace between 1704 and 1707. See Bodleian Library, Rawlinson Mss., D1399.

[125] LMA, Middlesex Sessions: 'Sessions rolls', MJ/SR/1972, R. 222–223 (Sept. 1701).

[126] *LL*, Middlesex Sessions: Sessions Papers, April 1709 (LMSMPS501050019). See also *LL*, set, 'Anne Dickins'.

[127] *LL*, Middlesex Sessions: Sessions Papers, April 1709 (LMSMPS501050014).

[128] LMA, Middlesex Sessions: 'Sessions rolls', MJ/SR/2136, R. 183 (Sept. 1709).

removed by habeas corpus to the Court of King's Bench, where it was ruled that simply being present in a brothel at a 'seasonable' (not late) hour was insufficient justification for the commitment.[129] As the judges recognised, the fact that she almost certainly *was* a prostitute, as can be seen in her subsequent commitments to Bridewell, was irrelevant. In the trial of the murderers of Dent in 1709, Chief Justice John Holt ruled that the initial arrest of Dickins on the basis that she had previously been convicted of prostitution, and was found in a street where they were known to frequent, was also illegal, thereby giving further succour to the reformers' opponents.[130]

As a result of these setbacks, prosecutions of the offence of 'lewd and disorderly' behaviour declined. Following Cooper's murder, the number of offences reported went down by 28.2 per cent between 1704 and 1707 (figures are missing for the intervening years) to 844, prompting the societies to switch the method of reporting in their accounts to include *all* persons 'prosecuted and proceeded against before the magistrates', rather than just those convicted. As a result, the figure for 1708 appeared much healthier at 1,255. Nevertheless, it continued its decline in 1709, the year of Dent's murder and Holt's judgement, falling by 36.7 per cent to 794. It may be significant that no published accounts of the societies' activities survive for 1710–14.[131]

In part the decline of the societies in the early 1700s can be attributed to the febrile political circumstances of these years and the poisonous religious dispute associated with the Sacheverell Riots.[132] Nevertheless, popular antagonism to the reformers was a key source of their difficulties. Supporters of the reformation of manners would have to await the arrival of the Hanoverian monarchy, and a new whig government, for an opportunity to regain the initiative.

New measures against crime

While the reformation of manners attacked the purported causes of crime, there were also efforts throughout the 1690s and 1700s,

---

[129] *LL*, set, 'Elizabeth Claxton'.

[130] *A Report of all the Cases Determined by Sir John Holt, Knt. from 1688 to 1710* (1738), pp. 406–7, 489–90; Shoemaker, *Prosecution and Punishment*, p. 261.

[131] *The Fourteenth Account of the Progress made in Suppressing Profaneness and Debauchery, by the Societies for Reformation of Manners* (1709).

[132] Craig, 'Reformation of manners', pp. 222, 271–91; Tina Isaacs, 'The Anglican hierarchy and the reformation of manners 1688–1738', *Journal of Ecclesiastical History*, 33 (1982), 401–2; Geoffrey Holmes, 'The Sacheverell riots: the crowd and the church in early eighteenth-century London', *Past & Present*, 72 (1976), 73–5.

particularly from 1697, to combat the apparently rising tide of crime directly through the passage of new legislation, both by encouraging more frequent prosecutions and by increasing the severity of punishments. While these statutes were national in scope, they were prompted by particular concerns about the extent of crime in London, especially the high level of female criminality, and they resulted directly from lobbying by City officials.[133] Some statutes effectively created new capital offences by removing 'benefit of clergy' from some of the most serious crimes (robbery, housebreaking in the daytime, and breaking into shops and warehouses and stealing goods to the value of five shillings), and from crimes that were thought to be increasing in London (shoplifting and theft from lodgings). There was also an attempt to encourage prosecutions of women by, paradoxically, awarding them benefit of clergy on the same terms as men (without a literacy test). Owing to concern that hanging women was discouraging victims from prosecuting, it was hoped this change would result in more women being tried. This statute also deemed those who received stolen goods (who were often women) accessories to a felony, meaning that they could be charged with a felony if the principal was convicted.[134]

The 1699 shoplifting statute, which was in part the result of pressure from London shopkeepers, was aimed specifically at the large number of female thieves in the capital. Almost half (23 of 48) of the defendants charged with shoplifting in the *Old Bailey Proceedings* in 1697–8 were women.[135] As a contemporary broadside, *The Great Grievance of Traders and Shopkeepers*, complained, shoplifting was a notorious and growing crime, committed by organised networks, backed by 'bullies' and receivers of stolen goods, and defended with 'craft and subtilty' when prosecuted. One recently executed female shoplifter, it alleged, 'had stolen to the value of twelve thousand pounds'.[136] This statute successfully led to an increase in prosecutions, with shoplifting doubling from 3.5 per cent of all offences in the five years leading up to the Act, to 7.1 per cent from 1700 to 1704. The proportion of female offenders also increased from 58.5 to 74.3 per cent of defendants accused of this offence.

Prosecutions were also encouraged by the offer of more generous rewards to prosecutors for the conviction of those who committed

[133] Beattie, *Policing and Punishment*, pp. 315ff.
[134] 3 & 4 William and Mary c. 9 (www.british.history.ac.uk, 30 Dec. 2013); Beattie, *Policing and Punishment*, p. 318.
[135] 10 & 11 William III c. 23 (www.british.history.ac.uk, 30 Dec. 2013); Beattie, *Policing and Punishment*, pp. 37, 67, 328.
[136] *The Great Grievance of Traders and Shopkeepers, by the Notorious Practice of Stealing their Goods out of their Shops and Warehouses* (1699).

serious crimes, an innovation which resulted in major changes in policing and, as an unintended consequence, opened up new possibilities for criminality. As early as 1692 a statute had established a permanent £40 reward for the conviction of highway robbers, and a 1695 statute offered a similar reward for coiners.[137] In 1699 a statute introduced new forms of reward: those who were responsible for convicting offenders of shoplifting, theft from warehouses, burglary and horse theft were to receive a 'Tyburn Ticket', which gave the owner an exemption from parish offices (and because it was transferable, amounted to a significant financial reward). More significantly, offenders who turned king's evidence and whose testimony resulted in the conviction of two or more accomplices were entitled to a pardon.[138] Together with a £40 reward for the conviction of burglars in 1706, these incentives encouraged the growth of thief-takers, men (and occasionally women) who turned arresting criminals into a profitable business.[139] While such mercenary activities date back to at least the sixteenth century, in the 1690s and early 1700s the number of thief-takers increased considerably.

John Beattie estimates that in the City of London alone, there were between thirty and forty active thief-takers in this period.[140] These include some of the most prominent reformation of manners informers, including James Jenkins and Bodenham Rewse.[141] From 1694 both were heavily involved in the prosecution of clippers and coiners, but Rewse also prosecuted thefts, at least one rape and someone accused of conspiring to assassinate the king. By 1699 he was employed by Isaac Newton at the Mint specifically to arrest coiners, and in 1701 he became deputy keeper of Newgate prison.[142] As with informers and the parallel development of deputy constables (who served for a fee in place of more respectable Londoners who were chosen to act as constables but preferred not to serve), the rise of these private detectives encouraged policing to become a mercenary activity.[143] However, rather than

---

[137] 4 & 5 William and Mary c. 8 (www.british.history.ac.uk, 30 Dec. 2013); 6 & 7 William and Mary c. 17 (www.british.history.ac.uk, 30 Dec. 2013).

[138] 10 & 11 William III, c. 23 (www.british.history.ac.uk, 30 Dec. 2013).

[139] 6 Anne c. 31, i.

[140] Beattie, *Policing and Punishment*, ch. 5, figure quoted from page 233. See also Tim Wales, 'Thief-takers and their clients in later Stuart London', in Paul Griffiths and Mark S. R. Jenner, eds., *Londinopolis: A Social and Cultural History of Early Modern London* (Manchester University Press, 2000), pp. 67–85.

[141] *LL*, set, 'James Jenkins'; and set, 'Bodenham Rewse'.

[142] Tim Wales, 'Rewse, Bodenham (d. 1725), thief-taker and prison warden', *Oxford Dictionary of National Biography* (2004) (www.oxforddnb.com, 30 Dec. 2013); Beattie, *Policing and Punishment*, pp. 237–46; Wales, 'Thief-takers and their clients', p. 76.

[143] Beattie, *Policing and Punishment*, pp. 134–6.

separate the worlds of policing and criminality, these developments encouraged a form of symbiosis between them, since thief-takers needed to be deeply acquainted with criminal networks and their activities in order to prosper. Those who participated in crime grabbed this opportunity to sell their knowledge for a price, whether as compensation for returning stolen goods or as rewards for providing information about the whereabouts of their accomplices.

For those, including criminals, who wished to manipulate the law for their own advantage, the introduction of rewards, therefore, provided lucrative new opportunities. Several thief-takers, notably John Gibbons, regularly extorted protection money from coiners in return for turning a blind eye to their activities.[144] Nevertheless, by increasing the number of prosecutions in the late 1690s, these measures also highlighted the problem of punishment. The authorities both struggled to punish the growing number of convicts and were confronted in these same numbers with evidence of the manifest failure of existing punishments to prevent crime from occurring. In considering the penal options at this time, it is remarkable that increasing the number of executions does not appear to have been a serious possibility, owing to concerns about the public reaction. As Beattie has argued, by the late seventeenth century with 'the unique crime problem emerging in the urban world of London ... too much violence in punishment could be seen as disruptive and counterproductive', particularly since so many of the convicts were women.[145] Despite the fact that these were years of considerable economic and social instability, the proportion of convicts sentenced to death at the Old Bailey during the prosecution wave from 1696 to 1702 (22.9 per cent) was significantly lower than in the previous seven years, when almost a third of convicts (31.4 per cent) were capitally convicted.

Convict defiance at the gallows may have contributed to this reluctance to respond to rising convictions with recourse to simple judicial murder. While convicts dying 'game' at Tyburn became much more common in the 1720s, this was already a recognised phenomenon in the late 1690s, when the Swiss visitor Henri Misson noted that the English 'look upon [hanging] as a Trifle'; they dress 'gayly, and go to it with ... an Air of Indifference'.[146] Even more worryingly for the authorities, the anonymous author of *Hanging, Not Punishment Enough, for*

---

[144] Wales, 'Thief-takers and their clients', p. 77; Beattie, *Policing and Punishment*, pp. 237, 241–2.

[145] Beattie, *Policing and Punishment*, p. 308.

[146] Henri Misson, *M. Misson's Memoirs and Observations in his Travels over England*, trans. M.Ozell ([1719]), pp. 124–5.

Murtherers, High-way Men and House Breakers (1701) complained that too many convicts made 'their *Exits* in Gay Clothes' like 'Men in Triumph', ridiculing hanging as nothing more than 'making a Wry Mouth'.[147] These observers had in mind convicts such as Charles Pynes, convicted of murder in July 1694, who 'kickt the Ordinary out of the cart at Tyburn, and pulled off his shoes, sayeing he'd contradict the old proverb, and not dye in them'.[148]

Rather than increase the number executed, or, as advocated in *Hanging Not Punishment Enough*, conduct those executions with even more brutality, the authorities experimented with various forms of secondary punishments, notably imprisonment and transportation, in addition to the traditional punishments of branding and whipping. There were, nevertheless, significant disadvantages to all these secondary punishments, not least owing to the ability of convicts to subvert or ignore them. In 1700 Timothy Nourse complained that

whipping or frizzing them a little in the fist, is a punishment of no great pain and of a short continuance; and such cauteriz'd or case-hardened rogues as soon as out of jail are but the more confirmed in their former practices.[149]

Branding was particularly ineffective, despite the fact that the location had been switched from the thumb to the cheek in 1699 in order to create more of a deterrent. In a presentment in November 1704, the City of London grand jury explained why the current laws against crime were ineffectual, pointing to, among other penal deficiencies, the impermanent nature of the mark left by branding:

the mark or burn in ye Cheek was to[o] small and Executed so imperfectly as to be scarcely visible, and by that meanes many of them had been burnt Five or Six times over ...

The grand jury went on to observe that

two of the most notorious Shopplifts that were Convicted the last Sessions have been taken Since in ye very act of Shopplifting in the late Dwelling House of Sr. Thomas Abney & tho. they were upon their last Conviction burnt in the Cheek the mark is not now to be discerned ...[150]

---

[147] *Hanging, Not Punishment Enough, for Murtherers, High-way Men and House Breakers* (1701), pp. 6, 21. See also Timothy Nourse, *Campania Foelix: Or, a Discourse of the Benefits and Improvements of Husbandry* (1706), p. 230.

[148] Narcissus Luttrell, *A Brief Historical Relation of State Affairs from September 1678 to April 1714* (Oxford University Press, 1857), III, p. 345. See also *LL*, set, 'Charles Pynes'.

[149] Nourse, *Campania Foelix*, p. 229.

[150] *LL*, City of London Sessions: Sessions Papers, 11 January 1703 – 24 November 1704 (LMSLPS150150024).

Another group of London citizens petitioned parliament, however, that this public mark of shame was *too* effective – as it prevented convicts from obtaining employment and 'made them desperate'.[151] Clearly, the permanence of the branding mark was variable, but either way, it did not prevent convicts from committing additional crimes.[152] Roderick Awdry, for example, whose first of several appearances at the Old Bailey occurred in 1710 at the age of no more than twelve, was, according to the Ordinary of Newgate, 'thrice Burnt in the Hand' as well as punished in the house of correction for his crimes, but he continued an active criminal career until he was finally executed in 1714. At the time of his execution, he confessed he had been responsible for thirty-eight substantial thefts over four years.[153]

Critics of branding advocated giving the judges the power to supplement it with a term of hard labour. This was authorised in a 1706 statute which allowed judges to sentence convicted felons who received benefit of clergy to hard labour in a house of correction or workhouse for between six months and two years.[154] This bill was passed in response to a campaign by City MPs in addition to a citizens' petition. The proposal appears to have attempted to capitalise on the perceived success of the London Workhouse; one of those who drafted the petition was Sir Robert Clayton, governor of the Corporation of the Poor. However, an additional factor was the need to find a punishment for several women who had been pardoned on condition of transportation, but who could not be transported because no merchant would take them.[155]

The choice of houses of correction and workhouses as places for putting felons to hard labour is significant in two respects. First, while the direct overlap between paupers and criminals was limited, the elision in provision for the poor and the criminal reflects the common belief that both groups were deemed in need of a period of hard labour, whether as a *punishment* in a house of correction for those guilty of crime, or as a prerequisite for *relief* (it was meant to reform both, by teaching them to be industrious). In the case of the London Workhouse, both were treated in the same institution. Second, institutions *not* designed for the

[151] Beattie, *Policing and Punishment*, p. 331, citing *PP*, *Journals of the House of Commons*, 19 December 1704, p. 463 (parlipapers.chadwyck.co.uk, 2 Jan. 2014).

[152] For a discussion of branding in a European context, see Valentin Groebner, *Who Are You? Identification, Deception, and Surveillance in Early Modern Europe* (New York: Zone Books, 2007), p. 105.

[153] *LL*, Ordinary of Newgate Prison: Ordinary's Accounts, 28 May 1714 (OA171405281405280005). See also *LL*, Molly Fisher, 'Roderick Awdry'.

[154] 5 Anne c. 6, i.

[155] John Beattie, *Crime and the Courts in England, 1660–1800* (Princeton University Press, 1986), p. 497; Beattie, *Policing and Punishment*, pp. 331–3.

punishment of serious criminals came to be used in lieu of the one London gaol designed to accommodate felons, Newgate. This was not only because of the perceived reformative potential of houses of correction and workhouses, but also owing to overcrowding and security problems at Newgate. As a result of the increase in prosecutions and the large number of convicts awaiting transportation, conditions in Newgate were at this time particularly unhealthy (a large number of prisoners in 1697 died of gaol fever) and the crowded inmates became rebellious.[156]

There were a series of escapes from Newgate dating from 1693. Robert Beames had been convicted of two thefts and of making a false charge of high treason and was arrested following the second theft 'in Bed betwixt two Women', with five picklock keys and a 'betty' (used to pry open doors).[157] He escaped from Newgate with an accomplice in April 1693 by the remarkably simple expedient of boring holes through the boards with augers, and 'by the help of a long Rope they slided down and got away'. In March 1696 Katherine Buckingham, who had been convicted of grand larceny the previous October, sentenced to death, and reprieved for pregnancy, also escaped.[158] According to the grand jury, this was a common problem: women acquired the time to engineer their escapes by 'pleading their bellies' before they were sentenced, and getting 'women of their own gangs' to sit on the matrons jury, 'who finding them quick wth Child they did by that means gaine time to escape'. In 1697 William Birkenhead, accused of participating in a conspiracy to assassinate the king, also escaped. The three men accused of assisting him allegedly told another man, 'we can soon get you out as we did Birkenhead', implying that escapes could be arranged on request. In 1712 Daniel Wells was accused of 'abetting and assisting several Prisoners to break her Majesty's Goal of Newgate, and make their Escape'. As one of the prosecutors, Bodenham Rewse, former reformation of manners informer and now turnkey, testified:

on Monday the eighth instant, he had private Information that there was a Design to break the Goal that Evening, which he communicated to Mr. Jeffreys; and thereupon they made a Search, and found a Hole cut in the Floor of the Hall 7 Inches broad, and 18 long, and also that the Irons of one Robert Wilks, a Highway-man, were saw'd off.

The scale of the security problems at Newgate was further illustrated by the fact that at the same trial 'It was also prov'd that the Prisoner was the

---

[156] See Luttrell, *Brief Historical Relation*, Vol. IV, p. 241; and Beattie, *Policing and Punishment*, pp. 363–5. For a similar development in the 1780s, see Chapter 7.
[157] *LL*, set, 'Robert Beames'.
[158] *LL*, set, 'Katherine Buckingham'.

Man who procur'd the Escape of Holloway, which was the Cause of three Persons Deaths.' William Johnson, alias Holloway, was a convicted thief awaiting transportation who broke out of Newgate and killed a man who attempted to re-arrest him. He was convicted of murder in September 1712.[159]

Escaping prisoners rendered any attempt to increase Newgate's role in the punishment of felons untenable. Other reasons were documented by the SPCK investigation of Newgate and other prisons in 1700. According to their report, 'the vices and immoralities of prisons' included the following:

- the personal lewdness of the keepers and under officers [and] their confederacy with prisoners in their vices, allowing the men to keep company with the women for money;
- the unlimited use of wine, brandy and other strong liquors;
- [the fact that] old and incorrigible criminals corrupt the new-comers.[160]

Prisoners could behave inside much as they would in the outside world.

Citing problems of disease and security, a statute in 1700 encouraged the building of new prisons to address overcrowding, but nothing happened in London.[161] Instead greater use was made of houses of correction. Commitments to the Middlesex, Westminster and City (Bridewell) houses of correction all increased significantly in the late 1690s and early 1700s, made up in part of prisoners summarily convicted of thefts which in different times might have resulted in commitment to Newgate followed by an Old Bailey prosecution for a felony. Further increases in house of correction commitments resulted from the 1706 statute authorising the use of hard labour for convicted felons. Between 1707 and 1713, 10.8 per cent of convicts at the Old Bailey were sentenced to hard labour in houses of correction.[162] While in numerical terms convicted felons in houses of correction were not significant (they were vastly outnumbered by the men and women committed directly by justices without trial for idle and disorderly conduct, vagrancy and petty theft), the character of these new prisoners and the length of their incarceration caused difficulties. Convicted felons stayed for up to two years, while most prisoners in houses of correction stayed for only a week, and

[159] *LL*, set, 'Bodenham Rewse'; *LL*, Old Bailey Proceedings, 10 September 1712 (t17120910-17).
[160] Edmund McClure, ed., *A Chapter in English Church History* (London: SPCK, 1888), pp. 48–51.
[161] 11 & 12 William III c. 19 (www.british.history.ac.uk, 30 Dec. 2013).
[162] Innes, 'Prisons for the poor', pp. 88–9, calculates that a fifth of defendants convicted of property crimes between 1707 and 1718 were committed to houses of correction.

no provision was made to pay for their support. Unsurprisingly they posed a substantial threat to security and sometimes formed criminal alliances with other prisoners. Moreover, they resisted the 'correction' to their character that the houses were supposed to achieve. Innes calculates that 'between 5 and 10 per cent (and perhaps even more)' of these convicts were ultimately rearrested for another offence.[163] Even those committed for petty offences proved recalcitrant. Not only had branding failed to keep Roderick Awdry from recidivism, but his five commitments to houses of correction were equally ineffective. According to the Ordinary, 'no sooner was he sent to those Houses of Correction, but he presently broke out, and return'd to his wicked Trade'.

A final penal option was transportation overseas. This had been used since 1615 and more frequently after 1660 as a condition of pardons given to prisoners sentenced to death.[164] Three-quarters of the convicts pardoned in the reign of King William were required to undergo transportation. However, it proved difficult to carry out this punishment owing to resistance from the colonies, disruptions to shipping and the fact that merchants, who bore the cost of the punishment, were only willing to transport fit young men whom they could sell into indentured labour. Given the absence of state funding and the inability to coerce the colonies, the number actually transported was low.[165] In an attempt to resolve this problem, convicts were encouraged to transport themselves, but as the City grand jury complained in 1704, although convicts had to provide security to ensure they would leave the country, some failed to do so and instead went 'at large comitting the like crimes and after all gett themselves into a generall pardon'.[166]

By the early eighteenth century, a combination of convict resistance, criminal recidivism and wider constraints had rendered all the available punishments for serious crime problematic in one way or another. The stalemate would only be broken by the passage of the Transportation Act in 1718.

Conclusion

The rising incidence of crime and growing demands for poor relief in the 1690s, exacerbated by population growth and immigration, supplemented

[163] Beattie, *Policing and Punishment*, p. 334; Innes, 'Prisons for the poor', pp. 89–90.
[164] Hamish Maxwell-Stewart, 'Convict transportation from Britain and Ireland 1615–1870', *History Compass*, 8 (2010), 1121, 1224–5; see also Peter Wilson Coldham, *Emigrants in Chains: A Social History of Forced Emigration to the Americas of Felons, Destitute Children, Political and Religious Non-Conformists, Vagabonds, Beggars and Other Undesirables, 1607–1776* (Baltimore: Genealogical Pub. Co., 1992).
[165] Beattie, *Policing and Punishment*, pp. 362–4.
[166] LL, City of London Sessions: Sessions Papers, 11 January 1703 – 24 November 1704 (LMSLPS150150024).

the impetus for reform arising from the Revolution settlement. While these pressures did not determine the content of the resulting changes in the administration of poor relief and criminal justice, they certainly forced their pace, and in some cases paupers and criminals determined the limits of the possible. In other ways the consequences of reform unintentionally empowered the poor, or particular groups outside the state (such as thief-takers), at the expense of local officials.

For the 'deserving' poor, support was increasingly tied to their parish of settlement, while the 'undeserving' poor were frequently put to hard labour, whether in a house of correction or a workhouse. In the process the balance of power between justices of the peace, parish officials and the poor was realigned. In this triangular relationship, overseers and churchwardens were substantially disempowered in their negotiations with the poor, who could now appeal more effectively to a justice. At the same time, settlement examinations, certificates and badges created a new technology of identity that gave to the settled poor evidence they could deploy in new ways in their negotiations with both parish officers and justices. A new kind of legal agency was created that was no longer in thrall to the discretion of the parish officers.

In relation to the activities of the reformation of manners campaign and in the development of penal policy, pressure from below limited what was possible, preventing both the systematic prosecution of vice and a bloodbath at the gallows. Although the growing number of Londoners tried at the Old Bailey or committed to a house of correction was ultimately the result of more systematic policing and prosecution, convict resistance shaped penal strategies. In addition, the poor could take advantage of the increasingly mercenary approach to policing, in which anyone could make an information and obtain a reward.

Although the poor were to some extent divided in terms of access to relief, and no doubt also in attitudes towards criminality, new alliances evolved, not only among criminals and the poor but also on occasion with those among their social superiors who also resisted change. These new alliances, already evident in the Sacheverell Riots of 1710, set the stage for the explosion of popular protest and resistance which accompanied the Hanoverian accession.

3   Protest and resistance: 1713–1731

Introduction

The arrival of peace with the Treaty of Utrecht in 1713, followed by the death of Queen Anne and the controversial accession of George I the following year, fuelled a crisis of law and order that had been brewing for half a decade. While wartime employment had to some extent mitigated the socio-economic difficulties caused by poor harvests, demobilisation set in train a new wave of crime and prosecution. Moreover, the disorder occasioned by the defence of religion and opposition to the Hanoverian succession, dating back to the Sacheverell Riots of 1710, allowed socio-economic grievances to be expressed through riot.

The new Hanoverian monarchy and whig government were not slow to respond to the pressures, not least with legislation including the Riot Act in 1715 and the Transportation Act in 1718. In part, these developments led to the creation of a more powerful central authority that found expression in the whig rule of Walpole and the Robinocracy. However, for poor Londoners, this was also a moment when divisions within the elite over church and politics gave them a voice. The corruption laid bare in the South Sea Bubble provided a new language that could be used to critique aggressive prosecution of crime and oppression of the poor. This politics threw into uneasy alliance the poor and the middling sort men who ran the parishes and sat on juries, setting them at odds with parliament and an increasingly powerful whig elite. But while central government grew in relative power, most new social policies were implemented at the local level. The most important poor law initiative of the period – the Workhouse Test Act of 1723 – was drafted as permissive legislation, leaving the initiative to the parishes, while responses to crime were dominated by the increasingly entrepreneurial activities of informers and thief-takers. For the next few decades, as parliament became more active, the character of change in London was markedly piecemeal, and open to challenge. For the city's poorest inhabitants, the 1710s and 1720s

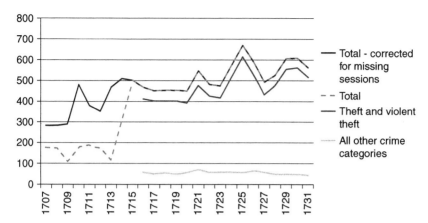

Figure 3.1 Offences prosecuted at the Old Bailey, 1707–1731. *Old Bailey Online*, Statistics: Offences by year, 1674–1913; Online data set: Crime Prosecutions.xlsx.

represented a moment of real, if still circumscribed, agency, in which the divided politics of the parish and the elite gave them a voice.

The challenge to public order

George I's accession to the throne was accompanied by a wave of crime and protest which threatened to undermine the new regime. In August 1714 the London poor were facing the worst economic conditions since the late 1690s, and crime prosecutions soared. Bad harvests leading to high bread prices had led to a fall in real wages of one-third between 1708 and 1711.[1] Just as real wages started to recover came demobilisation,[2] followed by the severe frosts of the winter of 1715–16 and the disruptions to trade caused by the Jacobite rebellion and cattle plague, such that 'the early years of the Hanoverian accession were … hard ones for many London trades'.[3] With adversity came increasing

---

[1] W. G. Hoskins, *The Making of the English Landscape* (Harmondsworth: Penguin Books, 1970), pp. 19, 30; E. A. Wrigley and R. S. Schofield, *The Population History of England, 1541–1871: A Reconstruction* (London: Edward Arnold, 1981), p. 643; John Broad, 'Cattle plague in eighteenth-century England', *Agricultural History Review*, 31:2 (1983), 104–15.

[2] At least 67,000 soldiers were discharged between 1711 and 1715, and with only two weeks' subsistence money in their pockets. Many went to London seeking work. H. C. B. Rogers, *The British Army of the Eighteenth Century* (London: Allen and Unwin, 1977), pp. 19–20; John Beattie, 'The pattern of crime in England 1660–1800', *Past & Present*, 62 (1974), 47–8.

[3] Nicholas Rogers, 'Popular protest in Early Hanoverian London', *Past & Present*, 79 (1978), 92–3.

theft prosecutions: between 1712 and 1714 the number of indictments tried at the Old Bailey increased by almost half.

It is of course impossible to determine whether crime actually increased in these years, or whether there was simply growing concern about crime which led to a greater propensity to prosecute. It is likely that both factors account for the surge in prosecutions. That disbanded soldiers (or at least male unemployment) contributed to the increase is suggested by the fact that indictments for robbery increased by 73.1 per cent over these years, and the gender balance of those accused switched from a narrow majority of female defendants (51.7 per cent) during wartime to a significant majority of men (62.5 per cent) from 1713 to 1715. Nevertheless, such was the increase in prosecutions, in a context of rising poverty, that the *number* of women tried from 1713 to 1715 also increased. There was also a significant increase in commitments for petty offences to the Middlesex and Westminster houses of correction, which rose from 1,244 in 1712 to 1,662 in 1717, when over a third of the prisoners in Middlesex were accused of petty theft and a further half of prostitution or loose, idle and disorderly behaviour.

Most worrying for the authorities was the hardened recidivism of many offenders, not least the women. Mary Knight, executed for picking a man's pocket in January 1716, had been committed to a house of correction and New Prison three times in 1715, and she confessed to the Ordinary of Newgate:[4]

That she had for these 12 Months past been a very loose Woman, a Night-walker, &c. and, That she had deluded as many Young Men, and others, as she met with in her Way, and could perswade to go along with her: That being sometimes taken by the Watch, she was carry'd to the Bridewell in Clerkenwell, from whence (after some slight Correction) being discharg'd, but not reform'd, she return'd to her former vicious Life.[5]

Mary Nichols, alias Trolly Lolly, executed in September 1715 following her second conviction in nine months at the Old Bailey for theft, claimed she had been driven to steal by 'extream poverty', and confessed to the Ordinary that over two years she had been guilty of 'several Felonies'.[6] Following the end of the war, male recidivism was no less of a problem. John Smith, alias Mackintosh, was executed in September 1715 at the age of twenty-one, following conviction on three burglary charges.[7]

---

[4] *LL*, Victoria Philpott, 'Mary Knight, *c.* 1685–1716'.
[5] *LL*, Ordinary of Newgate Prison: Ordinary's Accounts, 27 January 1716 (OA171601271601270002).
[6] *LL*, Ordinary of Newgate Prison: Ordinary's Accounts, 21 September 1715 (OA171509211509210006). *LL*, Edward Duncan, 'Mary Nichols, alias Trolly Lolly, *c.* 1685–1715'.
[7] *LL*, set: 'John Smith'.

He had previously served at sea in a 'Man of War'. He confessed to the Ordinary to having been involved in crime since the age of fifteen, and that he had been branded twice for theft and had also been convicted of participating in the violent attacks carried out by the 'Mohocks' in 1712. He escaped from prison twice, once from Bridewell and once from the Gatehouse.[8] His whole career seemed to illustrate the intractability of London's crime problem.

This crime wave, or at the very least prosecution wave, was exacerbated by the widespread popular protest which accompanied the Hanoverian succession. Since the 1690s, if not long before, Londoners had been developing a habit of taking to the streets to voice their grievances on any number of topics, such that by the early 1720s some form of riot occurred on average every other day in London. Encouraged by the 'rage of party', during which both whig and tory political leaders encouraged the wider population to take part in an annual round of street theatre, including burning effigies, bonfires, forced illuminations and processions, plebeian Londoners used traditional forms of licensed disorder to voice their own social and political concerns.[9]

As was evident in the Sacheverell Riots, by 1710 those grievances were increasingly cast in language supportive of the tories and the 'high church'. Following the accession of George I, Londoners had plenty of reasons to focus their discontent, exacerbated by economic hard times, on the new whig government. Many participated in the repeated tory-sponsored bonfires and processions which formed part of the calendar of political anniversaries throughout the first two years of George I's reign. On 29 May 1715, the anniversary of the Restoration of Charles II, a group of more than a hundred people marched between Bow Church and Queen Street, shouting 'no Hanoverian, no Presbyterian; High-Church for ever; High-Church and Ormond; High-Church and Sacheverel; a Second Restoration; no King George, but King James the 3d. High Church and Ormond, and the Race of the Steuarts for ever'.[10] Passersby were urged to join the procession, and those who declined were attacked. Few of the protesters were committed Jacobites (though they were not averse to using Jacobite language and symbolism), but most were firmly opposed to the whigs. Not only did the whigs have a history of supporting religious dissent, which many plebeian Londoners opposed, but there were fears that the king would take the country into a

---

[8] *LL*, Ordinary of Newgate Prison: Ordinary's Accounts, 21 September 1715 (OA171509211509210004).
[9] Robert Shoemaker, 'The London "mob" in the early eighteenth century', *Journal of British Studies*, 26:3 (1987), 273–304; Rogers, 'Popular protest', 100.
[10] *LL*, Old Bailey Proceedings, 13 July 1715 (t17150713-14).

new war, leading once again to excise taxes, profiteering and further disruptions to trade.[11]

The government was clearly unsettled by these disorders, and it was not slow to react. First, it prosecuted those who could be arrested, using prosecuting counsel to ensure convictions. Second, it passed the Riot Act in June 1715. While the Act failed to stop the disorder, by indemnifying those who suppressed riots it made it easier for the government to use the military to disperse crowds. The whig elite, notably the Duke of Newcastle, also responded forcefully by sponsoring 'loyal societies', composed of gentlemen and hired thugs, to defend the king, government and church on the streets. Based in taverns and coffee houses known as 'mughouses', these societies staged their own counter-demonstrations and bonfires, and armed with oak staves, launched violent attacks on tory crowds.[12]

The people frequently fought back, most dramatically in the attacks on Read's mughouse in Salisbury Court, off Fleet Street, on 23 and 24 July 1716. When a loyal society met on the night of the 23rd, a mob gathered and, according to one witness, 'hiss'd the Gentlemen as they went in and out; whereupon the Witness went out and ask'd them what they hiss'd at, but they threw Stones at him and at the Windows'.[13] The loyalists responded by breaking some windows of a rival tavern while denigrating the plebeian character of their opponents, shouting 'Down with the Butchers, Down with the Barbers … Down with the Pawnbrokers'.[14] The following morning the tory crowd returned to Read's mughouse armed with sticks. After pitched battles, the keeper of the tavern, Robert Read, acquired a gun and fired on the crowd, killing Daniel Vaughan.[15] Like many other Bridewell apprentices, Vaughan had a history of participation in Jacobite protests. Provoked, the crowd renewed its attack, forcing the gentlemen into the house where they barricaded themselves on the stairs, leaving the ground floor to the crowd's mercy. Following the time-honoured custom of 'pulling down a house', the crowd proceeded to demolish the interior. Eventually soldiers appeared and about thirty rioters were arrested, five of whom were the first in London to be convicted and hanged under the Riot Act.

In the short term the government and their loyalist supporters were victorious. The death sentences, the intervention of the military and the strength of the loyal societies all contributed to the restoration of order.

---

[11] Rogers, 'Popular protest', 91–4.
[12] James L. Fitts, 'Newcastle's mob', *Albion: A Quarterly Journal Concerned with British Studies*, 5:1 (1973), 41–9.
[13] *LL*, Old Bailey Proceedings, 10 October 1716 (t17161010-1).
[14] *LL*, Old Bailey Proceedings, 6 September 1716 (t17160906-1).
[15] *LL*, Dianne Payne, 'Daniel Vaughan, *c.* 1692–1716'.

As a correspondent observed the following month, 'there is an end of Tory mobbing here for the Whig mob being headed by officers and gentlemen has quite silenced them'.[16] But as Nicholas Rogers notes, the executions contributed to 'the persistent and deep-rooted hostility of Londoners to the new regime'.[17] Protests continued, but the focus became more explicitly social and economic. Worried that imported calico cloth would lead to the collapse of their trade, in 1719 and 1720 journeymen weavers waged a successful campaign against its use, culminating in the passage of a statute in 1721.[18] In addition to petitioning parliament and disseminating their case in print, groups of weavers roamed London's streets destroying calico clothing found in shops or worn by women, by slitting dresses with knives or throwing ink or nitric acid. The windows in the houses of those who opposed the weavers were smashed, and at one point they threatened to pull down New Prison, where four of the 'ringleaders' were incarcerated.[19] While there were attempts to label these protests as Jacobite, Justice John Lade reported that

the Vox Populi or the Rumor of the Mob was not disrespectful, to his Majesty or the Government, but the word was Must the Poor Weavers Starve, shall the Ingy (meaning the East India) callicoes be worn while the Poor Weavers and their Familys perish.[20]

At least one of the ringleaders, John Humphreys, did have experience in opposing the government.[21] On the same day that he was tried for 'Assaulting divers Women, and tearing their Gowns made of Callicoe' on 12 June 1719, he was also charged with seditious words, allegedly having said two years previously that 'King George was not Heir to the Crown, but King James the Third is the true Heir to the Crown'. One witness at the Old Bailey testified that 'Humphrey's [sic] was a Ringleader of the Mob at Salisbury-Court [and Read's mughouse], and that he heard him brag of what he had done.'[22] Another commentator suggested that it was no coincidence that the calico riots started on 10 June, the Pretender's birthday, and that Humphreys was not a weaver.[23]

---

[16] Quoted in Fitts, 'Newcastle's mob', 49.
[17] Rogers, 'Popular protest', 82.
[18] 7 Geo. I c. 7, 'An Act to Preserve and Encourage the Woollen and Silk Manufacturers of this Kingdom'.
[19] Alfred Plummer, The London Weavers' Company (London: Routledge, 1972), pp. 292–314; TNA, State Papers Domestic, 'George I', SP 35/16/114.
[20] TNA, State Papers Domestic, 'George I', SP 35/16/116.
[21] LL, set, 'John Humphreys'.
[22] LL, Old Bailey Proceedings, 8 July 1719 (t17190708-56).
[23] A Further Examination of the Weavers Pretences (1719), p. 4.

As this is the only evidence of Jacobite inclinations among the rioters, it seems likely that the anniversary was coincidental, but perhaps it was highlighted to alarm the authorities.

Riotous protests continued throughout the next decade. In 1720 a group of striking journeymen tailors attempted to pull down a master's 'house of call'.[24] In the following two years, crowds attacked reformation of manners informers who were making arrests. In 1724, in several riots involving up to sixty participants, the debtors of the New Mint defended their sanctuary by rescuing anyone of their number who was arrested, and subjecting bailiffs to the 'discipline' of the Mint, which involved harrowing physical humiliation. William Jones was drinking at an ale-house in Whitechapel, for example, when a group of minters

knock'd him down, and ... stript him naked, and wore Sixpenny worth of Rods to the Stumps in whipping of him, and ... threw him into a Pit fill'd with Human Excrement, and other Filth, in which they dipt the Rods when they whipt him. There they duck'd him several times, and as they took him out, [William Green] held him up by the Hair, and thrust a Turd into his Mouth.[25]

These riots are indicative of strong community solidarities among sections of the metropolitan population. The use of the traditional symbolic practices of shaming and ritual celebration underlines the rioters' claims to popular support and legitimation. The weavers paraded pieces of calico torn from women's dresses in triumph, wearing them on their hats and using them as flags. However, riots did not command universal support, even among plebeian Londoners.[26] As a newspaper reported of the weavers, 'in some parts they met with opposition, and several of them were severely beaten and wounded'.[27] Neither were mobs entirely plebeian. Analysis of their social composition suggests that while rioters were predominantly wage-earning labourers and petty craftsmen and tradesmen (the groups most likely to be accused of crimes or apply for relief), some more respectable tradesmen and gentlemen were also involved. The inclusivity of protest is emphasised by the large number of female rioters, particularly in non-political riots, where they accounted for almost half of the participants.[28] In the years following the Hanoverian accession, the habit of taking to the streets to protest became more deeply embedded in popular culture, and the 'mob', however composed,

---

[24] Shoemaker, 'London "mob"', 279–80.

[25] *LL*, Old Bailey Proceedings, 15 January 1725 (t17250115-67).

[26] Shoemaker, 'London "mob"', 299–301.

[27] *Weekly Journal, or Saturday's Post*, 12 September 1719 (Burney Collection: www. galegroup.com, 1 Jan. 2014).

[28] Rogers, 'Popular protest', 84–7; Shoemaker, 'London "mob"', 283–6.

became more assertive in defending its perceived rights, not least in response to innovations in social policy.

The law responds

The legal groundwork for the creation of a new relationship between the magistrates, the City of London, the parishes and the people had been laid in the years leading up to the Hanoverian succession, and included the passage of the 'Act for Fifty New Churches' in 1710 (discussed below). However, this relationship was consolidated, at least from the point of view of the state, in acts of parliament passed to address the challenges to law and order of the early years of the new reign.

The Riot Act is one of the most iconic pieces of legislation in the canon of British legal history, and yet it was passed through parliament in just three quick weeks in early July 1715. Entitled 'An Act for Preventing Tumults and Riotous Assemblies and for the More Speedy and Effectual Punishing the Rioters', it was not primarily a response to the problem of disorder in London.[29] Nevertheless, it did seek to reinforce the authority of justices of the peace, creating a new facet to the system of justice-led local governance that had been a characteristic of the developments of the 1690s and 1700s. The Act made it a felony subject to death without benefit of clergy for twelve or more people to assemble 'riotously and tumultuously', and continue for more than an hour after a justice had read out a proclamation which ordered the assembled crowd 'immediately to disperse themselves, and peaceably to depart to their habitations'. It also indemnified justices and the officers and soldiers under their command from being prosecuted if anyone in the crowd 'happened to be killed, maimed or hurt, in the dispersing, seizing or apprehending' of the rioters.

Despite its symbolic significance, the Act's impact was limited. The proclamation was frequently read, but few people were prosecuted under its authority: only thirty-six defendants were tried at the Old Bailey between 1715 and 1731 (almost half in 1715 and 1716). In part this is because crowds, having made their point, learned to leave the scene within the hour as instructed, such as the weavers who 'soon dispersed' after the proclamation was read on 13 June 1719.[30] Others treated the Act with contempt. After the proclamation was read during a riot precipitated by an attempt to arrest some gamblers in 1722, Edward

---

[29] 1 George I st. 2, c. 5; see Adrian Randall, *Riotous Assemblies: Popular Protest in Hanoverian England* (Oxford University Press, 2006), pp. 24–8.
[30] TNA, State Papers Domestic, 'George I', SP 35/16/122.

Galloway 'lifting up his left hand cry'd a T – d of your Proclamation, I have heard it twice already but don't value it'.[31] And during the celebrations of the election of Sir John Williams as an alderman in 1723, after the 'Proclamation was read three or four Times' the mob shouted 'No King George, No Hannoverian [*sic*] Proclamation'.[32]

The second major piece of legislation passed by the new government, the Transportation Act, had a much more substantial impact. Like the Riot Act, this was, according to Beattie, 'the product of a government under siege, and on the defensive'. Although with a national remit, the Transportation Act 'was also in no small measure a product of a crisis of crime in the capital'.[33] However, it was not only the very visible post-war wave of crime and disorder in the metropolis which provided a stimulus to action but also the fact that for some time criminal recidivism and convict resistance had rendered the existing punishments for felonies ineffective or unworkable. As the preamble to the Act states:

> it is found by experience, that the punishments inflicted by the Laws now in force against the offences of robbery, larceny and other felonious taking and stealing of money and goods, have not proved effectual to deter wicked and evil-disposed persons from being guilty of the said crimes.[34]

Between 1713 and 1717 the judges at the Old Bailey adjusted their penal strategy in an attempt to address this problem. Punishments deemed to be ineffectual, including branding and commitment to hard labour in a house of correction, declined, while the proportion of offenders sentenced to death increased dramatically, from 13.4 per cent of convicts in 1713 to 34.8 per cent in 1717.

However, to avoid a bloodbath, many of the condemned convicts were pardoned on condition of transportation, raising once again the problem of the lack of willing merchants to transport convicts, and the failure of offenders to honour commitments to transport themselves. As the preamble to the Act continued:

> many offenders to whom Royal mercy hath been extended, upon condition of transporting themselves to the West-Indies, have often neglected to perform the said condition, but returned to their former wickedness.

Consequently, the option of self-transportation appears to have been abandoned, and the growing number of convicts sentenced to

---

[31] *LL*, Old Bailey Proceedings, 28 February 1728 (t17220228-65).

[32] *LL*, Old Bailey Proceedings, 4 December 1723 (t17231204-52).

[33] John Beattie, *Policing and Punishment in London, 1660–1750: Urban Crime and the Limits of Terror* (Oxford University Press, 2001), p. 431.

[34] 4 George I c. 11.

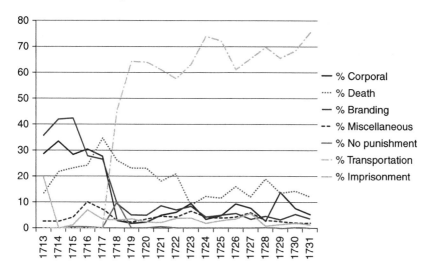

Figure 3.2 Old Bailey punishment sentences, 1713–1731. Online data set: *Old Bailey Online*, Statistics: Punishment sentences by year, 1674–1913; Online data set: Punishment Statistics, 1690–1800.xlsx.

transportation remained in Newgate awaiting ships, resulting in severe overcrowding.[35]

Convicts also seriously undermined the most recent experiment in punishing felons, commitment to a house of correction at hard labour for up to two years, authorised by an act in 1706.[36] Although the disadvantages of this punishment quickly became clear, judges continued to order it, and in 1713 dozens of men and women, convicted primarily of grand larceny, were given this sentence. However, prisoners such as Roderick Awdry repeatedly escaped and returned to a life of crime.[37] Other convicts who escaped in the early 1710s and committed further crimes include Jane Wells (alias Elizabeth Wells alias White alias Dyer), James Boswell, Robert Porter (alias Sandey), Ann Watts, Henry Sewell (alias Sweet alias Old Harry) and John Evans.[38]

The final straw occurred in September 1713 when 'a notorious Riott and Mutiny by severall of the Convicts comitted from Newgate' at the Clerkenwell house of correction led to the death of a turnkey, Edward

---

[35] Beattie, *Policing and Punishment*, p. 427.
[36] 5 Anne, c. 6, ii.
[37] LL, Molly Fisher, 'Roderick Awdry, *c.* 1698–1714'.
[38] LL, sets, 'Jane Wells'; 'James Boswell'; 'Robert Porter'; 'Ann Watts'; 'John Smith'; 'Henry Sewell'; 'John Evans'.

Perry, and the escape of several prisoners.[39] The riot started when the convicted felons Richard Keele, Charles Houghton, John Cullum and William Lowther were brought from Newgate to Clerkenwell to commence a twelve-month sentence at hard labour. When the governor of the house of correction, Captain Boreman, attempted to place them in fetters to ensure they would not escape, they rebelled. According to Lowther, 'he thought it a heavy thing to have Irons put upon him, and be obliged to hard Labour besides'.[40] Consequently, the convicts

swearing they would lose their Lives first, fell upon [Boreman] and his Servant, and with Irons beat and bruised them in a barbarous manner; Lowther biting off the tip of one Man's Nose, wounding him on the Head, and stabbing him twice with a Knife. And having thus used the Keepers, broke into the place where the arms lay, and forced them all out of the Prison; that being done, they swore they would never be iron'd, but die one and all.[41]

Outside the prison, the convicts, including Roderick Awdry and at least two others, attacked Perry, who later died of his wounds, and in the attempt to quell the mutiny Houghton was shot and killed. In the aftermath Keele and Lowther were found guilty of murdering Perry and hanged in Clerkenwell Green, next to the house of correction, on 23 December. But as a result of this mutiny, 1713 was the last year in which felons convicted at the Old Bailey were sentenced to hard labour at a house of correction.

With all the alternative secondary punishments undermined, the government opted to try and make transportation work. The key change implemented by the Transportation Act was the provision of a subsidy to ensure that all convicts sentenced would actually be transported. In choosing to invest in this punishment, various motives have been ascribed beyond the simple lack of feasible alternatives, including the benefits of providing forced labour for the development of the North American colonies (mentioned in the preamble to the Act). However, according to Roger Ekirch, the 'most compelling advantage, in the eyes of policymakers, lay in expelling from the British shores significant quantities of threatening offenders whose ways would not be mended by more mild penalties'.[42] For the most part, those 'threatening

---

[39] *LL*, Middlesex Sessions: Sessions Papers, January 1716 (LMSMPS501500009).

[40] *LL*, Ordinary of Newgate Prison: Ordinary's Accounts, 23 December 1713 (OA171312231312230003).

[41] *A Compleat Collection of Remarkable Tryals of the Most Notorious Malefactors*, 4 vols. ([1718]–21), III, p. 142. The edition of the *Old Bailey Proceedings* which contains this trial does not survive.

[42] A. Roger Ekirch, *Bound for America: The Transportation of British Convicts to the Colonies, 1718–1775* (Oxford: Clarendon Press, 1987), p. 19.

offenders' came from London, and it was the Recorder of London, William Thomson, who was principally responsible for the Act's passage.[43]

The Transportation Act took effect in the spring of 1718 and led to an immediate and long-lasting shift in sentencing patterns. At the Old Bailey twenty-seven of the fifty-one defendants convicted in April 1718 were sentenced to transportation, and by 1719 almost two-thirds of convicts were given this sentence. Over the entire period from 1719 to 1775, transportation accounted for 66.4 per cent of all sentences.[44] Even convicts found guilty of petty larceny, who might previously have been punished in a house of correction, were now often transported.[45] Consequently, the proportion of offenders sentenced to death decreased by more than half between 1719 and 1731 (despite continuing concerns about high levels of violent crime), and both branding and whipping fell dramatically.

The plebeian response to transportation is poorly documented. An unknown proportion of those exiled fulfilled the condition of their sentence and remained in America following its expiration, possibly rehabilitated and prosperous in the manner depicted in Daniel Defoe's novels *Moll Flanders* and *Colonel Jack* (both 1722). But many rebelled. There is evidence of at least four mutinies on board transport ships between 1720 and 1728, including one on the ship *Alexander* in 1722 in which the prisoners 'mutiny'd in their Passage, and would have kill'd the Master and Ship's Crew, and tied them back to back, and thrown them into the Sea'.[46] On board the ship was William Blewit, future member of Edward Burnworth's gang of robbers, who turned king's evidence and claimed he 'prevented it, and saved the Ship's Crew and Cargoe'.[47] Two years earlier, another criminal with a notorious future, the highway robber James Dalton, was on board the *Honour* when the prisoners mutinied and escaped from the ship in Vigo, on the Atlantic coast of Spain. Back in England the following year and sentenced to a further

---

[43] Beattie, *Policing and Punishment*, ch. 9.
[44] Old Bailey Statistics: Punishments, 1719 to 1775. To this should be added another 5 to 10 per cent of convicts who were initially sentenced to death and then pardoned on condition of transportation. In the City of London, 'roughly... half the men ... and about 70 per cent of the women' property offenders sentenced to death between 1714 and 1750 were pardoned on condition of transportation: Beattie, *Policing and Punishment*, p. 457.
[45] Beattie, *Policing and Punishment*, p. 446.
[46] *LL*, Old Bailey Proceedings, 16 January 1723 (t17230116-23).
[47] *LL*, Old Bailey Proceedings, 16 January 1723 (t17230116-23). See also *LL*, Mary Clayton, 'William Blewit d. 1726' and Mary Clayton, 'Edward Burnworth alias Frazier, d. 1726'.

sentence of transportation on the *Prince Royal*, an escape attempt was foiled when a file was discovered in a gingerbread cake in Dalton's possession.[48]

However, the most frequent means of resistance was the surprisingly easy expedient of simply returning to England before the expiration of the sentence. Both Blewit and Dalton did this (twice in Dalton's case), and the number of returnees captured and prosecuted at the Old Bailey (thirty-five between 1720 and 1731, or just under three per year) can bear little relationship to the number of convicts who actually returned. Most of the criminal gangs active in these years included such returnees, who would have found it difficult to return to normal life. Returning from transportation was a felony punishable either by death or fourteen years transportation, and with a £40 reward on offer, they needed assistance to avoid detection. The thief-taker Jonathan Wild used the possibility of arresting such returnees to control them. The Transportation Act thus forced returnees to embed themselves in a criminal subculture.

Criminal legislation formed one strand in a strategy to address the problem of disorder and political disquiet. The reorganisation of London's parishes was a parallel response, in this case to the increasing numbers of the poor. While City-wide projects such as the London Workhouse had fallen out of favour, parliament was still willing to intervene in the running of London's system of poor relief. On 21 January 1715/16, parliament noted the 'Miseries of the Poor in and about the Cities of London and Westminster' and, bracketing them with other forms of urban detritus, the 'Heeps of dirt, lee and snow' that obstructed the streets outside the Royal Exchange and Westminster Hall, ordered the justices of London and Middlesex to take the issue in hand.[49] Parliament also ordered a committee to investigate the system of poor and scavenger rates in the capital.[50] Confronted with 133 mini parochial bureaucracies of unknown complexity, the committee decided they could do no more than investigate a single parish, and chose as their exemplar St Martin in the Fields on the grounds that it had a reputation as the best managed parish in London. What they discovered was a system grown unmanageable as a result of both earlier reforms and

---

[48] Philip Rawlings, 'Dalton, James (bap. 1700?, d. 1730), street robber', *ODNB* (www.oxforddnb.com, 1 Jan. 2014); Gerald Howson, *Thief-Taker General: The Rise and Fall of Jonathan Wild* (London: Hutchinson, 1970), p. 139; *LL*, set, 'James Dalton'.

[49] *PP, Journals of the House of Commons*, 21 January 1715/16 (parlipapers.chadwyck.co.uk, 1 Jan. 2014).

[50] *PP*, 'The report of the committee to inspect the poor's rates and the scavenger's rates within the cities of London and Westminster, and weekly bills of mortality', March 1715, Numb. 201, p. 417 (parlipapers.chadwyck.co.uk, 1 Jan. 2014).

pauper demand. During the preceding three years, St Martin's had spent around £1,800 per year on the 'casual poor', the out of work, or out of luck, accident victims, and the simply miserable; compared to only around £1,250 on parish pensioners, the 'deserving' and settled objects of compassion. More difficult still, on interrogating John Eldridge, the clerk of the parish, and asking him to produce the justice's warrants that authorised each payment, he could not produce a single one.[51]

And if human tragedy needed to be added to the parish's overgenerous response to the insistent demands of the poor, the same committee found that parish children were 'inhumanly suffered to die by the barbarity of ... Parish Nurses, who are... hired by the Church wardens to take off a burthen from the parish at the cheapest and easiest rates they can'.[52] This conclusion was brought home to a wider London public a couple of years later through the case of Eleanor Gallimore, tried and acquitted on two occasions of starving and murdering the parish children put in her charge by St Andrew Holbourn, the first of several similarly horrific tales which surfaced during the century.[53]

It was not just in the west end and suburban parishes that the growing demands of the 'casual' poor loomed ever larger in the parish accounts. In the small City parish of St Dionis Backchurch, the list of 'pensioners' remained largely unchanged, but the casual payments evolved into growing paragraphs of serial hardship: 'to a distressed Family by Mr Travell 5s ...To a Poor Woman 1s: Goody Wills 2/6: To a poor Woman 2s: Daniell 2/6- 8 – To Goody Brett 2/6: Goody Williams 2/6: to a poor Family 10/5'.[54] For the parliamentary committee, and for rate-paying Londoners, the system seemed out of control.

Many assumed the solution was already in hand. The passage of the 'Act for Fifty New Churches' six years earlier had been intended to reshape the parochial landscape. This Act established a commission with authority to receive the income from a levy on coals imported to London from 1716 onwards, and use the funds to repair and build anew the churches of the capital.[55] The commission also addressed the problems of governance caused by the growing population of the suburban parishes

---

[51] *PP*, 'Report of the committee to inspect the poor's rates', March 1715, Numb. 201, p. 420.

[52] *PP*, 'Report of the committee to inspect the poor's rates', March 1715, Numb. 201, p. 420; Jeremy Boulton, 'Welfare systems and the parish nurse in early modern London, 1650–1725', *Family & Community History*, 10:2 (2007), 127–51.

[53] *LL*, Old Bailey Proceedings, 27 February 1718 (t17180227-41); *LL*, Old Bailey Proceedings, 10 September 1718 (t17180910-76); and set, 'Eleanor Gallimore'.

[54] *LL*, St Dionis Backchurch Parish: Churchwardens and Overseers of the Poor Account Books, 1689–1720 (GLDBAC300000555).

[55] 9 Anne c. 17; 3 George II c. 19.

by dividing some of London's largest parishes, making the provision of poor relief more manageable. Between the passage of the Act in 1710 and 1731, the commission was instrumental in the creation of eight new parishes, including St George Hanover Square, created from St Martin in the Fields in 1724, and St George Bloomsbury, carved from St Giles in the Fields in 1731. From the perspective of plebeian London, these developments were unfavourable in two respects. First, by separating off wealthier neighbourhoods from poorer ones (particularly in St Giles in the Fields), the wealthy escaped much of the responsibility for providing for those in need. Second, the new parishes were to be governed by 'select vestries', which severely limited popular participation in parish government.

Many of London's out-parishes, including St Martin in the Fields and St Paul Covent Garden, were already governed by select vestries by the end of the seventeenth century – created either under the authority of the Bishop of London or else by local act of parliament – but this form of vestry was made much more common by the 'Act for Fifty New Churches'. The commission was expressly ordered to specify 'a convenient number of sufficient inhabitants in each such new parish ... to be the vestrymen', and to direct each new vestry to constitute itself on the lines of the closed vestry which governed St Martin in the Fields.[56] Even when a new parish was carved from one with an open vestry, as happened when St John Clerkenwell was created from St James, the new parish was ordered to create a closed vestry. By mandating 'select vestries' for each new parish, the commission effectively normalised this form of parish government, creating self-perpetuating parish oligarchies, overseen by newly powerful justices and served by paid clerks and supernumeraries.[57]

To some extent the problem was simply one of population. Representations to the Commission for Fifty New Churches claimed that St Giles Cripplegate contained 4,600 houses (or around 27,600 people); St Andrew Holborn, 3,785 houses; St Clement Danes, 1,690; and Shoreditch, 2,278 houses. The commission calculated that twenty-six metropolitan parishes outside the City walls, including Stepney,

---

[56] Quoted in Sidney Webb and Beatrice Webb, *English Local Government*, Vol. I: *The Parish and the County* (London: Frank Cass, 1906; repr. 1963), p. 199.

[57] M. H. Port, ed., *The Commissions for Building Fifty New Churches, The Minute Books, 1711–1727: A Calendar* (London Record Society, vol. 22, 1986), pp. xxix–xxxi (www.british.history.ac.uk, 1 Jan. 2014). See also, M. Dorothy George, *London Life in the Eighteenth Century* (London, 1925; Harmondsworth: Penguin Books, 2nd edn, 1966), Appendix 3a.

  The most authoritative discussion of the evolution of the 'closed vestry', particularly in London, Webb and Webb, *Parish and the County*, pp. 194–9.

contained over 80,000 households, or around 513,000 individuals.[58] This was almost certainly an overestimate, but the much more reliable Bills of Mortality confirm that at least eighteen of London's out-parishes had populations in excess of 10,000, making each parish responsible for a population equivalent to one of the five largest cities in England, outside London.[59]

Populations of this size, containing thousands of householders with the right to attend an open vestry, made the closed variety seem an obvious, if highly divisive solution. Moreover, to service this number of inhabitants the parishes simply could not rely on the good will of annual volunteers and needed dedicated staff.

The creation of new 'select vestries' and the gradual bureaucratisation of parochial administration had three important consequences. First, the frequent inclusion of local justices of the peace as regular members of the vestry served to conflate the administration of criminal justice with poor relief, treating the poor and the criminal as one.[60] Second, select vestries effectively distanced parish government from not only the poor but also the vast majority of ratepayers, and third, the participation of those who were responsible for overseeing parish decisions, magistrates, in the actual administration of the parish opened up possibilities for corruption. A measure of the opposition to this change was the publication in 1719 of Daniel Defoe's vitriolic attack, *Parochial Tyranny, Or, Select Vestries Become the Plague of the People*. In this pamphlet, published on behalf of the out-parishes of London 'that find themselves Oppress'd by unjust Governours', Defoe complained that a small coterie of vestrymen, 'by the assistance and contrivance of corrupt M[agistrate]s, and their cormorant understrappers' had managed to 'ingross the Government of the Out-Parishes', to 'make the poor their Property'.[61] He was particularly critical of the new paid parish officers who were prone to corruption and the justices of the peace who countenanced 'new Schemes ... to bubble the Parish'.[62] Over the next decade, the scheme most of the out-parishes of London adopted was the workhouse, and the problems Defoe envisaged

---

[58] Port, *Commissions for Building Fifty New Churches*, p. xiii.

[59] In 1700, Norwich had a population of *c.* 30,000, Bristol, 21,000, Newcastle, 16,000, Exeter, 14,000 and York, 12,000. See Peter Borsay, ed., *The Eighteenth-Century Town: A Reader in English Urban History, 1688–1820* (London: Longman, 1990), p. 42, Table 1.

[60] The St Margaret Westminster petty sessions met in the parish vestry, and its minutes include discussions of poor relief business at virtually every meeting: WAC, St Margaret Westminster, 'Petty sessions minutes', E2554, 1719–23.

[61] Andrew Moreton [Daniel Defoe], *Parochial Tyranny: Or, The House-Keeper's Complaint Against the insupportable Exactions, and Partial Assessments of Select Vestries, &c.* (1719, 2nd edn, 1727), title page, pp. 2, 3.

[62] [Defoe], *Parochial Tyranny*, p. 5.

duly followed. Opposition to both workhouses and the management of select vestries dominated local politics.

With the exception of the Transportation Act, which reshaped the penal landscape for almost sixty years, the legislation passed in response to the outbreak of crime and protest which greeted the Hanoverian succession was undermined by opposition and had limited impact or unintended adverse consequences. The Riot Act failed to stop the rioting and led to few prosecutions. The creation of select vestries in the new parishes excluded many ratepayers from participation in local government as intended; however, as we will see, by limiting oversight and facilitating the hiring of paid parish officials, it encouraged extensive corruption and mistreatment of the poor, which the opponents of select vestries, in combination with the poor, did their utmost to expose.

Thief-taking

The official response to the widespread panic about crime in the post-war years also included the offer of a new series of rewards. A royal proclamation in 1720 stipulated a reward of £100 for the capture and conviction of highway robbers in the London area, *in addition* to the £40 statutory reward. Although this proclamation appears to have been explicitly designed to encourage thief-takers, the effect was not quite what the government intended. Not only did it make thief-taking considerably more lucrative, it also contributed to criminal activity. Since the threat of prosecution gave thief-takers almost complete power over thieves who (for the moment) they chose not to prosecute, they were able to effectively control entire criminal gangs, while the large rewards motivated them to encourage law-breaking.[63] Thief-takers in the 1720s, notably Jonathan Wild, distorted criminal justice so much to their own advantage that the authorities were finally forced to intervene. Wild's tactics also divided plebeian communities and encouraged London's criminals to develop new strategies for survival.

Thief-takers had flourished in London from well before the 1720s. Their development was encouraged by the growth of daily newspapers in which victims of crime advertised rewards for the return of stolen goods, and by the passage of statutes in 1702 and 1706 that made it easier to prosecute receiving stolen goods as a felony (making it more difficult for thieves to sell their loot directly to third parties).[64] Taking advantage of the on-going activities of the reformation of manners

[63] Beattie, *Policing and Punishment*, pp. 378–9.
[64] Beattie, *Policing and Punishment*, pp. 250–1. See also Howson, *Thief-Taker General*, ch. 4.

campaign, early thief-takers such as Charles Hitchen pretended to be reformers.[65] Hitchen blackmailed brothel keepers with the threat of a prosecution, and pickpockets to force them to bring their stolen goods to him. It is instructive that Hitchen does not appear as a prosecutor in the records of Bridewell or the Old Bailey: his interest was in *not prosecuting* offenders so that he could exploit them instead. Hitchen purchased the office of under-marshal in the City in 1712, and the following year he hired Jonathan Wild as his assistant.[66] The two soon quarrelled, and by 1714 Wild was acting independently as a thief-taker.

Wild's career and methods are well known.[67] From the start, he effectively combined the two sides of thief-takers' activities, the return of stolen goods to victims and the prosecution of thieves in return for a reward. He was not interested in petty crime, and only appears three times in the records of Bridewell, first early on in his career in October 1714, when he charged two men (or boys) with 'picking pocketts taken wth seven handkerchiefs upon one of them'.[68] Thereafter, he sought to control petty thieves rather than punish them, either so that they could steal goods which could profitably be returned to their owners, or until they could be prosecuted for a more serious crime for a reward. In this respect the Transportation Act helped Wild by establishing the offence of returning from transportation as a felony. Any convict who returned was therefore at the mercy of anyone (such as Wild) who knew of their previous conviction and sentence: if they misbehaved, they could quickly be arrested on a charge which was difficult to deny. Moreover, as convicted felons they could not turn on Wild and testify against him in court. When combined with the increased rewards available from 1720 and aided by his astute use of 'carefully planted "news reports"' and lawyers on 'permanent retainer', the stage was set for Wild to become the eighteenth century's most notorious thief-taker.[69]

---

[65] *LL*, set, 'Charles Hitchen'.

[66] Beattie, *Policing and Punishment*, pp. 253–5; Rictor Norton, *Mother Clap's Molly House: The Gay Subculture in England, 1700–1830* (London: GMP, 1992), pp. 131–7; Howson, *Thief-Taker General*, ch. 6. See also, *LL*, set, 'Jonathan Wild'.

[67] See especially Howson, *Thief-Taker General*, and Andrea McKenzie, 'Wild, Jonathan (bap. 1683, d. 1725), thief-taker', *ODNB* (www.oxforddnb.com, 1 Jan. 2014).

[68] *LL*, Bridewell Royal Hospital: Minutes of the Court of Governors, 26 June 1713–2 August 1722 (BBBRMG202040110). The other two times were in 1723 once when he and Quilt Arnold charged three men with picking pockets, and once, when he charged a man with threatening to kill him: *LL*, Bridewell Royal Hospital: Minutes of the Court of Governors, 26 December 1722–15 December 1737 (BBBRMG202050043) and *LL*, Bridewell Royal Hospital: Minutes of the Court of Governors, 26 December 1722–15 December 1737 (BBBRMG202050036).

[69] Howson, *Thief-Taker General*, pp. 115–17.

Between 1716 and 1724 Wild is reported testifying as a witness in forty cases at the Old Bailey, with his most active years between 1719 and 1723, when he broke up several London gangs.[70] The actual number of prosecutions he was responsible for is probably much higher. Together with his assistant Quilt Arnold, he was said to have apprehended 150 people, and Gerald Howson credits him with bringing 101 criminals 'to justice'.[71] We can be even less precise about the number of times he facilitated the return of stolen goods to their owners, but reports of the warehouses he kept full of stolen goods indicate that this was almost certainly a more substantial part of his business. In 1725, for reasons which are still not entirely clear, the authorities turned on him, and he was convicted of receiving money for the return of stolen goods and not apprehending or reporting the thieves. The case against him was managed on the orders of the Secretary of State, Charles Townshend.[72] While Wild had been useful to authorities desperate to curb violent crime and gangs, he had established a form of police acting outside the law which had grown intolerable. Once again, an innovative practice, encouraged by the state in response to a pressing social problem, was undermined by the opportunities for corruption which it opened up. Wild was executed on 24 May 1725.

Attitudes towards Wild were ambivalent. According to Howson, 'On the one hand, from 1719 until about 1724 [the "educated public"] regarded him as the man above all others able and always ready to deal with crime, wherever, and in whatever form it might occur.'[73] Juries, and by extension the courts, were remarkably supportive. Eighty-two per cent of the defendants he testified against between 1716 and 1724 at the Old Bailey were convicted, compared to 63 per cent of defendants overall, and all six defendants for whom he testified in favour were acquitted. 'On the other hand', Howson continues, the public 'knew that Wild's men were all rogues and gaol-birds ... and that the results he undeniably got were achieved by means it were better not to examine too closely'.[74]

Thieves depended upon Wild for both business and protection, but many also loathed him. It was not only Joseph 'Blueskin' Blake, who cut Wild's throat with a penknife outside the Old Bailey courtroom when

[70] Howson, *Thief-Taker General*, chs. 16–17.

[71] *LL*, Mary Clayton, 'Quilt Arnold, 1687 – c. 1726'; Howson, *Thief-Taker General*, Appendix 2.

[72] *LL*, Old Bailey Proceedings, 13 May 1725 (t17250513-55); Beattie, *Policing and Punishment*, p. 389.

[73] Howson, *Thief-Taker General*, pp. 124–5.   [74] Howson, *Thief-Taker General*, p. 126.

Wild refused to protect him, who resented his betrayals.[75] In February 1723, for example, John Bradshaw made 'a great noise in the streets last night threatening to kill [Wild] and other people being a very mischievous and disorderly person'.[76] Wild's response was to have Bradshaw committed to Bridewell. The attitudes of the rest of plebeian London are more difficult to fathom, but were frequently negative. Following Wild's arrest (when he was no longer a threat), he was the target of widespread popular hostility, in part owing to his role in the arrest and conviction of Jack Sheppard and Joseph 'Blueskin' Blake. Many commentators noted the crowd's antagonism towards Wild at his execution, in sharp contrast to the usual behaviour of the Tyburn crowd.[77]

This opposition was in part personal to Wild and not directed at thief-takers in general, who continued to prosper for decades. While there was some attempt to regulate the provision of rewards for conviction, the government continued to pay out large sums in rewards (£1,300 in December 1730 alone). More than a dozen thief-takers appear to have been working between 1730 and 1733, many of whom were constables. Yet their exploitation of the system continued: Beattie notes that 'the perjury and corruption that had fuelled many of Wild's prosecutions were clearly evident in the late 1720s and the early years of the next decade', and a major scandal concerning 'thief-making' erupted in 1754.[78]

Nonetheless, the activities of Wild and his successors appear to have had some important long-term repercussions. Most importantly, they stimulated thieves and others accused of crime to develop new means of defending themselves. Owing in part to the danger of wrongful convictions arising from corrupt prosecutions initiated by thief-takers, in the 1730s defendants accused of felony were allowed to employ counsel at the Old Bailey for the first time, an option they enthusiastically took up in the following decade. But faced with Wild's formidable success, it is likely that defendants in the 1720s were already obtaining legal advice from wherever they could find it. There are suggestions that some prisoners at this time were hiring 'Newgate solicitors' in order to pressure

[75] *LL*, Old Bailey Proceedings, 14 October 1724 (t17241014-43). See also, *LL*, set 'Joseph Blake'.
[76] *LL*, Bridewell Royal Hospital: Minutes of the Court of Governors, 26 December 1722 – 15 December 1737 (BBBRMG202050036).
[77] [Daniel Defoe], *The True and Genuine Account of the Life and Actions of the Late Jonathan Wild: Not Made Up of Fiction and Fable, but Taken from his own Mouth* (1725), p. 39.
[78] Beattie, *Policing and Punishment*, pp. 402, 404; Ruth Paley, 'Thief-takers in London in the age of the McDaniel Gang, c. 1745–1754', in D. Hay and F. Snyder, eds., *Policing and Prosecution in Britain 1750–1850* (Oxford University Press, 1989), pp. 301–42.

prosecutors to drop charges before trial.[79] Catherine Hayes, accused of the brutal murder of her husband, reportedly consulted a solicitor before pleading not guilty at her trial in 1726.[80]

Informal legal advice was also available inside Newgate prison. When in long-term incarceration there in the early 1730s, Roger Johnson, one of Wild's former accomplices, assisted the prisoners in preparing for their trials:[81]

> he tried the Thieves (as they call it) before they were carried down to the Sessions House to be tried, that is, he sate as Judge. The Prisoner told him the Truth of the Fact, and what he imagin'd would be swore against him, Roger then told him what to say, what Evasions and doubles to make, and told him whether he would come off or not.[82]

Faced with zealous prosecutors and constables responding to heightened pressures to deal with a perceived crime wave, and with exploitation by thief-takers and frequent betrayals by accomplices seeking pardons, London's thieves fought back with all means available. In the process, their attitudes towards the law hardened.

A culture of defiance

Taking advantage of the dramatic expansion of both print and public interest in crime in the 1720s, many thieves embraced their criminal identity and tried to exploit it for their own advantage. With newspaper proprietors, pamphleteers and clergymen (especially the Ordinary of Newgate prison) desperate for copy, 'many malefactors ... seemed willing enough to take an active part in their own self-mythologization'.[83] Because crime had become a reference point for many topics of public concern, there was no shortage of legitimising notions in the literature of crime, which thieves, particularly highway robbers, could draw upon to present themselves as 'social critics'.[84] Not least, they could draw

---

[79] *Directions for Prosecuting Thieves without the Help of those False Guides, the Newgate Sollicitors* (1728), pp. 10, 14. Similar complaints that solicitors were helping the accused avoid conviction were made in 1699 and 1747: *The Great Grievance of Traders and Shopkeepers, by the Notorious Practice of Stealing their Goods out of their Shops and Warehouses* (1699); Thomas DeVeil, *Observations on the Practice of a Justice of the Peace* (1747), p. vii.

[80] *A Narrative of the Barbarous and Unheard of Murder of Mr John Hayes* (1726), p. 25.

[81] *LL*, set, 'Roger Johnson'.

[82] *A Full and Particular Account of the Life and Notorious Transactions of Roger Johnson* (1740), p. 25.

[83] Andrea McKenzie, *Tyburn's Martyrs: Execution in England, 1675–1775* (London: Hambledon Continuum, 2007), pp. 106–7.

[84] Andrea McKenzie, 'The real Macheath: social satire, appropriation, and eighteenth-century criminal biography', *Huntington Library Quarterly*, 69:4 (2006), 581–605.

parallels with the political corruption of the whig oligarchy. The collapse of the South Sea Bubble in the autumn of 1720 may have had little economic impact on plebeian Londoners, but the evidence of sharp practices was there for all to see, as was the 1725 trial and conviction of the Lord Chancellor, Thomas Parker, Earl of Macclesfield, for taking £100,000 worth of bribes.[85]

The parallels which could be drawn between elite greed, the two-faced activities of thief-takers and the comparatively minor thefts committed by highwaymen, street robbers and pickpockets were missed by few. Not only could it be argued that the crimes of those brought before the Old Bailey were far less egregious than those of their governors, but at least *they* were willing to stand up and be held accountable for them. Moreover they could claim they robbed from exploitative lawyers and quack doctors, or, more generally, from those who could afford it, and, like Robin Hood, gave to the poor.[86] As Richard Steele commented when he read Alexander Smith's collection of the *Lives of the Most Noted Highwaymen* (first published in 1714), he had 'more respect for [these "great Men"] than for greater Criminals'.[87] The 1726 edition of Smith's collection included a quote from Samuel Garth's 1699 description of the Old Bailey as a court where 'little Villains must submit to Fate / While Great Ones do enjoy the World in State'.[88] While John Gay made the most of these comparisons in his *Beggars' Opera* in 1728, they were frequently drawn by others throughout the decade, not least by the more astute criminals.

These justifications may not have accurately described the motivations for crime, but they certainly helped explain even the most serious crimes after the event. While few publications failed to condemn crime, a space had been opened up for a language of mitigation, particularly in the *Ordinary's Accounts*. James Wright, a member of the Hawkins gang who was convicted of highway robbery in 1721 when William Hawkins turned evidence against him, told the Ordinary 'he generally aim'd at robbing Coaches, or those whose Equipage and Appearance show'd them best able to sustain a Loss: That he never would rob a poor

---

[85] Julian Hoppit, 'The myths of the South Sea Bubble', *Transactions of the Royal Historical Society*, 6th Series, 12 (2002), 145–56.

[86] Gillian Spraggs, *Outlaws and Highwaymen: The Cult of the Robber in England from the Middle Ages to the Nineteenth Century* (London: Pimlico, 2001); McKenzie, *Tyburn's Martyrs*, ch. 4.

[87] Richard Steele, *The Englishman: Being the Sequel of the Guardian* (1714), p. 381.

[88] [Alexander Smith], *Memoirs of the Life and Times of the Famous Jonathan Wild* (1726), title page (repr. New York: Garland Publishing, 1973); Andrea McKenzie, '"This death some strong and stout hearted man doth choose": the practice of *peine forte et dure* in seventeenth- and eighteenth-century England', *Law and History Review*, 23:2 (2005), 299.

Man, but pittied him, as much as himself'.[89] James Shaw, who according to Howson led a gang with at least thirteen known members and 'murdered several of the people he robbed', justified his choice of victims by the fact that, as he told the Ordinary, 'as it is more sinful to rob a poor Man or the Church of God, so it was less sinful to rob those who would have spent the Money taken in Gaiety and Luxury, or those who perhaps had unjustly acquired it by Gaming', drawing a parallel with contemporary efforts to suppress gaming houses.[90] The well-publicised collapse of the Bubble provided further arguments. Describing why he turned to robbing, John Hawkins (brother of William) told the Ordinary, 'he left the uncertain Way of dealing at Sea, to deal (he said) in the South Sea and the Bubbles from which he had recourse to bubbling in another Way, as some others besides have done'[91] Thanks to news coverage and the publication of several pamphlets, these justifications were widely disseminated.

While the Hawkins gang achieved significant notoriety, not least through their own publications,[92] the crimes and particularly the prison escapes of Jack Sheppard raised criminal celebrity to an entirely new level.[93] Although Sheppard was more 'used as a mouthpiece to denounce the hypocrisy and corruption of a society of which he was merely the mirror image' and did not make such claims himself, he did actively promote his public image as an anti-authority figure through his provocative comments to the Ordinary and in the pamphlet he wrote (with Defoe's assistance) just before his execution.[94] He told the Ordinary that it was 'no Crime in him to steal from those in better Circumstances

---

[89] *LL*, Ordinary of Newgate Prison: Ordinary's Accounts, 22 December 1721 (OA172112222112220002). See also, *LL*, set, 'James Wright', and set, 'William Hawkins'.

[90] Howson, *Thief-Taker General*, pp. 172, 183, 313; *LL*, Ordinary of Newgate Prison: Ordinary's Accounts, 8 February 1722 (OA172202082202080004). See also *LL*, set, 'James Shaw'.

[91] *LL*, Ordinary of Newgate Prison: Ordinary's Accounts, 21 May 1722 (OA172205212205210003). See also *LL*, set, 'John Hawkins'.

[92] William Hawkins, *A True and Impartial Account of all the Robberies Committed by William Hawkins* (1722); Ralph Wilson, *A Full and Impartial Account of all the Robberies Committed by John Hawkins, George Sympson (lately Executed for Robbing the Bristol Mails) and their Companions* (4th edn, 1722).

[93] *LL*, set, 'Jack Sheppard'.

[94] McKenzie, *Tyburn's Martyrs*, p. 102; *A Narrative of All the Robberies, Escapes, etc. of John Sheppard... The whole Published at the particular Request of the Prisoner* (1724). See also Hal Gladfelder, *Criminality and Narrative in Eighteenth-Century England: Beyond the Law* (Baltimore: Johns Hopkins University Press, 2001), pp. 90, 121–2.

than himself'.[95] Reluctant to follow the expected practice of showing repentance for his crimes, Sheppard instead voiced the ambition of taking revenge on those who had turned against him, saying 'he would increase the Number, as well as heighten the Quality of his Crimes'.[96] Arguing that criminals should support each other, he attacked both thief-takers, who 'deserve the Gallows as richly as any of the Thieves', and thieves who impeached their accomplices, and 'said that if all were but such Tight-Cocks as himself, the Reputation of British Thievery might be carried to a far greater height'.[97]

As a consequence of his incredible escapes from Newgate prison, Londoners became fascinated by Sheppard's story, and a veritable legion of hack writers produced biographies, ballads and newspaper reports. As Defoe wrote,

His Escape and his being so suddenly Re-taken made such a Noise in the Town, that it was thought all the common People would have gone Mad about him; there being not a Porter to be had for Love nor Money, nor getting into an Ale-house, for Butchers, Shoemakers and Barbers, all engag'd in Controversies, and Wagers, about Sheppard.[98]

He was reputedly visited in prison by crowds of elite men and women, and plebeian Londoners appear to have willed him on to succeed in his escapes. While there were struggles over the control of his corpse, however, there was no attempt to prevent his execution, suggesting that the crowd recognised the inevitability of his punishment.[99]

Other criminals, however, were encouraged by his story to commit their own acts of resistance. Defoe reported that 'The Felons on the Common Side of Newgate ... animated by Sheppard's Example, the Night before they were to be Shipt for Transportation ... cut several Iron Bars asunder, and some of them had saw'd off their fetters' in an attempt to escape. If they had had two hours more, Defoe wrote, 'near One Hundred Villians [sic] had been let loose into the World'.[100] Over

---

[95] LL, Ordinary of Newgate Prison: Ordinary's Accounts, 4 September 1724 (OA172409042409040005).
[96] LL, Ordinary of Newgate Prison: Ordinary's Accounts, 4 September 1724 (OA172409042409040004).
[97] A Narrative of All the Robberies, Escapes, etc. of John Sheppard, p. 15; The History of the Remarkable Life of John Sheppard (1724), p. 34.
[98] Remarkable Life of John Sheppard, p. 27.
[99] McKenzie, Tyburn's Martyrs, p. 101. For his execution, see Christopher Hibbert, The Road to Tyburn: The Story of Jack Sheppard and the Eighteenth-Century London Underworld (London: World Pub. Co., 1957), ch. 14.
[100] Remarkable Life of John Sheppard, p. 40.

the ensuing years several others successfully escaped, either en masse (Richard Scurrier 'with several others' in 1725), by following Sheppard's example and going through the roof (Roger Johnson, and accused murderer Henry Fisher in 1727) or by dressing in women's clothes (John Sherwin, accused of a libel and 'abusing the Bench of Justices at Hick's Hall' in 1731).[101]

Lewis Houssart, condemned for the murder of his wife, shared a cell with Sheppard shortly before both were executed, and also seems to have been inspired by his defiant attitude.[102] As the Ordinary reported,

After he was Convicted of the Murther ... his every Word and Look were full of Bitterness and venom against the Court and his Accusers ... he was not sorry that he had Arraigned the Justice of the English Nation, in the Face of the Court that Tried him, but sorry he had not done it more largely; ... But the Person with whom he seem'd the most pleas'd was John Sheppard; and while they were in the Condemn'd-Hold, they were sometimes very Merry and Jocose together.[103]

Refusing to meet conventional expectations that he should confess his crimes, Houssart denied murdering his wife when on the scaffold.

Whether or not highway robbers and footpads were motivated by their role as 'social critics' (and evidence of this is scarce), in their behaviour and publicity-seeking many thieves not only defied the law, as is evident in their repeated crimes, but also actively rejected the authority of the courts, notably by refusing to plead and thereby subjecting themselves to *peine forte et dure*. A historical remnant of the medieval transition from trial by ordeal to trial by jury, this form of torture had not been carried out at the Old Bailey since the 1680s, but from 1716 several defendants refused to plead and put themselves at risk of experiencing this horrific practice. Mary Andrews, for example, charged with highway robbery in 1721, 'was so obstinate as to suffer three Whipcords to be broke in tying her Thumbs, as the Law requires in such Cases', before she relented and entered her plea.[104] In the same year two highwaymen, William Spiggot and Nathaniel Hawes, and in 1726 Edward Burnworth, went so far as to endure the pain of being forced to lie flat, naked and spread-eagled on

---

[101] *LL*, Old Bailey Proceedings, 8 December 1725 (t17251208-12); *LL*, Old Bailey Proceedings, 16 October 1728 (t17281016-75); W. H. Sheehan, 'Finding solace in eighteenth-century Newgate', in J. S. Cockburn, ed., *Crime in England 1550–1800* (London: Taylor & Francis, 1977), p. 241; LMA, City of London: Repertories of the Court of Aldermen, COL/CA/01/01/131, 6 Nov. 1722 – 28 Oct. 1723, f. 295; *LL*, Old Bailey Proceedings, 8 December 1731 (t17311208-58).

[102] *LL*, set, 'Lewis Houssart'.

[103] *LL*, Ordinary of Newgate Prison: Ordinary's Accounts, 7 December 1724 (OA172412072412070004).

[104] *LL*, Old Bailey Proceedings, 25 May 1721 (t17210525-66).

the floor in Newgate prison and endure weights of up to 400 pounds placed on their chests before they finally agreed to plead.[105]

Those who refused to plead advanced several justifications, including demanding that possessions confiscated at the time of their arrest be returned (which was not legally possible). But as Andrea McKenzie has argued, 'the most likely motivations ... seem to have been the desire to preserve one's reputation or to express one's rejection of the tribunal, or both'. Not only was enduring the press and their willingness to die an 'implicit challenge to the legitimacy of the court', but it allowed these men, who were clearly playing to an audience both inside and outside the courtroom, to demonstrate their 'manly courage' and defiance of author-ity.[106] Hawes said his refusal 'was as became a Man of Courage and bold Spirit, and if the Court was so Uncivil as to deny him his own Cloths, he had no business to oblige the Court, in Pleading', claiming that the Old Bailey 'used to be a Court of Justice, but was now a Place of Injustice'.[107] He said in court that 'as he liv'd like a Man, he was resolv'd to die so' and acknowledged to the Ordinary that his primary motive for enduring the press was not to seek the return of his 'good Suit of Cloaths', but 'to evince his Boldness, and to gain Applause among the Gentlemen of the Highway, as he said, for being so brave a fellow'.[108] Burnworth was determined to remain longer under the press than Spiggot. He did so, lasting over an hour.[109]

Some defendants mocked the authority of the court during their trials. James Carrick, described as a member of 'the most villainous set about London', was finally tried in 1722 for robbing William Young, MP, as he travelled in a chair in Covent Garden between 1 and 2 in the morning on 1 July.[110] The *Proceedings* report that he made a 'frivolous defence' at his trial, but they do not explain what it consisted of.[111] As reported in the more complete *Select Trials*, an edition of trial accounts based on original shorthand notes from the trials but published twenty years later, he

[105] *LL*, set, 'William Spiggot'; *LL*, Emily Spencer, 'Nathaniel Hawes'; *LL*, Ordinary of Newgate Prison: Ordinary's Accounts, 8 February 1721 (OA172102082102080004).
[106] McKenzie, *Tyburn's Martyrs*, pp. 241–9. See also McKenzie, 'The practice of *peine forte et dure*'.
[107] *LL*, Ordinary of Newgate Prison: Ordinary's Accounts, 22 December 1721 (OA172112222112220005).
[108] *LL*, Old Bailey Proceedings, 6 December 1721 (t17211206-45); *LL*, Ordinary of Newgate Prison: Ordinary's Accounts, 22 December 1721 (OA172112222112220005).
[109] Howson, *Thief-Taker General*, p. 291.
[110] *Select Trials at the Sessions-House in the Old Bailey*, 4 vols. (1742), I, p. 204; Howson, *Thief-Taker General*, p. 172.
[111] *LL*, Old Bailey Proceedings, 4 July 1722 (t17220704-51).

aggressively cross-examined Young in a way which only further implicated him in the crime:

CARRICK: Pray Sir, which Side of the Chair was I on when you say
             I robb'd you?
MR. YOUNG: On the left Side.
CARRICK: Now that's a lie, for I was on the right side – I shall catch you
             again presently ... What sort of a Wig?
MR. YOUNG: A light Tye-Wig.
CARRICK: That's another damn'd Lie of yours ...[112]

While we do not know if anyone in the courtroom was impressed by this effrontery, we do know that, unsurprisingly, he was convicted and his defiance was omitted from the *Proceedings*.

Others steadfastly maintained their innocence even after conviction. John Hawkins 'defended himself and [George] Simpson to an extraordinary degree' at his trial, but was nevertheless convicted and sentenced to death in May 1722.[113] Hawkins then 'put on a Deportment suprizingly odd and bold, arraigning the Court and the Jury alternately, and discovering (as he fancy'd) several irregular Proceedings at his Trial'.[114] According to the *Select Trials*:

The Verdict being recorded, Hawkins exprest himself to this Purpose. I am altogether innocent of this Robbery; though I don't blame my Country-men for their Verdict, for their intentions were honourable, but they were over rul'd by a partial Judge.[115]

Similarly unreported in the *Proceedings* was James Dalton's behaviour following his conviction on a misdemeanour charge of attempted robbery in January 1730.[116] According to the *Universal Spectator*, 'he behaved himself with a great deal of Insolence while the Court were passing Sentence on him, and threatened to do Murder before long ... When that Part of his Sentence was pronounced of his Fine [40 marks, or about £26], he reply'd, Give me a Receipt for it, and I'll pay you now.'[117]

Awaiting execution, the condemned frequently resisted the ministrations of the Ordinary and played instead to the audience of fellow

---

[112] *Select Trials*, I, p. 198.
[113] *Tyburn's Worthies, or the Robberies and Enterprizes of John Hawkins and George Simpson* ([1722]), p. 23. See also *LL*, set, 'John Hawkins'.
[114] Ordinary of Newgate Prison: Ordinary's Accounts, 21 May 1721 (OA17220521220 5210003)
[115] *Select Trials*, I, pp. 167–8.
[116] *LL*, set, 'James Dalton'.
[117] *Universal Spectator and Weekly Journal*, 24 January 1730 (Burney Collection: www.galegroup.com, 1 Jan. 2014).

prisoners.[118] Martin Bellamy, one-time associate of James Dalton, and Benjamin Branch were described by the Ordinary as 'the most obstinate and obdurate Criminals I ever saw'.[119] Although the Ordinary claimed Bellamy eventually repented, the *London Journal* reported a rather different account of his behaviour the Sunday before his execution, when 'he publickly cursed the Ordinary and the whole Congregation, upon the Minister's taking a Text from St Matthew's Gospel against Thieves; and he continued so outrageous that there was no Sermon, the Ordinary not being able to proceed'.[120]

Although many convicts, like Bellamy, ultimately died penitent, for others the gallows provided an opportunity for a final act of defiance. The 1720s appears to have witnessed an escalation of the practice of common criminals dying 'game', by affecting a 'cheerful unconcern with [their] fate'.[121] Many of the condemned demonstrated their indifference to hanging by, at various times, wearing gay clothes, adopting a confident (rather than repentant) tone and demeanour, tossing their shoes into the crowd (so it could not be said that they 'died with their shoes on') and leaping off the scaffold rather than waiting for the hangman to act. By refusing to implicate their comrades, asserting their innocence and expressing their confidence of salvation, they rejected the gallows script in which they were expected to acknowledge their sins and place themselves at God's mercy.[122] Such behaviour was commemorated in Jonathan Swift's satirical poem, *Clever Tom Clinch Going to be Hanged* (1727), in which Tom told the execution crowd:

> Take Courage, dear Comrades, and be not afraid,
> Nor slip this Occasion to follow your Trade.
> My Conscience is clear, and my Spirits are calm,
> And thus I go off without Pray'r Book or Psalm.

The poem concludes, 'Then follow the Practice of Clever Tom Clinch / Who hung like a Hero, and never would flinch'.[123]

McKenzie suggests that dying like a hero was 'an ideal to which many real-life criminals aspired', and some convicts put on quite a show.[124] When the Minter Charles Towers, furious that he had been convicted of

---

118 McKenzie, *Tyburn's Martyrs*, ch. 5.
119 Ordinary of Newgate Prison: Ordinary's Accounts, 27 March 1728 (OA172803272803270001). See also *LL*, set, 'Martin Bellamy'.
120 *London Journal*, 23 March 1728 (Burney Collection: www.galegroup.com, 1 Jan. 2014).
121 McKenzie, *Tyburn's Martyrs*, p. 205.
122 McKenzie, *Tyburn's Martyrs*, ch. 7, quote from p. 206.
123 Jonathan Swift, 'Clever Tom Clinch Going to be Hanged', in *The Works of Jonathan Swift*, Vol. II: *Poetical Works* (Dublin, 1772), p. 223.
124 McKenzie, *Tyburn's Martyrs*, p. 192.

going in disguise when rescuing a fellow debtor, was on the scaffold, for example, he 'pull'd out a Paper' and demanded that it be read. While acknowledging that as a sinner he deserved death, he denied he had been in disguise or that he had committed any thefts, and 'inveigh'd against the Bailiffs'.[125] Others demonstrated contempt by their actions. At James Carrick's execution, he 'laughed and smiled upon all whom he there knew; gave himself genteel Airs in fixing the Rope aright about his Neck, and ... had continually some pretty Gesture or other when the People were silent and expecting of something from him'.[126] Stephen Barnham, convicted of highway robbery in 1728 and previously an associate of 'Blueskin' Blake, had already shown defiance in the courtroom when he and his accomplices seemed not to 'have the least Regret, but on the contrary, they all four laugh'd, and with the utmost Contempt despised the Witnesses who swore against them ... they stood at the Bar careless, negligent and confident'.[127] At Tyburn he 'laugh'd twice after he was ty'd up to the gallows' and took the Ordinary's prayer book and 'threw it up against the gallows with all the Passion and Folly imaginable'.[128]

Contemporaries worried that the bold behaviour of the condemned encouraged imitators. Bernard Mandeville wrote that during the procession to Tyburn, 'young Villains, that are proud of being so (if they knew any of the Malefactors) tear the Cloaths off their Backs ... [and] shake hands with [them] ... not to lose, before so much company, the Reputation there is in having had such a valuable Acquaintance'.[129] Similarly, Defoe commented:

One thing that increases the number of our Town Thieves, is to see the Criminals go to Execution as neat and trim, as if they were going to a Wedding. G-d D-mn, says one Rogue to another, Jack Such-a-one made a clever Figure when he went to Tyburn the other Day, and died bravely, hard, like a Cock.[130]

The 'game' criminal encouraged other acts of defiance. The crowd's behaviour in seeking to seize the corpses of those executed, to prevent them from being taken away for dissection by the surgeons, suggests that

---

[125] Ordinary of Newgate Prison: Ordinary's Accounts, 4 January 1725 (OA17250104250 1040006). See also LL, set, 'Charles Towers'.

[126] Ordinary of Newgate Prison: Ordinary's Accounts, 18 July 1722 (OA172207182 207180006). See also LL, set, 'James Carrick'.

[127] Old Bailey Proceedings, 16 October 1728 (t17281016-15). See also, LL, set, 'Stephen Barnham'.

[128] Fog's Weekly Journal, 16 Nov. 1728 (Burney Collection: www.galegroup.com, 1 Jan. 2014).

[129] Bernard Mandeville, An Enquiry into the Causes of the Frequent Executions at Tyburn [1725], pp. 23–4, 35.

[130] [Daniel Defoe], Street Robberies, Consider'd: The Reason of their being so Frequent ([1728]), p. 52.

they had developed a certain solidarity with the condemned.[131] As Mandeville commented, 'They have suffer'd the Law (cries the Rabble) and shall have no other Barbarities put upon them: We know what you are, and will not leave them before we see them buried.'[132]

These acts of defiance by thieves and their supporters at each stage of the judicial process failed to prevent executions, but together they reflect the evolution of a new culture, motivated in part by particular notions of social justice, which was sharply at odds with respectable London. More effective in eliciting support and sympathy, precisely because it appealed to a more respectable audience, was the development of the myth of the 'gentleman highwayman' – a robber whose elite aspirations and polite treatment of his victims made him appear less threatening than the violent street robber.[133] The term 'street robber' itself was only coined early in the decade, to denote (and condemn) a particularly violent form of theft, in contrast to older characterisations of highwaymen. In July 1722, citing robberies committed by James Carrick, the *Daily Journal* expressed concern about a gang of 'fifteen persons whose sole business is to rob about the streets of London'.[134] Owing to the danger of being apprehended, such robberies involved a higher degree of violence than those committed on country roads. According to a contemporary account of the Burnworth gang of 'Street Robbers',

this new Society of Robbers, more than any that ever went before them, at least in England, have been mark'd by this infamous Character, that they are Murtherers as well as Thieves, and that they have been more bent upon blood, than even the Gangs of Rogues among us have usually been.[135]

With the street robber receiving such bad press, some thieves began to cultivate an alternative persona, building on characteristics of the traditional highwayman. Nathaniel Hawes told the Ordinary that shortly after he arrived in London, he fell into 'expensive Company' and began wearing 'lac'd ruffles'.[136] Although he had to steal to support this

---

[131] Peter Linebaugh, 'The Tyburn riot against the surgeons', in Douglas Hay *et al.*, eds., *Albion's Fatal Tree: Crime and Society in Eighteenth-Century England* (London: Allen Lane, 1975), pp. 65–118.

[132] Mandeville, *Enquiry into the Causes*, p. 26.

[133] Robert Shoemaker, 'The street robber and the gentleman highwayman: changing representations and perceptions of robbery in London, 1690–1800', *Cultural and Social History*, 3 (2006), 381–405.

[134] *Daily Journal*, 3–4 July 1722 (Burney Collection: www.galegroup.com, 1 Jan. 2014).

[135] *A Brief Historical Account of the Lives of the Six Notorious Street-Robbers, Executed at Kingston* (1726), p. 4.

[136] LL, Ordinary of Newgate Prison: Ordinary's Accounts, 22 December 1721 (OA172112222112220005); LL, Old Bailey Proceedings, 12 October 1720 (t17201012-30). See also LL, Emily Spencer, 'Nathaniel Hawes, *c.* 1701–1721'.

lifestyle, he claimed he acted politely in his robberies, returning goods to the victims when they appeared to need them more than him: a ring with sentimental value to one victim and money to another when he discovered he only had 18 pence.

The image of the genteel and polite robber, which did not necessarily reflect actual conduct, was disseminated to the public not only through stories told to the Ordinary but also in separate tracts and biographies. In his *Full, True and Impartial Account of all the Robberies Committed by William Hawkins*, Hawkins exonerated his executed brother John by claiming he 'never did a barbarous Action, I mean in Relation to Bloodshed, which he always scorn'd' and was 'always too generous to destroy Papers and notes', when they were included in goods that they stole. Instead, they 'sent them back Gratis to the Owners, without any Reward', in implicit contrast to the normal practices of Jonathan Wild. And when 'mean rascally schemes of robbing Foot-Passengers' were proposed to the gang, they were dismissed as 'very base things ... we were too brave to attempt any Thing on Foot'.[137] Similarly, gang member turned informer Ralph Wilson denied claims that the gang raped the women they robbed, and wrote that while he was in prison 'several Gentlemen who have been robb'd by us ... who have been to see me, remember me for the great Civility I showed above my Companions'.[138]

All this did not prevent John Hawkins from being executed, though unusually the jury did have to 'withdraw several times to consult of their verdict' before convicting him of the capital offence of highway robbery.[139] However, there is some evidence that the general public warmed to the portrayal of Hawkins and his partner Simpson as gentlemen. The *Weekly Journal: or, British Gazeteer* described the pair as 'persons of a genteel and extraordinary behaviour, of good countenance and address, which renders them the objects of much pity and concern. A great concourse of people therefore daily resort to Newgate to see them.'[140] While highwaymen secure in their cells were safe to visit, even those still at large were sometimes treated with pity, and even respect. John Turner, tried four times for robbery between 1723 and 1727, adopted the title of 'Civil John', justified by his alleged polite treatment of his victims.[141] That there was at least some foundation to these claims

[137] Hawkins, *True and Impartial Account*, pp. 3, 7, 23.
[138] LL, set, 'Ralph Wilson'; Wilson, *Full and Impartial Account*, p. 28.
[139] *Tyburn's Worthies*, p. 23.
[140] *Weekly Journal: or, British Gazeteer*, 5 May 1722 (Burney Collection: www.galegroup. com, 1 Jan. 2014).
[141] LL, set, 'John Turner'.

is evident in the testimony of his last victim, Thomas Air, at Turner's 1727 trial: 'after I delivered [my purse], he asked my pardon, and said he could not help it'.[142] The Ordinary certainly appears to have been impressed by Turner:

> He appear'd to be a young Man of a civil complaisant Temper, whence it was, that his Acquaintance commonly call'd him, Civil John; others say, that he got this Appellation from the Gentlemen whom he robb'd, because of the civil Usage he gave them ...[143]

In 1728 the gentlemanly pretensions of highwaymen were given a significant boost with the staging and publication of John Gay's *The Beggar's Opera*, with its substantial references to plebeian London. Not only were many of its tunes derived from contemporary popular ballads, but the principal characters were clearly modelled on the thief-taker Jonathan Wild (Peachum, the villain) and criminal celebrities such as Jack Sheppard and James Carrick (Macheath). Yet unlike Sheppard and Carrick, Macheath is given gentlemanly status with the title 'Captain', and Mrs Peachum says 'there is not a finer gentleman upon the road than the Captain'. At the end the 'Beggar' observes that 'it is difficult to determine whether (in the fashionable vices) the fine gentlemen imitate the gentlemen of the road, or the gentlemen of the road the fine gentlemen'.[144] Its immense popularity (*The Beggar's Opera* was the most frequently produced play in the century) led commentators, including Daniel Defoe, to worry that it encouraged crime.[145] Certainly James Dalton suggests as much when in the *Narrative* of his crimes he reports that the gang went to see it and thought 'the whole seem'd to be an Encouragement of their Profession'.[146]

In the context of the increasingly genteel pretensions of highwaymen, however, a more important impact of the play may have been to make victims of such robberies more tolerant. The gentlewoman Gertrude Savile, who went to see it on the first night in January 1728 (and several more times), wrote in her diary that 'the top charicters [*sic*] were highwaymen and common whores and very exactly drawn and yet manag'd to be inofencive and very witty'. Overall, she found it 'wonderfully

---

[142] *LL*, Old Bailey Proceedings, 17 October 1727 (t17271017-22).
[143] *LL*, Ordinary of Newgate Prison: Ordinary's Accounts, 20 November 1727 (OA172711202711200002).
[144] John Gay, *The Beggar's Opera* (1728), act I, scene iv; act III, scene xvi.
[145] Daniel Defoe, *Augusta Triumphans: Or, the Way to Make London the Most Flourishing City in the Universe* (1728), p. 48.
[146] *A Genuine Narrative of all the Street Robberies Committed since October last, by James Dalton* (1728), p. 25; *LL*, set, 'James Dalton'.

entertaining and instructive, tho' the subject was so low'.[147] The light-hearted and sympathetic treatment of highwaymen in the play further distinguished them from the stereotypically violent conduct of street robbers. As a commentator, possibly Defoe, wrote in 1731, while victims of the latter are 'knock'd down and robb'd, nay, sometimes murther'd at their own Doors',

the English Highway-men generally rob with more Civility and good Manners than is practis'd abroad, and with something of generosity; not murdering those they attack, and frequently bidding the Ladies not to be frighted, and telling them they will do them no harm.[148]

The defiant culture of London's thieves in the 1720s thus had two main, if contradictory, consequences. On the one hand, the recidivism and rejection of authority evident in their crimes, courtroom behaviour and performance on the gallows encouraged the development of an oppos-itional plebeian culture and hardened elite perceptions of the threats posed by crime, contributing to more frequent prosecutions of ordinary thieves, and, in the 1730s, an increase in the powers given to the night watch. On the other hand, taking advantage of the opportunities accorded by the growth in printed literature about crime and the cultural resources of the traditions of courteous behaviour and social justice found among rural highwaymen, some robbers used print to reinvent themselves as a far less threatening form of criminal, the gentlemanly highwayman. Consequently, as would become more evident in later decades in cases such as that of highwayman James Maclaine, some victims became reluctant to prosecute, undermining the authorities' more punitive approach to crime and thereby exacerbating the challenge to law and order.

The debtors strike back

Just as criminal justice was challenged in the 1720s, so too was the administration of London's debtors' prisons. Prior to the passage of legislation in that decade, incarceration for small debt was a common misfortune suffered by many plebeian Londoners. Apprehended by often corrupt bailiffs (whose real interest was in extorting money from those whom they arrested in their 'sponging houses'), at the behest of real or fictional creditors, poor Londoners could find themselves left to rot on

---

[147] Alan Savile, ed., *Secret Comment: The Diaries of Gertrude Savile 1721–1757* (Thoroton Society Record Series, vol. 41, 1995), p. 100.
[148] *An Effectual Scheme for the Immediate Preventing of Street-Robberies* (1731), pp. 10, 30.

the 'common side' of any number of London's prisons, including Newgate. It has been estimated that debtors 'comprised more than half the prison population in the country' in the early eighteenth century, and that 'most were working poor, either artisans or shopkeepers'. In London, the most important prisons for debtors were the Fleet, King's Bench and the Marshalsea, with the Marshalsea holding an average of over 300 prisoners at any one time during the century.[149] Prisoners were divided by wealth between the relatively comfortable 'master's side' (where those who could afford it could live in their own apartments) and the frequently squalid 'common side', waiting for either a stroke of luck, or more realistically, the passage of one of the periodic acts 'for the relief of insolvent debtors', to open the prison gates. Six thousand debtors were released following the passage of one such act in 1712.[150] In between the passage of these acts, common side prisoners had to live in appalling conditions. In the Marshalsea in 1729, a single room, just sixteen feet by fourteen, housed thirty-two men: 'half are hung up in Hammocks', and all were obliged 'to ease Nature within the Room, the stench of which is noisome beyond Expression'.[151] Not entitled to any relief from county funds, prisoners were dependent for food on the 'groats' they could secure from their creditors, or the proceeds of begging at the prison gates.[152] In 1729 a parliamentary committee found that most of the 330 prisoners on the common side in the Marshalsea were 'in the utmost necessity' and that 'great Numbers ... appeared to have perished for Want'.[153]

Abuse of the prisoners was facilitated by the fact that the keepers' powers over them were only to a limited extent constrained by law, but paradoxically in practice the system of prison governance empowered the prisoners to run these institutions largely on their own terms. Debtors' prisons form an extreme example of the eighteenth century's unreformed system of prison governance, in which the position of

---

[149] Paul Haagen, 'Eighteenth-century English society and the debt law', in Stanley Cohen and Andrew Scull, eds., *Social Control and the State* (Oxford: Martin Robertson, 1983), pp. 223–4; Joanna Innes, *Inferior Politics: Social Problems and Social Policies in Eighteenth-Century Britain* (Oxford University Press, 2009), pp. 29, 227–78; Jerry White, 'Pain and degradation in Georgian London: life in the Marshalsea prison', *History Workshop Journal*, 68 (2009), 69–98; Roger Lee Brown, *A History of the Fleet Prison, London*, Studies in British History, 42 (Lampeter: Edwin Mellen Press, 1996), p. 154.

[150] Haagen, 'Eighteenth-century society', p. 223.

[151] *PP*, 'A report from the committee appointed to enquire into the state of the goals [*sic*] of this kingdom; relating to the Marshalsea prison' (London, 1729), p. 4 (parlipapers. chadwyck.co.uk, 11 Jan. 2014).

[152] Brown, *History of the Fleet*, pp. 198–9, 201.

[153] *PP*, *Journals of the House of Commons*, 14 May 1729, pp. 377–8 (parlipapers.chadwyck. co.uk, 11 Jan. 2014).

keeper was purchased and the prison was run for profit. To save costs, keepers were usually unwilling to hire the officers needed to run the prison and instead depended on the prisoners themselves, while at the same time providing a minimum standard of care. As Roger Brown describes the power dynamic in the Fleet, 'The warden needed the prisoners' consent to govern his prison with the minimum of resources, while the prisoners needed his favour in order that their traditional privileges [such as access to alcohol] could be continued.' In this prison the over 300 prisoners were supervised by a skeleton staff consisting of the warden and his deputy, a night warden, and two or three turnkeys. At night, the prisoners were simply locked in and left to their own devices.[154] The fact that prisoners for debt remained incarcerated for periods of years, rather than weeks as was more commonly the case with those charged with crime, and that they were sometimes able to transfer between prisons, meant that they could form close alliances with their fellow prisoners and develop more effective methods of resistance. We have already seen how the debtors of the New Mint defended their privileges through collective protest. The Fleet and King's Bench prisons were largely governed by a 'prisoners committee', with the latter's committee having printed a list of thirty-seven rules governing prisoner conduct. This system of self-governance had its own hierarchy, with common side prisoners excluded from decision-making, and prisoners subjected to punishments for breaking the rules.[155] It was supplemented by judicial oversight of the prisons, including the appointment of a prison 'visitor' at King's Bench prison, allowing prisoners to voice their complaints.[156] At crucial moments, in alliance with supporters outside the prison, this culture of both self-government and complaint allowed the prisoners to organise resistance to exploitation by the keepers.

In 1729 mistreatment of prisoners by the keepers of the Marshalsea and Fleet led to a parliamentary investigation. Occurring at a time when the whole interlocking system of local government, poor relief and criminal justice seemed, like the whig oligarchy itself, to be riven by corruption, these scandals touched a raw nerve. While MPs played a significant role in the investigations which eventually forced the keepers of these two prisons from office, it was the prisoners themselves who first brought the issue to public attention. In March 1728, when William Acton became

---

[154] Brown, *History of the Fleet*, pp. 132–3.
[155] Brown, *History of the Fleet*, p. 223. For self-governance and the 'debtor ethos' in the King's Bench prison, see Innes, *Inferior Politics*, pp. 234–5, 259–66.
[156] Innes, *Inferior Politics*, pp. 253–5.

Deputy Keeper of the Marshalsea, determined to make a profit on the £400 investment the position cost him, the death rate began to rise. In the first instance, some eight months after Acton took over, the prisoners on the common side simply 'rose up' against his regime. A prisoner named Anderson 'cry'd out One & all! and immediately they fell upon [Acton]', who eventually escaped with 'the Loss of a Little Blood and a torn Shirt' and what appears to be a renewed dedication to punishing his prisoners.[157] Acton had fetters, iron skull caps and stinking isolation cells, all the gruesome equipment of early modern incarceration, at his disposal. But the prisoners did not give up. In 1729, prompted by a parliamentary inquiry, the complaints of 'Several Persons now under Confinement' in King's Bench, the compters, Ludgate and the Marshalsea were published, including the testimony of one prisoner:

great Numbers of them [are] in Rags, and almost naked, starving for want of Bread ... [they are] Shadows, pale, and faint, without any the least Subsistence, and in all appearance, perishing for want of Relief, and daily seeing the dead Bodies of others carried out ...[158]

The parliamentary inquiry was established under the leadership of General James Oglethorpe, MP, philanthropist and founder of Georgia, to investigate conditions in the country's prisons. However, mired in the party politics, his inquiry initially failed to dislodge Acton. Although Acton was arrested and tried for the murder of four prisoners, including Thomas Bliss, who had died following a brutal round of what can only be described as torture, he was eventually acquitted of all charges at the Surrey Assizes in August 1729, following the intervention of powerful political figures. It took a further death and trial for murder to finally drive Acton from his position in September 1729, some eighteen months after his arrival.[159]

The committee also investigated the Fleet prison following the death of Robert Castell in squalid conditions. A debtor and friend of Oglethorpe, Castell had been transferred to the common side for failure to pay his fees, and his death formed the original catalyst for the inquiry. This investigation empowered the prisoners and their supporters to attempt to use the law against those who ran the prison. The leader of the

---

[157] John Gringer, ed., *Handel's Trumpeter: The Diary of John Grano* (Bucina: The Historic Brass Society Series, no. 3; Stuyvesant, NY: Pendragon Press, 1998), pp. 140–1, 18 Nov. 1728.

[158] *The Miseries of Goals, and the Cruelty of Goalers. Being a Narrative of Several Persons now under Confinement* (1729), p. 54.

[159] White, 'Pain and degradation in Georgian London', 89–90, 92.

prisoners, Roger Johnson, former accomplice of Jonathan Wild, accused the warden of the Fleet, Thomas Bambridge, of murder.[160] Both Bambridge and the former warden, John Huggins, were tried at the Old Bailey for the murder of different victims in May 1729, though the *Proceedings* failed to report the testimony in either trial. One prisoner, Elizabeth Barkley, also prosecuted Bambridge for the felonious theft of her household goods in December 1729. Although he was acquitted in both cases, and also in a suit of appeal for murder brought by Castell's widow, Bambridge was stripped of his post by Act of parliament.[161] Huggins, meanwhile, languished in Newgate while council wrangled over the text of a special verdict.

Although the failure of these prosecutions suggests the limits of prisoner resistance, both Acton and Bambridge did lose their posts and new rules were drawn up to regulate prison keepers' conduct and prohibit the sale of prison offices. When combined with elite support in the form of a parliamentary investigation, prisoner resistance had made a difference. Moreover, the very public nature of these scandals empowered other prisoners to complain. News of the committee's investigation prompted those in London's other prisons to 'draw up depositions against their keepers regarding impositions and extortions'.[162] In 1730, Newgate prisoners regained some control over the internal management of the prison when the powers of the 'partners', an elite group of four trusted prisoners who had been given a major role in running the prison and who subjected their fellow prisoners to theft and brutality, were reined in.[163] In 1733, a common side prisoner in the Fleet, Simon Wood, published a short pamphlet 'to represent to the Legislature, the Hardships of the distressed People' in the prison.[164]

In the longer term, owing to the passage of legislation which meant debtors could no longer be imprisoned before trial for debts below 40 shillings, the debtors' prison ceased to loom so large in the catalogue of misfortunes that might befall a plebeian Londoner. However, this pattern of abuse, public exposure, resistance and reform would be repeated over the course of the century. And as new forms of institutional care emerged, most notably the parish workhouse, this same pattern would become a dynamic process of inmate-led change.

---

[160] Howson, *Thief-Taker General*, pp. 289–90.
[161] A. A. Hanham, 'Bambridge, Thomas (d. 1741)', *ODNB* (2004).
[162] *St James Evening Chronicle*, 29 March 1729, cited by Brown, *History of the Fleet*, pp. 67–8.
[163] Sheehan, 'Finding solace', p. 234.
[164] Simon Wood, *Remarks on the Fleet Prison: or, Lumber-House for Men and Women* (1733).

Reforming divided communities

In addition to seeking a reformation of the prisons, reformers also sought to revitalise the reformation of manners movement in the 1720s, a less welcome development for most plebeian Londoners. The leadership of this movement in this period shifted from the original voluntary societies, which had been weakened by controversy over the involvement of dissenters and possibly also by simple generational change, to justices of the peace, who were newly empowered by statutes and subject to pressures both from central government and London householders seeking to clean up their neighbourhoods. Consequently, the targets of reform shifted, with disorderly houses now the chief focus. Such efforts divided communities, and once again the reformers encountered forceful resistance from men and women of all social classes.

Initially, the onslaught on streetwalkers continued. The number of offenders reported as prosecuted in the societies' annual reports peaked in 1717 at almost 3,000, almost two-thirds of whom were women accused of 'lewd and disorderly' conduct. In parallel, commitments to the Westminster and Middlesex houses of correction also peaked in 1715–17.

As with previous waves of prosecutions of prostitutes, this one did not go unchallenged. In February 1717, a reforming constable named Somes (possibly Daniel Soames, future assistant to Jonathan Wild) was arrested for having taken up 'some ill persons' at night in Fleet Street and taken them to Bridewell the previous May. Another constable by the name of Ingram, 'not satisfied with the legal authority which they shewed him' to justify the commitments, arrested Somes, leading him in turn to bring an action for false imprisonment before the Lord Chief Justice. The reformers won the case, with the Chief Justice expressing concern about 'the ill consequence that might attend discouraging so laudable a society', and Ingram was ordered to pay £20 damages.[165] But litigation against the reformers, often brought by plebeian Londoners, continued. In the same year, Charles Hitchen, City marshal, complained that peace officers were discouraged from making arrests owing to the frequent lawsuits brought against them by 'disorderly persons'.[166]

Eight years later a large number of similar commitments were challenged in Westminster, in a case which illustrates why justices of the peace sought to gain greater control over reformation of manners activities. In May 1725 Westminster justices John Troughton and Henry

---

[165] John Strype, *A Survey of the Cities of London and Westminster* (1720), II, Book V, ch. III, p. 32 (hrionline.ac.uk, 1 Jan. 2014).

[166] Charles Hitchen, *A True Discovery of the Conduct of Receivers and Thief-Takers* (1718), p. 17. See also *LL*, set, 'Charles Hitchen'.

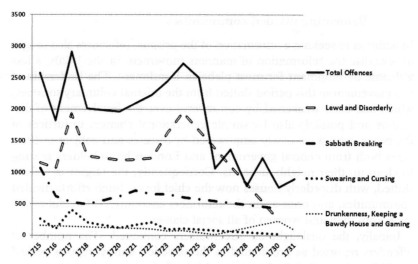

Figure 3.3 Societies for the Reformation of Manners prosecutions, 1715–1731. Robert Shoemaker, 'Reforming the city: the reformation of manners campaign in London, 1690–1738', in L. Davison *et al.*, eds., *Stilling the Grumbling Hive: The Response to Social and Economic Problems in England, 1689–1750* (Stroud: Alan Sutton, 1992), p. 105; Online data set: SRM Prosecutions, 1693–1738.xlsx.

Harpur issued a warrant 'To all Constables & other his Majesties Officers for the said County and Liberty whome these may concerne',

Whereas Complaint upon Oath hath been made unto us ... that Mary Ealey als Shase doth keep an Ill Governed & & Disorderly house Call'd Robinson's Coffee house at Charing Cross in the Parish of St. Martins in the feilds in ye County Aforsd & Doth Entertain Loose Idle Disorderly persons and women of Ill fame who Comitt Great Disorders in the sd. house to ye Disturbance of the Neighbourhood. These are therefore in his Majties. Name to will & require You on Sight hereof to make Deligent Search in the Sd: house & all other houses or parts that You Shall Suspect Such Disorderly persons As well men as Women to be harbour'd or Entertained in or persons Strouling in the Streets At an Unseasonable hour & Given no Good Acct. of themselves ...[167]

Over the following six months, on the basis of this 'general warrant', a subsequent investigation determined that a single constable, John Cameron, was responsible for 'not less than 169 Persons comitted by him to Bridewell & tenn to the Gatehouse and he has returned five & forty Recognizances to answer to this present Sessions'.[168]

---

[167] *LL*, Westminster Sessions: Sessions Papers, October 1725 (LMWJPS653740009).
[168] *LL*, Westminster Sessions: Sessions Papers, October 1725 (LMWJPS653740010). See also *LL*, set, 'John Cameron'.

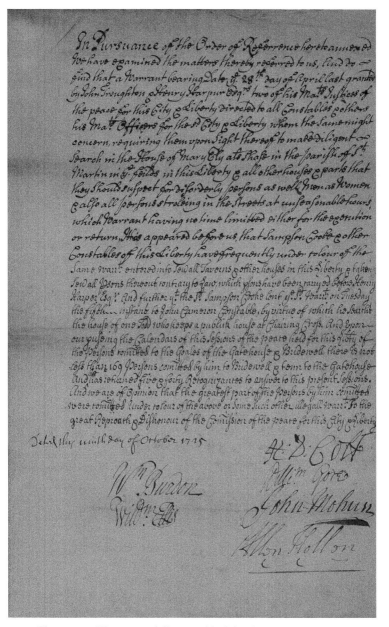

Figure 3.4 Warrant to 'all constables' for the arrest of 'disorderly persons' (1725). *LL*, Westminster Sessions: Sessions Papers, October 1725 (LMWJPS653740010).

It is not clear who objected, but a complaint to the Westminster justices about the allegedly illegal use by a constable of this single warrant to arrest so many persons for a wide range of offences prompted an investigation, after which the justices resolved 'that the granting the warrant mention'd in the Report in the General manner it appears to be framed and the not making it Returnable or calling for a Return thereof in due time, but suffering the same to be so many months in the hands of the Constable was irregular & illegal'.[169] While the legality of this ruling is questionable, the justices' expressed concern that the activities of rogue constables threatened to undermine their authority is notable.[170] As the justices concluded, the constables' actions had contributed to 'the great Reproach & Dishonour of the Commission of the Peace for this City & Liberty'.[171]

Consequently, in the 1720s a group of prominent Middlesex and Westminster justices sought to take control of the reformation of manners campaign. However, in throwing their weight behind the campaign the justices also changed its direction and narrowed its focus, prompting a new wave of opposition. The justices were not acting entirely on their own initiative; in concentrating on disorderly houses, they were responding to pressures from both above and below. As the focus of metropolitan concerns about crime shifted from the City of London to the rapidly growing parishes of Westminster and urban Middlesex, and the whig government sought to demonstrate it was in control, secretaries of state entered into more frequent correspondence with leading justices such as Nathaniel Blackerby, demanding concerted action against violent crime and its perceived causes.[172] But the justices also came under strong pressure from local inhabitants concerned to restore order in their neighbourhoods. Such pressure came particularly from householders in the inner west end parishes of St Giles in the Fields, St Paul Covent Garden and St Martin in the Fields, parishes located between the City of London and the new aristocratic developments in Westminster, and whose shifting social composition undermined the position of more prosperous long-term residents.[173] In 1716, for example, 'the Humble Peticon [sic] of the landlords and inhabitants of Little Wilde Streete in the Parish of St Giles in the Fields' named five women who kept coffee houses 'whereto dayly and nightly

[169] LL, Westminster Sessions: Sessions Papers, October 1725 (LMWJPS653740011).
[170] Robert Shoemaker, Prosecution and Punishment: Petty Crime and the Law in London and Rural Middlesex, c. 1660–1725 (Cambridge University Press, 1991), pp. 263–5.
[171] LL, Westminster Sessions: Sessions Papers, October 1725 (LMWJPS653740010).
[172] Beattie, Policing and Punishment, pp. 390–1.
[173] Shoemaker, Prosecution and Punishment, pp. 292–9.

resort many lewd women and other ill disposed people to the great terror and disturbance of your petitioners', thereby threatening to destroy the economy of this small street. Five houses were already empty, 'and the whole street [is] likely to be in a little time totally deserted'.[174]

These communities were divided between householders seeking to maintain a high standard of order and those who stood to benefit from 'disorderly' activities. Consequently, while the pressure to suppress vice was strong, there was also substantial opposition to such enforcement campaigns, not only from the 'disorderly', but also from those constables and justices who wished to maintain good relations with the members of their communities who tolerated (or made a living from) vice. Those responsible for law enforcement could be found on both sides, as can be seen in the extraordinary careers of two active informers, Phillip Cholmondley, a stationer, and Edward Vaughan, a basketmaker, both of St Martin in the Fields.[175] As a constable's assistant, Cholmondley had witnessed the murder of the reforming constable John Dent in 1709.[176] Over several years he and Vaughan participated in numerous prosecutions of artisans and shopkeepers for working on the Sabbath, as well as arrests of disorderly women.

In early 1719 both testified at King's Bench against two women from St Martin in the Fields who were accused of keeping disorderly houses. The extensive aliases of these women, Mary Evans wife of John alias Mary Carew alias Geary, and Elizabeth Whaley, alias Bource alias Connell, suggest a long career of evading the law. According to Vaughan, Evans's house 'was often complained of by the neighbourhood and reputed to be a common house of bawdry'. A neighbour, William Stagg, a victualler, testified that

murder has been frequently cryed out and many other disturbances and noises permitted to be carried on ... together with abundance of swearing, curseing and bawdy discourse to the great terror and disturbance of this defendant and the neighbourhood in so much that this deponent is afraid he and his neighbours houses may be set on fire.

Yet when attempts were made to arrest the women, the two constables and their assistants encountered violent resistance. According to Vaughan, 'they have been frequently insulted by the defendant [Evans] and the ill company in her house so much that they have been in danger of their lives'. Cholmondley testified that 'the company in the said house

[174] *LL*, Middlesex Sessions: Sessions Papers, December 1716 (LMSMPS501580039).
[175] *LL*, set, 'Phillip Cholmondley'; and, set, 'Edward Vaughan'.
[176] For Dent's murder, see section 'The reformation of manners renewed' in Chapter 2. See also *LL*, set, 'John Dent'.

[have] drawn their swords on the constables and their assistants for which reason they have oftentimes been obliged to leave disorderly persons in the said defendants' house ... [who have] often times beat out the said constables and their assistants'.[177]

Two years later it became clear that Cholmondley and Vaughan also provoked opposition from some justices of the peace. In August 1721, three reforming justices, John Mercer, Richard Gifford and John Gonson, sent for the two informers and told them they were concerned that 'clandestine practices' among constables and beadles were undermining attempts to suppress vice. Consequently, in company with a third constable the justices trusted, Cholmondley and Vaughan helped arrest several disorderly women on the streets late that evening. But the next day, when attempting to bring their prisoners before the three justices at the court house, they were confronted by a 'great mobb ... which could not but exceed a hundred people [which] seized Cholmondley and Mr Vaughan and said they must go before Justice Ellis'.[178] After insulting them in front of the mob, Justice John Ellis went to the courthouse and in front of the other justices told

Cholmondley he was a rascal and that he knew Cholmondley very well ... [and] did not doubt but he should have Cholmondley's eares nail'd to the pillory. And Justice Ellis turning to the three Justices said that Justice Milner and he had always strived to keep these fellows out of the parish.[179]

Then, in open court and in front of the accused women, Ellis instructed the constables that whenever they saw Cholmondley and Vaughan 'in St Giles Parish that they should carry them to New Prison'. Clearly concerned to keep a substantial proportion of the local population on his side, Ellis depicted the two informers as unwelcome interferers in local affairs, even though they lived in a neighbouring parish and were acting under the authority of three justices.[180]

This concern to prevent justices from interfering in each other's affairs, which had official recognition in orders from the Middlesex bench directing justices not to act outside their divisions, also caught out the prominent reforming justices Thomas Boteler and Nathaniel

---

[177] TNA, 'Crown side affidavits', Trinity 5 George I, KB 1/1/3/2. In February 1718, the constable of St Martin's was ordered to 'suppress Mrs Gerys Alias Evens her licence being that she keeps a disorderly house': LL, Middlesex Sessions: Sessions Papers, February 1718 (LMSMPS501680075).

[178] LL, Middlesex Sessions: Sessions Papers, August 1721 (LMSMPS501960006).

[179] LL, Middlesex Sessions: Sessions Papers, August 1721 (LMSMPS501960007).

[180] In other contexts, both Ellis and Justice John Milner (who was chair of the Middlesex justices in 1722) supported initiatives against vice. Shoemaker, *Prosecution and Punishment*, p. 259.

Blackerby.[181] In September 1720 both were summoned to appear before their fellow justices at the Middlesex sessions and 'shew cause why' they granted warrants against several persons who lived outside their divisions, contrary to the law, with Boteler threatened with a 'representation ... to ... the Lord Chancellor' if his answer was unsatisfactory.[182] Both justices had summoned offenders (their offences are unknown) from outside Westminster to appear at meetings of justices which took place in Westminster parish vestries. In Blackerby's case the warrants were granted against offenders living in Hammersmith, requiring them to appear at St Margaret's vestry. While both Blackerby and Boteler, as well as Cholmondley and Vaughan, survived these challenges and went on to further reforming activity, through these incidents they were made fully aware of the need to tread carefully.

In addition to prosecuting vice, reforming justices, together with the powerful select vestries of Westminster, sought to expand their power over constables and the night watch, which in Westminster remained in the hands of the Court of Burgesses, whose powers were essentially those of a manorial court. At this time watchmen were still drawn from local residents, or else were men hired to substitute for local ratepayers who did not want to serve. On 13 January 1720, the Middlesex bench petitioned parliament, claiming that 'severall Persons of Quality and others have been lately & in an unusual manner attackt in their Coaches and Chairs & some of them Robbed in the High Streets', and arguing that the current system of a nightly watch, as organised by the Court of Burgesses, was both expensive and ineffective.[183] An attempt to bring the watch under the direct control of the magistrates through a parliamentary act failed, but the struggle for power between the parish vestries and justices of the peace on the one hand and Court of Burgesses on the other would continue throughout the decade. It forms the backdrop to many reformation of manners activities during the 1720s and 1730s and the opposition they incurred, starting with the campaign against gaming houses between 1718 and 1722.[184]

Since 1690, if not before, proclamations against vice had routinely included gaming in their lists of sinful activities, but it was only in 1718 that explicit attention was called to the evils of gaming houses.

---

[181] Shoemaker, *Prosecution and Punishment*, pp. 257–8.
[182] *LL*, Middlesex Sessions: General Orders of the Court, 10 June 1713 – 17 October 1721 (LMSMGO400000227).
[183] *LL*, Middlesex Sessions: General Orders of the Court, 10 June 1713 – 17 October 1721 (LMSMGO400000191).
[184] Elaine A. Reynolds, *Before the Bobbies: The Night Watch and Police Reform in Metropolitan London, 1720–1830* (Basingstoke: Macmillan, 1998), pp. 10–15.

It is not clear where the impetus for this change came from, though gaming houses were known to be frequented by highwaymen, and there seems to have been some concern, as Whitelocke Bulstrode, chairman of the Middlesex justices, said to the grand jury in April 1718, about the effects of gambling on 'young gentlemen of fortune', whose losses 'ruin many worthy families'.[185] While, unusually, the impact of vice on the rich was singled out, Bulstrode expanded his comments six months later when he noted that gambling also caused 'ordinary Men, such as Day-Labourers, Apprentices, Servants, and Handy-Craft Tradesmen' to 'give themselves up to all Manner of Wickedness; and neglecting their Work, leave their Wives and Children a Burden to the Parish'.[186]

Justices played the leading role in this campaign. In October, Bulstrode noted that several 'common' gaming houses 'in the upper part of Westminster' had already been prosecuted. In fact, in July sixty-seven indictments were prosecuted at the Westminster sessions for keeping unlawful games such as 'ninepinns' and 'shovel board'.[187] These prosecutions appear to have had little impact, for two years later, prompted by a letter from the Lords Justices, the Westminster bench recommended that justices hold weekly petty sessions to put the laws in execution against the keepers of gaming houses and those who attended them.[188] The first meeting was to be held in Covent Garden, since 'there are more such public common gaming houses in the parish of St Paul Covent-Garden, and places adjacent, than in any other parts of this city and liberty'.[189]

In choosing to prosecute a vice in which many people had substantial financial interests, these justices bit off more than they could chew. Opposition came from several quarters: the Court of Burgesses (who benefited financially from the fines they imposed on gaming houses), other justices (it was alleged some even owned gaming houses) and of course the owners and clientele of the houses themselves and their friends. The Burgesses' officers undermined the justices' campaign at almost every turn. Constables refused to serve warrants, the grand jury at the Westminster sessions was packed with members who continually

---

[185] This was a result of some spectacular losses incurred by young heirs: Nicholas Tosney, 'Gaming in England, c. 1540–1760' (PhD dissertation, University of York, 2008), pp. 121–2.

[186] Georges Lamoine (ed.), Charges to the Grand Jury, 1689–1803, Camden Fourth Series, vol. 43 (London: Royal Historical Society, 1992), pp. 107, 124.

[187] LMA, Middlesex Sessions: 'Sessions rolls', MJ/SR/2312 (July 1718).

[188] LL, Middlesex Sessions: General Orders of the Court, 10 June 1713 – 17 October 1721 (LMSMGO400000228).

[189] LMA, Westminster Sessions: 'Orders of the court', WJ/O/C/001, April 1720 – April 1728, ff. 4–4d (5 Oct. 1720).

rejected the indictments (finding them 'ignoramus') and news of impending raids was leaked to gamblers in advance, even though the justices met secretly.[190]

The gamblers resorted to force. As the justices complained to the Lords, it was impossible to enter the houses since,

the Keepers of Such Gameing Houses have Strong Hatches to their Street doors and also to the doors of their Inner Rooms with Sharp Iron Spikes over the said Hatches, which Hatches are kept fast locked & are guarded by Soldiers who refuse to let the said Justices of Peace or any Constable enter the said Gameing Houses or Inner Roomes.[191]

The justices continued to meet on a regular basis to plan their raids, and tensions mounted, culminating in a raid on Vandernan's gaming house in Playhouse Passage, off Drury Lane, on 21 December 1721. Among those joining the raid as constables' assistants were none other than Edward Vaughan and Phillip Cholmondley.[192] Having managed to secure entry to the house as one of the patrons left, the constables and their assistants entered a room where around twenty gamblers were playing at hazard, an early and complex form of craps. Immediately the gamblers extinguished the candles and drew their swords, and the constables were forced to retreat. As a contemporary pamphlet sympathetic to the reformers explained,

This passage being full of gaming houses, and other houses that are frequented by disorderly people ... the mob assembled immediately; and being very numerous and outragious, the word was given, among the mob that were assembled out of doors, to murder the constables and their assistants.[193]

Divested of rhetoric, this text reveals that gamblers had substantial popular support, not least from the approximately 600 employees of gaming houses who worked in the area.[194] The Riot Act was read, but the gamblers shouted 'A T–d of your Proclamation' and 'you're a pack of informing dogs'.[195] Soldiers were called, but they were pelted with brickbats and pisspots. Thus provoked, one of the soldiers fired his musket, and Henry Bowes, a former tailor and now boxkeeper of the house, was killed.

---

[190] Shoemaker, *Prosecution and Punishment*, pp. 147, 265–6.
[191] *LL*, Middlesex Sessions: General Orders of the Court, 10 June 1713 – 17 October 1721 (LMSMGO400000228).
[192] *LL*, sets, 'Edward Vaughan'; and 'Phillip Cholmondley'.
[193] *An Account of the Endeavours That Have Been Used to Suppress Gaming-houses, and of the Discouragements That Have Been Met with* (1722), p. 22.
[194] Tosney, 'Gaming in England', p. 120.
[195] *LL*, Old Bailey Proceedings, 28 February 1722 (t17220228-65).

In the aftermath, the gamblers and their associates went on the offensive and, in the words of the reformers, 'attempted to throw the riot on the constables'.[196] In fact, it was their unpopular assistants, Cholmondley and Vaughan, who were indicted for the murder of Bowes at the Old Bailey in January 1722, for aiding and assisting John Hemlichen, the soldier who fired the shot.[197] At their trial, the prosecutors used language more commonly used by the reformers, describing the constables and assistants who attempted to enter Vandernan's house as a violent 'mob'. Vaughan was accused of telling the soldier to fire, saying 'I'll indemnify you'. The case for the defence, however, was bolstered by the presence of 'Several Justices of the Peace then on the Bench, [who] gave the prisoners a very good character.'[198]

Needless to say, the two were acquitted, and the following month the reformers got their revenge when three of the gamblers were tried and convicted at the Old Bailey on a misdemeanour charge of 'Riotously assaulting several Constables, in the execution of their Office'. They were sentenced to large fines and a period of imprisonment, and required to find security for their good behaviour.[199] Following this bruising but ultimately successful encounter, the reformers managed to prosecute large numbers of gamblers, with 104 prosecutions reported in the societies' account for 1722.

As was so often the case, however, the reformers won the battle, while ultimately losing the war. Although both Cholmondley and Vaughan appear in the records in 1722 and 1723 testifying against profane swearing and Sabbath breakers, these are their last appearances. There is no evidence that they continued to inform against prostitutes and gamblers.[200] More generally, the number of gaming houses prosecuted by the societies declined to forty-two in 1723 and twenty-three in 1724. Yet gaming houses continued to prosper, and the justices persevered. In 1723 a group of twenty-six Westminster and Middlesex justices, led by Sir John Gonson, 'entered into a society to suppress gaming houses ... [and] called themselves a convention'.[201] Yet when in 1725 Justice Samuel Ryder began his charge to the Westminster Grand Jury with an account of the offences 'abounding in this liberty', the first offence he

---

[196] *Account of the Endeavours*, p. 26.
[197] Probably because he was indemnified under the Riot Act, Hemlichen was not charged with the murder.
[198] LL, Old Bailey Proceedings, 12 January 1722 (t17220112-43).
[199] LL, Old Bailey Proceedings, 28 February 1722 (t17220228-65).
[200] WAC, St Margaret Westminster, 'Petty sessions records', SMW/E/99, 26 June 1723.
[201] LMA, Westminster Sessions: 'Orders of the court', WJ/O/C/001, April 1720 – April 1728, f. 127d.

mentioned was 'the keeping of gaming houses'.[202] In December of that year, the Middlesex justices complained that improperly selected grand juries had once again 'screened' those who kept 'common gaming houses, or disorderly publick houses' from prosecution.[203]

The opposition to the campaign against gaming houses was mixed. Many of the gamblers were described as 'well dressed', and both they and their hosts obviously needed considerable resources to gamble for the high stakes reported.[204] But as the riot at Vandernan's gaming house demonstrates, the keepers and their clients had considerable support from some of their less wealthy neighbours, and these groups combined to frustrate the reformers.

Efforts to suppress 'disorderly houses' were renewed at the end of the decade, when there were fresh concerns about rising crime, evident in increases in Old Bailey trials and commitments to Bridewell. In 1728, prompted by a letter from Secretary of State Townshend, the Middlesex justices resolved to 'to meet and hold Petty Sessions twice a week at least … to discover and Suppress all Such Persons who keep Night-Houses, Gaming-Houses, or other disorderly Houses, wherein Robbers or other Felons are harbour'd or incourag'd'.[205] A new cycle of enforcement began, now with a wider focus on 'disorderly houses', the inadequacies of the night watch and the sale of gin, which would in turn generate new forms of opposition.

The pressure for reform once again also came from local inhabitants in the west end.[206] In June 1730 the Westminster justices received a petition from eighteen shopkeepers, tradesmen and other inhabitants of St Martin in the Fields complaining that persons of the most 'notorious characters and infamously wicked lives and conversations' had taken up residence in the parish, in several streets and courts particularly in the neighbourhood of Drury Lane, which were 'infested with such vile people that there are frequent out crys in the night fighting robberies and all sorts of debauchery committed by them all night long'.[207]

In response to this and similar petitions, the Middlesex and Westminster sessions once again appointed committees of justices to investigate the

[202] Lamoine (ed.), *Charges to the Grand Jury*, p. 183.
[203] *LL*, Middlesex Sessions: General Orders of the Court, 22 February 1725 – 19 January 1734 (LMSMGO556000082).
[204] *Account of the Endeavours*, p. 22.
[205] *LL*, Middlesex Sessions: General Orders of the Court, 22 February 1725 – 19 January 1734 (LMSMGO556000316).
[206] LMA, Westminster Sessions: 'Orders of the court', WJ/O/C/002, June 1730, ff. 85–86d.
[207] *LL*, Westminster Sessions: Sessions Papers, 10 February 1731 – 8 July 1731 (LMWJPS653920032).

problem and oversee the work of constables in apprehending offenders. By April 1731 the Westminster justices reported that their committee had met forty-two times, extending their inquiry to five neighbouring parishes. They had bound over forty-eight persons for keeping disorderly houses, committed sixteen to prison and indicted twenty-four, and as a result twenty-six houses, including two of the most notorious ones, were 'suppressed and the persons that kept them gone away'. In addition, the justices had granted forty-two search warrants for apprehending rogues, vagabonds, sturdy beggars, and idle and disorderly persons, and apprehended 127 men and women, either in disorderly houses or on the streets, committing them to the house of correction. By these measures, they observed, 'we hope we have in great measure lessened the disorders compained of ... tho we have not as yet been able wholly to suppress them'.[208]

Indeed, even with the justices' support, the constables continued to find the going difficult. The committee reported that fourteen persons had been committed to prison or bound over for assaulting and insulting the constables in the execution of their office. Constables were also, according to the report of an earlier committee, subjected to 'causeless and vexatious anonymous suits and indictments brought against them ... and thereby ... put to great expence and charges which ... discouraged and deterred them from doing their duty'.[209] Such lawsuits, brought by those whom they prosecuted, were not, however, necessarily vexatious; they occasionally raised genuine legal issues. In a case brought before King's Bench in 1730, for example, Mary Freeman alias Talbott, assisted reportedly by five counsel, used a writ of habeas corpus to challenge her commitment by members of the committee to the Westminster house of correction 'to hard Labour till the first Day of the then next Quarter Sessions', on the grounds that she should not have been committed for a fixed time period, but until such time as a justice deemed her ready for discharge.[210] The reformers won this case, with all four King's Bench judges ruling in their favour.

Other opposition was more intractable. In their 1731 report, the Westminster justices singled out two particularly recalcitrant offenders, sisters Mary Harvey alias Mackeige and Isabella Eaton als Gwyn.[211] They were tried for theft several times between 1727 and 1732, often in

---

[208] *LL*, Westminster Sessions: Sessions Papers, 10 February 1731 – 8 July 1731 (LMWJPS653920035).

[209] LMA, Westminster Sessions: 'Orders of the court', WJ/O/C/002, July 1730, ff. 87–87d.

[210] Heather Shore, '"The reckoning": disorderly women, informing constables and the Westminster justices, 1727–33', *Social History*, 34:4 (2009), 421; *LL*, Westminster Sessions: Sessions Papers, 10 February 1731 – 8 July 1731 (LMWJPS653920034).

[211] *LL*, Heather Shore, 'Mary Harvey, fl. 1727–1733'; set, 'Isabella Eaton'.

the context of prostitution, and Harvey was prosecuted for keeping a disorderly house. As Heather Shore has demonstrated, these women were remarkably successful, both on the streets and in the courtroom, at resisting the reformers' efforts to close down Harvey's house and punish them. They resisted arrest and escaped from prison several times, and when tried in the courts they were only rarely convicted. With the assistance of counsel, they also initiated counter prosecutions against their accusers, including an indictment against the informing constables and thief-takers, brothers Michael and Thomas Willis, for highway robbery.[212] This accusation arose out of a disturbance which occurred when they attempted to arrest Eaton for keeping a disorderly house and encountered violent resistance. The case was tried at the Old Bailey in August 1730.[213] Although, following testimony from several reforming justices, the two constables were, as the *Evening Post* put it, 'honourably acquitted', Shore argues that this trial, as well as a failed perjury prosecution against Eaton and Harvey and a conviction of Thomas Willis for assaulting a gentleman in December 1731, sufficiently 'tarnished their reputations' that the Willis's reforming careers were over.[214] Neither Michael nor Thomas appears again in the records as an informer or constable, though Michael, and another brother, Robert, did manage to convict Eaton and Elizabeth Walker of conspiring to charge them with robbery in 1736.[215]

While Shore acknowledges that Harvey and Eaton were unusual in their success in resisting the reformers, she argues that the significant support both women received from friends and acquaintances (when they resisted arrest, escaped from prison and launched counter prosecutions) are indicative of 'plebeian communities attempting to assert their place in the [wider] local community'.[216] Like earlier reformation of manners activities, the disorderly house campaign divided neighbourhoods, pitting supporters of one definition of local 'order' against those whose livelihoods were embedded in alehouses and the activities (both licit and illicit) which took place there. Acts of resistance both grew out of, and contributed to, the culture of criminal defiance in the metropolis. They also substantially undermined the reformation of manners campaign.

---

[212] Thomas Willis was involved in the prosecution of sodomites and sabbath violators between 1725 and 1729; see *LL*, set, 'Thomas Willis'. Howson claims he was also involved in the arrest of Jonathan Wild: Howson, *Thief-Taker General*, p. 233. See also *LL*, set, 'Michael Willis'.
[213] *LL*, Old Bailey Proceedings, 28 August 1730 (t17300828-76).
[214] *Evening Post*, 29 August 1730 (Burney Collection: www.galegroup.com, 1 Jan. 2014); Shore, '"The reckoning"', 416, 419–24.
[215] *LL*, Old Bailey Proceedings, 10 December 1735 (t17351210-74).
[216] Shore, '"The reckoning"', 425–6.

Figure 3.5 William Hogarth, *A Harlot's Progress*, Plate 3 (1732). BM
1868,0822.1521. © Trustees of the British Museum.

While the disorderly house campaign, in spite of resistance from
people like Eaton and Harvey, succeeded in prosecuting large numbers
of offenders, the reputation of the reformers was undermined by the
constant accusations of misbehaviour that dogged their activities. As
one commentator, possibly Daniel Defoe, observed in 1731, while the
reformers had initially carried out 'great work', over time

less capable, and perhaps less sincere people, took the work, as it were out of their
hands, to the great scandal of the thing itself, and by their corruption, partiality
and at last, open connivances, they opened the doors to vice, which the first
zealous reformers had so happily shut.

'Reforming Constables', watchmen and magistrates were all accused
of 'Connivance, and more especially ... notorious Bribery and
Corruption'.[217] Even the magistrates were open to suspicion. William
Hogarth immortalised the disorderly house raids in Plate 4 of his *Harlot's*

---

[217] *An Effectual Scheme for the Immediate Preventing of Street-Robberies*, pp. 24, 14.

Progress (1732), in which Sir John Gonson is shown entering the prostitute Moll Hackabout's room with a puzzled, almost leering expression on his face. As a result of the opposition they encountered, the reformers were in a sense brought down to the level of their opponents. Shore suggests that in their desperate attempts to convict Mary Harvey, the Westminster justices resorted to methods of 'dubious legality' such as initiating malicious prosecutions. This is one reason why so many of the charges against her resulted in acquittals.[218]

By 1731, the cumulative result of a series of initiatives which achieved limited results at sometimes high cost, the reformation of manners campaign was on the wane. The number of prosecutions reported in their annual accounts fell dramatically after 1725, possibly as a result of the Westminster justices' ruling on 'general warrants', with prosecutions for the period 1726–31 averaging only 42 per cent of the average for the previous five years. In the first detailed report published after 1725, for 1730, prosecutions of lewd and disorderly conduct had fallen by 87.1 per cent and swearing and cursing by 79.6 per cent. Evidence that this decline in prosecutions was not just a result of less efficient reporting can be found in the fact that cases of vice in the Lord Mayor's waiting and charge books averaged only four per year between 1728 and 1733, compared to an average of over seventy-six per year between 1690 and 1705.[219] Owing to widespread opposition, the reformers had once again been forced to scale back their activities.

Workhouses and the poor

While the reformation of manners campaign addressed one form of disorder after another, the increasingly sophisticated and bureaucratic parishes, under the leadership of newly empowered justices of the peace, sought to address what many saw as the underlying causes of disorder. With advice from the SPCK, the parishes began to create workhouses for the poor designed to discipline them in both body and mind. Whereas the City-wide London Workhouse established in 1698 had foundered on the sea of City politics, the smaller institutions created by parishes in the 1720s rapidly became the second most common form of public building in London, outdone only by parish churches. From the perspective of the poor, the creation of a network of residential parish workhouses in the 1720s represents the single most significant development in the form and

---

[218] Shore, '"The reckoning"', 424.
[219] Faramerz Dabhoiwala, 'Prostitution and police in London, c. 1660–1760' (D.Phil. dissertation, Oxford University, 1995), p. 117.

nature of poor relief between the creation of a working system of settlement in the 1690s and the passage of the New Poor Law 140 years later. During the early years of development, the poor would do much to shape these new institutions.

From a standing start in 1719 (when Enfield established the first parish workhouse in greater London), the parishes of the metropolis created at least thirty-eight substantial institutions in the next dozen years, housing upwards of 5,000 paupers.[220] By 1730 there were five workhouses in Westminster, at least twenty in Middlesex and a further thirteen in the City of London itself.[221] Some of these were little more than parish houses in which high-dependency paupers were cared for by nurses and housekeepers, designed to save the cost of maintaining sick paupers in the hospitals of the capital. In many respects, these smaller houses formed a natural extension of the system of contracted residential nursing of the sort Jeremy Boulton has described for the period before 1720, and they form part of a substantial continuum in parish care.[222] However, others were massive institutions of stone-built bureaucracy that aspired to control every waking moment of the lives of all the dependent poor. The Westminster workhouses in particular housed hundreds of inmates of all sorts, subdivided into specialist wards.

Presented as a means of educating the poor to their religious duty of social subservience, enforcing a powerful work discipline, and as a disincentive that would prevent the workshy from applying for relief, workhouses seemed a panacea to many social problems. In 1720 the SPCK offered a premium to any town or parish setting up either a workhouse or working charity school and also began to put together an innovative pamphlet, *An Account of Several Workhouses*, that served to both publicise the idea and provide a template for new institutions.[223] But in the meantime the Society also ensured the take up of the new institutions by seeing to the drafting and probably the passage of the 'Workhouse Test Act' in March 1723.[224]

---

[220] The population figure is approximate, and based on the recorded population of eighteen of the thirty-eight houses in London and Middlesex included in the 1776 parliamentary report. *PP, House of Commons Sessional Papers*, 'Abstract of the returns made … by the overseers of poor', 1776 (parlipapers.chadwyck.co.uk, 1 Jan. 2014).

[221] Timothy Hitchcock, 'The English workhouse: a study in institutional poor relief in selected counties, 1696–1750' (D.Phil. dissertation, Oxford University, 1985), Appendix, pp. 258–81.

[222] Boulton, 'Welfare systems and the parish nurse'.

[223] Cambridge University Library (CUL), SPCK Archive, 'Standing Committee minute book, 1718–20', iii, p. 159; *An Account of Several Workhouses* (1725).

[224] 9 George I c. 7.

The Workhouse Test Act was in many respects unremarkable, neither exciting active comment at the time nor receiving a great deal of notice from the founders of later parish workhouses. It was a hodge-podge of poor relief clauses with little obvious direction and few new ideas. Nevertheless, it did give legislative expression to a new kind of workhouse and allowed parishes to 'test' whether a pauper was 'deserving' by presenting them with an 'offer of the house'. Anyone who refused to enter could be denied relief regardless of their need, a justice's order or settlement status. By authorising a 'workhouse test', the Act aimed to reconfigure the relationship between the parish, the bench and the poor – giving the parish the upper hand. As with the creation of closed vestries that included justices among their number, the Workhouse Test Act sought to realign the interests of the parish and the bench against a wider population of paupers. And in some respects it succeeded, at least in the short term. In most parishes where a new workhouse was opened, the number of dependent paupers fell by 50 per cent, before gradually rising again to pre-house levels over the following years.[225] But workhouses also required a huge level of expenditure both to build and to run. Ultimately, both workhouses and their inmates would be transformed in unintended ways. The parish poor were turned from partially dependent paupers, able to combine a pension or casual relief with begging, family support or perhaps medical care in the capital's charitable hospitals, into wholly dependent 'inmates'. At the same time, the houses themselves evolved to provide the substantial medical care demanded by the poor.

The parish workhouse opened by the new select vestry of St George Hanover Square in 1726 reflects the aspirations of the parishes which pursued this strategy. The house was designed by Nicholas Hawksmoor, and John Chamberlayne described it as being

contrived to lodge and diet above 250 men, women and children, 2 in a bed. There are in each wing 4 rooms on a floor provided with 3 lights so as to draw fresh air whenever it is wanted. Each room has a fire place and can receive 6 beds, which by curtains may be all private as occasion requires . . .[226]

The designers of parish workhouses attempted to create a total institution. Work, leisure, food and clothes would be both specific to the house and wholly contained within it, as publicised in SPCK pamphlets and endlessly rehearsed in vestry minutes. In the dull fabric of the workhouse uniform, the adequate if unvaried diet of the house, the timed

---

[225] Hitchcock, 'English workhouse', pp. 211–13.
[226] CUL, SPCK Archive, 'Special letters book', 18 May 1725 – 23 April 1726, pp. 55–6.

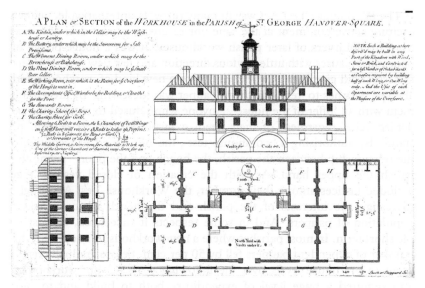

Figure 3.6 A plan and section of the workhouse in the Parish of
St George Hanover Square [1715–1731]. BM 1978, U.3654.
© Trustees of the British Museum.

labour of the inmates and the division of the house into wards and
sections, with their matrons and nurses, the environment of the house
was intended to create a regular way of life, both devout and virtuous,
industrious and contented. At the heart of these designs was a desire to
instil in the poor an unthinking desire to labour, a 'habit of industry'.

The response of the poor themselves to this innovation was immediate.
In the short term their only recourse was to refuse the house, and most
simply abandoned parish relief. At St Margaret Westminster, the vestry
set aside three days in November 1726 to gather in the parish poor.
There were 108 names on the parish books, but of these only 41 accepted
an offer of the house, and the rest, 67 in total, were struck from the parish
books.[227] In late April of the following spring, St Sepulchre's workhouse
was ready for its poor, and 26 children were brought before the workhouse committee. However, only 9 of them, children in the care of the
parish nurse who had no choice, accepted a place in the workhouse.[228]
Inevitably, as parish paupers had real and tangible needs, the numbers of

---

[227] WAC, St Margaret Westminster, 'Workhouse committee minutes', SMW/E/101/2632,
10, 14 and 16 November, 1726.
[228] LMA, St Sepulchre, Holborn, 'City of London, Workhouse committee book', 1727–9,
P69/SEP/B/071/MS03137/001, p. 12.

paupers dependent on the parish soon returned to their pre-workhouse levels, now often as workhouse inmates. However, in many parishes casual relief and pensions in exceptional circumstances would creep back in to the system in response to the claims of the poor.

Overall, the creation of these institutions had two immediate and substantial effects. First, it changed the social meaning of relief, pushing the settled poor into the same type of institution as the disorderly. In Defoe's emotive words, the workhouse served to

mix the Good and Bad; and too often make Reprobates of all alike. ... if an honest Gentleman or Trader should leave a Wife or Children unprovided for, what a shocking thing it is to think they must be mixed with Vagrants, Beggars, Thieves, Night walkers? To receive their Insults, to hear their Blasphemous and Obscene Discourse, to be suffocated with the Nastiness, and eat up with their Vermin.[229]

As importantly, the workhouses created a further layer of parish bureaucracy that demanded oversight.[230] Each of the larger parishes needed its workhouse master and its beadles, its clerks and rate-collectors, comprising a whole new cadre of salaried civil servants to keep the books and wink at the peculation and petty politics of the select vestries. They needed people who were willing and able to act on behalf of their social superiors in enforcing social policy and precept.

In the first decade of the workhouse movement, the person to whom the parishes of London overwhelmingly turned to lead this new bureaucracy was Matthew Marriott. Heavily promoted by the SPCK, he came to effectively monopolise the management of London's workhouses. By 1726 he can be identified as running at least five of London's largest houses: St Giles in the Fields, St George Hanover Square, St James and St Margaret Westminster and St Martin in the Fields.[231] Marriott's normal procedure was to contract for the care of the poor to be housed and employed in a building paid for by the parish. Unlike the specimen

---

[229] Defoe, *Parochial Tyranny* (2nd edn, 1727), pp. 33–4.

[230] For the sophistication of the parish administration of St Martin in the Fields, see Jeremy Boulton, 'Going on the parish: the parish pension and its meaning in the London suburbs, 1640–1724', in Tim Hitchcock, Peter King and Pamela Sharpe, eds., *Chronicling Poverty: The Voices and Strategies of the English Poor, 1640–1840* (Basingstoke: Macmillan, 1997), pp. 19–46; and Jeremy Boulton, 'The most visible poor in England? Constructing pauper biographies in early-modern Westminster', *Westminster Historical Review*, 1 (1997), 13–21.

[231] In total he can be identified as having sub-contracted at least seventeen different workhouses nationally, though he was entirely based in London from 1720 onwards. Hitchcock, 'English workhouse', pp. 182–3.

contract published in the *Account*, Marriott normally specified that poor relief should be denied to any applicant who refused the offer of a place in the workhouse, ensuring the application of a 'workhouse test'. Once the contract was signed, Marriott would then install an assistant, frequently drawn from his own family, to take care of day-to-day management, and he would also contract for the supply of furniture, clothing and foodstuffs. By taking on the whole operation, Marriott was able to make money on both the goods brought in to the house and the direct costs billed to the parish.

By employing Marriott, the select vestries distanced themselves from the delivery of poor relief – leaving both the standards of care and management to what rapidly became a de facto city-wide organisation. In the process, they created a new point of tension both with local ratepayers, who were now excluded from benefiting from parish expenditure, and with the poor, whose expectations of care and respect were dashed.

There is no evidence that Marriott was actively corrupt, or that he was less than a conscientious administrator. However, owing to concerns about both costs and the treatment of the poor, his moment as the single most important figure in the lives of thousands of London paupers lasted only a couple of years. Already in 1726 the SPCK complained about the excessive charges Marriott was levying for training provincial workhouse masters, and from that date the Society increasingly distanced itself from his activities. During 1727 he lost his contracts for the management of the four large workhouses he was then managing in Westminster. This turnaround in Marriott's fortunes resulted from a campaign directed specifically at him, and more generally at the workhouses of London, mounted by a powerful amalgam of the poor, local tradesmen and at least one justice. Starting with debates in vestries focused on the substantial costs he charged and his cruelty to the parish poor, this campaign mirrored the more public inquiry into the conditions in the debtors' prisons pursued in the same years. It finally surfaced more publicly with the anonymous publication of a ballad and associated broadside, called *The Workhouse Cruelty*, in 1731.[232]

Sung to the tune of 'Death and the Lady', the ballad gave what purported to be a 'full and true' account of Mrs Mary Whistle, who had recently died in the workhouse belonging to St Giles in the Fields. The ballad told of the cruel treatment of Mary Whistle by Matthew Marriott and his sister Mrs Underhood – master and mistress of the workhouse.

[232] *The Workhouse Cruelty: Workhouses Turn'd Goals; and Goalers [sic] Executioners . . . in the Parish of St. Giles's in the Fields* (n.d., [1731]); *The Workhouse Cruelty; Being a Full and True Account of One Mrs. M. W., . . . in the Parish of St. Giles's in the Field* (n.d., [1731]).

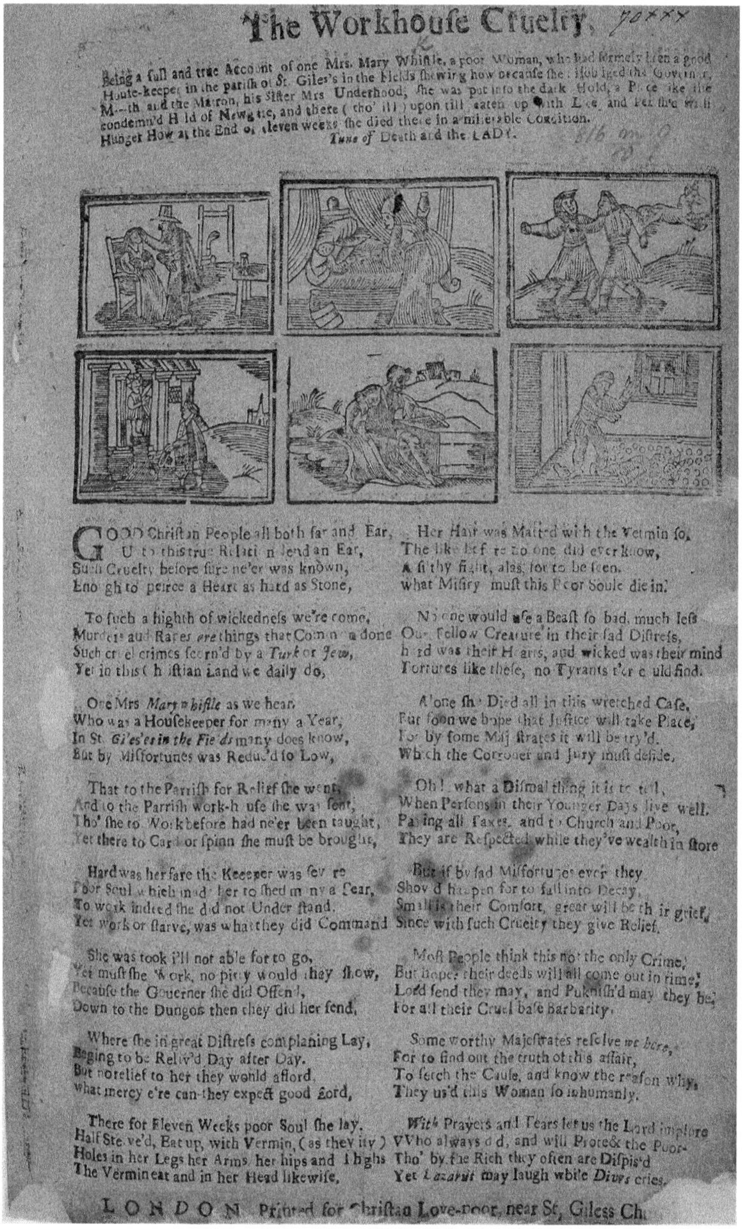

Figure 3.7 *The Workhouse Cruelty; Being a Full and True Account of One Mrs. Mary Whistle ... in the Parish of St. Giles's in the Fields* (n.d., 1731). © Trustees of the British Library.

To such a highth of wickedness we're come
Murders and Rapes are things that common done
Such cruel crimes scorn'd by a Turk or Jew
Yet in this Christian Land we daily do.
One Mrs. Mary Whistle as we hear,
Who was a housekeeper for many a year,
In St Giles in the Fields many does know,
But by misfortune was reduced so low,
That to the parish for relief she went
And to the Parish Workhouse she was sent.
Tho' she to work before had ne'er been taught,
Yet there to card or spin she must be brought.

And so the ballad went on, describing the coarse fare available in the workhouse, and the hard treatment of the master and mistress and how, in order to discipline Mary to work – to 'work or starve' – she was confined to the 'dark hole' for eleven weeks where she lay:

Half starved, eat up with vermin (as they say)
Holes in her legs her arms her hips and thighs,
The vermin eat and in her head likewise.

And so she died there – an object lesson in a new reality for the poor.

The ballad and broadside represent the culmination of a wider campaign against both Marriott and the model of workhouse organisation and parish care his approach entailed.

The massive St Giles workhouse had been built in 1725. On completion it was immediately passed into Marriott's hands. The house held some 300 people in a complex set of buildings made up of twenty-three wards, which aspired to serve as workhouse, hospital and burial ground. Despite its size, it was entirely typical of the new London workhouses.

As a result of the publication of a promotional pamphlet in 1725, the survival of one of the most extensive sets of rules and regulations for any workhouse in this period, and workhouse registers and minutes, we know a large amount about the poor of the parish and the conditions aspired to in the workhouse.[233] Immediately prior to its establishment, there had been some 841 paupers on the books, made up mainly of the halt, the lame, the elderly, the orphaned and those overburdened with children. In July 1728 the workhouse had a population of 238 inmates in its twenty-three wards, served by fourteen nurses and eight assistants. Some

---

[233] *Rules and Orders to Be Observed by the Officers and Servants in St. Giles's Work-house, and by the Poor Therein* (1726); *The Case of the Parish of St Giles in the Fields, As to their Poor, and a Work-House Designed to be built for Employing them* (n.d., 1725). A later Irish edition of the *Rules* is available on Open Access.

600 paupers had been forced off the parish books with the opening of the house. The pamphlet set out every aspect of the workhouse regime, including the number of horn books, primers, spelling books, psalters and testaments (twelve each) used to teach the workhouse children to read and write, the diet and the clothing the inmates received, and the number of beds (157) and quality of the sheeting (coarse) provided. It indicates when people were supposed to get up, and how long they were meant to spend getting dressed, brushing their hair and seeing to their toilet.

However, what looks well organised and rational in the plain prose of an eighteenth-century pamphlet is exposed as something entirely different in the series of scandals and the responses they evoked, recorded in the companion broadside to the *Workhouse Cruelty* ballad. Published in conjunction with the ballad, the broadside is also entitled *The Workhouse Cruelty*, but with the subtitle: *Workhouses Turn'd Goals and Goalers [sic] Executioners*, and it records, in addition to the case of Mary Whistle, a series of deaths in the workhouse with details of the characters of the victims.[234]

In concert with writers like Defoe, the *Workhouse Cruelty* emphasised the impact of workhouse care on decayed householders:

Here we'll suppose a poor housekeeper, he shall be obliged to pay to the poor, secondly he shall pay overates two or three in a year: thirdly, after this he shall pay towards the building of a workhouse; fourthly, thro' long mischance he shall fall to decay, and be brought to so low an ebb of fortune as to be obliged to ask relief; fifthly, instead of any comfortable relief he shall be then put into a workhouse, with little or no difference made between the whore, the thief, the pickpocket, the chimney sweeper, the japaner, the link boy and this, poor honest housekeeper.

In instance after instance, the respectability of such paupers – their distance from chimney sweeps and japanners – is emphasised, echoing the conflict between householders and those who made their living through vice. Sarah Jones 'once kept a good house in the parish of St Giles in the Fields', while an anonymous fellow pauper was robbed by the workhouse master of 'her money, upwards of three pounds, and good cloaths, all which they took from her'; and finally, Mary Whistle herself, 'having been a good sufficient housekeeper did refuse to work, as being unaccustomed to it'. In the words of the ballad:

Oh! What a dismal thing it is to tell,
When persons in their younger days live so well
Paying all taxes and to church and poor

[234] *Workhouse Cruelty: Workhouses Turn'd Goals.*

> They are respected while they've wealth in store.
> But if by sad misfortune ever they,
> Should happen to fall into decay,
> Small is their comfort, great will be their grief.
> Since with such cruelty they give relief.

Beyond the emphasis on the respectable nature of some of the paupers of St Giles, the author also raises the broader issue of the workhouse as a place which punishes those brought to poverty through mischance:

The tragical scene ... is one of the most cruel, dark and barbarous (in its nature) that ever mankind heard of ... unless speedy stop be put to the base, vile and wicked treatment of those knaves in power, called Governors of Workhouses, I mean such as M[arrio]th, the sufferings of these unhappy wretches who are obliged to go into them, will in all likelihood be as great, if not greater than those of unfortunate debtors.[235]

The horror of the workhouse to the mind of this author, and by extension to many poor Londoners, lay not simply in the cruelty which led to inmates' deaths but in its undifferentiated use for both decayed householders and the undeserving poor, which in turn implied a moral equivalence between the pauper and the pickpocket. Having established a secure system of identifying who belonged to the parish over the preceding three decades, the creation of workhouses broke down the subtle distinctions between less fortunate parishioners. The new parish employees and contractors could never be expected to understand and police the boundary between the 'deserving' and 'undeserving' poor, making a mockery of an older form of mutual social obligation.

What the *Workhouse Cruelty* reflects is the culture of the small householder, artisan and widow, of the everyday parishioner of St Giles in the Fields, and by extension numerous Londoners. Both ballad and broadside were published by 'The Christian Love-Poor' from a shop near St Giles' church, a group about which no further details can be found. However, what emerges is a world-view that made fine distinctions between moral culpability and virtuous poverty. What one sees in these broadsides is a self-conscious householder culture – within which the workhouse and parish community had very specific meanings.

Nevertheless, these householders came together with paupers and beggars to battle against this parochial innovation, exploiting the triangular relationship between the poor, the parish and magistrates established in the preceding decades. The *Workhouse Cruelty* forms the culmination

---

[235] *Workhouse Cruelty: Workhouses Turn'd Goals.*

of a series of complaints, dating from at least 1728, through which the poor, both in direct appeals to justices and in print, largely succeeded in changing the character of workhouse relief.

As a result of accusations such as the ones in the ballad and broadside, parish officers became increasingly vulnerable to pauper complaints. In part, this process entailed making common cause with a justice, in this instance John Milner, who had been instrumental along with Justice John Ellis in excluding the reforming constables, Phillip Cholmondley and Edward Vaughan, from the parish several years earlier.[236] The *Workhouse Cruelty* appealed to Milner by name, and while he had been instrumental in establishing the house, he used his influence with the parish vestry to ensure the complaints were addressed.[237]

The first substantial complaint had been aired in 1729:

That Mr Bull the apothecary at the workhouse had caused the arm & breast bone of a poor woman who dyed there to be cut off & carried away to a person who finishes skeletons, which being discovered had created great noise & disturbance ...[238]

The vestry resolved both to immediately dismiss the apothecary and to offer a reward, upon conviction, to any person who reported similar offences.[239] In the broadside a similar case was aired:

About that time nurse R[i]d[in]g understanding that a child was to have been made an anatomy of, after their common custom (for many are carried in sacks by night) Nurse R[i]d[in]g ... said she'd acquaint Justice Milner with it, upon which she was sent for by M[arrio]th, who kicked her for it, and ordered the doors to be shut, and threatened her with the hold, but finding she had friends M[arrio]th gave her a crown to hold her tongue.[240]

On her death, Mary Whistle was subject to a careful autopsy overseen by two doctors, two surgeons and an apothecary, which was almost certainly a result of the publication of the *Workhouse Cruelty*. The report was both carefully preserved (it is now in the Sloane manuscripts at the British Library) and published in the *Daily Post*.[241] But the outcome was probably a disappointment to the 'Christian Love-Poor', as it determined that Whistle had died of natural causes, 'little watery tumours' on the brain.

---

[236] *LL*, sets, 'Phillip Cholmondley' and 'Edward Vaughan'.
[237] See also 'Reforming divided communities', this chapter.
[238] *Workhouse Cruelty: Workhouses Turn'd Goals.*
[239] Camden Local Studies and Archives Centre (CLSAC), P/GF/M/1/2, 'St Giles in the Fields, vestry minutes, 1673–1771', 6 Nov. 1729, f. 531.
[240] *Workhouse Cruelty: Workhouses Turn'd Goals.*
[241] BL, Sloane Ms. 4078, f. 159; *Daily Post* (London, England), Saturday, 18 September 1731 (Burney Collection: www.galegroup.com, 1 Jan. 2014).

The 'dark hole' in the workhouse was also inspected, and found to be 'a clean place being free from damps or any offensive smell'.[242]

Nevertheless, these complaints, in combination with longer-term popular opposition, fundamentally changed the direction of workhouses in London. Marriott, whom the pamphlets roundly blamed for the abominations in St Giles, was driven from the management of all the large workhouses of Westminster and metropolitan London between 1727 and 1731. By 1729, when the first anatomy case was presented to the vestry of St Giles, he only managed this single London workhouse.[243] The anatomy cases and most especially the *Workhouse Cruelty* appear to mark the final push by a broad spectrum of plebeian London to rid the capital of this troublesome bureaucrat. He was excluded from St Giles within weeks of the autopsy (despite its conclusions), and died a few months later.

During the same few years, 1727 to 1731, in response to the large number of sick and pregnant paupers who appeared helpless at their doors, workhouses in the capital began to change their focus towards the provision of medical care. At St Giles the immediate upshot of the anatomy case of 1729 was a resolution of the vestry: 'That for the future the apothecary belonging to the workhouse do attend such out-patients belonging to this parish as the upper churchwarden … shall direct.'[244]

This effectively undermined the policy of applying a 'workhouse test' and recreated a restricted form of outdoor relief. More widely, as Kevin Siena has demonstrated, the larger houses of London refocused their efforts away from the imposition of labour discipline to the provision of medical care and accommodation for the elderly, orphaned and infirm. As Marriott was expelled from the workhouses, new provisions were established. Within months of St George Hanover Square dispensing with Marriott's services in 1727, a new infirmary was under construction. Similarly, at St Margaret Westminster, his departure was quickly followed by the conversion of six rooms into 'a ward … particularly assigned for the reception of the sick'.[245] A year later, six more rooms were added to the sick ward. At St Leonard Shoreditch, Marriott's dismissal was rapidly followed by the rebuilding of large parts of the house.[246]

---

[242] BL, Sloane Ms. 4078, f. 159.

[243] Hitchcock, 'English workhouse', pp. 282–3.

[244] CLSAC, 'St Giles in the Fields, vestry minutes, 1673–1771', 6 Nov. 1729, f. 531.

[245] Kevin P. Siena, *Venereal Disease, Hospitals, and the Urban Poor: London's 'Foul Wards', 1600–1800* (University of Rochester Press, 2004), p. 140.

[246] Hackney Archives Department, 'St Leonard Shoreditch, minute book of the select vestry and parish meetings', P/L/1, 5 Sept. 1727 – 5 Sept. 1771, 7 Aug. 1728, p. 13.

At St Martin's, one of the largest of London's workhouses, and the largest institution Marriott ran, the impact of his departure is less certain. In the years following 1727, he was replaced on an almost annual basis by a series of masters in much the same mould. But like the others, St Martin's was eventually forced to reconfigure its workhouse to provide more comprehensive medical care. In 1736, new wards were created 'for the sick, another for the smallpox and another for the lying in women'.[247] As for St Giles itself, even though it was being touted as an exemplar of workhouse management through 1731, like the rest it was forced to reconfigure its provision towards medical care and emergencies. By the end of the century, the parish officials were describing their workhouse as 'an Asylum for the aged, for orphans in an infant state, for idiots and the lame, blind, sick, or otherwise infirm and diseased'; for everyone except the able bodied.[248]

By 1731, clamorous paupers, with the assistance of a wider community and the connivance of at least one justice, had forced the parishes of London to substantially modify one model of workhouse organisation in favour of something that more fully reflected their needs.

Conclusion

In response to the substantial law and order problems which accompanied the Hanoverian accession, the new government responded aggressively, not only with the traditional method of adding additional capital crimes to the bloody code, and through encouragement of reformation of manners activities, but also with expensive innovations, signalling a new willingness of the state to devote financial resources to implement social policies. Two innovations in particular had a major impact of the lives of the poor and the deviant for more than a century. Now funded by the state, transportation became the dominant form of punishment for convicted felons until the early nineteenth century, when it was overtaken by imprisonment, but it continued in use until 1857. And, although the legislation was only permissive, the parish workhouse quickly became a regular feature of the London landscape for the poor. While policies changed, workhouses did not fully disappear until 1948. Less long lasting, but still influential for decades, was the royal proclamation of a £100 reward for the apprehension of highway robbers, which led to a

---

[247] WAC, St Martin in the Fields, 'Vestry minutes', STM/F/1/2006, 23 August 1736, p. 454.

[248] *Hints and Cautions for the information of the Churchwardens and Overseers of the Poor of the Parishes of St Giles in the Fields and St George Bloomsbury* (1797), p. 6.

significant increase in thief-taking. Despite the spectacular collapse of Jonathan Wild's network of thieves, thief-takers continued to flourish in London into the second half of the eighteenth century when they were gradually incorporated into official policing.

Not only did these innovations have a long-term impact on social policy, but they reshaped the personnel and power structures of local government. Justices of the peace acquired additional powers of law and order, both with the Riot Act and through their presence on parish vestries. Encouraged by the government, justices also took control of the reformation of manners. With new institutions to manage, parish vestries, increasingly restricted to elite residents, became not only more powerful but also more bureaucratic. However, the individuals who gained the most from these reforms were the private individuals who were hired by the state or individual parishes, or funded through the reward system – transportation contractors, workhouse managers and thief-takers – and who discovered numerous ways of profiting, often corruptly, at the expense of the poor, ratepayers and the state.

Yet plebeian Londoners, some of whom became thief-takers, were not simply the victims of change imposed from above. Often in alliance with their relatively wealthy neighbours, they actively shaped these innovations or set constraints on what could be achieved. As in the 1690s, reformation of manners prosecutions were continually sabotaged by popular resistance (not all of it plebeian in origin), and by 1731 the campaign was a pale reflection of its former self. Only the emerging crusade against gin seemed to offer supporters a potential lifeline. But even this would prove illusory following the failure of the 1736 Gin Act.

Resistance to the bloody code and the prosecution of felonies by thief-takers was less frequently successful. Nevertheless, London's thieves developed a defiant and confrontational culture in the 1720s which called the effectiveness of the law into question. Taking advantage of not only the huge public demand for stories about crime but also the prevailing critique of corruption in high places, some criminals successfully promoted themselves as celebrities, undermining the official crusade against highway robbers and blurring the line between settled communities and an anti-authoritarian criminal subculture.

Paupers, meanwhile, were obliged to respond to the harsh new world of the workhouse and the 'test', either by going without relief, or, with parish ratepayers, by calling attention to inhumane treatment within the houses. Through complaints to justices and in ballads and broadsides, they managed to discredit the most important workhouse contractor of the period, Matthew Marriott, effectively driving him out of London. As a consequence, new rules governing standards of provision in workhouses were adopted. Perhaps more importantly, with their constant demands for medical treatment, the poor forced a reformulation of workhouse provision. Together with the cost of outdoor relief, which re-emerged in spite of the 'workhouse test', this pressure meant that the creation of workhouses drove up, rather than down, the cost of looking after the poor.

However, these conflicts did not simply take the form of disputes between plebeian London and their social superiors. As we have seen, London's neighbourhood communities were often divided, particularly over responses to vice and the provision of poor relief. While many, often more respectable, residents living near 'disorderly houses' were keen to have such houses suppressed and order restored to their neighbourhoods, many others, dependent on the local economy of drink, prostitution and gambling, sought to protect them. And at times the aspect of workhouse provision which most seemed to alienate Londoners was not so much the mistreatment of inhabitants as the fact that respectable inhabitants who had fallen on to hard times were lumped together with whores and chimney sweeps in the same institution (and quite possibly the same beds). While non-elite London could effectively unite in its opposition to aspects of the new social policies, it remained divided on many other issues.

4 Vestries, justices and their opponents: 1731–1748

Introduction

When she stood trial at the Old Bailey for the theft of six pewter plates and an iron bedscrew (used to fasten bedframes together) in October 1736, Grace Powell must have seemed the embodiment of a disorderly Londoner.[1] Recently discharged from St Martin's workhouse, penniless, recently widowed, drunk and having apparently abandoned her only child, she sought temporary refuge at Samuel Pate's 'stand', or low lodging house in St Giles in the Fields, where for tuppence a night, he 'entertains Black-shoe-fellows, and sells Drams ... the House ... full of People, Men and Women, all lie[ing] together in the same Room'.[2] The worse for wear after drinking three or four drams of Pate's gin, Powell was caught with the iron bedscrew secreted in her petticoats, and when she attempted to escape down the back stairs to the cellar, Martha King watched as Powell 'dropp'd two Plates upon the Stairs, I saw her pull two more out of her Bosom, and two more she dropped down the Vault'. Despite the clanging pewter, and artfully hidden bedscrew, Grace Powell was acquitted by a sympathetic jury clearly willing to condone at least some types of disorder. They found her not guilty, following a simple plea that she had no 'Friends but God and my self'.[3] Grace was just one of the 3,805 defendants found not guilty at the Old Bailey in this eighteen-year period, bookmarked by years in which the acquittal rate was over 40 per cent.[4]

---

[1] *LL*, set, 'Grace Powell'.

[2] Grace Powell's settlement examination states that her husband Daniel, a shoemaker, had died some three months earlier, and that she was pregnant in December 1735. *LL*, St Martin in the Fields Settlement Examinations, 6 December 1735 (smdsset_22_2276). Our thanks to Jeremy Boulton for additional details on Grace's background.

[3] *LL*, Old Bailey Proceedings, 13 October 1736 (t17361013-33).

[4] In 1732, the rate reached 49.7 per cent, and in 1747, 40.4 per cent. The average for the period 1731 to 1748 was 37.6 per cent. See *Old Bailey Online*, Statistics: Verdicts by year, 1731–48 (counting by defendant).

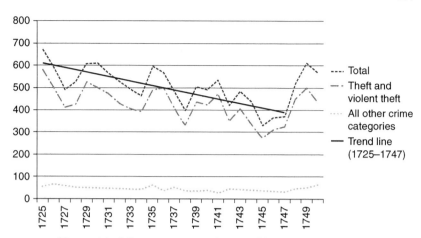

Figure 4.1 Offences prosecuted at the Old Bailey, 1725–1750. *Old Bailey Online*, Statistics: Offences by year, 1674–1913; Online data set: Crime Prosecutions.xlsx.

With one exceptional year, the 1730s and 1740s were characterised by relative calm and prosperity. The decade after 1729, in particular, witnessed a sustained series of good harvests driven by a unique series of mild winters and warm summers, resulting in high real wages.[5] Acquittal rates at the Old Bailey rose, while prosecutions and committals to Bridewell both slid gradually downward. Marginally fewer convicts were hanged or transported. Following the outbreak of war with Spain in 1739, the years between 1740 and 1748 also saw relatively good conditions. Many young men were drawn into the military, while prices and wages remained steady.

These halcyon decades were punctuated by one severe climatic event – the 'hard winter' of 1739–40, which recorded the lowest average temperatures for the whole century and resulted in the Thames freezing over from Christmas Eve 1739 to early March of 1740.[6] Some enjoyed the Frost Fair established on the river, but most struggled to make ends

---

[5] Brian R. Mitchell, *British Historical Statistics* (Cambridge University Press, 1988), pp. 754–6; E. A. Wrigley and R. S. Schofield, *The Population History of England, 1541–1871: A Reconstruction* (London: Edward Arnold, 1981), p. 432, Figure 10.12; and Leonard Schwarz, 'The standard of living in the long run: London, 1700–1860', *Economic History Review*, 2nd Series, 38:1 (1985), 24–41. This is not to suggest that the economy as a whole was necessarily thriving. The London building trades in particular stagnated in these decades. See Leonard Schwarz, *London in the Age of Industrialisation: Entrepreneurs, Labour Force and Living Conditions, 1700–1850* (Cambridge University Press, 1992), pp. 79–83.

[6] Tim Joslin estimates that in combination, the mild conditions of the 1730s and the harsh winter of 1739–40 represent a one in 10,000 year event. See '1740 and all that', 6 March

meet.[7] That winter and spring, workhouse numbers and wheat prices rose as the temperature fell. At St Martin's workhouse, January alone saw 163 new admissions, up 83 per cent on the same month a year before.[8]

Even accounting for the winter of 1739–40, for plebeian Londoners these decades were relatively prosperous. And yet, driven by continuing elite anxieties, the period also witnessed a series of major innovations in criminal justice and poor relief policies. Concern about the increasing cost of poor relief, driven ever upwards by the cost of the new workhouses and by the growing demands of the poor (in spite of relative prosperity), together with new anxieties about gin drinking by the poor and the role of criminal 'gangs', resulted in attempts to reorganise local government and policing. Through the Westminster Watch Acts and activities of the associated select vestries, and through the efforts of Thomas De Veil as 'court justice' and the creation of the first magistrates' court in the City, local government was reformulated.

These innovations were challenged at many levels, by ratepayers and tradesmen as well as by street sellers and members of 'gangs'. And there were some real victories. The 1736 Gin Act was rendered almost totally ineffective by popular resistance to the activities of informers, leading in turn to the collapse of the reformation of manners societies. And in the courts, the growing use of government-sponsored lawyers for the prosecution, together with the continued use of thief-takers, led to the admission and substantive use of defence counsel at the Old Bailey, partially rebalancing the scales of justice. Select vestries were forced to defend themselves against continuing charges of corruption and brutality, as revealed in the St Martin's roundhouse disaster, while parishes responded to the demands of the poor by largely abandoning their attempts to make a profit from their labour. The poor gradually forced parish workhouses to take on the character of general parish institutions run with the consent of the 'workhouse family', and they learned how to engage with the growing number of associational charities and hospitals.

2010 (unchartedterritory.wordpress.com, 1 Jan. 2014). These same conditions created a famine in Ireland in the subsequent year.
[7] The ice was thick enough to support dozens of tented businesses, including a printing press. See *British Museum Collection Online, An Exact Draught of Frost Fair on the River Thames as it Appear'd from White Hall Stairs in the Year 1740* (1889,0420.112); and *Printed Ticket from the 1739–40 Frost Fair on the Thames* (1880,1113.1802).
[8] Comparing admissions, 1–31 Jan. 1740, to admissions, 1–31 Jan. 1739. *LL*, St Martin in the Fields Workhouse Registers 1725 to 1819, gives a higher overall figure (397), but this has been corrected to account for duplicate entries in the registers. In 1739 wheat prices climbed 23.6 per cent above the thirty-one-year average, and the following spring of 1740 witnessed actual dearth (50.5 per cent above average): W. G. Hoskins, 'Harvest fluctuations and English economic history, 1620–1759', *Agricultural History Review*, 16:1 (1968), 31.

The poor

With the creation of workhouses by most of the large suburban parishes in the 1720s, supplemented by traditional 'outdoor relief', parish support for paupers had become more diverse. In the 1740s London's poor had an additional set of options, as the new associational charities, such as the Foundling Hospital, began to offer specialised services. Collectively, these innovations made poor relief more expensive, while allowing the poor, and to a lesser extent, the parishes, to play one source of relief against another. The ratepayers and householders who were expected to foot the bill became increasingly restive.

Who were the poor, and who was able to obtain relief? The most extensive and detailed surviving workhouse registers, those for St Martin in the Fields, record just over 10,000 workhouse admissions for the period from 1738 to 1748. Sources such as this reveal institutions dominated by women and children. At St Martin's, 51 per cent of inmates were adult women (aged 15 to 59), with children under 15 making up a further 26 per cent. The elderly, both men and women of 60 and over, made up a further 9 per cent, with adult men between 15 and 59 constituting just under 13 per cent of the total.

It was not simply adult women, but women of a child-bearing age who formed the largest group of admissions. While the number of girls and boys in the workhouse population was roughly equal, this diverged markedly from around the age of fourteen, with girls and young women becoming increasingly dominant, while young men either found the workhouse door firmly closed to them or chose not to attempt to enter.

Analysis of other London workhouses reinforces this basic pattern. In St Luke Chelsea, on the rural fringe of the capital and affected by the large number of 'out-pensioners' drawn to the locality by the Royal Hospital in Chelsea, the elderly component of the workhouse population was higher, but the dominance of adult women and children remained marked.[9]

However, this apparently consistent story of the prominence of women and children at the relative expense of men and the elderly is only part of a more complex pattern. It almost certainly holds true for the workhouses run by the forty-nine parishes that can be identified as either having a

---

[9] See Tim Hitchcock, 'Unlawfully begotten on her body: illegitimacy and the parish poor in St Luke Chelsea', in Tim Hitchcock *et al.*, eds., *Chronicling Poverty: The Voices and Strategies of the English Poor, 1640–1840* (Basingstoke: Macmillan Press, 1997), pp. 76, 84 (nn. 12 and 13). A similar pattern has also been identified in St Marylebone: Alysa Levene, 'Children, childhood and the workhouse: St Marylebone, 1769–1781', *London Journal*, 9:1 (2008), 41–60.

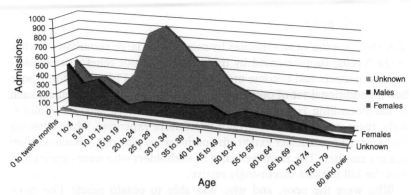

Figure 4.2 St Martin in the Fields workhouse admissions, 1738–1748. *LL*, St Martin in the Fields Workhouse Registers, 1725 to 1824 (86,489 admissions); Online data set: St Martins Workhouse Registers.xlsx. Note: these figures are based on 'admissions' rather than individual paupers, who frequently entered the house on several occasions. The quality of the registers also varied over time, with standards of record keeping rising and falling with the character of the parish staff. The registers are relatively weak for the decade up to 1738. The figures used here have been cleaned to eliminate repeated entries.

workhouse, or contracting out the care of the parish poor, by mid-century, but it reflects only a fraction of the broader parochial provision.[10] Almost no parish was able to maintain a strict 'workhouse test' for any extended period. Relatively quickly after establishing a workhouse, most parishes resumed providing at least some limited forms of casual and outdoor relief. Entirely typical was St Bride Fleet Street. After establishing a workhouse in the spring of 1727, the parish initially attempted to impose a strict test. But hard cases rapidly forced it to backtrack, and within a year the workhouse committee had begun to admit exceptions: 'no person should be allow'd any money unless the head of the family be sick'.[11] A few years later, in the nearby parish of St Ann Blackfriars, the workhouse committee attempted to make a virtue out of failure. In 1734 they declared that 'no person be relieved out of the

---

[10] See Timothy Hitchcock, 'The English workhouse: a study of institutional poor relief in selected counties, 1696–1750' (D.Phil. dissertation, Oxford University, 1985), Appendix, pp. 270–5. The London Workhouse has been excluded from this total.

[11] LMA, St Bride Fleet Street, 'Vestry minutes', 1715–27, P69/BRI/B/001/MS06554/004, 9 March 1726–7; St Bride Fleet Street, 'Vestry minutes', 1727–66, P69/BRI/B/001/MS06554/005, 25 April 1728, f. 4; and St Bride Fleet Street, 'Miscellaneous parish papers', 1666–1756, P69/BRI/B/012/MS06570/002, no. 181.

Workhouse ... except on emergent occasions' and went on to opine that relief of this sort should 'be Sparingly Granted and only upon Terms Evidently for the Benefit of the Parish'.[12] In most instances, it was hard cases that forced the parishes to relent. The head of a large household, ill and unable to work, if unsupported could bring four or five dependants onto the parish books. These poor, in need of a few pence to tide them over, would cost many times this amount if admitted to the workhouse. Compromise was almost always to 'the Benefit of the parish'.

It is also important to remember that although workhouses served over half of the metropolitan population, there remained over a hundred other parishes and liberties containing at least 250,000 people that continued to relieve the poor largely with cash doles and pensions.[13] In combination with the growing role of associational charities, and with the complex landscape of hospital and independent charitable provision, the settled poor of London, in particular, could choose between a patchwork of increasingly diverse relief opportunities.

The profound and evolving difference that the establishment of work-houses made for London's poor, and the complexity of the system as a whole, is reflected in the experience of those who continued to be relieved 'out of doors'. One of the few large London parishes that did not establish a workhouse in the 1720s and 1730s was St Clement Danes. In a rare compre-hensive census of its poor completed in 1745, the parish officers recorded the names, settlements and ages of their dependent poor, dividing them between the 'casual poor' (those who had a right to occasional relief as the need arose) and the 'monthly poor' (who received a regular income from the parish).

In total, the census provides details of 461 parish paupers, 344 of whom received a monthly pension, while the rest were in receipt of irregular or 'casual' doles. Of these, we know the ages of 301 individuals, from infants to the estimable and grey-haired Mary Curtis, who at ninety-four was the oldest person in the list.[14] This census is not entirely comparable with workhouse registers, as St Clement's continued to use a system of contract nursing for emergency and neo-natal care, and it is not clear whether the paupers cared for under contract in this way were included in the census,

---

[12] LMA, St Ann Blackfriars, 'Workhouse committee book', 1734–67, P69/ANN/B/074/ MS08690, 25 July 1734.

[13] The population of the parishes with a workhouse total some 339,000 according to figures calculated from the Bills of Mortality. This same source puts the overall population at 587,000 in the 1740s. Both figures are dubious and are probably underestimates, but they reflect a realistic order of magnitude and proportion. See *Locating London's Past*, Estimating London's Population. The underlying spreadsheet can be downloaded from the website (www. locatinglondon.org/static/population.html).

[14] *LL*, set, 'Mary Curtis'.

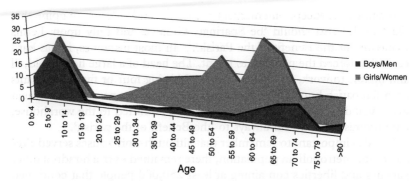

Figure 4.3 St Clement Danes, Pauper Census, 1745. *LL*, St Clement Danes Parish, Registers of the Poor, 1745 (WCCDRP36706RP36706); Online data set: St Clements Census of Pensioners 1745.xlsx.

but there remains a marked disparity between paupers in receipt of 'outdoor relief' and listed in the census, and those admitted to the capital's workhouses. In the St Clement Danes census, women and children continue to dominate the list, but here older women form the largest proportion of poor relief recipients, with women of sixty and over constituting 29 per cent of all paupers. The large bulge of younger women admitted to workhouses is entirely absent, and a wider population of paupers has become apparent.

Of the 228 individuals for whom we have information about the length of time they spent on the parish books, the average period of dependence prior to 1745 is sixteen years. In other words, while workhouse populations were dominated by short-term emergency relief, the pensions and doles provided 'out of doors' tended to go to those who had established a regular relationship with the parish, often spanning decades and constituting a substantial financial burden on the parish. Many had been passed on appeal from other London parishes, establishing an irrefutable 'settlement'. However, just as typical was sixty-year-old Hannah Davis, who was first admitted as a parish pensioner in 1713, thirty-two years prior to her appearance in the census, on the basis of 'her father's Renting a house of £18, a Yeare in Milford Lane [the] Strand'.[15] For at least the next three decades, Hannah received a pension of between 6 and 10 shillings a month.[16]

This same pattern of long-term support, focused particularly on elderly women, can also be seen in the records of the small and wealthy parish of

---

[15] *LL*, St Clement Danes Parish: Register of Fortnightly/Monthly Pensioners in 1733 (WCCDRP367060013). See also, *LL*, set, 'Hannah Davis'.

[16] There is also a mention of a sister Margaret for the first decade. See *LL*, St Clement Danes Parish: Minutes of Parish Vestries, 18 November 1716 – 3 June 1725 (WCCDMV362130035), 7 November 1717.

St Dionis Backchurch, straddling Fenchurch Street, deep in the heart of the City. St Dionis had a population of just under a thousand in the 1740s and provided regular and relatively generous relief for just a couple of dozen paupers. It attempted and failed to establish a workhouse in 1725, and again in 1730. In 1733 it subcontracted the care of a small subset of its dependent poor to John Thruckstone, who ran a workhouse at Tottenham High Cross.[17] This arrangement lasted only a year and collapsed in the face of pauper demands: 'They all Complain of the Hardship in the Winter by having no Fire, the Floor being of Loam & very cold.' A group of the most vocal were brought to give evidence to the vestry:

That such of the Poor as are now attending at the Door of the Vestry be called in and Frances Bunting, Mary Fairbrother & the Sister of Judith Rayner appearing were severally heard relating to the Hardships complained of.[18]

James Dorselt, 'a Boy', complained he was 'not taught to read'.[19] The parish transferred these paupers to a house run by the parish of St Mary Newington and continued to support a small proportion of its poor in a series of contract workhouses for the rest of the century.[20]

But most of St Dionis's dependent poor continued to receive outdoor relief according to a finely tuned hierarchy of merit and circumstances. The parish was responsible for distributing a range of charitable gifts amounting to approximately £32 a year to 'poor householders' and the 'deserving' poor.[21] It preserved the distinction between 'collectioners', relieved from funds generated from passing the plate at church on Sunday, and 'pensioners', relieved from the rates; and within this group, between weekly and quarterly pensioners. 'Collectioners' tended to be older and more established parishioners, while 'pensioners' were more likely to be disabled, foundlings (frequently identifiable by the use of 'Dionis' as their surname), or those temporarily out of work or overburdened with children.[22] In addition 'casual'

---

[17] *LL*, set, 'John Thruckstone'.
[18] *LL*, St Dionis Backchurch Parish: Minutes of Parish Vestries, 24 April 1712 – 20 February 1759 (GLDBMV305010220), 31 July 1734.
[19] *LL*, St Dionis Backchurch Parish: Minutes of Parish Vestries, 24 April 1712 – 20 February 1759 (GLDBMV305010220), 31 July 1734.
[20] *LL*, St Dionis Backchurch Parish: Minutes of Parish Vestries, 24 April 1712 – 20 February 1759 (GLDBMV305010220), 22 January 1734–5.
[21] In 1818 the parliamentary returns recorded the parish as being in receipt of £32 8s. 8d. per annum from its charitable holdings: *PP*, 'Abridgement of abstract of answers and returns relative to expense and maintenance of poor in England and Wales', 1818, pp. 266–7 (parlipapers.chadwyck.co.uk, 1 Jan. 2014).
[22] At least thirty people with the surname 'Dionis' appear in the parish records for St Dionis Backchurch. These include Timothy Dionis, a foundling baptised in 1704 who continued to receive parish relief until his death in 1765, and Charlotte Dionis, who was born in 1761 and disappears from the records in 1781, having received extensive

and emergency relief was also provided. The handful of people sent to the workhouse was drawn exclusively from among the 'pensioners'.

Typical of one sort of pauper was Elizabeth Yexley, whose settlement was based on her deceased husband's rental of a shop in the parish decades before she and her daughter were removed to St Dionis from St Giles Cripplegate after she threatened to become 'chargeable'.[23] The process of removal gave Elizabeth a secure legal right to relief, and she was supported on a casual basis over several years before finally being sent to the contract workhouse, where she was repeatedly reprimanded for her 'Elopement from the House and her infamous behaviour'.[24]

Equally typical was John Clifton.[25] In the 1730s Clifton was a householder in good standing and made regular contributions to the poor rates.[26] He also served as a 'Constable, Scavenger and Inquestman' in 1734, and sat on the vestry in the early 1740s.[27] However, following a period of declining fortunes during which he was regularly excused from serving in parish offices, he started to receive 'sacrament money' in November 1756, was subsequently included in the list of recipients for parish 'gifts' and began to receive extensive casual relief.[28] By 1759 he was an established collectioner, receiving a total of £23 7s. 9d. in parish relief, including £5 4s. contributed by his brother but distributed by the parish.[29] This included £4 in annual rent, a fortnightly allowance of 14s. and 18s. 9d. worth of coal.

All these forms of relief, both outdoor relief and in workhouses, responded to the demands of the poor. But their impact was felt most strongly on the newest, and most problematic form of relief, the workhouse. From the late 1720s, most London workhouses had evolved from institutions dedicated to putting the poor to work to care centres

support from the parish over the previous twenty years. See *LL*, Deirdre Palk, 'Timothy Dionis, 1704–1765', and Deirdre Palk, 'Charlotte Dionis, b. 1761'.

[23] *LL*, Hannah Wallace, 'Elizabeth Yexley, d. 1769'.

[24] *LL*, St Dionis Backchurch Parish: Workhouse Inquest (Visitation) Minute Books, 20 May 1761 – 29 April 1788 (GLDBIW30201IW302010018), 5 March 1763.

[25] *LL*, set, 'John Clifton'.

[26] He is listed, for, instance, as paying 13s. in 1730. *LL*, St Dionis Backchurch Parish: Churchwarden's Vouchers/Receipts, 7 May 1727 – 1 June 1748 (GLDBPP307000019), 30 October 1730.

[27] In the parish's comprehensive listing of ward and parish officers, Clifton is listed as having first served the ward from 18 December 1734; and to have last served the parish on 17 April 1740. See *LL*, St Dionis Backchurch Parish: Minutes of Parish Vestries, 24 April 1712 – 20 February 1759 (GLDBMV305010221), 18 December 1734; and St Dionis Backchurch Parish: Miscellaneous Parish and Bridewell Papers, 1 January 1708 – 4 May 1742 (GLDBPM306090027).

[28] *LL*, St Dionis Backchurch Parish: Churchwardens and Overseers of the Poor Account Books, 1729–62 (GLDBAC300060488).

[29] *LL*, St Dionis Backchurch Parish: Churchwardens and Overseers of the Poor Account Books, 1758–62 (GLDBAC300070119).

providing emergency and medical relief. In a large parish such as St Martin in the Fields, the workhouse served as a general homeless shelter, contained the parish morgue and housed the parish shell or stretcher. By the 1740s it also had specialised accommodation for the sick, those suffering from infectious diseases and women lying in.[30]

St Martin's was actually quite late in establishing dedicated medical wards in its workhouse, but in August 1736 the workhouse committee decided to buy a two-storey house adjacent to the main building and fit it up as a series of wards for the sick and pregnant:

in the Upper Floor there be a Ward for the sick, another for the Smallpox and another for the Lying in Women, and ... the House should be painted withoutside and Whitewashed within from Top to Bottom.[31]

Sixty new beech bedsteads were provided with new flock bolsters, coverlets and two blankets each. And eighty pairs of sheets were also purchased. In the words of Kevin Siena, developments of this sort were driven by the 'London poor simply ... turning up at the parish door, exercising... what they believed were legitimate demands for medical care'.[32]

This relationship is illustrated by the response to the opening of St Martin's new lying-in facility in the late autumn of 1736. The comprehensive registers of admissions for its workhouse date from the opening of the house in 1725, and for the first few years it admitted lying-in women in emergencies and also became home to the abandoned infants of the parish.[33] There is a significant gap in the records from 1731 to 1736, but when the register resumes in 1737 the impact of a new lying-in ward is evident. From 1737 the number of babies born in the house and of infants abandoned to its care increased significantly over the figures for the 1720s.

---

[30] For a comprehensive treatment of the role of the St Martin's workhouse in the provision of medical care, see Jeremy Boulton and Leonard Schwarz, 'The parish workhouse, the parish and parochial medical provision in eighteenth-century London', in *Pauper Lives in Georgian London and Manchester* (research.ncl.ac.uk/pauperlives, 1 Jan. 2014). See also Jeremy Boulton, Romola Davenport and Leonard Schwarz, "These ANTE-CHAMBERS OF THE GRAVE"? Mortality, medicine and the 'workhouse in Georgian London', in Jonathan Reinarz and Leonard Schwarz, eds., *Medicine and the Workhouse* (University of Rochester Press, 2013), pp. 58–85, and Kevin P. Siena, *Venereal Disease, Hospitals and the Urban Poor: London's 'Foul Wards' 1600–1800* (Rochester University Press, 2004), pp. 152–61.

[31] WAC, St Martin in the Fields, 'Vestry minutes', 1716–39, STM/F/1/2006, 23 August 1736, p. 454.

[32] WAC, St Martin in the Fields, 'Vestry minutes', 1716–39, 6 October 1736, p. 459; Siena, *Venereal Disease*, p. 142.

[33] For the impact of the establishment of the workhouse in 1725 on the provision of parish relief in St Martin's, see Jeremy Boulton, 'Welfare systems and the parish nurse in early modern London, 1650–1725', *Family & Community History*, 10:2 (2007), 127–51.

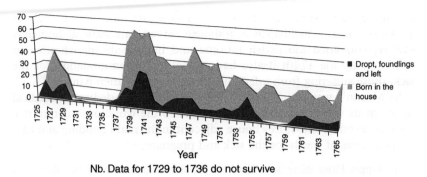

Nb. Data for 1729 to 1736 do not survive

Figure 4.4 St Martin in the Fields, Workhouse Registers, 'Dropt' and 'Born in the house'. *LL*, St Martin in the Fields Workhouse Registers, 1725 to 1824 (86,489 admissions); Online data set: St Martins Workhouse Registers.xlsx.

Between 1738 and 1741 the number of babies born in the house reached an average of fifty-nine per annum, or approximately 8 per cent of all parish christenings.[34] During the same years an average of almost twenty-three babies a year were described in the registers as being 'foundlings' or having been 'dropt' prior to their arrival at the workhouse door. This rise in abandoned children largely reflects the influence of the Foundling Hospital, whose charter was issued in 1739 and which opened in 1741. However, it also reflects real demand. Along with the sick, the ill and the injured, pregnant women and new mothers helped transform the workhouses of London into de facto hospitals for the poor. The provision of substantial resources in response to demand reinforced that process, hurrying along what Jeremy Boulton and Leonard Schwarz have described on the basis of the evidence from St Martin in the Fields as the 'medicalisation' of London's workhouse provision.[35]

In the nature of a dialogue, unmet demand from the poor had forced the parish to create new facilities for the ill and for lying-in women, which in turn generated a new demand for the provision of care. But having observed the health outcomes for babies and their mothers, it appears the poor decided to shift their demand elsewhere. Of the 184 babies born in

[34] This percentage is based on a birth rate of one child per thirty-five of the population, calculated from the Bills of Mortality for Westminster for the 1740s. This calculation gives an overall figure of approximately 786 births for a population of 27,502 for the parish as a whole. See *LL*, St Martin in the Fields Workhouse Registers 1725–1824, 'Westminster population estimates', 1740s (Online data set: St Martins Workhouse Registers.xlsx).

[35] Boulton and Schwarz, 'The parish workhouse'.

the house between January 1739 and December 1741, we know the immediate fate of 182: 68 were discharged from the house alive, while 114 were buried from it.[36] After 1741, the number of babies born in the house declined substantially.

There was another problem. The impact of rising demand for relief and the capital costs of moving from a system of universal outdoor relief, to one characterised by institutions supplemented by pensions and casual payments, generated conflict between the parish and the householders who were obliged to foot the bill. In two decades of relative prosperity during which real wages remained high, expenditure on poor relief nonetheless continued to grow. Workhouses were expensive. Where a new workhouse was created, this usually entailed the parish taking on substantial debt to raise the necessary capital and ensured it became wholly responsible for all the needs of those pensioners admitted to the house. A system of outdoor relief, in which most doles and pensions could be adjusted in light of the ability of the pauper to do at least some work in their own support, was replaced by one in which every need, from clean linen to the Christmas feast, was marked up to the parish account.

However, even in a parish such as St Clement Danes, which avoided the establishment of a workhouse and persevered with pensions and doles, the cost of poor relief grew substantially. In St Clement's the population declined by 6 per cent in the first half of the eighteenth century, but the cost of relief doubled in the two decades after 1730.[37] In 1731 the annual cost of relieving the poor came to £1,189, and by 1748 this had risen to £2,319.[38] In part the explanation for this growth in expenditure lay in the system of settlement and removal. As examinations and certificates – all the bureaucracy of identity and legal 'settlement' – came to encompass an ever-growing proportion of the population, it became more difficult to question the 'right to relief' of the supplicant at the overseers' door. The presence in Westminster of numerous 'trading justices' willing, at a moderate charge, to conduct an examination and sign a removal order inadvertently empowered the poor. At the same time, as evidenced in the new Watch Acts, tolerance for public begging was on the decline. For the poor, the alternative to casual door-to-door begging for broken food and small change – for the substance of neighbourliness – was frequently an appeal to the parish. Both the

---

[36] Based on all entries in the data set where the word 'born' is present, for the period 1 Jan. 1739 to 31 Dec. 1741. See *LL*, St Martin in the Fields Workhouse Registers: 'Born*'. These figures have been edited to eliminate duplicate entries.

[37] *Locating London's Past* – 'Estimating London's populations'.

[38] Poor Relief Expenditure for St Clement Danes, 1706–1803 (Online data set: St Clement Danes Poor Law Expenditure 1706–1803.xlsx).

demands of the poor and the perhaps unintended consequences of new policies drove up the cost of relief. This set the scene for new disputes over the organisation of local government and the role of poorer house-holders in parish administration.

The vestry closed and the watch reformed

At the same time as the cost of poor relief was rising, many householders found themselves increasingly excluded from parish government. The simmering disputes that characterised the 1710s and 1720s, the workhouse scandals and parliamentary investigations into peculation and corruption, laid the foundations for continuing conflict. When com-bined with the radical re-crafting of the administrative landscape of London through the creation of ten new parishes between 1720 and 1733 (with their select vestries) and at least thirty-two new poor relief institutions, these conflicts fuelled an on-going battle for control of local government that helped to redraw the lines of social class. In effect the new workhouses separated out the poor, even those who had once been householders, forcing on them a new identity as members of the 'work-house family', while select vestries, aided by 'select justices', grew ever more powerful.[39] Squeezed between were the 'Antient Inhabitants' of the parish, disenfranchised by the vestry and apparently taxed without end; householders Daniel Defoe characterised as 'the working or middling people who maintain not only those below, but those above them'.[40] The workhouses became a focus of ratepayer resentment and dispute, as both a financial liability and a feared resting place in old age.

The creation of closed or select vestries can be traced back to the sixteenth century and before.[41] However, the dominance of this form of government grew substantially in the 1720s and became the focus of vociferous opposition in the 1730s, in part as a result of their role in authorising the new workhouses.[42] On the eastern side of the City in

[39] The term 'select justice' is used by Joseph Phipps, *The Vestry Laid Open* (2nd edn, 1739), p. 26.

[40] Andrew Moreton [Daniel Defoe], *Parochial Tyranny: Or, The House-Keeper's Complaint Against the insupportable Exactions, and Partial Assessments of Select Vestries, &c.* (2nd edn, 1727), p. 36.

[41] N. J. G. Pounds, *A History of the English Parish: The Culture of Religion from Augustine to Victoria* (Cambridge University Press, 2000; paperback edn 2004), p. 193.

[42] These new parishes normally took the form of government that existed in the parish from which they were created. So St George Hanover Square, carved from St Martin in the Fields in 1724, simply reproduced the select vestry system in place in St Martin's and appealed to its mother parish for precedent and authority when defending its organisation in court.

St Botolph Aldersgate, for instance, the establishment of a workhouse by the select vestry led to the unprecedented move to create a separate 'general vestry' in February 1732. Having called a meeting, this general vestry in turn mandated a thorough-going investigation into parish finances.[43] The resulting sixty-page committee report led to the abolition of the select vestry and the creation of a body able to clean up parish politics. It was resolved 'That no business whatsoever ... be determined by any committee but by the General Vestry only'.[44] The remarkable aspect of this dispute lies in the vitriol and class hatred the campaign exposed. While the report itself is relatively tame, the manuscript notes and annotations made by the curate of the parish, William Freeman, reflect the depth of local feeling. Freeman notes the lowly occupations of the men who called the general vestry: soap boilers, shoemakers and tobacconists jostle for position with grocers and innkeepers. But he reserved his greatest ire for those supporting the workhouse and the closed vestry. One of the parish's long-serving churchwardens is described as, 'of a fiery temper, very Peevish & quarrelsome and bigoted to the Jacobite Party', whose untimely death was ascribed to 'overheating himself with passion, & quarrelling with Mr Scarr at the vestry'.[45] Freeman notes that another member of the select vestry, Samuel Smith, was publicly called a 'pickpocket' at a local alehouse by a supporter of the general vestry, and goes on to characterise him as 'a very saucy, Impudent Malicious Fellow, & was universally hated, he had neither judgement nor industry in any thing but frequenting Taverns, & Railing at his Neighbours'.[46] The transition from a select to a general vestry was the result of nothing short of a parochial revolution.

In Westminster the struggle for control of local government between the select vestries, the Middlesex bench and the Court of Burgesses that had rumbled on since the mid-1710s continued, but with the added complication of a new form of ratepayer activism in part motivated by the growing expenditure associated with the new workhouses. The dispute revolved most closely around the night watch, which did not seem to be doing enough to stop begging and crime. In the early spring of 1733, the Court of Burgesses petitioned parliament for an Act to reinforce its powers to

---

[43] *The Report of the Committee Appointed by a General Vestry of the Inhabitants of the Parish of St Botolph without Aldersgate, London: February 22d 1732. With some methods proposed to prevent abuses for the future* (1733), pp. 6–13.

[44] *Report of the Committee Appointed*, p. 47.

[45] Richard Scarr was active in the campaign for a general vestry. The manuscript elements are reproduced with a copy of the printed report as one of two copies available through *Eighteenth-Century Collections Online.* See *Report of the Committee Appointed*, image 98.

[46] *Report of the Committee Appointed*, image 97.

collect rates in support of the watch. They had recently discovered that while they had the power to set the rate, they could not collect it.[47] Although permission was granted to introduce the bill, it was killed stone dead on its second reading as a result of opposition from the select vestries of St George Hanover Square and St James Piccadilly, leaving the field open for the vestries of Westminster to step in directly.[48]

The two parishes had been created from St Martin in the Fields, and their select vestries included some of the most politically powerful men in the country. Promoted by these same parishes, the first parochial watch acts handed power to the vestries both to raise money for and to regulate the watch. This first Act was rapidly followed by legislation of an almost precisely similar character covering the other parishes of Westminster, first St Martin in the Fields, then St Margaret's and St John the Evangelist, followed by St Paul Covent Garden.[49] The only power left to the Court of Burgesses in relation to the policing of Westminster was the appointment of the high constable and his deputies, who as 'constables of the night' sat in preliminary judgement on the men and women arrested by the watch and confined in the roundhouses located in each parish.

Most historians have seen the flurry of Watch Acts passed in the mid-1730s as a response to violent crime.[50] However, the first Act primarily resulted from concerns about poverty and begging, and the querulous behaviour of ratepayers. The only crimes mentioned in justification of the Act were a series of thefts of lead from the roofs of new built houses, while debate focused on an account of a one-armed beggar who had discomforted the pregnant daughter of a 'Lady of Quality' by aggressively waving his stump hand in her direction.[51]

---

[47] PP, *Journals of the House of Commons*, 7–8 March 1733–4, p. 273 (parlipapers.chadwyck. co.uk, 1 Jan. 2014).

[48] PP, *Journals of the House of Commons*, 12–13 March, 1733–4, p. 278. For the role of the parishes in killing the bill, see Elaine A. Reynolds, *Before the Bobbies: The Night Watch and Police Reform in Metropolitan London, 1720–1830* (Basingstoke: Macmillan, 1998), p. 16.

[49] St Paul Covent Garden had an open or general vestry, in contrast to the others. St George Hanover Square and St James's, 8 George II c. 15; St Martin in the Fields, 9 George II c. 8; St Paul Covent Garden, 9 George II c. 13; St Anne, 9 George II c. 19; St Margaret and St John, 9 George II c. 17.

[50] The most comprehensive account of the politics and evolution of parochial government in Westminster in this period remains Sidney Webb and Beatrice Webb, *English Local Government*, Vol. I: *The Parish and the County* (London: Frank Cass, 1906; repr. 1963), pp. 227–62. For a recent account of the evolution of the watch, which identifies concerns about crime as a key motivating force, see Reynolds, *Before the Bobbies*.

[51] PP, *Journals of the House of Commons*, 18 March 1735, p. 420. This account appears to refer to the same individual who was arrested and sent to Bridewell on the orders of Sir John Gonson in September 1731. 'Philanthropos', writing in *The Daily Courant*,

Rather than crime, what motivated the passage of these Acts was the perception that 'the Streets have been every Day more and more pestered with idle vagrant Beggars, to the great Annoyance of Passengers', and that, as noted the previous year by the Court of Burgesses, 'the Methods hitherto practised, for raising Money to maintain the ... [watchmen and] Beadles, have been very precarious and unwarrantable'.[52] Most of the text of the first and subsequent Acts is taken up with issues of rating and taxation rather than with the watch itself, and had the effect of reinforcing the powers of the select vestries. At the same time, the Acts also encouraged the vestries to collaborate more closely with the justices of the Middlesex bench in pursuing their new rights of taxation and enforcement.

There is some evidence that the select vestries of Westminster began to adopt the practice of incorporating justices into their number and constituting themselves as a petty sessions as early as 1715.[53] Traditionally, petty sessions were held separately from the vestry, allowing two or more justices to meet and hear poor law appeals and a wide variety of criminal complaints.[54] In the normal course of events, justices rarely attended the vestry more than once a year, in order to audit the overseers' accounts at Easter. But the practice of justices regularly attending vestries became normalised in many suburban parishes in the 1730s, allowing the vestries in collaboration with justices to take direct control of setting and auditing their own rates, sit in judgement on poor law and vagrancy cases, and generally assume the full authority of the law.[55]

Described by his first biographer as the 'oracle of the vestry', Thomas De Veil, the single most significant justice of the period, attended the vestries of several west end parishes.[56] However, he was just one of a dozen or so justices who developed close relationships with individual

---

expressed the fear that allowing this beggar to go free would result in his disfigurement being passed onto the children of the aristocracy. *Daily Courant*, 20 September 1731 (Burney Collection: www.galegroup.com, 1 Jan. 2014).

[52] *PP, Journals of the House of Commons*, 27–28 February 1734, p. 395.

[53] In that year the vestry at St Clement Danes received a request from 'the Petty Sessions at St Martyn's Vestry' asking that the parish nominate an officer to attend this new hybrid institution. *LL*, St Clement Danes Parish: Minutes of Parish Vestries (WCCDM V362120238), 13 April 1715.

[54] Lee Davison *et al.*, 'The reactive state: English governance and society, 1689–1750', in Lee Davison *et al.*, eds., *Stilling the Grumbling Hive: The Response to Social and Economic Problems in England, 1689–1750* (Stroud: Alan Sutton, 1992), pp. xxxvi–xxxvii.

[55] The Webbs locate the origins of this practice in St Martin in the Fields in 1729. See Webb and Webb, *Parish and the County*, p. 231 n. 2.

[56] *Memoirs of the Life and Times of Sir Thomas De Veil, Knight, One of His Majesty's Justices of the Peace, for the Counties of Middlesex, Essex, Surrey and Hertfordshire, The City and Liberty of Westminster, The Tower of London, and the Liberties thereof, &c.* (1748), p. 46.

vestries. By 1742, activists seeking to reform the select vestry system in Westminster claimed it was normal for

> the Vestry [to] give Notice to the Justices, and order them to attend . . .; but that the Vestry attend likewise, and the business is done in a Vestry: That the Justices . . . are meer Cyphers, and that the Vestry govern and manage all these Matters . . . and that the Vestry do what they will in every Thing.[57]

In effect the Watch Acts had mandated this development, and in any case it was in the interests of the justices and vestrymen to work together, combining what Joseph Phipps described as 'select vestries' with 'select justices', who 'are so concurrent in their Dispositions and Judgments one with another, that they can't bear the Sight of one another's Failings'. This resulted in parishes where the 'Justices are one with the Rest, and share in devouring the Publick Money'.[58]

The problems generated by these acts are best illustrated in the experiences of St Martin in the Fields.[59] From 3 May 1736, the vestry took full control of the nightly watch and daily policing of the parish, appointing forty-one night watchmen, a principal watchman, a roundhouse keeper who was also charged with collecting the new watch rate, and eight beadles responsible for clearing the streets of beggars and nuisances. Many, such as Thomas Middleton, the rate collector and roundhouse keeper, simply continued in their existing role, doing what they had always done.

Nevertheless, each watchman was obliged to pay heed to a new set of rules: to arrive promptly at the roundhouse each evening, carrying his lantern and his staff, 'and keep watch and ward in his said walk or round from that hour till after five of the clock in the morning'.[60] Each beadle was expected to

---

[57] *Report of the Committee to whom the Petition of the Principal Inhabitants of . . . Westminster. . . was referred* (1742), p. 8.

[58] Phipps, *Vestry Laid Open*, p. 26. A similar Act for the City of London carefully located the right to rate householders for the nightly watch in the wards rather than in the parish vestries. John Beattie, *Policing and Punishment in London 1660–1750: Urban Crime and the Limits of Terror* (Oxford University Press, 2004), pp. 192–7.

[59] 'An Act for the better regulating the nightly watch and beadles within the parish of St Martin in the Fields', 9 George II c. 8. A manuscript version of the Act is contained in WAC, St Martin in the Fields Parish Records, 'Vestry draft minutes', F2028, 1736–54, pp. 1–5. For a sense of the sophistication of the parish administration of St Martin in the Fields, see Jeremy Boulton, 'Going on the parish: the parish pension and its meaning in the London suburbs, 1640–1724', in Hitchcock *et al.*, eds., *Chronicling Poverty*, pp. 19–46; and for a brief introduction to the variety of materials produced by the administration of this parish, see Jeremy Boulton, 'The most visible poor in England? Constructing pauper biographies in early-modern Westminster', *Westminster Historical Review*, 1 (1997), 13–21.

[60] WAC, St Martin in the Fields Parish Records, 'Vestry draft minutes', F2028, 1736–54, pp. 19–20.

every day constantly walk in the streets and other places ... and apprehend all idle persons as he shall find wandering and begging there or using any subtle craft or unlawful games or plays ...

and to

make an exact list of the names of all such persons as keep houses rented under ten pounds by the year and of all inmates entertained in such houses.[61]

These rules did not go unchallenged. Within a month one of the watchmen who had almost certainly been in post before the passage of the Act, William Morgan, 'endeavoured to foment an uneasiness among the rest of the watchmen appointed by this vestry and ... procured a scandalous writing to be drawn up for their signing'. We do not know the contents of the paper, but at least seven of Morgan's fellow watchmen added their names to it. All eight were summarily dismissed. That summer, the watchmen also found themselves at loggerheads with the wider population they were expected to police. Week after week they came to the vestry to complain about assaults by both householders and their servants, obliging the vestry to pass an explicit resolution that they would, 'stand by every watchman that shall be ill used'. Similarly, the beadles struggled to fulfil their obligations. Their returns listing all householders paying under £10 per year in rent were found to be inadequate, and when they were questioned on the matter, they 'alledged in excuse the great difficulty they met with in obtaining the names of such persons'.[62]

Even the keeper of the parish roundhouse, Thomas Middleton, struggled to make the new arrangements work. He began to question the legality of his role, letting various prisoners go on the grounds that the act of parliament did not give him the authority to hold them in the absence of the constable of the night, appointed by the Court of Burgesses.[63] The vestry stood on the authority of the Act, and in the end Middleton resigned his place as keeper of the roundhouse and was replaced by William Bird in July 1739.[64]

On the face of it, the role of keeper of the roundhouse was a good one, but by accepting this post at a time when the powers of the vestry were being challenged, Bird placed himself between several competing interests: the vestry, Court of Burgesses, local justices, householders who paid the watch rates and those who walked the streets. In particular, the householders were aggrieved at having to pay the cost of a service over

[61] 'Vestry draft minutes', 1736–54, p. 24.
[62] 'Vestry draft minutes', 1736–54, pp. 30, 34 5.
[63] 'Vestry draft minutes', 1736–54, p. 102.   [64] *LL*, set, 'William Bird'.

which they had no control. In 1740 a group of householders took the vestry to court in order to overturn the watch rate, a case which was eventually heard at King's Bench.[65] The householders observed 'that they were ... deprived of all hope of relief ... against this exclusive and excessive authority, void of all control, and privately conducted and vested in a few, who perpetuated their government by an arbitrary election of the members of their own body'.[66] Many householders simply refused to pay, leaving Bird, who was responsible for collecting the watch rate, in serious difficulties that would rumble on until the roundhouse disaster two years later.[67]

In St Martin's, what started as a new system under new authority quickly descended into a running battle, with the good order and the well-being of the parish the primary losers. However, it was not just in St Martin's that problems began to emerge, and they appeared not just in relation to the new night watch, or over questions of taxation. All of the parishes that had sought to reinforce the power of their select vestries, including St George Hanover Square, St Anne, St Margaret and St James, as well as St Martin's, became the objects of a concerted ratepayers' campaign focusing on both the corrupt practices of the vestrymen and the lack of representation of their interests.

To take the example of St James – one of the richest and least diverse parishes of the west end, with a powerful select vestry packed with elite men – running the new institutions of parish government, including both a workhouse and the watch, proved almost beyond their capacity.[68] A group of justices fell out with the select vestrymen and attempted to exclude them:

Several of the Justices of the Peace having taken upon them to give Directions concerning the Management of the Workhouse without the participation of the rest of the committee ... and having refused to meet ... though daily summoned thereto ... the affairs there run into disorder ...[and] Extreme bad conditions.[69]

---

[65] *Report of the Committee* ... (1742), pp. 5, 6, 14, 20. See also WAC, St Martin in the Fields, 'Vestry clerks bills', F2339, 1736–72, pp. 113–14.

[66] *Report of the Committee* ... (1742), p. 24.

[67] The case was eventually decided in favour of the vestry and against the parishioners. Webb and Webb, *Parish and the County*, p. 257.

[68] The vestry determined on building a house in December 1724, but it was not completed until three years later. The house was built on the local burying ground, over the objection that the putrid exhalations of the dead would harm the poor; and a few years later was described as housing 302 paupers, in a 'new spacious brick house'. WAC, St James Westminster, 'Vestry minutes', D1759, 1712–36, pp. 270–1; for discussion of the health issues associated with the burial ground, see pp. 272–5. See also *An Account of Several Workhouses* (2nd edn, 1732), p. 54.

[69] WAC, St James Westminster, 'Vestry minutes', D1759, 1712–36, pp. 343–4.

In the end, the parish had to take legal advice to secure the authority of the select vestry over that of the justices, but even this did not prevent the administration of the parish descending into chaos.[70] By April 1738, the 'early deaths of infants' in the workhouse reached an unacceptable level. The workhouse master was infirm, the mistress dead and the affairs of the house in 'great disorder'.[71] By March 1741 the house was 'in a very nasty condition, the stench hardly supportable, poor creatures, almost naked, and the living to bed with the Dead'. Even the governor refused to join the workhouse family in prayer, on the grounds that they were 'a rude, illiterate Rabble', while the health of everyone was affected by

a scorbutick distemper which hardly any young fresh persons escape ... and when they are discharged ... nobody will employ them; so that they pine and starve about the streets, till they are almost eaten up of it, and frequently die a lingering miserable death.[72]

St James had failed in its first duty of good management. While none of the parishes of Westminster could give up the night watch, St James eventually took the significant step of closing its workhouse in April 1742, certainly aware of the doleful conditions in the house, but also no doubt wary of the growing anti-select vestry campaign just reaching its climax in parliament.[73]

Two months before St James closed its workhouse, on 26 February 1742 at the Globe Tavern in the Strand, the ratepayers of Westminster met and sought to overturn the authority of their vestrymen.[74] Sixty-one men, mainly petty tradesmen, from the parishes of St James's, St Martin's, St George Hanover Square and St Anne Soho were constituted as a committee to petition parliament. The next week they were joined by twenty further representatives from St Margaret's.[75]

---

[70] WAC, St James Westminster, 'Vestry minutes', D1759, 1712–36, p. 339.
[71] WAC, St James Westminster, 'Vestry minutes', D1760, 1736–50, pp. 50, 115.
[72] WAC, St James Westminster, 'Vestry minutes', D1760, 1736–50, pp. 149–50.
[73] WAC, St James Westminster, 'Vestry minutes', D1760, 1736–50, pp. 177–8.
[74] The best account of these developments, and the basis for much of this discussion is Gillian Williamson, 'The nature of mid-eighteenth-century popular politics in the City of Westminster: the select vestry committee of 1742 and the parish of St George Hanover Square' (MA thesis, Birkbeck College, London, 2008). It is noteworthy that this was the same tavern used for meetings of the London Corresponding Society in the 1790s. See *The Address Published by the London Corresponding Society, at the General Meeting, Held at the Globe Tavern, Strand, on Monday the 20th of January, 1794 [London, 1794]*; and William Cobbett and David Jardine, *Complete collection of state trials and proceedings for ... 1794*, Vol. XXIII (1817), p. 1233.
[75] This campaign can also be seen against the backdrop of the febrile parliamentary politics of 1741 and 1742, but unlike most parliamentary activity, the anti-vestry committee was not apparently subject to elite patronage or direction. Williamson, 'Mid-eighteenth-century popular politics', pp. 16–20.

The resulting petition was submitted on 11 March and led to a series of detailed investigations in the House of Commons. What emerged were repeated examples of unfair rating practices, of vestrymen themselves being regularly undercharged and underrated, along with more serious accusations of outright corruption. Thomas Middleton, who had resigned from his post as keeper of the St Martin's Roundhouse, explained how (unlike William Bird) he had managed to retain the good opinion of the vestry only by varying the rates as they saw fit, with the support of the 'umpire of the vestry', William Godfrey, the clerk. At St Martin's the beginning of the rot in parish standards and accounting was traced back to the loan raised to finance the building of the parish workhouse in 1724, when the first 'illegal application of the parish money' was made at the 'caprice of the vestry'. This was followed by a tale of junketing, drinking and peculation. In a single year, £44 was spent on 'Account of Sacrament Wine', which on examination turned out to include, 'Sack, Hock, white Wine, or other Liquors, which . . . were never used in the Celebration of that solemn Ceremony'.[76]

In five separate inquiries, the select vestries of Westminster were exposed, and permission was given for a bill to be brought in designed to reform them all. The draft legislation mandated a thorough-going reconfiguration of the running of the vestry, with churchwardens and overseers to be chosen through an open poll, returning officers, an electoral register, voting by secret ballot and a franchise extending to everyone paying the poor rate. For a moment it seemed that the struggle for Westminster, the struggle between the select vestries and the wider population of householders, might be resolved in favour of the latter. However, in the end, the bill was voted down by 160 votes to 131, on May 28 1742.[77]

While in most parishes the select vestries and dependent justices retained their authority, the campaigns against them did not end. Eleven years after the householders of St Botolph Aldersgate had reclaimed their parish for a 'general vestry', St Anne Westminster followed suit. In this rich parish, many of the same individuals who had been involved in the wider anti-select vestry campaign of 1742 stormed a select meeting called to elect parish officers in January 1744 and asserted their right to an open vestry. At the all-important Easter meeting in 1745, when new parish officers were chosen and the accounts audited, at least ninety-nine householders attended an open meeting, wresting at least some authority

---

[76] PP, *Journals of the House of Commons*, 4 May 1742, pp. 196–7, 200–1.
[77] Williamson, 'Mid-eighteenth-century popular politics', p. 28 and fn. 94.

back from the select vestry to the wider community of householders.[78] And, in St Martin in the Fields a concerted effort to overturn the select vestry continued. In May 1744 a group of householders charged into a meeting, forcing the vestrymen to retire to the 'library'.[79] Justified in part as a response to the seemingly intractable problems of begging and crime, the select vestries experienced on-going opposition from a broad coalition of ratepayers.

The roundhouse disaster

Disillusionment with parish government was reinforced by each new scandal. In 1742 a tragedy once again helped expose the failings of both the parishes and the magistrates who oversaw them, prompting a direct response from plebeian London.[80]

William Bird, the ill-starred keeper of St Martin in the Fields round-house, whom the vestry had unsuccessfully attempted to dismiss for his failure to collect the watch rate in 1740, continued in place.[81] While he was not 'properly a constable', he was 'deemed the officer' responsible for the roundhouse by other parish employees.[82] On the evening of 15 July 1742, Bird, as usual, was sitting at a long table next to the constable of the night, overseeing the work of the parish's forty-three watchmen. On this particular hot Thursday, the roundhouse also hosted the constables of St Paul Covent Garden and the High Constable of Westminster, Booker Holden. They were there to check in before setting out on a 'midnight reformation', which had been authorised by a warrant signed by Justices Thomas De Veil and John Bromfield to arrest 'vagabonds, pickpockets, and other dissolute and disorderly persons'.[83]

Holden and his assistants targeted a range of houses and streets. Sarah Bland and Mary Maurice were picked up in the street 'just by

---

[78] Williamson, 'Mid-eighteenth-century popular politics', p. 34.

[79] Webb and Webb, *Parish and the County*, p. 259; King's Bench, Ferrers v. Nind, 1744. See James Manning and Archer Ryland, *Reports of Cases Argued and Determined in the Court of King's Bench* (1828), pp. 649–51.

[80] For more detailed accounts of the roundhouse disaster, see Tim Hitchcock, 'You bitches ... die and be damned: gender, authority and the mob in St Martin's roundhouse disaster of 1742', in Tim Hitchcock and Heather Shore, eds., *The Streets of London from the Great Fire to the Great Stink* (London: Rivers Oram Press, 2003), pp. 69–81; and Tim Hitchcock and Robert Shoemaker, *Tales from the Hanging Court* (London: Hodder Arnold, 2006), pp. 35–42.

[81] *LL*, set, 'William Bird'.

[82] *LL*, Old Bailey Proceedings, 9 September 1742 (t17420909-37).

[83] Robert Shoemaker, *Prosecution and Punishment: Petty Crime and the Law in London and Rural Middlesex, c.1660–1725* (Cambridge University Press, 1991), pp. 263–65.

the round-house'.[84] Elizabeth Amey, a prostitute who had previously worked at a notorious brothel, The Rose in Oxenden Street just west of Leicester Fields, was arrested in a cook shop.[85] Ann Norton was 'taken out of ... Bed from my Husband and carried to the Watchhouse'.[86] In total, twenty-six women and nine men were arrested that evening.[87]

The roundhouse was on St Martin's Lane just south of Duke's Court and opposite the parish church.[88] It was made up of three floors, and a set of stocks, capped by an ornate wooden carving depicting one man flogging another, stood in the street outside.[89] The lower ground floor contained two cells, one each for men and women. The women's cell, or hole, was 'about six Foot six Inches in Length, six Foot three or four Inches in Breadth'.[90]

By one o'clock in the morning, with almost twenty people in the women's cell, the heat was intense, and the drunken camaraderie which had earlier greeted the women as they came down the stairs was gradually transformed into desperation. Stripped down to their shifts or completely naked, they began to struggle for breath, while their clothes became soaked in sweat. Mary Cosier later testified that her handkerchief was as 'stiff as Buckram, with Sweat from the Heat of the Place'.[91] They beat on the low ceiling of the cell with their shoes trying to attract attention and cried out that one of them was in labour and needed relief. But mainly they cried out for water: 'for Christ's Sake let us have Water; for the Lord's Sake a little Water'.[92] The next morning, when the cell door was opened William Anderson found the place 'very nauseous, and the smell so strong, that I thought it would have struck me down'.[93] At least four people lay dead or dying.

De Veil, who had signed off on the original warrant, was also responsible for examining the survivors, and gradually realising the seriousness

---

[84] *LL*, set, 'Sarah Bland', and set, 'Mary Maurice'. See also *LL*, Old Bailey Proceedings, 9 September 1742 (t17420909-37).

[85] *LL*, set, 'Elizabeth Amey'. See *LL*, Old Bailey Proceedings, 13 October 1742 (t17421013-19). Amey claimed that she had worked as a waiter.

[86] *LL*, set, 'Ann Norton'; and *LL*, Old Bailey Proceedings, 13 October 1742 (t17421013-19).

[87] Hitchcock and Shoemaker, *Tales*, p. 38.

[88] The site is shown on a map included in *Survey of London*, Vol. XX: *Trafalgar Square and Neighbourhood*, ed. George Gater and Walter H. Godfrey (The Parish of St Martin-in-the-Fields, Part III, 1940), plate 2 (www.british-history.ac.uk/source.aspx?pubid=751&page=1&sort=1).

[89] Henry B. Wheatley, *London Past and Present*, 3 vols. (1891; repr. Cambridge University Press, 2011), II, p. 485.

[90] *LL*, Old Bailey Proceedings, 9 September 1742 (t17420909-37).

[91] *LL*, set, 'Mary Cosier'; *LL*, Old Bailey Proceedings, 9 September 1742 (t17420909-37).

[92] *LL*, Old Bailey Proceedings, 9 September 1742 (t17420909-37).

[93] *LL*, Old Bailey Proceedings, 13 October 1742 (t17421013-19).

Figure 4.5 Henry Fletcher, *A View of St Martin's Round-House* ('as tore to pieces by the enraged Multitude') (1742). © Trustees of the British Museum.

of the situation, he dismissed all the prisoners.[94] However, by the evening a crowd began to gather in St Martin's Lane. Stones and bricks were thrown at the house and by midnight a riot was in full progress. It took Justice James Frazier at least two hours to restore order.[95]

The situation for De Veil, the most prominent signatory of the warrant, was a delicate one, and he was 'greatly scared' by the likely popular reaction to the disaster.[96] A coroner's inquest convened the following day brought in a verdict of wilful murder against William Bird for the suffocation of Mary Maurice and three others.[97] De Veil attempted to deflect public outrage away from himself and the select vestries by publishing his own version of events early the next week. In his account, Booker Holden was named as the moving spirit behind the warrant, and De Veil went on to blame the constables (all appointees of the Court of Burgesses) for having 'greatly misbehaved' themselves, before offering up William Bird as a possible scapegoat.[98] No mention was made of the legion of parish employees who had participated in the arrests that night.[99]

Bird eventually stood trial at the Old Bailey on a charge of murder two months later. Counsel were just beginning to participate in trials, and four experienced attorneys were commissioned to make up the prosecution team. Bird's attempt to find a barrister to represent him, however, met a wall of indifference. By the day of his first trial in mid-September, Bird had failed to locate anyone willing to act – two claimed to be out of town, two others 'desired to be excused', while a fifth simply returned the brief without explanation. Bird, whom the trial records describe as a 'labourer', was forced to defend himself.[100] He was found guilty at his second trial and sentenced to hang.[101]

[94] *The Annals of Europe for the year 1742. Being a methodological and full account of all the remarkable occurrences which happened with that year either at home or abroad* (1745), p. 309.
[95] *LL*, set, 'James Frazier'. By the following morning the whole front of the roundhouse had been reduced to rubble. WAC, St Martin in the Fields, Parish Records, 'Vestry draft minutes', F2028, 1736–54, pp. 253–4.
[96] *The Letters of William Shenstone*, ed. Marjorie Williams (Oxford: Basil Blackwell, 1939), p. 56.
[97] *The Champion; or the Evening Advertiser*, 20 July 1742 (Burney Collection: www.galegroup.com, 1 Jan. 2014).
[98] *The London Evening-Post*, 15–17 July 1742 (Burney Collection: www.galegroup.com, 1 Jan. 2014). The same advertisement is reproduced in *The Annals of Europe for the year 1742*, pp. 307–11. At the trial De Veil disclaimed responsibility for this publication and challenged William Bird to 'prove... [he] put anything in the News'. See *LL*, Old Bailey Proceedings, 9 September 1742 (t17420909-37).
[99] At his trial Bird claimed that the advertisement purposely made him appear to be as 'cruel a dog as ever lived'. See *LL*, Old Bailey Proceedings, 9 September 1742 (t17420909-37).
[100] *LL*, Old Bailey Proceedings, 9 September 1742 (t17420909-37).
[101] *London Evening Post*, 14–16 October 1742 (Burney Collection: www.galegroup.com, 1 Jan. 2014). This was commuted to fourteen years transportation, and he was starved

In the months after the disaster, the parish rebuilt the roundhouse at a cost of £83 15s., adding piped water and a new set of iron palings, five feet, eight inches high.[102] But the roundhouse continued to be a target of regular popular attacks. The following year St Martin's spent a further £8 19s. repairing damage done to the house by a population that saw in it a continuing symbol of oppression, and in each succeeding year for the next decade a similar sum was spent on repairs.[103] This was no doubt one reason why the parish strengthened its watch and revised its Watch Act.[104] In addition, the role of the beadles was regularised, and they were given new uniforms at the cost of £36 17s.[105] Despite all the Watch Acts, the denigration of the Court of Burgesses and the newly powerful position of the select vestries, magistrates and vestrymen found it impossible to secure more than the grudging consent of the wider population to their policies and were continually forced onto the defensive.

The Mortmain Act and the rise of associational charities

While innovations in parish relief and governance stuttered forward in the face of householder and popular resistance, the new associational charities of the 1730s and 1740s seemed to provide welcome new resources for the poor and a new approach to social problems. Neither substantial charitable provision for London's poor nor subscription and associational charities, in which donors committed to making annual contributions, were entirely new in the 1730s. The charity school movement, led by the SPCK, had established subscription schools from the late 1690s, and the Westminster Infirmary, whose subscription charity was established in 1716, successfully used this model.[106] However, following the passage of the Mortmain Act in 1736, the next few decades

---

to death on the voyage. TNA, High Court of Admiralty, 'Criminal records', HCA 1/20, part 1, item 9: 'Indictment of Barnett Bond, for the murder of William Bird, 26 April 1744'. See also *Gentleman's Magazine*, xiv (1744), p. 226.

[102] WAC, St Martin in the Fields, 'Vestry draft minutes', F2028, 1736–54, pp. 274, 281.

[103] WAC, St Martin in the Fields, 'Watch rates, collectors book', F2676, 1735–57, pp. 153, 183, 241, 271, 273, 299, 323, 327, 351, 355, 381, 485.

[104] 23 George II c. 35, 'An Act for making a better ... provision for the relief of the poor... for keeping a nightly watch, within the parish of Saint Martin in the Fields'.

[105] WAC, St Martin in the Fields, 'Parish records, watch rates, collectors book', F2676, 1735–57, pp. 125–7.

[106] Notably, the leading figure in the establishment of the Westminster Infirmary was the SPCK supporter and banker, Henry Hoare, while its early publications were produced by the SPCK's printer, Joseph Downing. J. G. Humble and Peter Hansell, *Westminster Hospital 1716–1974* (London: Pitman Medical Publishing, 2nd edn, 1974), pp. 1–39.

witnessed the establishment of several new charities built around sociability and the contributions of living men and women.[107]

The Mortmain Act, meaning 'dead hand', was designed to discourage deathbed bequests of land to charitable uses. Instead, from 1736 most London charities were organised as associations of living donors, who contributed annually to the cause of their choice. In the 1740s alone, the London Infirmary, later the London Hospital (1740), the Foundling Hospital (1741), the Lock Hospital for venereal patients (1746) and the Lying-In Hospital for poor married women, later the British Lying-In Hospital (1749), were all established on this basis. At least twenty further London-based associational charities were created in the decades up to 1770.[108]

As well as responding to the provisions of the Mortmain Act, these new charities also reflected a wider disillusionment with parochial government and relief. As vestries became more 'select' and paupers shaped the distribution of parish relief, the subscription charity offered an alternative. The antagonism between these two very different charitable mechanisms was occasionally explicit. The Foundling Hospital justified its existence on the grounds that:

The [parish] Officers ... charged with the Care of the Poor, have been so negligent ... that some Infants have been suffered to perish with Cold and Hunger in the Streets, without any Attempt for their Relief.

And its regulations prominently declared:

That no ... [parish] officer ... shall have or exercise any Power or Authority in ... [the] Hospital ... nor shall have any authority to enquire concerning the Birth or Settlement of [the] ... children.[109]

The 1739 Act of parliament passed in support of the hospital authorised it to fine any parish officer interfering in the workings of the charity.[110]

As the parishes found their hands forced by pauper demands (in some measure taking advantage of the rules of settlement) to relieve a more

[107] 9 George II c. 36. The only sustained treatment of the Act is Gareth Jones, *History of the Law of Charity, 1532–1827* (Cambridge University Press, 1969), pp. 109–19.

[108] See Donna T. Andrew, *Philanthropy and Police: London Charity in the Eighteenth Century* (Princeton University Press, 1989), pp. 57–73; for the estimate of the number established to 1770, see Donna T. Andrew, 'Two medical charities in eighteenth-century London: The Lock Hospital and the Lying-In Charity for married women', in Jonathan Barry and Colin Jones, eds., *Medicine and Charity before the Welfare State* (London: Routledge, 1991), p. 82.

[109] *An Account of the Hospital for the Maintenance and Education of Exposed and Deserted Young Children* (1759), pp. 7, 28.

[110] Ruth K. McClure, *Coram's Children: The London Foundling Hospital in the Eighteenth Century* (New Haven, Conn.: Yale University Press, 1981), p. 39.

diverse group of the poor, associational charities gave their patrons the secure knowledge that only the most sympathetic of objects would benefit. This led to the creation of a newly competitive market for charitable giving as different organisations sought to attract wealthy benefactors – focusing charitable giving on paupers who made good advertising copy while encouraging the poor to present themselves in new ways.

To take a single example, the model for most associational charities, and the most influential of the 1740s foundations, was the Foundling Hospital. Captain Thomas Coram spent the 1730s working to establish a hospital for the reception of abandoned babies, justified by despair at the perceived inhumanity of the poor and concerns about population and national efficiency.[111] In the words of the charity's charter, the hospital's supporters were motivated by the terrible knowledge of the

frequent murders committed on poor miserable infants by their parents to hide their shame, and the inhuman custom of exposing new-born children to perish in the streets, or training them up in idleness, beggary or theft.[112]

The charity opened on 25 March 1741, and on the occasion of the first 'takings-in', some thirty babies were accepted before the doors were finally closed at midnight. While the demand for its services suggests it was fulfilling a real need, as is so often the case the unintended consequences of the opening of the hospital were substantial. Its immediate impact was to spark a murderous wave of child abandonment. In the year before it was awarded its royal charter in 1739, just nineteen deaths, overwhelmingly made up of abandoned infants, were recorded as 'found' on the streets in the Bills of Mortality. The 1730s as a whole saw 380 deaths of this sort. But in the two years following the award of the charter, during which the new charitable provision for abandoned babies was regularly discussed in the press, the bodies of some ninety-eight babies were found. And in the first full year following the opening of the hospital in 1741, the rate of abandonment reached an all-time peak. Seventy-one bodies were recorded in the Bills of Mortality as 'found'; while the 1740s as a whole witnessed a total of 526.[113] This pattern and

---

[111] See in particular, Andrew, *Philanthropy and Police*, pp. 57–64; McClure, *Coram's Children, passim*.

[112] *A Copy of the Royal Charter, Establishing an Hospital for the Maintenance and Education of Exposed and Deserted Young Children* (1739), p. 2.

[113] *A Collection of the Yearly Bills of Mortality, from 1657 to 1758 Inclusive. Together with several other bills of an earlier date* (1759), returns for 1741. The extent to which this category of the dead in the *Bills* is populated by abandoned infants is reflected in the dramatic fall in numbers recorded during the 'General Reception', when all foundlings brought to the hospital were admitted. In the four years between 1757 and 1760, just 19 deaths are recorded as 'found', compared to 102 deaths in the preceding four years.

impact extended to foundlings abandoned to parish care as well. As Figure 4.4 illustrates, at St Martin's workhouse thirty-one infants were given over to the parish as either 'dropt' or 'foundling' in 1740, and the following year saw twenty-nine – the two highest recorded figures for the whole of the eighteenth century.

For the first twenty years of its existence, the Foundling Hospital accepted children presented to them regardless of the background of the parents, 'with no Preference to any Person whatsoever'. In the process, it appears to have positively encouraged the abandonment of infants to the hospital, with parents choosing, if this did not work out, to leave unwanted babies on the streets. In part, this behaviour must have been a response to hardening social attitudes towards plebeian mothers. Employers faced with a pregnant servant could afford to take a tougher line in the knowledge that the child could be abandoned to the Foundling Hospital without bringing their own failure as householders and employers to the attention of the parish. Alternatively, perhaps simple elite patronage for the idea of abandonment was in itself enough to legitimate the process. In either case the prospect of public care for abandoned children generated its own demand, which the Foundling Hospital could not possibly meet. In the spring of 1741, at the first 'taking-in' where a system of balloting allows us to know the numbers of people who actually came in hope of leaving a child, forty-seven mothers arrived, seeking one of only 24 available places. The number of applicants grew as the decade advanced. In May 1746, seventy-nine mothers presented their children in hope of gaining access to one of 25 places.[114]

The increasingly complex landscape of charities multiplied the opportunities open to the poor for support, but each had its own admissions system which they needed to learn how to navigate. While at the Foundling Hospital monthly 'takings-in' involved an evening ballot and a largely random selection process, at St Thomas's Thursday mornings were set aside for admissions, when a sub-committee of the governors assessed the mandatory petitions and examined the medical needs of each patient.[115] St Bartholomew's and Guy's hospitals had different systems again, as did the Westminster Infirmary. The one-to-one relationship between a decayed householder and the parish overseer, in which needs were assessed and relieved (or not), was increasingly replaced by a pick and mix assortment of relief bodies, each designed

---

[114] See Adrian Wilson, 'Illegitimacy and its implications in mid-eighteenth-century London: the evidence of the Foundling Hospital', *Continuity and Change*, 4:1 (1989), 105–6.

[115] *LL*, St Thomas's Admission and Discharge Registers.

for a different malady – whether illness, infancy or simple poverty – and open to supplications from the poor, which then had to be evaluated.

The impact of these new institutions was at best ambiguous. While they undoubtedly provided additional resources, directed at real needs, they also complicated the relationship between paupers and the parish. In part, they made it possible for parish officers to evade their obligations, and allowed overseers to point to the charities as an excuse for denying relief. Some parishes actively sought to make use of these new institutions to offload their paupers. When the Foundling Hospital, for example, opened its doors to all comers in the following decade, the officers of St Martin's simply took the opportunity of dumping many of the newborn babies and foundlings in their care onto the hospital. But more fundamentally, the associational charities tended to create a new understanding of poverty. By defining poverty in terms of an abstract and compelling need, rather than as a normal part of the life cycle that deserved support from one's immediate neighbours, the charities subverted the role of the parish, and in the process, the poor's claim upon it. As the new charities responded to separate categories of headline-grabbing social problems among the 'deserving poor', whether abandoned babies, seduced girls or disabled soldiers, the parish was left to deal with an increasingly 'undeserving' residuum.

The poor learned how to navigate this new and complex landscape of relief but, as with the abandoned babies, the results were often cruel. Some twelve years after the Foundling Hospital opened, it received Mary Larkin, only a few weeks old.[116] The illegitimate child of Patrick Bourne and Mary Larkin, the baby was born in Rochester in April 1753.[117] The parish officers arrested the father, 'by a Warrant from a Justice of the Peace and … Comitted [him] to … his Majesty's Prison at Rochester … for the Space of Three Days', until he provided a bond for the support of the child – money that would normally have been used by the parish to support the mother and baby. To escape a continuing obligation, Bourne responded by taking the baby to London, with the connivance of the parish officers but without apparent reference to the mother, where he paid a guinea to Mary Thornton, a midwife, to secure its admission to the Foundling Hospital.[118] The child was dead within a few days, and because Bourne needed proof of the death in order for the parish to discharge his bond, Thornton was eventually tried for murder. She was acquitted in October 1753, and Bourne was discharged from his bond. He and the parish officers were no doubt satisfied, but the baby was dead.

---

[116] *LL*, set, 'Mary Larkin'.   [117] *LL*, set, 'Patrick Bourne'.
[118] *LL*, set, 'Mary Thornton'.

The fiddling magistrate

Sir Thomas De Veil, who sat uncomfortably as a principal participant in the roundhouse disaster, was at the centre of judicial reform and parochial politics in the 1730s and 1740s. He was appointed a justice of the peace in 1729 and was involved in the campaign against disorderly houses over the next two years. Unlike many justices, he adopted a proactive approach to the office, making himself available to hear criminal complaints, breaking up groups of high-profile criminals (notably the 'gang' led by William Wreathock) and pursuing murderers.[119] More than this, he took a particular interest in political dissent and from 1734 received a £250 government pension from the Secret Service Fund for his role in suppressing Jacobitism and anti-government sedition.[120] In 1738 he was given the sinecure of inspector-general of exports and imports (which provided a further £500 a year), he was knighted in 1744 and he was a colonel in the Westminster militia.[121] De Veil was 'court justice' – the chief metropolitan magistrate upon whom the government relied to convey its orders to the Middlesex bench.[122]

From his houses, first in Leicester Square, and then in Bow Street just east of Covent Garden (a house which would later be taken over by Henry and John Fielding), De Veil ran an extensive network of informers, thief-takers and spies.[123] Nonetheless, many of the poor appear to have brought their criminal complaints to him, hoping that his fierce reputation would bring their adversaries to justice. According to his posthumously published *Memoirs*, 'the readiness and facility with which he entered into all the branches' of the office of a justice, and the money he earned as a consequence, made him the 'envy' of the 'trading justices', since their normal clients, the poor, chose to bring their business before him instead.[124]

However, as the figure of authority publicly involved in almost every local controversy in Westminster in these years, De Veil repeatedly attracted popular hostility. With some exceptions, such as the day following the roundhouse disaster, he was happy to confront a mob,

---

[119] *LL*, set, 'William Wreathock'.
[120] Patrick Pringle, *Hue and Cry: The Birth of the British Police* (London: Museum Press, 1955), p. 61.
[121] Philip Sugden, 'Veil, Sir Thomas de (1684–1746)', *ODNB* (www.oxforddnb.com, 1 Jan. 2014).
[122] For 'court justices', see *Memoirs of the Life and Times of Sir Thomas De Veil*, pp. 21–5.
[123] *Memoirs of the Life and Times of Sir Thomas De Veil*, pp. 72–80; *Gentleman's Magazine*, 17 (1747), p. 563.
[124] *Memoirs of the Life and Times of Sir Thomas De Veil*, pp. 17–19.

and on several occasions read out the Riot Act and successfully dispersed crowds. Yet he also recognised the limitations of his powers. In 1738 an audience at the New Theatre in the Haymarket succeeded in preventing a performance by French players, at a time when English actors were unable to find work as a result of the Licensing Act of 1737. On this occasion De Veil's carefully choreographed plans failed. At the beginning of the performance, and in the face of a disorderly audience, De Veil claimed to have stationed troops outside and threatened to read the Riot Act. Nevertheless, he let himself be drawn into a debate with the audience and the hecklers won, with De Veil left impotently calling for candles by which to read the Act.[125] As reported in De Veil's purported *Memoirs*:

The Colonel then began to talk in the language of power, which is always out of season, when not immediately backed by superior force. The people in the pit thought they had power too, and began to exert it without farther ceremony, by pulling up benches and forms, and throwing all things into confusion, and it was in this temper of mind the company parted.[126]

De Veil was left 'pale and passive' as the audience yelled, 'No Treaties', and 'the mob in the streets broke the windows of the house all to pieces'.[127]

On this occasion De Veil avoided becoming the focus of the crowd's violence at the cost of finally giving in to popular opposition. And while he similarly managed to escape retribution following the roundhouse disaster, he was not always so fortunate. In May 1741, in response to his support for court candidates at the general election, a 'dreadful tumultuous mob' attacked his house. As he complained in a letter to the secretary of state asking that a reward be offered for the apprehension of the ringleaders,

the word was given, one and all, to pull down the House of the Manager (as they were pleased to call me) of My Lord Sundons and Sir Charles Wager's election, and at the same time a volley of large stones brought down the best part of all the windows of my House, which being often repeated has left me in a frightful condition.

His hope was that a quick, government-backed prosecution would demonstrate to the 'mob' that he had 'the honour to be under the safeguard

---

[125] Thomas Lockwood, 'Cross-Channel dramatics in the Little Haymarket theatre riot of 1738', *Studies in Eighteenth-Century Culture*, 25 (1996), 65; A. H. Scouten, ed., *The London Stage, 1660–1800: Part 3, 1729–1747* (Bloomington: Southern Illinois University Press,1961), pp. 735–6.

[126] *Memoirs of the Life and Times of Sir Thomas De Veil*, pp. 44–5.

[127] Benjamin Victor, *History of the Theatres of London and Dublin*, Vol. I (1761), p. 59; *London Evening Post*, 7–10 October 1738 (Burney Collection: www.galegroup.com, 1 Jan. 2014).

and protection of the government'.[128] De Veil, however, was eventually forced to prosecute the case himself at quarter sessions, and informers were found to give evidence against five men. But after a nine-hour trial and a stern direction from the bench to bring in a guilty verdict, the jury acquitted them all.[129] And when, in 1744, he arrested three men following an attempt to break up a meeting of footmen objecting to the employment of foreign servants, the crowd broke into his house and rescued them.[130] By way of xenophobia and Jacobitism, via theatres and the hustings, and through murderous disasters and simple miscalculations, De Veil's authority over the crowd had largely vanished by the mid-1740s. But the issue that did the most to undermine his reputation in the eyes of plebeian London was his role in the failed campaign against gin drinking.

Gin, gender and trading justices

In the late 1720s and early 1730s, the concerns about increasing levels of crime and disorder which had driven the campaign against disorderly houses in the previous decade found a new objective in an aggressive but ultimately futile campaign against gin. Justices of the peace and supporters of a reformation of manners had long been concerned about the constellation of social problems that seemed to emanate from excessive drinking and the sociable spaces where it was encouraged. But in the 1720s these wider concerns rapidly coalesced around the specific issue of 'Geneva and other Spirituous Liquors'.[131] In January 1726 this new emphasis is evident in a report to the Middlesex bench that implausibly concluded that in Middlesex and Westminster alone (excluding the City and Southwark), there were 'Six Thousand one Hundred and Eighty Seaven Houses and Shopps, wherein Geneva or other strong Waters are publickly sold by retail', amounting 'in some parishes [to] every Tenth House, in others every seventh, and in one of the largest every Fifth house'.[132] For the next twenty-five years, in an extended series of acts of

---

[128] TNA, State Papers Domestic, 'George II', SP 36/56, f. 48, 17 May 1741.
[129] *Daily Gazetteer* (London Edition), Tuesday, 2 June 1741; Monday, 29 June 1741 (Burney Collection: www.galegroup.com, 1 Jan. 2014).
[130] *Memoirs of the Life and Times of Sir Thomas De Veil*, pp. 60–1; Sugden, 'Veil, Sir Thomas de'.
[131] LL, Middlesex Sessions: General Orders of the Court, 13 October 1725 (LMSMGO556000070). See also Georges Lamoine, ed., *Charges to the Grand Jury 1689–1803*, Camden Fourth Series, vol. 43 (London: Royal Historical Society, 1992), p. 208.
[132] LL, Middlesex Sessions: General Orders of the Court, 14 January 1726 (LMSMGO556000091).

parliament and a major campaign of enforcement, gin took centre stage, but the attempt to dislodge it from plebeian culture failed.

Was gin drinking a problem? There was certainly an increase in the volume of spirits produced in these years, and gin was cheap and strong.[133] The 1730s saw rising real wages which meant working men and women could afford to drink more spirits than previously. However, it is impossible to prove that this led to either a significant increase in the consumption of gin by the poor in particular, or an increase in drunkenness. However, the actions of plebeian Londoners contributed to raising official awareness of gin drinking as a component of wider social problems in two ways. First, the legal provision exempting retailers of spirits from quartering soldiers 'put all sorts of inferior trades on Selling Strong waters'.[134] In effect, this legal loophole simultaneously encouraged poor households to add the sale of spirits to whatever other economic activities they were engaged in and brought the poor's gin-selling activities to the attention of the authorities attempting to organise the quartering of soldiers. Second, the profile of gin as a perceived cause of crime was raised by the growing tendency of defendants to cite drunkenness as an aspect of an 'amplified … language of mental excuse' in mitigation.[135] When asked in 1727 at her trial for petty larceny to explain her presence in someone else's house, Elizabeth Plat told the court that 'she had been that Afternoon a little too busy with Madam Geneva, and being intoxicated, tumbled in their [sic] by Accident'.[136] Although Plat was found guilty, drunkenness became a common defence strategy. The report of the trial of Rose Roberts for stealing a gold necklace a few months later notes that the prosecution was deemed to be malicious because 'upon Examination [the necklace] appeared only to be a gilt one, and the Assault no other than a Geneva Jostle', an accident prompted by drink and without malicious intent.[137] From 1728 onwards, the Ordinary of Newgate's biographies of the lives of the condemned occasionally cite gin as one of the causes that led them down the road towards Tyburn.[138]

---

[133] PP, 'Report of the commissioners of the Inland Revenue of the duties under their management', 1870 [C.82-1], II, pp. 4–6 (parlipapers.chadwyck.co.uk, 1 Jan. 2014). See also John Chartres, 'Food consumption and internal trade', in A. L. Beier and Roger Finlay, eds., *London 1500–1700: The Making of the Metropolis* (London: Longman, 1986), p. 175.

[134] LL, Middlesex Sessions: Sessions Papers, October 1721 (LMSMPS501980014).

[135] Dana Rabin, 'Drunkenness and responsibility for crime in the eighteenth century', *Journal of British Studies*, 44:3 (2005), 466–76, quote from 467.

[136] LL, Old Bailey Proceedings, 22 February 1727 (t17270222-50).

[137] LL, Old Bailey Proceedings, 5 July 1727 (t17270705-54).

[138] See, for example, the account of the life of George Weedon. LL, Ordinary of Newgate Prison: Ordinary's Accounts, 4 January 1728 (OA172802122802120003).

Following reports from the Middlesex justices and several pamphlets decrying the evils of gin, the first Act to regulate its sale passed swiftly through parliament in three weeks in the spring of 1729.[139] It placed a duty of 5 shillings per gallon on distilled gin, required retailers to acquire a licence costing £20 a year and, most importantly, legislated a complete ban on street selling – on the livelihoods of the dozens of mainly women who made a meagre living selling gin by the glass. However, banning the public sale of gin was to prove an impossible task, and Londoners quickly became adept at circumventing these legal controls.[140] This first Act, for example, could be avoided by switching from selling gin to raw spirits, which fell outside the scope of the Act and gained the ironic name of 'Parliamentary Brandy'. In the eyes of the reformers, the first Act was a failure and was replaced in 1733 by a second Act, which took established retailers out of the picture and concentrated on street sellers. But this was also largely a dead letter as the street sellers it made subject to draconian fines were next to beggars and unable to pay the fines levied upon them. Very few were actually prosecuted.[141]

As gin moved further up the reformers' agenda in the early 1730s, it also acquired a strong gender dimension. Women were prominent participants in the gin trade, both as street sellers (because this was an easy trade to enter) and as consumers (because they did not need to go into male-dominated alehouses to purchase it). A tendency to identify women, particularly single women and young mothers, as well as the poor more generally, as the chief consumers of gin was evident as early as 1726, but the theme that these groups were particularly adversely affected by the 'craze' became increasingly prominent in the 1730s. In 1736, a justices' report complained:

With Regard to the Female Sex we find the Contagion has Spread even among them, And that to a Degree hardly possible to be Conceived. Unhappy Mothers habituate themselves to these distill'd Liquors, whose Children are born weakly & Sickly and often look Shriveld & old, as tho they had Numbered many Years; Others again daily give it to their Children whilst young and learn them even before they can go to taste & approve of this Certain great Destroyer.[142]

[139] *The Charge of Sir John Gonson, Knt. to the Grand Jury of the Royalty of the Tower of London* (1728), reprinted in Lamoine, ed., *Charges to the Grand Jury*, p. 236; *The Historical Register, Containing an Impartial Relation of all Transactions, Foreign and Domestic* ([1729]), pp. 154–5; 2 George II c. 17.
[140] Lee Davison, 'Experiments in the social regulation of industry: gin legislation, 1729–1751', in Davison *et al.*, *Stilling*, pp. 25–48.
[141] 6 George II c. 17.
[142] *LL*, Middlesex Sessions: General Orders of the Court, 15 January 1736 (LMSMGO556010122).

Gin drinking came to be gendered female, with the sobriquet 'Madam Geneva' embodying the fear that gin threatened the gender, as well as the social, order.

The history of gin craze has been told many times, but traditionally the only agency ascribed to the targets of reform has been located in their facility for getting publicly drunk. Recent research, however, has problematized this story in two important ways. First, the scale of the actual social problems caused by gin has been questioned, suggesting that efforts to curtail gin drinking were at least as much the result of moral panic and social anxiety as they were a response to a genuine problem.[143] Second, historians have begun to give greater emphasis to the major role played by the poor in opposing the implementation of the gin legislation. Just as they successfully opposed other aspects of the reformation of manners agenda, the poor effectively prevented the legal regulation of gin consumption for more than two decades, until the 1751 Gin Act finally implemented a feasible compromise (though the impact of even this Act was limited).

Popular opposition was at its strongest following the passage of the 1736–7 Gin Acts. The first was promoted by a familiar group of reformers attached to the SPCK and the reformation of manners societies. Together with the London magistracy, they conducted an orchestrated campaign in support of more stringent regulation. In 1734 and 1735, magistrates in the City and Middlesex once again launched investigations into selling distilled spirits without a licence, and in January 1736 the Middlesex bench issued a new report outlining the 'pernicious' effects of gin drinking and petitioned parliament to do something about it. They told MPs:

That the drinking of Geneva & other Distill'd Spirituous Liquors has for some years last past greatly encreased, Especially among the people of Inferior Rank.

That the Constant & Excessive use thereof as now practiced, hath already destroyed thousands of his Majesties Subjects, and renders great Numbers of

---

[143] M. Dorothy George, *London Life in the Eighteenth Century* (London, 1925; Harmondsworth: Penguin Books, 2nd edn, 1966), p. 51; Peter Clark, 'The "Mother Gin" controversy in the early eighteenth century', *Transactions of the Royal Historical Society*, 5th Series, 38 (1988), 71–2; Jonathan White, 'The "slow but sure poyson": the representation of gin and its drinkers, 1736–1751', *Journal of British Studies*, 42:1 (2003), 35–64. The most recent survey of eighteenth-century London observes that 'it is very difficult to disentangle myth from reality when considering the place of gin in London life in these years': Jerry White, *London in the Eighteenth Century: A Great and Monstrous Thing* (London: Bodley Head, 2012), p. 329. Two important popular histories of this subject are Patrick Dillon, *The Much-Lamented Death of Madam Geneva: The Eighteenth-Century Gin Craze* (London: Headline Book Publishing, 2003) and Jessica Warner, *Craze: Gin and Debauchery in an Age of Reason* (London: Profile, 2003).

others unfitt for usefull Labour & Service, debauching at the [...] same time their Moralls & driving them into all Manner of Vice & Wickedness.[144]

The 1736 Act, sponsored by Sir Joseph Jekyll, Master of the Rolls, was passed in May.[145] It placed a duty on retailed gin of 20 shillings a gallon and required all retailers to take out an annual £50 licence. More significantly, it facilitated the prosecution of small-scale retailers by providing for fines of £10 for anyone found guilty of selling gin without a licence, including chandlers, alehouse keepers and apothecaries. The proceeds of these fines were to be divided equally between informers willing to provide sworn evidence and the local overseers of the poor. Anyone unable to pay the fine was to serve two months' hard labour in a house of correction. Initially this Act was just as ineffective as the two that preceded it, with the production of spirits dropping only marginally. Just twenty licences were issued to retailers, generating only £500 in duty.[146] Once again, it was easy to avoid prosecution, as there was little point in prosecuting sellers who were unable to pay the fines. However, in 1737 the excise office was empowered to pay the rewards for convictions in such cases, which suddenly made informing on a gin seller extremely profitable.[147] From this point the number of prosecutions increased dramatically. Reports in the press claiming that there had been some 12,000 convictions by August 1738 were wildly overstated, but 435 people were convicted following prosecutions by the excise in the months to March 1738, and several hundred more street sellers were punished by justices of the peace.[148]

Despite these prosecutions, the 1736–7 Acts failed to halt the sale and consumption of gin, as they were fatally subverted by a combination of subterfuge, legal action and popular protest. The Acts were evaded by creating various unregulated alternative strong alcoholic drinks such as sangree (created from Madeira wine), by purchasing two gallons (the minimum quantity which could legally be sold) on long-term credit (taking away a small amount at a time), or, most ingeniously, through the invention of a clever contraption, the 'puss and mew' – an automated dispenser of gin, set into a wall, that prevented informers and constables from identifying the seller.[149] As *Read's Weekly Journal* reported in February 1738:

---

[144] *LL*, Middlesex Sessions: General Orders of the Court, 15 January 1736 (LMSMGO556010125).
[145] 9 George II c. 23.
[146] Davison, 'Experiments in the social regulation of industry', pp. 35–6.
[147] 10 George II, c. 17.
[148] Davison, 'Experiments in the social regulation of industry', pp. 36–7, 39–40. The erratic survival of evidence of justices' summary convictions and commitments to houses of correction makes it impossible to determine the precise number.
[149] Dillon, *Much-Lamented*, pp. 150–2, 163–4.

The Way is this, the Buyer comes into the Entry and Cries *Puss*, and is immediately answer'd by a Voice from within, *Mew*. A Drawer is then thrust out, in which the Buyer puts his Money, which when drawn back, is soon after thrust out again, with the Quantity of Gin requir'd; the Master of this new Improvement in Mechanicks, remaining all the while unseen; whereby all Informations are defeated, and the Penalty of the Gin Act evaded.[150]

Popular opposition also took the form of frequent attacks on the informers, excise men and justices of the peace who enforced the Acts. The informers (almost 200), often poor men and women themselves, prosecuted thousands of their fellow Londoners.[151] Distaste for those who profited from prosecuting their neighbours had a long history, as was evident in the antipathy to reformation of manners informers in the 1690s and early 1700s. And like this earlier opposition, popular resistance to informers successfully undermined the efforts of parliament.

It was not simply the use of informers that attracted opposition, but also the underhand tactics they employed. To obtain evidence of the illegal activity of selling gin, informers needed to purchase spirits, trapping the gin seller. They had to enter unlicensed premises and prevail upon the owner to act illicitly by selling them gin, normally by playing to the owner's familiarity with the purchaser as a known member of the community. Another ploy was to claim that they needed the gin for medicinal use. Either way, the violations of trust evident in the subsequent prosecutions generated considerable hostility, both on the streets and in the courtroom.[152] Following her testimony against Mary Tidcomb for selling two glasses of 'Spirituos [*sic*] Liquor call'd Geneva' in 1739, Catherine Norton was shunned by others as 'one that laid Informations against People'.[153] She was tried (though acquitted) at the Old Bailey for perjury and conspiracy.

On 16 August 1738, Sarah Miller stood outside the home of Anne Adams and started screaming at the top of her lungs, 'Damn you, you informing Bitch!' She went on to describe Anne as an 'informing Bitch who goes partners with the Informers' and told her 'you had Share of the money ... which you bought your Scarlett cloack with'. Twenty or thirty passers-by joined the protest, and Anne was so frightened she

---

[150] *Read's Weekly Journal, or British Gazetteer*, 18 February 1738 (Burney Collection: www. galegroup.com, 1 Jan. 2014). Dudley Bradstreet identified himself as the inventor of this ruse in his 1755 autobiography. See *The Life and Uncommon Adventures of Captain Dudley Bradstreet* (Dublin, 1755), p. 79.

[151] Jessica Warner, Frank Ivis and Andreé Demers, 'A predatory social structure: informers in Westminster, 1737–41', *Journal of Interdisciplinary History*, 30:4 (2000), 617–34.

[152] Jessica Warner and Frank Ivis, '"Damn you, you informing bitch": *vox populi* and the unmaking of the Gin Act of 1736', *Journal of Social History*, 33:2 (1999), 308–9.

[153] *LL*, Old Bailey Proceedings, 17 January 1739 (t17390117-61).

miscarried.[154] Community disapproval was emphasised by the shaming nature of many similar attacks: informers were forced to ride on an ass, burned in effigy, dragged through the kennel or dunked in a muddy ditch or the Thames. However, the violence was not merely symbolic: informers were beaten and pelted with dirt and stones. During the lifetime of the 1736 Act, informers were subject to no less than fifty-seven reported attacks and were the object of seven riots. At least four were beaten to death.[155] Many of those arrested for selling gin were rescued, as when two persons who had been sentenced to a stint in the house of correction cried out 'Informers' and 'were rescued out of the Hands of the Constable, who with his Assistants narrowly escap'd the rough Discipline of the Rabble'.[156] As Jessica Warner concludes: 'for two years, from 1736 until 1738, hardly a day passed in which an informer was not attacked on the streets of London; during the same two years hardly a month passed without a major riot'.[157] By 1744, to be 'tossed about like a Gin Informer' had become proverbial in the mouths of Londoners.[158]

Justices of the peace and the excise officers who encouraged the informers were also targeted. On at least nine occasions, protesting crowds gathered in front of a justice's house or the Excise Office, including three times at the house of Thomas De Veil, the most active judicial supporter of the Acts.[159] The most serious of these riots occurred on 23 January 1738 after De Veil issued a warrant for the arrest of a man, Edward Arnold, who had threatened to kill an informer, Martha Beezley, for testifying against him. When a crowd formed to protect Arnold from arrest, Beezley and a fellow informer took refuge in De Veil's house, fearing retribution. The crowd outside the house grew to more than a thousand, and when De Veil read the Riot Act, Roger Allen allegedly stepped forward and urged the crowd to pull down the house and murder the two informers. In the end, the military was summoned, Allen was arrested and the protest suppressed, but the strength of feeling was clear. Perhaps in order to avoid letting Allen benefit from the sympathy of an Old Bailey jury, De Veil chose to prosecute him for violating the Riot Act at King's Bench. This tactic failed, however, as reported by the author of

---

154 LMA, City of London: Sessions, 'City sessions rolls', CLA/047/LJ/03, October 1738, quoted in Warner and Ivis, '"Damn you, you informing bitch"', 299.
155 Warner and Ivis, '"Damn you, you informing bitch"', 300, 309. See also Dillon, *Much-Lamented*, pp. 169–89.
156 *Read's Weekly Journal, or British Gazetteer*, 18 February 1738; Warner and Ivis, '"Damn you, you informing bitch"', 309–13.
157 Warner, *Craze*, p. 162.
158 *A Trip from St James's to the Royal Exchange: The Manners, Customs and Amusements of the Inhabitants of London and Westminster* (1744), p. 30.
159 Warner and Ivis, '"Damn you, you informing bitch"', 309–10.

De Veil's *Memoirs*. A 'prodigious mob' attended the trial, both inside Westminster Hall and in the Palace Yards, and when the jury, quite possibly influenced by the crowd, acquitted Allen, there was a 'universal huzza', and 'as soon as [he] was discharged', they 'sat him upon their heads and carried him off in triumph'. Allen told the crowd that his verdict had preserved 'the great liberty of mobbing a justice now and then'.[160] Edward Parker, an excise officer who had testified against Allen, later claimed that, 'Witnesses were so terrified on Allens Acquittal that he [Parker] could not prevail on many of them to appear as usual' against retailers.[161]

Informers were regularly subjected to successful counter prosecutions, many of which were probably vexatious. Just under a third (nineteen of sixty-three) of the most active informers under the 1736 Act were prosecuted, seven for extortion and twelve for perjury, and the prosecutors were frequently successful: seventeen of twenty-six informers charged with perjury, and fourteen of fifteen accused of extortion were convicted.[162] Mary Pocock, for example, was found guilty of perjury in October 1738 after testifying, along with Edward Parker, that Thomas Pepper had sold her a quarter pint of geneva. Pepper, supported by several witnesses, claimed he had never seen Pocock and never sold gin, while Pocock claimed that Pepper had a vendetta against her, having threatened her, 'I'll put you into the Half-Moon (the Pillory), and if I can't do your Business, I'll get others that shall.'[163]

With such widespread popular hostility, clearly shared by the propertied members of Old Bailey juries, law enforcement officers as well as informers grew reluctant to act. As Warner argues, 'by the end of 1738, ordinary Londoners had succeeded in cowing both the men who judged them and the men who governed them'.[164] Constables became unwilling to arrest gin sellers, the Commissioners of the Excise began to reduce their fines and obstruct the informers, and justices of the peace stopped encouraging prosecutions and made fewer convictions.[165] Parish vestries even started returning the fines levied on convicted gin sellers.

---

[160] *Memoirs of the Life and Times of Sir Thomas De Veil*, pp. 41–2; Warner and Ivis, '"Damn you, you informing bitch"', 317.

[161] TNA, PC/1/15/5, part 1, 1738; cited by Warner and Ivis, '"Damn you, you informing bitch"', 318.

[162] Warner *et al.*, 'Informers in Westminster', 631; Warner and Ives, '"Damn you, you informing bitch"', 316.

[163] LL, Old Bailey Proceedings, 11 October 1738 (t17381011-16).

[164] Warner, *Craze*, p. 162.

[165] Warner and Ivis, '"Damn you, you informing bitch"', 313–19.

The Middlesex sessions complained that, 'in Stead of applying Such Conviction money to the use of the poor of their parish', as required by law, some churchwardens and overseers of the poor 'have returned the Same back to the party or partys so convicted upon pretence of their being poor, which this Court doth adjudge to be a misapplication, and contrary to the meaning of the Said Act'.[166]

Together with their allies, plebeian London rendered the 1736–7 Gin Acts, which were specifically targeted against them, a dead letter. There was a temporary dip in overall gin consumption in 1737, but consumption then resumed its upward trajectory, surpassing the 1736 figure by 1740.[167] An attempt to bolster the law in May 1738, when a statute made it a felony to attack an informer,[168] encouraged a brief increase in convictions, but assaults against informers continued and prosecutions for gin selling declined, particularly after December 1738 when one of the most active excise men, Edward Parker, was exposed as corrupt. Instead of handing over half of the £10 fines to the local parishes for distribution to the poor, Parker had pocketed the money.[169] The Gin Acts were only lightly enforced after 1738 and were finally repealed in 1743, when a new Act, intended primarily as a money-raising measure, reduced licensing fees but increased the excise on gin. Crucially, the 1743 Act made no provision for the payment of rewards in cases where gin sellers were too poor to pay the fine; the government essentially admitted 'that dram drinking could not be eliminated'.[170] Without financial incentives for prosecution, and with popular opinion still strongly antagonistic to informers, few bothered to prosecute. As Patrick Dillon observes, 'the authorities had accepted that the war on gin had failed ... Never again would a British Parliament set out to eradicate gin-drinking.'[171]

Efforts to *regulate* the sale of gin, however, were renewed with another revenue-raising measure in 1747, and a more substantial Act in 1751. In this limited sense, the authorities eventually prevailed. However, the defeat of the 1736–8 campaign against plebeian gin drinkers and sellers had important consequences for the future of policing in the metropolis. Most directly, it further stained the reputation of informers, making it

---

[166] *LL*, Middlesex Sessions: General Orders of the Court, 13 April 1738 (LMSMGO556010225).
[167] *PP*, 'Report of the commissioners', p. 6.
[168] 11 George II c. 26.
[169] Dillon, *Much-Lamented*, pp. 198–9.
[170] 16 George II, c. 8; Nicholas Rogers, *Mayhem: Post-War Crime and Violence in Britain, 1748–1753* (New Haven, Conn.: Yale University Press, 2012), p. 151.
[171] Dillon, *Much-Lamented*, p. 228.

highly unlikely that any future effort to eradicate vice would rely on them, and rendering the wholesale prosecution of victimless crimes almost impossible. Related to this, the opposition to the Gin Acts provided the final nail in the coffin of the first reformation of manners campaign. Prosecutions initiated by the societies in the 1730s were already running at only a quarter of the number prosecuted in the first half of the 1720s, while the societies' sermons in these last years 'were full of disillusionment'.[172] The demise of this long-running campaign can be attributed to a number of causes, including a growing tolerance of sexual immorality.[173] But the loss of their chief weapon, the informer, in 1737–8, together with an associated loss of magisterial backing, proved to be the final straw.[174] The annual report of their activities for 1738 was to be their last.

In the longer term, this undermining of voluntary informers contributed to the bureaucratisation of metropolitan policing, which became ever more dependent on paid personnel, including watchmen and 'runners' attached to magistrates' offices, distanced from the communities they policed.[175] One facet of this transformation lay in the changing character of the relationship between some justices of the peace and their local communities. The Middlesex bench responded to accusations of corruption by encouraging justices to act more formally, by hearing violations of the Gin Acts 'only at their Meetings appointed for that purpose, and not at their own houses'.[176] In the City, this practice extended to all crimes and was formalised by the establishment of the first *rotation office*. In December 1737, building on the established practice of the Lord Mayor, the aldermen established a court 'for the public administration of justice' in the Guildhall, where they sat in their role as local justices, at regular hours in rotation, assisted by a clerk. It was this bureaucratic model that De Veil adopted when he purchased his house in

---

[172] Dudley W. R. Bahlman, *The Moral Revolution of 1688* (New Haven, Conn.: Yale University Press, 1957; repr. Archon Books, 1968), p. 66.

[173] Faramerz Dabhoiwala, *The Origins of Sex: A History of the First Sexual Revolution* (London: Allen Lane, 2012). See also G. V. Portus, *Caritas Anglicana: or, an Historical Inquiry into those Religious and Philanthropical Societies that Flourished in England between the years 1678 and 1740* (Madison: University of Wisconsin Press, 1912), pp. 182–90; Tina Beth Isaacs, 'Moral crime, moral reform, and the state in early eighteenth-century England: a study of piety and politics' (PhD dissertation, University of Rochester, 1979), pp. 310–18; Shoemaker, *Prosecution and Punishment*, pp. 270–1.

[174] Timothy Jollie, *A Sermon Preached to the Societies for the Reformation of Manners* (1739), p. 26.

[175] Dabhoiwala, *Origins of Sex*, p. 64.

[176] *LL*, Middlesex Sessions: General Orders of the Court, 29 June 1738 (LMSMGO556010237).

Bow Street in 1740. By establishing a courtroom in the house, and ensuring it was properly staffed, he set a pattern that would in its turn be adopted by the Fieldings.[177]

However, not all justices conformed to this new model, and many suffered for their unwillingness to do so. Justice Clifford William Phillips, who sat on the original committee of Middlesex justices which drew up the petition to parliament for the regulation of gin in January 1736, subsequently turned against the informers who enforced the Act.[178] Phillips allegedly told a fellow justice, Richard Farmer, who was active in hearing informations, 'that by encouraging such Rascally Scoundrell Fellows of Informers' he 'not only unjustly deprived a great many poor familys from honestly getting their Bread but likewise promised him the Curses of all poor persons'. That Phillips, in contrast, sought to retain the support of the poor in his east end neighbourhood is evident in a letter written by the minister, churchwardens and overseers of the poor of the parish of Whitechapel, who informed the Lord High Chancellor that 'by his knowledge and impartiality in the Discharge of his Duties', Phillips had 'acquired the Love and Esteem of the Inhabitants of our said parish'.[179] Nonetheless, Phillips was expelled from the commission of the peace in July 1738, along with forty-one other members of the Westminster bench and seventy-five members of the Middlesex bench (many men were on both commissions).[180] While there were many individual reasons for these expulsions (the Lord Chancellor did not have to justify his actions), the failure by some justices to navigate the pressures surrounding the enforcement of the Gin Acts was probably one of them.

In enforcing the Gin Acts, justices were forced to choose between adopting a systematic and formal approach to the law, as encouraged by the government, and siding with their poor neighbours, who repeatedly sought their assistance. By acting more discreetly, and less publicly, than Phillips, many of those who chose the latter avoided expulsion from the commission. However, because these justices sided with the poor, they were derided for their supposed low social status and became known as 'trading justices'. It was alleged that these magistrates lived off the fees they charged complainants and were corrupt. A satirical poem published

---

[177] Beattie, *Policing and Punishment*, pp. 107–10.
[178] *LL*, set, 'Clifford William Phillips'.
[179] BL, Add. Ms 35600, f. 105r; Warner and Ivis, 'Damn you, you informing bitch', 315; Rogers, *Mayhem*, pp. 149–50.
[180] *LL*, Westminster Sessions: Sessions Papers, October 1738 (LMWJPS654140014). For the Middlesex expulsions, see Norma Landau, *The Justices of the Peace, 1679–1760* (Berkeley: University of California Press, 1984), pp. 126–7.

in the *Gentleman's Magazine* celebrated the expulsions from the commissions as a victory over, paradoxically, both informers and trading justices:

> Tho' much too late. Sure this will purge the Bench.
> Informers now may find th' Employment bad;
> And Justice may from Justices be had.
> So sorely did the trading Harpies roast us,
> We suffer'd less by Spanish Guarda Costa's.[181]

But the trading justices were more enduring than informers, because they responded to the needs of their communities. As Norma Landau has shown, they offered important services to the poor, often mediating disputes for low fees. While such justices can be found dating back to at least the Restoration, they became an increasingly important feature of London justice from the 1730s.[182] Even De Veil was attacked for acting like a trading justice; Henry Fielding claimed that he 'used to boast' he earned £1,000 a year from the business he conducted as a justice.[183] In fact, according to De Veil's *Memoirs*, he was frequently *attacked by trading justices*, who it was claimed had lost their business to him, as they 'fell much beneath him in credit'. De Veil was a master of appearing all things to all people. In any case, this author's unsympathetic description of trading justices (the 'common people ... apply to them upon every trivial occasion, to gratify their own spleen and malice against their neighbours') demonstrates just how important they had become to the poor by 1748. As Landau argues, 'to some extent, the demands of the urban poor therefore created the trading justice'.[184] However, they also played an important role for the state, which explains why many were allowed to remain in the commission. Describing trading justices as 'necessary evils', the author of the *Memoirs* continued, 'if there were not such little magistrates, the laws could not be well put in execution, or the common people kept within any bounds in regard to their superiors, or to one another'.[185]

Conflicts over the enforcement of the Gin Acts opened up dramatic differences among justices of the peace in terms of their approach to the enforcement of the law. Responding to the growing demand among the poor for accessible justice, 'trading justices' offered an important

---

[181] *Gentleman's Magazine*, 8 (1738), 435.
[182] Norma Landau, 'The trading justice's trade', in Norma Landau, ed., *Law, Crime and Society, 1660–1830* (Cambridge University Press, 2002), pp. 64–70; Landau, *Justices of the Peace*, pp. 184–90; Shoemaker, *Prosecution and Punishment*, pp. 226–30.
[183] Henry Fielding, *The Journal of a Voyage to Lisbon* (1755), p. 23.
[184] Landau, *Justices of the Peace*, p. 203.
[185] *Memoirs of the Life and Times of Sir Thomas De Veil*, pp. 17–19.

counterpoint to the more bureaucratic justice attempted by Thomas De Veil, and later, and more successfully, by Henry and John Fielding.

'Gangs', thief-takers and the coming of the lawyers

In the aftermath of the failure of the Gin Acts to modify popular behaviour, the authorities focused on a new source of social anxiety: criminal gangs. In the modern, sociological sense of a group with a clear membership and rituals of collective identity, gangs did not exist in the eighteenth century.[186] Nonetheless, there were criminals in London who belonged to loose subcultures, in which thieves and their families, friends and neighbours defended each other against arrest and prosecution. These groups may have been weakly organised, but in shifting alliances they carried out crimes together over periods of months and even years. In the 1720s, gangs coalesced around prolific robbers such as John and William Hawkins, James Shaw, Edward Burnworth, James Carrick and others, and they form part of the defiant criminal culture of that decade.[187] In the following decade, other gangs came to the attention of the authorities and the press. Thomas MacCray, sometime solicitor and highwayman, led a gang in the early 1730s which allegedly planned to assassinate Thomas De Veil in retribution for his attempts to prosecute them.[188] And Mary Young, alias Jenny Diver, was portrayed as the leader of a large gang of pickpockets following her arrest in 1741.[189]

However, by far the most substantial and frightening gang active in these years was the Black Boy Alley gang, named after a turning off Chick Lane on the western edge of the City of London – one of the ill-policed boundary areas that surrounded the City. In the autumn of 1744, press reporting of the activities of this gang precipitated a 'moral panic' about highway robbery.[190] Even if the gang was depicted as a more formidable

---

[186] On modern 'gangs' and the complex ways in which reporting both defines and in some ways creates them, see Simon Hallsworth, 'Gangland Britain? Realities, fantasies and industry', in Barry Goldson, ed., *Youth in Crisis? 'Gangs', Territoriality and Violence* (Abingdon: Routledge, 2011), pp. 183–97; and for a wider historical account, see Heather Shore, *London's Criminal Underworlds, c. 1720 – c. 1930: A Social and Cultural History* (Basingstoke: Palgrave, 2015).

[187] John Beattie, *Crime and the Courts in England, 1660–1800* (Princeton University Press, 1986), pp. 252–63; Shore, *London's Criminal Underworlds*; Gerald Howson, *Thief-Taker General: The Rise and Fall of Jonathan Wild* (London: Hutchinson, 1970; repr. 1987), pp. 312–14. Howson exaggerates the coherence of these gangs.

[188] *Memoirs of the Life and Times of Sir Thomas De Veil*, pp. 34–8; John H. Langbein, *The Origins of Adversary Criminal Trial* (Oxford University Press, 2003), pp. 143–4.

[189] *LL*, set, 'Mary Young'.

[190] Richard Ward, 'Print culture, moral panic, and the administration of the law: the London crime wave of 1744', *Crime, History & Societies*, 16:1 (2012), 5–24.

threat than was actually the case, the crimes and acts of resistance committed by members of this group constituted a genuine threat to public order. Not only did they break the law with impunity, but they were also frequently successful in defending themselves from arrest and conviction.

The Black Boy Alley gang may have been active for years (one member, William Norwell, told the Ordinary of Newgate in December 1744 that 'he had been a Street-Robber for these seven Years past'), but its role in a spate of street robberies in September 1744 marked a significant escalation of its activities and attracted the attention of the authorities.[191] The gang was feared not simply for the number of crimes they committed but for their violence and audacity, and for the direct challenge they seemed to pose to authority. Over the course of that autumn, victims retailed horrific stories of violent assaults by members of the gang, who were often described as only 'boys'. One victim, Thomas Welldy, testified that he was walking in Moorfields in November, when Robert Carter, 'a little boy', and a woman came up to him, and said:[192]

D – n your eyes, what do you want? the little boy drew a knife at me, and said he would immediately let my puddings out, if I did not let him have what I had; the woman had a knife, and she threatened to rip me up.[193]

William Harper, who turned king's evidence, testified that William Billingsly and John Potbury 'were generally very cruel; for if a person did but turn about to look at them, they would knock them down'.[194] One identified gang member, Joseph Field, exposed what were thought to be its normal procedures by allegedly telling his confederates 'it was wrong to cut and slash People after they had robbed them'.[195]

The gang's apparently large size and willingness to rescue members who had been arrested also constituted a direct challenge to authority. Harper explained that the gang 'always helped one another, if they knew them ... If we met a man with a Constable in the Street ... we went to rescue him.'[196] Following the arrest of two boys accused of robbery in

---

[191] *LL*, set, 'William Norwell'; and *LL*, Ordinary of Newgate Prison: Ordinary's Accounts, 24 December 1744 (OA174412244412240007).

[192] *LL*, set, 'Robert Carter'.

[193] *LL*, Old Bailey Proceedings, 5 December 1744 (t17441205-24).

[194] *LL*, set, 'William Harper'; and set, 'John Potbury'. See *LL*, Old Bailey Proceedings, 5 December 1744 (t17441205-37).

[195] *LL*, set, 'Joseph Field'. See *LL*, Old Bailey Proceedings, 5 December 1744 (t17441205-48).

[196] *LL*, Old Bailey Proceedings, 5 December 1744 (t17441205-37).

September, their victims reported, 'up came four or five lusty fellows and said, D—n your eyes let them go, or we will cut you as small as sausages'.[197] After Joseph Field was apprehended picking a gentleman's pocket in 1742, his accomplice William Billingsly followed him as he was taken to Thomas De Veil's house for examination, and then put in a coach to be taken to Newgate prison. In the words of the Ordinary of Newgate, Billingsly,

seeing that, immediately makes the best of his Way to Black-Boy-Alley, in Chick Lane, to raise a Posse to rescue him; he got six of his own Gang, and all had got large Broomsticks; just at Holborn Bars they met the Coach, and one of them went to the Coachman and ordered him to stop his Horses, or else he would knock his Brains out, whilst the others got to the Coach-door, and let out their Companion, and carried him off in Triumph to Black-Boy-Alley, in Defiance of Justice.[198]

The challenge to authority was explicit. When Edward Jones, the City Marshall, attempted to arrest Billingsley in Drury Lane two years later, 'he made his Escape, and in 3 Minutes rais'd a Posse of twelve Villains, arm'd with Cutlasses, and two with Pistols, who all together attack'd Mr Jones' and his assistants. When the officers drew their guns and threatened to fire, they 'were so far from being intimidated, that they cried out, "We know what you have been about, and defy all Power"'. Returning fire, they wounded Jones and escaped.[199]

This was a group with a clear sense of collective opposition to authority, adept at using threatening language to manifest their power. Welldy reported that one of his attackers said to him in November, as 'he gave me a great blow, ... D – n your eyes, take that, all the black-boy-alley boys are not taken yet'.[200] Allegiance to the group was cemented by their 'custom', in the words of the Ordinary of Newgate, of giving 'foolish, insignificant Nick Names to one another'.[201] One trial in December 1744 included John Potbury, otherwise Jack the Sailor, William Billingsly, otherwise Gugg, and Henry Gadd, otherwise Scampey.[202] The accomplice who testified against them, William Harper, was known as Old Daddy or Old Man.

---

[197] *LL*, Old Bailey Proceedings, 12 September 1744 (t17440912-51).
[198] *LL*, Ordinary of Newgate Prison: Ordinary's Accounts, 24 December 1744 (OA174412244412240036).
[199] *General Advertiser*, 3079, 26 September 1744, 1 (Burney Collection: www.galegroup.com, 1 Jan. 2014).
[200] *LL*, Old Bailey Proceedings, 5 December 1744 (t17441205-24).
[201] *LL*, Ordinary of Newgate Prison: Ordinary's Accounts, 24 December 1744 (OA174412244412240003).
[202] *LL*, set, 'Henry Gadd'; *LL*, Old Bailey Proceedings, 5 December 1744 (t17441205-34).

As a result of the group's violence and resistance to authority, Black Boy Alley itself became a dangerous place for constables and the watch. When Alexander Forfar, thief-taker and headborough of the parish of St James Clerkenwell, along with five assistants including Robert Montgomery attempted to make an arrest at the house of Joseph Field, they were denied entrance, attacked by a mob, wounded and eventually driven off.[203] As a witness later reported, 'the people said that Montgomery and the constable were attacked by the people of Black Boy Alley'.[204] A few days later twelve men went to the house of one of the constables involved, William Body, a prominent thief-taker, who testified that they 'came to his house with drawn cutlasses in their hands, and pistols cocked, and said, D – n their Eyes and Blood, we will have him out of his house, for we will have his Head, and this Night his Brains shall be broiled in Black-Boy-Alley'.[205]

Sensationalist reporting of these attacks in the newspapers in the second half of 1744 stimulated public fears about street robbers and gangs, as Londoners came to believe they were under siege.[206] In response, the authorities increased the rewards for apprehending offenders. In September Portsoken Ward offered a reward for 'apprehending any of the persons concerned' in the attack on Alexander Forfar.[207] In the same month the vestry of St Clement Danes, noting that 'The Highways & Streets in this Parish being of late greatly infested by a Notorious Gang of Street Robbers & Pick pockets' and acting like other select vestries in a quasi-judicial capacity, offered a reward of ten guineas for the arrest of any gang member.[208] A month later, in November, the state reissued its proclamation offering the still larger reward of one hundred pounds, in addition to the statutory reward of forty pounds, for the conviction of robbers, while the City of London offered five pounds simply for the arrest of suspects.[209]

As intended, these rewards attracted the attention of thief-takers, and together with searches undertaken by the constables, this led to a

---

[203] *LL*, set, 'Alexander Forfar', and set, 'Joseph Field'.
[204] *LL*, Old Bailey Proceedings, 5 December 1744 (t17441205-61).
[205] *LL*, set, 'William Body'; *LL*, Old Bailey Proceedings, 17 October 1744 (t17441017-6).
[206] Ward argues that it was only from December that the Black Boy Alley gang was retrospectively blamed for the crime wave, which initially was attributed to wider concerns: 'Print culture, moral panic, and the administration of the law'.
[207] *LL*, Old Bailey Proceedings, 5 December 1744 (t17441205-61).
[208] *LL*, St Clement Danes Parish: Minutes of Parish Vestries, 18 September 1744 (WCCDMV362070280).
[209] *London Gazette*, 8378, 6–10 November 1744 (Burney Collection: www.galegroup.com, 1 Jan. 2014); LMA, City of London: 'Repertories of the Court of Aldermen', COL/CA/ 01/01/152, pp. 411, 419–20, 425, 446–9.

184 Vestries, justices and their opponents: 1731–1748

significant increase in the number of indictments for highway robbery tried at the Old Bailey.[210] While the first five meetings of the court in 1744 averaged 2.2 indictments per session, the next three sessions, in September, October and December, saw an average of 18 indictments each. Many of those charged that autumn were members of the Black Boy Alley gang: nineteen members, including four women, were tried at the Old Bailey for highway robbery in the last four months of the year.

Many of these prosecutions were initiated by thief-takers. Although in part discredited by the conviction of Jonathan Wild, 'thief-taking' had continued after his execution in 1725. Supported by rewards, the practice thrived on the back of both the authorities' desire to prosecute threatening criminals and the victims' desire to get their goods back. Judging by the distribution of rewards recorded in the City, John Beattie suggests there was a significant increase in the number of thief-takers active in the 1740s, explicitly encouraged by magistrates, including De Veil.[211] The rewards offered in late 1744 provided a lucrative new opportunity, and thief-takers, including Alexander Forfar and William Body, seized the moment. Both played a major role in prosecuting alleged members of the Black Boy Alley gang, often on the basis of dubious evidence. Of the forty-two individuals who shared in rewards for the conviction of purported members of the gang, amounting to £1,400 by December 1744, at least half were thief-takers or constables. These included John Berry and Stephen McDaniel, whose thief-taking activities date back to 1735 and 1741 respectively, and whose later involvement in thief-making scandals in 1747 and 1754 points to their direct involvement as active collaborators in crime.[212]

Some of the trials of the Black Boy Alley gang in 1744 were simple stitch ups. The ultimately unsuccessful prosecution of Ann Collier for assaulting Alexander Forfar and stealing a silk handkerchief, powder horn and pistol in December 1744, for example, was based on weak evidence and exposed the thief-takers' own criminal pursuit of rewards at

[210] Beattie, *Policing and Punishment*, pp. 406–8.
[211] Beattie, *Policing and Punishment*, pp. 410, 420.
[212] *LL*, set, 'John Berry', and set, 'Stephen McDaniel'; *LL*, Old Bailey Proceedings, 9 September 1747 (t17470909-1). See also Joseph Cox, *A Faithful Narrative of the Most Wicked and Inhuman Transactions of that Bloody-Minded Gang of Thief-takers, alias Thief-Makers* (1756), pp. 60–2; Beattie, *Policing and Punishment*, p. 411; Ruth Paley, 'Thief-takers in London in the age of the McDaniel gang, *c.* 1745–1754', in Douglas Hay and Francis Snyder, eds., *Policing and Prosecution in Britain, 1750–1850* (Oxford: Clarendon Press, 1989), p. 319. For an innovative recent study that locates thief-takers within a strongly local and gendered context, see Janice Turner, '"Ill-favoured sluts"? The disorderly women of Rosemary Lane and Rag Fair', *London Journal*, 38:2 (July, 2013), 95–109.

any cost.[213] Forfar had received £5 9s. for his part in the conviction of Ann Duck and Ann Barefoot in October, but appears to have fallen out with his fellow thief-takers over the distribution of this and other rewards.[214] In Collier's trial Forfar provided the only direct evidence implicating her, while the other prosecution witnesses refused to provide positive confirmation of her participation in the violent attack on Forfar. This not only undermined his testimony but also focused the legal spotlight on Forfar himself. John Blewmire, described by Forfar as 'my constable', turned on him and testified that the prosecution of Collier was motivated by greed alone. He reported that Forfar told him,'now is the time, 'tis near Christmas, if you have a mind for a piece of beef, we may keep Christmas well if Nan Collier was convicted, and a little matter will hang her'.[215] While this did not necessarily mean that the allegations against Collier were fabricated, the evidence of Robert Marcrost, a marshals' court officer, did. Referring to William Harper, who turned king's evidence following his own arrest, Marcrost told the court that Forfar had 'agreed to swear that Harper was at the riot, whether he was or was not, and that he had robbed him of the pistol', claiming that Harper would be convicted simply because he lived in Black Boy Alley: ''tis a bad place, the very sanction of Black-boy-alley will hang an hundred of them with very little evidence, no matter who swears'. With respect to Ann Collier, Marcrost testified that Forfar,

said it was worth while to prosecute her, and if he did not, some body else would, for there would be an hundred pieces for her by the late Proclamation. – I believe Forfar does this for the sake of the reward, and nothing else, for he is a very wicked man.

Despite the dubious quality of the evidence provided by the character witnesses called in her defence, including William Buckland's comment that 'she had the general character of keeping a very bad house, and harboured thieves; I have heard Murder cried out there', Collier was acquitted.[216] It is no wonder, in John Beattie's words, that thief-takers were 'hated by a large part of the population'.[217]

In response to this wave of often false prosecutions, members of the Black Boy Alley gang and others sought and obtained legal advice, from

[213] *LL*, set, 'Ann Collier'.
[214] *LL*, Old Bailey Proceedings, 5 December 1744 (t17441205-61); Old Bailey Proceedings, 17 October 1744 (t17441017-6); and Old Bailey Proceedings, 17 October 1744 (t17441017-22). See also, *LL*, set, 'Ann Duck', and set, 'Ann Barefoot'.
[215] *LL*, Old Bailey Proceedings, 5 December 1744 (t17441205-61).
[216] *LL*, Old Bailey Proceedings, 5 December 1744 (t17441205-61).
[217] Beattie, *Policing and Punishment*, p. 416.

both solicitors and barristers. This was not entirely new in 1744; we have already noted the use made of the law and lawyers by those accused of running disorderly houses in the 1720s, and Dabhoiwala notes that it 'was not uncommon for solicitors and barristers' to defend bawds and their associates in the 1730s.[218] Other accused criminals followed suit in the 1730s, with members of the MacCray and Wreathock gangs, both of which were actually led by solicitors, at the forefront of this development. As claimed in De Veil's purported *Memoirs*, some gang members

> were retainers to the law, who understood all the dark arts that qualified Newgate solicitors, and these fellows provided and managed everything, and that too with such dexterity, that there was nothing they could not prove, or disprove upon very short notice.[219]

While solicitors had been assisting defendants for decades, counsel for the defence in felony trials, however, were not allowed to appear at the Old Bailey until 1732 (prosecution counsel had been permitted from the 1720s). As John Langbein has argued, the 'epochal decision' to admit defence counsel was strongly influenced by two scandals involving perjured prosecution evidence given for the sake of obtaining rewards in 1732.[220] One involved the notorious informer John Waller, who was convicted of perjury in May for falsely charging John Edlin with highway robbery.[221] When, as his punishment, Waller was placed on the pillory he was violently attacked and killed by a mob led by Edward Dalton, brother of the executed highwayman James Dalton.[222]

To rebalance the legal process, the judges decided to allow defendants access to legal counsel to challenge precisely the kind of perjured evidence used in this case, although until 1836 defence counsel were not allowed to address the jury on matters of fact.[223] However, while it was the judges who agreed to allow this change in 1732, defence counsel would only begin to appear in significant numbers when defendants decided to hire them. This only happened in 1744, as criminal gangs began to rely on counsel to defend themselves. In this sense, while the judges *permitted* defence counsel to appear, it was the actions of those

---

[218] Dabhoiwala, *Origins of Sex*, p. 76.

[219] *Memoirs of the Life and Times of Sir Thomas De Veil*, p. 35; Langbein, *Origins of Adversary Criminal Trial*, p. 144.

[220] Langbein, *Origins of Adversary Criminal Trial*, pp. 136, 152–8.

[221] *LL*, set, 'John Waller', and *LL*, Old Bailey Proceedings, 25 May 1732 (t17320525-69).

[222] Edward Dalton was seeking revenge for Waller's perjured testimony in 1730 which led to James's execution. *LL*, Old Bailey Proceedings, 6 December 1732 (t17320906-69); and *LL*, set, 'James Dalton'.

[223] Stephan Landsman, 'The rise of the contentious spirit: advocacy procedure in eighteenth-century England', *Cornell Law Review* 75 (1990), 579.

accused of crime that actually led to the 'lawyerisation' of the criminal trial. While plebeian Londoners may have struggled to raise the minimum fee of half a guinea required to hire a barrister, evidence from the 1780s demonstrates that it was possible. Despite claims that 'only the affluent had defence counsel', defendants with legal representation included a significant number of artisans, labourers, servants and even prostitutes.[224]

Before the 1780s, reporting of the role of lawyers in the Old Bailey *Proceedings* was inconsistent, but the evidence available suggests that defence counsel were present in only a handful of trials in the 1730s, primarily in cases involving middle-class or elite defendants. Langbein identifies only nine trials involving defence lawyers in 1736, accounting for just 1.8 per cent of the trials that year, while Landsman counted fifteen the following year, or 3.4 per cent of all trials.[225] However, 1737 was atypical and the number of trials involving defence counsel remained in single figures until 1744. Including the four lawyers hired to prosecute him, and following three failed attempts to secure defence counsel, William Bird's trial probably exhausted the list of barristers willing to act in this capacity on both sides in 1742. The autumn of 1744 witnessed a step change in this pattern.

Of the at least twenty-four trials in 1744 where defence counsel appeared (accounting for 6.3 per cent of all trials), almost half (eleven) involved charges of highway robbery, and many of these involved members of the Black Boy Alley gang.[226] Before 1744 there are only two cases of highway robbery in the entire run of the *Proceedings* in which defence counsel were clearly present. In contrast, between 1744 and 1748 13.5 per cent of the defendants charged with highway robbery had counsel.[227] Thus, the significant increase in the presence of defence counsel in Old Bailey trials in 1744 was driven by the actions of defendants accused of highway robbery. Moreover, as the data from sample years in Figure 4.6 show, from the mid-1740s use of defence counsel

---

[224] Langbein, *Origins of Adversary Criminal Trial*, p. 318; David Lemmings, *Professors of the Law: Barristers and English Legal Culture in the Eighteenth Century* (Oxford University Press, 2000), pp. 213–15.

[225] John H. Langbein, 'The criminal trial before the lawyers', *University of Chicago Law Review*, 45:2 (1978), 311–12 (digitalcommons.law.yale.edu/yjlh, 2 Jan. 2014); Landsman, 'Rise of the contentious spirit', 607. The total number of trials in these years was calculated using the *Old Bailey Online* API.

[226] Because this methodology is based on keyword searching, with checking to determine whether the counsel present acted for the defence, it represents a minimum number of trials in which lawyers were present.

[227] Among these defendants in 1744–6, as reported in the *Proceedings*, were a tailor, street seller, cooper, breeches maker, cabinet maker and two tavern keepers.

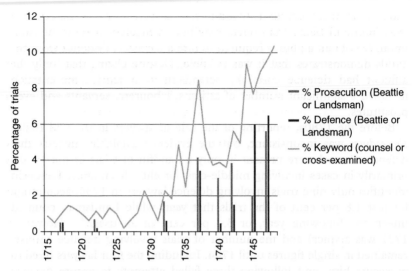

Figure 4.6 Legal counsel at the Old Bailey, 1715–1748. Online data set: Legal Counsel at the Old Bailey 1715–1800.xlsx. This database and chart are based on data for selected years collected by John Beattie ('Scales of justice: defense counsel and the English criminal trial in the eighteenth and nineteenth centuries', *Law and History Review*, 9 [1991], 227) and Stephen Landsman ('The rise of the contentious spirit: advocacy procedure in eighteenth-century England', *Cornell Law Review*, 75 [1990], 607); and the *Old Bailey Online*, keyword search for: *counsel, council, councel, counc** etc.; and *cross examined* and *cross examination*. NB: counsel were usually, but not always, present in trials which include the terms *cross examined* or *cross examination*. Where both Beattie and Landsman provide figures for the same years, the higher figure was used when calculating percentages. At the time of writing, Beattie is in the process of revising his figures.

exceeded that of prosecution counsel, further underlining the point that it was the former which drove the lawyerisation of the criminal trial. This pattern, though subject to fluctuations, was largely maintained into the following decade, with defence counsel making up an increasing proportion of the total number of counsel present.

These lawyers were effective, developing new strategies for challenging and cross-examining prosecution witnesses which began to alter the balance of power in criminal trials. Their presence may have encouraged the development of the 'corroboration rule', in which defendants were acquitted if the only evidence against them came from an accomplice turning king's evidence. Langbein notes the 'sudden' application of this practice in three trials at the height of the prosecutions of the Black Boy

Alley gang in December 1744, including that of street robbers Edward and John Hill (father and son).[228] Where thief-takers were involved, as we have seen in the trial of Ann Collier, counsel often discredited victims and witnesses by accusing them of being motivated by greed.[229] In the trial of Samuel Goodman for robbing Mary Footman, for example, Footman was aggressively cross-examined by an unnamed lawyer who asked her, "'Tis for the sake of the great reward, I suppose that you do this?' Similarly, her husband was asked, 'Did not you know of the reward which is promised for taking of street robbers?'[230] In other trials counsel went further and suggested that, like Jonathan Wild, thief-takers had staged the crimes in order to collect the reward. In the trial of the Hills for robbing Elizabeth Quaite, counsel asked the victim: 'Was not you directed to go into the King's Road in order to be robbed?', while her husband Francis was asked, 'Did not you go out that night on purpose to go a thief-taking?'[231] These and other defence strategies were remarkably successful, leading to a significantly higher acquittal rate when defence counsel was present. Of the twenty trials for highway robbery between 1744 and 1748 which demonstrably included defence counsel, fourteen (70 per cent), ended in acquittals. In comparison, when counsel were not present only 42 per cent were acquitted.

Unsurprisingly, defendants who did not have counsel began to use the same techniques. In December 1744, at his third trial at the Old Bailey in three months, Theophilus Watson challenged the evidence of his accomplice turned prosecution witness William Harper: 'Did not the thieftakers after you were taken up, threaten to hang you if you did not make a discovery of such and such things; and you said then you did not know any thing of them?'[232] When William Taylor was charged with pickpocketing the following month on the evidence of two thief-takers, Charles Remington and William Palmer Hind, Taylor attacked the thief-takers and attempted to shift the blame onto an accomplice who had turned king's evidence (and was in fact another thief-taker), Stephen McDonald (possibly an alias of Stephen McDaniel).[233] He told the court: 'McDonald is the person who took the handkerchief out of the gentleman's pocket, and now he wants to push it upon me. They [the

---

[228] LL, Old Bailey Proceedings, 5 December 1744 (t17441205-18); Langbein, *Origins of Adversary Criminal Trial*, p. 205.
[229] LL, Old Bailey Proceedings, 5 December 1744 (t17441205-61).
[230] LL, Old Bailey Proceedings, 5 December 1744 (t17441205-41).
[231] LL, Old Bailey Proceedings, 5 December 1744 (t17441205-17).
[232] LL, set, 'Theophilus Watson'; LL, Old Bailey Proceedings, 5 December 1744 (t17441205-34).
[233] LL, set, 'Charles Remington', and set, 'William Palmer Hind'.

prosecution] are the greatest rogues and thief-takers in the world; they do it for the sake of the reward.'[234] Tactics such as these, learned by Old Bailey defendants from their fellow prisoners at Newgate or from watching or reading about Old Bailey trials, were adopted by defendants even when they were unable to afford counsel. In this way the more vigorous efforts to combat crime in 1744 were matched by the growing sophistication of the strategies used by defendants in court.

Consequently, the Black Boy Alley gang survived the moral panic. Despite the execution of nine men and women associated with the gang in December 1744, the Alley continued to be a centre of criminal activity. In 1747 William Body testified at the Old Bailey that when he attempted to arrest two street robbers on nearby Chick Lane in July, 'there was so many of them, that we were afraid to attack them'. And when he accidentally encountered the two robbers the following Saturday between 10 and 11 in the morning, 'I was knock'd down; and I must speak it to the Praise of the House-keepers of Chick-lane, not one of them came to my Assistance.'[235]

In the first instance, the response at both local and national level to an apparent epidemic of gang-related crime in 1744 was to increase the rewards available for the prosecution and conviction of highway robbers. This, as we have seen, led to a significant expansion in thief-taking, and, like the gang itself, thief-takers continued active after 1744. Later in the decade, the activities of men such as William Palmer Hind, Charles Remington and Stephen McDaniel set the stage for Henry Fielding's only partially successful attempt to reform thief-takers through the creation of his influential group of 'runners' in 1749. Both corrupt thief-takers and gangs continued to plague London into the 1750s, when the McDaniel gang combined these two forms of criminality and caused a major scandal in 1754.

The anxiety generated by the Black Boy Alley gang may also have contributed to a change in the tone and content of the *Ordinary's Accounts*. In the 1730s, when the *Accounts* were published by John Applebee, they had expanded to include, in addition to the usual biographies of those convicted at Tyburn, 'lengthy appendices containing letters and supposed autobiographies of some of the most notorious criminals'. These included stories of highwaymen's 'pranks' and 'frolicks' involving thefts from misers, lawyers and quack doctors, which had 'the ring, if not exactly of verisimilitude, at least of popular appropriation and self-representation'. In some cases these sympathetic representations of criminal behaviour included highwaymen's justifications for their crimes,

---

[234] *LL*, Old Bailey Proceedings, 16 January 1745 (t17450116-19).
[235] *LL*, Old Bailey Proceedings, 9 September 1747 (t17470909-1).

such as Tom Easter's claim that he 'rob[s] the Rich to give to the Poor'.[236] Following the December 1744 issue of the *Account*, however, which included a lengthy if unsympathetic account of the crimes of the 'profligate Sett of audacious Bloodthirsty, desperate, and harden'd Villains' who comprised the Black Boy Alley gang, the Ordinary, James Guthrie, sacked Applebee.[237] Henceforth, the *Accounts* became more serious and less empathetic. When Mary Cooper took over as printer in June 1745, the title page announced that the tone would be raised. In contrast to the previous 'stile and language [which was] a little too gross and indelicate', the *Accounts* would now express a more censorious view of crime, in which criminals were described as 'poor wretches' and 'born thieves', and the *Account* itself was reframed as an attempt to educate the 'better kind of readers' in their obligations to devise more effective means of preventing crime.[238] The activities of the Black Boy Alley gang in 1744 and the responses they provoked resulted in significant changes, played out both in the short term and in ensuing decades, to policing, the criminal trial and the literature of crime.

Conclusion

In two decades marked by relatively high wages, low prices and generally fine weather, but also by concerns (and some real threats) about gin drinking, criminal gangs and the growing cost of poor relief (and the corruption of those who administered it), elite Londoners attempted to create a new system of governance. In the parishes the 'Antient Inhabitants' were increasingly excluded from the select vestries, which in turn took on the legal powers of a petty sessions. While many 'trading justices' resisted, Thomas De Veil and his allies sought to create a more systematic approach to policing. They sought to use informers, thief-takers and rewards to attack the problems of gin and gangs. The night watch in Westminster was put on a new legal footing, and the Court of Burgesses was finally eclipsed. In the City, the first rotation office, providing a

---

[236] *LL*, set, 'Tom Easter'; *LL*, Ordinary of Newgate Prison: Ordinary's Accounts, 7 April 1742 (OA174204074204070014). See also Andrea McKenzie, 'The real Macheath: social satire, appropriation, and eighteenth-century criminal biography', *Huntington Library Quarterly*, 69:4 (2006), 592–3.

[237] *LL*, Ordinary of Newgate Prison: Ordinary's Accounts, 24 December 1744 (OA174412244412240032); LMA, Court of Aldermen Papers, 'The humble complaint of James Guthrie, Ordinary of Newgate, read 19 Feb. 1744[/5]', COL/CA/05/01/0093; Andrea McKenzie, *Tyburn's Martyrs: Execution in England, 1675–1775* (London: Hambledon Continuum, 2007), p. 152.

[238] *LL*, Ordinary of Newgate Prison: Ordinary's Accounts, 7 June 1745 (OA17450607450 6070003).

regular system of justice, was opened for business. And finally, the associational charities created a system for relieving the most sympathetic forms of poverty to the exclusion of all others.

However, at almost every turn reformers were faced with opposition. Petty householders in the parishes opposed the select vestries, using petitions, rate revolts and simple force of numbers to try and hold them in check (albeit with limited success), while the justices were simply attacked. Their houses were mobbed, their prisoners rescued and informers and thief-takers were brutally assaulted with all the violence and shaming strategies of the early modern communal tradition. Using their strength in numbers as well as their new access to legal counsel, Londoners rose up in defence of the right of 'mobbing a justice now and then'.

To some degree these disputes can be mapped onto contemporary political divisions. The tradition of popular Jacobitism with its inchoate appeal to warm beer and neighbourliness provided one cultural context, while many justices and vestrymen were part of a culture of clientage, their actions motivated by a sycophantic dependency on the whig aristocracy.[239] Certainly the opponents of the Gin Acts rendered their message more potent when they shouted 'No Gin, No King', and highwaymen, smugglers and poachers sometimes justified their crimes in Jacobite language.[240] However, for plebeian London these battles were more closely concerned with the visceral and monetary issues of poverty and taxation, and a desire for community stability, rather than with the rights of distant princes, whether Stuart or Hanoverian.

By 1748, many aspects of the new systems of policing and parish governance had been challenged. The publication of two pamphlets seeking to defend the reputation of Thomas De Veil following his death in 1746 is just one measure of the extent to which he divided opinion.[241] The annual cycle of destruction meted out on the St Martin's roundhouse, the final collapse of the reformation of manners campaign and the abandonment of the attempt to suppress gin sellers all speak of an oppositional plebeian culture that left many, with De Veil, 'pale and

---

[239] For an overview of the role of Jacobitism in London politics, see Paul Monod, *Jacobitism and the English People, 1688-1788* (Cambridge University Press, 1993), pp. 225–32. For clientage relations in Westminster, see Nicholas Rogers, 'Aristocratic clientage, trade and independency: popular politics in pre-radical Westminster', *Past & Present*, 61 (1973), 70–106.

[240] According to Lord Egmont, this phrase was used by a mob that surrounded the Queen's coach in the autumn of 1736 (quoted in Dillon, *Much-Lamented*, p. 160). See also Monod, *Jacobitism*, pp. 111–19; Nicholas Rogers, *Crowds, Culture and Politics in Georgian Britain* (Oxford: Clarendon Press, 1998), pp. 50–1.

[241] Thomas DeVeil, *Observations on the Practice of a Justice of the Peace* (1747); *Memoirs of the Life and Times of Sir Thomas de Veil*.

passive' in the face of a wider population.[242] With the occasional support
of Old Bailey jurors and others, London's poor had achieved some
substantial victories. In the workhouses new medical provisions were
created to meet their demands for care, while in the courts they brought
in defence counsel to rebalance the scales of justice. Thief-takers walked
in fear, and the informers dared not accept their rewards. More problematically (because the poor were victims as well as perpetrators of
violence), a self-confident criminal culture survived the sporadic
attempts to suppress it. And if, in the end, many of the popular battles
fought against change were lost, the developments of these years had
created opportunities for plebeian Londoners to manipulate the system,
while enhancing their culture of opposition.

Faced with reform, many poorer Londoners, like the highwayman
Henry Simms and the ballad singer and thief Mary Cut and Come-again,
simply resisted. Simms was described by the Ordinary of Newgate, 'as
famous a Thief as ever yet adorn'd the Gallows'.[243] When he turned king's
evidence after his arrest in March 1745, he retracted in court all the
charges he had laid against his accomplices following his arrest, telling
the incredulous judges, while smiling, that 'not a word' of his previous
information was true and, in effect, challenging the judges to do something about it.[244] He was not prosecuted for perjury, and when he was
finally convicted and sentenced to death in February 1747, he apparently
assisted in the publication of a subversive pamphlet, *Hanging no Dishonour*,
which claimed that the corruption of kings, statesmen and ministers was a
far greater evil than the crimes of a small 'rogue' like 'Gentleman Harry,
[who] is but a Novice in Wickedness to one of them'.[245]

Also arrested in 1745, Mary Cut and Come-again similarly challenged
the court.[246] Mary refused to divulge her real name until just before her
death and declared that if she had to suffer a system that left her excluded
and powerless, well: 'D–n my eyes then I shall have a ride for the money'.[247]

---

[242] Victor, *History of the Theatres*, Vol. I, p. 59, quoted in Lockwood, 'Little Haymarket theatre riot', 65; and *London Evening Post*, 7–10 October 1738 (Burney Collection: www.galegroup.com, 1 Jan. 2014).
[243] LL, set, 'Henry Simms'; LL, Ordinary of Newgate Prison, Ordinary's Account, 17 June 1747 (OA174706174706170012).
[244] *The Proceedings at the Assizes of the Peace, Oyer and Terminer, and General Gaol Delivery for the County of Surry [sic]* (1745), pp. 7–8, 15.
[245] *Hanging no Dishonour. Being a modest attempt to prove that such persons as have the honour to make their exit at the triple-tree are not always the greatest Villains in the Nation* (1747), p. 14.
[246] LL, set, 'Mary Cut and Come-again'.
[247] LL, Old Bailey Proceedings, 24 April 1745 (t17450424-31). For a full account of Mary White, alias Mary Cut and Come-again, see Hitchcock and Shoemaker, *Tales*, pp. 50–4.

5   Reformers and their discontents: 1748–1763

Introduction

On Saturday 18 November 1750, Westminster Bridge was opened to the public for the first time. By linking Westminster to Southwark, it changed the character of the metropolis and laid the foundation for rapid expansion south of the river. Built of Portland stone in a plain neoclassical style, it was 'allowed by Judges of Architecture to be one of the grandest Bridges in the World'. That night a procession crossed the new bridge with 'Trumpets, Kettle-Drums, &c. with Guns firing during the Ceremony'. And on Sunday, 'Westminster was all Day like a Fair, with People going to view the Bridge and walk over it'. With twelve new salaried watchmen and thirty-two street lights, the bridge set the tone and style for a fifty-year period of civic building in the capital that would include many of the city's prisons and lock-ups, court houses and workhouses. And while 'The Pickpockets made a fine Market of it, and many People lost their Money and Watches', the bridge symbolised a new and more orderly London.[1] But it also reinforced the sometimes brutal character of the systems of justice and social care that governed the lives of London's working people. It became one of the specific and peculiar places where small crimes were made capital under statute law. Westminster Bridge joined the 'bloody code': 'Persons wilfully and maliciously destroying or damaging the said Bridge ... shall suffer Death as Felons without Benefit of Clergy.'[2] New and old architecture, new and old systems of police and punishment, new and old conceptions of community and social

---

[1] *Penny London Post or The Morning Advertiser*, 19 November 1750 – 21 November 1750, issue 1345 (Burney Collection: www.galegroup.com, 1 Jan. 2014).

[2] 9 Geo. II c. 29, 'An Act for building a bridge cross the River Thames', and 14 Geo. II c. 40, 'An Act to enable the commissioners for building a bridge cross the River Thames'. Lisa Cody has suggested that 'damage' in this instance extended to include 'graffiti'. Lisa Cody, 'Every lane teems with instruction, and every alley is big with erudition: graffiti in eighteenth-century London', in Tim Hitchcock and Heather Shore, eds., *The Streets of London from the Great Fire to the Great Stink* (London: Rivers Oram Press, 2003), p. 96. There is no evidence that this provision was ever actually used.

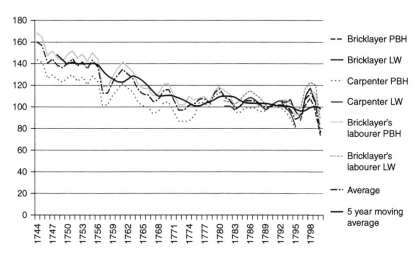

Figure 5.1 Real wage rates of London bricklayers, carpenters and their
labourers, 1744–1800. 'PBH' reflects data from E.H. Phelps Brown and
S.V. Hopkins; 'LW' data from P.H. Lindert and J.G. Williamson.
Leonard Schwarz, 'The standard of living in the long run: London,
1700–1860', Economic History Review, 2nd Series, 38:1 (1985),
39–40; Online data set: Wages and Prices.xlsx.

obligation jostled cheek by jowl in the 1750s, pitting innovation against
social cohesion and resulting in growing conflict.

London at mid-century was wet and miserable. A long series of damp
winters and soaking summers led to mildewed crops and rising food
prices.[3] After twenty relatively good years of high real wages and low
food prices, the economic well-being of London's workers was challenged year on year.[4] In 1756 the highest wheat prices for two gener-
ations and a significant drop in real wages were witnessed, the beginning
of a half-century-long decline that would reach its nadir only in the
1790s.[5] This decline in living standards exacerbated on-going conflicts
between plebeian Londoners and the ambitions of those who were
responsible for the building of Westminster Bridge.

[3] The period 1751–60 saw ten consecutive wet summers, producing an 'overall anomaly of
127% of the modern-era mean' (booty.org.uk/booty.weather, 1 Jan. 2014). For climate
data see J. H. Brazell, London Weather (London: HMSO, 1968), Appendix II, pp. 158–63.
[4] The spending power of a bricklayer's daily wage, for instance, fell by 9.5 per cent over the
course of the decade: Leonard Schwarz, London in the Age of Industrialisation: Entrepreneurs,
Labour Force and Living Conditions, 1700–1850 (Cambridge University Press, 1992),
pp. 172–3 and Table 6.1. See also Leonard Schwarz, 'The standard of living in the long
run: London, 1700–1860', Economic History Review, 2nd Series, 38:1 (1985), 24–41.
[5] This figure comes from the Winchester series of grain prices. See 'International Institute of
Social History: wheat prices in Winchester, 1657–1817' (iisg.nl/hpw/data.php, 1 Jan. 2014).

In the years following the end of the War of the Austrian Succession in 1748, the country's governors felt under siege. Not only were there concerns about a major crime wave in London, but there were violent confrontations with gangs of smugglers on the south coast, turnpike riots in the West Country and keelmen's strikes on the Tyne. It is against this backdrop of economic hardship and elite insecurity that the developments at mid-century must be read. While the comfortable middling sort were worrying about crime, and parliament was passing the Murder Act in 1752, mandating the immediate execution and dissection of those convicted of murder, artisans and labourers were beginning to struggle to make ends meet. And when Henry and John Fielding were designing a comprehensively reorganised system of poor relief and criminal justice, breathing new life into the discredited system of thief-takers and rewards, some of the working poor were going hungry. The gangs and criminals of the capital came into ever more open conflict with the authorities, while riots at Tyburn and popular disgust at the treatment of Bosavern Penlez cast a harsh light on the policies of the state and justices of the peace. Conflict on the streets and in the courtroom helped to define the growing gulf between self-styled reformers and their many enemies. Projectors and philanthropists used the new-fangled power of the associational charities to create the appearance of a more ordered metropolis where crime was not tolerated, and the poor were virtuous and hard working. However, through the Foundling Hospital they, in fact, inadvertently committed mass murder by neglect. In this difficult decade, plebeian London learned harsh lessons and in response refined their oppositional tactics and developed new ones, with varying degrees of success.

The crime wave and poverty's knock

In July 1748, as the hostilities of the War of the Austrian Succession waned and the peace negotiations leading to the Treaty of Aix-la-Chapelle accelerated (it was signed in October), London's elites grew anxious about rising crime and poverty. Many anticipated a post-war crime wave, in what turned out to be a self-fulfilling prophecy. From late 1747, long before the troops arrived home and during a period of low food prices and temporarily rising real wages, crime reporting in the press increased, and victims of crime and judicial officials began to press charges more regularly.[6] The same period witnessed renewed attempts by the City of London to control

---

[6] Richard Ward, 'Print culture and responses to crime in mid-eighteenth-century London' (PhD dissertation, University of Sheffield, 2010), pp. 51–3. See also his *Print Culture, Crime and Justice in 18th-Century London* (London: Bloomsbury Academic, 2014).

Figure 5.2 Prosecutions and commitments, 1745–1765: Old Bailey,
Bridewell and the London Workhouse. Online data set: Crime
Prosecutions.xlsx.

begging and vagrancy. At the beginning of February 1748–9, the
Common Council determined to publicise the awards available for apprehending vagrants and admonished constables and private citizens to do
their duty and prosecute the 'great numbers of beggars rogues and vagabonds' that pestered 'the streets & publick passages of this city'.[7] In the
autumn of 1749, the grand jury in the City followed with a presentment
that repeated the old claim that 'idle vagrants & common beggars' were a
particular danger 'to child-bearing women'.[8]

These concerns contributed to a wave of prosecutions at the end of the
1740s. The total number of offences tried at the Old Bailey increased by
84 per cent between 1745 and 1749, and while equivalent data from
Bridewell and the London Workhouse are missing for these years, there
was almost certainly a parallel growth in commitments for petty crimes,
particularly vagrancy. The number of vagrants removed northward
through the City grew substantially, rising by over 65 per cent, from
385 individuals in 1748 to 626 men, women and children in 1750.[9]

[7] LMA, City of London: 'Repertories of the Court of Aldermen', COL/CA/01/01/15610,
Nov. 1747 – 28 Oct 1748, 2 February 1747–8, p. 128.
[8] LL, City of London Sessions: Sessions Papers, 6 April 1748 – 13 December 1749
(LMSLPS150600040).
[9] LMA, City of London: Sessions, 'Account of the expenses of passing vagrants that was
passed from Southwark to St Magnus London Bridge . . . January the 12th 1747/8 to Jan.
1755', CLA/047/LR/06/034.

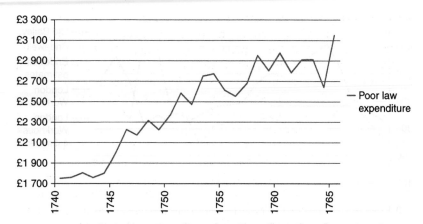

Figure 5.3 St Clement Danes, poor law expenditure, 1740–1765.
Online data set: St Clement Danes Poor Law Expenditure 1706–1803.
xlsx.

Expenditure by the City on vagrant rewards and removals increased even faster; rising from £35 3s. 4d. in 1747 to a new high of £131 11s. 9d. in 1751.[10]

The coming of peace heralded a period of real hardship. A fall in real wages came first: from 1745 to 1749 real wages fell substantially before temporarily levelling out. Subsequently, the arrival of demobilised sailors and soldiers (40,000 by October 1749) increased unemployment.[11] Increasing demand for relief led to a gradual increase in its cost; in Middlesex the years from 1748 to 1750 saw total expenditure rise from £79,181 in 1748 to £82,092 two years later.[12] Similar data for the following years are not available, but records for individual parishes suggest that for many this increase became more dramatic during the 1750s. In St Clement Danes, for example, after remaining relatively stable at between £2,100 and £2,300 per year from 1746 to 1750, expenditure grew rapidly after 1750, reaching £2,977 in 1760.

Reform and the anxieties that drove it were shaped by expectations of the behaviour of the poor and the criminal. Anticipated fears of a crime

[10] LMA, City of London: 'City's cash accounts', COL/CHD/CT/01/043, 1747–9, ff. 58, 199; LMA, City of London: 'City's cash accounts', COL/CHD/CT/01/044, 1750–2, ff. 61, 121, 192.
[11] Nicholas Rogers, *Mayhem: Post-War Crime and Violence in Britain, 1748–1753* (New Haven, Conn.: Yale University Press, 2012), p. 36.
[12] *PP*, 'Report from the Select Committee on the poor laws', 1818, with an appendix, p. 9 (parlipapers.chadwyck.co.uk, 2 Jan. 2014).

wave by demobilised soldiers and sailors meant that violent thefts received disproportionate attention in the press, accounting for half of all crime reports in the newspapers.[13] The result was that at the Old Bailey theft with violence accounted for a growing proportion of all prosecutions (rising from 3.8 per cent of all offences in 1747 to 13.0 per cent in 1750). At the same time, we cannot dismiss the possibility that the amount of actual crime committed, driven by the real hardship of the demobilised, unemployed and low paid, did increase.[14] Certainly growing demands for, and expenditure on, poor relief had a substantive basis in the needs of individual men and women; and while costs rose and fell with the price of grain, the overall trend was upwards. Poor relief was more 'demand led' than was criminal justice. In between, sharing characteristics of both crime and poverty, vagrancy encompassed both immediate responses driven by perceptions of a problem and changes in the actual life experiences of the poor. It was the combination of the real pressures generated by poverty and crime and the distinctive character of elite perceptions of these problems which shaped the ensuing responses. In turn, the actual impact of these new initiatives was significantly influenced by the responses of plebeian London.

The celebrity highwayman

One of the ways in which criminals actively shaped the distinct and growing anxiety about their activities can be found in the audacious, publicity-seeking practices of some highwaymen. Amplified by newspapers and other publications that were always keen to retail 'true crime' to a paying audience, accounts of robberies called attention to the apparent impunity with which crimes were committed, while raising the even more alarming possibility that, owing to the sympathetic manner in which they were portrayed, elite Londoners were not fully committed to bringing these criminals to justice. In the past, in addition to individual publications, highwaymen had taken advantage of the sympathetic attitudes of the publisher of the *Ordinary's Accounts* to get their story told. However, following the appointment of a new publisher of the *Accounts* in 1745 and a new Ordinary, John Taylor, in 1747, the *Accounts* became more closely guarded against attempts by criminals to justify themselves to the public.[15] Instead, they relied much more heavily on separately

---

[13] Ward, 'Print culture and responses to crime', p. 62.
[14] Rogers, *Mayhem*, pp. 43, 46, 51, argues for a real increase in crime, but this is impossible to prove.
[15] Ward, 'Print culture and responses to crime', p. 74.

published criminal biographies. Between 1747 and 1754, the lives of at least ten English (primarily London) highwaymen were published in separate printed pamphlets; in some cases in more than one version. Six of these lives were purportedly written by the robbers themselves, or at least compiled on the basis of information provided by them. While the criminal voices found in these pamphlets were certainly mediated, publishers went to great lengths to certify their authenticity. Readers of the *Memoirs* of Dennis Neale, for instance, were invited to view Neale's original manuscript at the printer's.[16] Priced at between 2 pence and 1 shilling, these pamphlets were available to a broad reading public, and they were popular. Several were published in multiple editions; those of William Parsons and Dennis Neale went into three editions within a year, while there were eleven editions of *The Discoveries of John Poulter* in just the first two years after publication.[17]

By retailing 'intrigues', 'extraordinary adventures' and 'pranks', these biographies provided light-hearted entertainment at a time of anxiety about violent crime. William Parsons, hanged at Tyburn in February 1751 for returning from transportation following his arrest for highway robbery, was described in his *Memoirs* as 'perhaps as great a Genius for Tricking as any Man in the World', and the *Memoirs*' publication was justified on the grounds that 'the artful manner he supplied himself from several young Ladies in Newfoundland, deserves the Publick's Notice'.[18] The text itself consisted largely of tales of his amorous adventures, rather than his crimes, the violence of which was markedly underplayed ('he robb'd several People, but always in the Night . . . but as nothing remarkable happened during these robberies, it is immaterial to give a Detail of the particular Circumstances').[19]

Highwaymen used these pamphlets as a form of self-justification, and a means of defending their reputations. Parsons claimed he had been denied support from his wealthy father, creating an 'errant necessity that urged him to [rob] for a subsistence', while others, including Thomas Munn, John Hall alias Rich, and William Farrer, claimed they had been corrupted by the bad influence of others, and/or that the robbery for which they had been condemned was their first and only offence.[20] Others, particularly Nicholas Mooney and Matthew Lee, claimed to have

[16] *LL*, set, 'Dennis Neale'; Dennis O'Neale, *Memoirs of the Life and Remarkable Exploits of the Noted Dennis Neale* (1754), 'Advertisement'.
[17] See John Poulter, *The Discoveries of John Poulter, alias Baxter* (1754).
[18] *LL*, set, 'William Parsons'.
[19] William Parsons, *Memoirs of the Life and Adventures of William Parsons* (1751), pp. 20, 57.
[20] William Parsons, *A Genuine, Impartial and Authentick Account of the Life of William Parsons* (1751), p. 39; Thomas Munn, *The Life of Thomas Munn . . . who was Executed*

been reformed following their arrests.[21] Lee was the subject of a biography attributed to John Wesley in which he repented all his sins following a conversion experience. Even this tale of apparent redemption was subject to spin. While Lee's biography claimed he pleaded guilty at his trial because he refused to lie following his conversion, in fact his plea was not guilty.[22]

More subversively, as in the 1720s, some highwaymen justified their crimes as acts of social justice, claiming they were prompted by the 'necessity' of maintaining their alleged gentlemanly status, and that their actions were no worse than the crimes of their social superiors. Some of these legitimising notions date from before the ideal of the 'gentleman highwayman' was first articulated. But that they remained current at mid-century can be seen in the ballad *The Flying Highwayman*, which celebrated the exploits of 'Young Morgan', 'a flashy blade', with both social aspirations and a social conscience:

> Soon he became a Gentleman,
> And left off driving Asses.
> I scorn poor people for to rob,
> I thought it so my duty;
> But when I met the rich and gay,
> On them I made my Booty.[23]

Morgan is arrested and sentenced to die, but like Macheath in the *Beggar's Opera*, he is reprieved at the last minute.

The mixed messages about robbery disseminated at this time are most fully embodied in publications about the most famous highwayman of this era. James Maclaine largely succeeded in portraying himself as a gentleman, with the *Gentleman's Magazine* reporting that he 'had handsome lodgings in St James's Street, at two guineas a week, and passed for an Irish gentleman at £700 a year'; the newspapers described him as 'genteel'.[24] Even before Maclaine emerged into the limelight following

---

with *John Hall* (1750), pp. 19–20; William Farrer, *A Genuine Account of the Confession and Dying Words of William Farrer* (2nd edn, 1747?), p. 9.

[21] *LL*, set, 'Nicholas Mooney', and set, 'Matthew Lee'.

[22] *LL*, Old Bailey Proceedings, 14 September 1752 (t17520914-38), and [John Wesley], *Some Account of the Life and Death of Matthew Lee* (2nd edn, London, 1752), p. 10.

[23] *The Flying Highwayman* (*c.* 1750), reprinted in John Holloway and Joan Black, eds., *Later English Broadsides* (London: Routledge & Kegan Paul, 1975), pp. 103–4, and online at *Outlaws and Highwaymen* (outlawsandhighwaymen.com/flying.htm, 2 Jan. 2014). Although Holloway and Black date this ballad *c.* 1780, the ESTC gives it the earlier (and more plausible) date of around 1750.

[24] *LL*, set, 'James Maclaine'; *Gentleman's Magazine*, 20 (1750), p. 391; *The Whitehall Evening Post Or, London Intelligencer*, 26–28 July 1750 (Burney Collection: www.galegroup.com, 1 Jan. 2014).

his arrest, his social aspirations were evident in the letter he wrote to Horace Walpole following his robbery of Walpole in Hyde Park in November 1749, during which Maclaine's pistol was accidentally fired. Written on gilt-edged paper (but poorly spelled and ungrammatical), the letter assured Walpole that no harm had been intended and justified the crime and the ransom he demanded for the return of Walpole's watch and seals on the grounds that 'we Are Reduced by the misfortunes of the world and obliged to have Recourse to this method of getting money', before promising to repay the small sum taken from Walpole's footman.[25] Similarly, when Maclaine and his accomplice William Plunket robbed the Salisbury coach, the crime for which Maclaine was arrested and tried, the two robbers made a great show of acting 'politely' and once again claimed 'that it was necessity [that] forced them upon those hazardous enterprizes'. Plunket put away his pistol in order to reassure the passengers, and, 'for fear of frightening the Lady, without forcing her out of the coach, took what small matter she offered without further search'.[26]

Following his arrest Maclaine achieved celebrity status by playing to the gallery during his preliminary examination and at his Old Bailey trial, thereby obtaining the attention of the press. Portraying himself as a gentleman who had fallen on hard times, he evoked the tears of watching gentlewomen and men, obtaining both their sympathy and their financial support.[27] By actively manipulating the public presentation of his case and his person, and through an account of his behaviour in prison penned by a sympathetic dissenting minister, he shaped the representation of his story and successfully generated widespread sympathy.[28] Some of his victims, including Horace Walpole and Lord Eglington, refused to testify against him in court (and were praised for doing so).[29] And at least nine 'gentleman of credit' and some ladies provided character witnesses at his trial.[30] The Sunday following his conviction 3,000 people visited him in prison, and Horace Walpole commented that

---

[25] *The Yale Edition of Horace Walpole's Correspondence*, ed. W. S. Lewis, 48 vols. (New Haven, Conn.: Yale University Press, 1980), XL, pp. 63–5 (images.library.yale.edu/ hwcorrespondence, 2 Jan. 2014).

[26] *A Genuine Account of the Life and Actions of James McLean, Highwayman* (1750), p. 11; *Complete History of James McLean, the Gentleman Highwayman* (1750), p. 52.

[27] *Complete History*, p. 53; British Museum, print, *Newgate's Lamentation or the Ladies' Last Farewell of Maclean* (1750), 1851,0308.411.

[28] [Fifield] Allen, *An Account of the Behaviour of Mr James Maclaine* (1750).

[29] *Walpole's Correspondence*, Vol. XX, p. 188; *Genuine Account*, pp. 12–14.

[30] The *Old Bailey Proceedings* failed to report the ladies' testimony, but see the text accompanying the image: BM, *James Macleane the Gentleman Highwayman at the Bar* (1750), 1935,0413.101.

Figure 5.4 *James Macleane, the Gentleman Highwayman at the Bar*, 1750. BM 1935,0413.101. © Trustees of the British Museum.

'you can't conceive of this ridiculous rage there is of going to Newgate'. Some of his elite visitors apparently attempted to secure him a pardon, but they were unsuccessful.[31]

[31] *Walpole's Correspondence*, Vol. XX, p. 199; *Genuine Account*, p. iii.

Not everyone was taken in. The case prompted concern that the popularity of gentlemen highwaymen was subverting attempts to crack down on robbery during the post-war crisis. As John Taylor, Ordinary of Newgate, observed of Maclaine:

> though he has been called the Gentleman Highwayman, and in his Dress and Equipage very much affected the fine Gentleman, yet to a Man acquainted with good Breeding, that can distinguish it from Impudence and Affectation, there was very little in his Address or Behaviour, that could entitle him to that Character.[32]

Similarly, *A Genuine Account of the Life and Actions of James Maclean, Highwayman*, a pamphlet written with the express purpose of seeing him hanged, complained that 'he has so far wrought himself into the esteem of persons of rank, that they have not only been induced to contribute to support him, but to solicit and use their utmost effort to save him', when in fact 'by the laws of this country he is undoubtedly to be deemed an enemy to society'.[33] Even Horace Walpole, one of his most sympathetic victims, was moved to observe that 'his profession is no joke'.[34]

In short, at the same moment that the wave of prosecutions which followed the peace in the autumn of 1748 signalled rising anxieties about violent crime, the activities of the 'gentlemen of the highway' evidenced continuing sympathy for a particular type of robber. This ambivalence could not be allowed to remain unchallenged. As Fifield Allen observed, 'robberies were so frequent, committed too by people of a genteel appearance like his', that Maclaine and others like him simply had to be hanged.[35] In one biography of the highwayman and robber William Parsons, the author felt obliged to defend the decision to prosecute him for returning from transportation, observing that bringing him to justice was 'absolutely necessary for the safety of the community'.[36] That this point even needed to be made suggests just how effective the self-presentation of these highwaymen had become. The publicity they achieved contributed to the growing sense of moral panic among the authorities, forcing them to develop new strategies to address the problem.

---

[32] LL, Ordinary of Newgate Prison: Ordinary's Accounts, 3 October 1750 (OA175010035010030003).
[33] *Genuine Account*, p. iii. See also *Complete History*, p. 65.
[34] *Walpole's Correspondence*, Vol. XX, p. 188.
[35] Allen, *Account of the Behaviour*, p. 14.
[36] LL, set, 'William Parsons'; *Genuine, Impartial and Authentick Account*, p. 42.

Henry Fielding's great plan

At the centre of the post-war response to crime was Henry Fielding, already a well-known dramatist and novelist and, from 1748, an active and ambitious justice of the peace. Fielding was already serving as a publicist for the government in 1748 when his patron the Duke of Bedford secured his appointment as justice of the peace in Westminster, and following Bedford's assistance in meeting the £100 property qualification, in Middlesex the following January. As Fielding told Bedford, 'without this Addition [appointment to the Middlesex bench] I can not completely serve the Government in that Office'.[37] From December 1748 Fielding was living in Bow Street, in the house formerly occupied by Thomas De Veil, and, like De Veil, he became 'court justice', the leading metropolitan justice charged with providing advice and support to the government, particularly on politically sensitive issues. As Malvin Zirker remarks, he was 'a political appointee whose voice could never be entirely his own'.[38]

Fielding hit the ground running immediately after he took the oath of office in January 1749. In March he was elected chairman of the Westminster sessions, and his first charge to the grand jury was delivered in June and published in July.[39] Fielding's ideas about poverty and crime are best known from his social policy writings, but these were informed by his day-to-day work at Bow Street. Evidence of his extensive judicial activity can be found not only throughout the Middlesex, Westminster and Old Bailey sessions records but also through his attempts at self-publicity, in reports he planted in newspapers such as the *Public Advertiser* and *Whitehall Evening Post*, and most substantially in his own *Covent Garden Journal*, published between 4 January and 25 November 1752. According to his more sympathetic biographers, Fielding 'exercised as much latitude as possible under the law' and 'temper[ed] justice with mercy', occasionally discharging or bailing prostitutes and petty thieves rather than committing them to prison, and sometimes relieving beggars rather than punishing them.[40] Fielding certainly promoted this

---

[37] Fielding to Bedford, 13 December 1748 (Ms. Letters, vol. xxii, fol. 95, Bedford Estates Office), transcribed in Martin C. Battestin and Ruthe R. Battestin, 'Fielding, Bedford and the Westminster election of 1749', *Eighteenth-Century Studies*, 11:2 (1977–8), 178.

[38] Henry Fielding, *An Enquiry into the Causes of the Late Encrease in Robbers and Related Writings*, ed. Malvin R. Zirker (Wesleyan edn, Oxford: Clarendon, 1988), p. xviii.

[39] Henry Fielding, *A Charge Delivered to the Grand Jury... on Thursday the 29th of June* (1749).

[40] Lance Bertelsen, *Henry Fielding at Work: Magistrate, Businessman, Writer* (New York: Palgrave, 2000), p. 16; Martin C. Battestin with Ruthe R. Battestin, *Henry Fielding: A Life* (London: Routledge, 1989), pp. 462–3, 551–2, 565. For examples of such

sympathetic view of his judicial practice, later suggesting that, unlike 'trading justices', his object was 'composing, instead of inflaming, the quarrels of porters and beggars', and claiming that he generally refused 'to take a shilling from a man who most undoubtedly would not have had another left'.[41]

Yet there was a darker side to Fielding's activities. He did show real sympathy for some young girls seduced into prostitution, as when he described the case of Mary Parkington in the *Covent Garden Journal*: she was 'a very beautiful Girl of sixteen Years of Age' who was 'seduced by a young Sea-Officer' and taken to a brothel run by Philip Church. However, his role was compromised by exposing her name and circumstances in print, thereby destroying her reputation.[42] Moreover, any sympathy Fielding may have shown for petty offenders was balanced by his merciless pursuit of more serious criminals. He led numerous raids against what he believed were 'gangs' of street robbers, highwaymen and housebreakers, including the 'Royal Family', led by Thomas Jones alias Harper in 1749, and worked tirelessly to ensure their conviction and execution.[43] Fielding also created the Bow Street Runners as an effective tool in his campaign against felons.

It is the severely judgemental side of Fielding's judicial personality which shines through in his social pamphlets. Despite the inclusion of many 'low' characters and scenes of licence in his fiction (including *Tom Jones*, published in February 1749, just as he began work as a justice), and the complicated and heart-breaking stories he heard on a daily basis at Bow Street, there is a noticeable lack of 'irony and ambivalence' in his other writings. In his widely read pronouncements on social policy, it was his role as a political appointee and self-appointed 'censor' of metropolitan morals that came to dominate.[44]

Famously addicted to chewing tobacco, profligate with his own money and that of his friends, gout-ridden from decades of self-indulgence, Henry Fielding knew precisely where the blame lay for the ills of society. He argued that the perfect ancient balance of the English constitution had been corrupted by the ever-growing luxury and power of the poor.

hearings, see Henry Fielding, *The Covent-Garden Journal and a Plan of the Universal Register-Office*, ed. Bertrand A. Goldgar (Wesleyan edn, Oxford: Clarendon Press, 1988), Appendix I, pp. 415, 422, 424, 426, 444.

[41] Henry Fielding, *The Journal of a Voyage to Lisbon* (1755), p. 23.

[42] *Covent-Garden Journal*, Appendix I, 7 (25 January 1752). As Bertelsen observes, 'such narratives not only provoke sympathy but also invite the reader to exercise and enjoy textual/sexual power over women': *Fielding at Work*, pp. 21–3.

[43] *LL*, set, 'Thomas Jones'; Battestin with Battestin, *Fielding*, pp. 464, 501, 511; Ronald Paulson, *The Life of Henry Fielding* (Oxford: Wiley, 2000), p. 583.

[44] Paulson, *Life of Henry Fielding*, p. 265.

He lay responsibility for the problems faced by London squarely at the feet of 'the mob'; of that 'very large and powerful body which form the fourth Estate in this Community', whose ambitious powers he believed extended to securing control over the execution of the laws, 'particularly in the Case of the Gin-Act some Years ago', and to 'stifling' the activities of informers.[45] In his most substantial work on social policy, *An Enquiry into the Causes of the Late Increase in Robbers*, published in 1751 at the height of the post-war panic over violent crime, he detailed how the 'Dregs of the People' had been transformed: 'The narrowness of their Fortune is changed into Wealth; the Simplicity of their Manners into Craft; their Frugality into Luxury; their Humility into Pride, and their Subjection into Equality.'[46] In Fielding's view, this doleful corruption, made possible by high wages, was manifest in their attendance at plays (some of which Fielding himself had written), pleasure gardens and masquerades, and in gin drinking and gambling; all of which led to crime via moral and financial bankruptcy. Moreover, Fielding believed the poor's 'wandering habits' placed them beyond the oversight of the magistracy. The 'mob' needed to be brought to heel and disciplined to unrelieved labour: 'throwing the Reins on the Neck of Idleness'.[47]

Fielding undoubtedly had a 'conservative social outlook', and many of his solutions were the nostrums retailed in social welfare pamphlets published over the preceding two centuries. However, there are two facets of Fielding's writings that are distinctive.[48] First, he constantly and self-servingly emphasises the role of the justice of the peace and the county bench as the layer of government to be entrusted with additional responsibility. Almost all of Fielding's solutions to social disorder involved shifting large amounts of power and expenditure from the parishes to the bench. And second, he takes an unusually draconian approach in advocating changes that would undermine the rights of defendants in court, and the poor to freedom of movement. He sought to reform the major systems of the social policy state – poor relief, felony prosecution and vagrancy – to ensure that those whose place it was to labour would suffer their poverty without cavil or complaint and without recourse to begging or theft.

---

[45] *Covent-Garden Journal*, 47 (13 June 1752), and 49 (20 June 1752).
[46] Fielding, *Enquiry into the Causes*, pp. 6, xxii.
[47] Fielding, *Enquiry into the Causes* (2nd edn, 1751), p. 102.
[48] Fielding, *Enquiry into the Causes*, p. xxii. See also Nicholas Rogers, 'Confronting the crime wave: the debate over social reform and regulation, 1749–1753', in Lee Davison et al., eds., *Stilling the Grumbling Hive: The Response to Social and Economic Problems in England, 1689–1750* (Stroud: Alan Sutton, 1992), pp. 82–7; and Rogers, *Mayhem*, ch. 7.

The earliest clear statement of the remedies Fielding advocated can be found in the draft of a bill he submitted to the Lord Chancellor, Philip Hardwicke, in 1749, some six months after he took up his role as 'court justice'. The bill advocated the creation of a 'commission' of justices empowered to oversee the night watch, and, if implemented, would have enhanced the powers of watchmen by providing them with arms and authorising them to arrest anyone found with a 'dangerous weapon', as well as 'all suspicious Persons ... standing in the streets Lanes or bye allys'.[49] Two years later, in 1751, Fielding extended his analysis and his solutions in the *Enquiry*, before rounding off his consideration of poverty and crime with his *Proposal for Making an effectual provision for the Poor*, published in 1753.[50]

Although historians have concentrated on his attitudes to policing and crime, the majority of Fielding's published work on social policy focused on the interwoven issues of poverty and vagrancy. He felt the main weakness in the system of poor relief lay in the inadequacies and failures of parish officers, who had neglected their legal obligation to set the poor to work,[51] and proposed a 'county house' able to accommodate 5,000 people, where the able-bodied and unemployed were to be set to work, while the vicious and workshy would be put to hard labour in a new 'county house of correction', able to imprison and set to hard labour some 600 vagrants.[52] And to make this pabulum of oppression work, he outlined a revision of the system of settlement and certificates to ensure that all migratory poor were subject to universal enforced labour, and advocated beefing up the laws against vagrants to ensure they received appropriate corporal punishment. None of these proposals was new, but Fielding's combined workhouse and house of correction did mark a new high point in relation to size and levels of complexity. It prefigured even the largest of nineteenth-century institutions and, if created, would have given the Middlesex bench an unprecedented budget and staff.

While poverty and vagrancy were the main focus of Fielding's pamphlets, he also included substantial proposals for the reform of arrest, felony prosecution and execution. Here Fielding was slightly more innovative, although he was 'preoccupied with the repressive aspects of penal policy'.[53] Receivers of stolen goods were to be prosecuted even when

[49] The full text of the bill is reproduced at Battestin, *Fielding*, pp. 706–11. For the original manuscript, see: BL: Add. Ms. 33054, ff. 406–13.

[50] Henry Fielding, *A Proposal for Making an Effectual Provision for the Poor* (1753).

[51] Fielding, *Enquiry into the Causes*, pp. 93–4.

[52] Fielding, *Proposal for Making*, p. 17.

[53] Leon Radzinowicz, *A History of English Criminal Law and its Administration from 1750*, Vol. I (London: Macmillan, 1948), p. 420.

the thief was acquitted; justices were to be given new powers to arrest suspicious persons; greater weight was to be placed on the role of pre-trial examination and interrogation; and in court the evidence of accomplices was to be given precedence over that of character witnesses. And once a defendant had been convicted, Fielding wished to limit the role of the royal pardon and to shift the place of executions from Tyburn to just outside the Old Bailey, and to conduct them in private as a means of eliminating the carnivalesque character of hanging days. Overall, he sought to make executions quicker, more certain and more terrible.[54]

Henry Fielding's great plan, including armed watchmen, forced labour for the poor and more frequent judicial murders, overseen by an increasingly powerful bench of magistrates, exemplifies one important strand in the thinking of elite Londoners in response to the post-war crisis and encompasses a set of ideas which would inform the evolution of social and criminal policy for the rest of the century. In the short term, its importance can be seen in the publishing success of the *Enquiry* – the first printing of 1,500 copies sold out quickly and a second of 2,000 was available within three weeks. It was 'more frequently cited than any other social pamphlet during the early fifties'.[55] But Fielding had his critics among Londoners of all social classes. While the long-term influence of his ideas on the evolution of policy was substantial, their direct and short-term effect was much more limited.[56] His reputation was undermined by his involvement in two scandals which raised questions about his competence and independence as a justice: the execution of Bosavern Penlez in 1749 and the Elizabeth Canning case four years later.

In early July 1749 thousands of sailors destroyed brothels on the Strand after two of their number had been robbed in one of the houses, but it was Fielding's zealous defence of the decision to execute one of the rioters which turned a traditional riot into a major crisis.[57] After a superficial examination of the first prisoners arrested (while a mob gathered outside his door), Fielding committed them to Newgate prison. Ultimately only three of the rioters were tried at the Old Bailey the following September, charged with violating the 1715 Riot Act. In spite of questionable prosecution evidence (one witness declared 'Upon my word . . . for my part I would not hang a dog or a cat upon their evidence') and good character references, two men were convicted: John Wilson

---

[54] Fielding, *Enquiry into the Causes*, pp. 145–99.
[55] Battestin with Battestin, *Fielding*, p. 521; Rogers, 'Confronting the crime wave', p. 82.
[56] Battestin with Battestin, *Fielding*, p. 521; Fielding, *Enquiry into the Causes*, p. lxviii.
[57] For the riots and subsequent prosecution at the Old Bailey, see Tim Hitchcock and Robert Shoemaker, *Tales from the Hanging Court* (London: Hodder Arnold, 2006), pp. 69–79.

and Bosavern Penlez.[58] Though the jury recommended mercy, both were sentenced to death. These sentences provoked widespread outrage: there was substantial sympathy for the rioters' aims (destruction of the brothels), and it was felt both Wilson and Penlez (a journeyman shoe-maker and perukemaker respectively) were men of good character who had been accidentally caught up in the riots. A substantial petitioning campaign led to a last-minute pardon for Wilson, but Penlez was hanged.

Even before the execution, Fielding was criticised for his role in the case, with some even suggesting that he was protecting the brothels because he accepted bribes from their owners.[59] More damning, how-ever, was the evidence that later emerged of his role in ensuring Penlez was refused a pardon. It was alleged that Penlez had originally been arrested in possession of a bundle of linen taken from one of the brothels, and although he had been indicted for burglary he had not been tried for this offence at the Old Bailey. At the last minute Fielding brought evidence of the theft to the attention of the Privy Council, and against the backdrop of the crime wave, Penlez's fate was sealed. Fielding's behind-the-scenes role became public when he published his *True State of the Case of Bosavern Penlez* in November, where he claimed, to his 'satisfaction', that his lobbying was responsible for the decision to pardon Wilson 'as an Object of Mercy' and execute Penlez as 'an Object of Justice'.[60]

The execution of Penlez proved to be crucial in the following month's Westminster by-election, which the government very nearly lost. Westminster had a broad franchise and a history of radical politics, and was both one of the most important and one of the most fiercely contested parliamentary constituencies in the country. The opposition candidate in 1749, George Vandeput, represented a faction which styled itself the 'Independent Electors of Westminster', and his supporters were typically middle-class householders of the sort who had opposed reforms of the night watch and defended open vestries in the preceding decades.[61] In contrast, Vandeput's opponent, the court candidate Gran-ville Leveson-Gower (Viscount Trentham), supported by Fielding, was tarred by his role in the Penlez affair (having failed to support the campaign for a pardon). Penlez featured frequently in the opposition's election literature, and his ghost even appeared in a procession, in which

---

[58] *LL*, set, 'Bosavern Penlez'; Old Bailey Proceedings, 6 September 1749 (t17490906-4).
[59] *Old England*, 15 July 1749, 25 November 1749 (Burney Collection: www.galegroup. com, 1 Jan. 2014).
[60] Henry Fielding, *A True State of the Case of Bosavern Penlez* (1749), p. 54.
[61] Rogers, *Mayhem*, pp. 76–7.

'he frequently sat up and harangued the populace for his unhappy fate'.[62] Some of Vandeput's strongest support came from the parishes where the brothels were located and the Penlez riots took place: St Clement Danes, St Paul Covent Garden and St Martin in the Fields.[63] Allying themselves with the sailors who attacked the brothels, these voters joined the public demonstrations in Vandeput's support. Worryingly for Fielding, these were the very parishes most directly served by his Bow Street office.

In the end Trentham narrowly won the election, but the events of that autumn led the Duke of Richmond, Sir Thomas Robinson, to worry about the increasing powers of the mob:

> I think in all future Elections the power of the Court is weakened & the lower Class of voters will determine Victory which ever side they take . . . [they] will be influenced from popular Cryes or Caprice or Money, for when we see what . . . *Penley's Ghost* has done at this Juncture, can any Juncture be without Scarecrows of such base materials[?][64]

Four years later Fielding embroiled himself in another very public controversy, this time over the validity of the claims by Elizabeth Canning that she had been kidnapped and held prisoner in a house of ill repute for four weeks.[65] Canning's claim initially resulted in the conviction of Mary Squires and Susannah Wells for robbery.[66] But eventually this verdict was overturned, and Canning herself was convicted of perjury.[67] The dispute over the truth of Canning's claims led to a major pamphlet war and debate in the newspapers lasting several months; the essayist Allan Ramsay claimed it was 'the conversation of every alehouse within the bills of mortality'.[68] This case has attracted substantial scholarly interest, but not enough attention has been paid to the damage to Fielding's reputation caused by his role in coercing Virtue Hall into testifying against Squires and Wells in the original trial, testimony which she later recanted, leading to the trial of Canning.[69]

---

[62] *T–t–m and V–d–t, A Collection of the Advertisements and Hand-Bills, Serious, Satyrical and Humorous, Published on Both Sides during the Election for the City and Liberty of Westminster* (Dublin, 1749), pp. 47–8.

[63] Rogers, *Mayhem*, p. 76. See also *LL*, Westminster Historical Database.

[64] Quoted in Rogers, *Mayhem*, p. 87.

[65] *LL*, set, 'Elizabeth Canning'.

[66] *LL*, Old Bailey Proceedings, 21 February 1753 (t17530221-47).

[67] *LL*, Old Bailey Proceedings, 24 April 1754 (t17540424-60).

[68] Allan Ramsay, *A Letter to the Right Honourable the Earl of – Concerning the Affair of Elizabeth Canning* (1753), p. 38.

[69] For the most comprehensive treatment of the case, see Judith Moore, *The Appearance of Truth: The Story of Elizabeth Canning and Eighteenth-Century Narrative* (Newark: University of Delaware Press, 1994).

Once again, Fielding's attempts to defend his actions in print only exacerbated the situation.[70]

Fielding was a divisive figure, and his behaviour in the Penlez and Canning cases, when combined with his aggressive approach to the office of justice of the peace, stimulated opposition. He was caricatured for 'his stern and arrogant demeanour on the bench, his habit of declaiming with his jaws crammed with tobacco, his way of favouring the rich and great while bullying the lower classes'.[71] As a result of these very public challenges to his authority, some of those who were summoned to appear before him were energised to fight back. In his early days as a justice, following the Penlez riot but before his execution, some defendants incarcerated on Fielding's warrants challenged their commitments under the Habeas Corpus Act, including Samuel Cross.[72] Fielding committed Cross to prison following a brawl in which James Burford died, but Cross petitioned 'that he may be either Tryed Bailed or Discharged' for 'the Said Supposed offence Pursuant to the Direction's of the Habeas Corpus Act'.[73] The following year Charles Pratt was more successful when, after he was accused of stealing a mourning ring and committed by Fielding to New Prison, he protested his innocence and lodged a similar petition (he was not tried).[74] In the next two years at least seven appeals were launched against Fielding's summary convictions, including those by four scavengers, who claimed their prosecution for not fulfilling their duties was itself 'illegal', and by Israel Walker, a housekeeper and dealer in brandy and other spirituous liquors.[75] Committed by Fielding to the house of correction as a 'Rogue & Vagabond', Walker claimed he had been 'unjustly charged' with breaking a watchman's lantern and playing at unlawful games.[76] These challenges to Fielding's authority may have provided him with additional motivation for reinforcing his powers through the promotion of the Bow Street Runners, but they may have also contributed to the popular opposition they encountered.

Parliament's response

Two days before the publication of Fielding's *Enquiry*, the king addressed the issue of rising crime and disorder in his speech opening parliament on

---

[70] *A Clear State of the Case of Elizabeth Canning* (1753); Fielding, *Enquiry into the Causes*, pp. cv–cvi, cxi–cxiii.
[71] Battestin with Battestin, *Fielding*, p. 529.
[72] *LL*, set, 'Samuel Cross'.
[73] *LL*, Middlesex Sessions: Sessions Papers, September 1749 (LMSMPS503970110).
[74] *LL*, Middlesex Sessions: Sessions Papers, October 1750 (LMSMPS504060016).
[75] *LL*, Middlesex Sessions: Sessions Papers, April 1751 (LMSMPS504100020).
[76] *LL*, Middlesex Sessions: Sessions Papers, February 1751 (LMSMPS504090023).

17 January 1751, exhorting the Lords and Commons 'to make the best use of the present state of tranquillity . . . for enforcing the execution of the laws, and for suppressing those Outrages and Violences, which are inconsistent with all good Order and Government'. In response, the Commons set up a committee (the 'Felonies Committee'), to investigate 'the Laws in being, which relate to Felonies, and other Offences against the Peace'. Six weeks later their remit was extended to 'the Defects, the Repeal, or Amendment of the Laws relating to the ... Poor'.[77] This committee was the first 'national, central investigation into the issue of crime and justice as a whole' ever conducted, and it was all the more remarkable for considering the issues of poor relief and settlement in the same report.[78] And yet the legislation which resulted was of limited consequence. Owing to both elite opposition and anticipated plebeian resistance to more ambitious measures, and actual plebeian opposition to the implementation of the statutes that were passed, the aspirations of the committee were not realised.

The committee worked fast and in April reported a series of twenty-five resolutions identifying the defects of the laws concerning criminal justice; adding a further two substantive resolutions on poor relief in June.[79] The most remarkable feature of these resolutions is that, like Fielding's *Enquiry* (which had little direct influence on the committee's findings), the responsibility for crime and poverty was placed firmly on the lower class, and measures were proposed to give magistrates greater control over 'suspicious' characters.[80] According to the committee, both 'the Increase of Thefts and Robberies of late' and the recent increase in the expense of poor relief resulted directly from the 'Habit of Idleness, in which the lower People have been bred often from their Youth'. The committee went on specifically to blame 'the Multitude of Places of Entertainment for the lower Sort of People' and 'Gaming amongst the inferior Rank of People' as 'incitement[s] to theft', before identifying the failure of the system of legal 'Settlement' to prevent the poor from wandering and poor parenting for propagating 'a new Race of Chargeable Poor, from Generation to Generation'.[81]

This was a good time for domestic legislation. It was peacetime and the government had firm control over the House of Commons. However, in

---

[77] *PP, Journals of the House of Commons*, 17 January 1750, p. 3, 1 February 1750, p. 27, 13 March 1750, p. 123 (parlipapers.chadwyck.co.uk, 2 Jan. 2014).

[78] Ward, 'Print culture and responses to crime', p. 145. For this committee, see also Richard Connors, '"The grand inquest of the nation": parliamentary committees and social policy in mid-eighteenth-century England', *Parliamentary History*, 14:3 (1995), 285–313; Rogers, *Mayhem*, pp. 173–81.

[79] *PP, Journals of the House of Commons*, 13 June 1751, p. 289.

[80] Henry Amory, 'Henry Fielding and the criminal legislation of 1751–2', *Philological Quarterly*, 50 (1971), 185; Battestin with Battestin, *Fielding*, p. 519.

[81] *PP, Journals of the House of Commons*, 23 April 1751, p. 190, and 13 June 1751, p. 289.

comparison with the breadth of the committee's recommendations, the legislative result was minimal, as 'the seamless web' of resolutions was chopped 'into legislative rags' and its radical poor law proposals were simply ignored.[82] In part this reflects the impediments to law making at this time, but it also reflects the specific pressures under which MPs were working. Not only were there concerns about the costs of implementing new legislation, and its impact on the vocal and competing interests of the parishes, counties, the City of London and justices of the peace, but MPs also anticipated that new measures would be subverted by plebeian opposition. This was particularly relevant in the case of the dockyards hard labour bill. Nonetheless, three important statutes were passed: the Gin Act (1751), Disorderly Houses Act (1752) and Murder Act (1752).

The 1751 Gin Act did not emanate from the work of the Felonies Committee, but it was a product of the same reforming impetus. The bill was discussed in the whole house the same day the recommendations of the Felonies Committee were presented, and it addressed many of the same issues. Following the passage of the 1743 Gin Act,[83] overall consumption of gin had been stable. Concern among reformers about its deleterious effects had nonetheless continued, and the perception of a post-war crime wave gave reformers a new opportunity to make their case. 'The strategy', as Patrick Dillon argues, 'was to tie gin-drinking in with the crime wave'.[84] In a coordinated campaign starting in early 1751, parliament was besieged by pamphlets and petitions, making arguments familiar from the 1730s that excessive drinking by the *lower class* was responsible for a spate of social problems.

Fielding's was the first high-profile intervention. In section two of his *Enquiry*, he identified drunkenness as a key manifestation of the problem of the 'Luxury of the Vulgar', because it led to 'so many temporal Mischiefs ... amongst which are very frequently Robbery and Murder itself'. A fortnight later, Isaac Maddox, the Bishop of Worcester, published a sermon, *The Expediency of Preventive Wisdom*, which made similar arguments, but paid more attention to gin's role in infant mortality while also arguing that if successful, plebeian resistance to the Gin Acts would lead to social levelling.[85] As if on cue, Hogarth's *Gin Lane* followed a

---

[82] Amory, 'Henry Fielding', 178.

[83] 16 Geo. II c. 8, 'An Act for repealing certain duties on spirituous liquors'.

[84] Patrick Dillon, *The Much-Lamented Death of Madam Geneva: The Eighteenth-Century Gin Craze* (London: Headline Book Publishing, 2003), p. 246.

[85] Fielding, *Enquiry into the Causes*, pp. 20–34; Isaac Maddox, *The Expediency of Preventive Wisdom. A Sermon Preached before the Right Honourable the Lord-Mayor, the Aldermen, and Governors of Several Hospitals of the City of London ... With a Dedication and an Appendix concerning Spirituous Liquors* (1751), p. 17; Isaac Maddox, *An Epistle to the Right Honourable the Lord Mayor, Aldermen and Common Council of the City of London* (1751), pp. 14–15.

Figure 5.5 William Hogarth, *Gin Lane*, 1751. BM S,2.122. © Trustees
of the British Museum.

fortnight later, with its evocative image of poverty, chaos and death
juxtaposed with the order and respectability of *Beer Street*.

Despite Hogarth's professed ambition to use his prints to reform the poor
directly, the real point of these prints and pamphlets was to bring the problem
to the attention of parliament and those responsible for governing London.[86]

---

[86] *General Advertiser*, 13 February 1751, quoted by Jenny Uglow, *Hogarth: A Life and a
World* (London: Faber and Faber, 1997), p. 494.

Figure 5.6 William Hogarth, *Beer Street*, 1751. BM S,2.122. © Trustees of the British Museum.

In this they succeeded: London's parish vestries, along with the Cities of London and Westminster and the Middlesex sessions, were prompted to petition parliament. The minutes of the vestry of St Clement Danes reveal that this was an organised campaign: the vestry met on 4 March to 'to take the Opinion of the Inhabitants whether they will Join with the rest of the

Inhabitants the City and Liberty of Westmr. in presenting a Petition to Parliament to Suppress the too common use of Spiritous Liquors'.[87] The motion was 'Carried in the Affirmative Nem Con'.[88]

When combined with extensive coverage in the press, the pressure on parliament was substantial.[89] And yet the ensuing bill was modest in its ambitions. The Act, against 'the immoderate drinking of spirits amongst the meaner and lowest sort', is generally perceived as having finally solved the gin problem, bringing to an end more than two decades of legislative failure.[90] However, the extent of its impact is debatable, and the reasons for the lack of popular opposition to the bill, when compared to the resistance which led to the abandonment of attempts to enforce the 1736 Act, need to be considered.

Cognisant of the failure of previous bills, the Act targeted those who were most able, and likely, to comply, while avoiding mechanisms for enforcement which were likely to generate popular opposition. Its provisions, described by Horace Walpole as 'slight ones indeed for so enormous an evil!', meant that it stopped far short of total prohibition.[91] As Patrick Dillon observes, 'there were plenty of politicians and commentators who could remember the lesson of 1736'.[92] Distillers were required to pay a substantially increased excise duty (up 4.5 pence a gallon) and prohibited from retailing gin, and retailers had to pay a higher licence fee (£2), while street selling remained prohibited. However, while informers, whose activities had provoked so much opposition in 1736, could still be used against retailers who sold gin without a licence, they were not given, as they were in 1736, any significant financial inducement to do so. Consequently, the Act led to few prosecutions.

Measured by levels of production, gin drinking fell in 1752 by over a third, but as with previous acts, levels of consumption rapidly recovered.[93] Gin remained part of the daily life of plebeian Londoners. The number of trials at the Old Bailey in which 'gin' and/or 'geneva' is

---

[87] *LL*, St Clement Danes Parish: Minutes of Parish Vestries, 5 June 1749 – 11 October 1754 (WCCDMV362090117).

[88] On 7 March, the Middlesex bench submitted a petition, followed by one from a sole East End parish, Christ Church Spitalfields. See *LL*, Middlesex Sessions: General Orders of Court, 19 May 1743 – 22 February 1753 (LMSMGO556020457); and *PP*, *Journals of the House of Commons*, 26, 12 March 1750, p. 117.

[89] Jessica Warner, *Craze: Gin and Debauchery in an Age of Reason* (London: Profile, 2003), pp. 202–3; Dillon, *Much-Lamented*, pp. 249–51.

[90] 24 Geo. II c. 40, 'An Act for granting to His Majesty an additional duty upon spirituous liquors'.

[91] Quoted by Dillon, *Much Lamented*, p. 260.	[92] Dillon, *Much Lamented*, p. 257.

[93] *PP*, 'Report of the commissioners of the Inland Revenue of the duties under their management' (1870) [C.82–1], II, pp. 8–9 (parlipapers.chadwyck.co.uk, 2 Jan. 2014).

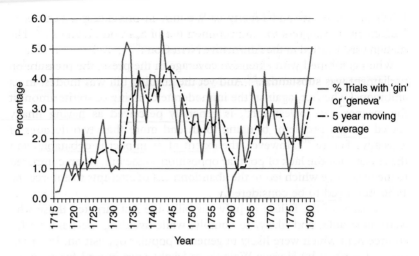

Figure 5.7 Old Bailey trial reports including 'Gin' or 'Geneva',
1715–1780. Online data set: Gin Geneva in Old Bailey Trials.xlsx.

mentioned, as a stolen good or a drink consumed by the defendant and/or
victim in the lead up to a crime, remained stable, averaging 11.7 a year
under the 1743 Gin Act (1744–50) and 10.6 following the passage of the
1751 Act (1752–6). While, as a result of the growing number of trials
heard in the 1750s, the percentage involving 'gin' or 'geneva' fell from a
peak in 1744, gin recovered its role in the records of crime in the 1760s and
1770s (Figure 5.7). In their biographies of the condemned, the Ordinaries
of Newgate continued to represent gin drinking as a lower-class curse:
Hannah Wilson, convicted in 1753 of stealing a coat and ribbon from a
child, 'had been drinking that cursed Liquor, called Gin, and was drunk,
or she had never have attempted to use the poor Baby ill'.[94] Following the
harvest failures of 1756–7 and a temporary ban on the domestic production of spirits, gin drinking declined temporarily, but judging by the
frequency of mentions in Old Bailey trials, it soon recovered. Overall
consumption did eventually decline, but this was due to the fact the price
of gin had risen and an alternative, cheaper, drink (porter) became available.[95] As Nicholas Rogers argues, 'the gin epidemic was ultimately
contained by changes in consumer taste, not by regulation'.[96]

[94] LL, set, 'Hannah Wilson'; Ordinary of Newgate Prison: Ordinary's Accounts, 1 October
1753 (OA175310015310010005).
[95] PP, 'Report of the commissioners', 1870 [C.82–1], II, pp. 8–9.
[96] Rogers, Mayhem, p. 157. See also Peter Clark, 'The "Mother Gin" controversy in the early
eighteenth century', Transactions of the Royal Historical Society, 5th Series, 38 (1988), 83.

The two Acts passed in the following year in direct response to proposals from the Felonies Committee were also targeted at, and in some
respects shaped by, plebeian London. The first, 'A Bill for the better
preventing Thefts and Robberies; and for regulating Places of publick
Entertainment; and punishing Persons keeping disorderly Houses',
better known as the Disorderly Houses Act, contained a number of
measures intended to make felonies easier to prosecute, in addition to
specific measures targeted at 'disorderly houses'.[97] These were thought
to harbour gaming, prostitution and excessive drinking, vices that were
considered to lead ineluctably to more serious crime. Consequently,
houses that provided 'Publick Dancing, Musick, and other public Entertainment of the like kind' within twenty miles of London would require a
licence, which could only be granted by four or more justices of the
peace, and anyone keeping an unlicensed house could be fined £100.
Prosecution of 'disorderly houses', including 'bawdy houses' and
'gaming houses', was made easier by rewards paid to informers, and a
legal injunction requiring constables to act on the complaints they
received (their expenses were paid).

Like the Gin Act, the Disorderly Houses Act was specifically targeted
at the poor. The measures were justified on the grounds that a

Multitude of places of Entertainment for the lower sort of People is a ... great
Cause of Thefts and Robberies, as they are thereby tempted to spend their small
Substance in riotous Pleasures, and in Consequence are put on unlawful
Methods of supplying their Wants, and renewing their Pleasures.

The Act was also designed to close various loopholes that had allowed
the owners and operators of such houses to evade prosecution, as had
occurred during the attempts to close down disorderly houses in the 1730s.
It outlawed the common strategy of removing a case by a writ of *certiorari*
to the Court of King's Bench, which added substantially to the cost of a
prosecution. The Act also closed the loophole which had allowed owners
to evade prosecution by ensuring that they were not directly connected
with running them.[98]

There is little evidence that the Act had any real impact. In the short
term, some pleasure gardens appear to have lost their music licences, and
there may have been an increase in the number of presentments against
disorderly houses in the City, but from 1753 presentments 'decline[d]
steadily', since 'the process of prosecution remained both expensive and

[97] 25 Geo. II c. 36, 'An Act for the better preventing thefts and robberies, and for regulating
places of public entertainment, and punishing persons keeping disorderly houses'.
[98] For the text of the Act see, John Collyer, *The Criminal Statutes of England: Analysed, and
Arranged Alphabetically* (1828), p. 412.

time-consuming'.[99] It appears there was little support for the new Act. Even the *Gentleman's Magazine* complained that the proposed bill would 'deny all amusements to the lower ranks of people', and potentially 'throw all those now engaged in exhibiting such amusement out of that way of getting their bread', resulting in an 'increase [in] robberies, instead of lessening them'.[100] In the end, owing to reluctance to prosecute partly due to concerns about its impact on the poor, as well as anticipated continuing opposition to prosecutions, the Act made little difference, such that later in the decade campaigners against vice found it necessary to launch a new society for the reformation of manners. In 1758, when Justice Saunders Welch complained that owing to 'the dread and terror every man is under of incurring the odious name of informer', the Act had failed to close down even the most 'bare-faced' brothels. It has been estimated there were only ten to fifteen successful convictions across the whole metropolis.[101] The problem of disorderly houses (and gin) remained in 1768, when John Fielding noted that they encouraged 'gaming and other disorders' and that many sold spirituous liquors, 'of which they vend treble the Quantity they do of Beer, which is absolutely establishing Gin-Shops'.[102] Neither is there any evidence that the provisions of the Act making felonies easier to prosecute had any impact – the number of offences tried at the Old Bailey in the subsequent decade fell by over a third (Figure 5.2).

If neither the Gin Act nor the Disorderly Houses Act had any substantive effect on plebeian behaviour, the Murder Act, also passed in 1752,[103] was more successful – at least in as much as it altered penal practice with respect to those convicted of murder. Crowd behaviour at executions also changed, but disorder did not disappear. Although not a direct response to any of the recommendations of the Felonies Committee, the Murder Act was passed with 'incredible speed' in 1752, urged on its legislative course by a spate of widely publicised murders, including horrific crimes committed by Mary Blandy and

---

[99] Robert Harris, *Politics and the Nation: Britain in the Mid-Eighteenth Century* (Oxford University Press, 2002), p. 303; Tony Henderson, *Disorderly Women in Eighteenth-Century London: Prostitution and Control in the Metropolis, 1730–1830* (London: Longman, 1999), p. 95.

[100] *Gentleman's Magazine*, 22 (1752), p. 31 (www.hathitrust.org, 2 Jan. 2014); Connors, '"Grand inquest of the nation"', 307.

[101] Saunders Welch, *An Essay on the Office of Constable* (1758), p. 32; Faramerz Dabhoiwala, *The Origins of Sex: A History of the First Sexual Revolution* (London: Penguin, 2012), p. 75.

[102] John Fielding, *Extracts from such of the Penal Laws, as Particularly Relate to the Peace and Good Order of this Metropolis* (1768), p. 414.

[103] 25 Geo II c. 37, 'An Act for better preventing the horrid crime of murder'.

Elizabeth Jefferies, collectively represented in the press as 'a pressing social problem'.[104] The Act modified the punishment for murder in order to add 'some further terror and peculiar mark of infamy to the punishment of death', by ensuring that convicted murderers were executed almost immediately following their conviction (two days later), and that their bodies were either hung in chains or handed over to the surgeons to be 'dissected and anatomized'. This made execution more certain, as few pardons could be organised in the short space between sentence and execution, and more horrible, by playing on popular beliefs about the significance of keeping the corpse intact. At one and the same time, the Act attempted to reduce disorder at Tyburn while securing a regular supply of fresh cadavers for the dissection tables at Surgeons' Hall.

In one respect this statute is most impressive for what it did not do. It did not follow the careworn pattern typical of early eighteenth-century legislation of extending capital punishment to a wider range of offences – there was no desire to increase the number of executions. This needs to be understood in the context of the dramatic increase in executions in the years 1749–52, driven by the post-war wave of prosecutions, and the disorder which accompanied them.[105] Despite the presence of strong guards and the sheriffs' attempts to negotiate with the crowd over control of the bodies of the executed, battles occasionally broke out between the crowd and the surgeon's men, with sailors and the Irish (who also figure frequently among the executed) prominent in the mêlée, often armed with bludgeons.

The presence of a contingent of foot guards as well as civil officers at the execution in 1748 of former sailor John Lancaster, for example, did not prevent a 'company of eight sailors with truncheons' rescuing the body from the surgeons' men after they left Tyburn and carrying it 'in triumph through London'.[106] The execution of the 'Gentleman Highwayman' James Maclaine, hanged with eleven other men in October 1750, unsurprisingly attracted a huge crowd: 'the greatest Concourse of People at Tyburn ever known at any Execution'.[107] In the chaos

---

[104] Ward, 'Print culture and responses to crime', pp. 146–70. Rogers sees the Act as a response to wider fears of plebeian violence: Rogers, *Mayhem*, p. 61.

[105] Simon Devereaux, 'Recasting the theatre of execution: the abolition of the Tyburn ritual', *Past & Present*, 202 (2009), Figure 3, 149.

[106] *LL*, set, 'John Lancaster'; Peter Linebaugh, 'The Tyburn riot against the surgeons', in Douglas Hay *et al.*, eds., *Albion's Fatal Tree: Crime and Society in Eighteenth-Century England* (London: Allen Lane, 1975), pp. 87–8.

[107] *LL*, set, 'James Maclaine'; *Penny London Post, or the Morning Advertiser*, 3–5 October 1750.

following the day's executions, the negotiated allocation of the bodies between friends of the deceased and the surgeons broke down. Maclaine's celebrity status meant that it was impossible to retain his body for dissection (though improbably his skeleton appears in the surgeons' hall in Plate 4 of William Hogarth's *Four Stages of Cruelty*). His body and that of William Smith (convicted of forgery) 'were taken away by their friends in Hearses, in order to be interred', while the surgeons were given the body of John Griffith (convicted of highway robbery). However, as the *London Evening Post* reported, while the bodies of 'the others, who had Friends or Relations, were taken care of by them', 'three or four were suffer'd to be carried off by the Mob, who dragg'd their naked Bodies about'.[108] After six men, including two Irishmen, were hanged in November 1751, the *London Evening Post* reported that the execution 'was performed with great Decency and Order', after 'a great Number of Sailors, and others, appearing arm'd with Bludgeons, under pretence of rescuing their Acquaintances from the Surgeons' were disarmed.[109] But this paper failed to report that a battle took place involving 'a quarter of a hundred chairmen and milkmen, [who] seemed to be all concerned in taking away the cart [and] horses, with the bodies' of two of the condemned.[110] The men, including Michael MacGennis, an Irish milkman, had seized the cart in order to carry away the bodies, but the cart's owner, Richard Shears, resisted, and in an ensuing scuffle Shears was fatally stabbed.[111] Subsequently, MacGennis and his accomplice drove the cart in triumph to Tower Hill, where they exhibited the bodies.

Elite concerns about the disorder at 'Tyburn Fair', given renewed impetus by William Hogarth's representation of Tyburn in Plate 11 of *Industry and Idleness* in 1747 and by Henry Fielding's comments in his *Enquiry* four years later, were not without foundation, though they failed to understand plebeian motivations.[112] Both forcibly suggested that the death penalty was not working because spectators had come to treat executions as a form of entertainment and were not learning the right lesson. Instead of recognising the consequences of sin, the terror of the gallows had become, in the words of another commentator, subject to 'the ridicule and mockery of an audacious vulgar'.[113] Contemporaries

[108] *London Evening Post*, 2–4 October 1750 (Burney Collection: www.galegroup.com, 1 Jan. 2014).
[109] *London Evening Post*, 9 November 1751.
[110] LL, Old Bailey Proceedings, 16 January 1752 (t17520116-28).
[111] LL, set, 'Michael MacGennis'; Hitchcock and Shoemaker, *Tales*, pp. 202–10.
[112] Fielding, *Enquiry into the Causes*, pp. 189–99.
[113] *Proposals to the Legislature for Preventing the Frequent Executions and Exportations of Convicts* (1754), p. 116, quoted by Randall McGowen, '"Making examples" and the

worried that at best the crowd treated executions as a holiday, while at worst they came to share in the defiance of those convicts who chose to die 'game'. They believed 'a bond had grown up between the condemned and the mob that the authorities were impotent to sever'.[114]

The authorities had no wish to exacerbate this disorder, whether prompted by disputes over taking bodies for dissection or a more general challenge to the forces of order, by staging more executions. Instead, in an attempt to intimidate the crowd, the Act added a further dimension of terror to the executions of those convicted of the most egregious crimes. In a subsidiary clause, it addressed the problem of the grotesque fights over corpses at the gallows by prescribing transportation for anyone convicted of attempting to rescue the bodies of those sentenced to dissection or hanging in chains. The Act also constituted a direct challenge to the culture of defiance among convicts and their supporters.[115] By requiring that condemned murderers be kept in solitary confinement during the much shortened interval between their sentence and their execution, the Act constrained the prison visits that contributed to the celebrity culture of crime and made the job of the criminal biographers more difficult.[116]

Nonetheless, these provisions applied only to those convicted of murder. Prison visiting did not end, and criminal biographies continued to be published. While the Murder Act is generally believed to have reduced disorder at Tyburn, a strong potential for conflict remained when non-murderers were executed, and some riots still occurred.[117] When five convicts were executed on 12 May 1755, for example, 'the Surgeons had got Possession of two of the Bodies, but the Mob soon deprived them of their Prize, and buried them in the Fields'.[118] To the extent that disorder did decrease after 1752, much of the explanation lies with the sharp fall in the number of executions between 1752 and the early 1760s, rather than in any change in the behaviour of surgeons and the crowd.[119]

crisis of punishment in mid-eighteenth-century England', in David Lemmings, ed., *The British and their Laws in the Eighteenth Century* (Rochester, NY: Boydell Press, 2005), p. 201.

[114] Andrea McKenzie, 'Martyrs in low life? Dying "game" in Augustan England', *Journal of British Studies*, 42:2 (April 2003), 67–205; McGowen, 'Crisis of punishment', in Lemmings, ed., *British and their Laws*, p. 200.

[115] Linebaugh, 'Tyburn riot', p. 115.

[116] Ward, 'Print culture and responses to crime', p. 193.

[117] Linebaugh, 'Tyburn riot', pp. 101–2; Devereaux, 'Recasting the theatre of execution', 145–8.

[118] *London Evening Post*, 10–13 May 1755.

[119] Devereaux, 'Recasting the theatre of execution', Figure 3, 149.

Rewards, thief-takers and the Bow Street Runners

The net result of the legislation passed in consequence of the post-war panic about crime was limited. The few Acts that made it onto the statute books were more significant for their aspirations to discipline plebeian London than for their impact in suppressing crime and vice or controlling the crowd. Several contemporary proposals which would have wrought substantial changes to policing were not adopted, including Henry Fielding's 1749 draft bill, while the proposals that emerged from the Felonies Committee giving justices of the peace greater oversight over the parish watch and poor relief, designed 'to induce Parishes to do their Duty', were quietly shelved.[120] The parishes won this battle for control of the watch and the workhouses, and the only legislation on policing passed took the form of additional watch acts, extending the system already in force in Westminster and the west end to the eastern and northern suburbs.[121] Instead, the most significant development in policing in these years was the initiative of Henry Fielding, reacting to the threats posed by highwaymen (particularly when in gangs) and the corrupt thief-takers who were supposed to apprehend them, to create the Bow Street Runners.

Despite the executions of several members of the Black Boy Alley gang in 1744, groups of criminals continued to act in concert, elites continued to construe these groups into ever more threatening 'gangs' and the authorities were forced to respond. In the introduction to his *Enquiry*, Fielding claimed:

> there is at this Time a great Gang of Rogues, whose Number falls little short of a Hundred, who are incorporated in one Body, have officers and a Treasury; and have reduced Theft and Robbery into a regular System.[122]

Fielding was referring to the 'Royal Family' – a large group centred around members of a privateering squadron which included former participants in the Black Boy Alley gang. The Royal Family became notorious in January 1749 when they staged an armed attack on the Gatehouse Prison to rescue Thomas Jones alias Harper.[123] Jones had been arrested for pickpocketing, and at least ten members of the gang were involved in the rescue.[124] The Royal Family may not have been as large and coherent as Fielding claimed, but it was nonetheless

---

[120] *PP, Journals of the House of Commons*, 1 April 1751, p. 159 (parlipapers.chadwyck.co.uk, 2 Jan. 2014).

[121] Elaine A. Reynolds, *Before the Bobbies: The Night Watch and Police Reform in Metropolitan London, 1720–1830* (Basingstoke: Macmillan, 1998), pp. 29–35.

[122] Fielding, *Enquiry into the Causes*, p. 4.   [123] *LL*, set, 'Thomas Jones'.

[124] Ruth Paley, 'The Middlesex Justices Act of 1792: its origins and effects' (PhD dissertation, University of Reading, 1983), pp. 329–31.

formidable, and they were willing to publicly challenge judicial authority. One witness described how following the attack, 'they made a terrible huzzaing; after they had got him out, I heard them say they would come back and pull down the goal [*sic*]'.[125] This was not the only gang active at this time: another, less well known (and unnamed), group was centred around Henry Webb and Benjamin Mason, alias Ben the Coalheaver.[126] This group contained at least thirteen men, who 'committed a great Number of Robberies together'.[127]

The government's response was the tried and failed one of offering rewards for the apprehension of the most notorious criminals. In February 1749 the £100 reward for the conviction of street robbers and highwaymen in London was reinstated (this remained available until early 1752), and in January 1750 a special £100 reward was offered for the capture of Thomas Jones. Other rewards were offered by parishes and individual victims.[128] Measured by the amount of money paid out, these rewards were a huge success: in 1750–2 the government proclamations cost the Treasury £11,100, indicating at least eighty successful prosecutions for robbery.[129] Many of the thief-takers who had been active in the 1740s were thereby enabled to continue or resume their activities, including William Palmer Hind, Charles Remington, John Berry and Stephen McDaniel, and many new ones became active.[130] Ruth Paley lists twelve 'leading thief-takers' and twenty-two 'less active ones' working in this period. As always, thief-takers relied not only on supportive local justices of the peace but also on their connections with criminals for information. Many had criminal records themselves: Edward Mullins had been a member of the Royal Family.[131]

Instead of preventing crime, the rewards encouraged it, as a result of thief-takers subverting their purpose. Taking advantage of the moral panic, it became easy for thief-takers to secure convictions, as their 'evidence was received with extraordinary credulity' in the courts.

[125] *LL*, Old Bailey Proceedings, 28 January 1750 (t17500228-41).
[126] *LL*, sets, 'Henry Webb' and 'Benjamin Mason'.
[127] *LL*, Ordinary of Newgate Prison: Ordinary's Accounts, 8 August 1750 (OA175008085008080010).
[128] John Beattie, *The First English Detectives: The Bow Street Runners and the Policing of London, 1750–1840* (Oxford University Press, 2012), p. 18; Fielding, *Enquiry into the Causes*, p. lvii; Ward, 'Print culture and responses to crime', p. 128.
[129] Beattie, *First English Detectives*, p. 22. This calculation assumes that the successful prosecutors claimed both the £100 reward offered by royal proclamation, and the £40 statutory reward.
[130] *LL*, sets, 'William Palmer Hind', 'Charles Remington', 'John Berry' and 'Stephen McDaniel'.
[131] *LL*, set, 'Edward Mullins'.

Consequently, thief-*making* gangs once again flourished, staging crimes and initiating false prosecutions in order to profit from the rewards. Through extensive use of perjury, extortion and blackmail, as well as violence, in Ruth Paley's assessment they turned 'the legal system into what was, in effect, a sophisticated offensive weapon', for profit as well as in order to persecute their enemies. This amounted to 'a systematic manipulation of the administration of the criminal law for personal gain'.[132] In the end, the thief-takers were as much of a threat to law and order as the robbers they were meant to apprehend.

It was in response to both the apparently unprecedented law-breaking of highwaymen and gangs and the corruption of the thief-takers that Henry Fielding introduced the Bow Street Runners. In 1749–50 he organised a group of men, comprising constables, ex-constables, prison officers and thief-takers, whom he could send out on a regular basis to apprehend serious offenders for examination at Bow Street.[133] While he paid these men a retainer (and thus maintained some control over them), they also kept any statutory rewards they were entitled to claim. According to many historians, these officers (they would not actually be called 'Bow Street Runners' for many years) mark the origins of the world's first modern police detective force. Indeed, Fielding made strenuous attempts to emphasise the novel character of his runners, and to differentiate them from the frequently corrupt thief-takers who came before. However, this proved impossible. Joshua Brogden, Fielding's clerk, had long-standing connections with thief-takers, and some of the men Fielding recruited in the early years were thief-takers themselves.[134] There is even some evidence that Stephen McDaniel and John Berry were among Fielding's recruits.[135] These two men had already been involved in a thief-making scandal in 1747 and would be even more sensationally caught out in another one in 1754. Fielding soon replaced the most corrupt and criminal of these men and claimed that his officers were restricted either to constables or ex-constables, but nonetheless he felt

---

[132] Paley, 'Middlesex Justices Act', *passim*, quotes at pp. 312, 327.
[133] Beattie, *First English Detectives*, pp. 17–20.
[134] Paley, 'Middlesex Justices Act', pp. 313–14, 336–7; Beattie, *First English Detectives*, pp. 32–3.
[135] LL, sets, 'Stephen McDaniel' and 'John Berry'. Historians disagree on this point. Compare Paley, 'Middlesex Justices Act', pp. 303, 336 with Beattie, *First English Detectives*, p. 33. Fielding attempted to distance himself from McDaniel and his activities: Paley, 'Middlesex Justices Act', p. 334; John Fielding, *A Plan for Preventing Robberies within Twenty Miles of London, with an Account of the Rise and Establishment of the real Thief-takers* (1755), p. 6.

the need to keep their names secret. Moreover, seeking to have it both ways, he justified the work of thief-takers in his *Enquiry*.[136]

In spite of their tainted origins, by creating this new body of organised detectives Henry Fielding and his half-brother John, who took over the Bow Street office in January 1754, had radical ambitions to change how London was policed. Henry advocated withdrawing government rewards, and in 1752 convinced the Privy Council to stop offering extraordinary rewards by royal proclamation. Instead, he argued for his force to be at least partly funded from central resources, and from 1753 obtained £200 per annum from the government, increased to £400 in 1757. While the runners continued to rely on rewards offered by victims, this funding change altered the character of the relationship between criminals and the police charged with their capture.[137]

Perhaps more importantly, victims of crime and the public were encouraged to rely on these officers to apprehend serious offenders, rather than attempt to capture them themselves. In newspaper advertisements from as early as 1749, the public were asked to send descriptions of thieves and stolen goods to Bow Street so they could be advertised, and from 1754 they were effectively requested to hand over responsibility for apprehending the culprits to the runners. This change was in part a response to the growing temerity of the public in seeking out and arresting criminals – something commentators including John Fielding frequently derided.[138] However, it also represents an attempt to gain greater direct judicial control over the processes of detecting and arresting suspects in order to prevent extra-legal negotiations between criminals and those who apprehended them. The Bow Street Runners were also given wider policing responsibilities. In particular high-risk areas or where local inhabitants demanded it, such as in Westminster squares and on highways leading into the city, the officers conducted patrols both on foot and on horseback.[139] As is clear from the accounts submitted by John Fielding to the Treasury, they also spent a substantial amount of time regulating and suppressing forms of popular recreation which were thought to lead to crime. As he explained in his *Account of the Origin and Effects of a Police Set on Foot by His Grace the Duke of Newcastle in the Year 1753,*

---

[136] Paley, 'Middlesex Justices Act', p. 337; Beattie, *First English Detectives*, pp. 31–2; Fielding, *Enquiry into the Causes*, pp. 161–3.

[137] Battestin with Battestin, *Fielding*, p. 578; Beattie, *First English Detectives*, pp. 23, 26, 55.

[138] Fielding, *Plan for Preventing Robberies*, pp. 7–9; Robert Shoemaker, *The London Mob: Violence and Disorder in Eighteenth-Century England* (London: Hambledon and London, 2004), pp. 41–9.

[139] Beattie, *First English Detectives*, pp. 34, 38, 41.

In large and populous Cities, especially in the Metropolis of a flourishing Kingdom, Artificers, Servants and Labourers, compose the Bulk of the People, and keeping them in good Order is the Object of the Police, the Care of the Legislature, and the Duty of the Magistrates, and all other Peace Officers.[140]

In sum, through their prominent role in apprehending criminal suspects throughout the metropolis as well as in regulating popular entertainments, the Runners, in the words of John Beattie, 'changed the face of official policing in London'. But since links with thief-taking were impossible to eliminate, the runners remained tainted by accusations of corruption (this was not helped by the fact that John Fielding continued to call them 'thief-takers'). Hostility was also prompted by their methods. Like thief-takers, the Bow Street officers relied on paid informers who passed on gossip and rumours picked up in alehouses and taverns, and, in a new departure, they used the records kept by Fielding at Bow Street 'about people suspected of committing offences and of those who had been charged but escaped conviction and punishment'. In some cases, 'the runners went after men and women on their lists of "known offenders" who seemed to fit the descriptions given by the victims'.[141] In the process, Fielding and the runners formalised the time-honoured police practice of 'rounding up the usual suspects'. Focusing on the 'usual suspects', however, provoked hostility leading in turn to a need for anonymity for the Runners. As Fielding recognised, 'as the thief-takers are extremely obnoxious to the common people, perhaps it might not be altogether politic to point them out to the mob'.[142]

Despite popular hostility, the Fieldings claimed their new methods were a success. They planted numerous reports in the newspapers of robbers apprehended and gangs broken up by their men. In December 1753 Henry claimed that in the few weeks since the Duke of Newcastle had begun to fund the runners: 'not one Robbery, or Cruelty hath been heard of in the Streets, except the Robbery of one Woman, the Person accused of which was immediately taken'.[143] This was a disingenuous exaggeration since there are four trials in the *Old Bailey Proceedings* alone for violent thefts committed between 10 November and 4 December. And while 1754 did see a decline in prosecutions for violent theft, there were still twenty-seven offences prosecuted at the Old Bailey. Neither individual nor gang crime could be crushed so easily. Despite the onset

---

[140] John Fielding, *An Account of the Origin and Effects of a Police Set on Foot by His Grace the Duke of Newcastle in the Year 1753* (1758), p. vii.

[141] Beattie, *First English Detectives*, pp. 24, 28, 61, 67–69; quotes from pp. 61 and 69.

[142] Fielding, *Plan for Preventing Robberies*, p. 24.

[143] *Public Advertiser*, 7 December 1753, see also 14 December 1753 (Burney Collection: www.galegroup.com, 1 Jan. 2014).

of the Seven Years War in 1757, which was expected to lead to a reduction in crime, John Fielding reported that new gangs had begun to operate. Under the guise of the 'Family Men' or the 'Coventry Gang', members of the Royal Family continued to commit crimes into the 1760s.[144]

There was also the continuing problem of thief-making. While the Bow Street officers appear to have pushed corrupt thief-takers out of Westminster, they continued to flourish in other parts of the metropolis throughout the 1750s, and, as Paley argues, 'not only [Henry] Fielding but also the whole of the contemporary legal establishment must have been well aware of what was going on'.[145] The most notorious scandal involved the thief-taker Stephen McDaniel, who had apparently acted as a Runner and participated in arresting a member of the Royal Family before he was dismissed from Bow Street by Fielding in 1751.[146] McDaniel continued to act as a thief-taker and his 'gang' engaged in numerous thief-making conspiracies throughout the early 1750s, though they seem to have avoided bringing cases to the Old Bailey (prosecuting cases outside London instead).[147] In August 1754 they were exposed at the Kent Assizes by Joseph Cox, high constable, who arrested McDaniel, John Berry, James Salmon and James Eagan and charged them with conspiracy to initiate a false prosecution against Peter Kelly and John Ellis for robbery in order to profit from the parliamentary reward. In February 1756 all four were tried and convicted of this conspiracy at the Old Bailey.[148] Cox also exposed several of the gang's other conspiracies.[149] In June, McDaniel, Berry and Mary Jones were tried and convicted for the murder of Joshua Kidden, whom they had falsely charged and convicted of robbing Jones in February 1754.[150] Kidden had 'declar'd his innocence to the last', and his friends and even the Ordinary of Newgate were entirely convinced.[151] Regardless, he was hanged on Monday 4 February 1754, while the crowd threw snowballs

---

[144] Beattie, *First English Detectives*, p. 38; Paley, 'Middlesex Justices Act', p. 329, n. 85.

[145] Paley, 'Middlesex Justices Act', p. 303 and *passim*.

[146] *LL*, set, 'Stephen McDaniel'.

[147] For a list of thief-making conspiracies involving this gang between 1738 and 1754, see Leon Radzinowicz, *A History of English Criminal Law and its Administration from 1750*, Vol. II (London: Stevens and Sons, 1956), p. 339.

[148] *LL*, Old Bailey Proceedings, 25 February 1756 (t17560225-48).

[149] Joseph Cox, *A Faithful Narrative of the Most Wicked and Inhuman Transactions of that Bloody-Minded Gang of Thief-takers, alias Thief-Makers* (1756).

[150] *LL*, Old Bailey Proceedings, 3 June 1756 (t17560603-16), and 16 January 1754 (t17540116-41).

[151] *LL*, Ordinary of Newgate Prison: Ordinary's Accounts, 4 February 1754 (OA175402045402040008).

and behaved as if they 'had been rather at a bear-baiting, than a solemn execution of the laws'.[152]

Although sentenced to death, the punishments of McDaniel, Berry and Jones were never carried out, owing either to concerns about the legal validity of the offence of 'murder by perjury' or to a desire on the part of the legal establishment not to put these thief-takers in a position where they might expose damaging information about official collusion in their activities. They were sentenced to the pillory instead, and the fact that McDaniel and Berry were heavily protected by the keeper of Newgate and one of the sheriffs, shielding them from understandable popular outrage at their crimes, suggests that the officials *were* worried. As Ruth Paley argues, 'the reason the thief-takers were tolerated for so long was that to make any move against them was to risk exposing the corruption of the whole system of the administration of the criminal law in the metropolis'.[153]

Thief-taking (and no-doubt thief-making) continued, but defendants acquired a useful card to play in their defence. The ill-disguised link between the Runners and thief-taking provided defendants with a tactic to use in court, where they could attempt to discredit the Runners by accusing them of acting like thief-takers. When one of the most active early Runners, William Pentlow, testified against Thomas Lewis and Thomas May in a highway robbery case in 1750, 'The two prisoners, especially May, much abused this headborough, as a person that would swear away any person's life for a trifle.' Henry Fielding was forced to rise to Pentlow's defence, saying 'he sincerely believed there was not an honester, or a braver man than he in the king's dominion', and the two defendants were convicted.[154] Others were more successful. When William Page,[155] a notorious highwayman zealously pursued by John Fielding, was finally tried at the Old Bailey in February 1758, he attacked the principal prosecution witness, his alleged accomplice William Darwell, suggesting that his association with Fielding undermined the validity of his testimony:

I know nothing of him, and why he should place this matter to my account, I don't know. He has had access to my lodgings, and has had a long connection with Mr. Fielding from his own testimony. He is every thing that is bad and infamous, in declaring himself a highwayman. He would have given testimony

---

[152] *LL*, Ordinary of Newgate Prison: Ordinary's Accounts, 4 February 1754 (OA175402045402040017).
[153] Paley, 'Middlesex Justices Act', pp. 334–5
[154] *LL*, Old Bailey Proceedings, 25 April 1750 (t17500425-14).
[155] *LL*, set, 'William Page'.

against any person that he should happen to fix upon, to save his own life. He glories in his wickedness.[156]

Page was acquitted. When the highwayman Paul Lewis was tried for robbing Mary Brook in 1762, he also conducted his own defence, carrying out robust cross-examinations of the prosecution witnesses.[157] In doing so, he suggested that the prosecuting attorney had framed him and that the constable was a 'hired constable' and a 'thief-catcher' (he, too, was acquitted).[158] These arguments were also used by defence counsel.

In response to the success of defence strategies like these, the Fieldings introduced a further innovation – more elaborate pre-trial hearings. Traditionally, the function of a preliminary hearing was limited, since justices were required to commit all accused felons to prison and forward the accusations against them for consideration by the grand jury. However, the Fieldings began to use their Bow Street office not simply to determine which of the accused to commit and take the necessary depositions but also to assess the evidence against suspects and solicit additional evidence where it was thought to be necessary to strengthen weak cases. As reports in his *Covent Garden Journal* suggest, Henry pioneered the practice of examining witnesses separately and waiting for the contradictions to emerge. While to modern eyes this seems like a natural detective practice, it was actually in contradiction of traditions of open justice in which all those involved in a dispute spoke to the same audience. Just as the introduction of counsel into criminal trials from the 1730s and 1740s had made the proceedings more 'adversarial', Fielding's innovations meant that pre-trial hearings began to acquire the character of an increasingly unequal interrogation.

In cases where the evidence was judged to be weak, suspects were held while new victims and witnesses were located through advertisements in the press, inviting anyone with potentially useful information (or a grudge) to come and view the prisoner, and participate in a 're-examination'. Although this system was perfected by John Fielding, it was probably initiated by Henry, based on a provision of the 1752 Disorderly Houses Act which allowed justices to hold persons accused of theft for up to six days without charging them.[159] Cases for the prosecution were thus potentially much stronger by the time they were forwarded to

---

[156] *LL*, Old Bailey Proceedings, 22 February 1758 (t17580222-28).
[157] *LL*, set, 'Paul Lewis'.
[158] *LL*, Old Bailey Proceedings, 8 December 1762 (t17621208-4).
[159] John Beattie, 'Scales of justice: defense counsel and the English criminal trial in the eighteenth and nineteenth centuries', *Law and History Review*, 9:2 (Fall 1991), 221–67; Beattie, *First English Detectives*, pp. 87–99, esp. p. 97.

the Old Bailey, where cases originating at Bow Street became increasingly common. In John's first decade in office (1756–66), 'more than a third of the accused felons sent for trial at the Old Bailey from Middlesex were committed as a result of proceedings at Bow Street, the vast majority conducted by Fielding himself'.[160] The pre-trial publicity Fielding generated by reporting these hearings in the newspapers provoked criticism in the 1770s, but from their beginning those subjected to the Fieldings' new methods of arrest and pre-trial hearings fought back. When the burglar William Tidd was examined by Henry Fielding, he 'd – d the justice, and said he was as big a thief as himself'.[161] Innovations at Bow Street evolved in a continuing dialectic with the challenges posed by the thief-takers, thief-makers and the accused thieves of plebeian London.

'The dogs of reformation'

Virtually the entire response to the post-war anxiety about crime can be seen as a renewed attempt at a reformation of manners, picking up where the previous campaign left off when it collapsed in 1738.[162] Understandings of the causes of crime remained firmly traditional, blaming irreligion, immorality and idleness. The 1750s approach to the reformation of manners, however, was different in two respects. First, this new campaign more clearly differentiated the vices of the poor from the forgivable failings of the well-to-do. Henry Fielding's social policy prescriptions explicitly focused on the poor and their supposed propensity for 'luxury'. While he occasionally criticised the vices of the rich in the *Covent Garden Journal* and set himself up as 'censor of the nation's morals', he did not think the wealthy needed judicial discipline.[163] Similarly, his half-brother John opined in 1763 that while all brothels were to be condemned, the ones that needed to be closed most urgently were the 'low, and common bawdy-houses, where vice is rendered cheap, and consequently within the reach of the common people'.[164] The second distinctive feature was the limited involvement of magistrates. Despite resolutions passed by justices of the peace in the early years of the post-war crisis and the passage of the Gin and Disorderly Houses Acts in 1751–2, there were

---

[160] Beattie, *First English Detectives*, p. 94.
[161] *LL*, David Gibbons, 'William Tidd, c. 1729–1750'; *LL*, Old Bailey Proceedings, 5 December 1750 (t17501205-19).
[162] Harris, *Politics and the Nation*, ch. 7.   [163] *Covent-Garden Journal*, pp. xxxiv–xxxv.
[164] John Fielding, *A Charge Delivered to the Grand Jury... Held at Guildhall, Westminster* (1763), reprinted in Georges Lamoine, ed., *Charges to the Grand Jury, 1689–1803*, Camden Fourth Series, vol. 43 (London: Royal Historical Society, 1992), p. 396.

few extra prosecutions in the early 1750s.[165] Magistrates were actively concerned about the opposition a new campaign would create. No doubt aware of the difficulties encountered during previous attempts to close down disorderly houses, particularly during the late 1720s, they treaded cautiously.

The only exceptions were the Fieldings, who, motivated by their ambitious redefinition of policing, defied the trend. In the early 1750s, Henry was involved in a campaign against gaming houses, and from 1755 John waged a battle against forms of popular culture which he believed encouraged vice.[166] The annual accounts of expenditure he submitted to the Treasury between 1755 and 1758 include sums for suppressing several types of plebeian recreation, including 'cock-scaling on Shrove Tuesday' and 'an illegal meeting of servants and apprentices at a dance at the Golden Lyon near Grosvenor Square'.[167] He devoted even more effort to prosecuting vice following the onset of war in 1757. He drafted a successful bill which prohibited gaming by journeymen, labourers and servants in public houses, and pursued a vigorous campaign against gaming houses.[168] While he attempted to avoid formal prosecutions, relying instead on warnings and threats to withdraw licences, his tactics, including paying large fees to secret informers (in one case he even paid for a 'disguise') and burning gaming tables in public, were deeply unpopular. As he himself recognised, he had become 'obnoxious to many Bodies of People'. This may explain rumours spread in the summer of 1758 that he had been suspended from the bench and committed to Newgate prison.[169]

Fielding did have some allies, particularly from August 1757 when a new society was formed to promote a 'reformation of manners'. Consciously based on the 'great' societies of the 1690s, this group had a religious focus and was composed of seventy dissenters, twenty members of the established church, twenty supporters of George Whitefield and fifty supporters of John Wesley, and was most directly concerned to act against 'the gross and open profanation of the Lord's Day'. Significantly, their first move was to visit Fielding 'for instruction'. With his approval

---

[165] Ward, 'Print culture and responses to crime', pp. 105–8 and appendices 4.1–4.4; Faramerz Dabhoiwala, 'Sex and societies for moral reform, 1688–1800', *Journal of British Studies*, 46:2 (April 2007), 316.

[166] Harris, *Politics and the Nation*, p. 303; Battestin with Battestin, *Fielding*, pp. 502–3, 522.

[167] TNA, Treasury Papers, Accounts for October 1755, November 1756, November 1758, T38/671.

[168] 30 Geo. II c. 24 (1757), 'An Act for the more effectual punishment of persons who shall attain, or attempt to attain possession of goods or money, by false or untrue pretence'.

[169] Beattie, *First English Detectives*, pp. 42–6; BL Add. Ms. 32876, f. 274; 32882, ff. 58–9.

and guidance, they sought and obtained approval from the City authorities, the county benches and the clergy.[170] While, as Joanna Innes observes, unlike the earlier reformers this campaign 'did not receive forceful backing from either the governmental or ecclesiastical elite' and did not involve the direct participation of justices of the peace, it 'clearly received enough support from metropolitan magistrates to flourish for some years'.[171]

The reformers' activities were initially focused on the dissemination of printed literature, including 'dissuasives from Sabbath-breaking, extracts from Acts of Parliament against it, and notices to the offenders'. However, prosecutions soon followed and eventually extended to include people accused of profane swearing, unlawful gaming, 'lewd women, and keepers of ill houses', sellers of obscene prints and men accused of sodomy. By August 1762 they claimed 10,588 persons had been 'brought to justice', and by 1765 they had reportedly spent £1,000 on these activities. But while the list of offences targeted was ambitious in scope, in fact the vast majority of the offenders were accused of two easily detected offences, Sabbath breaking and prostitution.[172]

The reformers quickly ran into a substantial barrage of opposition, similar to that experienced by the societies of the 1690s, 1700s and 1720s, and this time the campaign lasted only six years. The main reasons for opposition are familiar, but at mid-century the arguments had more purchase and the opponents (from all social classes) were stronger. First, the reformers were accused of hypocrisy because they only targeted the vices of the poor. As a letter to the *London Chronicle* complained, 'the dogs of reformation' were let loose only on those wearing 'a dirty gown, [and who] want shoes to [their] feet', while vice could be freely practised by those who 'wear a coronet, or subscribe [themselves] noble'.[173] In fact, the reformers readily admitted that they targeted 'the thoughtless poor'.[174] As before, the reformers were also accused of distorting normal judicial processes. With the advent of salaried night watchmen and the Bow Street Runners, the idea of private citizens taking the law into their own hands was becoming more

---

[170] John Wesley, *A Sermon Preached before the Society for the Reformation of Manners* (1763), p. 6; Moses Browne, *The Causes that Obstruct the Progress of Reformation* (1765), p. 29.

[171] Joanna Innes, *Inferior Politics: Social Problems and Social Policies in Eighteenth-Century Britain* (Oxford University Press, 2009), pp. 294–5.

[172] Wesley, *Sermon Preached before the Society*, p. 7; Browne, *Causes that Obstruct*, p. 29. For sodomy see Innes, *Inferior Politics*, p. 294, n. 60.

[173] *London Chronicle*, 21–24 Sept 1765 (Burney Collection: www.galegroup.com, 1 Jan. 2014).

[174] Browne, *Causes that Obstruct*, p. 30.

objectionable. As 'Persius' complained in a letter to the *London Chronicle*, 'For any number of individuals, to assume the place of the laws, to seize the sword of justice, and to arrogate a right both of ascertaining the degree of the crime, and affixing a punishment' was to engage in 'monstrous' conduct.[175]

However, as with previous antagonism to reformation of manners activities, the most effective opposition took place on the streets and in the courts. John Wesley complained that the informers who attempted to prevent tippling on the Sabbath 'were exposed to abundance of reproach, to insult, and abuse of every kind; having not only the tipplers, to contend with, but rich and honourable men ... all who gained by their sins'. In Wesley's view, this

> naturally encouraged 'the beasts of the people' to follow their example, and to use [those who 'laid informations'] as fellows not fit to live upon the earth. Hence they made no scruple, not only to treat them with the basest language, not only to throw at them mud or stones, or whatever came to hand, but many times to beat them without mercy, and to drag them over the stones or through the kennels.[176]

Those who attempted to arrest prostitutes were also targeted. In 1757 a military guard had to be summoned to protect constables attempting to clear prostitutes from the Strand after the constables were attacked 'by Soldiers and others, who swear they are their Wives'.[177] Similarly, an attempt to close some brothels and arrest prostitutes in March 1763 led to one thousand sailors assembling 'in a line of battle'. Military assistance was called in, but the crowd ignored three readings of the Riot Act and forced the soldiers to allow the release of the eight women who had been arrested.[178]

Despite the provisions of the Disorderly Houses Act which were intended to make prosecuting brothels easier, keepers were still able to use the law to stymie the reformers, primarily by filing malicious counter-prosecutions. A raid on the Sun Tavern in 1760, authorised by a warrant from John Fielding, failed to lead to a conviction when the keeper was acquitted and the headborough, William Payne, was charged in his place not only with assault and false imprisonment but also, incredibly, with planting 'an almost naked man and woman' in the house.[179] When, the

---

[175] *London Chronicle*, 21–24 Sept. 1765.
[176] Wesley, *Sermon Preached before the Society*, p. 8.
[177] *London Chronicle*, 20–22 October 1757.
[178] J. P. Malcolm, *Anecdotes of the Manners and Customs of London during the Eighteenth Century* (1808), pp. 277–8.
[179] *LL*, set, 'William Payne'; Innes, *Inferior Politics*, p. 295, and ch. 7 *passim* for an overview of Payne's career.

following year, James Braybrook, a thief-taker who had worked with Henry Fielding, was charged with keeping a disorderly house in Whitechapel, he conducted a war of attrition against his prosecutor, Mary Lowe.[180] Following advice from his attorney, he repeatedly forfeited recognizances and delayed his trial from session to session, while harassing her, calling out 'you Bitch i'll do for you for i'll never give it up to you ... and Sayd he would Spend two hundred Pounds before she should have her ends'.[181] Indeed, Lowe claimed she was subjected to several 'false and feigned Prosecutions that hath been wickedly and untruly raised Stirred up and Commenced agt. her', and had spent more than £30 defending herself. In the end, Braybrook was convicted, but Lowe was seriously out of pocket, and the bawdy house was 'still kept on in like manner and as Infamous as ever'.[182]

By 1765 the Society claimed it had spent almost £1,000 defending its members against malicious prosecutions.[183] This sum included the case which led to its final collapse, following a raid in 1761 on the Rummer Tavern in Chancery Lane. The constables were once again charged with assault and false imprisonment, and the tavern keeper, a woman named Leeman, won the case and was awarded £300 damages. The fine was upheld on appeal. The reformers described this case as vexatious, and that may have been true. Despite the fact that twenty prosecution witnesses described the house as a place of good repute, the tavern was, in fact, a brothel.[184] Nonetheless, there may have been real misbehaviour on the part of the 'reforming constables' when carrying out the initial arrest, and the judgement of the Chief Justice (Charles Pratt, Lord Camden) indicated a more principled objection to the reformers' activities. According to the legal report of the appeal, the constables, 'would not say what crime she was guilty of, or charged with; Allen the constable had a warrant but did not shew it ... the defendants never prosecuted the plaintiff'. The informer, Abraham Tristram, who provided the original information against the house, had 'fled for an abominable crime' and, although subpoenaed, failed to appear at the trial.[185] Chief Justice Pratt concluded his judgement, upholding the fine by saying 'I think the King's Bench would grant an information against these persons for setting themselves up as a kind of grand jury; an informer is a most odious

---

[180] *LL*, set, 'James Braybrook'.
[181] *LL*, Middlesex Sessions: Sessions Papers, July 1762 (LMSMPS505120080).
[182] *LL*, Middlesex Sessions: Sessions Papers, July 1762 (LMSMPS505120081).
[183] Browne, *Causes that Obstruct*, p. 31.   [184] Innes, *Inferior Politics*, p. 298.
[185] *LL*, set, 'Abraham Tristram'.

character; and I am glad of an opportunity of declaring my dislike towards these reformers.'[186]

Eventually, in 1765, the reformers managed to get their revenge when they successfully prosecuted the chief witness against them for perjury, but it was a pyrrhic victory. By that point legal costs and the £300 fine had forced the Society to close. Once again plebeian London, in alliance with more respectable Londoners who either profited from vice or objected in principle to the aggressive use of the law to prosecute it, had managed to defeat a reformation of manners campaign.

The costs of vagrancy

Part of the same basket of lower-class immorality, idleness and crime which was targeted by mid-century reformers, vagrancy was in many ways the easiest to prosecute. The flabby character of the statute law meant that a justice could define almost any plebeian man or woman outside their parish of settlement as a 'vagrant' and, once labelled, could use all the resources of the county to punish and remove them from the neighbourhood. The Vagrant Costs Act of 1699 had firmly located the administration of this system in the hands of the county bench, except in the City, where the punishment and removal of vagrants formed one of the main activities of the Lord Mayor and Aldermen, with the Guildhall and Mansion House justice rooms witnessing hundreds of vagrant removals every year. During the first half of the century, this became an increasingly lucrative activity. Starting at 2 shillings, rewards for apprehending vagrants rose to 5 shillings in 1744 and 10 shillings at the discretion of the justice.[187] In a petty version of the racketeering of the thief-takers, the constables for wards on the edge of the City who were responsible for removing vagrants made a substantial living. In 1751, just under a thousand vagrants were arrested and removed from the City,[188] and in Middlesex and Westminster the numbers were even higher. Between, 'July 1756 and July 1757', a total of 1,951 'Orders of Conveying' vagrants were issued, and rewards were distributed for the arrest of 498 people, at a cost of £246. And while these figures must be seen against the backdrop of a population of approximately 650,000, for a constable working with a justice willing to authorise a 10 shilling

---

[186] George Wilson, *Reports of Cases Argued and Adjudged in the King's Courts at Westminster* (2nd edn, 1779), pp. 160–2.

[187] Sidney Webb and Beatrice Webb, *English Poor Law History, Part I: The Old Poor Law* (London: Longmans, Green and Co., 1927; repr. 1963), p. 369.

[188] LMA, City of London: 'City's cash accounts', COL/CHD/CT/01/044, 1750–2, f. 192.

reward, the income could be substantial. In just six months in 1748, Thomas Sherratt, the constable for St Margaret Westminster, was paid £7 for the arrest of fourteen vagrants.[189]

While constables and justices of the peace certainly believed they knew a vagrant when they saw one, the legal definition, while broad, was also obscure. The 1714, 1740 and 1744 Vagrancy Acts simply repeated an apparently random list of under-specified categories of the undesirable, including:

all persons going about as Patent Gatherers or Gatherers of Alms under Pretence of loss by Fire or other Casualty or as Collectors for prisons Goals or Hospitals and all persons wandering abroad and Lodging in Alehouse Barns outhouses or in the open Air not giving a good account of themselves and all other persons wandering abroad and begging . . .

The Acts went on to list 'Fencers and bear wards . . . Common players of interludes . . . All minstrels, jugglers . . . All persons pretending to be Gypsies, or wandering in the habit or form of Egyptians', and so on.[190] In 1761 John Fielding included all these categories of the unacceptable under the general rubric of a 'Description of disorderly persons' in his *Extracts from . . . the Penal Laws*, justifying the vigorous prosecution of beggars, in particular, because in a phrase that echoed the discussion concerning the Westminster Watch Acts, they were 'offensive to Passengers in general, and . . . dangerous to pregnant women'.[191]

This lack of clarity allowed the system of vagrant removal to be applied to a wide range of people, including the settled poor (if deemed disorderly) and prostitutes and beggars, as well as migrant workers and itinerant chapmen. Typical of the variety of individuals labelled as vagrants were the five families and individuals arrested by William Andrews in the summer of 1757. They included:

Bazil Foster, a old man & his Wife Eliz:th & 4 children. . .

Mary & Sarah Stookes both publickly whipt & one child, all sent to . . . Stafford . . .

[189] LMA, Middlesex Sessions: 'Vagrant expenses: rewards', MF/V/1748.
[190] 13 Anne c. 26, 'An Act for reducing the laws relating to rogues, vagabonds, sturdy beggars and vagrants, into one Act of Parliament', 13 Geo. II c. 24, 'An Act for amending and enforcing the laws relating to rogues, vagabonds and other idle and disorderly persons' and 17 Geo. II c. 5, 'An Act to amend and make more effectual the laws relating to rogues, vagabonds and other idle and disorderly persons, and to houses of correction'. This same list was then reproduced in every justicing manual produced through the end of the century. See for example, Richard Burn, *The Justice of the Peace and Parish Officer*, Vol. IV (18th edn, 1797), pp. 410–11.
[191] Fielding, *Extracts from such of the Penal Laws*, p. 60.

Mary Lund, begging & acting as a Vagtt ... publickly whipt & sent by a Vagt pass to Newport in ye Isle of Wight ...

Mary Morse big with child & one small child a soldier['s] wife not permitted to go with her husband ... sent by a Vagtt pass to Bristoll ...

Sarah Gardiner acting as a vagtt ... having veneriall disease ye Itch & almost starved sent by a Vagt pass to ... Gloster ...

Eliz Jones a Soldier['s] wife & two small children laying in ye open air in ye high road sent by a vagtt pass to Gloster ...

For his efforts, Andrews was rewarded £3 10s., at a rate of 10 shillings per individual adult or married couple, all signed off by Justice Samuel Bever.[192]

A beggar or prostitute arrested by a beadle or watchman would have been taken first to the watch house, if it was night-time, or else directly to the justice's house, Bow Street, or the Guildhall or Mansion House for immediate examination. Without time to marshal character witnesses or evidence, the resulting hearing was little more than an exercise in social power. In *Amelia* (1751), Henry Fielding knowingly depicts the scene in Justice Thrasher's parlour as a travesty of prejudice, with the justice wielding his authority over a suspect on the basis of little more than bigotry: 'Sirrah, your tongue betrays your guilt. You are an Irishman, and that is always sufficient evidence with me'.[193]

According to statute, once arrested and examined by a justice, vagrants were to be 'publickly whipt by the constable ... or ... sent to the house of correction till the next session, or for any less time, as ...[the] justice shall think proper' – normally at least a week at hard labour. If the case was deemed to warrant it, they could then be committed to up to six months' further imprisonment on order of the quarter sessions; and if deemed to be an 'incorrigible rogue', either a further period of two years imprisonment, or else transportation.[194] However, it is not at all clear what facet of being a 'vagrant' differentiated those who were 'publickly whipt' from those simply removed, or privately whipped and imprisoned.

Vagrants taken to the house of correction were delivered to the porter who was required to enter their name and the details of their offence and punishment into the prison register, before escorting them to the prison yard. Jacob Ilive, a religious radical committed to the Clerkenwell house of correction in 1757 for blasphemy, published a first-hand account of the mixed composition of the prison population, composed of 'a great number of dirty young wenches, intermixed with some men; [and] some

---

[192] LMA, Middlesex Sessions: 'Vagrant expenses: rewards', MF/V/1757.
[193] Henry Fielding, *The History of Amelia* (1751), Bk 1, ch. 2.
[194] Burn, *Justice* (1755), p. 494.

felons, who had fetters on, sitting on the ground against a wall, sunning and lousing themselves'.[195] Conditions in houses of correction were tough for those with no money. Vagrants would have been hard pressed to provide the shilling required for a shared bed, or to supplement the county ration of a penny loaf of bread. For them, night would have been spent on straw with perhaps ten or twenty others, without sheeting under a rug provided by the master.

At the same time, it is clear that the community of prisoners made the best of a bad situation:

even while they are beating hemp, [they] sing the most lewd songs men or devils have invented ... They take great delight in sitting in a ring, and telling stories of their own adventures; – how many men they had bilked, what sums they had robbed 'em of, and how many watches they had masoned. Tell who had their M[aidenhea]ds; – how they were first debauched; ... As to their diversions, when they are not beating of hemp, they chiefly turn upon, Hunting the Slipper, Thread my Needle Nan and Prison and Bars. The men play at chuck-farthing, tossing up, Leap-Frog etc. They both take a particular delight in the Fairy Dance, called Rolly Powly, which is a very merry exercise, but abominably obscene.[196]

Overall, the system of vagrant arrest and removal put the authorities and a wider plebeian public at loggerheads, which in turn created substantial systemic problems which had to be addressed. Many Londoners struggled to see a 'vagrant' in the pitiable visage of a beggar or luckless prostitute, and there was widespread public tolerance of these pauper strategies. In Middlesex, the bench complained that

the common People have not a proper Idea of the Offence of begging and have in many instances by their Obstruction rendered it very dangerous for the Peace Officers to whip Sturdy Beggars.[197]

The tendency of Londoners to actively resist and resent the arrest of beggars and street entertainers as vagrants meant that the justices had to rely on rewards to motivate officers to undertake this unpopular task. However, this brought its own difficulties. As with felony prosecution, rewards led to corruption. The constables of Glass House Yard Liberty, for example, 'to whom the Vagabonds from the East and London and Southwark are generally delivered in their Passage to the North, ... have tried every Effort in their Power, to ... Artfully prevail... upon a

---

[195] LL, set, 'Jacob Ilive'; [Jacob Ilive], *Reasons Offered for the Reformation of the House of Correction in Clerkenwell* (1757), pp. 11–12; James A. Herrick, 'Ilive, Jacob (bap. 1705, d. 1763)', *ODNB* (www.oxforddnb.com, 1 Jan. 2014).

[196] [Ilive], *Reasons Offered*, pp. 38, 22–4.

[197] LL, Middlesex Sessions: General Orders of the Court, 3 May 1753 – 15 September 1757 (LMSMGO556030198).

Magistrate at upwards of Ten Miles Distant ... to sign such Orders [for rewards] to a large Amount'.[198] Following an investigation in 1759, it emerged that these constables had subverted the entire system by subcontracting the task of removing vagrants to the county border, and, by a 'Collusion between the Constable who delivers, and him that receives Vagrants', they had 'made a Sine Cure of upwards of £50 P Annum'.[199] In an ironic mirror of the language usually applied to supposedly professional beggars, the Middlesex bench complained that vagrant removal had become 'so lucrative that a kind of Trade has been made of it'.[200]

Further difficulties were created by the complex pattern of local administration, with its essentially arbitrary boundaries between the City, Middlesex and Westminster. Poor relief might set parish against parish, but vagrancy set both parish against county and counties against each other, and allowed beggars and street vendors to work the system. A committee of Middlesex justices reported in April 1757 that as a result of the division between the City and Middlesex, and also because of the individual Watch Acts which governed most of Westminster, 'putting the Vagrant Act into execution'

brings a large Expence upon the County without producing the designed Effect to the publick for ... [it is applied] only to one Species of Vagabonds, namely Beggars, those of them who are more the objects of Compassion than punishment feel the Lash of the Law, while the artificial Objects of Distress, who have reduced Begging into a Trade, well know how far the Whip of Justice extends and carefully avoid coming within its reach.[201]

More difficult still was the structural tension created between the parishes and the county. Removing a pauper under the auspices of the laws of settlement fell to the parish accounts, but removing a vagrant was chalked up to the county. At the same time, while a pauper removal was subject to appeal at quarter sessions, removal under the vagrancy legislation was not.[202] This essentially encouraged parish officers, with the

---

[198] *LL*, Middlesex Sessions: General Orders of the Court, 27 October 1757 – 9 December 1762 (LMSMGO556040257).

[199] *LL*, Middlesex Sessions: General Orders of the Court, 27 October 1757 – 9 December 1762 (LMSMGO55604GO556040257 and LMSMGO55604GO556040258).

[200] *LL*, Middlesex Sessions: General Orders of the Court, 3 May 1753 – 15 September 1757 (LMSMGO556030196).

[201] *LL*, Middlesex Sessions: General Orders of the Court, 3 May 1753 – 15 September 1757 (LMSMGO556030214).

[202] There is some confusion about when and if appeals to vagrancy orders could be taken to quarter sessions, but according to Audrey Eccles such appeals were legally impossible for much of the eighteenth century. This legal situation was regularised following the judgement in *Rex v. Ringwould* in 1777. See Audrey Eccles, *Vagrancy in Law and Practice under the Old Poor Law* (Farnham, Surrey: Ashgate, 2012), p. 56 (citing

connivance of local justices, to redefine paupers as vagrants, in order both to shift the expense of removing them to the county and to avoid a subsequent appeal – a redefinition made easy by the inchoate character of the statute law.

Mary Hyde, for example, was an inmate of the workhouse belonging to St Luke Chelsea. She was one of the migrant workers who 'usually come every year to or near London to work in the summer season'; however, she was forced to apply for relief when her eyesight began to fail in the autumn of 1755. The parish referred her to Hyde Park Hospital for treatment.[203] But when she was later 'discharged ... blind and incurable', she was reclassified as a 'vagrant' by the local justice, Samuel Bever, allowing her to be removed to Shropshire at county expense.[204] Bever's practices were eventually investigated, but his slapdash approach was ascribed to the 'Artifices of ... [parish] Officers', and no further action was taken.[205]

The almost unbridled authority of constables and justices to arrest whomever they felt fell within the definition of a 'vagrant' remained in place throughout the eighteenth century, and was probably most strongly experienced by London paupers struggling to make a living at the edges of the settled economy. Prostitutes, drunks and out of place servants and apprentices almost certainly made up the majority of 'vagrants', and their treatment effectively ended with a week's labour in a house of correction and a brief walk to a local parish of settlement, where they were handed over to the parish officers to be relieved. But, as with many of the 'vagrants' arrested by William Edwards, there were also those for whom being labelled a 'vagrant' formed the starting point for a long-distance relay race of removal from county to county, or indeed to Ireland. For these long-distance vagrants, the system changed significantly in 1757 when the county of Middlesex adopted a comprehensive system of 'farming' vagrant removal.

What had been a relatively informal system in which individual justices conducted examinations and issued removal orders, charging the constable to escort the named vagrant either to prison or the next parish became much more focused on the houses of correction and compters.

M. Nolan, *A Treatise of the Laws for the Relief and Settlement of the Poor*, Vol. II, 4th edn [London, 1825], pp. 238–40).

[203] LL, St Luke Chelsea Workhouse Registers, 12 September 1755 – 5 October 1755 (sldswhr_8_893).

[204] Tim Hitchcock and John Black, eds., *Chelsea Settlement and Bastardy Examinations, 1733–1766* (London Record Society, vol. 33, 1999), no. 307.

[205] LL, Middlesex Sessions: General Orders of the Court, 27 October 1757 – 9 December 1762 (LMSMGO556040265).

Theoretically, though not in practice, from 1757 all vagrants were processed through the prisons and delivered to the newly appointed 'vagrant contractor', James Sturges Adams. His contract with the county specified that he should

> provide himself with a Covered Cart and Proper Horses and Clear the Bridewells of all such Vagabonds ... twice every Week that is to say those whose destination is to the North on one day every Week And those to the South and West on some other day every Week.[206]

Two years later, the bench congratulated itself on having put an 'effectual Stop to the granting Vagrant Passes to the casual Poor, where no Act of Vagrancy had been committed'.[207] For the rest of the century, the vagrant cart could be seen making its regular journey, North, West, South and East, delivering thousands of men, women and children to their next staging post in the adjoining county. In many respects the action of the bench in sub-contracting vagrant removal reflected Henry and John Fielding's belief that the effective administration of the laws against vagrancy, by preventing the 'wandering' of the poor, would contribute to social order. What is much less clear is who these vagrants and vagabonds were, and how they responded to their treatment.

We know that those processed as 'vagrants' were overwhelmingly women. In 1757 they outnumbered men by three to one among those removed from the City and Middlesex. Of the 189 female vagrants removed from Middlesex that year, 38.6 per cent were married or widows, many with small children in tow.[208] As with workhouse populations, women of childbearing age made up the majority of vagrants, reflecting a powerful overlap between the simply poor and the vagrant. Like Mary Hyde, most vagrants were just unlucky.

The changes to vagrant removal outlined in this section were largely the result of a struggle between parishes and the county to control rapidly escalating costs; the role of the poor in this process was confined to the sheer weight of their rising demands for relief and their perceived disorder and criminality. It is unclear how the poor responded to these changes, and to what extent they were able to manipulate the system

---

[206] *LL*, Middlesex Sessions: Sessions Papers, July 1757 (LMSMPS504630003).
[207] *LL*, Middlesex Sessions: Sessions Papers, July 1757 (LMSMPS504630029). NB: this report is filed out of order, among an earlier set of documents.
[208] Nicholas Rogers, 'Policing the poor in eighteenth-century London: the vagrancy laws and their administration', *Histoire Sociale–Social History*, 24 (1991), 133–4 and Table 1 (pi.library.yorku.ca, 2 Jan. 2014). The gender balance changed significantly in the 1780s.

for their own ends. By separating them even more completely from their parish officers, these new arrangements forced accused vagrants, like accused felons, to develop new tactics for survival, but the limitations of the surviving evidence mean that those tactics are difficult to detect. One possibility was to exploit their newly determined legal settlement (which resulted from a formal vagrancy examination) to demand more extensive poor relief when they arrived at their settlement parish. Another was to take advantage of corrupt officials, as some vagrants did in the 1760s, to escape from the removal cart and return to their familiar haunts in London. But perhaps the most likely outcome was simply a lingering resentment against a system which had the power to forcibly transport so many paupers back to places which they no longer called home.

The penal stalemate

Punishments for felons had not changed substantially since the 1718 Transportation Act. At mid-century there were growing concerns that the present system was not working; concerns exacerbated by the growth in the number of felons convicted from 1748 and by continuing attempts by convicts to subvert existing punishments. The 1751 Felonies Committee expressed substantial reservations about the existing penal regime, identifying problems with the death penalty, transportation and imprisonment. Despite their concerns, and owing in large part to worries about anticipated plebeian responses, no major changes were implemented, with the exception of the Murder Act.

Despite calls, including from Henry Fielding, for more frequent executions, the number of felons executed, and the proportion of those sentenced to death who were actually executed, rose only briefly during the prosecution wave before returning to their previous level.[209] The number of executions peaked at sixty-three in 1751, and the following year the proportion executed increased to 90.4 per cent of those sentenced; both figures then declined, to only fifteen executions (60 per cent of those sentenced) in 1762, before a new crime wave following the end of the Seven Years War led to more executions, though not an increase in the proportion executed.

Corporal punishment also declined, from 20.6 per cent of all felons sentenced at the Old Bailey in 1747 to just 3.1 per cent in 1762. Instead, an increasing number of convicts were sentenced to transportation, not only at the Old Bailey, where the proportion of convicts sentenced

---

[209] Fielding, *Enquiry into the Causes*, pp. 182–8.

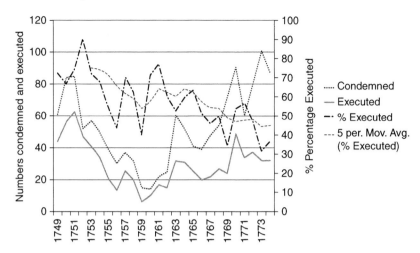

Figure 5.8 Old Bailey death sentences and executions, 1749–1774. Online data set: Death Sentences and Executions 1749–1806.xlsx.

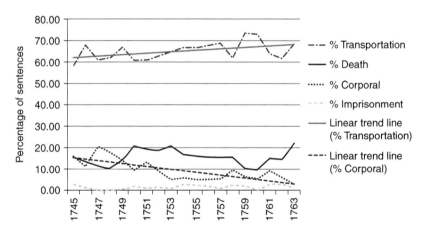

Figure 5.9 Old Bailey punishment sentences, 1745–1763. Online data set: Punishment Statistics 1690–1800.xlsx.

increased from 62.5 per cent in 1747–51 to 67.8 per cent in 1759–63, but also at quarter sessions.

Those convicted of the most serious offences were still hanged, and parliament continued to pass laws removing benefit of clergy (thus mandating a death sentence) from offences which were deemed to be particularly serious and threatening, such as the theft of goods worth more than 40 shillings from a ship or wharf, a crime which was thought to undermine trade.[210] The passage of the Murder Act in 1752 demonstrates the continuing appeal of this ultimate sanction to law-makers, but it did not increase the number of capital offences, and as we have seen its impact was limited. There were increasing concerns expressed by commentators that hanging convicts was simply not working. Even the Felonies Committee resolved 'That it would be reasonable to exchange the Punishment of Death, which is now inflicted for some Sorts of Offences, into some other adequate Punishment'.[211] Yet, while the advent of the Seven Years War in 1756 accelerated the decline in executions, the approach of peace from 1761 reversed the trend. Once again judges and the Privy Council resorted to capital punishment as a means of addressing an anticipated post-war crime wave. Death had not yet been abandoned as the punishment of last resort, not least because all the alternative sanctions could, like Tyburn, be undermined by convicts and the crowd.

While the number of hangings fluctuated depending on perceived levels of crime, the Old Bailey judges appear to have substantially lost faith with whipping at mid-century. While to some extent the decline in sentences was due to the diversion of a substantial number of lesser larceny cases to the Middlesex sessions of the peace, there were also growing concerns about the practice of conducting whippings in public.[212] From the 1730s, a new form of whipping, private whipping, emerged. According to the sheriff's cravings (lists of fees claimed), between 1746 and 1759 more than half of the defendants whipped in London were punished privately, inside a prison or house of correction, or at a stationary post outside a prison or court house, in contrast to the traditional practice of being whipped at a cart's tail along one hundred yards of a public street.[213] While few reservations were openly expressed, judges and justices appear to have become increasingly concerned that public whipping was no longer effective. In part, this may have reflected concern that the crowds on London's streets were no longer paying attention to the spectacle, but the issue of public order was also involved. As we have seen, at the height of the prosecution wave in 1751, a

---

[210] 24 Geo. II c. 45 (1751), 'An Act for the more effectual preventing of robberies and thefts upon any navigable rivers, ports of entry or discharge, wharfs and keys adjacent'; John Beattie, *Crime and the Courts 1660–1800* (Oxford University Press, 1986), p. 524.

[211] *PP, Journals of the House of Commons*, 23 April 1751, p. 190. For two different interpretations of this statement, see Beattie, *Crime and the Courts*, pp. 522–4; McGowen, '"Making examples"', pp. 182–205.

[212] Ward, *Print Culture*, ch. 3.

[213] Robert Shoemaker, 'Streets of shame? The crowd and public punishments in London, 1700–1820', in Simon Devereaux and Paul Griffiths, eds., *Penal Practice and Culture, 1500–1900: Punishing the English* (Basingstoke: Palgrave Macmillan, 2004), pp. 237–40.

committee of Middlesex justices investigating the laws against 'rogues and vagabonds' resolved that it was 'dangerous for the Constables to whip Vagrants in the publick streets' and that they should instead be whipped in a house of correction.[214] There were clearly also concerns that it was inappropriate to whip women in public, since only one-third of the women whipped in this period suffered their punishment in public, compared to almost two-thirds of men.[215] This shift towards private whipping removed one of the most important characteristics of corporal punishments, their publicity.

Despite the widespread attraction of hard labour to those responsible for setting penal policy, the replacement for the declining proportion of convicts sentenced to death or whipping at the Old Bailey was not to be imprisonment, with or without hard labour.[216] Despite the Felonies Committee's concern to address the problem of idleness, the attempt, in the Felons Confinement in the Dockyards Bill in 1752, to introduce hard labour in the naval dockyards as a punishment for felons failed. As Nicholas Rogers observed, there were fears 'that the concentration of convicts in the yards would simply generate a criminal sub-culture rather than a reformative atmosphere'.[217] Among the objections raised against the bill were that 'being in numbers [the convicts] may plot together', 'they may fire the yards and do other mischief', and 'they will escape'.[218]

Experiences with disease and periodic escapes in London's existing prisons made the authorities wary of incarcerating more convicts. Particularly during the post-war prosecution wave, London's prisons were seriously overcrowded and insecure. Newgate could hold 150 prisoners, including debtors, yet that maximum was regularly exceeded, particularly in the days before each Old Bailey sessions. In the period from 1748 to 1751, an average of 1,020 accused criminals and 176 debtors were committed to the prison each year.[219] Almost inevitably, given the poor sanitary conditions, epidemics followed, and this was forcefully

---

[214] *LL*, Middlesex Sessions: Sessions Papers, May 1751 (LMSMPS504110044). For the argument that crowds lost interest in public punishments, see Shoemaker, 'Streets of shame?', pp. 248–9. In contrast, Greg Smith suggests that concerns about public order were more important: Greg T. Smith, 'Civilised people don't want to see that kind of thing: the decline of public physical punishment in London, 1760–1840', in Carolyn Strange, ed., *Qualities of Mercy: Justice, Punishment and Discretion* (Vancouver: UBC Press, 1996), pp. 21–51.

[215] Shoemaker, 'Streets of shame?', p. 242.

[216] Beattie, *Crime and the Courts*, pp. 548–53; Fielding, *Proposal for Making*.

[217] Rogers, 'Confronting the crime wave', p. 89.

[218] BL, Add. Ms 33053, Papers of Thomas Pelham-Holles, Duke of Newcastle, ff. 45–6. We are indebted to Richard Ward for this reference.

[219] W. J. Sheehan, 'Finding solace in eighteenth-century Newgate', in J. S. Cockburn, ed., *Crime in England 1550–1800* (Princeton University Press, 1977), pp. 231–2.

brought home to the authorities in April 1750 when an outbreak of 'gaol fever' (typhus) spread from the prisoners on trial to those present in the Old Bailey courtroom, killing the Lord Mayor, two judges, an alderman, and several lawyers and members of the jury. Almost immediately, plans for the rebuilding of Newgate were drawn up, though disagreements and the difficulty of obtaining funding meant that the actual rebuilding did not commence until 1769. In the short term, the only improvement was the addition of a windmill on the roof (for ventilation) in 1752, but this made little difference. Between 1755 and 1765, 132 prisoners died.[220]

Another consequence of overcrowding was a regular pattern of escapes, not only from Newgate but from virtually all of London's prisons, houses of correction and lockups. In 1748–9, at the height of the prosecution wave, there were escapes from New Prison, Bridewell, and the Wood Street and Poultry Compters, as well as two foiled escapes from Newgate. This problem was acknowledged by the Felonies Committee, which included among its resolutions that 'persons breaking, or attempting to break, any Prison, should be made liable to some severer Penalties'.[221] What is remarkable is how easy it seems to have been to effect an escape, owing to the poor state of the buildings and relatively open access given to visitors. Shortly before the execution of Bosavern Penlez in 1749, it was reported that 'the convicts under sentence of Death in Newgate, having got a Quantity of Gunpowder, Chips and other Combustibles, convey'd to them, design'd to attempt an Escape, by Setting Fire to, or blowing up Part of the said Gaol'.[222] That plan was foiled, but earlier that year John Stanton, committed for pilfering a linen handkerchief, escaped from Bridewell with the help of a 'spring saw' brought into the prison by Sarah Stanton and Marshe Dickenson.[223] He was able 'to saw off his feet lock & make his Escape', while William Taylor, Elford Mills and Thomas Kempton escaped from New Prison in their irons by climbing over the wall 'with the help of Ropes and other Instruments'.[224] Three years later William Carney was able to break out of New Prison with the assistance of William Harvey, who smuggled in a disguise.[225] Similarly, in 1762 Bartholomew Place

---

[220] Harold D. Kalman, 'Newgate Prison', *Architectural History*, 12 (1969), 50–1.

[221] *PP, Journals of the House of Commons*, 23 April 1751, p. 190.

[222] *Whitehall Evening Post*, 5 October to 7 October 1749; also cited by Linebaugh, 'Tyburn riot', p. 98.

[223] *LL*, set, 'John Stanton'.

[224] *LL*, Bridewell Royal Hospital: Minutes of the Court of Governors, 12 January 1738 – 4 April 1751 (BBBRMG202060437); Middlesex Sessions: Sessions Papers, September 1749 (LMSMPS503970109).

[225] *Covent-Garden Journal*, Appendix I, p. 421.

brought William Place (perhaps his brother), detained for burglary in Bridewell, 'a certain fustian frock ... being a dress for the disguising the sd. Wm. Place without the Privity of the Keeper with intent to Aid & assist the Escape of the sd. Wm. Place', as well as 'a certain Instrumt. Made of Iron & Steel called a Punch (being an Instrumt. proper to facilitate the Escape of Prisoners)'.[226] Although unsuccessful, the attempted escape of a group of felons awaiting transportation in June 1758 (they 'had sawed through eight iron bars, each as thick as a man's wrist') provided a further reminder of the insecurity of London's prisons.[227]

As the escapes from Bridewell suggest, houses of correction were no better: the Felonies Committee reported that they suffered 'great Defects ... and Abuses'. These can be summarised as, in addition to the problems of overcrowding, disease and disrepair which affected all prisons, the prisoners' poverty, and their defiance and recalcitrance in the face of attempts (unique in this period to houses of correction) to put them to hard labour and religious duty.[228] Prisoners in London's four houses of correction were some of the poorest in the metropolis. In 1741 the keeper of the Middlesex house in Clerkenwell observed that

the Persons in his Custody are even lower in Life & poorer than those committed to New Prison & often have not one Friend come near them during the whole Time they are confined ... many of the Prisoners are in a dismall Condition near unto starving ... they are often very ill and unable to be bro't up to Court when sent for ... & that he verily believed their Illness was often occasioned by their great Necessities & Want of Provision.[229]

Although some money was provided to support such prisoners, the problem remained. Jacob Ilive, whose observations about vagrants in the house of correction have already been cited, observed in 1757 that 'many persons die here, in the course of a year, for want of food and care', in part because the keeper refused to discharge prisoners who could not pay their fees.[230]

Among the prisoners who were able to feed themselves, through their own labour or from charity, the prison culture was debauched and defiant. Ilive described a 'scene of debauchery', as men went into the Clerkenwell house of correction to find prostitutes, and Henry Fielding

---

[226] *LL*, set, 'William Place'; Middlesex Sessions: Sessions Papers, December 1762 (LMSMPS505170006).

[227] *Gentleman's Magazine*, 28 (1758), 285 (www.hathitrust.org, 2 Jan. 2014).

[228] *PP, Journals of the House of Commons*, 23 April 1751, p. 190.

[229] *LL*, Middlesex Sessions: General Orders of the Court, 28 February 1734 – 14 April 1743 (LMSMGO556010461).

[230] *LL*, set, 'Jacob Ilive'; [Ilive], *Reasons Offered*, pp. 30, 56.

dismissed 'Bridewells' as 'Schools of Vice, Seminaries of Idleness, and Common-shores of Nastiness and Disease'.[231] But house of correction prisoners did not simply descend into a riot of vice and debauchery; they conspired to resist their prosecutions and punishments. In April 1752 the Middlesex justices noted that prisoners in New Prison and the house of correction who had been accused of felonies 'or some other Grand Misdemeanor' had devised a scheme for escaping prosecutions. Before they were examined by a justice of the peace in front of their prosecutors, they 'changed their Apparell and put on different Cloathing and so disguised themselves that the prosecutors have not known whether they were the same persons against whom they complained or not, By which Artifice such Offenders have escaped a prosecution'.[232]

In addition, prisoners such as Ilive (admittedly atypical) used print (two pamphlets, published in 1757 and 1759) to highlight conditions in houses of correction, thereby forcing the justices to act.[233] In 1760 the Middlesex bench asked a committee of justices to examine prisoners in the house of correction and New Prison 'to inform themselves from the Prisoners what sort of Beds are provided for them and whether they are incommoded by any Sort of Vermin as has in print been asserted'. The court further recognised the power of prisoners' complaints by resolving that prisoners should 'be properly kept from hard usage to prevent Reflection either to the Magistracy or Keepers of the said Prisons'.[234] Inadvertently, this and earlier justices' orders helped make prisoners aware of the potency of their complaints through their power to influence the keepers and excuse their own misbehaviour. Sarah Griffith, charged with escaping from the Westminster house of correction in 1756 by using a knife to prise off an iron grate and climbing over a fifteen foot wall, justified her actions by claiming 'I was there 3 weeks, and for four days without victuals, being obliged to eat the cabbage stalks off the dunghill, because there is no allowance for us'.[235] Although the keeper claimed that he would have provided for her if she had only asked, Sarah was acquitted.

As in the past, felons in houses of correction presented a particular problem. Overcrowding at Newgate occasionally meant that felons could

---

[231] [Ilive], *Reasons Offered*, p. 15; Fielding, *Enquiry into the Causes*, p. 96.
[232] *LL*, Middlesex Sessions: General Orders of the Court, 19 May 1743 – 22 February 1753 (LMSMGO556020517).
[233] [Ilive], *Reasons Offered*; [Jacob Ilive], *A Scheme for the Employment of all Persons Sent as Disorderly to the House of Correction in Clerkenwell* (1759).
[234] *LL*, Middlesex Sessions: General Orders of the Court, 27 October 1757 – 9 December 1762 (LMSMGO556040108 and LMSMGO556040109).
[235] *LL*, set, 'Sarah Griffith'; *LL*, Old Bailey Proceedings, 14 July 1756 (t17560714-1).

be found in these other prisons, which were intended only for the punishment and reform of petty offenders. Incarcerating felons in houses of correction had been tried before following an Act of 1706, but this policy had been subverted by prisoner behaviour, including a mutiny over the use of fetters in 1713. The experiment was briefly tried again in July 1750, when seven convicted thieves were sentenced to the Clerkenwell house of correction for six months, but there were similar problems. Fielding reported the following year that he had been informed by the keeper that it had been impossible to put the felons to hard labour 'with any heavy or sharp Instruments of Work, lest they should be converted into Weapons'; and Ilive claimed that houses of correction were simply not suitable for felons because they were so easy to escape from.[236]

With significant reservations over the use of hanging, whipping and imprisonment, many of which reflected convict resistance, the judges increased the number of sentences of transportation in the 1750s, although this punishment also generated both convict subversion and elite doubts. As we have seen, at the Old Bailey transportation accounted for a large and growing proportion of all punishments (Figure 5.9). From late 1749 the Middlesex justices also used transportation for those convicted of petty larceny at quarter sessions, drastically reducing the number of convicts who were whipped or sent to a house of correction. Between 1749 and 1754, 48 per cent of these convicts were sentenced to transportation.[237]

Despite its popularity with judges and justices, substantial criticisms of transportation remained. It was thought that life in the American colonies had become too easy for transportation to act as a deterrent, that it could lead to depopulation and that returning from transportation was relatively straightforward for those who could afford to buy their freedom and a passage home.[238] These concerns were exemplified by the case of John Poulter, alias Baxter, convicted at the Old Bailey of receiving stolen goods and sentenced to fourteen years' transportation in 1746.[239] A frequently republished account of Poulter's multiple crimes demonstrated how easy it was to return from transportation (while not admitting that he had done so). Convicts only needed to purchase their freedom from the merchant or captain of the transport ship, and they would then be released 'unmolested' when they arrived in America. They were then

---

[236] Fielding, *Enquiry into the Causes*, p. 97; [Ilive], *Scheme for the Employment*, p. 45.
[237] Not only did this policy reflect an attempt to increase the severity of the punishment for petty larceny, but it was also intended to reduce the pressure on houses of correction: Ward, 'Print culture and responses to crime', pp. 83–5, 92.
[238] Beattie, *Crime and the Courts*, pp. 538–43.
[239] *LL*, set, 'John Poulter'; *LL*, Old Bailey Proceedings, 5 December 1746 (t17461205-11).

able to return to England on any other ship ('if they can pay their passage they are refused no ship'). Those unable to purchase their freedom could run away from their masters and travel to Philadelphia, New York or Boston, 'in which places no Questions are asked them'. Poulter claimed, therefore, that transportation was 'but four or five months pleasure'.[240]

Although it is impossible to determine how many convicts actually returned home (one estimate suggests the number was 'relatively modest'), those who did so nonetheless constituted a headache for the authorities.[241] Many became members of gangs, and returnees were surprisingly difficult to convict. Between 1748 and 1762, twenty-seven defendants were charged with returning from transportation at the Old Bailey, seventeen during the prosecution wave of 1748–53. Despite the relative ease of proving the offence (all that was required was proof of the defendant's original conviction and sentence), seven were acquitted, owing to flaws in the indictments, lack of positive identifications or defendants' successful arguments that they had been brought back to Britain against their wishes (e.g. as a prisoner of war). Consequently, the Felonies Committee proposed that 'the method of convicting such Offenders should be rendered more easy and less expensive'.[242]

The penal system in the 1750s had therefore reached a stalemate. Owing to both elite concerns and potential disorder at Tyburn, it was not thought politic to execute more convicts, but the alternatives of whipping and hard labour were also rejected due to fears that they, too, were both ineffective and easily subverted. While transportation was increasingly used, concerns were mounting that it suffered from similar disadvantages. This situation would not fundamentally change until transportation was interrupted by the outbreak of the American War two decades later.

London's lost children

If policing and punishment struggled to cope with what seemed like a rising tide of disorder, the increasing number of associational charities

---

[240] Poulter, *Discoveries*, p. 28; Gwenda Morgan and Peter Rushton, *Eighteenth-Century Criminal Transportation: The Formation of the Criminal Atlantic* (Basingstoke: Palgrave Macmillan, 2004), pp. 98–100.

[241] Gregory Durston, 'Magwitch's forbears: returning from transportation in eighteenth-century London', *Australian Journal of Legal History*, 9:2 (2005), 157 (search.informit.com.au, 2 Jan. 2014).

[242] *PP, Journals of the House of Commons*, 23 April 1751, p. 190.

such as the Foundling Hospital must have appeared to point the way towards a more orderly London. The metropolis had long been plagued by high levels of infant mortality. According to the *Bills of Mortality*, the death rate of children under ten typically stood at over 500 deaths per thousand christenings in the first half of the century. While in the 1740s the existence of the hospital appears to have reduced this by 5 per cent (largely by shifting the place of death from the town to the countryside), in the 1750s the mortality rate began to climb again, and it soon returned to half of all babies born in the capital, before finally starting a long slow decline in the second half of the century.[243] The situation was particularly bad in the new workhouses. In 1750 a committee of the vestry at St Margaret Westminster reported on 'all the children that have been born' in their workhouse, 'or sent in under the age of twenty months', between February 1746 and May 1750. Fifty-six babies and toddlers had been delivered or admitted, of whom twelve had been discharged to friends or parents, their eventual fate unrecorded. Only six were reported as still living and in the house, and of these, five had been born in the house and were still under the age of twenty months. The committee could find only a single child above the age of twenty months who had been admitted as an infant and was still alive and in the house.[244] St Margaret's workhouse was quite simply a place of death. And the Foundling Hospital, which carefully screened the babies it admitted for signs of illness and poor health, and which developed a comprehensive system of rural nursing, managed little better. The first half of the 1750s saw the hospital experiencing a mortality rate of over 72 per cent. This figure rose to over four out of every five babies during the latter half of the decade, during the 'General Reception' (1756–60) when all infants were admitted.[245]

---

[243] Corbyn Morris, *Observations on the Past Growth and Present State of London* (2nd edn, 1758), Table II, reproduced as part of *A Collection of the Yearly Bills of Mortality, from 1657 to 1758 Inclusive. Together with several other bills of an earlier date* (1759). These figures form a crude guide only. For a more nuanced analysis of infant mortality in London that incorporates corrections for under-registration, see John Landers, *Death and the Metropolis: Studies in the Demographic History of London, 1670–1830* (Cambridge University Press, 1993), pp. 98–101. Unfortunately Landers does not factor in the role of the Foundling Hospital in his analysis. See also, Alysa Levene, 'The mortality penalty of illegitimate children: foundlings and poor children in eighteenth-century England', in Alysa Levene, S. Williams and T. Nutt, eds., *Illegitimacy in Britain, 1700–1920* (Basingstoke: Palgrave Macmillan, 2005); and Alysa Levene, *Childcare, Health and Mortality at the London Foundling Hospital, 1741–1800* (Manchester University Press, 2007), ch. 3.

[244] WAC, St Margaret Westminster, 'Orders of vestry', E2420, 1738–55, pp. 249–52.

[245] Ruth K. McClure, *Coram's Children: The London Foundling Hospital in the Eighteenth Century* (New Haven, Conn.: Yale University Press, 1981), Appendix III, p. 261.

For the elite men who ran the parishes, managed the charities and sat in judgement in the courts, it was clear enough who was to blame: the gin-soaked mothers of their imagination. When, in February 1751, William Hogarth published *Gin Lane*, he put centre stage a drunken crone, absent-mindedly dropping her unnaturally plump and healthy baby boy (Figure 5.5).[246] Just as the apparent disorder associated with gin consumption was used to justify new controls, so the new associational charities and government policies that came in their wake – the 'General Reception' at the Foundling Hospital and Jonas Hanway's Registration Acts (1761 and 1767) – identified concerns for the health of newborn Londoners as justification for exercising an intrusive civic authority over both the bodies of mothers and the lives of their children. In these initiatives can be found a concerted form of what Patricia Crawford has characterised as 'civic fatherhood'.[247] When parliament failed to legislate in response to what the Felonies Committee described as the propagation of 'a new Race of chargeable Poor, from Generation to Generation', the associational charities took on the challenge.[248] Despite professed humanitarian aims, the impact of these new institutions and policies was both stark and divisive. For the babies left in the hands of the Foundling Hospital, the most likely outcome was a quick death, while effectively breaking up families and leaving a trail of heartbreak. At the same time, initiatives such as the new lying-in hospitals, the Marine Society and John Fielding's Asylum for Orphan Girls, designed to support the production of healthy and useful children, redirected charitable resources to the settled poor by creating a complex series of admission tests designed to filter the moral and healthy from the dissolute and gin soaked. Collectively, the new policies of the 1750s both reinforced the division between the settled poor and a desperate residuum, and directly led to the deaths of thousands of babies and very young children.

A new procreative agenda had stuttered into life in the late 1730s and 1740s, and came to fruition in the 1750s. The response to alarmingly high rates of infant mortality was largely to remove the care of many expectant mothers from the parishes, and of the children of the poor from their parents. Just as the Foundling Hospital was being established, Richard Manningham founded the 'Charitable Infirmary for the Relief of Poor Women Labouring of Child'. The next decade and a half witnessed the

---

[246] Mark Hallett, *Spectacle of Difference: Graphic Satire in the Age of Hogarth* (London: Yale University Press, 1999), pp. 206–9.

[247] Patricia Crawford, *Parents of Poor Children in England, 1580–1800* (Oxford University Press, 2010), pp. 193–239.

[248] *PP, Journals of the House of Commons*, 13 June 1751, p. 289.

establishment of five further charities aimed at expectant mothers.[249] In 1747 new lying-in wards were built at the Middlesex General Hospital, and in 1749 the British Lying-in Hospital in Brownlow Street was established. Next came the City of London Lying-in Hospital in 1750, followed by the General Lying-in Hospital, later Queen Charlotte's in 1752, and finally, in 1757, the Lying-in Charity for Delivering Poor Married Women in their own Habitations.[250] These mother and baby centred initiatives were mirrored by a series of charities aimed at older children, seeking to steer their youthful paths in the way of useful lives. Both Jonas Hanway's Marine Society (1756) and John Fielding's Asylum for Orphan Girls (1758) sought to capture the hearts and minds of the children of London, by removing them from the baleful influence of pauper parents. And finally, using state resources, the 'General Reception' at the Foundling Hospital was mandated by parliament in the spring of 1756, sparking the most expensive and murderous experiment in social welfare in British history, while encouraging widespread parental abandonment of their small children.

In combination with the evolution of workhouses into centres for the care and relief of younger women of child-bearing age, and the passage of Hardwicke's Marriage Act in 1753, which rendered most traditional forms of irregular marriage illegal, these charities and initiatives created a new reproductive regime in London.[251] Elite male control was enhanced by the gradual introduction, from the 1730s, of male midwives into this traditionally female area of care.[252] The state and the elite men who managed reproduction claimed a kind of collective oversight of pauper women's bodies, and the children they produced. Working Londoners were largely excluded from this discussion, but the way they interacted with these new institutions would shape their development.

Each of these charities added a new landmark to the already complex landscape of relief and support which Londoners in desperate circumstances needed to navigate, and each had a different impact on their lives. The lying-in charities, for example, appear to have been reasonably popular, despite suspicion of the 'man-midwifery' associated with them.

---

[249] Lisa Cody, *Birthing the Nation: Sex, Science and the Conception of Eighteenth-Century Britain* (Oxford University Press, 2005), pp. 172–6. For St James, see WAC, St James Westminster, 'Vestry minutes', D1760, 1736–50, p. 192.

[250] The best overview of these developments is Lisa Foreman Cody, 'Living and dying in Georgian London's lying-in hospitals', *Bulletin of the History of Medicine*, 78:2 (2004), 309–48. See also Donna T. Andrew, *Philanthropy and Police: London Charity in the Eighteenth Century* (Princeton University Press, 1989), pp. 65–8, 105–9.

[251] 26 Geo. II c. 33, 'An Act for the better preventing of clandestine marriages'.

[252] John Gillis, *For Better, For Worse: British Marriages, 1600 to the Present* (Oxford University Press, 1988), pp. 140–2; Adrian Wilson, *The Making of Man-Midwifery: Childbirth in England, 1660–1770* (London: UCL Press, 1995).

As Lisa Cody has demonstrated, they provided relatively good conditions for the settled poor. Even specialised parish provision of the sort provided by St Martin's attracted a willing clientele, at least in the short term. At institutions such as the British Lying-in Hospital in Brownlow Street, conditions were of an even higher standard, with individual beds, clean clothing and nutritious food. Perhaps most significantly, the hospital ensured that most births were overseen by traditional midwives, and supported a full month of post-delivery rest and recuperation.[253] Gin and gambling were forbidden, and a gruelling regime of religion was demanded. But all told, the lying-in hospitals represented a substantial financial and material contribution to the lives of the poor. The only problem was that they were difficult to access. As Cody relates, to gain admission to the British Lying-in Hospital, each prospective patient

needed to locate a governor who could give her a recommendation; she had to have proof of her marriage, or go to the Old Bailey to have an affidavit made out; and then she was interviewed at a Thursday board meeting, where she was asked about her menstrual cycle and other matters, examined by the matron, and, if determined a clean, proper object of charity, was allowed to ballot for a place.[254]

These procedures effectively excluded the unsettled, the unmarried and the desperate. In effect, the existence of these new institutions pushed these mothers towards parish provision (or the Foundling Hospital), while the charities took on the care of more established women and their children. This in turn reinforced the association of parish relief with extreme poverty and moral turpitude, while ensuring that the capital's workhouses would continue to be dominated by women of childbearing age who were excluded from the lying-in hospitals.

In order for even the respectable poor to obtain the benefit of the new charities, they needed to learn how to write petitions and secure the support of their richer neighbours. At the Asylum for Orphaned Girls, or Lambeth Asylum, founded in 1758, the requirements for admission included that

each object applying for Admission will be required to produce ... a Certificate of their Age & Necessity as shall be satisfactory to the Guardians then present; each Certificate to be sign'd by two substantial House Keepers of the Parish where the Objects resides.[255]

[253] Cody, 'Living and dying', 323. At Brownlow Street there was an early and murderous outbreak of puerperal fever that dented this rather rosy picture.
[254] Cody, 'Living and dying', 343, n. 148.
[255] University of Pennsylvania Archives, Ms. Codex 1623, Asylum for Orphan Girls, Minutes and records of the Guardians, p. 15, Wednesday, 21 June 1758 (hdl.library. upenn.edu/1017/d/medren/5456346, 2 Jan. 2014).

While the advertisements and rules were clear that the Asylum was intended to provide housing, care and education to orphaned and poor girls between the ages of eight and twelve who, in the words of Donna Andrew, were in danger of being 'sold into prostitution', the inevitable result of the selection process was that most of the girls accepted by the Asylum were much less at risk than the Society's advertising suggested.[256] Of the fifty-four girls admitted in the first three years to 1761, only eight were actually orphans; the rest had one or both parents still living. Many applicants were excluded on the grounds that they had a legal settlement, and several others on the grounds that their parents were 'very well able to maintain them'. But overall the charity appears to have evolved into a support for established families seeking help with the costs of education and training, rather than as a facility for street children.

The poor seeking to benefit from this charity essentially colluded in a process of directing resources to the settled poor in direct contradiction to the objectives of the trustees. When in August 1759, Sarah Carpenter, Sarah Gelder and Mary Morris 'got out at the Window and went home to their Parents, but returned in a few hours', they were making the most of resources which were not actually intended for them.[257]

Many of the other mid-century charities came to support precisely this same settled community, even when they claimed to be directed at the marginal and desperate, and in the process they had a similar effect on the wider population of the poor. Besides the half-dozen lying-in charities, this selectivity is also apparent in the workings of the Marine Society. This Society was and is dedicated to supporting recruitment to the Navy, and from its foundation in 1756 was primarily concerned with fitting out men and boys with the clothes and equipment they needed to serve at sea. Some basic training was also provided, and a subset of boys was trained to play the fife. Like the lying-in hospitals, this was a popular charity that provided substantial resources of clothing and bedding to the poor. The rhetoric associated with the Marine Society was about the problem of 'vagabond boys who are in filth and rags and have no means of support but theft and beggary', and its express purpose was to relieve London 'from the burden of Idle and useless boys'.[258] But as a result of

---

[256] Andrew, *Philanthropy and Police*, p. 118.
[257] Mitch Fraas, *The Records of the Asylum for Orphan Girls (Part II)*, 2 May 2012 (uniqueatpenn.wordpress.com, 2 Jan. 2014).
[258] National Maritime Museum, Greenwich, Marine Society Fair Minutes, MSY/A/1, 7 January 1762, quoted in Dianne Payne, 'Rhetoric, reality and the Marine Society', *London Journal*, 30:2 (November 2005), 80; Jonas Hanway, *An Account of the Marine Society, Recommending the Piety and Policy of the Institution* (1759), p. 73.

the large number of boys presented, and the refusal of ship's captains to take on vagrant and sickly children, the charity quickly abandoned its concentration on the very poor and became a resource for settled families looking to place their male children without the expense of a formal apprenticeship. Consequently, despite the fact Fielding had helped found it, the charity largely stopped accepting the children sent by him in July 1757.[259] Instead, most of the Society's recruits could read, were in stable employment and from settled backgrounds.

Thus, most of the charities established at mid-century appear to have evolved to support a form of settled poverty, with families figuring out how to use them as a way of securing care in childbirth and education for their children. To this extent, working Londoners learned how to exploit these charities, providing much-needed resources in support of families at two of the most difficult times in the life cycle. In effect these charities stepped into the breach left by the creation of parish workhouses, which sought to discourage applications from all but the most marginal Londoners. However, in order to generate the income from benefactors needed to provide this service, the hospitals and charities strove vigorously, one against the other, in 'open competitions' for resources that threatened to bring them all into disrepute, and which were built on a damning indictment of the London poor.[260] In pursuit of charitable donations, and while it continued to recruit 'stout lads' of good parts from settled backgrounds, the Marine Society, for instance, constantly pointed up the criminal and feral character of London's children. Similarly, the Lambeth Asylum depicted its own charges as preternaturally addicted to sex and gin.

The irony underpinning the hard work of even well-meaning philanthropists such as Jonas Hanway was that in order to provide what were generous conditions for London's poor, they needed to paint women and children as vicious and libertine. In the short term, the respectable poor, who learned how to obtain these resources by presenting themselves as victims and personal failures, struck this bargain, despite the unflattering light it cast upon them. But in the longer term, the charities' strategy effectively made working Londoners appear both in the guise of a problem in need of an elite solution and as a class of people beyond redemption or real empathy.

If the actions of the charitable and well-meaning tended to demean the poor in the course of providing them with much-needed support, the development of state policy in these same years, promoted by many of

[259] Payne, 'Rhetoric, reality and the Marine Society', 68.
[260] *Gentleman's Magazine*, May 1758, p. 215.

the same people, tended to actively destroy families and increase the murderous rate of infant mortality. By far the most expensive state intervention in the lives of poor Londoners between the establishment of the Old Poor Law and the creation of the modern welfare state, the 'General Reception' at the Foundling Hospital was mandated by parliament in March 1756, in response to a petition from the hospital. Motivated by the expectation that caring for foundlings would contribute to building up the armed forces, between June 1756 and March 1760 the Foundling Hospital was charged by parliament to accept all children offered to it under the age of two months. Over the next five years, 14,982 babies were admitted to the hospital at a direct cost of over £500,000.[261] By comparison, at mid-century the parishes of London and Middlesex were spending in total between £80,000 and £90,000 per year on poor relief, and the annual national cost of parish relief was just under £700,000.[262]

The babies admitted during the General Reception were brought by their mothers or fathers, or by parish officers, occasionally in cahoots with the fathers of illegitimate babies. For their parents, the hospital offered hope that their infants would obtain the secure upbringing they were unable to provide. As the testimony of Giuseppe Ricciardelli alias Joseph Geraldine, a poverty-stricken Italian immigrant sentenced to hang at Tyburn for murder, suggests, even in 1752 the hospital's facilities seemed to offer the promise that someone would care for his child, when he himself faced oblivion.[263] Just before his death, he wrote to a friend, to

recommend to you my unfortunate Wife, lately brought to Bed of a Son in Brownlow-Street Hospital ... and particularly beseeching you, if possible, to get the Child to be admitted into the Foundling-Hospital, and educated in the Protestant Religion.[264]

Many of the notes left with the children express real gratitude for the care provided, and a belief that the child 'could be plac'd no where safer, than under yr wise & good Government'.[265]

[261] McClure, *Coram's Children*, p. 116; James Stephen Taylor, *Jonas Hanway, Founder of the Marine Society: Charity and Policy in Eighteenth-Century Britain* (London: Scholar Press, 1985), p. 68.

[262] See *PP*, 'Report from the Select Committee on poor rate returns', 1821, pp. 9, 14 (parlipapers.chadwyck.co.uk, 2 Jan. 2014).

[263] *LL*, set, 'Giuseppe Ricciardelli'.

[264] *LL*, Ordinary of Newgate Prison: Ordinary's Accounts, 23 March 1752 (OA175203235203230012).

[265] LMA, A/FH/A09/1/53, Margaret Hall, child no.4338, 1 May 1757; quoted in Alysa Levene (general ed.), *Narratives of the Poor in Eighteenth-Century Britain*, Vol. III: *Institutional Responses: The London Foundling Hospital* (London: Pickering & Chatto, 2006), p. 139. Margaret died on 6 February 1763.

However, the system was open to abuse. Even Jonas Hanway recognised that many infants were 'torn by the Parish-Officers from the Breast of a shrieking Mother, with a View to save Expence to the Parish'.[266] At least forty-three babies, for example, were sent to the hospital from St Martin's workhouse.[267] These included children such as Prudentia Miller, the illegitimate daughter of Anne Miller, born in the workhouse and sent unbaptised to the hospital at just six days old: 'with a desire for her to be named Prudentia'.[268] Anne Miller, a widow, had recently been removed to St Martin's as a vagrant from Ealing along with her two older children, four-year-old James Edward and two-year-old Mary.[269] It is unclear what happened to James Edward, but Anne and Mary left the workhouse a month after Prudentia's birth, with '3 Shill[ing]; to Carry her into ye. Cuntry'.[270] The parish officers had indeed been saved a deal of trouble and expense.

The most substantial effect of this essentially mercantilist attempt to break a perceived pattern of intergenerational poverty was simply thousands of dead children. From 24 June 1758 to 29 September 1760, 81 per cent of the 7,000 admitted, or just under 6,000, died, the vast majority under the age of one year. Of the children kept at the hospital itself (as opposed to those sent out to nurse), this figure rose to 94 per cent of the total.[271] The Governors were fully aware of the problem, but kept the wider public largely in ignorance. The deaths continued through the summer of 1760, when parliament finally withdrew its financial support primarily because of the growing costs.[272]

Of course, infant mortality was also high outside the hospital, and the governors of the Foundling Hospital were largely well-meaning; the 10,000 children whose deaths they facilitated in the first twenty years of the hospital's operation were unintended consequences of simple hubris.

---

[266] Jonas Hanway, *A Candid Historical Account of the Hospital for the Reception of Exposed and Deserted Young Children* (1760), p. 34.

[267] *LL*, St Martin in the Fields Workhouse Registers, 1756–60, keyword: foundling.

[268] *LL*, set, 'Prudentia Miller'; St Martin in the Fields Workhouse Registers, 17 March 1757 – 21 March 1757 (smdswhr_367_36711).

[269] *LL*, set, 'Anne Miller'. For this kind of 'family fragmentation', see Jeremy Boulton, '"It is extreme necessity that makes me do this": some "survival strategies" of pauper households in London's West End during the early eighteenth century', *International Review of Social History*, Supplement 8 (2000), 47–70.

[270] Anne returned to the workhouse on four further occasions and left her second child, Mary, in the care of the house two years later – where she died of a fever on 28 September 1757. *LL*, St Martin in the Fields Workhouse Registers, 2 June 1757 – 25 June 1757 (smdswhr_367_36724).

[271] See McClure, *Coram's Children*, pp. 102, 104, Appendix III, p. 261.

[272] McClure, *Coram's Children*, p.105. Declining annual payments for 'Parliamentary children' continued through 1771.

However, the real impact of this initiative was on the families torn apart by the policy. Many contemporaries regretted the doleful effects of the General Reception on family relationships. Joseph Massie, for instance, worried that the policy would erode, 'those natural Obligations' upon which 'the Happiness of Individuals, and the Welfare of Society, do very much depend', leaving no one to 'Maintain their Parents when they grow Old', and leaving each foundling with no one 'to give them good advice, to assist them when they behave well, or restrain them from doing Ill'.[273]

More telling was the experience of Mary Hindes, hanged and anatomised in June 1768 for the murder of eighteen-month old John Smith.[274] Mary was a widow living in St George Hanover Square workhouse, who regularly visited John's parents in Green Street. On 17 April, Mary volunteered to take 'Joe', as his father called him, out to buy a cheesecake; and from there went from pub to pub, before eventually drowning him in the Serpentine. In her own estimation, she was

wearied of life, she had had a great many disquietudes ... and ... a couple of children [taken] from her, and put ... into the Foundling-hospital, which had given her a great deal of anxiety; she concluded with saying, she was desirous of dying, and that led her to do that sort of an act, for which she said she knew she should receive no mercy of the jury ...[275]

It rapidly emerged that 'Joe' Smith was not Mary's first victim and that she had been tried and acquitted of an almost identical crime seven years earlier, when she was accused of drowning five-month-old Edward Mulby, the son of Malachi and Sarah.[276] Once again, she had taken an infant child from its mother as a favour, fed it and drowned it in a pond – this time near Knightsbridge. Theft was not the motive in either case, and it is clear that Mary Hindes was insane, gripped by a pathological interest in small children of an age with those taken from her. Just before she was turned off at Tyburn, on Wednesday 29 June 1768, she admitted to the hangman that she was also responsible for 'destroying several other children' in addition to Joe and Edward.[277] Mary Hindes was a serial killer, the victim of a system that paid little heed of her emotional attachment to her own children.

By the end of the General Reception, even the Hospital's most fervent proponents recognised that, in the words of Jonas Hanway, it was 'the cause of the deaths of many thousands', particularly among rural infants

---

[273] Joseph Massie, *Farther Observations Concerning the Foundling-Hospital* (1759), p. 1.
[274] *LL*, set, 'Mary Hindes'.
[275] *LL*, Old Bailey Proceedings, 18 May 1768 (t17680518-39).
[276] *LL*, Old Bailey Proceedings, 9 December 1761 (t17611209-26).
[277] *St. James's Chronicle or the British Evening Post*, 28 June 1768 – 30 June 1768, p. 3 (Burney Collection: www.galegroup.com, 1 Jan. 2014).

brought to London.[278] Public charities as a whole were also brought in to disrepute. When the anonymous author of *Some Considerations of the Fatal Effects . . . of the Present Excess of Publick Charities* published his views in 1763, he directed his particular ire at recent London foundations, including 'The Magdalene, Asylum, Foundling, Hospitals for Sick and Lame, Lying-in Hospitals, Charity Schools, and the Dissenting Fund'. The mid-century experiment in the foundation of new associational charities was largely finished.[279]

London's poor did not create these charities, though they were a response to growing poverty and its associated perceived and real social problems. Nor, for the most part, did they shape their form and direction. In many respects, as the case of Mary Hindes suggests, these policies were an unmitigated disaster for the poor. However, in their encounters with the gatekeepers of these charities, the poor did learn valuable lessons. They discovered how to manipulate the available resources for their own purposes, colluding with parish officers and charity officials where it was in their interests to do so, and in other circumstances playing them off against each other. Using petitions, letters of reference and personal lobbying, the poor, especially the more respectable poor, learned how to exploit these charities to get the support they needed. And by the sheer level of demand, they forced these charities into making what sometimes turned out to be disastrous policy choices. While, as in the case of the General Reception, the results of the policies were manifestly not in their interests, neither were they ultimately in the interests of the charities themselves.

However, to Jonas Hanway's way of thinking, these failures did not invalidate his efforts to intervene to protect pauper children from both their parents and the parish officers. He knew the value of every child lost to gin and parochial greed, and calculated it at precisely £151 11s. 4d. per baby.[280] And in the early 1760s, he determined to take the lessons he believed he had learned from the operation of the Foundling Hospital and apply them to the regulation of London's parishes and workhouses. The result was *An Act for the keeping regular, uniform and annual Registers, of all Parish Poor Infants under a certain Age*, which formed the starting point for an increasingly aggressive assault on the right of pauper parents to care for and direct the lives of their children.[281]

---

[278] Jonas Hanway, *Serious Considerations on the Salutary Design of the Act of Parliament for a Regular, Uniform Register of the Parish-Poor* (1762), pp. 6–7.
[279] *Some Considerations of the Fatal Effects . . . of the Present Excess of Publick Charities* (1763), title page.
[280] Hanway, *Serious Considerations*, p. 5.
[281] 2 Geo. III, c. 22, 'An Act for the keeping regular, uniform and annual registers of all parish poor infants under a certain age'.

The resilient highwaymen

Collectively, the policy changes of the 1750s sought to transform the culture of idleness, immorality and crime that elite commentators thought characterised the lives of the labouring poor. However, as with the initiatives of the associational charities, the real outcomes were seldom straightforward and rarely conformed to the expectations of those who implemented them. Many aspects of popular culture, including the belief in polite highway robbery as a legitimate form of social mobility, were more resilient than this, and some more respectable Londoners remained sympathetic.

Despite growing criticisms, highwaymen continued to claim the label of gentlemen throughout the late 1750s and early 1760s, and to use it to their advantage.[282] Victims continued to report that highwaymen treated them with politeness and civility, and the reading public continued to consume stories involving the gentlemen of the highway.[283] The *General History of the Lives and Adventures of the Most Famous Highwaymen, Murderers, Pirates, Street-Robbers, and Thief-Takers* was republished in 1758, along with pamphlet accounts of the lives of highwaymen including William Page, Isaac Darkin and Paul Lewis (published between 1758 and 1763).[284] As they had been doing since the 1720s, this public profile allowed robbers to style themselves as gentlemen highwaymen, claiming that role through their dress, activities on the road and behaviour in public and in prison. When Page, the son of a bargeman, and his accomplice William Darwell robbed John Webb, they emphasised their social pretensions and 'scorned to take any silver', while Webb actively participated in what feels like a ritual between social equals by 'desir[ing] him to take a crown for a bowl of punch'. Webb's servant called the robbers 'Gentlemen'.[285] In an account of the trial of Isaac Darkin, the son of a corkcutter and a widowed gentlewoman, he is described as having 'made no small figure in Publick: He frequented Places of

---

[282] Robert Shoemaker, 'The street robber and the gentleman highwayman: changing representations and perceptions of robbery in London, 1690–1800', *Cultural and Social History*, 3:4 (October 2006), 381–405; Andrea McKenzie, 'The real Macheath: social satire, appropriation, and eighteenth-century criminal biography', *Huntington Library Quarterly*, 69:4 (2006), 581–605.

[283] In 1763 alone, there were seven such reports in the *London Evening Post*.

[284] Capt. Mackdonald, *A General History of the Lives and Adventures of the Most Famous Highwaymen, Murderers, Pirates, Street-Robbers, and Thief-Takers* (1758). *A Genuine Narrative of the Life and Surprising Robberies and Adventures of William Page* (1758) went into a second edition and an abridged edition.

[285] *LL*, Old Bailey Proceedings, 22 February 1758 (t17580222-28).

Diversion, drove his Phaeton, and constantly appeared upon the Turf'.[286] He was credited with having 'a high Notion of Honour'.[287]

Having attempted to play the gentleman on the road, these three robbers followed the example of highwaymen such as James Maclaine earlier in the decade and cooperated with authors and printers to ensure that sympathetic accounts of their stories reached a wider public. Although no copies have survived, the *Genuine Life of Isaac Darking, alias Dumas* was published, 'Collected from his own Papers, and signed by himself the Day before his Execution'.[288] Paul Lewis, who knew the Ordinary would not portray him in a sympathetic light, sold his story to another printer, who described him as 'brave', and as 'a person of good natural parts, [with] a just sense of the Christian Religion'.[289] Some newspapers repeated these claims: Page was 'the gentleman highwayman', and Lewis, a former sailor, was 'Captain Lewis ... the famous highwayman'.[290]

Prison continued to afford highwaymen opportunities to publicise their genteel pretensions and recruit support from visitors and their fellow inmates. While imprisoned in Salisbury, Darkin's

Sufferings made a deep Impression upon the tender Hearts of the Ladies, some of whom having visited him in his Confinement, his obliging Manner, genteel Address, lively Disposition, and whole Deportment, so struck them, that his Fame soon became the Discourse of the Tea Table.

He had 'constant visitors' in Newgate and Oxford prisons.[291] While in Newgate, Paul Lewis 'was surrounded by a croud of curious spectators', whom he entertained with 'his talent of prophane ribaldry' and references to the *Beggar's Opera*:

he affected to be a real M'Heath, 'tis said he boasted to a visitor that he could, like that hero, buy off the Old Baily; and merrily sang: If gold from law can take out the sting, &c. – as in the Beggar's Opera.[292]

---

[286] *LL*, set, 'Isaac Darkin'.

[287] *The Authentic Trial, and Memoirs of Isaac Darkin, alias Dumas, Capitally Convicted for a Highway-robbery, near Nettlebed ... at Oxford* (Oxford, 1761), pp. 5, 26.

[288] This title was printed for booksellers in London, Gloucester, Oxford, Salisbury and Leicester and advertised in the *Old Bailey Proceedings*: *LL*, Old Bailey Proceedings, 1 April 1761 (a17610401-1).

[289] *A True, Genuine and Authentic Account of the Behaviour, Conduct and Transactions of John Rice, the Broker, and Paul Lewis, the Famous Highwayman, who were Executed at Tyburn May 4, 1763* (1763), pp. 18, 22.

[290] *Genuine Narrative of the Life and Surprising Robberies ... of William Page* (1758), p. 41; *London Evening Post*, 22–24 March 1763. See also *London Chronicle*, 3–5 May 1763.

[291] *Authentic Trial*, pp. 9, 27.

[292] *LL*, Ordinary of Newgate Prison: Ordinary's Accounts, 4 May 1763 (OA176305046 305040012).

Darkin also entered 'thoroughly into the Spirit of Mackheath's Part'.[293] This behaviour continued at the scaffold, where both men, as well as Page, died 'game'. During Lewis's journey to Tyburn, according to the *London Chronicle*, 'several officers and some of distinction ... showed their respect to him as he passed along'.[294]

The continuing power of the gentleman highwayman stereotype is reflected in its effect on James Boswell, who visited Paul Lewis in prison after his trial and went to see his execution. He recorded in his journal:

Paul, who had been in the sea-service and was called captain, was a genteel, spirited young fellow. He was just a Macheath. He was dressed in a white coat and blue silk vest and silver, with his hair neatly queued and silver-laced hat, smartly cocked. An acquaintance asked him how he was. He said, 'very well'; quite resigned. Poor fellow![295]

These highwaymen were ultimately executed, and to that extent their strategies of self-promotion clearly failed. However, this was only after pursuing sometimes long careers on the highway (Page: twelve years; Darkin: three years; Lewis: two years). Their ability to remain at large and prosper, despite the efforts of Henry and John Fielding and their Bow Street officers, resulted from a combination of marked public sympathy and their ability to manipulate the legal process. Some victims were reluctant to prosecute: Lord Ferrers, for instance, who was robbed by Page, refused to either pay the prosecution costs or give evidence at his trial.[296] And just as had been the case in the 1740s, those accused of highway robbery between 1755 and 1763 were more likely than other defendants to hire counsel and to be acquitted. The introduction of more concise reporting of trials in the Old Bailey *Proceedings* in December 1749 means that the presence of counsel was even less consistently reported in the 1750s, but evidence from the trial notes of Chief Justice Dudley Ryder indicates that counsel (prosecution, defence or both) were present in 9 per cent of trials in 1754–6.[297] In contrast, according to the limited reporting in the trial accounts, 13.4 per cent of accused highway robbers between 1755 and 1763 had defence counsel.[298] This could be worthwhile: those charged with highway robbery were somewhat more

---

[293] *Authentic Trial*, p. 26.   [294] *London Chronicle*, 3–5 May 1763.

[295] James Boswell, *Boswell's London Journal 1762-1763*, ed. Frederick A. Pottle (New York: McGraw-Hill, 1950), pp. 251–2.

[296] Beattie, *First English Detectives*, p. 40.

[297] David Lemmings, *Professors of the Law: Barristers and English Legal Culture in the Eighteenth Century* (Oxford University Press, 2000), pp. 208–10.

[298] For all but two of these twenty-five defendants, the evidence of defence counsel is based on the 'cross examination' of prosecution witnesses.

likely to be acquitted than other defendants (41.2 per cent of verdicts, compared to 34.6 per cent for defendants as a whole).

While the trope of the gentleman highwayman became the subject of some scepticism in the 1750s, highwaymen still found a receptive audience. They used their claims to gentility and knowledge of the legal process to promote their interests successfully, avoiding some of the harsh treatment accorded to other robbers. Their use of print, and behaviour in the courts and in prison, demonstrate that they continued to constitute a substantial challenge to authority, which would eventually force further changes to the evolving system of police.

Conclusion

The period from 1748 to 1763 started with a prosecution wave and, following the Treaty of Paris, ended with one; in the intervening years, the real and perceived crimes and demands of London's poor prompted multiple new disciplinary policies initiated by parliament, the Middlesex bench, the Fieldings and philanthropists. Many of the institutions that would come to characterise London in the next half-century can locate their origins to this period, including the Bow Street Runners and the associated system of 'rotation offices' (modelled on Bow Street). Efforts to both make hanging more terrible and rid Tyburn fair of its populist cast started here. London was beginning to turn into the kind of city that would justify the sleek neoclassical lines of Westminster Bridge. But in the process the authorities were often confronted by a plebeian London that had its own agenda and aspirations. Some highwaymen continued to stride the boards of Newgate and the Old Bailey to widespread acclaim, dying 'game' to the applause of an audience that was meant to cringe in fear of the power of state retribution.

As defendants, prisoners and convicts, and as vagrants, parish paupers and subjects of the new charities, poor Londoners often suffered under new policies, but they also learned how to navigate and manipulate the system. Their strategies of self-presentation became more sophisticated in dialogue with the new demands placed upon them, and in the process they were often able to constrain and deflect the fondest aspirations and most damaging intentions of men such as Henry and John Fielding, Jonas Hanway and Thomas Coram. Plans for grandiose prisons and houses of correction in which the poor were to be taught their place and set to labour were abandoned (at least for the time being). Defence counsel and corrupt thief-takers undercut attempts to institute a new style of detective policing and encourage more regular convictions for theft, while renewed attempts to prosecute vice were systematically undermined through violence and vexatious prosecutions.

While the initiatives of the 1750s set London's elite against its poor, the decade's innovations also divided plebeian London, labelling the unsettled and unemployed as gin-soaked and immoral, uncaring and workshy, while providing new charitable resources for the settled and working poor. In response, the latter formed temporary communities of interest with the parish and charity officers who relieved them, while at other times, such as in defence of Bosavern Penlez, plebeian London was united, in alliance with middling householders, against efforts to impose more rigorous standards of order. It was through shifting alliances that the poor and the criminal influenced social policy.

Ultimately, despite the building of new sites of civility such as Westminster Bridge, plebeian disorder, sometimes exploited by those of a higher class, proved difficult to shift. In May 1763 a 'low wretch' of a prostitute took James Boswell to the bridge to satisfy Boswell's 'brutish appetite' in exchange for a few pence. Despite the twelve night watchmen stationed on the bridge and its thirty-two street lights, no one seems to have disturbed this commercial transaction.[299]

---

[299] *Boswell's London Journal,* pp. 255–6. John Black argues that this kind of alfresco encounter was very unusual. John Black, 'Illegitimacy, sexual relations and location in metropolitan London, 1735–85', in Hitchcock and Shore, eds., *The Streets of London,* pp. 101–34.

6 Finding a voice: 1763–1776

Introduction

In the late autumn of 1762, Robert Munro was admitted to St George's Hospital, 'very Melancholy & dejected'. He was disappointed in his search for work, owed money to a great many and had recently undergone an unsuccessful salivation to cure his venereal disease at the Lock Hospital. His head throbbed with pain. But in his despair, the event that finally drove him over the edge was the casual cruelty of his fellow patients, who 'told him Fielding was after him'. Munro asked a hospital porter, Roderick McKinnon, if he had spotted Justice John Fielding on the wards, and in response McKinnon advised him that he 'had better think of his maker'. In the early hours of the next morning, Robert Munro took a razor and cut his own throat. He died six hours later. The subsequent coroners' inquest found that he had, 'Cut his throat being a Lunatick'.[1] However, in the hard decades of the 1760s and 1770s, many Londoners must have felt the rising despair that moved Munro's hand.

The second half of the eighteenth century saw a dramatic decline in real wages for working Londoners (Figure 5.1). From a high point in 1744, wages for bricklayers and carpenters, for example, fell 38 per cent by the end of the century. Much of this decline was concentrated in the period between 1761 and 1774, during which real wages fell by 24 per cent for these same occupations.[2] In part, this was the result of harvest failure and rising food costs, and it was national in scope. The years 1767 and 1768 and the winter of 1775/6 all witnessed extreme weather events

---

[1] *LL*, City of Westminster Coroners, Inquests into Suspicious Deaths, 8 January 1762 – 20 December 1762 (WACWIC652020355, WACWIC652020348).
[2] Leonard Schwarz, 'The standard of living in the long run: London, 1700–1860', *Economic History Review*, 2nd Series, 38:1 (1985), 40. See also E. A. Wrigley and R. S. Schofield, *The Population History of England, 1541–1871: A Reconstruction* (London: Edward Arnold, 1981), p. 643; Brian R. Mitchell, *British Historical Statistics* (Cambridge University Press, 1988), pp. 754–6.

that affected the harvest and the cost of living.[3] However, these climatic phenomena were essentially temporary in character, and the fall in real wages was exacerbated in London by a growing labour supply fed by in-migration, particularly following demobilisation at the end of the Seven Years War in 1763, and the fact London employers sought to lower their costs in order to respond to new competition from manufacturers operating in the North and overseas. With employers reducing their wages and introducing new working practices, plebeian Londoners found themselves squeezed between lower incomes and periodic sharp increases in the cost of living.

The years between 1763 and 1776 also witnessed the evolution of a more aggressive policy of policing and punishment. John Fielding consolidated his influence over the administration of justice in Middlesex and Westminster, while his 'Runners' extended their detective work, perfecting the art of rounding up the 'usual suspects', and working hard to ensure that once identified and arrested they were duly convicted at the Old Bailey. While Fielding concentrated on pursuing felony crime, constables and the watch launched new campaigns to clear the streets of that vast category of minor offenders that could be deemed to fall within the scope of the vagrancy laws. In parallel, and despite the failure of his early charitable ventures, Jonas Hanway, in pursuit of his goal of reforming poor relief, pursued a new strategy of assembling evidence and creating statistics that could be used to force the parishes to break up families and institutionalise more paupers, ensuring that the system of relief and care that had evolved over the preceding two hundred years was brought into contempt. At the same time, the gruesome deaths of a series of vulnerable parish apprentices reinforced the perception that the system was broken and needed to be reformed.

Plebeian Londoners were not, however, passive objects of change. Through violence and tactic, playing the system and occasionally employing professionals to play it for them, Londoners honed strategies developed in the previous decades, with some long-lasting consequences. They pursued increasingly well-trodden paths through a complex legal system and forced the parishes to relieve them in times of need. Strikes and riot and a new politics of 'liberty' provided another set of options, as did shopping for justice from among the growing number of 'trading' magistrates, and employing counsel to ensure the system worked in a defendant's favour. Others intimidated witnesses from testifying in court and subverted punishments. For paupers, the petition and the pleading

---

[3] J. H. Brazell, *London Weather* (London: HMSO, 1968), p. 9. See also 'Historical weather events' (booty.org.uk/booty.weather/climate/wxevents.htm, 1 Jan. 2014).

letter, the appeal to a magistrate and the artful presentation of distress to parish officers and associational charities became an increasingly important set of skills in making the system work in their favour. As settlement regulations became more bureaucratic, and legal disputes more onerous for the parishes, the balance of authority between the beggar's plea and the parish officers' parsimony gradually shifted, with rising costs the inevitable result.

These thirteen years saw the governors of London – the secretaries of state, Lord Mayors and magistrates – become ever more ambitious in their struggle to control three-quarters of a million souls, while plebeian Londoners themselves became ever more resourceful. The fuel that would explode in the 1780s was piled high in the 1760s and 1770s.

A crime wave with a difference

The Treaty of Paris was signed in February 1763, bringing to an end the Seven Years War. With the peace came the seemingly inevitable increase in prosecutions at the Old Bailey. The number of offences tried started to increase in April 1763 and continued to rise through most of the following year. In previous post-war 'crime waves', prosecutions fell relatively quickly after a demobilisation-induced peak, but in this instance, and with the exception of a slight decrease in the mid-1760s, they continued high and rising for the next decade, reaching a new peak in 1773, the busiest year to date at the Old Bailey, up 136 per cent since 1762.

This unusual pattern of prosecutions cannot be entirely attributed to the hardship of these years – the proportion of trials for theft increased only marginally. Instead, this increase was driven by more intense policing of felony crime by John Fielding and his Bow Street Runners, and of minor offences by constables and the night watch. The latter led to a dramatic rise in commitments to Bridewell, where the numbers in 1772 and 1775–6 were almost twice as high as they had been in the early 1760s. The majority resulted from police-initiated arrests for vagrancy and related offences.[4]

One stimulus for this increasing level of policing may have been the continuing visibility of celebrity criminals, who seemed to flout the law

---

[4] Based on all commitments listed in the Bridewell Court of Governors Minute Books from July 1772 to January 1774 (224 prisoners): *LL*, Bridewell Royal Hospital: Minutes of the Court of Governors, 9 July 1772 – 6 January 1774 (BBBRMG202080389 to BBBRMG202080446). These minute books list only those prisoners who happened to be in the prison on the days when the governors had their meetings.

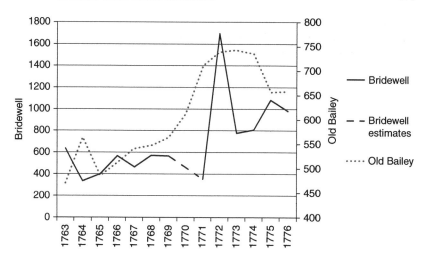

Figure 6.1 Crimes prosecuted, 1763–1776: Old Bailey and Bridewell.
Online data set: Crime Prosecutions.xlsx.

with impunity. In the early 1770s both William Cox, executed for theft in 1773 at the age of nineteen after a criminal career lasting over five years, and John Rann, a highwayman executed the following year at the age of twenty-four, attracted the attention of the public and the authorities.[5] With their widely reported previous acquittals, they appeared to be able to avoid conviction with ease. It was reported that they had each been tried at the Old Bailey over a dozen times. Although Cox appears in only eight trials and Rann in four in the *Proceedings*, the names of both men can be found on many more gaol calendars, suggesting that other charges against them had been dropped before trial. With the exception of the trials leading to their executions, all but one case resulted in an acquittal, owing to the failure of the prosecutors to appear (sometimes out of mercy), a lack of sufficient evidence against them or their own stratagems (it was claimed that Cox had 'often been obliged to fee council to bring him off').[6]

More active policing, together with growing concerns about recidivism, signalled a significant change in attitudes towards crime. Before the 1760s, as evidenced by the popularity of publications such as the *Ordinary's Accounts*, many people believed that crime was the result of sins which all men and women were in danger of committing. But in the decades after the publication of Henry Fielding's *Enquiry*, this approach

[5] *LL*, set, 'William Cox' and *LL*, Edward Duncan, 'John Rann, d. 1774'.
[6] *A Genuine Account of the Life, Robberies, Trial and Execution of William Cox* (1773), p. 9.

was gradually replaced by a more censorious view of criminals as a distinct and threatening under-class needing ever more aggressive control. As Simon Devereaux argues:

> there were clear signs from the late 1760s onwards, that the notion of an inveterate criminality, one that could not be checked or reduced by deterrent punishments of the worst offenders, was acquiring a more decidedly central place in the discursive continuum of explanations for English criminality.[7]

Symptomatic of this change was the decline and disappearance of the *Ordinary's Accounts*, as readers lost interest in the details of men who no longer seemed to be like them. Only six editions were published after 1767, the last one in October 1772.[8]

A parallel decline in the publication of standalone biographies underlines this point. While both Cox and Rann were the subjects of multiple biographies, these were less sympathetic than similar publications about highwaymen such as James Maclaine produced in the 1750s. Although both Cox and Rann, like Maclaine before them, aspired to present themselves as 'genteel', in their cases the claim was met with widespread scepticism. Their behaviour was described as 'artful', 'audacious' and the result of 'mistaken vanity'.[9] It was no doubt his lack of polish and obvious lower-class demeanour that ensured that when Rann attempted to blag his way into elite company at the Bagnigge Wells spa, he was challenged and forced to leave.

As importantly, Cox and Rann were described as belonging to a distinct criminal fraternity. Cox grew up 'trained in the ways of thieving', and his mother was described as 'the only honest person in the family'. He allegedly drank toasts to 'all thieves', and the fact that he once shared his booty with a companion who had not participated in the crime was used to demonstrate that 'There is Honour among Thieves'.[10] Rann's lower-class origins and style of speech were highlighted in the account of his final trial in the *Proceedings*, when, unusually, the publisher reported his defence statement *'verbatim et literatim'*:

[7] Simon Devereaux, 'From sessions to newspaper? Criminal trial reporting, the nature of crime, and the London press, 1770–1800', *London Journal*, 32:1 (2007), 12–16, quote at 18.
[8] LL, Ordinary of Newgate Prison: Ordinary's Accounts, 14 October 1772 (OA17721014721014001); Andrea McKenzie, *Tyburn's Martyrs: Execution in England 1675–1775* (London: Hambledon Continuum, 2007), p. 265; Andrea McKenzie, 'From true confessions to true reporting? The decline and fall of the Ordinary's Account', *London Journal*, 30:1 (2005), 55–70.
[9] *The Genuine Life of William Cox, who is Now Under Sentence of Death, in Newgate* (5th edn, 1773), title page; *The Only Authentic Life and Trial of William Cox* ([1773?]), p. 31; *A Genuine Account of the Life of John Rann, Alias Sixteen-String Jack* ([1774?]), p. 3.
[10] *Genuine Account of ... William Cox*, pp. 7, 22, 25.

I knows no more of it than a child does unborn, nor I never seed Mr. Bell before he came to Sir John's, which Mr. Bell must be certain of, for to think for me, for to come to him in the middle of the day, for to rob him, which I was never guilty of; I know no more of the affair what these gentlemen, that belongs to Sir John [Fielding], that wants to do things to swear my life away, for I don't know what.[11]

In contrast to earlier popular criminal figures, Rann was also depicted as having entered into 'solemn engagements to be true and stedfast' with other thieves. His moniker, 'Sixteen-String Jack', was awarded by his fellow criminals, rather than the press, after his habit of wearing breeches with eight silver-tipped strings on each knee. And while, like previous criminal celebrities, Cox and Rann received many visitors in prison, these were depicted in print as being decidedly lower class, including several prostitutes.[12] By the 1770s, respectable London had come to view criminal celebrities with increasing disdain, as part of a criminal under-world in need of urgent attention.

These changing perceptions of celebrity criminals, together with the real threats posed by violence and theft, shaped elite responses and helped drive the development of policing and punishment discussed in the remainder of this chapter. However, just as importantly, the evolution of policing was a response to the demand-driven rising cost of poor relief, and, more directly, to explicit and dramatic challenges to public order and authority in the form of labour disputes, rioting and political agitation.

The 'mob' challenges the law

Though the public disorder witnessed on London's streets between 1763 and 1771 would soon be eclipsed by the Gordon Riots of 1780, it was nevertheless on an unprecedented scale. Against a background of demobilisation, declining real wages and a series of trade-specific crises, London experienced protests by workmen in defence of pay and working conditions in at least twenty separate trades. These industrial disputes combined with political protests in support of the radical critic of the government John Wilkes to create a uniquely threatening mix. While there exists a rich literature on these events, historians have largely failed to appreciate the interconnections between the industrial and political

[11] *LL*, Old Bailey Proceedings, 19 October 1774 (t17741019-50).
[12] John Villette, *The Annals of Newgate; or Malefactors Register*, 4 vols. (1776), IV, pp. 379, 384; *Genuine Account of ... William Cox*, p. 24; *An Account of John Rann, Commonly Called Sixteen-String Jack* ([1774?]), p. 23.

protests, or to explore their significance in terms of the evolution of the relationship between the 'mob' and those who aspired to govern them.[13]

Throughout the 1760s there were demonstrations in all parts of the metropolis, often involving thousands of participants, and the protesters were at once well-organised, threatening and occasionally violent, leading at times to panic among London's ruling elite. The 1765 weavers' riots led Horace Walpole to fear a 'rebellion' was in prospect, owing to the 'general spirit of mutiny and dissatisfaction in the lower people'.[14] Three years later, in May 1768, a month which witnessed at least eleven industrial disputes and the largest of the Wilkite demonstrations, Benjamin Franklin observed:

this capital ... is now a daily scene of lawless riot and confusion. Mobs patrolling the streets at noonday, some knocking all down that will not roar for Wilkes and Liberty; courts of justice afraid to give judgement against him; coal-heavers and porters pulling down the houses of coal merchants that refuse to give them more wages; sawyers destroying saw-mills; sailors unrigging all the outward bound ships, and suffering none to sail till merchants agree to raise their pay; watermen destroying private boats and threatening bridges; soldiers firing among the mobs and killing men, women and children.[15]

The coalheavers were particularly violent, attacking the exploitative 'undertakers' who organised the trade. Their all-night armed attack on the house of one undertaker, John Green, on 20 April 1768 (the same night Wilkes was temporarily discharged from King's Bench prison) led to several deaths, a murder trial and seven executions. According to George Club:

by nine [pm] there was a vast crowd of people before his [Green's] house; there were stones and brickbats throwed at his house ... I heard the people many times

---

[13]   The key secondary works on the protests associated with Wilkes are George Rudé, *Wilkes and Liberty: A Social Study* (Oxford: Clarendon Press, 1962); John Brewer, *Party Ideology and Popular Politics at the Accession of George III* (Cambridge University Press, 1981), ch. 9; Arthur Cash, *John Wilkes: The Scandalous Father of Civil Liberty* (London and New Haven, Conn.: Yale University Press, 2006). For the labour unrest, see C. R. Dobson, *Masters and Journeymen: A Prehistory of Industrial Relations, 1717–1800* (London: Croom Helm, 1980); Walter J. Shelton, *English Hunger and Industrial Disorders: A Study of Social Conflict during the First Decade of George III's Reign* (University of Toronto Press, 1973). Good surveys are provided by John Stevenson, *Popular Disturbances in England: 1700–1832* (Harlow: Longman, 1992); Adrian Randall, *Riotous Assemblies: Popular Protest in Hanoverian England* (Oxford University Press, 2006).

[14]   *The Yale Edition of Horace Walpole's Correspondence*, ed. W. S. Lewis, 48 vols. (London: Oxford University Press, 1937–83), XXXVIII, p. 560, Walpole to Earl of Hertford, 20 May 1765 (images.library.yale.edu/hwcorrespondence, 2 Jan. 2014).

[15]   *The Works of Benjamin Franklin: Containing Several Political and Historical Tracts not Included in any Former Edition*, ed. Jared Sparks, 10 vols. (1840), VII, pp. 401–2.

swear they would have his heart and liver, and cut him in pieces and hang him on his sign-post.[16]

In defending his house (one man attempted to break down the front door with an axe), Green shot and killed two men. The coalheavers retaliated by throwing stones and shooting into both the front and rear of the house. In the aftermath, Green reported there were 'about 260 shot in the front, that is bullet marks', and 'a wheelbarrow full of stones of a heap now that were throwed into my room'.[17]

In the case of the journeymen silkweavers, violence was accompanied by conspiracy and secrecy. Because their protests had been explicitly criminalised by the passage of the Spitalfields Act in 1765, making participation in their 'combinations' a capital offence, the weavers were driven underground, meeting in clubs with names such as the 'Independent Sloop' and 'Bold Defiance'.[18] By the latter half of the 1760s, the silkweavers were actively enforcing their edicts, setting wages and working practices on both other journeymen and masters with clandestine violence. Disguising themselves and forcing their way into masters' houses in the middle of the night, armed with swords and pistols, and destroying both work in progress and the looms on which the work was set out, they earned themselves the name of 'cutters'.[19]

Supporters of John Wilkes were less likely to use weapons, but their language and actions were just as threatening and violent. During a demonstration at King's Bench prison on 10 May 1768 in which soldiers fired a volley into a stone-throwing crowd, the mob cried out:

Wilkes and Liberty. No Wilkes, no King. Damn the King, Damn the Government, Damn the Justice ... This is the most glorious opportunity for a Revolution that ever offered.[20]

Later that day, at the Mansion House in the City, a crowd of a hundred or more 'were very riotous in flinging stones and d – ning my Lord Mayor, wishing they had him out, saying they would kill him'.[21]

Despite some historians' claims to the contrary, the political and labour disputes of these years *were* significantly connected, and not

---

[16] *LL*, Old Bailey Proceedings, 18 May 1768 (t17680518-38).
[17] *LL*, Old Bailey Proceedings, 6 July 1768 (t17680706-46).
[18] 5 Geo. III c. 48, 'An Act for prohibiting the importation of foreign silk stockings [etc.]'.
[19] TNA, Treasury Solicitors Papers, TS11/818, *King vs Doyle and Valline, King vs Horsford*; Catherine Swindlehurst, 'Trade expansion, social conflict and popular politics in the Spitalfields silkweaving community, *c.* 1670–1770' (PhD dissertation, University of Cambridge, 1999), pp. 269–304 *passim*.
[20] BL, 'Correspondence and papers of John Wilkes', Add. Ms. 30884, f. 73 (August 1768).
[21] *LL*, Old Bailey Proceedings, 6 July 1768 (t17680706-62).

simply by a coincidence of chronology.[22] The protests shared both personnel and purpose. In George Rudé's assessment, the Wilkite crowds 'while by no means drawn exclusively from the wage-earners, were, like the industrial protests, overwhelmingly composed of "the lower orders of people"'.[23] Wilkes, by claiming he was fighting for *their* liberties, both attracted the support of ordinary Londoners and gave them a language of protest which they used in ways he never intended. Plebeian Londoners were able to follow Wilkes's example in challenging the government by attaching their economic and labour issues to his cause.

On an evening in August 1769, when John Fitzharris was drinking in the Well and Bucket tavern near Old Street with two weavers, they talked about 'several things', including 'Wilkes and trade'.[24] There is considerable evidence that the weavers, the most active rioters, were sympathetic to Wilkes. During the Middlesex election in March 1768, weavers from Spitalfields demonstrated their support for him in Piccadilly, and the following month, when Wilkes's carriage, which was supposed to take him to King's Bench prison, was diverted by the crowd, they took it to Spitalfields, where most of the weavers lived.[25] According to Middlesex Justice Ralph Hodgson, coalheavers also caught 'the infection, [and] began to join the senseless roar of Wilkes and Liberty'. During the attack on John Green's house, they called out 'Wilkes and coal-heavers for ever'.[26] Even criminals showed their support for Wilkes. Prisoners illuminated their cell windows to celebrate Wilkes's release from King's Bench prison, while the condemned wore Wilkite cockades on their way to their executions at Tyburn.[27]

There is also evidence that groups of workers in the different trades coordinated their efforts. In May 1765 the Sheriffs of London reported that journeymen weavers had threatened 'to collect at a general rendezvous in Moorfields ... with as many others as they can collect of Shoemakers, Dyers, Taylors etc.' unless the government prevented the importation of French silks. When asked why other trades were also involved, the weavers explained, 'because if the weavers are oppressed,

[22] Stevenson, *Popular Disturbances*, p. 90; Cash, *John Wilkes*, p. 224; Rudé, *Wilkes and Liberty*, pp. 94–104; Shelton, *English Hunger and Industrial Disorders*, p. 162.
[23] Rudé, *Wilkes and Liberty*, p. 183.
[24] *LL*, Old Bailey Proceedings, 6 December 1769 (t17691206-34).
[25] *Walpole's Correspondence*, Vol. XXIII, p. 6 ; Rudé, *Wilkes and Liberty*, pp. 42, 48.
[26] *LL*, Old Bailey Proceedings, 18 May 1768 (t17680518-38).
[27] Cash, *John Wilkes*, p. 266; *Worcester Journal*, 9 June 1768, cited in John Brewer, 'The Wilkites and the law, 1763–74: a study of radical notions of governance', in John Brewer and John Styles, eds., *An Ungovernable People: The English and their Law in the Seventeenth and Eighteenth Centuries* (London: Hutchinson, 1980), p. 170.

other trades are consequently so'.[28] Three years later striking sailors issued a proclamation calling on 'all watermen, lightermen, ballast men, ballast heavers, coalheavers, etc. to leave their duty and not to go to work till our wages be settled', claiming 'fifteen or twenty-thousand Spitalfields weavers' were ready to join them; on one occasion sailors and coalheavers patrolled the riverside, forcing a general work stoppage.[29] And in April 1773, handbills were distributed among several different bodies of workers, including weavers, coalheavers, watermen, porters and carmen, inviting them to march together to Westminster to 'show the king our distress'. A few days later, an anonymous letter warned justices of the peace and other figures of authority that workmen in all trades had been invited to assemble in Moorfields.[30] While on a few occasions different groups of workers clashed, most notably in violent confrontations between the coalheavers and strike-breaking coastal sailors, London's wage-earners showed an unprecedented degree of solidarity during these disputes. Even the confrontation which led to the murder of the sailor John Beattie (or Beatty) by coalheavers began with groups of sailors and coalheavers shaking hands, as they 'reasoned the affair before they began' to fight.[31]

Faced with these unprecedented threats to public order, those responsible for maintaining the peace mounted a vigorous response. There were some attempts by justices at mediation and accommodation, but the authorities' use of the army and capital punishment against the most violent protesters is notable and had long-term consequences. Soldiers had been used before to put down outbreaks of disorder, but the extent of the army's involvement in dispersing rioters and arresting offenders in the 1760s was unprecedented. By the middle of May 1768, seven regiments were camped in and around London.[32] Soldiers could not be summoned, or ordered to fire, without the consent of a justice of the peace, but the justices were given strong encouragement to use the army. As demonstrations in support of Wilkes intensified in April, Lord

[28] BL, 'Collections, historical, antiquarian, etc., made by Thomas Astle', Add. Ms. 34712, f. 109, Saunders Welch, JP, to Lord Halifax (1765).

[29] William Petty, 1st Marquis of Lansdowne, 2nd Earl of Shelburne papers, vol. 133, ff. 363–74, cited by Shelton, *English Hunger and Industrial Disorders*, pp. 188, 190; Richard Sheldon, 'The London sailors' strike of 1768', in Andrew Charlesworth *et al.*, eds., *An Atlas of Industrial Protest in Britain 1750–1990* (Houndmills: Macmillan, 1996), p. 15.

[30] TNA, State Papers Domestic: Letters and Papers, SP37/10, ff. 63, 68, 73, 97, 108 (13–23 April 1773), quote from f. 108.

[31] LL, Old Bailey Proceedings, 6 July 1768 (t17680706-57). For this dispute, see Shelton, *English Hunger and Industrial Disorders*, pp. 176–7.

[32] Tony Hayter, *The Army and the Crowd in Mid-Georgian England* (London: Macmillan, 1978), p. 140.

Barrington, Secretary of War, wrote to Daniel Ponton, chairman of the Surrey justices, advising him of the military forces available and encouraging him to use them: 'I hope you will not delay a Moment calling for their Aid, and making Use of them effectually where there is Occasion'. Ponton was assured that a military force could never 'be employed to a more constitutional Purpose, than in the Support of the Authority and Dignity of Magistracy'.[33]

This was an unfortunate comment in light of what followed on 10 May in front of King's Bench prison. Thousands had gathered in support of Wilkes, who was due to be released, and papers expressing Wilkite sentiments were plastered to the walls of the prison. When magistrates ordered these to be removed, the crowd began to throw stones. In response Justice Samuel Gillam ordered the soldiers to fire on the crowd, killing between five and twelve people in what became known as the 'St George's Fields Massacre'.[34] The crowd responded by attacking two justices' houses in Southwark. That evening there were also riots outside the Mansion House in the City, while weavers, coalheavers and sawyers marched through other parts of London. Despite the fact that most of those shot by the soldiers were innocent bystanders and had nothing to do with the stone throwers, Gillam was acquitted of murder, and none of the soldiers was held to account for the deaths.[35]

In August of the following year, there was further military violence when a group of foot guards raided a secret meeting of the cutters at the Dolphin public house and two weavers were killed. Two months later troops killed another five.[36] In 1770, the Wilkite John Horne-Tooke complained about the stationing of soldiers in response to the activities of the cutters:

It is pretended that the civil power is too weak to keep the peace in the neighbourhood of Spitalfields: a barrack has been therefore built, and soldiers have regularly mounted guard there for a long time past; they have likewise been employed as constables to apprehend offenders.[37]

---

[33] John Wilkes subsequently obtained a copy of this letter and sent it to a newspaper: *St James's Chronicle*, 8–10 December 1768, issue 1214 (Burney Collection: www.galegroup.com, 2 Jan. 2014).

[34] P. D. G. Thomas, 'The St George's Fields "massacre" of 10 May 1768: an eye witness report', *London Journal*, 4:2 (1978), 221; Rudé, *Wilkes and Liberty*, p. 51.

[35] *LL*, Old Bailey Proceedings, 6 July 1768 (t17680706-58); Cash, *John Wilkes*, pp. 223–4, 227.

[36] *Annual Register*, 12 (1769), pp. 136, 138 (bodley.ox.ac.uk/ilej, 2 Jan. 2014).

[37] *Genuine Copies of all the Letters which Passed Between the Right Honourable The Lord Chancellor, and the Sheriffs of London and Middlesex ... Relative to the Execution of Doyle and Valine* (1770), p. 38.

This murderously heavy-handed policing was accompanied by attempts to secure exemplary punishments for the rioters in court. Ministers were keen to convict as many of the leading participants as possible and ensured that the prosecution counsel they employed were provided with extensive briefs.[38] Of the twenty-seven defendants tried at the Old Bailey as a result of Wilkite and labour conflicts, seventeen were convicted and sentenced to death. Only three were pardoned, and unusually, in an attempt to intimidate the local population, nine of the fourteen executions were staged in the east end neighbourhoods where the defendants lived.

The seven coalheavers executed for shooting at John Green, for example, were hanged near his house by Sun-Tavern Fields in Shadwell, just north of the riverside where they worked. Widespread resentment about their punishment meant that a detachment of the guard and 300 soldiers were sent to maintain order.[39] There is no evidence of any misbehaviour on this occasion, but the execution of two cutters, John Doyle and John Valloine, in Bethnal Green on 6 December 1769 was much more problematic.[40] Recognising the distress and disorder staging the executions in the weavers' neighbourhood would cause, the Wilkite sheriffs of London, James Townshend and John Sawbridge, appealed unsuccessfully to the king to change the place of execution.[41] The sheriffs were right to be apprehensive. According to *Lloyd's Evening Post*, when the condemned

came to the place of execution, the mob grew extremely outrageous, which obliged the proper Officers to order the offenders to be turned off immediately; this so irritated the multitude, that they threw stones, brickbats, etc. at the Sheriffs, and, after the men had hung about half an hour, [the crowd] pulled up the gallows, and carried it to the house of a Gentleman near Spitalfields Church, whose windows they broke, and tore part of his furniture to pieces.[42]

The 'Gentleman', was Lewis Chauvet, a master weaver who was rumoured to have offered a substantial reward for information about the cutters and had provided lodging for the officers of the soldiers

---

[38] These survive in Treasury papers for the years 1768–9 and include briefs against six Wilkites, twelve cutters and seventeen coalheavers, mostly for capital offences. TNA, Treasury Papers, 'King vs. Greenwood and Hipgrave' (August 1768), T1/468, ff. 261–73; Treasury Solicitors Papers, 'Re: Prosecutions of the Spitalfields weavers re attacks on Spitalfields silk manufacturers' (1768–9), TS11/818.

[39] *Public Advertiser*, 26 July 1768, p. 2 (Burney Collection: www.galegroup.com, 2 Jan. 2014).

[40] *LL*, sets, 'John Doyle' and 'John Valloine'   [41] *Genuine Copies of all the Letters*.

[42] *Lloyd's Evening Post*, 4–6 Dec. 1769 (Burney Collection: www.galegroup.com, 2 Jan. 2014).

quartered in Spitalfields.[43] According to Captain Thomas Taylor, there were 'four or five thousand' men outside Chauvet's house, and 'They were hallooing out, Pull the house down – Hang him. . . . They said, the Sheriffs hanged the men up like dogs, they would not let them have time to say their prayers'.[44] The riot ended only after reinforcements were sent from the Tower. Both Doyle and Valloine had maintained their innocence to the end, and Valloine's scaffold speech, reproduced verbatim in several papers, contained a powerful condemnation of the men who connived at his death: 'Let my Blood lay to that wicked Man who has purchast it with Gold and them notorious Wretches who swore it falsely away'.[45]

On the same day that Doyle and Valloine were executed, the December sessions of the Old Bailey began, and three more weavers were convicted and sentenced to hang: William Horsford, William Eastman and John Carmichael.[46] This time they were executed at Tyburn, but as with Doyle and Valloine, Horsford maintained his innocence to the last.[47] The strong sense of injustice and betrayal caused by these executions persisted in Bethnal Green and Spitalfields for years.

At the centre of the judicial response to the disorder was John Fielding. When it came to riots and industrial protest, Fielding's natural instinct was to mediate, as he had done previously with strikes by tailors and cabinetmakers, and would do again with other trades.[48] However, he was forced to change his approach following a mass lobby in Westminster in May 1765, in which several members of parliament were jostled and the Duke of Bedford's coach was wrecked. Later that day Bedford's house was besieged and nearly destroyed. Fielding was summoned to the House of Lords, ordered to kneel and reprimanded for not responding to the riot more forcefully. The House resolved that 'Sir John Fielding is particularly blameable; having (as he himself acknowledged) thought that this was not such a Mob as by their Insolencies authorized him to read the Proclamation'.[49] From this point onwards, Fielding and his runners were actively involved in suppressing industrial and political disorder and arresting leading figures.

[43] Rudé, *Wilkes and Liberty*, p. 102.
[44] *LL*, Old Bailey Proceedings, 6 December 1769 (t17691206-23).
[45] *London Chronicle*, 5–7 December 1769 (Burney Collection: www.galegroup.com, 2 Jan. 2014).
[46] *LL*, sets, 'William Horsford', 'William Eastman' and 'John Carmichael'.
[47] *Lloyd's Evening Post*, 18–20 December 1769. (Burney Collection: www.galegroup.com, 2 Jan. 2014)
[48] Dobson, *Masters and Journeymen*, pp. 67–8, 78, 84–5.
[49] *PP, Journals of the House of Lords*, 22 May 1765, p. 214 (parlipapers.chadwyck.co.uk, 2 Jan. 2014).

He was particularly determined to prosecute the cutters. John Carmichael, for example, was accused of participating in an attack on Robert Cromwell's house in Moorfields on 25 September 1769.[50] He was arrested in Coventry in early October, returned to London and brought before Fielding. Over the course of the next month, Fielding examined him no less than 'six times', but was forced to discharge him because he could find no one willing to break the wall of silence that had descended on Spitalfields.[51] It was only when Carmichael was rearrested on a separate charge that Fielding was able to locate witnesses willing to testify to his role in the original attack. He also personally participated in the violent raid on a secret meeting of the cutters at the Dolphin tavern.

Fielding was assisted by other justices, notably David Wilmot (attached to the Whitechapel Rotation Office). However, the justices' headlong pursuit of the leaders of the weavers and coalheavers was in sharp contrast to the long-standing tradition of justices of the peace, particularly trading justices, seeking to mediate disputes, and it undermined the relationship between the bench and the local community. Some justices made a different choice. In 1769 Ralph Hodgson, an experienced justice who had been active for more than a decade, set up an alternative employment office to help the coalheavers escape their dependence on the undertakers.[52] But this strategy was also problematic. The office he established operated as a closed shop, and the coalheavers subjected fellow workers who refused to join to ritual punishments. And when, following a strike, rival undertakers such as John Green set up alternative 'houses of call' offering higher wages, Hodgson was drawn into the violent protests that followed. When he marched at the head of a St Patrick's Day procession of coalheavers (many of whom were Irish) wearing a shamrock, and then failed to prevent the violent attack on Green's house that followed, members of the coal trade lost their patience and 'a great number of the Inhabitants of Shadwell and the parts adjacent[,] men of property and respectable characters' petitioned the Middlesex bench to investigate.[53] A committee of justices found that Hodgson had acted illegally in setting up the employment office and had responded to the riots with 'Inactivity & supineness'.[54]

[50] *LL*, set, 'John Carmichael'.
[51] *LL*, Old Bailey Proceedings, 6 December 1769 (t17691206-37).
[52] *LL*, set, 'Ralph Hodgson'.
[53] *LL*, Middlesex Sessions: Sessions Papers, September 1768 (LMSMPS505870068).
[54] *LL*, Middlesex Sessions: Sessions Papers, September 1768 (LMSMPS505870066).

The committee resolved that Hodgson should be removed from the commission of the peace.[55]

Hodgson responded to these charges in a pamphlet setting out an alternative conception of justice, drawn up to contrast with the views of Fielding and Wilmot. Hodgson claimed he was trying to help the coal-heavers combat the 'oppression and extortions' they suffered from the 'avarice of a set or combination of men, known by the designation of coal-undertakers' and explained that the undertakers had provoked the rioting by their unreasonable behaviour. And while he acknowledged that there had been 'illegal excesses', he expressed his 'constant desire of keeping peace, by lenient, healing expedients'. Thus, when one of the principal rioters in the attack on Green's house, David Grammer, was brought before him, the magistrate 'insisted on the Prisoner being discharged on Asking pardon and acknowledging he was drunk'.[56] Hodgson contrasted his approach to that of an undertaker, who had wished to see 'nineteen of [the coalheavers] hung up before his door'.[57]

The Middlesex justices were divided about how to respond. A petition to the Lord High Chancellor to remove Hodgson from the commission passed, but only after eight justices, including John Hawkins, chairman of the sessions, abstained. He 'did not vote in this Business' – a fact pointedly recorded in the Orders of the Court.[58] Noticeable by their apparent absence from the meeting were both John Fielding and David Wilmot, who, while no doubt opposed to Hodgson, must have believed that pursuing Hodgson would damage their reputations and paint the law as partial and unfair. Their refusal to condemn Hodgson's behaviour was probably part of an attempt to maintain the respect of these communities in spite of their role in the prosecutions of rioters. It reflects the continuing importance of community justice as a form of managed social relations as practised by Hodgson, and evident in the growing popularity of trading justices in this period. Nonetheless, in December 1768 Hodgson was removed from the commission.

Not for the first time, judicial attitudes fractured, and plebeian attitudes towards the law shifted. As they always had done, journeymen continued to seek magisterial assistance in negotiating and enforcing wage agreements, and some justices, including Fielding, played their

---

[55] Norma Landau, 'The trading justice's trade', in Norma Landau, ed., *Law, Crime and Society, 1660–1830* (Cambridge University Press, 2002), pp. 55–6, who states that the petitioners were members of the coal trade. See also Shelton, *English Hunger and Industrial Disorders*, pp. 172–5.

[56] LL, Middlesex Sessions: Sessions Papers, May 1768 (LMSMPS505830056).

[57] *The Conduct of Ralph Hodgson, Esq. ... in the Affair of the Coal-heavers* (1768), pp. 3, 16.

[58] LL, Middlesex Sessions: General Orders of the Court (LMSMGO556050141).

part.[59] However, no doubt influenced by the Wilkites' successful use of the law, those accused of crimes more frequently obtained professional legal advice in defence of life and freedom.[60] Like other defendants prosecuted by Fielding, a high proportion of the weavers (eleven of seventeen) and all sixteen coalheavers tried at the Old Bailey for riot, murder and related offences between 1765 and 1771 employed legal counsel in their defence, no doubt paid for with the support of their clubs. While the widespread use of prosecution counsel in these trials ensured a relatively normal conviction rate (eight of the eleven weavers, and nine of the sixteen coalheavers), this extensive use of counsel reflects the defendants' desire to use all the tools available within the legal system.

Others came to treat justice with contempt. With several of those convicted claiming to their last breath that they were innocent, many weavers and coalheavers sought to avoid the courts altogether by preventing witnesses against them from coming forward. Intimidation was common, which meant that several trials of the cutters could only be held many months after the crimes they were accused of committing. They also exacted revenge on those who testified. Following the acquittal of John Green for murdering one of the men who attacked his house in 1768, the coalheavers 'grew if possible more outrageous, threatening to murder and pull down the house of every inhabitant who appeared at the Old Bailey' in his defence.[61] Officers and justices who were responsible for arresting the coalheavers and weavers were also attacked. In April 1768 a 'large body of coalheavers' armed with cutlasses attempted to pull down the house (which was also a tavern) belonging to James Marsden, a headborough who had arrested Thomas Farmer, one of the coalheavers accused of murdering a strike-breaking sailor. They broke into the house and demolished partitions, shelves, windows and boxes. Some of the men 'were heard to swear they would murder Marsden, and cut his heart out, and broil it'.[62] Mobs in support of Wilkes also attacked houses and symbols of justice. Following the St George's Fields 'massacre', while the justices were attempting to disperse the mob outside King's Bench prison hundreds of people marched to London Bridge and attacked the houses of two justices, including that of Edward Russell, which was also a distillery. In a series of events that foreshadowed the Gordon Riots of a

<hr/>

[59] Dobson, *Masters and Journeymen*, chs. 6 and 9, *passim*.
[60] Brewer, 'Wilkites and the law', pp. 128–71.
[61] TNA, 'King vs. Murphy' (1768), TS11/818, f. 10.
[62] TNA, 'King vs. Byrne and Dignam' (1769), TS11/818. These two coalheavers were tried and convicted for participation in this riot at the Middlesex sessions.

decade later, they broke into the house and opened the casks of spirituous liquors, letting them run as they used their hats to collect the drink. Later, drunk beyond control, they threatened to set fire to the house and murder Russell's family.[63]

In Spitalfields and Bethnal Green, the community rejection of official justice was almost total, as can be seen in the case of Daniel Clarke, a master weaver and pattern drawer whose testimony was blamed for the executions of Eastman and Horsford.[64] As a result of repeated harassment, Clarke was advised by justices to carry pistols in his pockets, but he did not have them when he was attacked by a crowd on a snowy day in April 1771. Calling him a 'blood-selling rascal' and 'saying they had got Clarke who Swore agt. the Cutters', he was stripped to his waist and whipped, and then chased by a stone-throwing mob to a nearby pond.[65] A crowd of two or three thousand proceeded to duck him while pelting him with earth and brickbats.[66] While ducking was a traditional form of popular justice, being attacked by brickbats was not, and the assault proved fatal.

At this point the community closed ranks and shut out the law. Some of the crowd had tried to save Clarke, but once this became a murder case distrust of the judicial system and fears of retaliation silenced potential witnesses. Immediately following the riot, Justice Wilmot advertised a reward for information, but although he reported to the government that he had sat every day at the rotation office, 'no person has given us any information'. Informers, he claimed, refused to come forward, fearing 'the revenge of a bandita ... as most certainly they would'.[67] Eventually two men, Henry Stroud and Robert Campbell, and one woman, Anstis Horsford, the widow of William Horsford, were tried for the murder, but it is remarkable how many witnesses who testified at this Old Bailey trial failed to name any of the participants, and two female witnesses had to be told by the court that they might give 'evidence without being frightened'.[68] Nonetheless, the man who arrested Campbell, a constable employed in the Whitechapel Rotation Office, was only identified in the *Proceedings* as 'the Man', despite the fact his identity must have been known in the courtroom.[69]

[63] TNA, 'King vs Greenwood and Hipgrave' (1768), T1/468, ff. 261–4; Rudé, *Wilkes and Liberty*, p. 52.

[64] *LL*, set, 'Daniel Clarke'.

[65] *LL*, Old Bailey Proceedings, 3 July 1771 (t17710703-59); Old Bailey Sessions: Sessions Papers, 1771 (LMOBPS450170235).

[66] *LL*, Old Bailey Proceedings, 3 July 1771 (t17710703-59).

[67] TNA, SP37/8, ff. 110, 114 (1771).

[68] *LL*, sets, 'Henry Stroud' and 'Robert Campbell'.

[69] *LL*, Old Bailey Proceedings, 3 July 1771 (t17710703-59).

Stroud and Campbell were convicted, hanged in Bethnal Green in chains and their bodies taken for dissection. Anticipating disorder, the execution was attended by the sheriffs and a large number of constables, with a body of soldiers on standby. The sheriffs, worried that the presence of the military might incite the crowd, ensured that the soldiers remained a quarter of a mile from the hanging, standing guard outside Justice Wilmot's house. Like some of the hanged cutters, Stroud maintained his innocence to his death and was widely believed. Several newspapers published a letter he wrote the night before his execution in which he claimed that he was only convicted on the perjured testimony of a man who had 'swore, if I would not give him a pot of beer, or a shilling, he would take my life away'. Some of the papers added, 'it is now generally believed that Stroud was innocent'.[70] With the decline of the 'sacramental' view of execution as a necessary purging of man's sinfulness (regardless of whether one was guilty as charged), these assertions of innocence became increasingly subversive.[71] Once again, a large body of Londoners was left nursing a grievance against criminal justice, a fact which would have significant consequences for attitudes towards the law over the next two decades.

In 1773 the weavers achieved their goal of obtaining a parliamentary Act regulating their wages.[72] The bill was passed only as a result of heavy extra-parliamentary pressure, which included not only the cutters' attacks and mass lobbies of parliament but also the distribution of an anonymous letter to figures of authority. In it they were warned not to obstruct 'the poor people [who] go in large bodies'. Workmen in all trades had been invited to assemble in Moorfields, where they thought they would have the protection of the City magistrates, but, in an opaque warning to the Middlesex bench, the letter went on to chastise the 'ill-timed zeal of neighbourhood justices'.[73] The fact that the Middlesex magistrates lobbied for the bill's passage is indicative of the effectiveness of this pressure.[74] The other political and industrial grievances of these years remained unresolved. Nevertheless, out of this crucible of conflict the crowd had learned its own lessons. Even though some executions

---

[70] *Westminster Journal and London Political Miscellany*, 13–20 July 1771; *Middlesex Journal*, 11–13 July 1771 (Burney Collection: www.galegroup.com, 2 Jan. 2014).

[71] For the earlier view, see Andrea McKenzie, 'God's tribunal: guilt, innocence and execution in England, 1675–1775', *Cultural and Social History*, 3:2 (2006), 121–44.

[72] 13 Geo. III c. 68, 'An Act to impower magistrates therein mentioned to settle and regulate the wages of persons employed in the silk manufactures'.

[73] TNA, SP37/10, f. 108 (23 April 1768).

[74] R. Leslie-Melville, *The Life and Work of Sir John Fielding* (London: Lincoln Williams Ltd, 1935), pp. 181–4. We are grateful to Joanna Innes for this point.

could not be prevented, working Londoners had grown more powerful in the confident knowledge that they could challenge the forces of criminal justice.

'Brownrigg-like cruelty'

If plebeian Londoners learned the hard lessons of how to confront the law in these years, they were also becoming ever more adept at manipulating the increasingly bureaucratic and complex system of poor relief. As one author complained in 1771:

> The churchwarden or overseer is perpetually harassed, either for some weekly allowance in money, or for admission to the workhouse, by poor people who will take no denial; and who, if refused, may have their complaints heard before a magistrate, and the overseer or churchwarden is summoned to attend. If the necessity of the complainant appears to the Justice, and it always does, if their tale is believed, they are relieved in their own way.[75]

Both in London and in the nation as a whole, the third quarter of the eighteenth century witnessed a substantial increase in expenditure on poor relief. At mid-century the average annual expenditure for London and Middlesex was £81,030.[76] By 1776, this had risen 65 per cent to £125,206, against a background inflation rate of only 1.5 per cent per annum. Much of this increase was concentrated in the 1760s and early 1770s.[77] Even in a small, wealthy City parish such as St Dionis Backchurch, with a falling population and few social problems, the poor law accounts gyrated upwards, rising from £324 in 1763 to £419 in 1776 after reaching a peak expenditure of £529 in 1773.[78] In the larger and more diverse parish of St Clement Danes, the cost of relieving the poor rose from £2,916 in 1763 to £5,343 16s. in 1776.[79]

In some measure these growing costs reflected simple need. The decline in real wages in these decades left many struggling to maintain

[75] 'To the author of the police', *The Oxford Magazine, Or Universal Museum*, 5–6 (1771), p. 46.

[76] *PP*, 'Report from the Select Committee on the poor laws', 1818, with an appendix, p. 9 (parlipapers.chadwyck.co.uk, 2 Jan. 2014).

[77] *PP*, 'Abstracts of the returns made by the overseers of the poor', 1777 (parlipapers.chadwyck.co.uk, 2 Jan. 2014). This figure includes Middlesex and Westminster, and excludes the City. For England as a whole, the equivalent figure had grown by 122 per cent, reaching £1,529,780 in 1776. Inflation as measured by a retail price index, i.e. the cost of living, rather than wages, rose by 40 per cent in these years (safalra.com/other/historical-uk-inflation-price-conversion/, 15 Feb. 2014).

[78] These figures are drawn from parish records. National returns for 1776 for this parish record a higher expenditure of £476.

[79] Parliamentary returns record a slightly lower figure of £4,972 for this year.

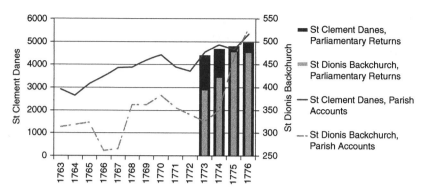

Figure 6.2 Poor relief expenditure 1763–1776: St Clement Danes and St Dionis Backchurch. Online data set: Poor Relief Expenditure 1690–1800.xlsx

an independent life.[80] At workhouses such as that belonging to St Martin in the Fields, the number of admissions grew in response. In the 1750s the house was admitting between 700 and 800 a year. By the mid-1770s, following some rebuilding, this had risen, albeit temporarily, to an average of well over 1,000.[81] But the growing costs, particularly for smaller parishes, also reflect both the administrative burden created by the increasingly bureaucratic character of the system of settlement and the ability of paupers to effectively manipulate that system. Although a relatively rare procedure, even removing a family across the short distance between two City parishes could entail crippling expense. In the autumn of 1775, for instance, on the orders of the then Lord Mayor, John Wilkes, and George Hayley, Thomas and Ann Bloodworth and their four children were removed just a few hundred yards from St Michael Cornhill, near the Royal Exchange, to the much smaller parish of St John the Evangelist, just east of St Paul's.[82] Following a petition and appeal by the churchwardens and overseers of St Michael's, this case cost both parishes dear.[83] The total cost to St John the Evangelist was £14 19s. 6d., making up a full third of the parish's expenditure on poor relief that year. But even for the larger parish of St Michael Cornhill, the cost of

---

[80] Schwarz, 'The standard of living in the long run', 24–41. Real wages reached a high point in 1744, before falling by 38 per cent over the course of the rest of the century.

[81] The number of admittances reflects a complex amalgam of demand and supply, and does not reflect the number of people in the house at any one time. The admissions for the period were 1772: 1,212; 1773: 1,368; 1774: 1,021; 1775: 1,026 and 1776: 1,069.

[82] *LL*, sets, 'Thomas Bloodworth' and 'Ann Bloodworth'.

[83] *LL*, City of London Sessions: Sessions Papers, 2 June 1773 – 22 February 1776 (LMSLPS150860582 and LMSLPS150860583).

this single removal and appeal amounted to £15 4s., some 3 per cent of that year's budget.[84] The possibility that a removal order and a dispute might follow a refusal of relief effectively empowered paupers in relation to parish officers.

At the same time as costs were spiralling, the parishes faced an additional challenge. The system of parochial care itself was brought into disrepute in the eyes of both paupers and the wider community by a series of deaths of paupers in care, publicised through the concerted black propaganda of 'reformers' such as Jonas Hanway.

The rising chorus of criticism began with the brutal murders of Ann Nailor and her sister Mary at the hands of Sarah Metyard and her daughter.[85] In 1762 the daughter

confessed that her ... Mother had Cruelly used and Starved two of her apprentices to Death vizt. Ann and Mary Nailor and that she Cut the Body of the former in Pieces and carried it to the Gulley hole [gutter] in Chick-Lane; ... one hand which She Burnt for fear of a discovery it having a Stump Finger, and that she kept the Body in a Box in the House upwards of two Months.[86]

The two sisters had been apprenticed by the parish of Tottenham High Cross, and the tale of beatings and starvation that emerged at the trial was harrowing. However, the failure of either Tottenham High Cross or St George Hanover Square (where the Metyards kept house) to maintain any oversight of conditions also emerged clearly. Jeremiah Brown, the milkman who served the house, reported the situation to the parish overseer.[87] Having done so, he expected something to be done, but he 'never heard that any step was taken'. He later recalled that the 'Child was like an Otomy and appeared as if she had Actually been Starved'.[88] Following their convictions for murder, both the mother and daughter were hanged at Tyburn on Monday 19 July, their bodies handed over to the surgeons for dissection. Unusually, the Tyburn crowd was hostile: 'the mob were so rude as to throw Stones, &c as the Bodies were hanging'.[89]

Within eighteen months a new scandal emerged. In November 1763 a prospective buyer was looking over a house in Stonecutters Street, which

---

[84] PP, 'Report from the committee appointed to inspect and consider the returns made by the overseers of the poor, in pursuance of Act of last session', 1777, p. 399 (parlipapers. chadwyck.co.uk, 2 Jan. 2014).

[85] LL, sets, 'Ann Nailor', 'Mary Nailor', and 'Sarah Metyard'.

[86] LL, Middlesex Sessions: Sessions Papers, July 1762 (LMSMPS505120049).

[87] LL, Old Bailey Proceedings, 14 July 1762 (t17620714-30).

[88] LL, Middlesex Sessions: Sessions Papers, July 1762 (LMSMPS505120056 and LMSMPS505120055).

[89] Public Advertiser, July 20, 1762, issue 8645 (Burney collection: www.galegroup.com, 2 Jan. 2014).

ran between Fleet Market and Shoe Lane, just north of St Bride's Churchyard in the City, and found the emaciated bodies of three nearly naked women on the ground floor, and two more women and a girl almost starved but still alive in the garret. Two of the bodies were of women who had worked as casual porters in Fleet Market just a few yards down the road, but the figure that exercised public opinion was sixteen-year-old Elizabeth Surman, and once again, the failure of parish government was held to blame for her condition. *Lloyd's Evening Post* devoted a long paragraph to her tragic biography. Her parents had died when she was six years old. After that she lived with a neighbour, a Mrs Jones, who herself died a few years later, leaving Elizabeth destitute. She then undertook what work she could get, eventually finding a place with a washing woman in Spitalfields Market, where she stayed for six years, before falling ill and losing her place. At this point she appealed to her parish of settlement, St Stephen Coleman Street, without knowing what she needed to say.

She then went to the Churchwarden of the parish where her father had been housekeeper many years, to desire relief, but he refus'd, without so much as expostulating with her about her legal settlement, or informing her, that she had gained a settlement by servitude. She being very ill and weak, lay all night at the Churchwarden's door, but it had no effect upon him; and this girl was obliged to lie about in the streets ...[90]

A parish had once again failed a vulnerable teenager.

However, the most infamous case of the century came to light in 1767 and involved the death of Mary Clifford at the hands of Elizabeth Brownrigg, her husband James and son John.[91] Like Ann Nailor before her, Mary Clifford was a parish apprentice who was starved and beaten by a mistress more interested in strict obedience and cheap labour than child welfare. And like the Metyards, this abuse was a family affair of long standing, with both parish and Foundling Hospital apprentices being placed with the family as trusted partners in charge of a large and superficially well-regulated household. Unlike the Metyards, only one of the perpetrators was actually hanged, the mother, Elizabeth Brownrigg, while James and John Brownrigg were acquitted. There is a substantial modern literature on this case that emphasises its use to discipline middle-class domestic arrangements and reinforce an evolving heterosexuality.[92] However, to eighteenth-century eyes, it once again

---

[90] *Lloyd's Evening Post*, 21–23 November 1763, issue 993 (Burney Collection: www.galegroup.com, 2 Jan. 2014).

[91] *LL*, sets, 'Mary Clifford' and 'Elizabeth Brownrigg'.

[92] See in particular, Patty Seleski: 'A mistress, a mother and a murderess too: Elizabeth Brownrigg and the social construction of the eighteenth-century mistress', in Katherine

reflected the failure of both the parish and the parish community to care effectively for the next generation.

At heart these were simple crimes of personal cruelty; however, they were also tragedies compounded by economic pressure and neglect. Families like the Metyards and the Brownriggs took on pauper apprentices in the expectation of at least saving the cost of a servant, and ideally of turning a profit on their labour. And parish officers, eager to restrain costs, asked fewer questions as the pressure on their budgets mounted. But these high-profile scandals undermined the relationships between the parishes, the poor and a wider public.

'Brownrigg-like cruelty' soon became proverbial in the mouths of Londoners, and even as Elizabeth Brownrigg waited to hang, London's poor incorporated her story in to their begging (and thieving) strategies.[93] Four days before Brownrigg's execution the *Public Advertiser* reported how a young girl played on the case. She was about eleven years old and was

sitting at a Door, and bemoaning herself after a very piteous Manner; ... [a gentleman], making Enquiry after the Reason of it, she replied, that she had broke a Bottle, which her Mistress had given her to fetch some Oil in, and that she dare not go home, she should be so cruelly beat, for that the Person she lived with was not a Degree better than the Woman in Newgate (meaning Brownrigg). The Gentleman gave her Sixpence ... but having watched which Way her Benefactor took, she was again at his Heels presently, and still incessantly crying. The Gentleman turning about, seeing the same Girl, asked her what she cried for then; she told him that she should certainly be murdered by her Mistress for staying so long, unless he would be so good to go with her ... [She said she] was a poor helpless Foundling, who had been apprenticed by the Parish, and that she was beat most unmercifully many Times every Day, without any Provocation, and half starved into the Bargain. The Gentleman, actuated by Compassion, went along with her.

Predictably, he was led to a ruinous building off Tottenham Court Road where two of the girl's accomplices expertly fleeced him of his remaining valuables.[94]

In parallel with concerns about the fate of parish apprentices was a growing anxiety about newborn children. This was founded on the

---

Kittredge, ed., *Lewd and Notorious: Female Transgression in the Eighteenth Century* (Ann Arbor: University of Michigan Press, 2003), pp. 210–34; and Kristina Straub, 'The tortured apprentice: sexual monstrosity and the suffering of poor children in the Brownrigg murder case', in Laura J. Rosenthal and Mita Choudhury, eds., *Monstrous Dreams of Reason: Body, Self, and Other in the Enlightenment* (Lewisburg: Bucknell University Press, 2002), pp. 66–81.

[93] For use of this phrase see *Middlesex Journal or Chronicle of Liberty*, February 22–24, 1770 (Burney Collection: www.galegroup.com, 2 Jan. 2014).

[94] *Public Advertiser*, September 10, 1767, issue 10251 (Burney Collection: www.galegroup.com, 2 Jan. 2014).

insistent critique of plebeian parenthood promoted in print by supporters of the Foundling Hospital over the preceding twenty years. However, this argument, larded with ever more detailed statistics, reached a new crescendo of condemnation in the decade following the disaster of the General Reception. Based on statistics gathered by Jonas Hanway and focusing on the care of newborns and infants by parish nurses and in workhouses, Hanway and his supporters held up parishes as well as the poor to detailed censure. Most famously, Hannah Poole, who ran a large nursing home providing full-time care for pregnant women, children and adult paupers in St Clement Danes, was traduced in print as an angel of death available for hire at 2 shillings per week, per child.[95]

In Hanway's estimate:

She is certainly not qualifyed for a nurse, to keep children alive, though she seems to understand the art of lulling infants to their everlasting rest ... This woman began to prepare shrowds on the 19th of March 1765, and her last burial was on the 25th of Jan. 1766.[96]

Hanway claimed that Poole had the care of twenty-three children in the year ending January 1766, of whom eighteen died in her care, while a further five were discharged to their parents, meaning that not a single infant survived her ministrations for a whole year. In part this onslaught was a rhetorical device aimed to retrieve the Foundling Hospital's financial position following the collapse of the General Reception, by encouraging parliament to employ it to nurse parish children. But it effectively coloured parish poor relief in the dark hues of murder.

It is impossible to verify Hanway's statistics as the relevant registers for St Clement Danes for 1765 have not survived, but the equivalent figures for two years later suggest that he substantially misrepresented Poole's record. Among the paupers housed at parish expense with Hannah Poole that year were twenty-six children aged 15 or under. Most were long-term residents of the house. Thomas Taylor had lived with Hannah Poole for eight years, since 1760, and was 15 years old.[97] John Smith and William Jones were also 15, and were apprenticed from the house after around a year's residence.[98] Of the other children in the house, ten were between the ages of 7 and 15; and a further thirteen were under the age of 3. None of the older children are recorded as having died during

[95] *LL*, set, 'Hannah Poole'. Although largely concerned with the early eighteenth century, the best account of the role of the parish nurse is Jeremy Boulton, 'Welfare systems and the parish nurse in early modern London, 1650–1725', *Family & Community History*, 10:2 (2007), 127–51.
[96] Jonas Hanway, *An Earnest Appeal for Mercy to the Children of the Poor* (1766), pp. 138–9.
[97] *LL*, set, 'Thomas Taylor'.   [98] *LL*, sets, 'John Smith' and 'William Jones'.

the course of the year. Of the infants and toddlers, three did die; two of whom had been born in the house to mothers lying in at parish expense. A 'B' by their names in the registers reflects their status as bastards.[99] The third death was of an illegitimate child who came into Poole's care at 18 months, abandoned by its parents. A fourth illegitimate child born in the house, Charlotte Sirr, died soon after being transferred to a country nurse.[100] In this single year of 1767, there were also at least three births in Hannah Poole's establishment. But more significantly, the bastardy examinations for the parish for the 1760s mention only one parish nurse as providing facilities for women lying in at parish expense, and that nurse was Hannah Poole. In other words, Hannah Poole was providing care for a uniquely vulnerable group of babies, illegitimate children born to pauper mothers, and her success in doing so was at least similar to that achieved by other institutions catering for similar children, such as the Foundling Hospital.

Typical of the mothers and children Nurse Poole accommodated was Margaret Bedward and her child Thomas, who was born in Hannah Poole's house on 17 March 1765, meaning that Thomas formed one of the babies that made up Hanway's damning statistics.[101] Margaret Bedward was a pauper who had been passed three years earlier from St Andrew Wardrobe in the City, and who at that time had two older illegitimate children, Mary and John.[102] Thomas was her third illegitimate child, and she stayed with him and cared for him throughout his very short life, meaning that Thomas's mother, rather than Nurse Poole, was responsible for his immediate care. Thomas died within a month of birth, but Margaret's other children continued in parish care and Mary, her older daughter, in particular seems to have thrived in the process – or at least when she was later apprenticed to a Margarett Le Batt, she had the support of her mother and the self-confidence to use the criminal justice system to pursue a charge of assault against her mistress.[103] Both Mary and her mother appeared at quarter sessions to lodge a complaint and succeeded in overturning her apprenticeship.

Hannah Poole's nursing home cared for a much more diverse crew of paupers than newborn babies and children. Surviving coroners' inquests concerning two adult deaths at Mrs Poole's give details of the internal management of her house. These suggest that it was a reasonably well-

[99] *LL*, St Clement Danes Parish: Registers of Poor Children under 14 years in Parish Care (WCCDRC365000008).
[100] *LL*, set, 'Charlotte Sirr'.
[101] *LL*, sets, 'Margaret Bedward' and 'Thomas Bedward'.
[102] *LL*, set, 'Mary Bedward'; St Clement Danes Parish: Pauper Settlement, Vagrancy and Bastardy Exams, 20 June 1757 – 5 October 1763 (WCCDEP358190350).
[103] *LL*, set, 'Margarett Le Batt'.

run and humane establishment. One death was the result of a suicide by a middle-aged man, Richard Raine, and the other the result of a drunken brawl in the street outside, instigated by Margaret Burgis, who was recovering from a fever at the time. She was nevertheless free to go out when she wanted – and to get drunk, presumably at parish expense.[104]

Despite his problematic evidence, Hanway's public ridicule brought the parishes into disrepute, reinforcing the perception that neither the churchwardens and overseers nor working Londoners could be trusted to care for the next generation. In a popular play published in 1768, *The Bastard Child, or a Feast for the Church-Wardens*, the 'dramatis personae' include 'Old nurse Careless', who could be relied upon 'for the daily allowance of one poor quart of juniper water' to kill off any parish child within three days; while the churchwardens, 'Greedy' and 'Tearfowl', working in cahoots with 'Justice Hog' and the constable, 'Daniel Love-fee', were all depicted as working the system for personal profit.[105]

However, Hanway's efforts had more serious repercussions. They resulted in the passage of two Acts of parliament which would help reshape the character of London poor relief. His first legislative intervention was *An Act for Keeping Distinct and Regular Accounts of the Poor under a Certain Age*, which came in to force in early June 1762.[106] It specified that the parishes within the *Bills of Mortality* should collect detailed monthly returns on the fate of all parish children under the age of four and report them to the Worshipfull Society of Parish Clerks. The explicit intention was to highlight the failings of parochial relief and more particularly the care provided in the capital's workhouses. In some respects the Act reflects the wider experience of the new associational charities, which were dependent on their ability to present a compelling, humanitarian case for whichever particular object of charity they hoped to relieve, by discrediting other types of care.[107] The innovation here was that Hanway's 1762 Act used the authority of parliament to collect and publish information about social problems as a device to generate concern, which could in turn be used to drive the evolution of a wider social policy. Compliance was patchy, but sufficient returns were generated to allow Hanway to begin to build a larger case directed at both ensuring

[104] *LL*, sets, 'Richard Raine' and 'Margaret Burgis'.
[105] Sir Daniel Downright, *The Bastard Child, or a Feast for the Church-Wardens* (1768), pp. ii, 5.
[106] 2 Geo. III c. 22, 'An Act for the keeping regular, uniform and annual registers of all parish poor infants under a certain age, within the bills of mortality'.
[107] See Dianne Payne, 'Rhetoric, reality and the Marine Society', *London Journal*, 30:2 (2005), 66–84; Sarah Lloyd, *Charity and Poverty in England, c. 1680–1820: Wild and Visionary Schemes* (Manchester University Press, 2009), ch. 5.

parish children were boarded in the countryside – far from the doleful influence of their family and 'friends' – and that parishes were held to stricter account in relation to the apprenticeship of older children.

Hanway's second Act was passed in 1768.[108] This extended the requirement for parishes to maintain a precise register of parish children and apprentices. More significantly, it required that all children below the age of four years should be nursed in the country at least three miles from London and Westminster (five miles in certain circumstances). The length of time a London parish child could be apprenticed was also lowered to a maximum of seven years or until the age of twenty-one for both boys and girls. The Act also stipulated that the minimum fee given with a parish apprentice should be £4 2s. and that this fee should be paid in two instalments – the second half three years into the apprenticeship. Finally, the Act established committees of 'Guardians of the Poor', drawn either from the nobility or the highest-ranking members of the parish community, to oversee and inspect the workings of poor relief. To Hanway's disappointment, the ninety-seven parishes within the City of London were excluded from the provisions of the Act, as were four further urban parishes from Middlesex and Surrey. But the vast majority of the large urban parishes that circled the old City, including Hanway's favourite example of dysfunctional parish government, St Clement Danes, were brought within the new regulatory framework.

Hanway's two Acts drew significant attention to the issue of infant mortality in the parishes of London and the plight of parish apprentices, and led to some improvements in the conditions experienced by some parish children. The registers produced as a result of the two Acts formed the basis for an optimistic analysis produced ten years after the second Act came into force. In a parliamentary report authored by Owen Bereton, the returns were surveyed and 9,727 children under the age of six were recorded as having been given up to parochial care in fifteen large urban parishes, of whom *only* 2,042, or 21 per cent, were dead at the end of the period.[109] Bereton concluded that the registration Acts had 'produced very salutary effects', though not in the way Hanway had originally envisaged, as few of the new committees of 'Guardians of the Poor' had ever met, and those that had were 'very little attended to'. Many of the same 'black spots' for infant and child mortality remained. Despite falling into line by building a workhouse and sending its children to nurse in the country, St Clement Danes continued to suffer a higher

[108] 7 Geo. III. c. 39, 'An Act for the better regulation of the parish poor children'.
[109] *PP*, 'Report of the committee on the state of the parish poor children', 1 May 1778, p. 7 (parlipapers.chadwyck.co.uk, 2 Jan. 2014).

than average child mortality rate with 113 deaths among the 257 children under the age of six placed in the care of the parish.

In many respects, Hanway's Acts set the tone for parliamentary inquiries in subsequent decades. The emphasis on clear and well laid out statistics can be seen in the extensive parliamentary reports on poor relief published in 1776 and 1786, which were in turn followed by a series of exhaustive inquiries by both private individuals such as Frederick Morton Eden in the 1790s, and several long-standing parliamentary commissions in the first decades of the nineteenth century.[110] And as James Stephen Taylor has observed, Hanway's aspirations were 'remarkably like' those of 'the Poor Law Commissioners' 1834 *Report*'.[111] However, while Hanway could influence legislators, he could not control how the poor, or even the parishes, responded to his demands.

Parish and pauper strategies

Just as the Foundling Hospital encouraged child abandonment, Hanway's 'reforms' had unintended consequences, and these were exploited by the poor. The parishes, faced with growing demands for relief and ever more bureaucratic requirements to keep records and abide by precise legal diktats, looked for alternatives. They adopted new practices which significantly transformed key aspects of the support provided to paupers. In response the poor learned further lessons in the art of how to use the letter of the law for their own ends.

One parochial strategy that became popular from at least the early 1770s was to seek informal and hence inexpensive agreements with other parishes in respect of providing for individual paupers, as an alternative to removing them under the laws of settlement. These 'friendly' passes or orders were essentially extra-legal agreements between two or more parishes whereby the receiving parish agreed to accept paupers believed to be settled there without contest, initally bypassing the justices and collectively saving all the participants the cost of a legal removal. These agreements eventually grew into substantial consortia of parishes covering large parts of London.[112] The informal character of these passes

---

[110] For a discussion of these returns as they relate to London in particular, see David Green, *Pauper Capital: London and the Poor Law, 1790–1860* (Farnham, Surrey: Ashgate, 2010), chs. 1 and 2.

[111] James Stephen Taylor, *Jonas Hanway: Founder of the Marine Society: Charity and Policy in Eighteenth-Century Britain* (London: Scholar Press, 1985), p. 104.

[112] Green, *Pauper Capital*, p. 46. The relatively few appeals between parishes evident in county records suggest that these kinds of informal agreements could have been in operation from as early as the 1720s.

means that very few have been preserved in parish archives, and it is possible that they substantially predate the mid eighteenth century. However, by at least 1772 they were common enough to justify the creation of blank forms for the purpose. Typical of these passes was that printed for St Botolph Bishopsgate. One completed form was addressed to the churchwardens or overseers of the parish of St Dionis Backchurch:

Gentlemen, Upon examination it appears that Elisth Crocker belongs to your Parish by her Husband Benjn. Crocker Serving his time to Mr Wm. Wright a glaiser in Philpot Lane Fenchurch Street. Please to accept the same without a pass, and the Favour shall be returned by, Gentlemen, Your very humble Servant, Wm Woodcock Church-Warden of St. Botolph Bishopsgate.[113]

By their nature 'friendly passes' left few traces in the archive. Not being legal documents, they had little administrative value, but their existence reflects a new activism on the part of the parishes in the face of an ever more demanding legal system.[114] More importantly, they also effectively gave paupers a veto over the process. An appeal to a justice against a 'friendly pass' could cost both parishes dear.

Other parish responses to the growing demands of the poor were less benign. Contract workhouses, often located on the edge of the metropolis, had been in operation from the 1720s, taking on paupers from urban parishes for a weekly or yearly fee. From the 1760s these institutions became both more commonplace, and more specialised. The small parishes of the City were particularly dependent upon them, with most using them to warehouse high-dependency paupers, or as a form of punishment for the recalcitrant and the merely awkward. But it was not just small City parishes that used these private institutions to discipline the unruly poor. St Botolph Aldgate, which straddled the City's border with Middlesex, despite running two parish workhouses containing upwards of 450 paupers, chose to house its disorderly poor and the insane at two different large pauper farms on the outskirts of the

---

[113] *LL*, St Dionis Backchurch Parish: Miscellaneous Parish and Bridewell Papers, 3 December 1701 – 27 August 1817 (GLDBPM306050119). The earliest example of a 'friendly pass' that we can identify is on a printed form and dated 21 September 1772. LMA, St Peter Cornhill, 'Removal orders, pass warrants and settlement examinations', P69/PET1/B/029/MS04198.

[114] This informal system also probably helps to explain the relatively low legal costs for London parishes recorded in the mid-1780s, when only 1.5 per cent of parish expenditure was spent on the administration of legal settlement. These figures are most easily consulted using the 1804 cumulative returns. See *PP*, 'Abstract of the answers and returns ... relative to the expence and maintenance of the poor in England', 10 July 1804 (parlipapers.chadwyck.co.uk, 2 Jan. 2014).

metropolis.[115] As a result of growing demand for these services, Hoxton, Bethnal Green and Mile End, all just outside the three-mile limit specified by Hanway's second registration Act, became veritable pauper suburbs.[116]

However, the complex interrelationship between the new legislation and the operation of parochial relief is perhaps best captured in the evolution of poor relief in St Clement Danes. Unlike other large Westminster parishes, St Clement's did not establish a workhouse until 1773 – relying instead on outdoor relief and a string of parish nurses (including Hannah Poole). This was largely the result of the settled opposition of the wider community. Attempts had been made to establish a workhouse in the 1730s and early 1740s, but these were unsuccessful. In both June 1754 and August 1759, the issue was once again canvassed, leading to fierce debate and a series of public votes by householders in a general vestry that, unusually, both gave authority to a wide swathe of the population and provided a mechanism for recording the outcome.[117]

Eventually the minister, churchwardens and overseers, and a select band of parishioners went over the heads of the population and applied to parliament for a private Act authorising both the reform of the nightly watch and the creation of a parish workhouse. From 1764 a group of up to twenty-four substantial inhabitants were incorporated as Directors or Governors of the Nightly Watch and Beadles, while the vestry, churchwardens and overseers of the poor were given authority to build and manage a workhouse, inflict corporal punishment on the inmates (unusually), and arrest and train children under ten years old found begging in the streets.[118] Regardless of the Act, opposition continued, and it was not until a further Act was passed in 1771, explicitly authorising the parish to buy land for a workhouse and enforce a rate in support of it, that work was begun.[119] The parish workhouse was eventually opened in 1773 with accommodation for some 350 paupers.[120]

[115] LMA, St Boltoph Aldgate, 'Vestry minute books for the Middlesex part of the parish', P69/BOT2/B/003/MS02642-43, cited by Pam Cross, 'The operation of the workhouse in the parish of St Botolph Aldgate, c. 1734–1834' (BA dissertation, Fitzwilliam College, Cambridge, 1990), p. 40.

[116] For the distribution of these workhouses, see Green, *Pauper Capital*, pp. 66–8.

[117] LL, St Clement Danes Parish: Minutes of Parish Vestries, 5 June 1749 – 11 October 1754 (WCCDMV362090349) and 11 October 1754 – 18 December 1760 (WCCDMV362100322).

[118] 4 Geo. III c. 55, 'An Act for making compensation ... and for other purposes therein mentioned'.

[119] Hanway, *Earnest Appeal*, p. 3; 11 Geo. III c. 22, 'An Act to amend and render more effectual several acts made relating to ... places within the City and liberty of Westminster and parts adjacent'; *PP, Journals of the House of Commons*, 32, 8 March 1770 (parlipapers. chadwyck.co.uk, 2 Jan. 2014).

[120] PP, *House of Commons Sessional Papers*, 'Abstract of the returns made by the overseers of the poor', 1776, p. 105 (parlipapers.chadwyck.co.uk, 2 Jan. 2014).

As in other parishes, in the short term the impact was simply to increase expenditure on the poor – with total costs rising by some 20 per cent in the year after the house opened. However, the creation of a workhouse also led to the dismantling of the local system of nursing homes and a more thorough implementation of the policy of sending children under the age of four to the country. From at least 1773, most infants from St Clements were dispatched to one of several nurses at Low Layton, five miles from the parish, just beyond Hackney Wick and around two hours walk away. As a result, parish children under four were put largely beyond the possibility of 'Sunday visiting'. As Jonas Hanway noted:

> If you send your Infant-Poor to be nursed in Places remote from the Metropolis, you will not only avoid the Perplexity occasioned by the Visits of such Parents, as can do their children no good, but this measure will ... [ensure] the most Abandoned, or the real Distressed will chuse to part with their Children for the few Years which may be necessary.[121]

The parish then further undermined any remaining local connections to family or friends through a new system of apprenticeship. St Clement Danes was one of the earliest parishes to explore the possibility of large-scale industrial apprenticeships to the new factories of the North. Following an infancy far from friends and family, raised by a wet nurse in the country, a child born in the parish by the mid-1770s was likely to spend the next five or six years living in the parish workhouse, before being shipped, at around the age of apprenticeship (eleven or twelve) from one kind of institution to another – this time a factory hundreds of miles away. Most parish children in St Clement's spent their adolescence at John Birch's cotton mill, in Cartmel, Lancashire.[122]

Despite the fact the poor were subjected to new forms of control and exploitation, as London's landscape of parish relief and charity grew ever more complex and as the legal ramifications of settlement gradually came to be normalised within the cultures of relief, the poor were able to identify cracks in the system which provided new opportunities. Some learned the art of petitioning and letter writing – of both throwing oneself on the mercy of the charities and of threatening the parish with untold expense if immediate relief was not provided. Others, perhaps from a middle-class or elite background, advertised for charity in the columns of

---

[121] Jonas Hanway, *Serious Considerations on the Salutary Design of the Act of Parliament for a Regular, Uniform Register of the Parish-Poor* (1762), pp. 27–8.

[122] The parish first started advertising its apprentices in 1785: Katrina Honeyman, *Child Workers in England, 1780–1820: Parish Apprentices and the Making of the Early Industrial Labour Force* (Aldershot: Ashgate, 2007), pp. 36, 59.

the press, while some became more adept at combining one form of relief and authority with another.[123] A few attempted to navigate the choppy waters of the law, either by appealing to a local magistrate for an order of relief or, more problematically, by seeking removal under the vagrancy laws, which established a prima facie settlement that could not be challenged by a direct appeal. And finally, the mothers of illegitimate children used the interests of the parish to force the fathers of their children to provide the resources they needed. The bureaucracy of belonging that lay at the heart of the system of parish relief and settlement was turned to account by the needy and the desperate.

Perhaps the most significant driving force in the creation of a new literate culture of plaint and petition were the associational charities. Many, including the Foundling Hospital after the end of the General Reception, required that applicants produce a formal petition in order to gain admission for themselves or their child. The hospital also required a detailed petition before a child could be reclaimed. Illiteracy remained a problem for some, but by the 1760s most plebeian Londoners were able to deploy written language as part of their engagement with authority, and if not, it was usually possible to hire someone who could act as a scribe.[124] And they did not simply petition single organisations. The policies of the associational charities forced supplicants to find a way to write persuasively about their predicament, and to use this and other tactics to navigate between different institutions.

A measure of the scale of the effort devoted to these activities can be found in the extensive records of the Foundling Hospital. In one ten-month period between March 1763 and January 1764, the hospital received 160 petitions from parents and friends hoping to reclaim a child. The vast majority (103) of the children were, of course, dead, but the process of petitioning demonstrates how paupers learned to work with the authorities in new ways. Entirely typical was the petition received from Mary Marshall née Hobs. In order to reclaim the child Mary had given up to the hospital at the height of the General Reception, she needed to both write a petition and procure a certificate

---

[123] See Thomas Sokoll, ed., *Essex Pauper Letters, 1731–1837* (Oxford University Press, 2001); Donna T. Andrew, '"To the charitable and humane": appeals for assistance in the eighteenth-century London press', in Hugh Cunningham and Joanna Innes, eds., *Charity, Philanthropy and Reform from the 1690s to 1850* (Basingstoke: Macmillan Press, 1998), pp. 87–107.

[124] Historians have become increasingly sceptical about measuring literacy rates and have instead focused on the varied practices of using pen and print. See Susan Whyman, *The Pen and the People: English Letter Writers, 1660–1800* (Oxford University Press, 2009), pp. 104–11.

authenticating her story from the General Lying-In Hospital where the child had been born. Remarkably, six-year-old 'Thorncroft, 10269' was still alive and after the petition was 'Read at the Gen[era]l Comm[itt]ee [on] 30th May 1764', she was delivered to her parents, despite their inability to afford the steep charges the hospital normally made in such cases.[125]

For those living outside their parish of settlement, writing to one's parish was also increasingly commonplace. The earliest recognisable 'pauper letters' requesting relief date from the 1730s, but there was little incentive to preserve these documents and few survive before the first decades of the nineteenth century.[126] Nevertheless, the full mix of tactics that characterise nineteenth-century pauper letters can be found in the few that survive from mid-century, including those preserved among the records of St Dionis Backchurch.[127] Letters written between the late 1750s and the early 1770s by Catherine Jones, a disabled pensioner whose undisputed settlement lay in the parish of St Dionis Backchurch, for example, demonstrate, despite her limited literacy skills, a comprehensive understanding of how her requests for relief would be read by the parish officers.[128] Jones appealed to her rights as an ex-householder. She played on the sympathy of the churchwardens, and most effectively, she used the threat of the cost of her return to St Dionis, from her present home some 200 miles away in Shrewsbury and Wrexham, to move their hands.

An early letter reflects the pattern:

For Mr Piter phope in Fan church street London.
  September the 2 1758
  onerd sir I … am very soray to be so trubelsum to you, but I canot help it for I am in gret want of relief from my parch … Heir everything is at gret prise but watter. Their is none knows what paines I do baer in my limes and I can not stire sum time for the ruptor, but I do keep my contyenas [countenance] as well as I can or eles I should be sent to my parch before now. And if … I must go the ofissers of this parch … they will hunt me from heer as the did from Wrechame. Then I must come to london. But I do raether have to gunyes [two guineas] heir. No more from a poor poper Catherine Jones.[129]

[125] LMA, Foundling Hospital, 'Register of children claimed, 28 March 1764 – 23 Jan. 1765', A/FH/A/11/001/001.

[126] Sokoll, ed., *Essex Pauper Letters, 1731–1837*.

[127] *LL*, St Dionis Backchurch: Letters to Parish Officials Seeking Pauper Relief, 1758–9 (GLDBPR308000002).

[128] *LL*, Deirdre Palk, 'Catherine Jones'.

[129] *LL*, St Dionis Backchurch: Letters to Parish Officials Seeking Pauper Relief, 1758–9 (GLDBPR308000006 and GLDBPR308000007).

In later correspondence, Jones informed the churchwardens that both her arms were bad and that she needed constant personal care, and threatened to put the parish to 'six pound Carish, in bringing of me up' to London, praying repeatedly for more and regular relief.[130] These letters were remarkably successful: through these years, Catherine typically received between £2 2s. and £4 4s. per year.[131] Eventually she was brought back to London and supported in a contract workhouse for a number of years before once again entering into negotiations with the parish. This time she asked the parish to facilitate her return to Wrexham:

Catherine Jones applied for leave to return home to Wrexham in Denbighshire upon condition of paying her two guineas in hand and two guineas per annum, which was agreed, to also give her a pair of shoes.[132]

Maintaining Catherine Jones at a pauper farm in Hoxton cost the parish approximately £5 8s. per year, so sending her back to Wrexham where she had friends was a pragmatic response which suited both parties.

Most pauper letter writers mixed claims to a right to relief based on their settlement and a sense of belonging to the parish with appeals to simple humanity. A somewhat more dangerous tactic was to play magistrates and other figures of authority against the parish officers. This was the route pursued by Paul Patrick Kearney.[133]

Born and raised in Ireland, but with a secure settlement in St Dionis Backchurch at the heart of the City, Kearney, unlike Catherine Jones (whom he would have known), was well educated and highly literate. After a long career in commerce, but which also included an appearance at the Old Bailey (he was convicted of forgery) and correspondence with a secretary of state, Kearney fell into severe need in 1761.[134] By the winter of 1764, barefoot and ragged, he formally applied for relief from the parish but was summarily turned down.[135] Kearney's next step was open to any pauper. He appealed to the Lord Mayor, William Bridgen,

---

[130] *LL*, St Dionis Backchurch: Letters to Parish Officials Seeking Pauper Relief, 1758–9 (GLDBPR308000019).

[131] *LL*, St Dionis Backchurch: Churchwardens and Overseers of the Poor Account Books, 1758–62, p. 122 (GLDBAC300070234) and 1729–62, p. 265 (GLDBAC300060536).

[132] *LL*, St Dionis Backchurch: Workhouse Inquest (Visitation) Minute Books, 20 May 1761 – 29 April 1788, 7 July 1772 (GLDBIW302010079).

[133] *LL*, Tim Hitchcock, 'Paul Patrick Kearney'.

[134] For a comprehensive treatment of Kearney's career, see Tim Hitchcock, *Down and Out in Eighteenth-Century London* (London: Hambledon and London, 2004), pp. 125–31.

[135] Unless otherwise noted, material on Kearney is drawn from the LMA, 'Papers relating to an application for parish poor relief by Paul Patrick Kearney, 1771', P69/DIO/B/082/MS11280C; and LMA, St Dionis Backchurch, 'Miscellaneous parish papers, vouchers, 1766–72', P69/DIO/B/099 (old ref: Ms 11280 box 6).

sitting as a magistrate in the Mansion House Justice Room. At Kearney's request William Kippax, the parish overseer, was summoned to appear to explain why relief had been refused. According to Kearney's account, 'Mr Kippax ... vindictively attempted to shew cause to his Lordship why ... [he] should not be relieved [and] told his Lordship several untruths'. In response, Kearney 'justly and truly contradicted' the claims and demanded that Kippax swear an oath. At this point Kippax refused to cooperate and was given short shrift by the Lord Mayor, who declared, the 'parish can get no credit by giving this [man] such treatment ... and ordered [Kearney] to be ... relieved'. 'Kippax then and there promised his Lordship to relieve [Kearney, and gave him] a note in his ... own handwriting directed to one Richard Birch in Rose Lane' in Spitalfields, gaining him admittance to the workhouse.

Kearney, however, was worried that by being sent outside the City, beyond the jurisdiction of the Lord Mayor, he would be disadvantaged. In his words, the note he received:

instead of being an order for [his] relief was a warrant of commitment of [his] body to imprisonment, labour or work in an infected filthy dungeon called a workhouse kept by ... Richard Birch, containing near one hundred poor victims to parish cruelty, but not capacious enough healthily to hold forty ...

Kearney was forced to accept accommodation in Rose Lane, but he very quickly set about manoeuvring the parish into supporting him elsewhere. This took him just three weeks, after which he was initially supported outside the workhouse with both money and clothing, until on 7 August he gained admission, at parish expense, to Guy's Hospital. Here, in Kearney's words, he was put 'under the care of an eminent physician surgeon and apothecary who did all they could to cure him'. He was eventually discharged in early December and over the next three years received substantial relief from the parish. In 1766 alone he was given a new great coat, a pair of breeches and a new pair of shoes, which with accommodation and medical care cost £10 4s. 4d.[136] After a further encounter with the Lord Mayor in 1767 – this time instigated by the parish – Kearney eventually turned his back on London and for the next few years 'languished a long time at Bath and elsewhere' and 'went to Ireland', only to return in early 1771, when he once again went to the Mansion House in order to force the hand of the parish.

Kearney's final negotiation came in the following year, and it took almost exactly the same form as Catherine Jones's. Kearney wrote to the

---

[136] *LL*, St Dionis Backchurch Parish: Churchwardens and Overseers of the Poor Account Books, 1764–1770 (GLDBAC300080115).

churchwardens of St Dionis Backchurch in March 1771. He explained that he had secured a position with a Captain Scot and offered the parish a deal: 'that I never would demand, ask or claim any relief of St Dionis's parish if you would furnish me now with about forty shillings to get my things to fit me for that place'. He signed his note, 'Your afflicted and abused neighbour, P. Kearney'. Pragmatism once again trumped all other considerations, and the parish paid up.

Very few paupers had the skills and sheer brio Kearney deployed in his negotiations with St Dionis Backchurch. Moreover, his strategy was in some ways less effective than Catherine Jones's more humble, if quietly threatening, appeals. While Jones secured a promise of lifelong support at the rate of £2 per year, Kearney apparently exchanged his parish rights for a single one-off payment of the same amount.[137] But more common than either tactic was an attempt to collaborate with the overseer against better-off parishioners or, better still, the wealthy inhabitants of some other parish.

The relationship between the mothers of illegitimate children and parish officers was always fraught. Mothers faced punishment if they failed to name the father, and the known instances of overseers colluding in the abduction and murder by neglect of bastard children taken by force from their mothers and delivered up to the Foundling Hospital speak of an unequal landscape of power and motive. However, two fundamental assumptions of poor law practice ensured that the mothers of illegitimate children could negotiate with the parish from a position of relative strength. In the words of Richard Burn, it was clear both that:

A bastard child is 'prima facie' settled where born: and this was the ancient genuine settlement.

And that:

if the mother and the child have different settlements ... the bastard child ... shall go with the mother for nurture until the age of seven years ... as a necessary appendage of the mother, and inseparable from her.[138]

Despite the attempts of 'reformers' such as Jonas Hanway to denigrate plebeian parenthood, the Old Poor Law put an uncompromising obliga-tion on ratepayers and parish officers to provide care for illegitimate children and by extension their mothers. This obligation, in its turn,

---

[137] Of course, it is unlikely this agreement would have stood the test of legal challenge, so Kearney was not giving anything up.
[138] Richard Burn, *The Justice of the Peace, and Parish Officer*, 4 vols. (12th edn, 1772), III, pp. 306, 310.

frequently ensured that parish officers and pauper mothers shared a common interest in securing support from feckless fathers.

The process of forcing the father of a bastard child to support it, and indemnify the parish for any expenses incurred, was complex and bureaucratic. Richard Burn devoted some thirty-six pages to the topic in the 1772 edition of his *Justice of the Peace*.[139] Following a voluntary examination of the mother on oath before two magistrates, declaring that the father had 'carnal knowledge' of the examinee leading to pregnancy, a warrant was issued for apprehending the father, who could then be forced to provide a bond to the parish, under threat of immediate punishment in the house of correction, normally to guarantee support for the child to the sum of £100 by the 1770s.[140] To provide a bond of this sort, the father would normally have to rely on employers and relatives as sureties, and the bond remained in force until the child reached the age of fourteen, was apprenticed or died. The father would also be obliged to comply with a 'filiation' and maintenance order, normally at a rate of 2s. 6d. a week. From the mother and child's perspective, the process ensured that the settlement of both would be securely determined and that they would have access to parish relief, even if the substance of that relief was supplied by the child's father.

As had long been true, for many young women the first step in securing relief of this sort was to establish the child's settlement by giving birth in the parish workhouse. Between 1770 and 1775, at least 67 women entered the the workhouse belonging to St Martin in the Fields while actually in labour, and a further 205 in the later stages of pregnancy. Many more came in with a bastard child in tow. The experience of someone like the seventeen-year-old prostitute Mary Brown, who gained admission to the St Clement Danes workhouse in 1786 having simply turned up at the workhouse door deep in labour, reflects the strategies available to young women and the willingness of many to make full use of them.[141]

Despite the often unfavourable innovations introduced by 'reformers' such as Jonas Hanway and the parishes, paupers possessed the skills to release real resources. Crafting a powerful petition, combining approaches to more than one institution, working with the overseers against an ex-lover or knowing which magistrate to approach on what

---

[139] Burn, *Justice of the Peace*, Vol. I, pp. 179–215.

[140] *LL*, St Clement Danes Parish: Pauper Settlement, Vagrancy and Bastardy Exams, 27 October 1772 – 17 May 1776 (WCCDEP358070248); St Clement Danes Parish: List of Securities for the Maintenance of Bastard Children, 14 April 1755 – 15 June 1779 (WCCDRR368000054).

[141] *LL*, set, 'Mary Brown'.

business were all valuable means of extracting support. But while workhouses, weekly pensions and the provision of clothes and medical care
form the meat and gristle of eighteenth-century poor relief, and were
provided increasingly frequently in response to the demands of the poor,
it is important to remember that parishes also controlled access to more
substantial resources, such as the almshouses that pauper residents could
aspire to occupying in old age. When Westminster Abbey decided to tear
down its almshouses in Dean's Court in 1779, it was obliged to pay
compensation of £5 5s. per year to each resident in exchange for their
agreement to vacate the houses.[142]

Clearing the streets

In attempting to reduce the growing cost of poor relief, and building on
the development of a comprehensive system of vagrant contracting in
1757, the men who governed the City and Middlesex adopted an additional strategy: they stepped up efforts to punish the casual and informal
components of the London poor, expelling thousands to their parishes of
settlement outside the metropolis. Women and men deemed disorderly,
whose begging was too aggressive, who worked as prostitutes or who
were deemed unwilling to work for a living, were arrested and prosecuted
for vagrancy, including all the ill-defined 'crimes' of 'wandering and
begging' and of being 'loose, idle and disorderly'. In what might be
described as an official reformation of manners campaign, and echoing
the increasingly systematic prosecution and removal of vagrants in the
1750s, officers in both Middlesex and the City renewed and expanded
their efforts to clear the streets of vagrants, especially in the tense years
between 1768 and 1773.[143] Large numbers were arrested, committed to
houses of correction and in many cases removed, but many of those
prosecuted were able to undermine the authorities' efforts, and ironically, some managed to use the system to secure a legal settlement.

Starting in 1765 in Middlesex, and 1767 in the City, the money spent
on vagrant removals, and by extension the numbers of vagrants apprehended and passed, increased significantly, so that by 1768 the cost of
policing vagrancy in Middlesex had doubled since 1764, and City
expenditure had risen eight times (Figure 6.3).

Expenses declined between 1768 and 1770–1, before dramatically
increasing, especially in the City. In 1773 expenditure amounted to

[142] Westminster Abbey Muniment Room, 13 May 1799, Ms. 66000.
[143] Although prosecutions strongly imply this change in policy, no trace of a specific order
to launch such a campaign has been identified.

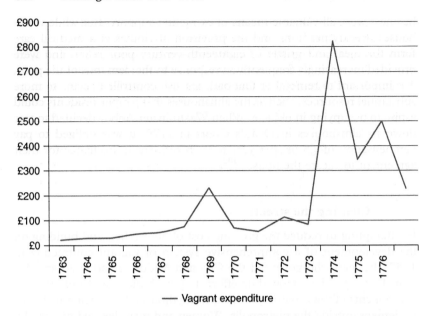

Figure 6.3 City of London vagrant expenditure, 1763–1776. Online data set: City of London Vagrant Expenditure 1738–1792.xlsx.

£827 14s. 5d., ten times higher than the average of the previous four years and almost twice as much as in Middlesex. Many of those apprehended in the City were committed to Bridewell, where commitments soared to 1,755 in 1773, the highest level in almost 150 years.[144] They remained high, at over 800 per year, until 1777 (Figure 6.1).

Not everyone committed to houses of correction was accused of vagrancy, but most were tarred with one or more of the long list of offences that made up this rag-tag category of crime. Records of less than 10 per cent of those committed to Bridewell survive, but of the 224 men and women committed from July 1772 to January 1774 for whom we have information, 37.9 per cent were described as rogues, vagrants and beggars, 11.6 per cent as loose, idle and disorderly persons, and 21.9 per cent as prostitutes.[145]

[144] Faramerz Dabhoiwala, 'Summary justice in early-modern London', *English Historical Review*, 121:492 (2006), 808–18. The figures Dabhoiwala reports for 1772 and 1773 are wrong, as is clear from the Minutes of the Court of Governors which indicate higher figures (*LL*, Bridewell Royal Hospital: Minutes of the Court of Governors, 7 January 1762 – 15 March 1781 (BBBRMG20208)). The alternative figures he reports from the *Annual Register* for 1773 and 1774 are correct (*Annual Register*, 16 [Dec. 1773], p. 94; 17 [Dec. 1774], p. 108).

[145] Each commitment to Bridewell was numbered in sequence from the start of the year, but the complaint and process that led to the commitment was only recorded when the

(Of the remainder, the largest category by far was petty theft at 24.6 per cent.) Edward Hamleeter, for example, was arrested for being a 'Rogue and Vagabond and an Idle and disorderly Person having no Visible way of living and not giving a good Account of himself and found Asking Alms in the Parish of St. Michael le Querne', and Mary Myler and three other women were accused by one of the constables of Farringdon Ward Without 'for being Rogues and Vagabonds wandring Abroad lodging in the open Air in the Parish of St. Brides and not giving a good Account of themselves', all in December 1772.[146] Only summary statistics survive of commitments to the Middlesex house of correction, but they show that a substantial proportion of the more than fifteen hundred prisoners committed annually between October 1769 and September 1772 were accused of vagrancy-related offences. Of the 4,987 prisoners, 21.8 per cent were accused of being 'disorderly'. Between 1772 and 1774, an average of 531 vagrants a year were sent to the county's houses of correction.[147]

We do not know precisely how many of those arrested for vagrancy were removed to their parish of settlement, as opposed to, or in addition to, being committed to a house of correction (many of the arrested were actually apprehended in their own parish of settlement). Nevertheless, the number of those passed was certainly substantial: in 1775 the Middlesex clerk of the peace estimated that an average of 'near Twelve hundred' vagrants a year were passed at county expense.[148]

The rewards offered to constables for the arrest of vagrants encouraged some to be particularly active. The City's cash accounts reveal that two men received the bulk of the payments in the late 1760s and 1770s: John Sharp was paid £204 6s. 3d. for apprehending vagrants and filling out passes in 1768, and £216. 4s. for passing and clothing vagrants in 1773, while James Morgan received a total of almost £793 for apprehending vagrants, filling in passes and taking examinations between 1774 and 1776.[149] Also active was William Payne, who cut his teeth as an informer and parish officer in the 1757–63 reformation of manners campaign and in 1771 was appointed deputy constable of Farringdon Ward

Court of Governors was actually in session, and the Court met infrequently in this period. Since most prisoners were discharged before the Court met, we know the numbers committed, but the reason for the commitment in only a fraction of cases.

[146] *LL*, Bridewell Royal Hospital: Minutes of the Court of Governors, 7 January 1762 – 15 March 1781 (BBBRMG202080399).

[147] *PP*, 'Report from the committee appointed to make enquiries relating to the employment, relief and maintenance of the poor, fourth schedule', 21 May 1776, p. 67 (parlipapers.chadwyck.co.uk, 2 Jan. 2014).

[148] *LL*, Middlesex Sessions: Sessions Papers, April 1775 (LMSMPS506520137).

[149] LMA, City of London: 'City's cash accounts', COL/CHD/CT/01/050, f. 126; COL/CHD/CT/01/051, ff. 91–2; COL/CHD/CT/01/052, f. 203; COL/CHD/CT/01/053, ff. 107, 231.

Without.[150] Five years later he was given a reward of 20 guineas 'for faithful discharge of his duty', shortly after two other men earned similar gratuities for 'being very active in bringing to justice several notorious rogues and offenders'.[151]

The loose definition of vagrancy led many officers to arrest vulnerable individuals on little more than a whim. When Susannah Everitt was committed to Bridewell in May 1773, she was accused of 'Wandring abroad Lodging in the Open Air and not giving a good Account of herself and for Asking Alms in this City'.[152] But when the men who arrested her failed to appear against her, she told the court:

she got her living by sticking Pins for Pinmakers that she was going on a Sunday Evening with her Child in her Arms to See her Sister who lived at Westminster and having put down her Child at the Corner of a Passage to make Water she was taken into Custody carried before the Lord Mayor and Committed to this House for no other offence as she knew of.

She was discharged, and the men who arrested her were reprimanded for failing to appear and testify against her. Four other men were similarly censured for not giving 'evidence against sundry persons taken up by them and Committed by the Lord Mayor as Vagrants'.[153]

Those apprehended for vagrancy had some opportunities to evade removal. In Middlesex, the system of vagrant removal was subcontracted to James Sturges Adams, and later his son, Henry Adams, but despite their extensive experience many of those removed did not end up back in their parish of settlement. In 1774 John Lay, 'a Cripple [taken] in the act of begging' in the parish of St George Hanover Square, was ordered to be removed north to Hertfordshire on his way to York, but about a week later he was seen about the streets of neighbouring London parishes. He told the parish beadle, 'there was a boy come with a Cart to Bridewell and took him the sd. Lay a little way and then told him he might go where he like'.[154]

Even those who were properly removed frequently made their way back to the parish where they were arrested. Elizabeth Holland's settlement was in Bethnal Green, but in 1773–4 she was arrested three times for vagrancy in Westminster and passed to Bethnal Green.[155] On each occasion,

---

[150] *LL*, set, 'William Payne'.
[151] LMA, 'Journals of Common Council', COL/CC/01/01/064, 15 February 1776, ff. 294–5; 14 March 1776, f. 298.
[152] *LL*, set, 'Susannah Everitt'.
[153] *LL*, Bridewell Royal Hospital: Minutes of the Court of Governors, 7 January 1762 – 15 March 1781 (BBBRMG202080429 and BBBRMG202080430).
[154] *LL*, Middlesex Sessions: Sessions Papers, October 1774 (LMSMPS506450198 and LMSMPS506450199). See also the case, in the same document, of Edward Maclauchlin.
[155] *LL*, set, 'Elizabeth Holland'.

however, she was back in Westminster within days, because, she said, the overseers of the poor in her parish 'would not do any thing for her'.[156]

Lay and Holland were not alone in subverting attempts to remove them back to their parish of settlement, or, if they were apprehended in their own parish, to force them to change their behaviour. Several similar examples of recidivism can be identified in the records of Bridewell. Some names, such as Anne Sparkes, occur repeatedly.[157] A prostitute, Sparkes was arrested on 19 December 1771, 6 August 1772, 17 February 1773 and 9 June 1774. Others, such as Mary Gardiner and Michael Burke, can be found listed in the records both of the Middlesex house of correction at Clerkenwell and of Bridewell in the City.[158] In 1775 the Middlesex justices resolved to keep records of the vagrants they passed so that 'if such persons should return and be found committing the like offence', they could be more severely punished – though there is no evidence that they ever did so.[159]

There were other ways of undermining the system. By employing a false or counterfeit pass, beggars were able to move about unimpeded, and without fear of arrest.[160] Since most passes were pre-printed and certified with the signature of a magistrate from a distant neighbourhood, such frauds were difficult to detect. Of the six women charged with this offence that can be identified in this period, three were discharged without punishment.[161] However, even legitimately removed paupers could force the hands of parish officers. While it is impossible to demonstrate that individuals 'chose' to be arrested and removed as a vagrant, the process created a prima facie claim to a settlement that was almost impossible for the parishes to challenge. Implicit in the laws themselves, and legally explicit following two test cases heard at King's Bench in 1777, a vagrancy removal order could not be subject to an appeal, even if the examination upon which it was based proved to be inaccurate. Because an appeal of this sort would shift responsibility for the vagrant from the supposed parish of settlement to the parish of arrest, it was thought unreasonable. Instead, the named parish of settlement had to

[156] LL, Middlesex Sessions: Sessions Papers, October 1774 (LMSMPS506450200).
[157] LL, set, 'Anne Sparkes'.
[158] LL, sets, 'Mary Gardiner' and 'Michael Burke'. The uncertainties of record linkage make it difficult to be certain that in all these and similar cases the same names refer to the same individual, but it is very likely that this is true in at least *some* of these cases.
[159] LL, Middlesex Sessions: Sessions Papers, December 1755 (LMSMPS506590123).
[160] LL, Middlesex Sessions: Sessions Papers, December 1768 (LMSMPS505900003); LL, City of London Sessions: Sessions Papers, 7 December 1765 – 17 December 1766 (LMSLPS15077PS150770154).
[161] For more on false passes, see Hitchcock, Down and Out, p. 148.

either accept the vagrant as a settled pauper or seek to remove them at parish expense under the poor law.[162]

While some may have actively manipulated the system, others challenged the legal basis under which they were apprehended and punished. Acquiring the financial resources needed to mount a legal challenge was beyond the capacity of most of those accused of vagrancy, but enough accused prostitutes were able to hire lawyers and challenge their prosecutions that the very basis of policing prostitution came under threat. As Faramerz Dabhoiwala argues, 'by the middle of the eighteenth century the idea had become firmly established that street-walking by prostitutes was not itself punishable'; proof of specific misconduct was necessary.[163] In April 1770 John Fielding blamed the large number of prostitutes in Westminster on

the great Difficulty, as the Law now stands, to punish those Offenders, they being, as common Prostitutes, scarce, if at all, within the Description of any Statute now in being: And he added, that this subjects Watchmen, Roundhouse-keeprs, Constables, and even the Magistrates themselves, to Prosecutions from low Attorneys.[164]

Fielding experienced these difficulties first-hand later the same year. Two women, Frances York and Jane Fielding, used a lawyer named Bearcroft, supported by a Mr Wallace and Mr Dunning, to bring a case to King's Bench. The case, brought in the same legal term in which the Wilkite printer John Almon appealed his conviction for libel, directly challenged the commitment of the two women to the Westminster house of correction at Tothill Fields for 'being loose idle and disorderly persons, of evil fame, and common nightwalkers' in Covent Garden. They had been convicted on the oath of the Bow Street Runner William Haliburton, on a warrant signed by John Fielding. The women made three objections. Most worryingly for the authorities, they claimed the terms 'loose idle and disorderly ... are too loose and inadequate'. Perhaps to avoid looking too closely at the broader issues involved, Chief Justice Mansfield quashed their conviction on a narrow and technical

[162] Audrey Eccles, *Vagrancy in Law and Practice under the Old Poor Law* (Farnham, Surrey: Ashgate, 2012), p. 56; and *Decisions of the Court of King's Bench, upon the Laws Relating to the Poor*, 2 vols. (1793), II, pp. 788–91, *Rex* vs. *Ringwould* and *St Lawrence Jewry* vs. *Edgeware*. It is important to note that this judicial policy also allowed the counties to effectively wash their hands of any financial responsibility for vagrants once they had been delivered to the parish of supposed settlement.
[163] Faramerz Dabhoiwala, *The Origins of Sex: A History of the First Sexual Revolution* (London: Penguin, 2012), pp. 72–6.
[164] PP, *Journals of the House of Commons*, 32, 10 April 1770, p. 882 (parlipapers.chadwyck.co.uk, 2 Jan. 2014).

ground that in signing the warrant Fielding had failed to identify himself as a justice of the peace with the authority to make such commitments.[165] However, this did not prevent the issue of principle being raised in the press. Robert Holloway, a staunch critic of Fielding and the rotation offices, set himself up as an 'advocate for ... oppressed women' following the commitment of fifty women to Clerkenwell house of correction in a short period in 1773.[166] Attacking the justices responsible (from the Litchfield rotation office), he questioned the moral and legal basis of the commitments:

> how could you, in the face of day, commit such an atrocious outrage against natural liberty, and without compunction cast your fellow-creatures into the very bowels of wretchedness? What! Send fifty poor women to a loathsome prison, without regard to age, condition, or situation, on a presumption, or mere suspicion, that they might commit an offence, which if committed, is not cognizable by law?[167]

Holloway also reported his extensive correspondence with 'Arabella', a woman in the Clerkenwell house of correction who had allegedly been seduced by a justice, and who claimed that prostitutes were committed there only if they were unable to pay tribute to justices of the peace.[168]

As a result of these and other challenges, and perhaps also owing to an increase in prostitution resulting from falling real wages, by the mid-1770s it had becoming increasingly difficult to suppress street prostitution and related offences in London.[169] While hundreds of men and women continued to be punished and removed as vagrants every year, some of the more savvy, sometimes assisted by sympathetic officers, lawyers and others, had found effective ways to subvert the process.

---

[165] [James Burrow], *Reports of Cases Argued and Adjudged in the Court of King's Bench, during the Time of Lord Mansfield's Presiding in that Court*, 5 vols. (Dublin, 5th edn, 1794), V, pp. 2484–6.

[166] *LL*, set, 'Robert Holloway'.

[167] *Morning Chronicle*, 4 January 1773, issue 1129 (Burney Collection: www.galegroup. com, 2 Jan. 2014).

[168] Robert Holloway, *The Rat-Trap: Dedicated to the Right Hon. Lord Mansfield... Addressed to Sir John Fielding* [1773], pp. 68–96.

[169] In 1772, another woman hired an attorney to bring a charge of false imprisonment against a justice 'for committing her to Clerkenwell bridewell to peal hemp for the space of twelve days without any lawful cause or reason whatever', but the case collapsed when the woman appeared in court drunk. TNA, King's Bench, 'Crown side records: affidavits', KB 1/19/2/1, bundle for Michaelmas 1772, #43, cited by Joanna Innes, 'Statute law and summary justice in early modern England' (unpublished paper, May 1986), p. 32. For the policing of prostitution in the City in the late eighteenth century, see Drew Gray, *Crime, Prosecution and Social Relations: The Summary Courts of the City of London in the Late Eighteenth Century* (Houndmills: Palgrave, 2009), pp. 126–35.

John Fielding, Bow Street and contested notions of justice

Frustrated in his efforts both to prosecute prostitutes and to control industrial and political unrest, John Fielding focused most of his efforts in the 1760s and 1770s on the policing and prosecution of felony. Knighted in 1761, Fielding's practices and outspoken opinions were undoubtedly innovative, but they attracted praise and ridicule in almost equal measure, and prompted other justices and litigants to adopt different strategies. Ambivalence towards Fielding's approach to the law was reflected in his appearance before a parliamentary committee in 1770. Formed to 'enquire into the several Burglaries and Robberies that of late have been committed in and about the Cities of London and Westminster', the committee summoned only three witnesses. For his part, Fielding 'presented statistics to show the extent and growth of property crime in recent years, commented on the causes of such increases, and noted some of the difficulties magistrates faced in carrying out their functions'. His suggestions for remedying the problems, however, fell on deaf ears. His by now careworn proposal to place the night watch under the control of a committee of magistrates was ignored by MPs, and his complaint 'That Ballad-singers are a greater nuisance than Beggars, because they give Opportunity to Pickpockets, by collecting People together: That the Songs they sing are generally immoral and obscene' was literally laughed at.[170] When a new committee returned to the issue of the watch two years later, Fielding was not even called to testify, and a set of reforms for Westminster was adopted that left control firmly in the hands of the parish vestries.[171]

Fielding was left to concentrate on the detection of felons and on ensuring their convictions through the preparation of detailed case materials. Following his 'General Preventative Plan' of 1772, he extended his efforts to collect information about crimes and suspects to the entire country. As John Styles notes, Fielding 'saw a vast pool of fugitives from justice waiting to be trawled' and believed that if information was collected efficiently, they could be located and prosecuted.[172] Under his

---

[170] *The Parliamentary History of England from the Earliest Period to 1803*, Vol. XVI (1813), p. 935.

[171] Elaine Reynolds, 'Sir John Fielding, Sir Charles Whitworth, and the Westminster Night Watch Act, 1770–1775', in Louis A. Knafla, ed., *Policing and War in Europe* (Westport, Conn.: Greenwood Press, 2002), pp. 1–19, quote from p. 4; 14 Geo. III c. 90, 'An Act for the better regulation of the nightly watch and beadles within the City and liberty of Westminster, and parts adjacent'.

[172] John Styles, 'Sir John Fielding and the problem of criminal investigation in eighteenth-century England', *Transactions of the Royal Historical Society*, 33 (1983), 127–49, quote

direction and using methods he had established in the 1750s, the Bow Street Runners continued to pursue suspects, both in London and the provinces. According to John Beattie, as a result of the regular reports of their activities in the newspapers and the Old Bailey *Proceedings*, the Runners gradually came to be 'regarded as perhaps more respectable than they had been earlier'. But their reliance on lists of suspects and anonymous paid informers continued to generate popular opposition.[173] Passers-by were frequently stopped in the streets simply for being 'suspicious characters', and once arrested they could find themselves roughly searched on the basis of dubious legal authority in the increasingly notorious Brown Bear pub, across the street from Fielding's office. Some offenders were framed: Beattie notes that the Runners 'almost certainly helped to convict men innocent of the charges they faced by rigging identity parades and encouraging hesitant prosecutors'. Nonetheless, the Runners were increasingly trusted by Old Bailey jurors. In cases where they testified, defendants were more likely to be found guilty.[174]

An early arrest of the highwayman John Rann illustrates some of the Runners' methods.[175] Following a series of robberies on the road to Hampstead on the night of Saturday 13 November 1773, Fielding dispatched two of his more experienced Runners, John Clarke and Richard Bond, in search of the culprits. As Clarke testified,

we went on the road that night, but finding nobody. . ., we went and searched disorderly houses; at the Three Tuns near Knave's Acre, we found the four prisoners, and another man whose name is Scott. On searching Monro I found some shot in his pocket.[176]

Without any particularly damning evidence, or obvious reason to suspect them, the five men were arrested as 'disorderly' under the vagrancy laws and taken before Fielding the next morning. There, threatened with the possibility of being charged with a capital offence, one of the five turned king's evidence and testified against the others. It was only the inability of the victim to provide a positive identification that prevented the remaining four from being convicted and possibly sentenced to death.

The Runners inspired fear and loathing among plebeian Londoners. When John Davis, who claimed he had gone to a house to collect some money for mending a step in March 1774, heard that 'Sir John

---

from 148; John Beattie, *The First English Detectives: The Bow Street Runners and the Policing of London, 1750–1840* (Oxford University Press, 2012), p. 85.

[173] Beattie, *First English Detectives*, p. 51; for the Runners' methods, see ch. 4.

[174] Beattie, *First English Detectives*, pp. 75, 105–7, 117, 133.

[175] LL, Edward Duncan, 'John Rann, d.1774'.

[176] LL, Old Bailey Proceedings, 8 December 1773 (t17731208-1).

Fielding's men' had come to the house, he ran 'down stairs' in panic, later explaining to the court that 'I did not care to be in their mess; I should not like to meet them any where, much less in a house'.[177] His fear is understandable: the house in question was full of coiners, and Davis was arrested and convicted along with six others. Not surprisingly the Runners always worked in pairs or larger groups, both to avoid attack and to ensure that any evidence given in court could be confirmed by a witness who could be trusted to tell a consistent story.[178]

Fielding also attracted criticism in the public press. Robert Holloway, his embittered critic, highlighted the Runners' tendency to make arrests on inadequate evidence in his 1773 polemic, *The Rat-Trap*. When a crime was reported to a rotation office, he claimed, 'the lucky incident gives opportunity for our cautious magistrates to suspect whom they please ... what is infinitely more oppressive, this hideous power is delegated to every runner and thief-taker in the office'. As a result, four out of ten suspects were 'wrongly committed, of course unlawfully; and most of these commitments under the pernicious pretext of suspicion'.[179] More damagingly, Holloway claimed that some of these innocent men were actually convicted and executed, citing the cases of Thomas Grear and Thomas Younger. In September 1773 the *Morning Chronicle* reported that these two men, executed on 11 August, were in fact innocent, following the information on oath of a man named Lane, a 'very old offender', that he and his accomplices had committed the horrific burglary of which Grear and Younger were convicted (both female victims were woken and threatened by a 'gang' of armed robbers).[180] Claiming that such executions of the innocent were not unusual, the paper concluded that this was a case 'so defenceless, bloody and cruel, that we can call it no other than an absolute murder'.[181]

In addition, in a series of anonymous articles on 'The Police' in the *Oxford Magazine* between 1769 and 1772 written by a supporter of John Wilkes, Fielding was criticised for focusing only on the most serious offences, while ignoring the vice and petty misdemeanours which encouraged crime: 'Sir John Fielding's is a transporting and hanging system of Police'.[182] Pulling no punches, the author identified the area around Fielding's Bow Street office as one of the worst in London:

Covent Garden, the applauded seat of justice, where his worship is so hurried with informations, pursuits, commitments, compromises and discharges, ... is

---

[177] *LL*, Old Bailey Proceedings, 13 April 1774 (t17740413-90).
[178] Beattie, *First English Detectives*, p. 80.   [179] Holloway, *The Rat-Trap*, pp. 19, 21.
[180] *LL*, Old Bailey Proceedings, 7 July 1773 (t17730707-1).
[181] *Morning Chronicle*, 6 September 1773.   [182] *Oxford Magazine*, 8 (Feb. 1772), p. 43.

the most abominable, the most detestable sink of iniquity, that ever disgraced any reputable city.[183]

Four years later, in *A Letter to Sir John Fielding* (criticising his request to David Garrick to stop staging the *Beggar's Opera* because it allegedly encouraged crime), William Augustus Miles made the same complaint. He told Fielding he was 'up to your very chin ... in all manner of vice ... It is generally imagined, Sir, that a reformation in your neighbourhood would be the means of lessening the number of public executions, and, in my opinion, you ought to have begun with Bow Street.'[184]

In his testimony to the 1770 parliamentary committee, Fielding had acknowledged the proliferation of brothels and prostitutes in Covent Garden as a problem, but he blamed the failure to suppress them on deficiencies in the law and resistance from those prosecuted. However, the author of 'The Police' attributed Fielding's failure to act to baser motives, alleging that both Fielding and his patrons in government profited from vice: 'the civil magistrate is pensioned by bawds, pimps, whores, vintners, and gamblers'.[185] It was also alleged that he allowed disorderly houses to remain open so that his Runners could use them as sources of information about the perpetrators of more serious crimes.[186] More damning still was the implication that he allowed petty offenders to become increasingly delinquent until their crimes were serious enough for the Runners to obtain rewards for their convictions. This was the explanation given by one of his biographers for why John Rann was allowed to commit so many crimes before he was eventually arrested: he was 'the constant prey of a set of miscreants' (the Runners) and 'had been a long time marked down by them for Blood Money'.[187]

These criticisms effectively bracketed the Bow Street Runners with the independent thief-takers who continued to practise in other parts of the city. In 1772 Holloway observed, 'The world, in general, conceive no very favourable opinion of the morals or humanity of a thief-taker, and from this notion the rotation-office in Bow-street is held some little distance from a tabernacle of righteousness'.[188] These accusations left Fielding and his Runners open to challenge, and some of the defendants he prosecuted at the Old Bailey used this tactic to attempt to undermine the cases against them. Direct accusations of corruption proved largely

---

[183] *Oxford Magazine*, 3 (Sept. 1769), p. 81.
[184] William Augustus Miles, *A Letter to Sir John Fielding* (1773), pp. 9, 12.
[185] *Oxford Magazine*, 3 (July 1769), p. 5.   [186] Beattie, *First English Detectives*, p. 69.
[187] *Genuine Account of the Life of John Rann*, p. 3.
[188] Robert Holloway, *A Letter to Sir John Fielding, Knight. Illustrated with a Portrait of a Monster* (1772), p. 5. See also *Oxford Magazine*, 8 (Feb. 1772), pp. 42–3.

unsuccessful in court, but arguments that Fielding and his officers had used improper means to obtain evidence were given more credence.[189] Samuel Stevens was charged with receiving a stolen 'swish whip' in 1767. In his defence, he testified that the Runners told him:

you may as well tell where it is, you have put it out of the way. They . . . took me to a public-house, and wanted to get something out of me. They are some of Sir John Fielding's people, and live by what they can make that way.[190]

He was acquitted, as was Christopher Broaders, who had been taken to the Brown Bear the previous year by the Runner John Heley. At Broaders's trial, Heley testified that he told him, 'I must search him; at first he refused it; we were forced to tie him to search him'.[191]

In spite of the criticisms levelled against him, Fielding's focus on convicting serious offenders, rather than on preventing crime through the prosecution of minor offences, intensified in the 1770s when he stopped signing large numbers of recognizances for petty crimes.[192] In the 1750s he and his brother Henry had pioneered the use of extensive pre-trial hearings and re-examinations of suspected felons at Bow Street as a means of sifting out weak cases and building up those which had the potential to result in a conviction. These procedures were further elaborated in the 1760s when John Fielding began to advertise re-examinations of suspects, held each Wednesday, as a means of encouraging additional witnesses to come forward. In 1772 he built a courtroom at Bow Street incorporating substantial galleries designed to attract both the public and the press. The claim that 'above a thousand people had assembled at Bow Street' to see John Rann examined in 1774 was no doubt an exaggeration, but it reflects the publicity these hearings achieved.[193]

These practices, as Beattie has argued, created 'a new stage in pre-trial procedure', bypassing the 300-year-old Marian bail statute and creating a magistrate-led investigatory hearing firmly within Fielding's control. In the process he subverted the role of the jury in the subsequent Old Bailey trial. This innovation raised the hackles of some contemporary commentators, who objected that jurors could be swayed by the press reports, that defendants were forced to reveal their defence strategies in advance of

---

[189] See, for instance, the case of William Halliburton (LL, Old Bailey Proceedings, 11 December 1765 (t17651211-6)).

[190] LL, Old Bailey Proceedings, 29 April 1767 (t17670429-71).

[191] LL, Old Bailey Proceedings, 17 December 1766 (t17661217-36).

[192] R. Paley, 'The Middlesex Justices Act of 1792: its origins and effects' (PhD dissertation, University of Reading, 1983), p. 397.

[193] An Account of John Rann, p. 20.

Figure 6.4 The Public Office, Bow Street. *The Malefactor's Register; or the Newgate and Tyburn Calendar* (1779), vol. III, frontispiece. © Trustees of the British Library.

their trials and that prosecutors were able to fine-tune their testimonies to ensure a conviction.[194] In 1773 William Augustus Miles questioned Fielding's 'impartiality', and the propriety of erecting a tribunal in your own house'. He suggested that by devoting his efforts to seeking convictions, rather than justice, Fielding had 'degraded' his office 'into that of a petty-fogger' and had become an 'inquisitor general' who treated the 'miserable objects' who appeared before him as 'the sport of your unfeeling auditors and an abandoned rabble'.[195]

Many victims and prosecutors, however, responded to the perceived success of this new orchestration of justice by bringing their complaints to Bow Street, ensuring that Fielding became 'the most active magistrate in Middlesex'. Between 1767 and 1773, his office accounted for half of all commitments to trial at the Old Bailey.[196] No doubt buoyed by his popularity among the victims of crime, Fielding continued these practices until his death in September 1780, though his successors were forced to abandon them shortly thereafter.

Some of Fielding's procedures, particularly having justices attend his 'office' by rotation, keeping it open for long hours and using regular 'runners' to make arrests, were imitated by justices in other parts of the metropolis. Saunders Welch, a protégé of Henry Fielding and rival of John, established a short-lived office in Litchfield Street, just west of Bow Street, in the late 1750s. And in 1763, at the urging of John Fielding and in response to a petition from fifty-seven Middlesex justices, the Middlesex bench established offices for justices in Clerkenwell, Shoreditch, Whitechapel and Shadwell.[197] Known as 'public offices' or 'rotation offices', these had no government funding and were entirely dependent on the fees charged for executing judicial business. Instead of hiring men to serve as 'runners' to carry out detective work and apprehend suspects, they relied on unpaid thief-takers, who depended on rewards for their income (they were nevertheless called 'runners').[198]

However, this model of justice did not appeal to everyone. In spite of attempts by some justices to channel all judicial business to the rotation offices, others refused to cooperate.[199] Charles Palmer, an enthusiastic

---

[194] Beattie, First English Detectives, pp. 87–103.
[195] Miles, Letter to Sir John Fielding, pp. 18–24.
[196] Beattie, First English Detectives, pp. 87, 94–6.
[197] LL, Middlesex Sessions: General Orders of the Court, 24 February 1763 – 13 January 1774 (LMSMGO556050008).
[198] Beattie, First English Detectives, p. 88; LMA, 'Rotation Committee papers', MC/SJ-1, 1763–4; Paley, 'Middlesex Justices Act', chs. 3–7.
[199] The Tower Division office resolved 'not to transact any of the Business relating to the Office of a Justice of the Peace in or for the above Division at any of their Houses or any Office of a Justice of Peace or other Place than the place now agreed upon except Parochial Business

supporter, complained in a series of private letters that several of his colleagues defied the resolutions in order to continue profiting from judicial business: 'where a shilling is to be got Law and Gospel is forgot'.[200] But these justices in their turn argued that the plaintiffs who brought their complaints to them preferred to conduct their business in a more private manner, beyond the public gaze, because this privacy allowed the justices to tailor their judgements to the specific circumstances of each case. Ironically, in this case it was the rotation offices, with their reliance on thief-takers, that rapidly attracted a reputation for corruption.[201] Even the Middlesex bench came to recognise that there were serious problems. Prompted by the misbehaviour of Justice John Gretton, who attended a 'public office' on Cambridge Street, the justices reported to the Lord High Chancellor in 1778 concerning

sundry Instances of Oppression illegal practice and other misbehaviour in certain of the acting Magistrates keeping Public Offices in those parts of the County that are adjacent to London and therefore the most populous ... the said Magistrates with the assistance of their Clerks and a number of infamous persons called Runners ... had a considerable time past been raising a Revenue to themselves to the great Disgrace of Justice.[202]

In the course of their petition to have Gretton removed from the commission, the justices outlined several instances where they claimed Gretton had extracted fines from people for 'Breach[es] of and Disobedience to Statutes that never were enacted and Laws that do not exist'.

At stake were not only actual corruption and competition over the profits of judicial office but also fundamentally contrasting notions of justice, and of the relationship between magistrates and plebeian London. On the one side was Fielding's 'transporting and hanging' system of police, and the rotation office justices and runners who followed in his footsteps. On the other were those justices, long known as 'trading justices', who in response to demands from plebeian Londoners chose to follow traditional justicing methods and, like Ralph Hodgson in his relations with the coalheavers, to cater for the needs of their poorer neighbours.[203] These justices, often men of lower status than the gentlemen who traditionally served, adopted a flexible and local approach to

and on emergent Occasions'. *LL*, Middlesex Sessions: General Orders of the Court, 24 February 1763 – 13 January 1774 (LMSMGO556050014).

[200] LMA, 'Rotation Committee papers', 28 June 1763.

[201] *Oxford Magazine*, 5 (Dec. 1770), p. 201.

[202] *LL*, Middlesex Sessions: General Orders of the Court, February 1774 – December 1780 (LMSMGO556070178).

[203] Fielding was actually labelled a trading justice, but his approach to justice was in fact antithetical to the description: Landau, 'The trading justice's trade', p. 63.

the administration of justice, welcoming complaints from the poor and resolving them informally wherever possible. As one observer complained in 1758, Middlesex justices 'are no sooner appointed than some of them open shops, contiguous to their trade and employments, for the distribution of justice'.[204] With so many justices acting in such a small geographical area, complainants were able to choose justices who offered the cheapest and most flexible services, avoiding rotation office justice in favour of that offered by magistrates sympathetic to their circumstances and complaints. While these justices were often accused of encouraging disputes (to create business) and corruption, recent research suggests that few acted illegally and that in fact 'what contemporaries found troubling in the trading justices was their devotion to judicial business'. In any case, their understanding of justice was markedly different from Fielding's.[205]

Even some of the actions of the disgraced John Gretton can be seen as responses to the demands of the often poor plaintiffs who appeared before him. When he issued an apparently illegal summons (because there was no statutory basis for the offence) to Elizabeth Jones 'for unlawfully refusing to give the complainant a Character', the victim was her servant, Ann Drury, whose future employment depended on the character Gretton sought to force from the reluctant hand of Jones.[206] While their detractors saw in the dramatically increasing activity of trading justices from the mid-1760s little more than venality and corruption, it should be viewed instead as a reflection of a growing demand for personalised judicial services from a population alienated from the new variety of justice being dispensed at the rotation offices and Bow Street.[207] Norma Landau has demonstrated that the recognizance, a simple legal instrument which bound over the accused to appear at sessions to answer charges, was used by the trading justices to settle disputes informally, and thus the number of recognizances issued represents a crude measure of the volume of such judicial activity.[208] In this context, the fact that the total number of recognizances issued by Middlesex justices began growing rapidly in the early 1760s is significant.

[204] BL, Add. Ms. 33053, f. 223 (1758).

[205] Landau, 'The trading justice's trade', p. 49; Paley, 'Middlesex Justices Act', ch. 3, esp. pp. 93–4.

[206] LL, Middlesex Sessions: General Orders of the Court, February 1774 – December 1783 (LMSMGO556070182).

[207] Sidney Webb and Beatrice Webb, The Parish and the County, Vol. I: English Local Government (London: Frank Cass & Co., 1906; repr., 1963), pp. 329–30.

[208] Norma Landau, The Justices of the Peace, 1679–1760 (Berkeley: University of California Press, 1984), pp. 184–6, 190.

By 1775 this number had increased by more than half since 1760 and stood at over 2,000 per year, a pattern of growth that continued almost without interruption until the passage of the Middlesex Justices Act in 1792.[209] As Fielding and his imitators adopted an increasingly strident approach to punishing crime, many Londoners, and particularly the poor, opted for a different form of justice, thereby encouraging the growth of trading justices. This was particularly true in the east end, an area where both rotation offices and trading justices prospered and the competition for judicial business (as we have seen in the case of labour disputes) was intense.[210]

For those apprehended by the Bow Street Runners and subjected to Fielding's public examinations, however, going to another justice was not an option. Since almost half of all Old Bailey trials in this period resulted from Bow Street commitments, and since convictions were much more likely when the Runners testified, those targeted by them increasingly resorted to desperate measures to avoid arrest.[211] In response to the Runners' new tactic of using 'Post Chaises . . . to apprehend Highwaymen & footpads', for instance, it was claimed that 'the robbers fearful of being apprehended by such Thief takers have lately made it a Practise first to fire into the Carriages they intend to stop, tending . . . to Introduce Murder to Robbery'.[212]

However, for men and women caught up in Fielding's systematic methods of prosecution, the only effective theatre of resistance was at the Old Bailey. As we have seen, some defendants attempted to discredit their accusers by accusing them of mercenary motives and corruption, or by playing on procedural irregularities. In addition, and continuing a now well-established trend, the early 1770s saw a significant number of defendants employing legal counsel. In response to Fielding's aggressive examinations at Bow Street, many suspects began to have legal representation at their pre-trial hearings, where lawyers 'ask[ed] questions and in other ways [became] involved on behalf of defendants'.[213] Unsurprisingly, many of these same defendants were subsequently represented by counsel at their formal trials. While the published *Proceedings* did not routinely report the presence of counsel until the next decade, and virtually never explicitly named them in this period, the proportion of

[209] Landau, 'The trading justice's trade', p. 68; Paley, 'Middlesex Justices Act', p. 394.
[210] Paley, 'Middlesex Justices Act', pp. 119–20.
[211] Beattie, *First English Detectives*, pp. 95, 117.
[212] LL, Middlesex Sessions: Sessions Papers, May 1773 (LMSMPS506300065).
[213] Beattie, *First English Detectives*, pp. 125–7; John Beattie, 'Sir John Fielding and public justice: the Bow Street Magistrates' Court, 1754–1770', *Law and History Review*, 25:1 (2007), 99–100.

trials where there is clear reference to the presence of defence counsel was 5.3 per cent between 1770 and 1776; the real figure was undoubtedly considerably higher.[214] Among defendants, legal representation was becoming an expectation. When defending herself in court against an accusation of shoplifting in 1777, Sarah Armstrong, a washerwoman, plaintively asked the court, 'As I have no counsel, will your lordship please to hear what I have to say?'[215] In response to new policing strategies, plebeian Londoners encouraged the growth of two alternative forms of justice: the primarily discretionary private decision-making of trading justices, and the public, adversarial contests at the Old Bailey.

Transportation's decline and prisons rebuilt

If one response to the crime wave following the Seven Years War was to introduce new methods of policing, we might expect these to be accompanied by new penal strategies. However, the only substantial developments, in fact, were an increase in the use of the traditional punishment of whipping, and a gradual and incremental drift away from transportation and towards greater use of imprisonment. In 1765 the proportion of convicts sentenced to transportation reached one of its highest levels in the century, 73.1 percent of all sentences, but this gradually declined over the next decade, with the exception of a short-lived peak in 1771. By 1775 transportation accounted for little more than half, 55.1 per cent, of all sentences.[216]

Even *before* transportation was interrupted by the outbreak of war with the colonies, judges were losing faith in it, at least in part owing to the contempt with which some convicts treated the sentence. In 1766 Elizabeth Martin explained her motives for 'stealing a silver spoon' to a servant in Newgate: 'I'll tell you the reason of it; I have a husband that is to be transported from Maidstone, and I want to know how I can go along with him.'[217] Her first attempt to secure a sentence of

---

[214] These statistics dramatically underestimate the true number of trials where defence counsel were present: Robert Shoemaker, 'Representing the adversary criminal trial: lawyers in the Old Bailey *Proceedings*, 1770–1800', in David Lemmings, ed., *Crime, Courtrooms and the Public Sphere in Britain, 1700–1850* (Farnham, Surrey: Ashgate, 2012), pp. 77–8.

[215] *LL*, Old Bailey Proceedings, 14 May 1777 (t17770514-4). For other examples, see Stephen Landsman, 'The rise of the contentious spirit: adversary procedure in eighteenth-century England', *Cornell Law Review*, 75 (1989–90), 648, n. 268.

[216] An even more dramatic decline occurred in neighbouring Surrey: John Beattie, *Crime and the Courts in England, 1660–1800* (Oxford University Press, 1986), p. 546.

[217] *LL*, set, 'Elizabeth Martin'; *LL*, Old Bailey Proceedings, 3 September 1766 (t17660903-69).

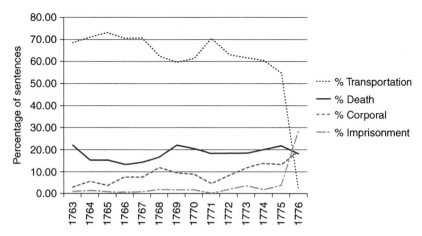

Figure 6.5 Old Bailey punishment sentences, 1763–1776. Online data set: Punishment Statistics, 1690–1800.xlsx.

transportation failed, resulting instead in whipping and a rebuke from the Recorder of London. Undeterred, however, she appeared at the following sessions under a different name, Elizabeth Strut, and was convicted of stealing a pair of linen sheets.[218] This time she had her wish and was duly sentenced to transportation. Strut, of course, was atypical; most convicts had no desire to be sent to America, but the punishment no longer induced fear. According to Robert Stephens, the turnkey of Maidstone gaol, when John Smith stood trial in the summer of 1773 and was sentenced to fourteen years' transportation, he told him 'he did not care, America should not hold him fourteen years, nor two neither'.[219] He was true to his word, and within eighteen months Smith was back in London and on trial for returning from transportation.

The number of convicts who were tried at the Old Bailey for returning from transportation in the years 1763–76, forty-seven, may not seem large, but they formed the tip of an iceberg of returnees and, at 3.4 defendants per year, amounted to almost double the annual average (1.8) for the period 1748–62. Ekirch has argued that 'a great majority of fugitives succeeded in escaping detection', and there is some evidence that, as the number and speed of ships crossing the Atlantic increased, so did the problem of returned convicts. In 1773 John Hewitt observed that 'there are more returned transports at this time in the Kingdom than

[218] *LL*, Old Bailey Proceedings, 22 October 1766 (t17661022-14).
[219] *LL*, Old Bailey Proceedings, 18 February 1775 (t17750218-49).

known before'.[220] Some convicts even returned twice, taking advantage of the fact that most of those sentenced to death for returning were subsequently pardoned on condition of an even longer period of transportation. William Hughes, for instance, was transported for seven years for stealing a silk handkerchief in 1771, but then arrested in London a year later.[221] Convicted of returning, he was once again transported, on this occasion for fourteen years, but he made his way back to London within two. By this time the authorities had lost patience and he was executed.

Others found that transportation could be avoided altogether. Six of those tried for 'returning' in these years had never actually made it to America, having escaped before leaving the country. Others exploited the apparent ease of obtaining pardons for their original offences or for the crime of returning from transportation.[222] John Fielding complained to the secretary of state that 'free pardons for offenders under sentence of transportation' and 'the mercy lately shown to several notorious offenders convicted of returning from transportation' had 'to his certain knowledge [led to] some very daring robbers [having] been let loose to the terror of society'. Fielding went on to claim that these pardons resulted from 'strong application[s] (deceitfully obtained)'.[223] John Hawkins, chairman of the Middlesex sessions from 1765 to 1781, made a similar complaint two years later. The Middlesex justices, Hawkins told the secretary, were 'frequently defied by those whom they commit for Offences', who told them 'You may do your worst for I know how to get a pardon'.[224] Hawkins claimed that it was widely recognised that 'your Lordship's Office has been the fountain and well Spring of forgiveness; this the Newgate Solicitors and other agents for convicts have found out'.

One of the cases Hawkins cited to substantiate his assertion concerned Thomas Erskine, convicted of fraud at the Middlesex sessions and sentenced to transportation in 1772.[225] When he returned, he was

---

[220] A. Roger Ekirch, *Bound for America: The Transportation of British Convicts to the Colonies, 1718–1775* (Oxford: Clarendon Press, 1987), p. 214; Hewitt quoted by Douglas Hay, 'War, dearth and theft in the eighteenth century: the record of the English courts', *Past & Present*, 95 (1982), 143.

[221] *LL*, set, 'William Hughes'.

[222] According to John Howard, of thirty-one people found guilty at the Old Bailey of returning from transportation between 1749 and 1771, 29 per cent were either pardoned or died in gaol: *An Account of the Principal Lazarettos in Europe* (Warrington, 1789), p. 255.

[223] *Calendar of Home Office Papers of the Reign of George III: Preserved in the Public Record Office*, Vol. IV (London: HMSO, 1899), pp. 10–12.

[224] *LL*, Middlesex Sessions: Sessions Papers, November 1774 (LMSMPS506460008).

[225] *LL*, set, 'Thomas Erskine'.

'pardoned upon condition of transporting himself' again, but, Hawkins wrote, 'as I and everyone else expected' he returned a second time.[226] Following his arrest in March 1774, Erskine's trial was postponed twice owing to the absence of a key witness, and when he was finally tried for returning from transportation in July 1774, he was acquitted and walked free. It is very likely that the growing reluctance to sentence convicts to transportation in the 1770s resulted from a recognition of convicts' ability to subvert the punishment, even before the North American colonists rendered the system unworkable in 1776. From 1769 the authorities began to look for new destinations for transported convicts, in order to make it more difficult for them to return home.[227]

The judges may also have been influenced by the arguments of penal reformers for the use of imprisonment as an alternative punishment, for *reforming* convicts. In the 1760s and 1770s, Jonas Hanway and others began advocating the use of solitary confinement, hard labour and religious instruction to reform criminals, in part reflecting beliefs and practices that had become commonplace in contemporary discussions of the role of workhouses in reforming the idle poor, and houses of correction in punishing minor offenders. Also influenced by evangelical beliefs and the work of Cesare Beccaria, several commentators appealed to the possibility of inculcating labour discipline among more serious offenders, and engendering 'a true sense [of their] duty to God and Society'.[228]

These ambitions could not be realised in existing prisons, and yet for the most part the prison rebuilding that marked these years was more concerned with keeping prisoners alive and secure than in reforming them. Problems of poor sanitation had been highlighted by the outbreak of 'gaol fever' in Newgate prison in April 1750, while regular escapes by prisoners repeatedly raised the problem of security. More fundamentally, prison culture clearly stood in the way of any programme of reform. Ultimately, the conditions and behaviour of prisoners had more influence than the reformers over the character of the rebuilding programme.

In the first instance, concerns about the health of prisoners provided the driving force behind the City's efforts to rebuild Newgate prison. These began almost immediately after 1750, but made little progress until prompted by a new outbreak in 1763, which killed between fourteen and twenty-two people (reports differ). The distemper was 'all over the Gaol', and in April 1764 the City petitioned parliament for

---

[226] *LL*, Middlesex Sessions: Sessions Papers, November 1774 (LMSMPS506460009).
[227] Ekirch, *Bound for America*, pp. 228–9.
[228] Jonas Hanway, *The Defects of Police the Cause of Immorality* (1775), p. 214; Beattie, *Crime and the Courts*, pp. 548–59, 568–72.

funding.[229] In 1767 it obtained £50,000, and in 1769 work began. Plans for the new prison included an infirmary, reflecting the role of health concerns even before the passage of the Health of Prisoners Act of 1774.[230]

However, with its massive hundred-metre-long windowless external façade composed of large rusticated stones, the design of the new prison suggests security and the prevention of escapes was also a driving force behind the design of the new building. There had been attempted escapes from the old prison in 1762 and 1763 (when groups of prisoners sawed through their irons),[231] and November 1769, when Thomas Dunk, charged with multiple highway robberies, 'formed a design to break the goal open, and set the prisoners at liberty; which they partly executed, and would in a very short time have compleated, were it not for the great attention, and watchful care of the master of the prison'.[232] The prisoners had made a copy of a key to an unused room, and then, using a 'small crow or tool of iron' brought into the prison by Dunk's mother, 'filed and cut almost every bar in the window'.[233]

In Middlesex, where the justices downplayed health issues, security was an even greater concern. The lesser-known Gatehouse prison in Westminster, which held state prisoners, felons and petty offenders, had even more commitments 'than to Newgate' and was the subject of several complaints in this period.[234] Its dilapidated state in 1763 allowed Edmond Collins and William Matthison to escape by breaking 'through the Stone wall of the said Prison under the Gateway', and in April 1770 John Fielding told a House of Commons Committee that the prison was 'too small for the Number, and too weak for the safe Custody of Prisoners'.[235] It was pulled down in 1776, and the prisoners transferred to the Westminster house of correction in Tothill Fields.

Outside Westminster, Middlesex prisoners were committed to two adjoining prisons in Clerkenwell: New Prison and the county house of

---

[229] LL, Middlesex Sessions: Sessions Papers, April 1765 (LMSMPS505470113).

[230] Simon Devereaux, 'Convicts and the state: the administration of criminal justice in Great Britain during the reign of George III' (PhD dissertation, University of Toronto, 1997), pp. 131–3; 14 Geo. III c. 59, 'An Act for preserving the health of prisoners in gaol'.

[231] Gentleman's Magazine, 32 (Feb. 1762), p. 89, and 33 (May 1763), p. 255.

[232] LL, set, 'Thomas Dunk'.

[233] LL, Ordinary of Newgate Prison: Ordinary's Accounts, 14 February 1770 (OA177002147002140014 and OA177002147002140015).

[234] LL, Middlesex Sessions: Sessions Papers, April 1765 (LMSMPS505470111). For Samuel Johnson's diatribe against the Gatehouse prison, see Ben Weinreb et al., The London Encyclopedia (London: Pan Macmillan, 2010), p. 321.

[235] LL, Middlesex Sessions: Sessions Papers, May 1763 (LMSMPS505220041); PP, Journals of the House of Commons, 32, 10 April 1770, p. 880.

correction. By this period both included a substantial number of felons awaiting trial, accounting for 55 per cent of the commitments to New Prison and 36 per cent of those to the house of correction, and these prisoners were considered particularly likely to escape.[236] Both buildings dated back to the previous century, and in 1772 the Middlesex justices resolved that:

The two gaols of New Prison and the House of Correction at Clerkenwell are greatly out of repair and in so weak and insecure a state as not to be sufficient for the safe custody of felons and others necessarily from time to time confined therein.[237]

Continuing a pattern dating from at least the 1750s, there were a number of escapes and attempted escapes from both prisons. In 1766 Martha Pitt smuggled in 'one Iron Chissell one large Gimblet one Flint & Steel one Iron Tobacco Box with Tinder & six Matches (being Instrumts proper to facilitate the Escape of Prisoners)' to Edward Hempston, then held in the house of correction on suspicion of felony.[238] Hempston's escape attempt appears to have failed, but in 1775 Thomas Green alias Smart, a bucklemaker accused of coining, used 'two spring saws, and a woman's dress', smuggled in by his wife, to saw through his irons and leave the jail in disguise.[239] That same year seven prisoners, including serial escapee Michael Swift, escaped by 'breaking through a brick wall into the Governor's garden'.[240]

In May 1772, ambitious plans for new buildings covering a much larger site were drawn up. Although they incorporated a reforming agenda in the guise of facilities for 'every fitting kind of hard labour', the justices eventually rejected these in favour of a less ambitious plan designed to address security issues alone.[241] A new committee of justices was appointed to oversee these repairs and ensure they were 'sufficient for the safe Custody of the Felons', with the proviso that 'no additional

---

[236] *LL*, Middlesex Sessions: Sessions Papers, October 1772 (LMSMPS506240151–LMSMPS506240152).

[237] LMA, Middlesex Sessions: 'Minutes of the committee for repairing the house of correction, Clerkenwell, and the New Prison, Clerkenwell', MA/G/GEN/0001, vol. 1, p. 1 (22 April 1773).

[238] *LL*, Old Bailey Sessions Papers, 9 December 1765 – 23 December 1766 (LMOBPS450100267).

[239] *LL*, set, 'Thomas Green'; Old Bailey Proceedings, 6 December 1775 (t17751206-74). He was recaptured and tried on the coining charges at the Old Bailey almost a year later. *LL*, Old Bailey Proceedings, 16 October 1776 (t17761016-40).

[240] *LL*, set, 'Michael Swift'; *Morning Post and Daily Advertiser*, 30 October 1776 (Burney Collection: www.galegroup.com, 2 Jan. 2014).

[241] *LL*, Middlesex Sessions: Sessions Papers, October 1772 (LMSMPS50624PS506240143).

building be made or more ground covered than at present'.[242] The justices tackled New Prison first, as the prison most in need of repair, and, in order to increase security, the committee almost immediately exceeded its brief by proposing (and securing permission) to enlarge the building. The 'felons room' was placed two stories higher and extended by ten feet, and the keeper's apartment was extended by twenty feet, in order to 'more Effectually tend to the safe Custody of the prisoners confined therein'. In addition, fetters were purchased for 'the security of such felons as are committed to New Prison there being none at that Gaol belonging to the County'.[243]

These changes were completed by September 1775, when the justices were advised to 'commit in future all persons charged with felony or suspicion thereof' to New Prison, so that 'the House of Correction may be solely appropriated to the punishment of the Idle and disorderly'. The committee was 'the more earnest in this recommendation',

as it will be a means of preventing the greater Offenders having intercourse with those committed for lesser crimes and thence avoid that contamination of manners and morals which is but too frequent in those Goals in which the Prisoners are promiscuously confined.[244]

The desire to prevent prisoners from associating with those who might corrupt them is another theme running through the prison reforms of this period, as attempts were made to make prison culture less subversive. In part, this issue was elided with health concerns about 'contagion', but it also related to the security problem because when prisoners congregated they planned illegitimate activities. To address this issue, the anonymous author of the letters on 'The Police' in the *Oxford Magazine* recommended in 1770 that the rebuilt Newgate prison should include 'a reasonable number of separate cells for criminals, that the evil consequences to society of their associating together, and living merrily in Newgate, as some of the hardened wretches have termed it, may be prevented'.[245] Some advocates of solitary confinement focused on its supposed spiritual benefits, but the reformer John Howard echoed the opinion of this correspondent in also citing the importance of preventing escapes: 'The separation I am pleading for, especially at night, would

---

[242] *LL*, Middlesex Sessions: Sessions Papers, April 1773 (LMSMPS50629PS506290110–LMSMPS50629PS506290111).

[243] LMA, 'Minutes of the committee for repairing', pp. 2–7 (28 April to 27 May 1773), pp. 38–9 (8 Dec. 1774).

[244] LMA, 'Minutes of the committee for repairing', p. 73 (13 Sept. 1775).

[245] *Oxford Magazine*, Dec 1770, p. 203.

prevent escapes, or make them very difficult: for that is the time in which they are generally planned, and effected'.[246]

However, the open nature of the unreformed prisons facilitated the evolution of a culture that went well beyond the plotting of escapes or further crimes; it provided a context for mutual support. At its most extreme, in the debtors prisons, inmates banded together to challenge the very legality of their incarceration.[247] In other prisons, they devised and shared survival strategies and tactics for courtroom defence. During the visits to London's prisons which resulted in his 1776 book, *State of the Gaols in London, Westminster, and Borough of Southwark*, William Smith noted the 'mixture of generosity and some traces of goodness in some of the most wretched of the human species', evident in the fact that felons shared their food with one another. While Smith was impressed with this form of prisoner association, he also worried about the consequences of prisoners congregating, as 'by such means they form into companies, and become more formidable to society... under no pretence whatever should any two or more felons be suffered to associate, even for one minute'.[248]

With the exception of the condemned cells in Newgate used for those awaiting execution, there were no solitary cells in London until the opening of a new Middlesex house of correction, Cold Bath Fields, in 1794. But in the early 1770s some efforts were made to separate prisoners by type of offence and sex, as is evident in the attempt to exclude felons from the Clerkenwell house of correction. Although the rebuilt Newgate prison would not include individual cells (except as replacements for the existing condemned cells), there were separate quadrangles for debtors, male felons and female felons. Southwark house of correction, rebuilt in 1773, had separate wards for men, women and apprentices.[249] Prisoners awaiting trial at the Old Bailey were kept separate from the public by the construction in 1774 of 'a Screen upon the Circular Wall of the [rebuilt] Sessions House intended to prevent Communication between the Publick and the Prisoners'.[250]

---

[246] John Howard, *The State of the Prisons in England and Wales* (Warrington, 1777), p. 43.

[247] Joanna Innes, *Inferior Politics: Social Problems and Social Policies in Eighteenth-Century Britain* (Oxford University Press), pp. 270–8.

[248] William Smith, *State of the Gaols in London, Westminster, and Borough of Southwark* (1776), pp. 12–13, 35–6, 76.

[249] H. D. Kalman, 'Newgate Prison', *Architectural History*, 12 (1969), 52; C. W. Chalklin, 'The reconstruction of London's prisons 1770–99: an aspect of the growth of Georgian London', *London Journal*, 9:1 (1983), 27–8.

[250] LMA, City of London: Sessions, 'Committee for carrying into execution so much of the Act of parliament lately passed as relates to the rebuilding of the gaol of Newgate', COL/CC/NGC/04/01/001, 20 April 1774, f. 140.

As a result of financial concerns, but also owing to more pressing worries about escapes, London's governors largely failed to implement, or even fully discuss, a substantial programme of prison reform in this period. Instead, they beefed up security in new or rebuilt prisons and adopted relatively simple systems of segregating prisoners. Perhaps in consequence, and despite a gradual shift in sentencing practices, the Old Bailey judges remained reluctant to sentence convicts to incarceration. Imprisonment continued to be rarely imposed; as a proportion of all sentences it only increased from 0.6 per cent in 1763 to 3.7 per cent in 1773–5, before the suspension of transportation forced a radical shift in sentencing strategies. Judges were still unwilling to use this punishment on its own, or for the most serious offences. Imprisonment was typically only imposed in combination with a fine or branding, and the offences involved (grand larceny, 16.85%; fraud, 15.7%; coining, 12.4%; and manslaughter, 11.2%) were not the most threatening. With hindsight these sentencing patterns appear to herald an important shift in penal strategy, but advocates of reformatory imprisonment had as yet had little impact. A traditionally restive prison culture made existing prisons problematic places for punishment and demanded more immediate fixes to security problems. Through escapes and the threatening 'contagion' of a shared prison culture, the prisoners helped ensure that reform was delayed.

Conclusion

In the spring of 1776, two of the men hanged at Tyburn were Thomas Henman and Benjamin Harley.[251] Both were coalheavers from Deptford, who had lived in lodgings on Church Street and supplemented their meagre earnings by hurrying smuggled goods on their way. There is no evidence that either participated in the industrial unrest or riots of the preceding decade, and their employers provided character witnesses at their trial. However, in May 1776 they were found guilty of the brutal murder of a customs officer, Joseph Pierce, who had been beaten to death by a gang of men including Edward or Gypsy George Lovell, and two brothers, Benjamin and Robert Harley, in company with Henman.[252] One of the gang, Samuel Whiting, turned king's evidence and ensured that first Henman and Benjamin Harley, and later Gypsy George and Robert Harley, were convicted and sentenced to hang and to be dissected. Much of the trial evidence concerned the discussions between

---

[251] *LL*, sets, 'Thomas Henman' and 'Benjamin Harley'.
[252] *LL*, William Young, 'George Lovell, alias Gypsy George, *c.* 1742–1772'.

Figure 6.6 William Pink, after Agostino Carlini, 'Smugglerius'
(1776, 1834). © Royal Academy of Arts, London.

prisoners in Newgate and the Clerkenwell house of correction, in which
one or other of the main witnesses were shown to have retracted and
changed their stories. Whiting had once allegedly declared that Henman
and Benjamin Harley were as 'innocent as the ... iron bars' of Newgate.
Nonetheless, they would hang. But just like some convicted thieves and
cutters, and the alleged murderers of Daniel Clarke, the two men maintained their innocence to their dying breath.[253]
    Despite the confusion of evidence and retractions, the governors of
London were confident enough in their authority and fearful enough of
the threat posed by smugglers to execute these men, and then to go one
step further. The lifeless body of one of them was first handed over to
William Hunter and his students at the Royal College of Surgeons,
before being passed on to the Royal Academy of the Arts, just around
the corner from Bow Street. Here, Agostino Carlini turned judicial
murder into art. As the body was seized in rigor mortis, Carlini, with
Hunter's assistance, stripped the skin from the flesh and posed the lifeless
corpse as a gruesome caricature of a famous statue, before casting the
figure in plaster of Paris. The pose Carlini chose was one many
eighteenth-century connoisseurs were familiar with from Rome and the
Grand Tour, and which they knew as the 'dying gladiator' – a slave, killed
for entertainment.

---

[253] *LL*, Old Bailey Proceedings, 22 May 1776 (t17760522-32).

Sitting at the centre of a worldwide empire, with the first third of the rebuilt Newgate prison ready to receive its cargo of malefactors, an emerging salaried police force managed by ambitious justices, and their parish workhouses and established bureaucracy of migration and labour control, London's governors had a lot to be confident about. However, the forces that would forge a different trajectory were already in place, in the form of escapes from prison and in plebeian Londoners' willingness to use large-scale collective action to pursue better conditions and an ill-defined 'liberty'. They could be found in the strategies that leveraged increasing resources from reluctant parishes and in the self-confidence and anger of defendants willing to shop around for justice, to strategise and employ counsel in their defence or simply to intimidate witnesses. In these conflicts can be seen the beginnings of a crisis that would both bring down Newgate and force the pace of change in unanticipated directions. As implied by Samuel Whiting, the iron bars of Newgate prison may well have been 'innocent', but they could not entirely hold in check the aspirations and power of plebeian Londoners.

Introduction

During the 1760s and early 1770s, plebeian Londoners nursed an accumulating sense of grievance. Innovations in policing and prosecution placed those suspected of crimes at a growing disadvantage, while new poor relief policies created an ever widening chasm between parish worthies and the dependent poor. Yet through both legal and illegal means, individually and collectively, plebeian Londoners had developed and refined effective tactics for challenging authority. In this febrile context, war with America broke out in 1775, a war whose far-reaching consequences would include not only an ideological crisis over the state of English liberties but also a fundamental renegotiation of social policy in the metropolis. The interruption of criminal transportation caused unprecedented chaos in the penal system and the creation of Britain's first mass prison population. The hardships suffered by prisoners held for years in buildings designed for short-term incarceration, or in rotting hulks on a stinking Thames, laid the foundations for keenly felt grievances. Thousands of Londoners experienced, for the first time, the pressured boredom of long days spent in powerless proximity with people just like themselves: marked, like the vast majority of criminals, by their youth, poverty and ill-luck. In the process, and despite relatively favourable climatic and economic conditions (except following demobilisation in 1783), new patterns of resistance developed.

This chapter describes these new communities of resistance, solidified through long-term imprisonment and shared suffering following 1776; communities created at a time of intense political debate. It argues that it was the new-lived, and by 1780 widely shared, experience of mass imprisonment that transformed the Gordon Riots from an anti-Catholic protest into an organised proto-revolutionary series of attacks on the prisons of London. The origins of the reconfigured system of criminal justice and poor relief that followed can be found most fully in the experience of plebeian men and women forced into desperate dialogue with judges and turnkeys, overseers and churchwardens.

Punishment in crisis

The suspension of transportation, caused by the outbreak of war with America in 1775, followed the growth of elite dissatisfaction with transportation over the previous decade. It nonetheless created an unprecedented penal crisis. A criminal justice system that for sixty years had shipped hundreds of London felons to North America each year was suddenly confronted by the need to guard and care for a population of convicts that grew month by month, with each meeting of the courts. And while some of the prisons which held them had been rebuilt or remodelled, all prisons remained inadequate to the task of securely holding large bodies of prisoners. The scale of the problem can be seen in the fact that in the previous decade, transportation had accounted for two-thirds of all sentences at the Old Bailey, amounting to an average of 263 convicts a year.[1] The prisons quickly became overcrowded with convicts awaiting transportation, and new (it was hoped, temporary) arrangements had to be made. In justifying this to Edmund Burke in March 1776, the penal reformer William Eden said, 'The fact is, our prisons are full, and we have no way at present to dispose of the convicts.'[2] This overcrowding prompted the passage of the 'Hulks Act' in 1776, which authorised alternative punishments for those sentenced to transportation and currently languishing in prison.[3] Male convicts were to be put to hard labour 'improving the navigation of the Thames', while female convicts, and men incapable of performing such physical work, were to be committed to houses of correction. The place where the men ordered to work on the Thames were to be incarcerated was not specified, but Duncan Campbell, the man awarded this contract (who had formerly contracted to transport convicts to America) decided to house them in disused ships, which became known as the hulks. The first two ships, the *Justicia* and the *Censor*, took on their first prisoners in August 1776. They too soon became crowded: Campbell reported in April

---

[1] The national figure for 1775 was approximately 900: Peter Wilson Coldham, *Emigrants in Chains: A Social History of Forced Emigration to the Americas of Felons, Destitute Children, Political and Religious Non-Conformists, Vagabonds, Beggars and Other Undesirables, 1607–1776* (Baltimore: Genealogical Pub. Co., 1992), p. 183, Appendix viii.

[2] Charles William et al., eds., *The Works and Correspondence of the Right Honourable Edmund Burke*, 8 vols. (1856), I, p. 305.

[3] 16 Geo. III c. 43, 'An Act to authorise, for a limited time, the punishment by hard labour... for certain crimes'.

1778 that there were 370 men on board these vessels; the following year this had increased to 510, divided almost equally between them.[4]

Conditions on the hulks were intentionally poor. Despite the fact the prisoners were put to gruelling labour shifting gravel and soil on the banks of the Thames, the Act specified that the convicts were to be 'fed and sustained with bread and any coarse or inferior food, and water or small beer', and nothing else.[5] When combined with the crowded conditions, the fact that some of the prisoners were already infected with gaol fever when they arrived, and the absence of a surgeon or apothecary on board ship, this poor nutrition led to frequent illness and death. In the first twenty months, over a quarter of the prisoners died (176 of 632); and 138 more perished in the following year.[6] This high mortality attracted widespread criticism. When the prison reformer John Howard visited the convicts on the *Justicia* in October 1776, 'he took two walks round them, and looked in the face of every individual person, and saw by their sickly looks, that some mismanagement was among them'. He inspected the food and reported that 'all the biscuits were mouldy and green on both sides', and noted that the convicts had no bedding. The resulting 'depression of the spirits' among the prisoners was frequently remarked upon by visitors to the ships, and Dodo Ecken, an assistant surgeon, reported 'that he had known eight or ten of the convicts die merely of lowness of spirits'.[7]

Conditions improved in subsequent years, partly owing to pressure from the prisoners, who were able to communicate their grievances to visiting magistrates and doctors. Their escapes and mutinies also played a part. Campbell reported that following a mutiny of the prisoners in 1778 he increased the allowance of bread and other foodstuffs for the prisoners such that, he claimed, 'the provisions allowed to the convicts were ... better than laboring men usually had'.[8] In order to address the problem of morale, pardons were offered to well-behaved prisoners, and in 1779 sick prisoners were removed to a separate hospital ship. But the hulks remained crowded, mortality rates remained high and the prisoners remained rebellious.

---

[4] PP, *Journals of the House of Commons*, 36, 15 April 1778, p. 927; and 'Report from the committee ... to consider ... persons convicted of felonies or misdemeanors, and now under sentence of imprisonment ...', 1 April 1779, p. 9 (parlipapers.chadwyck.co.uk, 2 Jan. 2014).

[5] 16 Geo. III c. 43, 'An Act to authorise', s. 7.

[6] PP, *Journals of the House of Commons*, 15 April 1778, p. 927; and PP, 'Report from the committee', 1 April 1779, p. 10.

[7] PP, *Journals of the House of Commons*, 15 April 1778, p. 929; and PP, 'Report from the committee', 1 April 1779, p. 11.

[8] PP, 'Report from the committee', 1 April 1779, pp. 9–10.

Figure 7.1 Carver & Bowles (publishers), 'A view near Woolwich in Kent, shewing the Employment of the convicts from the Hulks' (1779). NMG PAJ0774. © Trustees of the National Maritime Museum at Greenwich.

Stewart Erskine, the captain of the hulks, claimed that prisoners from the country were more likely to be 'very much dejected' than the London felons, and this makes sense. Prisoners from London had more friends, both on the hulks and outside, and were probably more able to organise resistance.[9] When on board prisoners were confined below deck in large undivided spaces, while the small number of guards stayed above, giving prisoners plenty of opportunities to plot escapes.[10] Left to their own devices, and experiencing horrific conditions, this is just what they did. There were four mass escapes in the first few months of the hulks, at least one more in 1777, and a mutiny in September 1778 called the 'insurrection' by contemporaries. Perhaps consciously following in the tradition of riverside labour unrest last seen ten years earlier, about 150 prisoners working on the shore of the Thames armed themselves and attempted to force their way past the guards to escape. In the ensuing battle two were

[9] *PP*, 'Report from the committee', 1 April 1779, p. 12.
[10] Charles Campbell, *Intolerable Hulks: British Shipboard Confinement 1776–1857* (London: Fenestra Books, 2001), p. 56.

killed and seven or eight more were wounded.[11] While none got away, Treasury papers indicate that between 1778 and 1780 forty prisoners did manage to escape.[12] Although many were not recaptured, between 1776 and 1780 seventeen escapees were put on trial at the Old Bailey, including one, John White alias Stephen Broadstreet, who escaped twice, in 1777 and 1780, and who would later be active in the Gordon Riots. In their defence, the prisoners justified their actions by the terrible conditions on board.[13] Thomas Farmer, who escaped on 7 November 1776, pleaded with the court to sentence him to service in the navy rather than return him to the hulks, since he was 'afraid I shall be cruelly used on board this ship again'.[14] More explicitly, Michael Swift, convicted of shooting at boatswain Charles West during the 'insurrection', justified his actions by telling the court that 'The usage of the place is enough to make any man try to escape; they not only starve them, but murther them'.[15]

The interconnections between the escapees testify to the development of a culture of resistance on the hulks. Charles Drake, described in the *Public Advertiser* as an American by birth, who had a long criminal record and had escaped from one of the hulks in December 1777, shared experiences with, and probably knew, three other escapees.[16] When he was first convicted of the theft of a silver watch in April 1776, he, along with several other prisoners convicted of grand larceny, was sent back to Newgate to remain until the May sessions, while the government worked out what to do with prisoners who would previously have been sentenced to transportation. One of the prisoners who shared that experience, and who was also sentenced to branding in May, was Thomas Farmer, who, following another conviction which resulted in his commitment to the hulks, escaped in November of the same year.[17] Michael Swift and John Jones, who were sentenced along with Drake to the hulks in January 1777, were also past and future escapees.[18] Swift had escaped from Clerkenwell house of correction in October 1776, and would later escape from the hulks in June 1778. Soon recaptured, his rebellious mood was no doubt contagious; four months later, as noted, he was a participant in

[11] William Branch-Johnson, *The English Prison Hulks* (London: Phillimore, 1970), p. 6.
[12] Simon Devereaux, 'Convicts and the state: the administration of criminal justice in Great Britain during the reign of George III' (PhD thesis, University of Toronto, 1997), p. 183.
[13] *LL*, set, 'John White'.
[14] *LL*, set, 'Thomas Farmer'; Old Bailey Proceedings, 4 December 1776 (t17761204-39).
[15] *LL*, set, 'Michael Swift'; Old Bailey Proceedings, 21 October 1778 (t17781021-39).
[16] *LL*, set, 'Charles Drake'; *Public Advertiser*, 12 July 1776 (Burney Collection: www.galegroup.com, 2 Jan. 2014).
[17] *LL*, set, 'Thomas Farmer'.   [18] *LL*, sets, 'Michael Swift' and 'John Jones'.

the 'insurrection', while Jones may be the same John Jones referred to in Figure 7.3, who escaped from the hulks in April 1781.

While the hulks would continue to be used into the nineteenth century to meet the continuing need for extra prison accommodation for those awaiting transportation, this convict resistance was one of the reasons, in addition to disease, why the authorities rapidly lost faith in them as anything other than an unsatisfactory stopgap and sought to limit their use.[19] In 1779 the Penitentiary Act restricted the power to sentence offenders to the hulks to judges at the Old Bailey and the assize courts. The Middlesex justices, who had sentenced 86 prisoners to the hulks between July 1776 and February 1779, mostly for petty larceny, lost this option.[20] Felons also became less likely to be committed there, as the average population of the hulks, which peaked at 508 in 1779, declined steadily to only 199 in 1783.[21] The last convict sentenced directly to the hulks at the Old Bailey in the 1780s was Charles Manning, convicted of highway robbery in April 1784.[22] The House of Commons committee which met in the spring of 1779 to consider the fate of convicts previously transported noted recent improvements to the hulks, but recommended the resumption of transportation for the most serious offenders as soon as it became feasible, and imprisonment at hard labour for 'the class of convicts heretofore liable to transportation' who were not strong enough for 'any severer punishment'. Having marked the many deficiencies of the hulks, the committee recommended that these convicts should instead be kept in 'solitary confinement ... [with] well-regulated labour, and instruction'; essentially in a new form of prison – a penitentiary.[23]

Even when the hulks were still an acceptable penal option, not all convicts could be accommodated on them. In addition to female convicts and the men deemed incapable of hard physical work, both of whom were sentenced to houses of correction, many other men were incarcerated in London's prisons simply because the hulks did not have space for them. The same House of Commons committee reported that in April 1779 243 convicts were incarcerated in the city's prisons, including 84 in Newgate, 114 in the Clerkenwell house of correction and 10 in New Prison. When Richard Akerman, keeper of Newgate, was asked 'how it came to

---

[19] Devereaux, 'Convicts and the state', p. 225.
[20] LMA, 'Account of people convicted and confined on a prison ship', MA/G/GEN/1301.
[21] Devereaux, 'Convicts and the state', p. 183.
[22] LL, set, 'Charles Manning'.
[23] 19 Geo. III c. 74, 'An Act to explain and amend the laws relating to the transportation, imprisonment and other punishment of certain offenders'; PP, 'Report from the committee', 1 April 1779, pp. 25–6; Simon Devereaux, 'The making of the Penitentiary Act, 1775–1779', Historical Journal, 42:2 (1999), 428–30.

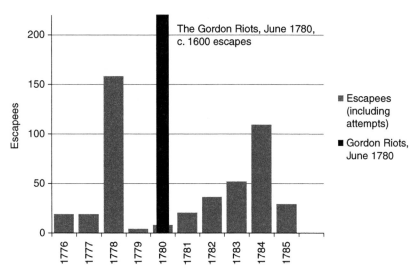

Figure 7.2 Escapees (attempted and actual) from prisons, hulks and transports, 1776–1786. Online data set: Escapes, 1776–1786.xlsx. This database and graph do not include reports of 'several persons' escaped from Newgate prison in 1778; 'divers prisoners' from New Prison twice in 1781; and 'several' escapees from Newgate prison in 1782. No systematic record of escapes survives, and these figures, derived from a wide range of sources, should be considered as indicating a minimum.

pass that many who were sentenced to the hulks remained in Newgate', he answered, 'there was no room on board the vessels to receive them'.[24]

When these prisoners were added to those awaiting trial and convicts sentenced to terms of imprisonment, the resulting overcrowding led to conditions not dissimilar to those found on the hulks. Never before had London's prisons been forced to accommodate so many long-term prisoners, placing new demands on their keepers. In October 1777 Thomas Gibbs, surgeon and apothecary to both New Prison and the house of correction at Clerkenwell, petitioned the Middlesex justices, asking for an increase in his salary owing to the higher level of medical care required in both prisons. Referring to the prisoners who 'have been sentenced to imprisonment in the said jails', he claimed that many came in 'diseased and frequently continue so from their poverty and long confinement not to mention the many infected prisoners who from time to time are sent to remain in these jails from Newgate'.[25] In

[24] *PP*, 'Report from the committee', 1 April 1779, p 7
[25] *LL*, Middlesex Sessions: General Orders of the Court, October 1777 (LMSMGO 556070150).

Newgate itself, Akerman found the same 'dejection of spirits among the prisoners' which others had found on the hulks, and he reported that 'many had died broken-hearted'.[26]

There were, however, two important differences between the hulks and the prisons. First, those on the hulks had to subsist on the food provided, while those in the prisons relied primarily on food and drink brought in by friends and family, supplemented by prison charities. Duncan Campbell reported that initially he had allowed friends to bring provisions to the convicts on the hulks, but he was forced to forbid the practice 'as they conveyed saws and other instruments for their escape'.[27] Thus, the second difference was that the prisoners incarcerated on land were able to receive frequent visitors, a practice made possible by the relatively lax visiting rules in the still unreformed prisons. Not only might tools be smuggled in to assist with a break-out, but visitors also brought ideas and messages. In Newgate, as Akerman reported, 'all the male prisoners, accused of felonies and misdemeanours, associated together in the day times' (as did female prisoners, but in a separate yard).[28] London prisoners, particularly the convicts incarcerated for years as the war dragged on, had plenty of time, opportunity and grievances about prison conditions to encourage them to conspire in pursuit of escapes and insurrections. As a result the numbers of prison escapes rose to a new level.

Between 1776 and the Gordon Riots in June 1780, with their wholesale release of up to 1,600 prisoners, there were group escapes from the Clerkenwell house of correction (7 prisoners, including Michael Swift in October 1776), and New Prison (despite the fact it had been significantly rebuilt only a few years earlier), where 'several persons' escaped 'by cutting their way through the walls' of the prison in July 1778.[29] There were also individual escapes from Wood Street Compter, the house of correction at Clerkenwell, and New Prison. Edward Hall, keeper of the house of correction, made the connection explicit between the presence of convicted felons in his prison and these escapes, telling a committee of justices 'he is thence more liable to escapes'.[30] While the new buildings of

[26] PP, 'Report from the committee', 1 April 1779, p. 7.
[27] PP, Journals of the House of Commons, 15 April 1778, p. 927.
[28] PP, 'Report from the committee', 1 April 1779, p. 7.
[29] LL, set, 'Michael Swift'; Morning Post, 30 October 1776 (Burney Collection: www. galegroup.com, 2 Jan. 2014); LL, Middlesex Sessions: General Orders of the Court, September 1778 (LMSMGO556070213).
[30] LMA, Middlesex Sessions, 'Minutes of the committee for repairing the house of correction, Clerkenwell, and the New Prison, Clerkenwell', MA/G/GEN/0001, vol. 2, p. 58.

(a)   (b)

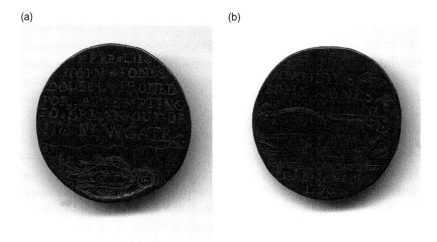

Figure 7.3 'Here Lyeth John Jones, doubel ironed for attempting to break out of Newgate, 1776'. ©Tim Millet.

Newgate prison proved almost invulnerable, it witnessed a substantial riot in August 1777, when a group of prisoners led by Patrick Madan caused considerable damage: 'all the windows were broke, and iron casements thrown into the yard, together with innumerable brickbats which had been broke from the inside of their wards; and one of the other wards began to be demolished, in which business they continued all night'.[31] The prisoners were encouraged by 'the famous Miss West', who repeatedly shouted 'Go it lads, go it, dash away, don't spare them! Liberty! Liberty! Liberty!'. Once order was restored, the prisoners justified their actions by saying 'the length of their imprisonment, some of them being for seven years, and others five years, together with their poverty, had made them desperate'.[32]

A simple physical marker of the newly rebellious mood of the prison population can be found in the existence of 'convict love tokens'. These were fashioned from coins, pounded flat and carved with a simple message, usually recording the date a prisoner was convicted and their name, and a plea that they should be remembered by loved ones. The

[31] *LL*, set, 'Patrick Madan'. For an extended account of Madan's experience, see Emma Christopher, *A Merciless Place: The Lost Story of Britain's Convict Disaster in Africa* (Oxford University Press, 2011), ch. 2.
[32] *London Chronicle*, 19 August 1777 (Burney Collection: www.galegroup.com, 2 Jan. 2014).

earliest known example of these mementos is dated 1776 and commem-
orates John Jones, 'doubel ironed for attempting to break out of Newgate'.[33] Over the course of the next decade, these tokens became a
physical reminder of the chasm that imprisonment, and later transportation to New South Wales, created between those convicted of crime and
the communities which supported them. That they were made by
hammering smooth a coin decorated with the face of the king and all
the symbols of state power simply added significance to these love tokens
as a marker of popular hostility.[34]

The overcrowding and security challenges posed by the presence of so
many convicts after the suspension of transportation prompted the
authorities to make changes to the Clerkenwell house of correction and
New Prison.[35] In 1777 iron spikes were ordered to be fitted to the walls
of the house of correction, to render it 'more secure against the attempts
of the convicts therein confined', and the following year it was recommended that all the walls of the wards in New Prison be 'secured with
iron hoops and sheathed with oak . . . in order to prevent the possibility of
an escape in the future'.[36] Other improvements addressed the unsanitary
conditions which the overcrowding exacerbated: 'air holes lights or
windows' were cut in the walls of the women's gallery of the house of
correction to improve circulation and a bathing tub was provided for the
female prisoners. In New Prison a separate ward was created to accommodate sick prisoners.[37]

Nevertheless, conditions remained dire, and it is likely that the convicts who served long terms, often at hard labour, both on the hulks and
in the prisons, accumulated deep feelings of resentment which were
communicated to their families and friends and no doubt remained even
after they were discharged. This resentment flared into active and violent
resistance to the institutions of policing and punishment in June 1780.

---

[33] *LL*, set, 'John Jones'. This is very possibly the same John Jones, mentioned above, who
was sentenced to imprisonment on the hulks in January 1777, participated in the
'insurrection' the following year and escaped from the hulks in April 1781, but this
cannot be confirmed.

[34] Michele Field and Tim Millett, *Convict Love Tokens: The Leaden Hearts the Convicts Left
Behind* (Wakefield Press, 1998). For a discussion of the symbolism and meanings
associated in popular culture with coins, see Deborah Valenze, *The Social Life of Money
in the English Past* (Cambridge University Press, 2006).

[35] C. W. Chalklin, 'The reconstruction of London's prisons, 1770–1799: an aspect of the
growth of Georgian London', *London Journal*, 9:1 (1983), 35.

[36] *LL*, Middlesex Sessions: General Orders of the Court, October 1777
(LMSMGO556070146); September 1778 (LMSMGO556070213).

[37] *LL*, Middlesex Sessions: General Orders of the Court, September 1778
(LMSMGO556070215); LMA, 'Minutes of the committee for repairing', MA/G/
GEN/001, vol. 3, pp. 7, 12 (28 Jan. 1780).

The Gordon Riots

The Gordon Riots erupted on a hot Friday, 2 June 1780, and within a week at least 285 men and women were dead, and a further 173 seriously injured.[38] Some estimates put the dead and wounded as high as 700.[39] The damage wreaked on the fabric of the city in a full week of rioting is estimated to have run to £200,000, with thirty-two private homes destroyed as well as numerous businesses and public buildings.[40] Although several detailed narratives are available, the events of that week have not been effectively integrated into a larger analysis of the evolution of plebeian resistance to criminal justice.[41]

Undoubtedly the immediate trigger for the riots was the parliamentary agitation associated with Lord George Gordon, who, as leader of the Protestant Association, sought the repeal of the Catholic Relief Act of 1778.[42] This Act ameliorated the laws restricting the legal position of Catholics in England, and although it had faced little active opposition in parliament when it was initially passed, it rapidly became the focus of an extensive extra-parliamentary campaign to have it repealed. An effective measure of the kind of respectable support the Protestant Association attracted is the high-profile participation of men such as William Payne, the 'Protestant Carpenter' and an active figure in the reformation of manners campaign of 1757–63.[43] Payne expressed strongly anti-Catholic views throughout his life, in conjunction with an equally strong commitment to a rigid social order, based on the preservation of a coherent Protestant community. According to Gordon, it was Payne who insisted

---

[38] For this section, see also Tim Hitchcock, 'Renegotiating the bloody code: the Gordon Riots and the transformation of popular attitudes to the criminal justice system', in Ian Haywood and John Seed, eds., *The Gordon Riots and Eighteenth-Century British Culture* (Cambridge University Press, 2012), pp. 185–203.

[39] J. Paul de Castro, *The Gordon Riots* (London: Oxford University Press, 1926), p. 236; Tony Hayter, *The Army and the Crowd in Mid-Georgian England* (London: Macmillan, 1978), p. 186. The often repeated estimate of 700 is derived from N. William Wraxall, *Historical Memoirs of My Own Time* (Philadelphia, Penn., 1836), p. 138.

[40] George Rudé, 'The Gordon Riots: a study of the rioters and their victims', *Transactions of the Royal Historical Society*, 5th Series, 6 (1956), 100.

[41] The best narrative account remains de Castro, *Gordon Riots*; see also Christopher Hibbert, *King Mob: The Story of Lord George Gordon and the Riots of 1780* (London: Longman, 1959); and John Nicholson, *The Great Liberty Riot of 1780* (London: BM Bozo, 1985). The most intellectually ambitious analyses of the riots include Rudé, 'The Gordon Riots'; and Peter Linebaugh, *The London Hanged: Crime and Civil Society in the Eighteenth Century* (London: Allen Lane, 1991), ch. 10, 'The delivery of Newgate'; and, more recently, Haywood and Seed, eds., *The Gordon Riots*.

[42] 18 Geo. III c. 60, 'An Act for relieving His Majesty's subjects professing the popish religion from certain penalties and disabilities imposed on them'.

[43] *LL*, set, 'William Payne'.

on marching en masse to present the petition for repeal to parliament, who led the City of London division and who was identified as inciting the mob outside parliament itself.[44] That Gordon could garner some 100,000 signatures to his 'monster petition', and marshal between 40,000 and 60,000 people to attend, in military formation, his public meeting on St George's Fields, reflects the extent to which he had touched a significant nerve among a wider populace, made up of many of the same men who served as overseers and constables, vestrymen and clerks, and the householders who had contested the powers of the select vestries. But the events that followed the delivery of that monster petition helped to expose the divisions between Payne's world of parish feasts, seasonal charity and moral policing and that of an emerging self-consciousness among criminals and the poor.

The afternoon of Friday 2 June was given over to a heated debate in parliament, with Lord Gordon attempting to use the milling crowds of excitable Associationers outside to drive through the repeal of the Act. But as parliament prevaricated and delayed, finally adjourning its decision to the following Tuesday, and as a hot day turned into a torrid evening, events rapidly moved beyond the control of Gordon and his associates. By evening, Lords Hillsborough, Stormont and Townsend found themselves attacked by a crowd that was rapidly becoming a mob; their wigs pulled from their heads, 'hair flowing on their shoulders', they were forced to flee down side streets in hackney coaches and sedan chairs.[45] The wheels were taken off the carriage belonging to the Bishop of Lincoln, Lord Mansfield was forced to run from his coach as the mob smashed its windows, and the Archbishop of York was cornered in Parliament Street and forced to chant 'No Popery!' in 'a pitiable and enfeebled voice'.[46] Gordon attempted to calm the crowds, but it was only at eleven in the evening that a troop of guards was able to free the politicians who remained in parliament.

That evening the rioting began in earnest, with the firing of the Catholic chapel belonging to the Sardinian ambassador in Lincoln's Inn Fields, and later the chapel attached to the Bavarian embassy in Warwick Street. Thirteen arrests were made that night by troops arriving late on the scene, following 'much scuffling' in which several people were slightly wounded by the bayonets wielded by the soldiers.[47] However,

---

[44] Joanna Innes, 'Payne, William (1717/18–1782)', *ODNB* (www.oxforddnb.com, 1 Jan. 2014); BL, Add. Ms. 42129, f. 8.

[45] *General Evening Post*, 3–6 June 1780 (Burney Collection: www.galegroup.com, 2 Jan. 2014).

[46] Thomas Holcroft, *A Plain and Succinct Narrative of the Late Riots and Disturbances* (3rd edn, 1780), pp. 16–17.

[47] Holcroft, *A Plain and Succinct Narrative*, pp. 16–17.

while the anti-Catholic objectives of these early riotous events are self-evident, the beginnings of a new focus on attacking the institutions of criminal justice can be found. Outside the Sardinian Chapel, Sampson Rainsforth,[48] a man closely associated with Bow Street and its policing of Westminster, and who had testified against some of the arrested rioters, was spotted, and the mob yelled 'Damn him! He ... is the late High Constable [of Westminster]; knock him on his head'.[49] In that moment, the riots began to turn from a Protestant outcry voiced by respectable householders into an assault on the judicial system. 'Anti-popery' was a shibboleth that could unite Londoners of all social classes, drawing on 250 years of shared politics.[50] Policing and criminal justice, in contrast, divided communities along very different lines.

The composition of the crowds that filled London's streets over the ensuing week and the motives of the rioters have been hotly contested ever since. George Rudé, on the basis of a detailed analysis of those prosecuted following the riots, agreed with Charles Dickens, who in *Barnaby Rudge* characterised the rioters as for the most part 'sober workmen' and apprentices.[51] If we take the example of William Winterbotham, one of the few people who admitted to participating in the riots of his own volition, this description seems apt. A seventeen-year old apprentice silversmith from Aldgate, given to both 'evil ways' and 'much false zeal', Winterbotham admitted he had 'entered warmly into the ... senseless cry of "No Popery"'.[52] However, the list of people eventually tried as a result of the riots also includes the ragged edge of London society: beggars and prostitutes, casual labourers, and Black refugees from the American Revolution.[53] Overall, it is clear that individual riots drew their personnel from all the varied communities of London. For the most part, people rioted on their doorsteps. Their motivations were similarly mixed, local and constantly changing. Certainly anti-Catholicism remained important, and attacks on Catholic

---

[48] *LL*, set, 'Sampson Rainsforth'.
[49] As recalled by Rainsforth in a deposition given at Bow Street, and reproduced in de Castro, *Gordon Riots*, p. 44. See also John Beattie, *The First English Detectives: The Bow Street Runners and the Policing of London, 1750–1840* (Oxford University Press, 2012), p. 148.
[50] Colin Haydon, *Anti-Catholicism in England: A Political and Social Study* (Manchester University Press, 1993).
[51] George Rudé, *Paris and London in the Eighteenth Century: Studies in Popular Protest* (New York and London: Viking Press, 1971), pp. 282–3. See also Linebaugh, *London Hanged*, p. 341.
[52] *The Rev. William Winterbotham: A Sketch* (London: Printed for private circulation, [1893]), p. 9.
[53] See, for instance, Merika Sherwood, 'Blacks in the Gordon Riots', *History Today*, 1 December 1997, 24–8 (www.historytoday.com, 2 Jan. 2014).

houses and institutions can be found throughout – though as Rudé has demonstrated these were focused on rich Catholics to the exclusion of the poor majority of Irish Catholic immigrants.[54] But there were also many, to follow James Gillray's assessment made during the riots and published on 9 June, who had ulterior motives:

> Tho' He says he's a Protestant Look at the Print
> The Face and the Bludgeon will give you a hint.
> Religion he cries in hopes to deceive.
> While his practice is only to burn and to thieve.[55]

A constant and insistent strand discernible throughout the course of the riots was a powerful hostility towards criminal justice and its institutions, and not simply those which contained prisoners arrested in the riots. Two days of relative calm followed the events of Friday the 2nd, but the riots caught flame on Monday, when Sampson Rainsforth's house in Clare Street was attacked and pulled down, causing £624 worth of damage. On Tuesday Justice William Hyde's house in St Martin's Street was attacked, with the eventual cost of the night's mayhem amounting to £2,062. Hyde was a prominent justice and had read the Riot Act in Palace Yard the preceding Friday. This anti-criminal justice focus rose to a new pitch of concerted activity with attacks on the house of the Lord Chief Justice, Lord Mansfield, in Bloomsbury Square, where over £5,700 worth of damage was caused in a few short hours, before taking in the administrative epicentre of new policing, John Fielding's house in Bow Street.[56] In addition to causing over £1,000 worth of damage to the fabric of the house, the rioters were also careful to destroy Fielding's registers of known and suspected offenders.[57] By contrast, at £472, the cost of the damage inflicted on the Bavarian Chapel in Golden Square ran to less than half of that inflicted on Bow Street.[58] Rioters seeking revenge also totally destroyed the Bethnal Green house of Justice David Wilmot, who had been active in prosecuting the 'cutters' during the weavers' disputes a decade earlier. The next day John Gamble was heard

---

[54] Rudé, *Paris and London*, pp. 285–6.

[55] James Gillray, *No Popery, Or Newgate Reformer* (1780), Lewis Walpole Library, 780.06.09.01+ (images.library.yale.edu/walpoleweb, 2 Jan. 2014).

[56] *LL*, Middlesex Sessions: Sessions Papers, February 1782 (LMSMPS507510098, LMSMPS507510105, LMSMPS507510125).

[57] *LL*, Middlesex Sessions: Sessions Papers, February 1782 (LMSMPS507510097), (LMSMPS507510098), (LMSMPS507510105), (LMSMPS507510125); Philip Rawlings, 'Fielding, Sir John (1721–1780)', *ODNB*; and Anthony Babington, *A House in Bow Street: Crime and the Magistracy: London 1740–1881* (Chichester: Barry Rose Law, 1999), p. 161. Lord Mansfield had taken a leading role in obstructing the prosecution of Catholics, so the attack on his house might have been partly motivated by anti-Catholic sentiment.

[58] *LL*, Middlesex Sessions: Sessions Papers, February 1782 (LMSMPS507510127).

Figure 7.4 James Gillray, *No Popery, Or Newgate Reformer* (1780).
Lewis Walpole Library, 780.06.09.01+ (images.library.yale.edu/
walpoleweb, 2 Jan. 2014). ©Trustees of the Lewis Walpole Library.

bragging that the rioters had, 'done Davy ... they had done the Doctor
on the green'.[59]

Attempts to rescue rioters previously arrested were a traditional component of many eighteenth-century riots, as were attacks on the houses of

---

[59] *LL*, Old Bailey Proceedings, 28 June 1780 (t17800628-22).

Figure 7.5 *The devastations occasioned by the rioters of London firing the new goal of Newgate ... June 6, 1780.* © London Metropolitan Archives, ref. SC/GL/PR/446/OLD/2/q8038930.

those who attempted to suppress disorder, but by Tuesday only three rioters remained in custody – all in Newgate – and John Fielding, who was ill, was not directly involved in suppressing the riots. The crowd was wreaking revenge on a system of justice whose policies of arrest and prosecution amounted to a 'transporting and hanging system of police'. Despite the fact that Bow Street had held some of the arrested prisoners, the destruction of Fielding's records and the attacks on the houses of other justices and Lord Mansfield cannot be seen as simple acts of rescue, but instead took on the character of revenge. The high level of destruction (not looting) inflicted on them – amounting to over £10,000 in total – reflects a distinctive and different pattern of behaviour from that found in typical London riots.[60]

---

[60] Of the thirteen men arrested on Friday, one was bailed and eight were released following a re-examination at Bow Street on the Monday. See de Castro, *Gordon Riots*, pp. 58–9. For Bow Street, see Babington, *House in Bow Street*, p. 161. For the low levels of destruction and violence traditionally associated with riot, see Robert Shoemaker, *The London Mob: Violence and Disorder in Eighteenth-Century England* (London: Hambledon and London, 2004), pp. 113–33, *passim*. The figure of £10,000 incorporates the damage done to the homes of William Hyde, Lord Mansfield, Sir John Fielding and Robert Cox (£10,062 in total compensation). It excludes Sampson Rainsforth's house, as he was not a serving justice at the time.

It was only on Tuesday, five days into the riots, that we come to the famous set piece at their heart, with the attack on Newgate prison itself. According to one witness, the mob was led by James Jackson, a sailor recently returned from sea:

he cried out 'Newgate, a-hoy'. That was about six o'clock, as near as I can recollect. He went down Orange Street coming towards Newgate. Great numbers of the mob followed him.[61]

It sometimes seems as if half of London was either in the crowd before Newgate or looking down on the scene from the windows above. However, what is beyond doubt is the destructive fury unleashed. The fabric of the newly completed prison was almost entirely destroyed, and 117 prisoners, from petty thieves to murderers, were set loose on the streets.[62] In the words of the clerk of the works:

the new Gaol of Newgate and ... the chapel and keeper's house etc thereto belonging ... were totally destroyed and several of the external parts considerably damaged by fire, the loss sustained by this means ... could not be made good for a less sum than £30,000.

The prison would not be fully operational again until July 1784, more than four years later.[63]

Fanny Burney, watching from the roof tops on Tuesday evening, identified four separate major conflagrations, all associated with criminal justice: 'Our square was light as day by the bonfire from the contents of Justice Hyde's house ...; on the other side we saw flames ascending from Newgate, a fire in Covent Garden which proved to be Justice Fielding's house, and another in Bloomsbury Square which was at Lord Mansfield's.'[64] And this was just the start. The attack on Newgate was quickly followed by attacks on King's Bench and Fleet prisons, New Prison and the house of correction at Clerkenwell. 'The cause', in the words of Thomas Haycock, sentenced to hang for his role in the destruction of Justice Hyde's house and Newgate prison, was not religion, or even the courts, but to ensure that 'there should not be a prison standing ... in London'.[65]

---

[61] *LL*, Old Bailey Proceedings, 28 June 1780 (t17800628-112).
[62] The most detailed account of these specific events is Linebaugh, *London Hanged*, ch. 10.
[63] LMA, City of London: Sessions, 'Committee for carrying into execution so much of the Act of parliament lately passed as relates to the rebuilding the gaol of Newgate', COL/CC/NGC/04/01/001, ff. 355 (29 Nov. 1780), 533 (13 July 1784).
[64] Quoted in de Castro, *Gordon Riots*, p. 84.
[65] *LL*, Old Bailey Proceedings, 28 June 1780 (t17800628-34). Thomas Haycock's role and background are substantially explored in Linebaugh, *London Hanged*, pp. 346–7.

One after another the prisons fell, or their keepers meekly opened their gates in hopes of preserving their private carceral fiefdoms. Contemporaries began to fear that it was not simply the prisons that were under assault but also the law itself. The barristers and students of the Inns of Court certainly felt themselves likely objects of attack. John Grimston reported to his friends in Yorkshire what he purported to be the common knowledge that 'there was a plan laid to burn all the Law Societies'. And indeed, the residents of the Inns were issued government arms with which to protect themselves, and the Temple and Barnard's Inn were actually assaulted.[66] Tellingly, the destructive force of the riots was also remarkably selective. In contrast to the extensive destruction visited on Bow Street and Newgate, the Sessions House at the Old Bailey (next door to Newgate, and home of the jury trial), while attacked, was relatively little damaged, with only some of the furnishings destroyed. Repairs cost just under £170, and ironically the building was sufficiently intact to host the trials of the first rioters on 28 June.[67] On the day Newgate was attacked, at least one rioter also tried to rally the crowd for an attack on the nearby Bridewell (one of the oldest and most traditional of London's prisons), calling, 'Now my lads, for Bridewell', but no one chose to follow him.[68]

We should not understate the profound significance of these assaults on the prisons, or the extent to which they heralded a desperate, if inchoate, revolutionary moment. The Bank of England came under sustained attack in the twenty-four hours following the burning of Newgate, and was only preserved from sacking by brute military force. Lord Gordon attempted and failed to convince the mob outside the Bank to desist – a clear measure of the profound distance between the crowds of the previous Friday and those assembled before the Bank. More tellingly, John Wilkes, hero of the mob in the 1760s but now ex-Lord Mayor of London, resorted to arms. Acting in his capacity as a Buckinghamshire militiaman, in combination with the 534 soldiers stationed at the Bank under the command of Lt Col. Thomas Twisleton, he 'Fired 6 or 7 times on the rioters at the end of the Bank ... Killed two rioters directly opposite to the great gate of the Bank; several others in Pig Street and

[66] East Riding Records Office, DDGR/42/30, John Grimston letters, f. 58, 8 June 1780. Our thanks to Katrina Navickas for this reference. For the issuing of arms, see Anthony Babington, *Military Intervention in Britain from the Gordon Riots to the Gibraltar Incident* (London: Routledge, 1990), p. 27.

[67] LMA, 'Committee for carrying into execution ... the rebuilding of Newgate', COL/CC/NGC/04/01/001, f. 361, 29 Nov. 1780.

[68] Edward G. O'Donoghue, *Bridewell Hospital: Palace, Prison, Schools*, 2 vols. (London: John Lane, The Bodley Head, 1929), II, pp. 203–8.

Cheapside.'[69] The battle of Fleet Street alone resulted in sixty dead or wounded rioters shot at close range – though the actual number may have been much higher, as contemporaries believed that many of the dead were unceremoniously pitched into the Thames to save them from being identified.[70] A simple measure of the sense of crisis induced by the rioters, and the extent to which their objectives extended beyond the religious policies of the state, is contained in the list of buildings which desperately sought military defenders over these days. Besides the prisons and the Bank of England, they included the South Sea Company, East India Company, Excise Office and Customs House, Navy Pay Office, Victualing Office, Freemasons' Hall, and Coutts', Thelusson's and Drummond's Banks.[71] These institutions represented a broad range of power and authority. It is worth noting that not a single workhouse, hospital or parish church was attacked.

The riots were finally suppressed through concerted military action on Thursday 8 June. By this time three interwoven changes had occurred. First, the refusal of the Lord Mayor and many of the justices of peace of London and Middlesex to sanction the direct use of military force against the rioters, arising from their traditional conception of law and order as best achieved through negotiation and mediation (and previously seen in their unwillingness to have executions policed by the military), forced the government to step in. This fundamentally changed the relationship between civilian government and the military. On Wednesday the 8th, the Privy Council passed a general order sanctioning the use of military force without the prior consent of a local justice, and vested the management of the military response to the riots in the hands of Lord Amherst as commander-in-chief. In the process the Council effectively undermined the role of justices of the peace, who even following the passage of the Riot Act had been a civilian check on the use of troops against rioters.[72]

Second, the parish worthies who had signed the petition, who saw in a common defence of a confessional Protestant community a defence of their own liberties, were made to look at their fellow Londoners and found in the rioters harbingers of disorder and chaos, rather than co-religionists and loyal subjects. During the riots themselves, and in the months and years that followed, inhabitants' associations and parish patrols were organised to police the streets and to ensure that the parish

[69] Quoted in de Castro, *Gordon Riots*, p. 142. For the numbers stationed at the Bank, see Hayter, *Army and the Crowd*, p. 154.
[70] Wraxall, *Historical Memoir*, p. 139.   [71] Hayter, *Army and the Crowd*, p. 160.
[72] Babington, *Military Intervention*, pp. 26–30.

community was protected against its own less respectable members.[73] By 27 June, William Payne, who began the month leading the crowd outside parliament, was writing to the Lord Mayor setting out plans for the recapture of the prisoners released on the storming of Newgate.[74]

And finally, the riots both reflected and contributed to a transformation in the attitudes of the poor. Changes to the systems of police and punishment were a motive force behind the unprecedented scale of the riots. The anger that was unleashed was then exacerbated by the response of the judicial authorities to the events of that June, ensuring that the same motives and agenda that stirred the rioters would continue to influence plebeian actions and attitudes.

The aftermath

Now back in control, the authorities were quick to exact retribution. Of the 450 rioters who were arrested, 160 would eventually appear at trial.[75] Of these men and women, mainly social outcasts offered up by their own communities as exemplary culprits, 62 received sentences of death, of whom 26 were eventually hanged. In the long weeks of July and early August, the neighbourhoods that had seen the riots' most destructive violence played host to executions designed both to allow plebeian Londoners to witness the retribution meted out by their social superiors and to ensure that not so many bodies swung from any single gibbet that public tolerance was stretched beyond endurance.[76] Policed by the new parish associations (the uniformed military assiduously kept out of sight, if not out of reach), these executions drew crowds of up to 12,000 people, and were marked by a quiet solemnity.

In the same months London took on the feel of a military encampment. While troops stayed away from the executions, they were stationed at the prisons and courts, and the parks were filled with over 10,000 soldiers. The overt military presence was gradually withdrawn and preference was given to parish associations and local militia, who radically

---

[73] Matthew White, '"For the safety of the City": the geography and social politics of public execution after the Gordon riots', in Haywood and Seed, eds., *The Gordon Riots*, pp. 204–25.

[74] Innes, 'William Payne', *ODNB*.

[75] Rudé, *Paris and London*, p. 275. For a detailed analysis of the state trials, see Uwe Böker, '"The people that the maddest times were ever plagued with": English justice and fair trials after the Gordon Riots (1780)?', *Erfurt Electronic Studies in English*, 6 (2003) (webdoc.gwdg.de, 2 Jan. 2014).

[76] Rudé, *Paris and London*, p. 275; White, '"For the safety of the City"', pp. 209–16. Rudé states that the number eventually hanged was twenty-five, but as White points out (p. 219) the addition of Henry Penny, executed on 22 August, raises this to twenty-six.

increased the personnel available for police duties; but by the autumn, as the last of the rioters were hanged and the military were increasingly confined to barracks, a new dispensation emerged. Respectable Londoners had become more distrustful of their social inferiors, while a stronger sense of opposition to authority could be found among prisoners and defendants.

In part this can be seen in the business of the Old Bailey. In the years following the outbreak of hostilities in North America, the number of crimes tried remained level or declined, but following the mass prosecution of rioters in June and September 1780, the number of trials began to increase. This marked the beginning of a period of significant increase, peaking in 1784 following demobilisation. Unusually, the first phase of this increase, between 1779 and 1782 when the number of offences increased by more than half, occurred during wartime and affected men and women equally. A similar increase occurred at Bridewell, where commitments increased by 43.6 per cent between 1780 and 1782. Prosecutions increased more dramatically following the end of the war when, as normal, men accounted for a higher proportion of defendants.[77] Between 1782 and 1784, the number of offences at the Old Bailey grew by 72.2 per cent, reaching a century-high total of 1,104 in 1784 when 80.8 per cent of the defendants were men. At Bridewell the growth in business was even more dramatic: the 385.6 per cent increase between 1782 and 1784 led to a century-high total of 2,956 commitments.

The first part of these increases did not occur during a period of economic hardship, and the most likely explanation is that in the tense period of insecurity following the riots, victims, neighbours and officers were more likely to prosecute suspected offenders formally, rather than rely on widely used traditional informal procedures. The activities of voluntary associations like the Honourable Artillery Company may also have contributed.[78] It is also possible, though impossible to substantiate, that London's alienated working poor became more willing (or felt more compelled) to break the law in these years.

In the early 1780s more Londoners than ever before found themselves in prison and before the courts. Around 1780 the house of correction in Clerkenwell received approximately 2,000 prisoners annually, and New Prison around 1,650.[79] In the City, the compters received approximately

[77] For the post-war crime wave, see John Beattie, *Crime and the Courts in England 1660–1800* (Princeton University Press, 1986), ch. 5, *passim*.

[78] William Blizard, *Desultory Reflections on Police* (1785), *passim*. We are grateful to Joanna Innes for this reference.

[79] In October 1778, the keeper of the Middlesex house of correction, Edward Hall, estimated that approximately 2,000 persons a year were committed to his custody:

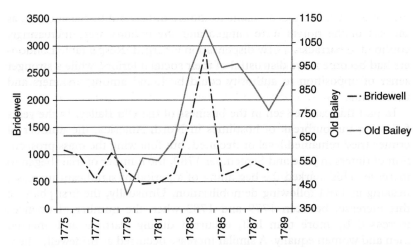

Figure 7.6 Prosecutions and commitments, 1775–1789. *Old Bailey Online*, Statistics: Crime by year, 1775–1789 (counting by offence); Faramerz Dabhoiwala, 'Summary justice in early modern London', *English Historical Review*, 121:492 (2006), appendix (committals); Online data set: Crime Prosecutions.xlsx.

4,000 commitments a year.[80] Even allowing for double counting and recidivism, if we include the Newgate and Bridewell the number of Londoners who were incarcerated in the years around 1783–4 exceeded 11,000 a year, or approximately 1.3 per cent of London's total population.[81] Since these figures do not include the Westminster or Surrey houses of correction and all those indicted at the City, Middlesex, Westminster and Surrey sessions (most of whom were bound over rather than imprisoned), the actual number brought before the authorities and accused of some form of criminal activity in these years must have

LMA, 'Minutes of the committee for repairing', MA/G/GEN/0001, vol. 2, p. 58 (13 Oct. 1778). Three surviving 'turnover' calendars from around this time include an average of 267 prisoners committed since the last sessions, and there were eight sessions a year: LMA, Middlesex Sessions: 'House of correction calendars', MJ/CC/B/ 079–90 (Feb. 1778 and April 1781); LMA, 'Minutes of the committee for building the new house of correction', MA/G/CBF/1 (January 1784); LMA, 'List of prisoners committed to New Prison', MJ/CC/V/002 (January 1778 – October 1780).
[80] LMA, City of London: Sessions, 'Miscellaneous papers from the Compter Committee', CLA/032/02/006, figures for 1771–82.
[81] Assuming a population of 820,000: John Landers, *Death and the Metropolis: Studies in the Demographic History of London, 1670–1830* (Cambridge University Press, 2006), Table 5.7, p. 179. Evidence collected as a result of the authorities' new-found interest in prison conditions allows us to estimate for the first time the total number of Londoners affected.

amounted to around 3 per cent of the population. Not only does this figure betoken a significant increase in the desire of Londoners to prosecute deviance, it is also a measure of the unprecedented pressures the machinery of criminal justice faced in the early 1780s, at a time when the prisons were still overcrowded due to both the damage sustained in the Gordon Riots and the suspension of transportation.

The consequences for London's prisoners and prisons were profound. After years of policy chaos, the prison population was becoming both more experienced and more recalcitrant. A simple snapshot of the inmates of Newgate on 15 January 1783 – when the prison was still only partly repaired – reveals some of the prisoners' characteristics. In addition to the traditional complement of prisoners awaiting trial (145), there were 211 'on orders', primarily either sentenced directly to imprisonment or held from session to session awaiting transportation, all mixed together and free to argue and plan.[82]

The 'Mother of Newgate' was Lea Joseph Solomons, a widow and receiver, who had attempted to recoup her declining fortunes through arson and insurance fraud.[83] In August 1779 she set fire to her rented house in hopes of claiming £400 in insurance on her working capital and clothes. At her trial she was convicted and sentenced to two years' imprisonment at Newgate, and to pay a £100 fine. Following her release during the Gordon Riots and eventual recapture, she was simply left 'to remain' for years after. Among the men was Thomas Mooney, who had led a mob of between 300 and 400 people during the Gordon Riots and, although found not guilty of that offence, was later incarcerated in Bridewell for a minor offence, where he assaulted the keeper, earning himself a transfer to Newgate and years of uncertain imprisonment.[84] There was also John Martin, described in the *Proceedings* as 'a negro', a sailor and probably a refugee from the American Revolution.[85] He spent the whole of the summer and autumn of 1782 and the spring of 1783 in Newgate following his conviction for stealing a bundle of clothes. Sentenced to seven years' transportation to the coast of Africa, he only escaped this fate by virtue of suffering from typhus. Essentially left to rot in prison, he was eventually sent to New South Wales on the First Fleet.[86]

These were desperate men and women, thrown together in desperate circumstances. Their experiences, and those of their numerous fellow

---

[82] LMA, City of London: 'City sessions rolls', CLA/047/LJ/01/1107 (January 1783).
[83] *LL*, set, 'Lea Joseph Solomons'.
[84] *LL*, set, 'Thomas Mooney'; LMA, 'City sessions rolls', CLA/047/LJ/01/1107.
[85] *LL*, set, 'John Martin'.
[86] Christopher, *A Merciless Place*, pp. 215, 217, 304.

inmates, contributed to the development of new attitudes, and new strategies of self-preservation.

Lawyering up

The place, the theatre of justice, in which these new attitudes are most evident is the Old Bailey itself. These were the years when the 'adversarial trial' reached maturity with a dramatic increase in the number of defence counsel, which contributed to the development of new legal procedures and defendant rights.[87] While we have seen that defence counsel were first allowed to appear at Old Bailey trials in 1732, and in the ensuing decades had frequently represented highwaymen, members of gangs and rioters, from the late 1770s there was a further step change in the number of defence counsel appearing. In part the evidence for this reflects the reporting in the *Proceedings*, since the presence of counsel was not routinely reported prior to the appointment of Edmund Hodgson as publisher in 1782.[88] However, the sheer magnitude of the increase provides evidence that a change in the use and role of counsel took place in these years. According to Allyson May, these changes were 'rooted in client behaviour rather than any theoretical imperatives on the part of the legal profession'.[89] And as Figure 7.7 demonstrates, it was defendants rather than prosecutors who led the way. The growing number of defendants who appeared at the Old Bailey from the late 1770s came to realise that with the help of defence counsel they could challenge the courts and their prosecutors more effectively.

The Gordon Riots, and the wave of prosecutions that followed, played a key role in advancing these changes. An examination of the sessions on either side of the riots makes it clear that it was precisely in these trials – held at the sessions beginning 28 June, just weeks after the riots – that counsel first appear in large numbers. In the May sessions prosecuting counsel is mentioned in one trial, and defence counsel in a further three. By contrast, in the June sessions thirty-three prosecuting counsel are

[87] John H. Langbein, *The Origins of Adversary Criminal Trial* (Oxford University Press, 2003).

[88] John Beattie, 'Scales of justice: defense counsel and the English criminal trial in the eighteenth and nineteenth centuries', *Law and History Review*, 9:2 (1991), 228; Robert Shoemaker, 'Representing the adversary criminal trial: lawyers in the Old Bailey Proceedings, 1770–1800', in David Lemmings, ed., *Courtrooms and the Public Sphere in Britain, 1700–1850* (Farnham, Surrey: Ashgate, 2012), pp. 71–83.

[89] Allyson May, 'Advocates and truth-seeking in the Old Bailey courtroom', *Journal of Legal History*, 26:1 (2005), 85. See also T. P. Gallanis, 'The mystery of Old Bailey counsel', *Cambridge Law Journal*, 65:1 (2006), 159–73; and Allyson May, *The Bar and the Old Bailey, 1750–1850* (Chapel Hill: University of North Carolina Press, 2003).

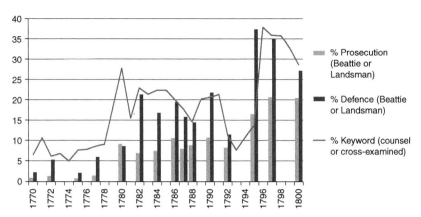

Figure 7.7 Percentage of Old Bailey trials with legal counsel,
1770–1800, as reported in the *Proceedings*. Online data set: Legal
Counsel at the Old Bailey 1715–1800.xlsx. Beattie, 'Scales of justice',
227 (the figures for 1780 have been recalculated to include trials
associated with the Gordon Riots); Landsman, 'Rise of the contentious
spirit', 607. At the time of writing Beattie is in the process of revising his
figures. NB: Figures for the early 1790s are incomplete, as trials
resulting in an acquittal were eliminated from the published *Proceedings*
between October 1790 and December 1792.

explicitly mentioned (reflecting the state's desire to convict the rioters)
and twenty-one for the defence.[90] Never before had counsel appeared at
so many trials in a single Old Bailey sessions.

To some extent this particular meeting of the court is anomalous – in
subsequent sessions the number of defence counsel gradually but briefly
declined to a level not much higher than in the years prior to the riots –
but a new and clear pattern quickly emerged that saw the proportion of
trials with counsel reach unprecedented levels for the remainder of the
decade. As well as acting as a catalyst for new attitudes to prosecution
and imprisonment on the part of victims and the authorities, the riots and
their aftermath also represent a significant escalation in the role of
defence lawyers in the courtroom. It is the Gordon Riots that mark the
moment when defendants en masse at the Old Bailey decided it was time
to get lawyered up against a system they perceived as rigged against them.
And if convicted and sentenced to death, some members of this same
cohort of men and women decided, by refusing the royal pardon, that it
was worth the risk of death to challenge the judges.

[90] See *LL*, Old Bailey Proceedings, 10 May 1780 and 28 June 1780.

While these changes were well in train before William Garrow came to the bar in November 1783, Garrow's presence was nonetheless transformative. The most prominent defence lawyer of the eighteenth century, from his first trial at the Old Bailey he proved himself a master of cross-examination and judicial attack. In the next ten years Garrow is estimated to have acted in over a thousand cases, about three-quarters for the defence. It has been argued that he laid the foundation for the notion that the defendant was innocent until proven guilty, and that the guilt or innocence of the defendant should be proven through an adversarial procedure.[91] But what historians have yet to explore is the nature of the group of men and women who were paying Garrow to act in this capacity.

As already noted, in the decade after the creation of the first hulks there was a generation of men and women who found themselves held for long periods in unreformed prisons organised in such a way as to allow both social interaction among prisoners and (with the exception of the hulks) the incorporation of a wider group of visitors into prison culture. These men and women lived together for years on end, many under the shadow of the gallows. And it is their shared knowledge of criminal justice and its officers that led to a growing sophistication in the courtroom and a viral enthusiasm to deploy Garrow and other counsel in their defence.

A simple measure of the origins of this change in attitudes can be found in the characteristics shared by Garrow's first fifty defence clients. All but seven individuals (86 per cent) had been previously tried at the Old Bailey, and hence held for a time in New Prison or Newgate, on at least one occasion prior to the trial in which Garrow was involved. Typical of Garrow's clients was Richard alias Jonas Wooldridge, who, without benefit of counsel, and with three others, had been found guilty of counterfeiting in September 1781.[92] He was fined one shilling and sentenced to twelve months imprisonment in Newgate, which he served in New Prison while Newgate was out of commission.[93] Three years later, when he was again tried for the same offence, Wooldridge employed Garrow as his counsel, and as Wooldridge looked on, Garrow attacked the prosecutor for being motivated by a desire to secure her husband's acquittal on a similar charge, raised a technical point of law and argued with the judges. In the end, Garrow left the court consumed

[91] On Garrow, see John Beattie, 'Garrow and the detectives: lawyers and policemen at the Old Bailey in the late eighteenth century', *Crime, History and Societies*, 11:2 (2007), 5–24 (chs.revues.org, 2 Jan. 2014); and John Hostettler and Richard Braby, *Sir William Garrow: His Life, Times and Fight for Justice* (Hook, Hampshire: Waterside Press, 2009).
[92] *LL*, set, 'Richard Wooldridge'.
[93] *LL*, City of London Sessions: Sessions Papers, December 1781 (LMSLPS150920303).

by laughter at the prosecutor's expense, with Wooldridge a free man.[94] The benefits of obtaining a lawyer, and a desire to employ Garrow, were part of the expertise that circulated through New Prison and Newgate in these years.

The significance of this change in defendant behaviour is reinforced by an appreciation of the costs involved. Between prison garnish, living expenses and gaol fees, being accused of any crime in the eighteenth century was an expensive proposition that required the support of friends. Hiring defence counsel, which could easily cost £1 or more per trial, substantially increased the cost.[95] And yet, lower-class Londoners managed to raise this money: among Garrow's first fifty clients were seven servants (plus a servant's wife), four labourers, a laundress, a broker and dealer in old iron and rags, a buyer and seller of old clothes, a chandler, a porter and several craftsmen (cooper, gardener, hair dresser, ivory turner, shoemaker, silk throwster, stone mason).[96] We do not know how prisoners managed to secure this money, but with their lives at stake (as the number of hangings increased) desperation became the mother of invention. Funds are likely to have come from some combination of charity (including from fellow prisoners), possible reduced charges from lawyers keen to make a name for themselves in the courtroom, the proceeds of crime, and family and friends. Patrick Madan, for example, received financial support from his sister. In his letters home, among the details of his attempts to escape from Newgate, the problems he was encountering in smuggling gaol-breaking equipment in a pie and the idle gossip of the prison community, he reported how, with his sister's assistance, he had, 'procured [a] lawyer', an 'Old Bailey Solicitor'.[97] The fact that several hundred were able to pay counsel in the 1780s, many of whom were in lower-class occupations and including for the first time many who were accused of non-capital offences, is testimony to both the desperation and the combativeness of Old Bailey defendants in these years.[98]

Garrow's most successful defence strategy is also revealing of the attitudes of prisoners in the aftermath of the riots. His most common rhetorical device was to question the financial interests of the prosecution, and, despite John Fielding's attempts to make the Bow Street

[94] *LL*, Old Bailey Proceedings, 25 February 1784 (t17840225-95).
[95] May, *Bar and the Old Bailey*, p. 84.
[96] For the complete list, see the group of 'GarrowsClients' on the *London Lives* website.
[97] *Authentic Memoirs of the Life, Numerous Adventures, and Remarkable Escapes, of the Celebrated Patrick Madan* (1782), p. 46.
[98] David Lemmings, *Professors of the Law: Barristers and English Legal Culture in the Eighteenth Century* (Oxford University Press, 2000), pp. 212–15.

Runners respectable, to paint the varied officers of the law in the lurid and corrupt colours of a thief-taker. Garrow aggressively raised this long-standing defence tactic to a new level. Again and again he asked what the prosecution hoped to get out of a conviction. In the process, and on behalf of hundreds of prisoners, he held to account a system that was perceived as out of control, and he questioned the very basis of the evolving system of police. For the most part, he avoided using this tactic when cross-examining senior Runners from Bow Street, who with vast courtroom experience, quickly developed the ready defence of asking Garrow what he himself earned.[99] But Garrow was confident enough of the jury's dislike of the other Runners to characterise them in open court as the 'myrmidons', or hired ruffians 'that attend at the Brown-bear'.[100] In making this kind of case, Garrow cut with the grain of public opinion about the new system of police, an opinion that encompassed both his clients and at least some members of the jury.

There is some evidence that those who were defended by counsel were more likely to be found not guilty: over half of Garrow's clients were acquitted, compared to just 35 per cent of all defendants in the same years.[101] And the ability of some offenders such as Charlotte Walker to avoid conviction for long periods with the assistance of counsel is indeed impressive.[102] However, with prosecution counsel also increasingly present, the balance of power in the courtroom had not dramatically changed. Overall, the new frequency with which defence counsel were employed was as likely to have been motivated by fear as by hubris. Many of Garrow's clients would likely have agreed with Benjamin Brown, who despaired when his counsel failed to appear: 'I thought I was prepared with a counsel, but am entirely lost'.[103]

According to John Langbein one of the consequences of the growing use of barristers for the defence was the silencing of the defendant, as lawyers shifted the focus of the trial to whether the prosecution had proved its case, and defendants let their counsel make their case for

[99] Runners like Charles Jealous regularly appeared, frequently several times, at sessions of the court. In the five years before Garrow came to the bar Jealous appeared in at least forty-two separate trials. For a wider discussion of Garrow's attitudes towards the Runners, see Beattie, 'Garrow and the detectives'.

[100] LL, Old Bailey Proceedings, 25 February 1784 (t17840225-29); Oxford English Dictionary, 'Myrmidon', definition no. 3 (www.oed.com, 2 Jan. 2014).

[101] John Beattie, 'Garrow for the defence', History Today, February 1991, 51, 53 (www.historytoday.com, 2 Jan. 2014).

[102] LL, Mary Clayton, 'Charlotte Walker', and Mary Clayton, 'The life and crimes of Charlotte Walker, prostitute and pickpocket', London Journal, 33:1 (2008), 3–19.

[103] LL, Old Bailey Proceedings, 15 September 1779 (t17790915-46).

them.[104] But perhaps encouraged by the development of a more adversarial tone in criminal trials, those defendants who did speak began to do so in an increasingly confident tone, justifying their crimes with claims that they had been driven to steal by 'starvation', 'necessity' and 'distress'. Despite the dangers associated with admitting culpability (such testimony only increased the chance of conviction, and punishments tended to be no lighter), defendants challenged the court to convict them in the face of increasingly eloquent pleas for mercy. Thomas Archer, accused in 1784 of stealing two loaves of bread worth 15 pence from the basket of a journeyman baker making deliveries, told the court:

I have a wife and three children, and I could get no work, I was drove to great distress, I had no bread for three or four days; I come from Norfolk to seek for work; I am a baker by trade, I have applied at a number of places, but none of them wanted a journeyman.

Nonetheless, he was convicted, sentenced to be publicly whipped and passed back to his parish. Mary Smith received a little more mercy. Charged in 1783 with stealing two linen shirts from 'a poor woman' in the house in which she lodged, she told the court:

Sir, I was in great distress, I was a widow with two small children, I buried my husband out of her house … I meant to return them again, she knows I have worked at several places; I have no friend in the world.

Although she was also convicted, the jury recommended her to mercy, and the court ordered her to be privately whipped and discharged, telling her, 'You will have favour shewn to you this time; but if you are not able to maintain yourself by honest industry, apply to your parish'.[105] While this growing practice of defendants justifying their crimes may often have been ineffective or even counterproductive, their growing willingness to stand up to the court and make such pleas, even without the aid of a lawyer, is indicative of a new assertiveness among prisoners.

The impact of legal counsel was even wider. Those who acted at the Old Bailey, or the solicitors they worked with, also practised in other London courts, defending the accused, prosecuting counter-accusations and challenging poor law orders. Lawyers had been involved in hearings at Bow Street since at least 1772, when John Fielding had begun conducting regular 're-examinations'.[106] One such attorney, Thomas Ayrton, 'an attorney at King's Bench', brought a suit which successfully

---

[104] Langbein, *Origins of Adversary Criminal Trial*, pp. 266–73.
[105] *LL*, Old Bailey Proceedings, 20 October 1784 (t17841020-23), 30 April 1783 (t17830430 18).
[106] Beattie, *First English Detectives*, p. 127.

challenged Fielding's practices. Following an illness which lasted a few months, Fielding died in November 1780, but the hearings continued under a justice with less clout, William Addington. Ayrton brought his suit in December following an altercation at a hearing conducted at Bow Street by Addington of a suspected highway robber, in which Ayrton, as usual, was not permitted to cross-examine the prosecutor. The resulting legal challenge, tried in front of Lord Mansfield, ended with a strong censure of the Bow Street practice of pre-trial hearings, particularly the extensive pre-trial publicity they received. As a consequence of this case, newspapers stopped reporting the hearings, and defendants were no longer expected to disclose their evidence in advance of the trial. It is likely that the growing practice of solicitors representing accused felons at such pre-trial hearings resulted in further challenges to the procedures in the ensuing decades.[107] Solicitors also increasingly aided the poor in cases of poor law appeals, vagrancy and debt. John Silvester, one of the most active Old Bailey counsel, regularly appeared on briefs for settlement and vagrancy cases in the 1770s, although we know little about the nature of his practice.[108] Just as counsel hired by defendants forced legal innovations which worked to their advantage in the courts, solicitors may have stimulated changes in poor law practice which benefited the poor.

Punishment transformed

During these same years punishment was further transformed, driven by both social anxiety and the behaviour of convicts. Following the Gordon Riots, more defendants were convicted and punishments became harsher. Between 1770–81 and 1782–6, the conviction rate at the Old Bailey (both full and partial verdicts) increased, despite the increased presence of defence counsel, from 55 to 61 per cent.[109] With transportation unavailable until 1787 (although sentencing resumed in 1781), there were substantial increases in the number and proportion of convicts who were whipped, imprisoned and sentenced to death.

Following the suspension of transportation, the authorities initially relied on traditional punishments. The number of sentences of branding per year increased from an average of 17.7 between 1750 and 1775 to 100.5 between 1776 and 1779, when it was abolished as a punishment for

---

[107] John Beattie, 'Sir John Fielding and public justice: The Bow Street magistrates' court, 1754–1780', *Law and History Review*, 25:1 (2007), 93–100.

[108] May, *Bar and the Old Bailey, 1750–1850*, p. 66.

[109] *Old Bailey Online*, Statistics: Verdicts by year, 1770–86 (counting by defendant). Unknowns and multiple defendants excluded.

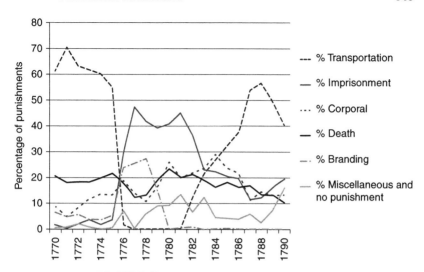

Figure 7.8 Old Bailey punishment sentences, 1770–1790. *Old Bailey Online*: Statistics: Punishments by year, 1770–1790, counting by defendant. Online data set: Punishment Statistics, 1690–1800.xlsx.

crimes subject to benefit of clergy.[110] Similarly, following a decline in the use of whippings in the 1750s, the punishment was substantially revived in the late 1770s. As recorded by the Sheriff of London, the number of whippings carried out (including those sentenced at quarter sessions) increased from 40 offenders in 1779 to 164 in 1785, the largest annual total in the century. Similarly, whereas 60 felons were sentenced to death in 1779, this figure almost tripled to 173 in 1783. Executions increased even more dramatically. Whereas 23 were executed in 1779, there were 97 executions in 1785, the bloodiest year in the century. Not only were more convicts hanged, but they formed a growing percentage of all those sentenced to death, reaching 64.2 per cent of the condemned in 1785 and 81.4 per cent in 1787. This was a direct result of a decision by the Home Secretary in September 1782 to refuse to grant pardons (as had often occurred previously) to those convicted of robberies and burglaries 'attended with acts of great cruelty'.[111] All told, 500 people were hanged in London in the seven years following 1780, almost a third of all those hanged in the eighteenth century.

---

[110] Beattie, *Crime and the Courts*, pp. 88–9.
[111] Quoted by Simon Devereaux, 'Recasting the theatre of execution: the abolition of the Tyburn ritual', *Past & Present*, 202 (2009), 127.

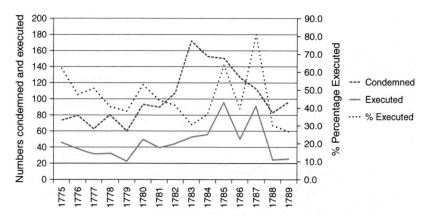

Figure 7.9 Old Bailey death sentences and executions, 1775–1790. *PP, House of Commons Sessional Papers*, 1818, xvi, 185–7 and 1819, xvii, 295–9; Online data set: Death Sentences and Executions, 1749–1806.xlsx.

The increasing severity of punishment in response to the twin crises of the Gordon Riots and the post-war crime wave was accompanied by changes in implementation. Both whippings and executions were carried out in new ways which served to reduce the role of the watching crowd and ensure that the authorities retained control of the ritual, addressing concerns raised by Henry Fielding in 1751. Accelerating a long-term trend which had begun in the 1730s, whippings were primarily conducted in private. Rather than being carried out along a street for a hundred yards 'at the cart's tail', whippings were increasingly staged at a stationary whipping post or inside prisons. The proportion of whippings carried out in public (whether sentenced at the Old Bailey or quarter sessions) declined by almost half, from 42.8 per cent in the 1770s to just 23.1 per cent in the 1780s.[112] As noted previously, the motivations for this shift in penal strategy are unclear. While there is no direct evidence that the authorities were concerned about potential disorder among the crowds which witnessed whippings, this is suggested by the fact that from 1785 the City of London began to use large numbers of 'extra constables' to police public punishments.[113]

---

[112] Robert Shoemaker, 'Streets of shame? The crowd and public punishments in London, 1700–1820', in Simon Devereaux and P. Griffiths, eds., *Penal Practice and Culture, 1500–1900: Punishing the English* (Basingstoke: Palgrave Macmillan, 2004), pp. 238–40 and Table 9.1.

[113] Andrew T. Harris, *Policing the City: Crime and Legal Authority in London, 1780–1840* (Columbus: Ohio State University Press, 2004), pp. 64–5.

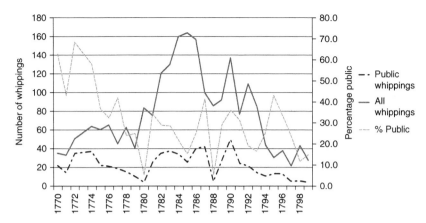

Figure 7.10 London whipping punishments, 1770–1799. TNA,
Sheriff's Cravings, T64/262, T90/165-168; Online data set: London
Whipping Punishments, 1770–1799.xlsx.

Similar concerns lay behind the decision in the autumn of 1783 to
move public executions from their traditional location at Tyburn on the
western edge of the metropolis to immediately outside Newgate prison
(whose reconstruction following the Gordon Riots was nearly complete).
As a result, the sometimes disorderly procession carrying the condemned
in a cart from Newgate to Tyburn was abandoned, executions were held
earlier in the day and the size of the crowds which were able to watch
executions was reduced. Furthermore, the introduction of the 'drop'
speeded up hangings, making it difficult for the condemned to make a
show of dying 'game' and giving the crowd less of an opportunity to
sympathise with their suffering. Executions would now take place in front
of the rebuilt Newgate's sober facade, with the condemned brought out
onto the scaffold only shortly before their actual executions.

The motivations for this significant change in the execution ritual have
been variously ascribed by historians to a desire to protect property values
in the west end, concerns to enhance the impact of prospective executions
on the convicts' imaginations and, in the latest article on the subject,
attempts to improve the deterrent effect on the attending crowd.[114] As
Simon Devereaux argues, 'the most compelling impetus for the abolition

---

[114] Steven Wilf, 'Imagining justice: aesthetics and public executions in late eighteenth-
century England', *Yale Journal of Law & the Humanities*, 5:1 (1993–4), 51–78
(digitalcommons.law.yale.edu/yjlh, 2 Jan. 2014); V. A. C. Gatrell, *The Hanging Tree:
Execution and the English People 1770–1868* (Oxford University Press, 1996), pp. 602–4;
Devereaux, 'Recasting the theatre of execution'.

of Tyburn was a penal crisis of unprecedented proportions', with the existing regime manifestly failing to stop the apparently relentless increase in crime. Immediately before the decision to transfer executions to Newgate was taken, twenty-six men who had mutinied on a transport ship they believed was destined for Africa had been convicted, and six were hanged.[115] In this context the decision to stage executions at Newgate was made in an attempt, much like the multiple locations of the executions of the Gordon rioters, to re-establish control over an increasingly intransigent criminal population. But the authorities also sought to stop the crowd disorder which still sometimes accompanied processions to Tyburn and subsequent executions. As the sheriffs Thomas Skinner and Barnard Turner (who had been involved in suppressing the Gordon Riots) argued in their pamphlet justifying the change:

The Croud of Spectators will probably be more orderly, because less numerous; and more subject to controul by being more confined; and also because it will be free from the accession of stragglers whom a Tyburn procession usually gathers in its passage, and who make the most wanton part of it.[116]

The problem of crowd disorder nonetheless persisted, contributing to the scaling back of the number of prisoners executed in London after the peaks in 1785 and 1787. In 1788 this figure dropped from 92 to 25, and the number stayed low for the rest of the century: between 1789 and 1800 executions averaged 22 per year. This is because the bloodbath in the mid-1780s placed capital punishment 'under attack to a degree never before experienced'.[117] Opposition to large-scale executions can already be seen in 1780, when Edmund Burke unsuccessfully lobbied for the number of Gordon rioters to be executed to be limited to six, since, he wrote: 'a very great part of the lower, and some of the middling people of this city, are in a very critical disposition ... [and] may very easily be exasperated, by an injudicious severity, into desperate resolutions'.[118] In 1784 the housekeeper at the Old Bailey was worried that 'evil minded people would gain access to the yard where the scaffold was kept between executions and set fire to it'.[119] Changing the location of executions had

---

[115] Devereaux, 'Recasting the theatre of execution', 133–4.
[116] White, '"For the safety of the City"', pp. 216–17; *An Account of Some Alterations and Amendments Attempted in the Duty and Office of Sheriff of the County of Middlesex and Sheriffs of the City of London, during the Shrievalty of Sir Barnard Turner and Thomas Skinner, Esq.* (1784), p. 29.
[117] Devereaux, 'Recasting the theatre of execution', 171.
[118] Edmund Burke, 'Some thoughts on the approaching executions', in *The Works of the Right Honourable Edmund Burke*, 2 vols. (London: Samuel Holdsworth, 1846), II, p. 417.
[119] LMA, 'Committee for carrying into execution ... the rebuilding of Newgate', COL/CC/NGC/04/01/001, f. 533 (13 July 1784).

not allayed concerns about the behaviour of both the crowd and the condemned: a correspondent to the *Gentleman's Magazine* in 1784 complained that 'Our executions seem to have lost all their good effects ... the only solicitude too many of [the crowd] discover is, whether the criminals *die hard*'.[120] That concern about the impact of frequent executions was shared at the highest levels of government is indicated by the worry expressed by the prime minister, William Pitt, in 1789 that they would create the wrong 'public impression'.[121]

If both public attitudes and crowd behaviour rendered large-scale executions no longer feasible, it was necessary to increase the use of secondary punishments. Whipping was deemed adequate only for minor offences, leaving imprisonment and transportation (if a new destination could be found) as the only alternatives. But owing to the trail of destruction left by the Gordon rioters, London's prisons in the early 1780s were in a state of chaos. Newgate had suffered most and was only gradually brought back into use, one section at a time. It would not be fully repaired until the summer of 1784. Most London prisoners were therefore crowded into the hastily repaired New Prison and Middlesex house of correction in Clerkenwell, where convicts serving sentences of imprisonment joined those arrested and waiting to stand trial, petty offenders committed by summary jurisdiction to short terms of hard labour, and debtors. Since it was necessary to house convicts who previously would have been transported as well as those displaced from Newgate, the crowding was intense. The resulting poor conditions and inevitable intermingling among different classes of prisoners contributed to the further evolution of a culture of resistance among London's prison populations. Managing both prisons became the main item of business discussed by the Middlesex justices at their meetings throughout the early 1780s.

The scale of the problem can be seen in the fact that between May and September 1780 a total of 678 prisoners were committed to New Prison.[122] The number committed to the house of correction is not known, but by October the Middlesex justices expressed concern that 'a far greater number of persons is now in general imprisoned there than what the building is capable of containing with safety and convenience'. In 1781–2, the number of prisoners held at any one time ranged from 134 to 233; there were 130 more in New Prison. We have seen that prison crowding was a serious issue in the years between the suspension

---

120 *Gentleman's Magazine*, 54, part 1 (1784), 18–19.
121 Devereaux, 'Convicts and the state', p. 383.
122 LMA, 'List of prisoners committed to New Prison', MJ/CC/V/002.

of transportation and the Gordon Riots; the difference now was that London's strongest prison was temporarily unusable, and prisoners were forced into buildings not designed to hold large numbers of felons. To prevent escapes, a military guard was placed at both prisons.[123] When Newgate fully reopened in 1784 the poor conditions and overcrowding were simply transferred. In November, the keeper reported that the prison contained 362 felons and 167 debtors, and about 300 of the 529 prisoners lacked rugs to sleep on and keep themselves warm.[124] A year later the prison held 680 prisoners, and in October 1788 almost 750.[125]

The presence of so many long-term prisoners (convicts serving sentences of imprisonment, and those awaiting transportation) continued to be problematic. Reports from 1781 indicate that the Clerkenwell house of correction held between 55 and 65 convicted felons, while a list of the prisoners in February 1783 included 77 prisoners who had been convicted at the Old Bailey, and a further 18 convicted at the Middlesex sessions.[126] Some had been there since April 1781. The previous month the keeper of New Prison voiced concern about 'the capital convicts now in his custody who are very numerous and licentious and continually endeavouring to escape', and a week later a committee of justices reported that convicts who 'continue there months and for years [are] in an idle and worse than an useless state corrupting each other and forming confederacies dangerous to the public ... [they are] ever making disturbances and riots within the goale and encouraging others to misbehave'.[127] Similar concerns were apparently present at the City of London Bridewell, where the number of commitments increased dramatically between 1781 and 1784. In December 1782 the General Prison Committee issued new regulations restricting visitors, ordered that cutlasses be kept in a case in the watch house and stipulated that 'a Rattle be Provided ... in Case of any Disturbance [an officer] may Alarm the

---

[123] LMA, 'Minutes of the committee for repairing', MA/G/GEN/0001, vol. 3, pp. 40, 42, 67 (27 Oct. 1780, 10 Nov. 1780, 26 April 1781); LMA, Middlesex Sessions: 'House of correction calendars', MJ/CC/B/080; LMA, 'Justices' reports to sessions on the state of New Prison and Middlesex Bridewell', MA/G/GEN/0010 and MA/G/GEN/0013 (1781); LMA, 'Minutes of the committee for building the new house of correction', MA/G/CBF/001 (27 Jan. 1784).

[124] LMA, City of London: Sessions, 'Miscellaneous papers from the Compter Committee', CLA/032, Nov. 1784.

[125] Devereaux, 'Convicts and the state', pp. 232, 254.

[126] LMA, 'Minutes of the committee for repairing', MA/G/GEN/0001, vol. 3, p. 67; LMA, 'Justices' reports to sessions', MA/G/GEN/0010; LMA, Middlesex Sessions: 'House of correction calendars', MJ/CC/B/81.

[127] LMA, 'Minutes of the committee for repairing', MA/G/GEN/0001, vol. 3, pp. 56–7 (13 and 21 March 1781).

Beadle at the Lodge that the Gate of the Hospital may be immediately Locked to Prevent Escapes'.[128]

Despite these precautions, including the presence of military guards, the rebellious mood among the prisoners led to a rash of escapes and mutinies. We have already seen that there was no shortage of escapes in the five years leading up to the Gordon Riots. But in the chaotic years which followed, leading to the decision to establish a penal colony in Australia, escapes multiplied, and London's prisons and transport ships became a seething cauldron of discontent (Figure 7.2).

In the prisons alone, the seven multiple escapes and three attempts between July 1780 and June 1785 demonstrate both the desperation and the new-found confidence of convict prisoners, particularly at the recently rebuilt New Prison. In December 1780, three convicted felons, William Mackenzie, Joseph Caddy and George Bartington, escaped. Their recapture cost £60 and earned the keeper a harsh rebuke from the Middlesex justices.[129] Four months later, on 29 April 1781, a further escape attempt from the same prison was mounted by the inmates, who

in an unlawful, riotous and tumultuous manner assembled themselves together and attempted to break out of and escape ... and with force and arms assaulted [the guards] stationed to keep the said prison.[130]

The guards were issued with guns and in the mêlée that followed William Bell, a thief a few months into a year-long sentence of hard labour, was shot and killed.[131] Five months later still, on 3 September 1781, once again the prisoners 'assembled themselves together and attempted to break out of and escape from the ... prison'.[132] Again, guns were issued, and this time, three prisoners were shot and killed: Benjamin Lees, William Trenter and George Hutton.

Later the same month, and in direct response to this incident, the keeper, Samuel Newport, petitioned the Middlesex justices, who incorporated his observations in a further petition of their own to the judges at the Old Bailey, describing the mood of the prisoners.

That since the late Dreadful Riots ... those confined in the ... Prison ... have become most licentious and dissolute, are unruly and riotous to a very daring degree, continually committing the most outrageous acts, endeavouring to effect

---

[128] *LL*, Bridewell Royal Hospital: Minute Books of the General Prison Committee, 23 December 1782 (GLBRMB201000021).

[129] *LL*, Middlesex Sessions: General Orders of the Court, 7 December 1780 (LMSMGO556070311).0

[130] *LL*, Middlesex Coroners' Inquests, 1 May 1781 (LMCOIC651010007).

[131] *LL*, set, 'William Bell'.

[132] *LL*, Middlesex Coroners' Inquests, 5 September 1781 (LMCOIC651010009).

their escape, and encouraging others to join with them in their desperate designs... In such an attempt lately [made] three Prisoners [were] unfortunately killed and three more wounded.

Newport concluded his plea with the observation that the prisoners were possessed of a 'determined Resolution... [for a] General Escape'.[133] In response, a troop of soldiers was stationed in the gaol for two years, at a cost of £16 per quarter, in an attempt to calm what the local commander would later describe as the 'riotous and dangerous state of the prisons'.[134] And as a carrot to counterbalance this stick of military authority, the daily allowance of food provided to each prisoner was doubled, and for the first time shoes and clothes were made available for poor prisoners.[135]

Samuel Newport's fears were nonetheless realised. In February 1782 he informed the justices 'that several prisoners had attempted a break out of one of the wards and had destroyed some part thereof'.[136] Seven months later, 'two prisoners ... made their escape' from Newgate.[137] And in November of the same year, William Wood, a prisoner at the house of correction at Clerkenwell, directly next door to New Prison, put a pistol to the head of Thomas Mumford and threatened to blow his head off if he did not deliver the keys; while John Fitzgerald, his legs still in irons, threatened to cut John Brown's throat if he did not cooperate. In total, thirty-one people, all classified as 'vagrants', escaped that night.[138]

A clear measure of the fear and anxiety created in the minds of the administrators of criminal justice by this new spirit of rebellion and escape can be found in the reactions of the keeper of New Prison to a riot, perhaps an attempted escape, perhaps just a scuffle, that occurred on 1 August 1784. Some stones were thrown and a complaint was made by the women prisoners because their victuals were not delivered as normal at the open gate to their yard, but through a serving hatch. A broomstick was pushed through the gate in a threatening manner, and someone yelled that they would burn the prison. In a desperate

---

[133] *LL*, Middlesex Sessions: Sessions Papers, September 1781, 'Petition of Samuel Newport' (LMSMPS507440060).

[134] *LL*, Middlesex Sessions: General Orders of the Court, September 1782 (LMSMGO556070380).

[135] *LL*, Middlesex Sessions: Sessions Papers, Sept. 1781, 'An account of money paid by James Crozier... for the poor convicts' (LMSMPS507440064).

[136] LMA, 'Minutes of the committee for repairing', MA/G/GEN/0001, vol. 4, p. 133 (2 Feb. 1782).

[137] *LL*, Old Bailey Proceedings, 16 October 1782 (t17821016-35).

[138] *LL*, Middlesex Sessions: General Orders of the Court, December 1783 (LMSMGO556070403).

response to what most witnesses described as a relatively minor affray, the keeper broke open the arms cabinet and distributed weapons to both his own staff and a couple of soldiers who happened to be visiting. In the confusion that followed Sarah Scott, seven months pregnant and mother of two, was shot in the face and killed. No escape was effected, but the fear of one, and the pride of prisoners in being able to create that fear, was fully reflected in the trial for murder that followed, when the prisoners' testimony reveals a remarkable self-confidence. When called to testify against William Stevenson, the man who fired the fatal shot, each prisoner seemed more keen than the last to claim a reputation as an escape artist and rabble- rouser. Daniel Hopkins claimed he was only in New Prison in consequence of 'breaking out of that [same] gaol', while Thomas Jones claimed to have escaped from Newgate. The counsel for the defence suggested that Jones 'was so bad a fellow, that the keeper got some of his own people to bail [him], that [he] might not corrupt the whole gaol'. To this Jones heartily concurred, 'Right, Sir! Very right, Sir! Very right, Sir!'.[139]

A similar narrative was played out on the hulks. Owing to prison overcrowding and the renewal of court sentences of transportation (despite the fact no destination had been identified), convicts continued to be kept there. Their continuing use from 1782, despite their known limitations, was justified as a stop-gap measure until transportation could resume. In December the removal of additional prisoners to the hulks was justified in a Treasury minute by the fact 'that the Gaol of Newgate is crowded with prisoners to a very inconvenient degree'.

However, conditions on the hulks were at least as bad as in the prisons, and once again some of the convicts escaped. And once again, those re-arrested justified their actions by the harsh treatment they had received. Charles Peyton told the court in 1785 'I have only to say, I had very hard usage on board the hulk'.[140] George Morley, tried for escaping for a second time, said 'I cannot disown the charge of being guilty, the reason of my making my escape, was the ill treatment I received after my first escape'. Morley elaborated:

I was run over across my loins, I am lame, I was always struck without a cause, when I tried to do the utmost of my endeavour, and I hope the merciful Jury will take it into consideration, and send me to any other place: the allowance [of food and drink] is but two pints of barley water, from three in the morning, till six in the afternoon, and there is half a brown loaf, and half an ox cheek for six hearty

---

[139] *LL*, Old Bailey Proceedings, 15 September 1784 (t17840915-66).
[140] *LL*, Old Bailey Proceedings, 23 February 1785 (t17850223-75).

young men, and the ballast that I heaved up, weighs a ton weight, and is fit for a horse to do, and I am entirely a cripple now, and an object [of mercy].[141]

Memories of such harsh treatment were not easily erased. Charles Peat spent some time on one of the hulks before being taken on the transport ship the *Mercury* in 1784, from which he escaped following a prisoners' mutiny. At his trial for returning from transportation he told the court 'Whilst I was on board the hulk, I had the mortification of seeing my fellow sufferers die daily, to the amount of two hundred and fifty'.[142] Joseph Morrell had extensive experience of the hulks between 1784 and 1789.[143] Convicted of grand larceny in 1784 and sentenced to transportation, he was committed to the hulk the *Censor*, moved to the *Justicia* and then to a hospital ship, from which he escaped in 1786. Indicted for returning from transportation, he told the court 'I suffered such hardships, that I made my escape'. Convicted and sentenced to death but with a recommendation for mercy from the jury, Morrell was apparently sent to Newgate. Before he was sentenced, he pleaded 'I hope I shall not go on board any more hulks; I accept my sentence very freely, only not to send me on board the hulks'.[144]

Throughout the century there was a persistent pattern of prison escapes, and prisoner collusion in devising defence strategies for their trials. But the 1780s witnessed a significant escalation of oppositional behaviour among London prisoners, defendants and convicts, both at the Old Bailey and in the prisons. More than a simple, and perhaps understandable rejection of the carceral chaos that characterised London in these years, the mutinies and mass escapes, and confident behaviour in court, constituted a newly self-confident plebeian challenge to the institutions of criminal justice. The authorities were forced to respond.

Transportation in name only

The resistance to the hulks reminded the authorities (should any doubt have remained) of their serious limitations. Pointing out the deficiencies not only of the hulks but also of the prisons and the increased number of executions, in 1784–5 a House of Commons committee emphasised the need to return to transportation as soon as possible. With respect to the prisons, the committee noted 'that the extraordinary fullness of the gaols makes a separation of offenders impracticable, and that by constant

---

[141] *LL*, Old Bailey Proceedings, 6 April 1785 (t17850406-81).
[142] *LL*, Old Bailey Proceedings, 7 July 1784 (t17840707-6).
[143] *LL*, set, 'Joseph Morrell'.
[144] *LL*, Old Bailey Proceedings, 9 September 1789 (o17890909-6); see also 13 December 1786 (t17861213-31).

intercourse they corrupt and confirm each other in every practice of villainy'. But the hulks were no better: 'however necessary they may have been as a temporary expedient, [they] have singularly contributed to these mischievous effects... [the prisoners] form distinct societies for the more complete instruction of all new comers'. Although the committee did not put it this way, those incarcerated had discredited the hulks and the prisons as effective means of punishment. But increasing the number hanged was no longer possible. While refraining from directly criticising the increase in executions, the committee also noted that 'these sacrifices to public justice have produced no other effect than the removal of the offenders in question; and crimes ... still multiply'.[145]

Through both plebeian resistance and public opinion, the pressure to do something was irresistible, and the judges began sentencing offenders to transportation again as early as October 1781. The American War was coming to an unsatisfactory end and the usual post-war crime wave was in prospect, but an alternative destination had not yet been identified. In a futile attempt to resolve the problem, in 1782 and 1785 four transport ships were sent abroad, to the African coast, America (twice) and Honduras.[146] However, the newly mutinous spirit among the convicts helped ensure a rocky road for these experiments. Robert Hill, ordered to go to Africa, refused because he had been granted a pardon on condition he went to the East Indies. When this failed, he, together with Patrick Madan and two others, attempted to scuttle the ship by piercing a hole in the bottom and was given 175 lashes and imprisoned.[147] Thomas Limpus, whose life story began this book, made the voyage to Goree on the West Africa coast, but conditions were so poor when he got there that, he claimed, 'the soldiers were drawn up in a circle on the parade, the Lieutenant of the island ordered us all into the middle of it, and told us we were all free men, and that we were to do the best we could, for he had no victuals'.[148] Having managed to work his passage home, Limpus was tried for returning from transportation and sentenced to be transported to America for life. While in Newgate awaiting trial, Limpus intermingled with other prisoners who were about to board the transport ship the *Swift*. Although the ship's stated destination was Nova Scotia, it was actually destined for Maryland.[149] Perhaps sensing the deception

[145] *PP, Journals of the House of Commons*, 40, 28 July 1785, p. 1161.
[146] Christopher, *A Merciless Place*, chs. 10–15.
[147] *LL*, set, 'Patrick Madan'; Old Bailey Proceedings, 9 January 1782, Supplementary Material (o17820109-2); *London Chronicle*, 28 July 1781.
[148] *LL*, set, 'Thomas Limpus'; Old Bailey Proceedings, 10 September 1783 (t17830910-41).
[149] A. Roger Ekirch, 'Great Britain's secret convict trade to America, 1783–1784', *American Historical Review*, 89:5 (December 1984), 1285–91.

involved, many convicts worried that they would actually be taken to Africa, the horrors of which had been retailed by Limpus.

When the *Swift* set sail on 28 August 1783, her 143 prisoners were fearful and rebellious; and as she beat her way down the Channel they rose up in mutiny. As Charles Keeling later testified, 'the reason of our first opposition' was 'that we were to go to Africa'.[150] Having taken over the ship, the convicts sailed it close to shore and cast anchor. Forty-eight felons escaped onto the smugglers' coast of Kent, sparking one of the largest manhunts in the history of eighteenth-century crime, only surpassed by that which had followed the Gordon Riots. Thirty-nine were eventually captured, and twenty-six were tried at the Old Bailey for returning from transportation. Restocked with food, the *Swift* did eventually make it to North America, landing in Baltimore in December. However, the convict population still harboured a visceral distrust of those responsible for their punishments, and when a second transport ship, the *Mercury*, headed to America the following year with 179 prisoners, they once again mutinied, this time off the coast of the Scilly Isles. At least 108 prisoners, including Thomas Limpus, escaped, but most were recaptured before reaching land and the ship continued on its way, only to be rejected by the newly independent Americans and forced to sail to Honduras, where the colonists also wanted to have nothing to do with it.[151] Faced with stiff rejection by both the convicts and the destination populations, the authorities were forced to find a new destination for transportation, eventually deciding on Botany Bay in 1786.

The First Fleet, comprising eleven ships holding almost 700 convicts, set off for Australia in May 1787, commencing an episode of forced migration that would ultimately ship 164,000 convicts from the UK to Australia over the next eighty-one years. While in numerical terms the reintroduction of transportation was clearly successful, it is important to note that it would never again dominate the penal system for felons the way it had prior to 1776. Whereas sentences of transportation account for just under two-thirds of all Old Bailey punishments between 1718 and 1776, transportation to Australia accounted for only a third of sentences between 1787 and 1800. This is not only because transportation to Australia was expensive and there was a new desire to attempt to reform those convicted of less serious offences in prisons but also because the underlying discontent among the convict population

---

[150] *LL*, Old Bailey Proceedings, 10 September 1783 (t17830910-20).
[151] Tim Hitchcock and Robert Shoemaker, *Tales from the Hanging Court* (London: Hodder Arnold, 2006), pp. 216–24; Ekirch, 'Great Britain's secret convict trade', 1290.

continued. An attempted mutiny on the Second Fleet was perhaps inspired by men who had participated in those on the *Swift* and *Mercury*. Parodoxically, it was only foiled through the intervention of a fellow transportee, Samuel Burt.[152]

The limits of policing

The authorities also addressed the crisis of order by attempting to beef up the policing of the metropolis. While the need for enhanced security for property was self-evident, the options for action and reform were limited. Immediately following the Gordon Riots, the military were given the primary responsibility for maintaining order, supplemented by neighbourhood associations. But the military were a target of popular hostility and were quickly withdrawn to their camps. In addition to largely middle-class concerns about infringements on English liberties, hostility among plebeians resulted from memories of the soldiers' violent repression of the riots, which did not fade quickly. In February 1782, twenty months after the riots, two soldiers from the guards (which had been deeply involved in the army response) were committed to New Prison on suspicion of stealing lead. As soon as they entered the prison, they were attacked by Patrick Madan and several other prisoners.[153] According to one of the soldiers, William Stobbart:

as soon as he went in among the other prisoners Patrick Madan seized hold of him and put him in to a large tub of filthy Urine & kept him there until he was near being suffocated declaring they would serve every soldier in like manner for preventing them getting out of Goal.[154]

This traditional community shaming punishment was often used against informers. We have seen that earlier, out of concern that a show of military force might result in a much more violent popular response, the military were kept out of sight when the executions of twenty-six convicted Gordon rioters took place not much more than a month after the riots ended. Instead, policing was carried out by voluntary associations such as the London Volunteers Association, and supernumerary constables.

---

[152] *LL*, set, 'Samuel Burt'; *London Chronicle*, 16 October 1790.
[153] *LL*, set, 'Patrick Madan'.
[154] *LL*, Middlesex Sessions: Sessions Papers, February 1782 (LMSMPS507510013). Emma Christopher suggests this was an individual response on Madan's part to the role of soldiers in thwarting his own escape attempts, but he appears to have had the support of other prisoners in targeting these men. Christopher, *A Merciless Place*, p. 210.

Figure 7.11 Patrick Madan (1782). Frontispiece: *The Life of Patrick Madan* (London: Alexander Hogg, [1782]). ©Trustees of the British Library.

Over the ensuing years, as anxiety about crime mounted, the need for improved policing in the metropolis was keenly felt, but the military were clearly not the answer. Nor was the creation of a metropolitan-wide police force, as proposed in the 'radical and in some ways extreme' London and Westminster Police Bill, a response to the crisis of order revealed by the Gordon Riots which was presented to parliament in 1785. The bill was scuttled owing to objections from City officials and the Middlesex justices, both of which wanted to preserve their traditional autonomy from central government interference.[155] Instead, reforms took place at the local level, in ways intended to prevent an escalation of the penal crisis. In the City, a city-wide night 'patrole' was created in 1785 for the purpose of moving on vagrants and loose, idle and disorderly men and women, quelling minor disturbances and preventing serious crime. Significantly, this preventative function meant that the patrole made few arrests. As Andrew Harris argues, the City authorities had no wish to add to the pressures on the overcrowded prisons.[156]

A similar reduction in ambition and focus on prevention was evident in changes at Bow Street, which had suffered both the physical destruction of Fielding's office and its records and substantial damage to its reputation. At hearings conducted during the riots, the names of witnesses who testified against the rioters were retailed to the press, which subsequently published them, allowing the rioters to take revenge. A few months later, following the death of John Fielding in September, a ruling at King's Bench in a suit brought by Thomas Ayrton led to the end of both press reporting of preliminary hearings and, apparently, the practice of holding regular 're-examinations' of suspects.[157] Forced to change its policies, Bow Street, now under the direction of Sampson Wright, returned to its original focus on prevention and detection, rather than prosecution. Nevertheless, the Runners continued to be treated with hostility or suspicion in parts of plebeian London; as one Runner, John Sayer, recalled in 1816, in the 1780s 'An officer could not walk in Duck-lane, Gravel-lane, or Cock-lane, without a party of five or six men along with him', or else gangs 'would have cut him to pieces if he was alone'.[158] While the Runners continued to be respected, and used, by many Londoners, they were distrusted by the poor. Perhaps the introduction of a government-funded armed foot patrol in 1782 to discourage highway robbery on the streets leading into London encountered less opposition, focused as it was on the periphery of the metropolis. As Beattie observes, the 1780s witnessed 'something of a

[155] Beattie, *First English Detectives*, pp. 147–59, quote at p. 159.
[156] Harris, *Policing the City*, pp. 38–52.
[157] Beattie, *First English Detectives*, pp. 101–2, 148.
[158] *PP*, 'Report from the committee on the state of the police of the metropolis', 1816, p. 212 (parlipapers.chadwyck.co.uk, 2 Jan. 2014).

transition in London policing' towards a new focus on prevention, 'in opposition to what some were coming to regard as the brutality of Fielding's catch-and-punish policing'.[159]

Supplementing these limited reforms of official policing, there was a return to voluntary policing in 1787 in the form of yet another reformation of manners campaign, launched by the Proclamation Society. Founded by William Wilberforce with substantial elite backing, the immediate stimulus for the new Society was a proclamation issued by the king against drunkenness, gaming, profane swearing and cursing, lewdness, profanation of the sabbath and 'other dissolute, immoral, or disorderly practices'.[160] However, while a campaign against vice was an entirely conventional response to a perceived growth in crime and disorder, lessons had been learned from the opposition encountered in earlier campaigns and the tactics used this time were far less dependent on the aggressive use of criminal justice. As Joanna Innes has commented, the campaign 'was marked by tactical caution', as efforts were targeted at convincing sinners to reform or, if that failed, encouraging existing legal officials to carry out their responsibilities more rigorously. Unlike previous societies, informers were used sparingly.[161] Rather than prosecute large numbers of offenders, supporters relied on high-profile prosecutions of a small number of 'examples' as a means of discouraging vice. Nonetheless, once again the reformers encountered substantial opposition, including vexatious prosecutions, from the middle and lower classes, and by the end of the century its campaign against vice had ended. As Innes concludes, 'the cause of moral reform, as the Proclamation Society had implemented it, had failed to win the hearts and minds of the people'.[162] Despite widespread concerns about public order, plebeian resistance helped ensure that changes in policing in the 1780s were limited. Not only was the military isolated and the powers of Bow Street and the new City 'patrole' constrained, but popular and legal opposition to the systematic prosecution of vice also meant that a traditional reformation of manners campaign was no longer feasible.[163]

---

[159] Beattie, *First English Detectives*, pp. 9, 140–3.

[160] *London Gazette*, 29 May 1787 (Burney Collection: www.galegroup.com, 2 Jan. 2014).

[161] Joanna Innes, 'Politics and morals: the reformation of manners movement in later eighteenth-century England', in Eckhart Hellmuth, ed., *The Transformation of Political Culture: England and Germany in the Late Eighteenth Century* (Oxford and New York: German Historical Institute, 1990), p. 75. See also M. J. D. Roberts, *Making English Morals: Voluntary Association and Moral Reform in England, 1787–1886* (Cambridge University Press, 2004).

[162] Innes, 'Politics and morals', p. 118.

[163] Faramerz Dabhoiwala, 'Sex and societies for moral reform, 1688–1800', *Journal of British Studies*, 46:2 (2007), 290–319.

Poor relief contested

The parish system of poor relief was to some extent shielded from the direct impact of the crisis of order and punishment. There is little evidence that the elderly and infirm men and women who formed the majority of workhouse populations engaged in active resistance or political violence. The systems of relief and judicial policy were nevertheless intertwined, and as policing and punishment evolved, so too did parochial policies. The role that ensured that Sampson Rainsforth would be an early and prominent victim of the Gordon Riots was his past service as the high constable of Westminster, and his testimony against the rioters at Bow Street.[164] But also important was his service as a vestryman, then churchwarden, and by June 1780, upper or senior churchwarden of St Clement Danes, where he acted in the interests of the ratepayers. Indeed, Rainsforth spent the early part of the evening of 5 June chairing a committee of churchwardens and overseers for the parish, to arrange contracts for supplying the workhouse with 'Forty Chaldron of the best Windsor Ponton Tanfield Moor Coals'.[165] He went home after this meeting, only to be dragged from his bed later the same night and forced to watch his furniture and stock in trade torched by the rioters.[166]

Rainsforth went on to serve the parish as senior overseer of the poor throughout much of the early 1780s and was intimately involved in the reformulation of poor relief during these years. These multiple roles, also evident in the mixed business of select vestries, reflect the uncertain boundary that existed between criminal justice and parish poor relief, and the extent to which many people were obliged to fill roles in both systems as they progressed through a series of annual appointments. Poor relief and criminal justice were perhaps divided by their perceived objects: the deserving and the disorderly respectively. However, they were tied into a single whole both by personnel like Rainsforth, with their desire to defend the social order in a time of upheaval, and by the needs, behaviour and expectations of London's working population.

We have seen in previous chapters that from at least mid-century expenditure, both per pauper and per capita, in London on poor relief increased significantly, and that from the 1720s poor relief in the capital was characterised by a remarkably high reliance on institutional provision, both in parish-run and in private-contract workhouses. In

---

[164] de Castro, *Gordon Riots*, p. 44; Beattie, *First English Detectives*, p. 101.
[165] LL, St Clement Danes Parish: Minute Books of Parish Vestry Sub-Committees, 5 June 1780 (WCCDMO361030027).
[166] Hibbert, *King Mob*, p. 73.

particular, driven by both pauper demand and statutory 'reform', relief levels grew substantially from the mid-1760s through the middle of the following decade. But from the mid-1770s, across the capital, parish authorities made great efforts to reduce expenditure and generally succeeded in stabilising costs, despite the static or falling living standards of these years for London workers.[167] In this same period (1775–87), a series of parliamentary enquiries spearheaded by Thomas Gilbert into the state of poor relief and workhouses called attention to London's relatively high level of expenditure and extreme reliance on institutional care. Like Jonas Hanway, Gilbert was essentially sympathetic to the plight of the parish poor, but his inquiries exposed a system of relief that must have appeared increasingly expensive to vestrymen and ratepayers.[168]

The resulting dialogue between parish bureaucrats and the poor was unequal and led to a series of policy innovations that substantially disadvantaged the latter. Some parishes, such as St Dionis Backchurch, became ever more reliant on contract workhouses, gradually withdrawing from the provision of outdoor relief and the provision of annuities for elderly widows. In a small parish like St Dionis, these changes both physically removed parish pensioners from a tightly knit community and, in the minds of the poor at least, threatened their ability to appeal to the Lord Mayor. Significant for more Londoners were developments concerning the relief provided to thousands of paupers in the extensive workhouses of Westminster and Middlesex.[169] Here, the same pressures to reduce parochial obligations to the poor led to the creation of a more bureaucratic system of relief. In turn, these changes exacerbated the problems faced by the system of vagrant removal (which substantially overlapped with poor relief).

Sampson Rainsforth's parish of St Clement Danes was in many respects typical of these large extramural parishes. Following ten years of dramatically increasing parish expenditure (rising from £2,645 per annum in 1764 to an average annual expenditure of £4,592 in the mid-1770s), and the establishment of a new workhouse (finally) in 1773, St

---

[167] See Leonard Schwarz, 'The standard of living in the long run: London, 1700–1860', *Economic History Review*, 2nd Series, 38:1 (1985), 28, Fig. 1 and 36–40, Appendix 1.

[168] The best recent analysis of the returns generated by Gilbert's activities is David Green, *Pauper Capital: London and the Poor Law, 1790–1870* (Farnham, Surrey: Ashgate, 2010), ch. 2.

[169] The 1776 inquiry found that London as a whole had at least eighty workhouses with spaces for over 16,000 paupers: *PP*, 'Abstract of the returns made by the overseers of the poor, 1776' (15 May 1777) (parlipapers.chadwyck.co.uk, 2 Jan. 2014); Green, *Pauper Capital*, pp. 57–64.

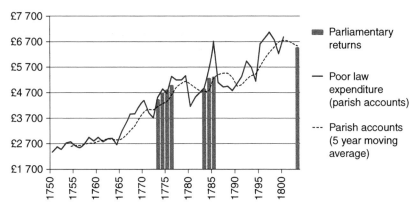

Figure 7.12 St Clement Danes, poor law expenditure, 1750–1803.
Online data set: St Clement Danes Poor Law Expenditure 1706–1803.
xlsx. See also *PP*, 'Abstract of the answers and returns made ... relative
to the expense and maintenance of the poor in England', 1803–4,
p. 724.

Clement's was faced with both public criticism of its care for the over
300 paupers maintained in its workhouse and growing demands that
expenditure should be kept within bounds.

In some respects, the establishment of a workhouse in 1773 had left
the parish open to the demands of the poor – institutional relief systems
were uniquely dependent on the good will of inmates to function
effectively. However, in the first instance, it was the care of dependent
children that provided the driving force in the evolution of relief, and a
touchstone issue for the parish, and for poor parents. St Clement Danes
had been singled out for public opprobrium by Jonas Hanway in the
1760s for the apparently high death rates suffered by children in parish
care, but despite significantly improving its system of record keeping
and sending children to nurse in Enfield, the parish continued to suffer
a high mortality rate. Removing infant children to nurse in the countryside might have been marginally healthier, but it disadvantaged both the
children and their parents by making it more difficult for them to keep
in contact.

In company with many other London parishes, and driven at least in
part by a desire to shift long-term parochial obligations to distant communities, St Clement Danes decided to take this policy of separating
parents and children even further. In 1782 the parish contracted to send
girls to work at a silk mill in Hampshire. Ten girls, the youngest six-year-
old Ann Benzie, were dispatched on 2 July. At the same meeting, the

parish sought to limit its responsibility for the care of even younger children by boarding them with the Foundling Hospital.[170]

This was the first of a series of decisions taken in the crisis years of the early 1780s which attempted a thorough reconfiguration of the system of relief provided by St Clement Danes at the expense of the poor. In the first instance, these changes were precipitated by rising costs and the issue of the work expected of the workhouse inmates. Almost precisely a year after the children were first sent to Hampshire, Sampson Rainsforth led the way in seeking to find some way of making a profit from the poor. In July 1783, at Rainsforth's behest, a committee was created to investigate other workhouses, and to seek the 'most effectual means to Employ the Poor'.[171] In most parishes with large workhouses, this kind of inquiry was set on foot every few years in the vain hope of finding ways of squeezing advantage from the poor (the most common occupation was spinning mop yarn, which could be produced with the minimum of care and effort). For the most part, and given the limited power of workhouse administrators to force the poor to work, these kinds of inquiries ran into the ground.

Unusually, however, on this occasion workhouse inmates themselves appear to have become involved, and, in the words of the parish clerk, 'agitated', with regard to their employment.[172] The inmates posted a petition in the workroom, which has not survived but appears to have been precipitated by a threatened loss of earnings to the poor. In most workhouses a proportion of the tiny income generated through manufacturing was distributed as 'encouragement' money. In this instance, the 'agitation' led to a rapid response: 'Ordered that the Petition in the Mop Room be forthwith taken down and the Machine for Opening the Wool be immediately put into repair so as to Employ the Poor in spinning Mop yarn as heretofore'.[173]

Over the next twenty months, as workhouse expenditure rose to unprecedented heights, a new labour contractor was brought in and desperate attempts were made to secure cheaper supplies – to little purpose. Finally, in the autumn of 1784 the parish decided on a comprehensive review of its provision and, as a first step, ordered the creation of a unique workhouse census to record the details of all the inmates in the house – 'their Christian and Sir Names – Their Age – the time and

[170] LL, St Clement Danes Parish: Minute Books, 22 July 1782 (WCCDMO361030051).
[171] LL, St Clement Danes Parish: Minute Books, 1 July 1783 (WCCDMO361030066).
[172] LL, St Clement Danes Parish: Minute Books, 2 September 1783 (WCCDMO361030073).
[173] LL, St Clement Danes Parish: Minute Books, 8 July 1783 (WCCDMO361030067).

Manner of their gaining Settlements in this Parish' – all of which was designed to remove the unsettled and the disorderly from the house and thus reduce expenses.[174] The resulting document listed 393 individuals, and a measure of its significance can be found in the numbers in the house by August of the same year – only 280.[175] Over a hundred people had been shunted onto the streets, or removed to another parish, either as a pauper or a vagrant. Some had no doubt left voluntarily to take up seasonal work in the spring, but many others were forced to leave.

For the children of the workhouse, however, a different fate awaited them. At the same meeting that determined the creation of the census, a further resolution was passed 'That an Advertizement be inserted in the Daily Advertizer that there are several Children, Boys and Girls in the Workhouse of a fit Age to be placed out Apprentices'.[176] After several months' negotiations, the parish agreed to supply a steady stream of parish apprentices, as young as eight, to the new mills of Lancashire and Yorkshire. In the next five years, twenty-two girls and sixty-one boys were apprenticed by the parish. Most went to John Birch's Backbarrow Mill, near Lake Windermere in Lancashire (now part of Cumbria).[177]

While small City parishes sent their paupers to contract workhouses on the edge of the metropolis, beyond the reach of the Lord Mayor and community oversight, parishes such as St Clement's sent pauper children hundreds of miles away to large factories where they had no friends and no family, where Sunday visiting would be unknown, and where, however supportable the food and labour might be (and the parish regularly inspected conditions), each child was incalculably disadvantaged by mere distance.

In one step, St Clement's reduced the likelihood of future demands on its resources, drove the marginal poor from its doors and attempted to gain a new control over its costs. In pursuing these initiatives, it was not alone. While the parish's workhouse census is unique, its decision to apprentice its pauper children to factory labour put it at the centre of a metropolitan-wide transformation. Following early experiments in apprenticing children to silk weaving in the south-east, from the spring

---

[174] *LL*, St Clement Danes Parish: Minute Books, 1 February 1785 (WCCDMO 361030102).

[175] *LL*, St Clement Danes Parish: List of Workhouse Inmates in 1785.

[176] *LL*, St Clement Danes Parish: Minute Books, 1 February 1785 (WCCDMO 361030104).

[177] In total the parish sent 99 girls and 180 boys in the three decades up to 1815. Katrina Honeyman, *Child Workers in England, 1780–1820: Parish Apprentices and the Making of the Early Industrial Labour Force* (Aldershot: Ashgate, 2007), Table 4.1, pp. 59–60.

of 1785 most of the larger London parishes settled on industrial apprenticeships in Yorkshire and Lancashire. The first group of five young boys left the workhouse of St Martin in the Fields for the mill owned by Thomas and William Douglas at Eccles in Lancashire on 28 May 1785.[178]

St Clement's was not far behind. Its first wagon full of twelve- and thirteen-year-old boys left for the same mill on 25 November of the following year. Among their number, was twelve-year-old James Vobe.[179] He was the fourth of six children, the son of Jane and Thomas Vobe, who had kept the Indian Queen alehouse in Holywell Street until the family fell into crisis in 1781 and were forced to seek parish support. In being sent north, James was effectively separated from a large family, including his older brother Thomas, who was by this time gainfully employed outside the workhouse as a waiter, his older sisters Elizabeth and Ann, and his younger sister Jane.[180] It is unlikely he ever saw any of them again; least likely his older brother Thomas, who was sentenced to seven years transportation in 1788 and shipped to Australia on the *Surprise*, as part of the Second Fleet, in 1790.[181] In 1786 the example set by St Martin's and St Clement's was followed by St Giles in the Fields, St Mary Lambeth, and St James Piccadilly.[182]

However, the new policies of exclusion and industrial apprenticeship could not stop the demands placed on the parish by the poor. When in 1786, Mary Brown, a seventeen-year-old prostitute, went into labour, the discussion that ensued between her, Mrs Davies (who kept the lodging house from which she worked), and Ann Pope reflected the continuing self-conscious manipulation of the parishes of London by the poor. First, and despite living in Jackson's Alley, in St Paul Covent Garden, they discussed which parish workhouse was the best place to give birth – St Martin in the Fields or St Clement Danes – and quickly determined that the latter was the best 'casualty parish' in London and that Mary should apply there. When Mary presented herself at the door, deep in labour, the workhouse mistress had no choice but to admit her to the lying-in ward, where she rapidly gave birth to an illegitimate boy named

---

[178] *LL*, St Martin in the Fields Workhouse Registers, May 1785: Charles Stuart (smdswhr_582_58254), Joseph Barnes (smdswhr_591_59117), Jeremiah Sparks (smdswhr_622_62244), Hughes Twendale (smdswhr_624_62431) and John Hughes (smdswhr_628_62863).

[179] *LL*, set, 'James Vobe'.

[180] *LL*, Edward Duncan, 'Thomas Vobe, b. 1775'; Edward Duncan, 'Jane Vobe, b. 1775'.

[181] *Convict Stockade: A Wiki for Australian Convict Researchers* (historyaustralia.org.au/twconvic, 2 Jan. 2014).

[182] Honeyman, *Child Workers*, pp. 59–77.

John. The child automatically gained a settlement in the parish by virtue of being born illegitimate. But Mary likewise was able to tell a story that gave her a legal claim to stay. In a long and revealing settlement statement recorded several days after the birth, she claimed 'she was born on board ship coming from Ireland', meaning that she was settled in neither Ireland nor England, and therefore impossible to remove from St Clement's.[183]

Just as accused criminals and convicts sought new ways of working an increasingly oppressive system, so paupers were able, in the face of substantial cost-cutting measures and new initiatives, to find imaginative means of securing the relief they needed. Despite the best efforts of Sampson Rainsforth and his fellow parish officers, the cost of relieving the poor of St Clement's, which had briefly stabilised around 1780, renewed its upward trajectory, indicating the success of paupers like Mary Brown in frustrating every attempt to save on the rates.

New approaches to vagrancy

At the awkward intersection between poor relief and criminal justice, the treatment of vagrancy also substantially evolved in these years, reflecting not simply harsher official attitudes but also the demands and expectations of the poor. Rates of committal to Bridewell (and probably London's other houses of correction) soared in the first few years of the 1780s, reflecting both a new intolerance of minor street disorder following the Gordon Riots and the fears created by the arrival of newly demobilised soldiers at the ragged end of the American War. Almost 3,000 men and women were committed to Bridewell in 1783, by far the largest annual total in the century, despite long-running concerns about the prison's corrupting influence on those incarcerated. Many were vagrants of one description or another, sentenced to suffer the usual punishment of a week or a month at hard labour and a whipping. But by 1784 the resulting overcrowding, in combination with the pressures created by the demobilisation of soldiers and sailors in the winter and spring of that year, seems to have contributed to a fundamental change in the system of vagrant punishment and removal. In that year the number of commitments to Bridewell fell to 612, while the number of vagrants passed from the City to Middlesex for removal to their place of settlement grew. This reached 2,231 individuals in the twelve months following October 1784. While continuing to arrest and remove

---

[103] *LL*, St Clement Danes Parish: Pauper Settlement, Vagrancy and Bastardy Exams, 26 January 1786 (WCCDEP358000216).

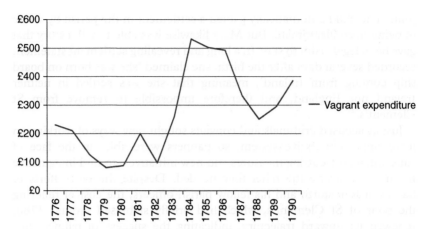

Figure 7.13 City of London vagrancy expenditure, 1776–1790. NB:
Includes the cost of apprehending and passing vagrants, as well as
rewards and miscellaneous costs. LMA, City of London: 'City's cash
accounts', 1699–1801, COL/CHD/CT/01/023-068; Online data set:
City of London Vagrant Expenditure 1738–92.xlsx.

vagrants in large numbers, the City had abandoned its legal obligation
to punish them in Bridewell and directly passed them instead. Like
many of the dependent poor, and (eventually) convicts, those labelled
as vagrants were simply expelled from the metropolis.[184] However, the
difference in this case is that some 'vagrants' apparently chose to be
removed.

When Henry Adams succeeded his father as the 'vagrant contractor'
for Middlesex in 1774, the average number of vagrants carried from the
houses of correction to the county border numbered around 1,300 per
year. But with this change in City policy, in early 1783 Adams was
overwhelmed by the number of vagrants passed into his hands. When
the total reached over 4,000 in the twelve months after October 1784,
Adams complained bitterly to his paymasters, the Middlesex sessions,
and presented evidence that the vast majority of this increase came from
the City of London. He complained that the individuals passing through
his hands 'do not appear to be Objects of the Vagrants Laws' and many
were 'dangerously Ill some of which have died in his Hands'.[185]

---

[184] Tim Hitchcock, 'The London vagrancy crisis of the 1780s', *Rural History*, 24, special
issue 1 (2013), 59–72.
[185] *LL*, Middlesex Sessions: General Orders of the Court, April 1786
(LMSMGO556090234).

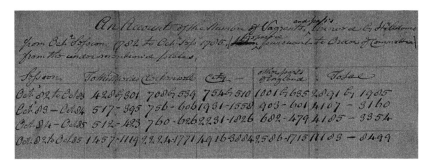

Figure 7.14 Vagrants removed via Henry Adams, broken down by place passed from, October 1782 – October 1785. *LL*, Middlesex Sessions: Sessions Papers, April 1786 (LMSMPS508090267).

Adams concluded that the reason the number of vagrants passed from the City had increased exponentially 'arose from the ease with which passes were obtained from the Magistrates of the City of London' and that 'the City Magistrates never ... Cause the Vagrants to Be Whippd or Imprisoned ... previous to their being passed'.[186] This sparked a furious letter to the Lord Mayor, who promised to investigate – although there is no evidence that he ever did so.

Thus, vagrant removal in the City changed in the 1780s. In part, this may have resulted from changes in policing, including more aggressive regulation of street traders from 1784 and the creation of the more preventative-focused City patrole in 1785.[187] More generally, it may reflect a combination of a short-term crisis resulting from demobilisation and increasing intolerance of the less savoury inhabitants of the streets.[188] However, it may also reflect a recognition that the City simply did not have the facilities to punish vagrants as the law directed. Concern about prisoner unrest may have discouraged its officials from continuing to commit large numbers of vagrants to Bridewell.

There is evidence that the poor took advantage of this change. Some Londoners appear to have used a vagrancy conviction as a relatively painless pathway to free transportation, medical care and accommodation. Being arrested as a vagrant required a certain wilfulness, and the

---

[186] *LL*, Middlesex Sessions: General Orders of the Court, April 1786 (LMSMGO556090233); Middlesex Sessions: Sessions Papers, April 1786 (LMSMPS508090268).
[187] Harris, *Policing the City*, pp. 45–6.
[188] Douglas Hay suggests that 130,000 men were discharged in the spring of 1783: 'War, dearth and theft in the eighteenth century: the record of the English Courts', *Past & Present*, 95 (1982), 139.

growing numbers being passed through the City suggest that its policies made arrest for this offence attractive for seasonal migrants and the Irish poor, once it became clear that they would not be punished in Bridewell before being removed.[189] Others, as Adams's complaint suggests, simply went to the Lord Mayor and requested a pass. Given the absence of first-person evidence from those concerned, these are difficult points to prove, but they are supported by both a demographic change among those removed (now more often single adult men, perhaps travelling in search of work) and a reminiscence of James Dawson Burn from the early nineteenth century.[190] As a child, Dawson recalled having been taken by his mother to the Mansion House in the City to apply 'for a pass to Hexham, in Northumberland ... which she had no difficulty in obtaining'. Armed with this pass, the family travelled northwards, bene-fiting from the support parishes were obliged to provide removed vagrants:

> As my mother preferred taking the journey at her ease, and her own time, she frequently had the benefit of the cash that the overseers would have had to pay for sending us forward in a conveyance, and at the same time she had the advantage of the intermediate relieving officers, who were often glad to get clear of us at the expense of a shilling or two.[191]

This system could also be used by paupers to obtain medical support. When Adams began to refuse to accept vagrants who were ill, the City was forced to provide medical care for any vagrant it wished to pass, until they were well enough to be able to endure a long journey in a cart. As a result, the City's medical costs began to increase in the late 1780s, reaching almost £1,800 per annum in the 1790s, for the care of hun-dreds of vagrants who appear to have simply presented themselves at the Mansion House and Guildhall Justice Rooms with a demand for a pass.[192]

Just as the pressure on the prisons eased with the departure of the First Fleet and the waning crime wave, the immediate crisis of vagrant removal eased in the latter years of the 1780s. However, the City never returned to a comprehensive policy of punishing vagrants. In 1790, when a com-mittee of the Middlesex bench examined a group of three vagrants passed

---

[189] Tim Hitchcock, *Down and Out in Eighteenth-Century London* (London: Hambledon and London, 2004), ch. 7.

[190] Tim Hitchcock, Adam Crymble and Louise Falcini, 'Loose, idle and disorderly: vagrant removal in late eighteenth-century Middlesex', *Social History*, Vol.39, 4, 2014, 509–27.

[191] James Dawson Burn, *The Autobiography of a Beggar Boy*, ed. David Vincent (London: Europa, 1978), p. 58.

[192] Hitchcock, 'The London vagrancy crisis', 62.

from the City, it ruefully observed in its report that they had been 'advised to go to the Lord Mayor for passes which they did, and had them of course'.[193] As with parochial poor relief, the City's attempt to reform its procedures for apprehending vagrants in the tense years following the Gordon Riots failed to prevent the poor from exploiting the system for their own ends. Consequently, vagrancy would remain an item of concern to the authorities in the early 1790s.

Refusing the royal pardon

The culmination of this escalating pattern of plebeian resistance was played out at the Old Bailey in the second half of the decade. The case which made William Garrow's name was that of Henry Aikles, who was tried for returning from transportation in 1785 and whose case demonstrated that a transportee could return if conditions forced him to (in this case, illness prevented Aikles from even embarking).[194] This was also the first case in which Garrow asserted that the court could not 'extend the law beyond the letter of it'.[195] It was a complex case that brought to the public's attention both the dubious legality of the legal fiction the court was attempting to impose through the use of the hulks (that prisoners were being transported 'beyond the sea') and the ability of a smart brief to cut a swath through the apparently secure authority of the crown. The implications of Aikles's case exercised the court through the late 1780s, and it was later referred to as a precedent for others caught returning from transportation or escaping from the hulks. For those awaiting trial, it must have exposed a weakness in the court's armour which would become more evident as the plans for the new penal colony in New South Wales developed in just these years.

Nonetheless, by this point there was no question but that transportation would be resumed, despite the setbacks on the voyages to Africa and America. Simon Devereaux has argued that from the point of view of the authorities transportation remained an ideal punishment because it appeared to fulfil all the potentially contradictory expectations of the purposes of punishment at this time: severity, deterrence and reform.[196]

---

[193] *LL*, Middlesex Sessions: General Orders of the Court, January 1791 (LMSMGO556100109).
[194] *LL*, set, 'Henry Aikles'.
[195] *LL*, Old Bailey Proceedings, 14 September 1785 (t17850914-181).
[196] Simon Devereaux, 'In place of death: transportation, penal practices, and the English State, 1770–1830', in Carolyn Strange, ed., *Qualities of Mercy: Justice, Punishment and Discretion* (Vancouver: UBC Press, 1996), pp. 52–76.

At the same time, it also addressed the continuing pressures caused by prisoners in London's overcrowded prisons and hulks. In the 1786 letter from Lord Sydney which finally announced the choice of Botany Bay in Australia as the new destination, the first justification given for the resumption of transportation was that 'the several gaols and places for confinement of felons in this kingdom being in so crowded a state that the greatest danger is to be apprehended, not only from their escape, but from infectious distempers, which may hourly be expected to break out amongst them'.[197]

While disease was a problem, the 'distemper' of convict rebellion also worried the authorities. That rebellious attitudes among convicts were still present in Newgate in the late 1780s can be seen in the phenomenon of 'refusing the royal pardon' – the dramatic refusal by nineteen men and women in the spring and autumn of 1789 to accept transportation to New South Wales in preference to death.[198]

The first refusenik, however, was not among the men and women who stood before the court in 1789, but appeared three years earlier. His name was Samuel Burt and his defence counsel was once again William Garrow.[199] In court it emerged that he had determined to forge an order to pay £100 with the precise intention of being caught, tried and executed. He was a lovelorn apprentice who was denied the object of his love. Garrow understandably entered a defence of insanity, but Burt was convicted nonetheless. At the next session his sentence was respited to transportation for life – an offer which Burt eloquently turned down, so that he would still be hanged. He only finally accepted transportation to New South Wales after the object of his affection died from a fever contracted while visiting him in Newgate. At the session starting 22 February 1787, Burt accepted his fate in a long-winded speech, before making room for Henry Aikles to stand up immediately after him to hear the outcome of his own case. Both Burt's initial refusal and the legal

---

[197] 'Lord Sydney to the Lords Commissioners of the Treasury, 16 August 1786', in A. Aspinal, ed., *English Historical Documents 1783–1832* (London: Routledge, 1996), p. 781.

[198] See Lynn MacKay, 'Refusing the royal pardon: London capital convicts and the reactions of the courts and press, 1789', *London Journal*, 28 (2003), 21–40; Simon Devereaux, '"Death is more welcome to me than this pardon": execution, transportation, and convict resistance in London during the 1780s', *Proceedings of the University of Queensland History Research Group*, 13 (2002), 53–65 (espace.library.uq.edu.au, 2 Jan. 2014); Simon Devereaux, 'Imposing the royal pardon: execution, transportation, and convict resistance in London, 1789', *Law and History Review*, 25:1 (2007), 101–38; Hitchcock and Shoemaker, *Tales*, pp. 225–33.

[199] *LL*, set, 'Samuel Burt'.

changes implied by the precedent set by Aikles sent strong messages to the prisoners next door.[200]

The first news of the progress of the settlement in Australia by the First Fleet reached London in the last week of March 1789, and throughout April the newspapers were full of optimistic accounts of the landing at Botany Bay, while possibly less rosy accounts drawn from direct experience circulated through the waterside communities of London.[201] At the end of the April sessions, twenty-three women who had been sentenced to death were brought before the bar at the Old Bailey, where they received the news that they were to be pardoned on condition of transportation to New South Wales as part of the Second Fleet, which was just then in preparation. Of these women, seven simply refused to accept their pardons. They proclaimed their innocence and, in the words of Sarah Mills, declared they 'would rather die than go out of my own country to be devoured by savages'.[202]

After furious negotiations with the court, and under the threat of almost immediate execution, the women held out over the course of two more sessions. It was only after being held in solitary confinement in Newgate on bread and water, and following the desperate intervention of William Garrow, ferrying messages between the women and the judge, that they were finally compelled to accept transportation.[203]

At the September sessions that year, as the Second Fleet continued its preparations for departure, a further twelve men refused the king's pardon. Some claimed innocence, questioning their treatment at the hands of the court. John Durham complained bitterly of his conviction on the basis of uncorroborated evidence and declared: 'I think I ought to suffer as a man; I am very sorry I must refuse it'.[204] In this instance, it was not until the October sessions that all the men could be convinced to accept transportation.

The majority of these seven women and twelve men who refused pardons that year had been in prison for many months – many for as

---

[200] Burt was initially tried in July 1786, and found guilty and sentenced to death, though both the jury and prosecutor recommended the court give him mercy. His sentence was respited until January, at which time Burt refused the pardon and was remanded in custody. At the next sessions he finally accepted transportation to New South Wales. *LL* Old Bailey Proceedings, 19 July 1786 (t17860719-31 and s17860719-1), 10 January 1787 (s17870110-1) and 21 February 1787 (o17870221-2).

[201] *The Times*, March 27, 1789, 4; and April 13, 1789, 1; *The Times Digital Archive* (thetimes.co.uk/tto/archive/, 2 Jan. 2014).

[202] *LL*, set, 'Sarah Mills'; Old Bailey Proceedings, 22 April 1789 (o17890422-1).

[203] Hitchcock and Shoemaker, *Tales*, pp. 229–32.

[204] *LL*, set, 'John Durham'; Old Bailey Proceedings, 9 September 1789, Punishment Summary (s17890909-1).

long as two years between arrest, trial and the final offer of transportation – and must have been familiar with Burt's case, and with the state of preparation of the Second Fleet. Of the twelve men who refused the royal pardon in 1789, four had been defended by Garrow at their original trials.

Eventually, all the convicts caved in and accepted their pardons – though several did eventually avoid transportation. However, no one in the courtroom (or in the wider population of plebeian London) could fail to have marked the apparent impotence of the judges at the Old Bailey in the face of this concerted opposition. When Judge Rose declared to Mary Burgess on 22 April that 'you certainly will be ordered immediately for execution', and she answered, 'Well, I am very glad to hear it. I do not care how soon', and yet the threatened order was not given, the balance of authority in the courtroom had changed.[205]

Conclusion

The fundamental transformations in criminal justice and the evolution of poor relief that marked the 1780s cannot be understood without acknowledging the crisis of obedience precipitated by the Gordon Riots. Reforms were driven not only by bureaucratic impetus, cost-cutting and (at times) humanitarian concerns but also by a fundamental fear of rebellion and disorder. Nor should we underestimate the impact of wider plebeian pressure and resistance in shaping social policy. The demands of the poor forced City and parish officials to change their approaches to poor relief and vagrancy, while the growing number of defendants obtaining legal representation enhanced the role of counsel in the criminal trial and increased its impact. Each official initiative to address the crises caused by the interruption of transportation, the Gordon Riots and the post-war crime wave, whether it was the introduction of the hulks, the surge in executions and whipping, the increase in incarceration or the attempts to implement new forms of policing and new strategies for removing vagrants, was circumscribed by plebeian behaviour, both actual and anticipated.

By 1789 the two most common punishment sentences at the Old Bailey were imprisonment and transportation, the public punishments of death and whipping having declined precipitously since their peaks in the mid-1780s. As these public punishments declined in part owing to concerns about the disorder they might occasion, rebuilt prisons and

---

[205] *LL*, Old Bailey Proceedings 22 April 1789 (o17890422-1).

transportation to Australia came to dominate punishment strategies. This dominance resulted from the crisis created by the overcrowding of prisons and hulks and the ensuing escapes and mutinies, which forced London's judicial authorities to accelerate the pace of penal reform.

As the increased use of transportation to a faraway continent and imprisonment, often with hard labour, suggests, the consequences of this transformation did not necessarily work to the advantage of plebeian Londoners, but they had nonetheless played a fundamental role in shaping it. Without the pressures generated in these years, the pace and the trajectory of change in both penal reform and poor relief would have been very different. Even the refusals of the royal pardon had significant consequences. While in the end the convicts accepted their pardons and most endured transportation, the experience prompted the authorities to revise the processes of sentencing and pardoning in order to reduce the amount of discretion exercised, both by the courts and by convicts. From 1797 conditional pardons were tantamount to orders: it was no longer necessary for convicts to accept a pardon in order for it to take effect.[206]

By the end of the decade, transportation to Australia and improved economic conditions had reduced the pressures on criminal justice and the poor law, but the relationships between authority and deference, governors and governed, had been transformed. The new dispensation is epitomised in the 1789 refusals, when a group of convicts momentarily challenged the very foundations of the penal system. However, these men and women formed only a vocal and visible fragment of a wider community. If the prisons and transport ships formed the debating chambers in which the terms of new attitudes and loyalties were hammered out, those attitudes soon spilled beyond the prison walls. As the numbers hanged grew temporarily to unsupportable levels, as the children of the poor were shipped beyond the love of a parent, as a generation of young men and women pined in prison and rotted on shipboard and as parish worthies turned a hardened face to the suffering of their neighbours, a new anger was created. That anger was not informed by fine words or clearly articulated programmes for change, but it formed a new caesura which divided many plebeian Londoners from those who governed them. The government's crackdown, following the French Revolution, on suspicious behaviour and dissent in the 1790s further exacerbated these divisions, but Londoners now possessed an array of tactics which would allow them to fight back and to continue to shape social policy.

---

[206] Devereaux, 'Imposing the royal pardon', 101–38.

8 Epilogue: The 1790s

Lives

Thomas Limpus, with whom this book began, spent the 1790s in Australia.[1] While attempts in the previous decade to transport him and others 'beyond the seas' – to Africa, revolutionary America, Canada and Honduras – had been stopgap and incompetent measures that collapsed in the face of plebeian resistance and settler opposition, his transportation to Australia was permanent. Sheer distance, combined with military power, limited indigenous opposition and a colonialist agenda that placed a new positive value on his life and labour, ensured that he would stay put. He died on Norfolk Island sometime before 1801.[2]

Many of the other men and women who had stymied the best efforts of the judicial establishment over the course of the 1770s and 1780s also ended their lives in Australia. Robert Sideaway had been first convicted and sentenced to the hulks soon after Thomas Limpus in 1778.[3] Like Limpus, he was later charged with returning from transportation, in his case following a daring escape from Newgate prison dressed in women's clothes.[4] Despite his counsel's attempt to secure his release on a technicality, Sideaway was transported on the First Fleet. He went on to establish a successful bakery, and opened Australia's first theatre in 1796. He died there in 1809.[5] So did Mary Burgess, whom the clerk at the Home Office described as: '5 f[oot] 4 in[ches, with] Grey Eyes, Brown hair [and a] Sallow Complexion'.[6] In the spring and summer of 1789, she had been one of the

---

[1] *LL*, set, 'Thomas Limpus'.
[2] For more on Limpus, see Emma Christopher, *A Merciless Place: The Lost Story of Britain's Convict Disaster in Africa* (Oxford University Press, 2011), *passim*.
[3] *LL*, set, 'Robert Sideaway'.
[4] *LL*, Old Bailey Proceedings, 16 October 1782 (t17821016-35).
[5] Vivien Parsons, 'Robert Sideaway 1758–1809', in *Australian Dictionary of Biography*, Vol. II (Manchester University Press, 1967) (adb.anu.edu.au/biography, 2 Jan. 2014).
[6] *LL*, set, 'Mary Burgess'; Home Office: Criminal Registers of Prisoners in Middlesex and the City, September 1793 – September 1794 (NAHOCR700070012).

men and women who had publicly challenged the court at the Old Bailey by refusing the royal pardon. Following an escape from her transport ship, the *Lady Juliana*, the night before it was due to weigh anchor, she spent the next three years selling old clothes in Petticoat Lane before she was finally recaptured. She arrived in Australia on 4 October 1794.[7]

However, if these rebels were finally forced into exile, many others remained in the capital, continuing to successfully play the system. Sarah Cowden, for instance, had stood beside Mary Burgess when they refused their pardons in 1789 and then escaped with her from the *Lady Juliana*. But unlike Burgess, Cowden made a successful fist of her freedom. She had been raised a parish pauper in St Botolph Aldgate and appeared together with her three sisters in the local version of Jonas Hanway's 'Register of Parish Children'. Her experience of dealing with authority was deep. Following her escape from the transport ship she made a successful living in the Spitalfields silk industry. She was 'Five foot 3", [with] dark hair [and] Hazel Eyes', and when she was finally rearrested in September 1794 (just a month after Burgess's trial), Cowden was able to use her experience of the law to her advantage.[8] Even the guard who testified to her previous conviction volunteered that 'she has behaved very well'. While her performance in court and a string of convincing character witnesses could not prevent a guilty verdict in an open and shut case, they were compelling enough to move both the jury and the court to 'Recommend [her] to mercy'.[9] In the end she convinced a jury of matrons that she was with child, and her sentence of death was 'Respited on account of Pregnancy'. She was given a 'free pardon'.[10]

Lives of poverty remained on their frequently tragic course, but paupers continued to wrest necessary resources from the parish, driving up the cost of poor relief in the process. When, in the autumn of 1793, Mary Dyson felt she was being ill-treated by St Clement Danes she knew what to do.[11] Fifty years old and mired in poverty, Mary summoned her friends and demanded the support she needed by 'abusing the [parish] officers at their own Houses & ... putting the officers at defiance and parading the Strand with a Number of people after her and by her

---

[7] Tim Hitchcock and Robert Shoemaker, *Tales from the Hanging Court* (London: Hodder Arnold, 2007), p. 351.

[8] *LL*, Home Office: Criminal Registers of Prisoners in Middlesex and the City, September 1792 – September 1793 (NAHOCR700060023).

[9] *LL*, Old Bailey Proceedings, 31 October 1792 (t17921031-7).

[10] *LL*, Home Office: Criminal Registers of Prisoners in Middlesex and the City, September 1792 September 1793 (NAHOCR700060023).

[11] *LL*, set, 'Mary Dyson'.

intimidations, extorting Money'.[12] The parish punished her defiance, but they could not escape responsibility for her support.

Just as transportation to Australia resulted in lifelong exile for many, London's pauper children and their parents were also forced to confront new systems of exile. Between 1784 and 1814, some 4,414 of the country's most vulnerable children were apprenticed to the new industrial mills of the North, the vast majority from the capital.[13]

Harriet Russell, for instance, born in December 1779, spent her first decade in the care of St Clement Danes, mainly with nurse Thurling in Low Layton.[14] She was the illegitimate child of Elizabeth Russell and William Augustus Howard, and her father, a doctor, put up a bond for £40 to indemnify the parish for the expense of caring for her.[15] When she was eleven years old, the overseers ensured that she would have no future claim on the parish by apprenticing her hundreds of miles away. She was one of the at least 99 girls and 180 boys sent north by St Clement's in the three decades after 1786. Most were sent to John Birch's cotton mill in Cumbria, but Harriet and two other girls were sent to Wells and Middleton's cotton mill in Sheffield. According to Katrina Honeyman, the mill was below standard on almost every measure except the quality of the medical provision, but between 1789 and 1808 the proprietors were nevertheless allowed to take on precisely 100 London apprentices – 56 girls and 44 boys.[16] With an apprenticeship went a settlement that overrode place of birth or parental connection, and with the exception of Harriet Russell we can locate none of the children from St Clement's in the parish records following their industrial exile, suggesting that few if any returned.

However, on completion of her term Harriet headed 'home', and in early September 1797 the vestry was confronted by 'A girl by the name of Harriet Russell' and forced to listen.[17] A special meeting of the church-wardens and overseers was 'called for the Purpose' of hearing her story,

---

[12] *LL*, St Clement Danes Parish: Minutes of Parish Vestries, 13 July 1787 – 6 August 1795 (WCCDMV362050278).

[13] Katrina Honeyman, *Child Workers in England, 1780–1820: Parish Apprentices and the Making of the Early Industrial Labour Force* (Aldershot: Ashgate, 2007), Table 5.2, pp. 100–1. See also Joanna Innes, 'Origins of the factory acts: The Health and Morals of Apprentices Act, 1802', in Norma Landau, ed., *Law, Crime and Society, 1660–1830* (Cambridge University Press, 2002), p. 236.

[14] *LL*, set, 'Harriet Russell'.

[15] *LL*, St Clement Danes Parish: Pauper Settlement, Vagrancy and Bastardy Exams, 26 January 1779 – 29 March 1783 (WCCDEP358090076); St Clement Danes Parish: Enfield Books – Parish Children Put Out to Nurse (WCCDBE356030047).

[16] Honeyman, *Child Workers*, pp. 59–60 (Table 4.1), 242, 290.

[17] *LL*, St Clement Danes Parish: Minutes of Parish Vestries, 1 December 1796 – 4 December 1800 (WCCDMV36201MV362010042).

together with 'Reading Letters from Backborrow from some boys there'.[18] In the end Harriet's complaints of mistreatment did not directly change parish policy. Nevertheless, it was difficult for even the most patronising of vestrymen and magistrates to entirely dismiss the voice of experience. Paupers like Harriet and the boys of Backborrow contributed to the perception of the mills as unhealthy and miserable, feeding a wave of concern that resulted a few years later in an 'Act for the Preservation of the Health and Morals of Apprentices ... employed in ... Mills and ... Factories' (1802).[19] Consequently parishes, including St Clement's, were forced to develop a more comprehensive regime of inspection.[20]

Despite attempts to control costs, as a result of harvest failures driving up prices, and trade disruption leading to under-employment and poverty, the cost of poor relief in the metropolis increased substantially in the 1790s, outstripping both inflation and the rate of increase in the country as a whole. By 1803 Londoners were spending £525,261 a year on relieving the parish poor and administering the system, over two and a half times the figure twenty-five years earlier.[21] In the City expenditure on apprehending and removing vagrants also rose substantially – only in part as a result of more aggressive policing, as the poor learned how to turn this system to their advantage. What in 1690 had been a decentralised and relatively inexpensive system of policing migration ended the eighteenth century as a powerfully bureaucratic, county-based regime which was passing thousands of vagrants a year through a complex system of independent contractors and way stations. In the decade after 1789, the cost of apprehending and removing vagrants from the City rose from £293 to over £1,800 a year.[22] However, most of the money was not spent on removing vagrants – instead, it went on caring for the sick, as those liable to removal sought medical care from some of the country's best hospitals. The poor were increasingly skilled at securing support from their parishes and the City – and they needed it. Wheat prices reached a new high in 1795 following harvest failure, and real wages

---

[18] *LL*, St Clement Danes Parish: Minute Books of Parish Vestry Sub-Committees, 31 August 1790 – 27 February 1798 (WCCDMO361040145); St Clement Danes Parish: Minutes of Parish Vestries, 1 December 1796 – 4 December 1800 (WCCDMV362010047).

[19] 42 Geo. III c. 73, 'An Act for the preservation of the health and morals of apprentices'.

[20] Innes, 'Origins of the factory acts', pp. 230–55.

[21] *PP*, 'Abstract of the answers and returns made ... relative to the expense and maintenance of the poor in England', 1803–4 (parlipapers.chadwyck.co.uk, 2 Jan. 2014).

[22] See Figure 7.13. For the equivalent figure in 1799, see LMA, City of London: 'City's cash accounts', COL/CHD/CT/01/068, 1799, ff. 263–6.

reached a new low in 1800 – down over half on their eighteenth-century peak fifty-six years earlier.[23] In 1795 and 1800 London experienced the rare phenomenon (for the metropolis) of food riots.[24]

From the point of view of the authorities and elite Londoners, the 1790s experienced what must have felt like unprecedented social and political challenges from below. In addition to the more confident behaviour of plebeian London, whether in securing poor relief, defending themselves in court or protesting on the streets, the radicalism stimulated by the French Revolution raised the threat to the established order to a new level. While hardly a typical criminal, the moral panic over the minor violence committed by the 'Monster', Rhynwick Williams, between 1788 and 1790 reflects the febrile state of public opinion.[25] Even before local and national government embarked on a period of substantial political repression in 1792, a concerted effort was under way to subject those considered prone to crime, immorality and poverty to new forms of control.

The attack on suspicious London

By 1789 plebeian Londoners were adept at defending their interests, but in the following decade they were confronted by rapidly changing systems of poor relief and criminal justice. Unprecedented numbers of boys and girls were being shipped to an unknown life in the factories of the North, while, if convicted of a felony, their older brothers and sisters, if not executed on the new gallows outside Newgate, were vulnerable to being transported beyond ken to the other side of the world.[26] Against this backdrop the French Revolution sparked the development of both a new radicalism and a conservative backlash. Many Londoners concluded with Thomas Paine that, 'When ... we see age going to the workhouse, and youth to the gallows, something must be wrong in the system of

---

[23] Real Wage Rates of London Bricklayers, Carpenters and their Labourers, 1696–1800 (Online data set: Wages and Prices); based on Leonard Schwarz, 'The standard of living in the long run: London, 1700–1860', *Economic History Review*, 2nd Series, 38:1 (1985), 28, Fig. 1 and 36–40, Appendix 1.

[24] John Stevenson, *Popular Disturbances in England: 1700–1832* (Harlow: Longman, 1992), pp. 214, 220–1.

[25] *LL*, set, 'Rhynwick Williams'; Jan Bondeson, *The London Monster: A Sanguinary Tale* (Philadelphia: University of Pennsylvania Press, 2001); Robert Shoemaker, *The London Mob: Violence and Disorder in Eighteenth-Century England* (London: Hambledon and London, 2004), ch. 10.

[26] In the decade after 1789, 1,781 children were apprenticed to northern factories from London in this way. Katrina Honeyman, *Child Workers*, Table 5.2, pp. 100–1.

government'.[27] The co-evolution of plebeian resistance with radical politics precipitated the development of additional new forms of policing, punishment and surveillance.

The creation of the London Corresponding Society (LCS) in January 1792, open to 'members unlimited' and with its goal of universal male suffrage and annual parliaments, set in train the first wave of political repression. Described by Boyd Hilton as the 'first time ordinary working people took part in organised political activity entirely on their own initiative', the LCS attracted thousands of supporters drawn primarily from among the artisans of the capital.[28] Most members were of a higher social standing than those involved in many of the acts of plebeian resistance identified in this book, but they were frequently shoemakers, tailors, weavers and clockmakers; men of the class who had earlier fought for the right to speak at an open vestry and sought to defend the parish pension against the creation of workhouses.[29]

In response – both to the French Revolution itself (as it descended into the Terror) and the rise of the LCS – the government embarked on a period of sustained political repression. Seditious meetings and publications were outlawed, and loyalist associations were promoted (and encouraged to disrupt radical meetings). Habeas Corpus was suspended, radicals were prosecuted for sedition and treason, and new Combination Acts were passed prohibiting trade union activity.[30] At the same time, and motivated by similar concerns, policing and punishment were strengthened. Innovations that had been designed to address the plebeian challenges to public order of the preceding decades, but had been deemed too ambitious, could now be justified on account of the crises of revolution and radicalism.

One measure of this co-evolution of anti-radicalism and a heightened concern to control public disorder can be found in the passage of the Middlesex Justices Act in 1792. This implemented key provisions of the failed London and Westminster Police Bill of 1785, in the context of both the crackdown on radicalism and concerns about the 'alarming

---

[27] Thomas Paine, *The Rights of Man, for the Use and Benefit of All Mankind,* Vol. II (1792, 1795 edn), p. 124.

[28] Boyd Hilton, *A Mad, Bad, and Dangerous People? England 1783–1846* (Oxford University Press, 2006), p. 66. In 1795 Francis Place estimated that the LCS had 2,000 members: Mary Thale, ed., *The Autobiography of Francis Place (1771–1854)* (Cambridge University Press, 1972), p. 140, n.

[29] Mary Thale, ed., *Selections from the Papers of the London Corresponding Society, 1792–1799* (Cambridge University Press, 1983), p. xix.

[30] For a general survey of these developments, see Hilton, *A Mad, Bad and Dangerous People?*, ch. 2.

increase' of crime.[31] Building on the precedent established decades
earlier at Bow Street, the Act created a system of stipendiary magistrates
covering the whole of the metropolis apart from the City. Based in seven
police offices, each staffed by three magistrates, two clerks and six
constables paid on a retainer, these 'rotation offices' were funded
through fees charged to those who attended. In effect (and intent), the
Act suppressed the activities of 'trading justices'. Following its passage
the number of recognizances issued by Middlesex justices, a legal instrument frequently used when mediating disputes, plummeted by over
60 per cent, from 7,322 in 1791 to 2,752 in 1793.[32] As one supporter
of the Act commented, it 'contributed to quell a spirit of litigation among
the lower classes' – the poor had lost a vital source of redress.[33] But not
only did this Act remove a form of inexpensive and independent justice
for the poor, it also empowered constables and watchmen to arrest them
if they fitted a loose definition of suspicious behaviour. The Act allowed
officers to apprehend 'divers ill-disposed and suspected persons, and
reputed thieves' as vagrants on the oath of 'one or more credible witnesses', if there was 'just ground to believe that such person' had intent to
commit a felony and was unable 'to give a satisfactory account of
himself ... and of his ... way of living'.[34] The contemporaneous
1792 Vagrancy Act further broadened this already wide definition of
suspicious behaviour, while attempting to impose more consistent
punishments, whipping for male offenders and a week in a house of
correction for both men and women.[35] In 1802 these principles were
embodied in the first 'sus' law, where the definition of those who could

---

[31] 32 Geo. III c. 53, 'An Act for more effectual administration of the office of a justice of the
peace in such parts of the counties of Middlesex and Surrey as lie in and near the
metropolis'. For the political impetus behind the bill, see Hilton, *A Mad, Bad, and
Dangerous People?*, p. 68, and Elaine A. Reynolds, *Before the Bobbies: The Night Watch and
Police Reform in Metropolitan London, 1720–1830* (Basingstoke: Macmillan, 1998),
pp. 85–6; for the 'alarming increase' of crime, see David Philips, '"A new engine of
power and authority": the institutionalization of law-enforcement in England
1780–1830', in V. A. C. Gatrell, Bruce Lenman and Geoffrey Parker, eds., *Crime and
the Law: The Social History of Crime in Western Europe since 1500* (London: Europa
Publications, 1980), p. 170.
[32] Norma Landau, 'The trading justice's trade', in Landau, ed., *Law, Crime and Society,
1660–1830* (Cambridge University Press, 2002), p. 68; Ruth Paley, 'The Middlesex
Justices Act of 1792: its origins and effects' (PhD dissertation, University of Reading,
1983), p. 394.
[33] Cited by Landau, 'The trading justice's trade', p. 69.
[34] 32 Geo. III c. 53, 'An Act for more effectual administration of the office of a justice of the
peace', s. 17; see also Bruce P. Smith, 'The presumption of guilt and the English law of
theft, 1750–1850', *Law and History Review*, 23:1 (2005), 164.
[35] 32 Geo. III c. 45, 'An Act to explain and amend an Act ... relating to rogues, vagabonds
and other idle and disorderly persons'.

be arrested for vagrancy was extended still further.[36] In the context of previous plebeian legal challenges to arrests for vaguely-defined offences, the provisions of these statutes represent attempts to establish firmer statutory foundations for police powers. However, the result was that the poor's civil liberties were substantially eroded.

The City of London, which by consent was excluded from the Middlesex Justices Act, pursued a similar policy without parliamentary interference. The duties of the City patrole were expanded to include daytime patrols, and officers were encouraged to arrest 'Pick Pockets known Thieves and suspected Persons'. In addition, from 1793 the City beefed up its policing in response to fears of public disorder, substantially increasing the number of constables deployed at public gatherings such as notorious trials and executions. Between 900 and 1,200 extra constables were employed during the 1794 treason trials.[37]

One of the leading new stipendiary justices in Middlesex was Patrick Colquhoun, a maverick reformer who contributed to the expansion of police powers, motivated by his profound belief in the essential criminality of the lower orders. Colquhoun employed an extensive network of spies and informers to report on weavers who embezzled silk, and was criticised for violating suspects' rights in his examinations.[38] He was the leading proponent of the development of the Marine Police, established in 1798 with funding from West India merchants. Not only did this office employ a substantial body of officers (almost twice as many as employed by all the other rotation offices combined),[39] but it sought to extend direct control over labour by setting itself up as an employment agency for the 'lumpers' who unloaded ships. The office regulated their pay and working conditions, and constables searched the men every day when they finished work.[40] The fact that even Colquhoun estimated the losses in the port at less than 1 per cent of the value of the goods exported and imported suggests that the main purpose of the scheme was to control the

---

[36] 42 Geo. III c. 76, 'An Act for repealing two Acts … for the more effectual administration of the office of a justice of the peace'; Nicholas Rogers, 'Policing the poor in eighteenth-century London: the vagrancy laws and their administration', *Histoire sociale – Social History*, 29:47 (1991), 145.

[37] Andrew T. Harris, *Policing the City: Crime and Legal Authority in London, 1780–1840* (Columbus: Ohio State University Press, 2004), ch. 3, quotation from p. 76.

[38] Paley, 'Middlesex Justices Act', pp. 336–7; Peter Linebaugh, *The London Hanged: Crime and Civil Society in the Eighteenth Century* (London: Allen Lane, 1991), p. 409. See also Leon Radzinowicz, *A History of English Criminal Law and its Administration from 1750*, Vol. III (London: Stevens and Sons, 1957), ch. 9.

[39] Leon Radzinowicz, *A History of English Criminal Law and its Administration from 1750*, Vol. II (London: Stevens and Sons, 1956), p. 365.

[40] Reynolds, *Before the Bobbies*, p. 76; Paley, 'Middlesex Justices Act', pp. 349–50; Harris, *Policing the City*, p. 73; Linebaugh, *London Hanged*, pp. 430–1.

labour force rather than reduce theft.[41] In 1800 the Thames Police Office (minus control over the lumpers' pay and conditions but with a strong 'suspected persons' clause) was given statutory backing as the eighth magistrates' office in the metropolis.[42]

As a part of this campaign against radicalism and disorder, the magistrates themselves were subjected to greater control by the Home Office. Established in 1782 and given responsibility for the magistracy, in the early 1790s the Home Office used its authority to involve JPs in its campaign of spying on and suppressing the radical societies as well as controlling crime. From 1792 the new stipendiaries were required to provide the Home Office with regular reports of crime in their areas.[43] Following the death of Sampson Wright, John Fielding's successor, in 1793, the Home Office also took more direct control of Bow Street, which had been excluded from the 1792 Act. The Runners were used in 'the government's programme to suppress the radical societies and counter threats of sedition', while one Bow Street magistrate, Richard Ford, effectively acted as a 'third under-secretary', attending the Home Office on a daily basis.[44]

For those accused of crime, there were attempts to limit the possibilities of mounting an effective defence by, among other policies, censoring the Old Bailey *Proceedings*. In the 1780s, under the proprietorship of Edmund Hodgson, the *Proceedings* had included ever more detailed trial accounts, including some of the longest reports of the century, with particularly detailed evidence reflecting the role of defence counsel. They also reported at length episodes such as the nineteen men and women who refused the royal pardon. However, this generated growing concern that criminals were being given too much information. In 1787 a City committee complained that the 'very extensive publication of all the trials indiscriminately' taught criminals both new law-breaking strategies and the 'manner of fabricating defences, especially alibis', while the Recorder of London complained that reporting 'the arguments of counsel' had been 'the occasion of the prisoners being acquitted'. In response, in October 1790 the City eliminated all reports of trials that ended in acquittals (comprising about 40 per cent of verdicts). This is the only

---

[41] Radzinowicz, *History of English Criminal Law*, Vol.II, pp. 359, 487.

[42] 39 and 40 Geo. III c. 87, 'An Act for the more effectual prevention of depredations on the River Thames'.

[43] Philips, '"A new engine of power and authority"', pp. 168–9; Reynolds, *Before the Bobbies*, p. 86; Radzinowicz, *History of English Criminal Law*, Vol.II, p. 416.

[44] Paley, 'Middlesex Justices Act', p. 286; John Beattie, *The First English Detectives: The Bow Street Runners and the Policing of London, 1750–1840* (Oxford University Press, 2012), pp. 168, 184–9; Radzinowicz, *History of English Criminal Law*, Vol.II, p. 407.

time in the 239-year history of the *Proceedings* that there was such a substantial attempt at censorship. The policy backfired as sales plummeted, and trial reports resulting in acquittals were restored in December 1792. Nonetheless, particularly from 1796, the activities of counsel were frequently 'bleached out' in the reports.[45]

Many defendants, however, never made it to the Old Bailey, as the creation of magistrates' courts circumvented the evolving legal protection available to those represented by counsel in felony trials. While the poor could occasionally use summary justice to their advantage, Bruce Smith has argued that in many of the statutes enforced by these courts there was no presumption of innocence, and in its place there was a 'statutory presumption of guilt'.[46] In particular, men and women charged with possessing stolen goods on the basis of, in Colquhoun's words, 'circumstantial evidence ... and in default of regular Proof', were obliged to prove their ownership and their innocence in an often hostile context, shaped by his and others' beliefs in the fundamental criminality of the poor.[47] Those arrested for vagrancy faced a similar disadvantage, being obliged to give a 'satisfactory account' of themselves, including their settlement and how they earned their living, if they were to avoid punishment and removal. Although, like the prostitutes who challenged commitments by John Fielding, those convicted sometimes appealed to King's Bench or by petition to the Home Office, the high courts were extremely reluctant to overturn magistrates' summary decisions.[48]

The 1790s also witnessed a sea change in penal strategies, as imprisonment finally became the sentence most frequently imposed on felons. Between 1789 and 1799 the proportion of imprisonment sentences at the Old Bailey doubled from 16.4 per cent of all sentences to 32.4 per cent, more than half of which involved a commitment to a house of

---

[45] Robert Shoemaker, 'Representing the adversary criminal trial: lawyers in the Old Bailey *Proceedings*, 1770–1800', in David Lemmings, ed., *Courtrooms and the Public Sphere in Britain, 1700–1850* (Farnham, Surrey: Ashgate, 2012), pp. 83–90; John H. Langbein, *The Origins of Adversary Criminal Trial* (Oxford University Press, 2003), p. 190.

[46] Drew Gray, *Crime, Prosecution and Social Relations: The Summary Courts of the City of London in the Late Eighteenth Century* (Houndmills: Palgrave, 2009); Smith, 'Presumption', 133–71, quote from 135 (see also the subsequent debate in the same issue).

[47] Patrick Colquhoun, *A Treatise on the Commerce and Police of the River Thames* (London, 1800), pp. 279, 674–5.

[48] Douglas Hay, 'Dread of Crown Office: the English magistracy and King's Bench, 1740–1800', in Landau, ed., *Law, Crime and Society*, pp. 19–45; Hay, 'Legislation, magistrates and judges: high law and low law in England and the empire', in David Lemmings, ed., *The British and their Laws in the Eighteenth Century* (Woodbridge: Boydell Press, 2005), pp. 59–79.

correction.[49] Convict resistance to the unreformed prison and alternative forms of punishment had forced the hands of the authorities in London, who started building prisons on the penitentiary model, with solitary confinement and the provision of more onerous forms of hard labour. In 1791 the City opened Giltspur Street Compter, which included separate sections for different categories of offenders and individual cells for felons.[50] From 1794 felons in Middlesex were incarcerated in the new Cold Bath Fields prison (although a 'house of correction', the prison also held felons), built according to designs originally drawn up for the 1779 Penitentiary Act. Cold Bath Fields held 384 prisoners, 232 of whom were held in solitary confinement. Prisoners were subjected to mandatory religious instruction and put to hard labour. In practice, exploitation and mistreatment by the first keeper, Thomas Aris, ensured that they suffered cold, starvation and disease as well.[51] Five years later, a new Surrey county gaol at Horsemonger Lane opened with 'every reformed requisite' of a new prison, including 177 cells and a centrally located keeper's house from which eight separate courtyards could be surveyed.[52]

During these same years the growing cost of poor relief constituted a further headache for the authorities, but owing in part to fears of insurrection there was little innovation. In rural England, new ways of subsidising inadequate wages were implemented – the Speenhamland system – but in the metropolis parishes and paupers just got by as best they could. A new poor law, passed in 1795, limited the ability of parishes to remove paupers prior to their becoming 'chargeable', but overall in London, in stark contrast to developments in policing and punishment, these years were characterised more by drift and argument than by real change.[53] In public discourse, however, there were important developments that prefigure the 1834 New Poor Law. Colquhoun published

---

[49] Old Bailey Punishment Sentences, 1690–1800 (Online data set: Punishment Statistics 1690–1800.xlsx); Old Bailey Online, Statistics: Punishment Category by Year, 1789–99, Punishment Subcategories: Imprisonment, 1799.

[50] C. W. Chalklin, 'The reconstruction of London's prisons, 1770–1799: an aspect of the growth of Georgian London', *London Journal*, 9:1 (1983), 24–5; Richard Byrne, *Prisons and Punishments of London* (London: Harrap, 1989), pp. 47–50.

[51] Michael Ignatieff, *A Just Measure of Pain: The Penitentiary in the Industrial Revolution, 1750–1850* (New York: Columbia University Press, 1978), pp. 127–8; *Rules, Orders, and Regulations for the Management of the New House of Correction for the County of Middlesex* (1795).

[52] Robin Evans, *The Fabrication of Virtue: English Prison Architecture, 1750–1850* (Cambridge University Press, 1982; repr. 2011), p. 185; Byrne, *Prisons and Punishments of London*, pp. 113–14.

[53] 35 Geo. III c. 101, 'An Act to prevent the removal of poor persons, until they shall come actually chargeable'.

long *Treatises* in an attempt to colour working people in the darkest shade of immorality and scare the public, while T. R. Malthus achieved the same end by raising the spectre of unsustainable population growth and starvation, and Jeremy Bentham added his own redesigned workhouses to his penitentiary prisons.[54] But for the moment, the old poor law stood, and these pamphlets and panaceas largely remained fodder for the coffee house fire.

Perhaps the most important developments at the end of the century involved the first substantial glimmerings of a new 'information state'. Anxiety concerning political radicalism and public disorder, as well as the rising costs of poor relief and vagrancy, all contributed to a change in the character of policy-making that in the longer term would profoundly affect how plebeian Londoners interacted with the authorities. Many late eighteenth-century innovations were the result of a new impetus to collect and compare information about the poor and the criminal in order to control them. The convening of a national convention of magistrates, organised by the Proclamation Society, for example, allowed a national picture of vagrancy to emerge for the first time and led directly to the passage of the 1792 Vagrancy Act.[55] But more substantially, the sheer volume of documentation collected about the lives of plebeian Londoners grew exponentially. One of the arguments of this book has been that the increasing use of settlement examinations, and to a lesser extent certificates and trial reports, created a bureaucratic system that enabled plebeian Londoners to escape the system of deference that invested so much authority in parish officers and magistrates. However, in the last decade of the eighteenth century, that scaffolding of paperwork was increasingly put to a new use by the authorities.

The origins of this new ecology of information can be traced back to the middle of the eighteenth century. John Fielding's files of suspected criminals (destroyed by the mob in the Gordon Riots) and the Jonas Hanway-inspired registers of parish children were just two instances of a broader data-gathering exercise that in itself helped to focus public attention on the criminal and the poor as a distinct and supposedly knowable group. The rise of parliamentary commissions, encouraged by the work of Jonas Hanway, Thomas Gilbert and John Howard among a host of others, created a new pattern of collecting and publishing often highly problematic data about social problems that would justify

---

[54] For an overview of this literature, see Lynn Hollen Lees, *The Solidarities of Strangers: The English Poor Laws and the People, 1700–1948* (Cambridge University Press, 1998), ch. 3.

[55] Joanna Innes, *Inferior Politics: Social Problems and Social Policies in Eighteenth-Century Britain* (Oxford University Press, 2009), pp. 45, 208–9.

legislation and become a normal part of both parliamentary practice and social investigation in the next century. We have seen how Hanway used questionable statistics about infant deaths to discredit parochial nursing and pass new legislation requiring pauper infants to be nursed in the country. Similarly, Colquhoun relied on detailed, but highly dubious, statistics to justify his proposals for greater police powers.[56] When, in 1782, parliament demanded that gaol calendars include details of each prisoner – their sex, age, conduct and literacy, as well as their crime and punishment – a new way of representing and understanding a specific social problem was created.[57]

However, it was in the late 1780s and 1790s, with the creation of the Criminal Registers, initially covering only London and Middlesex, and with national surveys of the cost of poor relief and vagrancy, that these trends in collecting and analysing information about plebeian Londoners were first used to real effect.[58] It was the Criminal Registers (lists of prisoners accused of crimes, which include a physical description, place of birth, occupation, evidence of previous convictions, as well as details of the subsequent judicial process) which finally doomed the long-term recidivist Charlotte Walker to transportation in 1799.[59] As a result, the literary stereotypes and well-understood narratives that lay behind understandings of poverty and crime in the early eighteenth century were replaced by an esoteric knowledge recorded in tables, which could easily be restricted and used against individuals and groups of criminals and paupers. An entry in the Criminal Register, available to the judge but not the defendant, or comparative figures for local poor relief expenditure, privileged elite knowledge over personal experience. Jeremy Bentham's proposed panopticon prisons and workhouses were merely an architectural expression of a wider transition in which elite reformers developed a technology for the comprehensive oversight of criminals and paupers, including the distant perspective of statistics.[60]

When Matthew Martin began interviewing London's street beggars in 1796 in order to lay a solid statistical foundation for his *Plan for the Suppression of Beggary*, he combined both old and new forms of gathering

[56] Radzinowicz, *History of English Criminal Law*, Vol.III, p. 243; Patrick Colquhoun, *A Treatise on the Police of the Metropolis ... The Sixth Edition* (1800), *passim*.
[57] Innes, *Inferior Politics*, ch. 4, esp. p. 163.
[58] Tim Hitchcock, Sharon Howard and Robert Shoemaker, 'Criminal registers', *London Lives, 1690–1800* (www.londonlives.org/static/CR.jsp).
[59] *LL*, Mary Clayton, 'Charlotte Walker'.
[60] Sandra Sherman, *Imagining Poverty: Quantification and the Decline of Paternalism* (Columbus: Ohio State University Press, 2001), *passim*.

knowledge about the poor. By paying his informers a few pence each for their stories, he purchased thousands of well-crafted narratives that had allowed beggars and paupers to survive on the streets of London against the letter of the law and principles of parish relief for decades. Some were true, and all were credible, but when Martin incorporated the information gathered into simplified statistical tables that would help inform state policy towards the poor over the next twenty years, the potency of the beggars' side of the story was lost.[61] In the 1790s the power of systematically collected data and statistics was increasingly set against the power of narrative, to the disadvantage of the poor.

The evolution of plebeian tactics

The implementation of new regimes of surveillance and discipline was a response to the pressures generated by plebeian London over the previous decades, as well as the political challenges precipitated by the French Revolution. If we trace the story of plebeian agency past 1789, we find that Londoners responded to the increasing powers of the state with a combination of old and new tactics. Building on the skills and methods developed over the preceding hard decades and taking advantage of the development of radicalism, they found new ways to challenge authority. As a result plebeian Londoners would continue to play a central role in shaping the development of social policy, even as the locus of policy formation moved to a national arena.

Old patterns of behaviour remained useful in many circumstances. The continuing roles of riot and legal argument, for instance, are exemplified in the opposition to the short-lived reformation of manners campaign, founded in 1787 by the Proclamation Society.[62] The Society's attempt in June 1792 to suppress a servants' dance in Mayfair was countered by five days of rioting. The watchhouse and house of the constable who served the warrant were attacked, and soldiers were repeatedly summoned to disperse the rioters.[63] Consequently, the magistrates were forced to dismiss most of those arrested. Later in the decade attempts to prosecute the publishers of indecent literature were stymied

---

[61] Innes, *Inferior Politics*, p. 165; Tim Hitchcock, *Down and Out in Eighteenth-Century London* (London: Hambledon and London, 2004), pp. 3–5; Lynn MacKay, *Respectability and the London Poor, 1780–1870: The Value of Virtue* (London: Pickering & Chatto, 2013), pp. 108–9. See also Matthew Martin, *An Appeal to Public Benevolence for the Relief of Beggars: With a View to a Plan for the Suppression of Beggary* (London, 1812).

[62] Shoemaker, *London Mob*, pp. 146–8.

[63] BL, Add. Ms. 51020, ff. 37 9; *The Times*, 6–9 June 1792, *The Times Digital Archive* (thetimes.co.uk/ttto/archive/, 2 Jan. 2014).

by defence lawyers who repeatedly challenged the use of paid informers. As a result of these and other forms of opposition, once again an attempted reformation of manners campaign was undermined. The Society responded by diversifying into other reforming activities which were less likely to encounter resistance, such as inspecting prisons and setting up a separate society, the 'Society for Bettering the Condition and Increasing the Comforts of the Poor'. By 1801 the original Society was 'effectively out of action'.[64]

Defendants' use of legal advice in felony trials continued to increase significantly, making the presence of defence counsel almost the norm at the Old Bailey. Between 1795 and 1800 defence counsel are recorded as present in more than a third of Old Bailey trials, 70 per cent more than the number of trials with prosecution counsel and by far the highest levels in the century.[65] In light of the selective reporting in the *Proceedings*, it is likely that the real figure was even higher. In 1793, the Home Secretary was warned of the existence of a large criminal gang that 'have a Treasury for the necessary expences of evading Justice, feeing Counsel, Support in Prison, and other Incidents'.[66] Although it is not possible to determine how the presence of defence counsel affected trial outcomes, defendants clearly expected an increased chance of acquittal. We have seen that cross-examinations raised the standards of evidence needed to convict and helped to establish the idea that the defendant was innocent until proven guilty. Counsel may have also, as Colquhoun believed, encouraged acquittals through greater use of false alibis.[67] In addition, as Sir John Hawkins worried in 1787, the fear of aggressive cross-examinations may have discouraged some victims from prosecuting crimes in the first place.[68] Two decades later Thomas Rowlandson included being cross-examined at the Old Bailey among the 'Miseries of Human Life'.[69]

The increased presence of counsel for the defence in felony trials may have been partly motivated by political concerns, as it certainly was in the case of the radicals tried in 1794 for treason.[70] Thomas Erskine was hired

---

[64] M. J. D. Roberts, *Making English Morals: Voluntary Association and Moral Reform in England, 1787–1886* (Cambridge University Press, 2004), pp. 52–3, 63–4, 71.

[65] See Figure 7.7: Legal Counsel at the Old Bailey, 1770–1800, as reported in the *Proceedings*.

[66] TNA, Home Office, 'Letters and Papers', HO42/25, ff. 622–3. We are indebted to Joseph Cozens for this reference.

[67] Colquhoun, *Treatise on the Police of the Metropolis*, pp. 20, 424.

[68] John Hawkins, *The Life of Samuel Johnson* (Dublin, 1787), p. 522.

[69] Thomas Rowlandson, 'More miseries', *Miseries of Human Life* (1807–8), British Museum, 1869,0213.100.

[70] David Lemmings, *Professors of the Law: Barristers and English Legal Culture in the Eighteenth Century* (Oxford University Press, 2000), pp. 216–17, 225.

to defend all twelve defendants, but the trials were abandoned after the first three, including that of Thomas Hardy, a shoemaker and the secretary of the LCS, resulted in acquittals. As David Lemmings has observed, these 'triumphs ... tended to inhibit government prosecutions of radicals which depended on the constructive extensions of the law of treason', and Erskine's actions helped inspire 'the next generation of defence counsel'.[71] There is some evidence that legal representation was being extended to the summary courts, where as we have seen a presumption of innocence was often absent. In 1800 Patrick Colquhoun noted that those prosecuted under the 'Bumboat Act', which allowed dockers to be searched for pilfered goods at the end of the working day, had formed a 'general Subscription Club, for the purpose of defraying all expences arising from the detections, penalties, and forfeitures'. These expenses are likely to have included taking professional legal advice. Bruce Smith has noted that 'during the second quarter of the nineteenth century, a smattering of attorneys – and persons claiming to be attorneys — emerged to offer legal services to defendants tried in the police offices of London'.[72]

Another tactic honed by plebeian Londoners over the eighteenth century was letter writing. As the system of settlement in the provision of poor relief accommodated itself to labour mobility (the 1795 Poor Law Act was explicitly directed to this end), the role of pauper letters, demanding support under the threat of returning to the settlement parish at much greater cost, grew. Examples can be found dating from the late 1730s (those of Catherine Jones, and Paul Patrick Kearney in the 1760s, discussed in Chapter 6, are particularly good ones), but the heyday of the pauper letter was the last three decades of the Old Poor Law, from when thousands of letters survive.[73] From 1795 one's home parish could be charged for the cost of medical care even if that care was provided by another parish. This added role of pauper letters (as evidence of potential parish liabilities) helps explain their greater survival after 1795, but the continuity in the kinds of narratives and language used by paupers over the course of the eighteenth and early nineteenth centuries reflects the on-going effectiveness of this tactic.[74]

---

[71] David Lemmings, 'Erskine, Thomas, first Baron Erskine (1750–1823)', *ODNB* (www. oxforddnb.com, 2 Jan. 2014).

[72] Colquhoun, *Treatise ... River Thames*, p. 48; Smith, 'Presumption of guilt', 171.

[73] *LL*, Deirdre Palk, 'Catherine Jones'; *LL*, Tim Hitchcock, 'Paul Patrick Kearney'; Thomas Sokoll, ed., *Essex Pauper Letters, 1731–1837* (Oxford University Press, 2001), pp. 19–20.

[74] Steven King, Thomas Nunn and Allannah Tomkins, eds., *Narratives of the Poor in Eighteenth-Century England*, Vol. 1: *Voices of the Poor* (London: Pickering & Chatto, 2006), pp. xxxiii–liv.

In a similar way, petitioning retained both its power to leverage resources from charities and parishes, and its central role in the workings of criminal justice. The growing number of private charities in London ensured that the skilful crafting of a petition for admission to a hospital or an almshouse would remain a central attribute of a successful pauper. However, petitioning was even more vital for those convicted of crimes, since it allowed convicts to plead to have their sentences reduced from death or transportation to a lesser punishment by means of a conditional pardon. Since, as Edmund Burke noted in 1780 in the context of the Gordon Riots, staging too many executions would 'exasperate' the people, the state needed reasons to pardon a significant proportion of capital convicts. When transportation was resumed in 1787, it was used for a much smaller proportion of convicts than previously, leading to the significant possibility of avoiding this punishment. Convicts grew more adept at providing justifications for such remissions. V. A. C. Gatrell has noted a significant increase in the early nineteenth century in the number of petitions 'submitted by or on behalf of felons sentenced to death, transportation, or rotting years on the prison hulks'; these were 'sent in by a high proportion even of those who could not realistically hope for redress'. While historians have debated whether the language of these texts was deferential, the key point is that plebeian letter writers and petitioners, often with the aid of professional writers and legal advice, learned to express the right combination of sentiments (including not only submission, but also anger and implied threat) to create the best chance of achieving the desired outcome. Tactics included complaining about 'over-hasty trials and indifferent judges, perjured evidence, unexamined witnesses, unheard alibis, and misunderstood motivations'; all plausible defects in trials whose length at the Old Bailey could still be measured in minutes rather than hours. By the early 1820s, 'even rather obscure people were learning to challenge the more dubious sentences with new confidence and sophistication'.[75]

Some letters, as E. P. Thompson demonstrated, took the form of anonymous threats of damage to persons and property. While such letters can be found throughout the eighteenth century, Thompson found the number increased dramatically in the 1790s and 1800s, and their tone changed: 'seditious or levelling threats became more

---

[75] V. A. C. Gatrell, *The Hanging Tree: Execution and the English People 1770–1868* (Oxford University Press, 1996), pp. 197–8, 204, 207. For the pardoning archives in TNA, see Home Office, 'Judges' reports on criminals', HO47, and 'Criminal petitions, series I', HO17.

general'.[76] In 1810 a London criminal prosecutor received a letter complaining that his actions had led to two men being sentenced to transportation, and demanding that he secure them a pardon:

> If I had known that you & your Cleark would have prosecuted them I would have put them & you & your Cleark out of the way I am determined on killing you both . . . if you do not get them both off.[77]

The literacy skills evident in plebeian letters were also put to good use in writing and reading (and hearing) printed literature. The explosion in cheap print from the 1780s, in the form of ballads, handbills, small books and pamphlets, provided the opportunity for plebeian views to achieve wider circulation.[78] The perceived power of cheap print is evident in the fact that in response conservatives such as Hannah More published her moralising *Cheap Repository Tracts*. She described her publications as 'substituting something better [than] ballad singing', but plebeian readers preferred other texts.[79] Handbills and posters were used to recruit support for public protests, including the food riots in 1800. During the 1794 'Crimp' riots (which involved attacks on houses where men were allegedly forced to enrol in the military), the most serious disturbances in London since the Gordon Riots, printed handbills were used to encourage the crowd and turn the riots into an attack on Colquhoun and his 'informers, spies and agents'.[80] Ballads had long expressed qualified admiration for highwaymen and 'game' criminals, and continued to do so.[81] Others expressed a new defiance. In the 1790s and into the nineteenth century, a number of ballads addressed transportation.[82] 'The Convict Maid' complains 'My punishment is most

---

[76] E. P. Thompson, 'The crime of anonymity', in Douglas Hay *et al.*, eds., *Albion's Fatal Tree: Crime and Society in Eighteenth-Century England* (London: Allen Lane, 1975), pp. 255–308, quote from p. 281.

[77] *London Gazette*, issue 16341, 10 January 1810, p. 221 (www.thegazette.co.uk, 2 Jan. 2014).

[78] While the number of titles published increased substantially at the end of the century, their average page length decreased: Michael Suarez, 'Towards a bibliometric analysis of the surviving record, 1701–1800', in Michael F. Suarez and Michael L. Turner, eds., *The Cambridge History of the Book in Britain*, Vol. V: *1695–1830* (Cambridge University Press, 2009), pp. 43, 60.

[79] Quoted in Gatrell, *Hanging Tree*, p. 125; Robin Ganev, *Songs of Protest, Songs of Love: Popular Ballads in Eighteenth-Century Britain* (Manchester University Press, 2009), pp. 201–8.

[80] Stevenson, *Popular Disturbances*, pp. 220–1; *idem*, 'The London "Crimp" riots of 1794', *International Review of Social History*, 16:1 (1971), 45; Paley, 'Middlesex Justices Act', p. 337.

[81] Gatrell, *Hanging Tree*, pp. 156–68.

[82] Roly Brown, 'Glimpses into the 19th century broadside ballad trade, number 20: Transports', *Musical Traditions* (23 May 2006) (mustrad.org.uk, 2 Jan. 2014).

severe / My woe is great and I'm afraid / That I shall die a convict maid'.[83] But in contrast to the convicts who refused the royal pardon in the late 1780s, by the following decade many convicts (or at least ballads about them) refused to take transportation seriously. In 'The Jolly Lad's Trip to Botany Bay' (c. 1795?), the transportees reassure each other that they are going to a place where there may be 'many a pretty lass'. The key stanza ends, 'A fig for transportation little do we care'.[84]

To these more traditional forms of plebeian literature, the decades after 1790 added a new genre. Taking a variety of forms – political lives designed to influence policy, brief epilogues to published poetry, religious narratives of redemption and simple stories intended to raise money – working-class autobiography flourished. Robert Blincoe was a London pauper raised in the St Pancras workhouse in the 1790s, and apprenticed, like so many others, to a cotton mill in the North. His classic *Memoir of . . . An Orphan Boy* formed a piece of campaigning literature specifically designed to expose the 'Horrors of a Cotton-Mill' to a national audience.[85] Just as instrumental, but in an entirely different way, Ann Candler's account of her life and experience in the Tattingstone House of Industry, when appended to her cottage poetry, formed what amounted to a sophisticated petition for help, and it provided her with a passport to a secure and respected old age.[86] While Mary Saxby's *Memoirs of a Female Vagrant*, published in 1806, had the external form of a conversion narrative, it was explicitly dedicated to demonstrating the proverb: 'One half of the world does not know how the other half lives'.[87]

Many of the methods in the increasingly sophisticated armoury of plebeian Londoners were in evidence during the campaign against solitary confinement and the mistreatment of prisoners in Cold Bath Fields that raged from 1798 to 1800. As a result of the confinement of the Nore mutineers and LCS members in 1798, radicals became aware of the appalling conditions inside this new 'reformed' prison, demanding a parliamentary investigation and using it as an election issue. The campaign included plebeian voices and traditional tactics: echoing the escapes which had long marked the history of imprisonment, eleven Nore

---

[83] Mark Gregory, *Australian Folk Songs* (folkstream.com/026, 2 Jan. 2014).

[84] John Holloway and Joan Black, *Later English Broadside Ballads*, Vol. I (London: Routledge & Kegan Paul, 1975), pp. 145–6.

[85] Robert Blincoe, *A Memoir of Robert Blincoe, An Orphan Boy; sent from the Workhouse of St Pancras, London, at seven years of age to Endure the Horrors of a Cotton-Mill* (Manchester, 1832; repr. Caliban Books, 1977).

[86] Ann Candler, *Poetical Attempts by Ann Candler, a Suffolk Cottager with a Short Narrative of Her Life* (Ipswich, 1803).

[87] Mary Saxby, *Memoirs of Mary Saxby, A Female Vagrant* (1806; repr. 1827).

mutineers broke out, and there were riots inside and outside the prison. New tactics were also used: petitions were sent to the Middlesex magistrates, the coroner and MP Sir Francis Burdett calling attention to conditions in the prison, and in 1800 a pamphlet was published describing the atrocious treatment of Mary Rich, a fourteen-year-old girl who was raped while a prisoner. The issue was taken up by Burdett in the parliamentary election of 1802, in which he narrowly defeated Charles Mainwaring, the chairman of the Middlesex bench. Although the keeper of the prison, Thomas Aris, continued in his post and the regime at Cold Bath Fields did not dramatically change, the resistance to solitary confinement was enduring and 'was one major reason why penitentiary ideas spread so slowly in England after the years of innovation in the 1780s'.[88]

By the turn of the nineteenth century, plebeian Londoners, both individually and collectively, had developed a wide range of skills and tactics for defending themselves and pursuing their interests in ways which forced the authorities to respond.[89] In relation to criminal justice, continuing pressure ensured that the policing and punishment of crime would remain on politicians' agendas throughout the first half of the new century, while poor relief gradually built to a powerful systemic crisis. By 1800 plebeian tactics were more politically aware, evident in the protests over Cold Bath Fields, providing a new language in which to express grievances and militate for resources. Plebeian agency was by no means solely responsible for driving social policy in these or earlier decades; nor were plebeian Londoners likely to have been satisfied with the reformed institutions and policies which resulted. Nevertheless, the pressures and demands we have described were instrumental in forcing change. In the new century, with the effective abandonment of the bloody code and the creation of the Metropolitan Police, with the passage of the New Poor Law and the 1832 Reform Act, plebeian demands and challenges would combine with a new politics to quicken the pace of change, both locally and nationally. Plebeian Londoners continued to play a key role in the development of the modern state.

---

[88] Ignatieff, *Just Measure of Pain*, pp. 126–42; Innes, *Inferior Politics*, pp. 225–6.

[89] Using a similar definition of 'plebeian London', Lynn MacKay has recently argued that between 1780 and 1870 plebeian Londoners resisted, or reached their own accommodation with, prevailing notions of 'respectability': MacKay, *Respectability and the London Poor*.

Bibliography

ARCHIVAL SOURCES

Bodleian Library, Rawlinson Ms., D1399
British Library (BL)
   Add. Ms. 30884, 32876, 32882, 33053, 33054, 34712, 35600, 42129, 51020
   Sloane Ms. 4078
Cambridge University Library (CUL)
   SPCK Archive, 'Standing Committee minute book', 1718–20
   SPCK Archive, 'Special letters book', 1725–1726
Camden Local Studies and Archives Centre (CLSAC), 'St Giles in the Fields,
   vestry minutes', P/GF/M/1/2, 1673–1771
East Riding Records Office, 'John Grimston letters', DDGR/42/30
Edinburgh University Library (EUL), Laing Ms., III, 394
Hackney Archives Department, 'St Leonard Shoreditch, minute book of the
   select vestry and parish meetings', P/L/1, 1727–71
London Metropolitan Archives (LMA)
   City of London: 'City's cash accounts', COL/CHD/CT/01
   City of London: 'Lord Mayor's waiting books', CLA/004/01/01
   City of London: 'Mansion House charge books', CLC/286/MS00487
   City of London: 'Repertories of the Court of Aldermen', COL/CA/01/01
   City of London: Sessions, 'Account of the expenses of passing vagrants that
      was passed from Southwark to St Magnus London Bridge ... January the
      12th 1747/8 to Jan. 1755', CLA/047/LR/06/034
   City of London: Sessions, 'City sessions rolls', CLA/047/LJ
   City of London: Sessions, 'Committee for carrying into execution so much of
      the Act of parliament lately passed as relates to the rebuilding the gaol of
      Newgate', COL/CC/NGC/04/01/001
   City of London: Sessions, 'Miscellaneous papers from the Compter Commit-
      tee', CLA/032/02/006
   Court of Aldermen Papers, 'The humble complaint of James Guthrie, Ordin-
      ary of Newgate, read 19 Feb. 1744[/5]', COL/CA/05/01/0093
   Foundling Hospital, 'Register of children claimed, 28 March 1764 – 23 Jan.
      1765', A/FH/A/11/001/001
   Middlesex Sessions: 'Account of people convicted and confined on a prison
      ship', MA/G/GEN/1301

Middlesex Sessions: 'House of correction calendars', MJ/CC/B/079–90
Middlesex Sessions: 'Justices' reports to sessions on the state of New Prison and Middlesex Bridewell', MA/G/GEN/7–18 (1781)
Middlesex Sessions: 'List of prisoners committed to New Prison', MJ/CC/V/ 002
Middlesex Sessions: 'Minutes of the committee for building the new house of correction', MA/G/CBF/1
Middlesex Sessions: 'Minutes of the committee for repairing the house of correction, Clerkenwell, and the New Prison, Clerkenwell', MA/G/GEN/0001
Middlesex Sessions: 'Rotation Committee papers', MC/SJ-1, 1763–4
Middlesex Sessions: 'Sessions books', MJ/SBB
Middlesex Sessions: 'Sessions papers', MJ/SP/1689/08/010
Middlesex Sessions: 'Sessions rolls', MJ/SR
Middlesex Sessions: 'Vagrant expenses: rewards', MF/V/1748, MF/V/1757
'Minutes of the Court of the President and Governors for the Poor of London', CLA/075/01/007, 1702–5
St Ann Blackfriars, 'Workhouse committee book', P69/ANN/B/074/MS08690
St Boltoph Aldgate, 'Vestry minute books for the Middlesex part of the parish', P69/BOT2/B/003/MS02642-43
St Bride Fleet Street, 'Miscellaneous parish papers', P69/BRI/B/012/ MS06570/002
St Bride Fleet Street, 'Vestry minutes', P69/BRI/B/001/MS06554/004–005
St Dionis Backchurch, 'Miscellaneous parish papers, vouchers, 1766–72', P69/ DIO/B/099
St Dionis Backchurch, 'Papers relating to an application for parish poor relief by Paul Patrick Kearney, 1771', P69/DIO/B/082/MS11280C
St Peter Cornhill, 'Removal orders, pass warrants and settlement examinations', P69/PET1/B/029/MS04198
St Sepulchre, Holborn, 'City of London, Workhouse committee book', P69/ SEP/B/071/MS03137/001
Westminster Sessions: 'Orders of the court', WJ/O/C
The National Archives (TNA)
High Court of Admiralty, 'Criminal records', HCA1/20, 1744
Home Office, 'Criminal petitions, series 1', HO17
Home Office, 'Judges' reports on criminals', HO47
Home Office, 'Letters and papers', HO42/25
King's Bench, 'Crown side affidavits', KB1/1/3/2, Trinity 1719
King's Bench, 'Crown side affidavits', KB1/19/2/1, Michaelmas 1772
State Papers Domestic, 'George I', SP35
State Papers Domestic, 'George II', SP36
State Papers Domestic, 'George III', SP37
Treasury Papers, Accounts, T38/671, 1755–8
Treasury Papers, 'Sheriff's cravings', T64/262
Treasury Papers, 'King vs Greenwood and Hipgrave', T1/468
Treasury Solicitors Papers, 'Re: prosecutions of the Spitalfields weavers re attacks on Spitalfields silk manufacturers', TS11/818

Westminster Abbey Muniment Room, '13 May 1799', Ms. 660000
Westminster Archives Centre (WAC)
   St James Westminster, 'Vestry minutes', D1759–1760, 1712–50
   St Margaret Westminster, 'Orders of vestry', E2420, 1738–55
   St Margaret Westminster, 'Petty sessions minutes', E2554, 1719–23,
   St Margaret Westminster, 'Petty sessions records', SMW/E/99, 1723
   St Margaret Westminster, 'Workhouse committee minutes', SMW/E/101/
      2632, 1726–7
   St Martin in the Fields, 'Vestry clerks bills', F2339, 1736–72
   St Martin in the Fields, 'Vestry draft minutes', F2028, 1736–54
   St Martin in the Fields, 'Vestry minutes', STM/F/1/2006, 1716–39
   St Martin in the Fields, 'Watch rates, collectors book', F2676, 1735–57

SOURCES FROM *LONDON LIVES, 1690–1800: CRIME,
POVERTY AND SOCIAL POLICY IN THE METROPOLIS*
(www.londonlives.org)

Bridewell Royal Hospital: Minute Books of the General Prison Committee,
   1775–1800
Bridewell Royal Hospital: Minutes of the Court of Governors, 1689–1800
City of London Sessions: Sessions Papers, 1690–1796
City of Westminster Coroners: Inquests into Suspicious Deaths, 1761–1800
Home Office: Criminal Registers of Prisoners in Middlesex and the City,
   1791–1800
Middlesex Coroners: Inquests, 1781–1799
Middlesex Sessions: General Orders of the Court, 1713–1800
Middlesex Sessions: Sessions Papers, 1690–1799
Old Bailey Proceedings, 1674–1800
Old Bailey Sessions: Sessions Papers, 1771
Ordinary of Newgate Prison: Ordinary's Accounts, 1680–1772
St Botolph Aldgate Parish: Churchwardens and Overseers of the Poor Account
   Books, 1683–1800
St Clement Danes Parish: Registers of the Poor, 1745
St Clement Danes Parish: Enfield Books – Parish Children Put Out to Nurse,
   1787–98
St Clement Danes Parish: List of Securities for the Maintenance of Bastard
   Children, 1755–79
St Clement Danes Parish: List of Workhouse Inmates, 1785
St Clement Danes Parish: Minute Books of Parish Vestry Sub-Committees,
   1771–1800
St Clement Danes Parish: Minutes of Parish Vestries, 1703–1800
St Clement Danes Parish: Pauper Settlement, Vagrancy and Bastardy Exams,
   1739–1800
St Clement Danes Parish: Register of Fortnightly/Monthly Pensioners in 1733
St Clement Danes Parish: Register of Pauper Settlement and Bastardy Examin-
   ations, 1703–7
St Clement Danes Parish: Registers of Poor Children under 14 years in Parish
   Care

St Dionis Backchurch Parish: Churchwardens and Overseers of the Poor Account Books, 1689–1798

St Dionis Backchurch Parish: Churchwardens Vouchers/Receipts, 1683–1782

St Dionis Backchurch Parish: Letters to Parish Officials Seeking Pauper Relief, 1758–9

St Dionis Backchurch Parish: Minutes of Parish Vestries, 1690–1800

St Dionis Backchurch Parish: Miscellaneous Parish and Bridewell Papers, 1722–97

St Dionis Backchurch Parish: Workhouse Inquest (Visitation) Minute Books, 1761–88

St Luke Chelsea Workhouse Registers, 1743–99

St Martin in the Fields Settlement Examinations, 1725–93

St Martin in the Fields Workhouse Registers, 1725–1819

St Thomas's Hospital Admission and Discharge Registers

Westminster Historical Database

Westminster Sessions: Sessions Papers, 1690–1799

ONLINE DATA SETS CREATED FOR THIS BOOK

Located at www.cambridge.org/9781107639942

City of London Vagrant Expenditure, 1739–92 (City of London Vagrant Expenditure 1738–1792.xlsx)

Crime Prosecutions, 1680–1800 (Crime Prosecutions.xlsx)

Escapes and Attempted Escapes from Prisons, Hulks and Transports, 1776–85 (Escapes, 1776–1786.xlsx)

Legal Counsel at the Old Bailey, 1715–1800 (Legal Counsel at the Old Bailey 1715–1800.xlsx)

London Whipping Punishments, 1770–99 (London Whipping Punishments, 1770–1799.xlsx)

Old Bailey Death Sentences and Executions, 1749–1806 (Death Sentences and Executions 1749–1806.xlsx)

Old Bailey Punishment Sentences, 1690–1800 (Punishment Stats 1690–1800. xlsx)

Old Bailey Trials which Include 'Gin' or 'Geneva', 1715–80 (Gin Geneva in Old Bailey Trials.xlsx)

Poor Relief Expenditure for St Clement Danes, 1706–1803 (St Clement Danes Poor Law Expenditure 1706–1803.xlsx)

Poor Relief Expenditure, 1690–1800 (Poor Relief Expenditure, 1690–1800.xlsx)

Prosecutions Initiated by the Societies for the Reformation of Manners, 1693–1738 (SRM Prosecutions, 1693–1738.xlsx)

St Clement Danes, Pauper Census, 1745 (St Clements Census of Pensioners 1745.xlsx)

St Dionis Backchurch Poor Law Expenditure 1688–1803 (St Dionis Backchurch Poor Law Expenditure 1688–1803.xlsx)

St Martin's Workhouse Registers, 1725–1834 (St Martins Workhouse Registers. xlsx)

Vice Offences Recorded in Lord Mayor's Waiting and Charge Books, 1686–1733 (LM Waiting and Charge Books 1686–1733.xlsx)

Wages and Prices, 1696–1800 (Wages and Prices.xlsx)

OTHER INTERNET PRIMARY SOURCES

Online sources last consulted 15 July 2015

17th–18th Century Burney Collection Newspapers (www.galegroup.com)

Annual Register (www.bodley.ox.ac.uk/ilej)

British History Online (http://www.british-history.ac.uk/), *Statutes of the Realm*, vols. 5–7, 1628–1701

British Museum Collection Online (www.britishmuseum.org/research/collection_online/collection_object_details.aspx)

Eighteenth-Century Collections Online (www.galegroup.com)

English Short Title Catalogue (estc.bl.uk)

John Strype's A Survey of the Cities of London and Westminster (1720) (hrionline.ac.uk/strype/)

International Genealogical Index (IGI) (familysearch.org)

Locating London's Past (www.locatinglondon.org)

Parliamentary Papers (PP) (parlipapers.chadwyck.co.uk):

'A report from the committee appointed to enquire into the state of the goals of this kingdom; relating to the Marshalsea prison', 1729

'Abridgement of abstract of answers and returns relative to expense and maintenance of poor in England and Wales', 1818

'Abstract of the answers and returns made ... relative to the expense and maintenance of the poor in England', 1803–4

'Abstract of the returns made by the overseers of the poor, 1776', 15 May 1777

House of Commons Sessional Papers, 'Abstract of the returns made ... by the overseers of poor', 1776

Journals of the House of Commons, 1692–1800

Journals of the House of Lords, 1698–1800

'Report from the committee appointed to inspect and consider the returns made by the overseers of the poor, in pursuance of Act of last session', 1777

'Report from the committee appointed to make enquiries relating to the employment, relief and maintenance of the poor', Fourth Schedule, 21 May 1776

'Report from the committee on the state of the police of the metropolis', 1816

'Report from the committee ... to consider ... persons convicted of felonies or misdemeanors, and now under sentence of imprisonment', 1 April 1779

'Report from the Select Committee on poor rate returns', 1821

'Report from the Select Committee on the poor laws', 1818

'Report of the commissioners of the Inland Revenue of the duties under their management', 1870

'Report of the committee on the state of the parish poor children', 1 May 1778

'Report of the committee to inspect the poor's rates and the scavenger's rates within the cities of London and Westminster, and weekly bills of mortality', 1715

Proceedings of the Old Bailey Online, 1674–1913 (oldbaileyonline.org)

Portcullis: Parliamentary Archives Catalogue [authoritative list of statutes] (portcullis.parliament.uk/)

The Times Digital Archive (thetimes.co.uk/tto/archive/)

University of Pennsylvania Archives, Ms. Codex 1623, 'Asylum for Orphan Girls, minutes and records of the Guardians', 1758–83 (dla.library.upenn. edu/dla/medren)

The Yale Edition of Horace Walpole's 12 *Correspondence* (images.library.yale.edu/ hwcorrespondence)

PRINTED PRIMARY SOURCES

(Place of publication is London unless otherwise stated.)

An Account of John Rann, Commonly Called Sixteen-String Jack ([1774?])

An Account of Several Workhouses (2nd edn, 1732)

An Account of Some Alterations and Amendments Attempted in the Duty and Office of Sheriff of the County of Middlesex and Sheriffs of the City of London, during the Shrievalty of Sir Barnard Turner and Thomas Skinner, Esq. (1784)

An Account of the Endeavours That Have Been Used to Suppress Gaming-houses, and of the Discouragements That Have Been Met with (1722)

An Account of the Hospital for the Maintenance and Education of Exposed and Deserted Young Children (1759)

The Address Published by the London Corresponding Society, at the General Meeting, Held at the Globe Tavern, Strand, on Monday the 20th of January, 1794 ([1794])

Allen, [Fifield], *An Account of the Behaviour of Mr James Maclaine* (1750)

The Annals of Europe for the year 1742. Being a methodological and full account of all the remarkable occurrences which happened with that year either at home or abroad (1745)

Antimoixeia: or, the Honest and Joynt Design of the Tower-Hamblets for the General Suppression of Bawdy Houses, As Incouraged by the Publick Magistrates (1691)

Authentic Memoirs of the Life, Numerous Adventures, and Remarkable Escapes, of the Celebrated Patrick Madan (1782)

The Authentic Trial, and Memoirs of Isaac Darkin, alias Dumas, Capitally Convicted for a Highway-robbery, near Nettlebed... at Oxford (Oxford, 1761)

Blincoe, Robert, *A Memoir of Robert Blincoe, An Orphan Boy; sent from the Workhouse of St Pancras, London, at seven years of age to Endure the Horrors of a Cotton-Mill* (Manchester, 1832; repr. Caliban Books, 1977)

Blizard, William, *Desultory Reflections on Police* (1785)

Bradstreet, Dudley, *The Life and Uncommon Adventures of Captain Dudley Bradstreet* (Dublin, 1755)

Bray, Thomas, *The Good Fight of Faith... Exemplified in a Sermon Preached the 24th of March 1708/9* (1709)

A Brief Historical Account of the Lives of the Six Notorious Street-Robbers, Executed at Kingston (1726)

Browne, Moses, *The Causes that Obstruct the Progress of Reformation* (1765)

Burke, Edmund, 'Some Thoughts on the Approaching Executions', in *The Works of the Right Honourable Edmund Burke*, 2 vols. (1846)

Burn, Richard, *The Justice of the Peace, and Parish Officer*, 4 vols. (1755; 12th edn, 1772, and 18th edn, 1797)

[Burrow, James], *Reports of cases Argued and Adjudged in the Court of King's Bench, during the Time of Lord Mansfield's Presiding in that Court*, 5 vols. (Dublin, 5th edn, 1794)

Candler, Ann, *Poetical Attempts by Ann Candler, a Suffolk Cottager with a Short Narrative of Her Life* (Ipswich, 1803)

The Case of the Parish of St Giles in the Fields, As to their Poor, and a Work-House Designed to be built for Employing them (n.d., 1725; a later Irish edition of the *Rules* is available on Open Access)

The Charge of Sir John Gonson, Knt. to the Grand Jury of the Royalty of the Tower of London (1728)

A Clear State of the Case of Elizabeth Canning (1753)

Cobbett, William and David Jardine, *Complete Collection of State Trials and Proceedings for . . . 1794*, Vol. XXIII (1817)

A Collection of the Yearly Bills of Mortality, from 1657 to 1758 Inclusive. Together with several other bills of an earlier date (1759)

Collyer, John, *The Criminal Statutes of England: Analysed, and Arranged Alphabetically* (1828)

Colquhoun, Patrick, *A Treatise on the Commerce and Police of the River Thames* (1800)

A Treatise on the Police of the Metropolis. . . The Sixth Edition (1800)

A Compleat Collection of Remarkable Tryals of the Most Notorious Malefactors, 4 vols. ([1718]–21)

Complete History of James McLean, the Gentleman Highwayman (1750)

The Conduct of Ralph Hodgson, Esq. . . . in the Affair of the Coal-heavers (1768)

A Copy of the Royal Charter, Establishing an Hospital for the Maintenance and Education Of Exposed and Deserted Young Children (1739)

Cox, Joseph, *A Faithful Narrative of the Most Wicked and Inhuman Transactions of that Bloody-Minded Gang of Thief-takers, alias Thief-Makers* (1756)

Decisions of the Court of King's Bench, upon the Laws Relating to the Poor, 2 vols. (1793)

Defoe, Daniel, *Augusta Triumphans: Or, the Way to Make London the Most Flourishing City in the Universe* (1728)

[Defoe, Daniel], Andrew Moreton, *Parochial Tyranny: Or, The House-Keeper's Complaint Against the insupportable Exactions, and Partial Assessments of Select Vestries, &c.* (1719, 2nd edn, 1727)

[Defoe, Daniel], *Street Robberies, Consider'd: the Reason of their being so Frequent* ([1728])

The True and Genuine Account of the Life and Actions of the Late Jonathan Wild: Not Made Up of Fiction and Fable, but Taken from his own Mouth (1725)

DeVeil, Thomas, *Observations on the Practice of a Justice of the Peace* (1747)

Directions for Prosecuting Thieves without the Help of those False Guides, the Newgate Sollicitors (1728)

Downing, Joseph, *A New Catalogue of Books and Small Tracts Against Vice and Immorality; and for Promoting the Knowledge & Practice of the Christian Religion. . .* ([1708])

Downright, Sir Daniel, *The Bastard Child, or a Feast for the Church-Wardens* (1768)

An Effectual Scheme for the Immediate Preventing of Street-Robberies (1731)

An Excellent New Copy of Verses, Being the Sorrowful Lamentation of Mrs Cooke (1703)

Farrer, William, *A Genuine Account of the Confession and Dying Words of William Farrer* (2nd edn, 1747?)

Fielding, Henry, *A Charge Delivered to the Grand Jury... on Thursday the 29th of June* (1749)

  The History of Amelia (1751)

  The Journal of a Voyage to Lisbon (1755)

  A Proposal for Making an Effectual Provision for the Poor (1753)

  A True State of the Case of Bosavern Penlez (1749)

Fielding, John, *An Account of the Origin and Effects of a Police Set on Foot by His Grace the Duke of Newcastle in the Year 1753* (1758)

  Extracts from such of the Penal Laws, as Particularly Relate to the Peace and Good Order of this Metropolis (1768)

  A Plan for Preventing Robberies within Twenty Miles of London, with an Account of the Rise and Establishment of the real Thief-takers (1755)

  The Fourteenth Account of the Progress made in Suppressing Profaneness and Debauchery, by the Societies for Reformation of Manners (1709)

Fowler, [Edward], *A Vindication of a Late Undertaking of Certain Gentlemen* (1692)

A Full and Particular Account of the Life and Notorious Transactions of Roger Johnson (1740)

A Further Examination of the Weavers Pretences (1719)

Gay, John, *The Beggars Opera* (1728)

A Genuine Account of the Life and Actions of James McLean, Highwayman (1750)

A Genuine Account of the Life of John Rann, Alias Sixteen-String Jack ([1774?])

A Genuine Account of the Life, Robberies, Trial and Execution of William Cox (1773)

Genuine Copies of all the Letters which Passed Between the Right Honourable The Lord Chancellor, and the Sheriffs of London and Middlesex ... Relative to the Execution of Doyle and Valine (1770)

The Genuine Life of William Cox, who is Now Under Sentence of Death, in Newgate (5th edn, 1773)

A Genuine Narrative of all the Street Robberies Committed since October last, by James Dalton (1728)

Genuine Narrative of the Life and Surprising Robberies and Adventures of William Page (1758)

The Great Grievance of Traders and Shopkeepers, by the Notorious Practice of Stealing their Goods out of their Shops and Warehouses (1699)

Hanging no Dishonour. Being a modest attempt to prove that such persons as have the honour to make their exit at the triple-tree are not always the greatest Villains in the Nation (1747)

Hanging, Not Punishment Enough, for Murtherers, High-way Men and House Breakers (1701)

Hanway, Jonas, *An Account of the Marine Society, Recommending the Piety and Policy of the Institution* (1759)

  A Candid Historical Account of the Hospital for the Reception of Exposed and Deserted Young Children (1760)

  The Defects of Police the Cause of Immorality (1775)

An Earnest Appeal for Mercy to the Children of the Poor (1766)

Serious Considerations on the Salutary Design of the Act of Parliament for a Regular, Uniform Register of the Parish-Poor (1762)

Hawkins, John, *The Life of Samuel Johnson* (Dublin, 1787)

Hawkins, William, *A True and Impartial Account of all the Robberies Committed by William Hawkins* (1722)

Hints and Cautions for the information of the Churchwardens and Overseers of the Poor of the Parishes of St Giles in the Fields and St George Bloomsbury (1797)

His Majesties Letter to the Lord Bishop of London (1689)

The Historical Register, Containing an Impartial Relation of all Transactions, Foreign and Domestic ([1729])

The History of the Remarkable Life of John Sheppard (1724)

Hitchen, Charles, *A True Discovery of the Conduct of Receivers and Thief-Takers* (1718)

Holcroft, Thomas, *A Plain and Succinct Narrative of the Late Riots and Disturbances* (3rd edn, 1780)

Holloway, Robert, *A Letter to Sir John Fielding, Knight. Illustrated with a Portrait of a Monster* (1772)

   The Rat-Trap: Dedicated to the Right Hon. Lord Mansfield . . . Addressed to Sir John Fielding (1773)

Howard, John, *An Account of the Principal Lazarettos in Europe* (Warrington, 1789)

   The State of the Prisons in England and Wales (Warrington, 1777)

[Ilive, Jacob], *Reasons Offered for the Reformation of the House of Correction in Clerkenwell* (1757)

   A Scheme for the Employment of all Persons Sent as Disorderly to the House of Correction in Clerkenwell (1759)

Jekyll, Thomas, *A Sermon Preach'd at St Mary-le-Bow, June 27, 1698. Before the Societies for Reformation of Manners* (1698)

Jollie, Timothy, *A Sermon Preached to the Societies for the Reformation of Manners* (1739)

Luttrell, Narcissus, *A Brief Historical Relation of State Affairs from September 1678 to April 1714*, 5 vols. (Oxford, 1857)

Mackdonald, Capt., *A General History of the Lives and Adventures of the Most Famous Highwaymen, Murderers, Pirates, Street-Robbers, and Thief-takers* (1758)

Maddox, Isaac, *An Epistle to the Right Honourable the Lord Mayor, Aldermen and Common Council of the City of London* (1751)

   The Expediency of Preventive Wisdom. A Sermon Preached before the Right Honourable the Lord-Mayor, the Aldermen, and Governors of Several Hospitals of the City of London . . . With a Dedication and an Appendix concerning Spirituous Liquors (1751)

Malcolm, J. P., *Anecdotes of the Manners and Customs of London during the Eighteenth Century* (1808)

Mandeville, Bernard, *An Enquiry into the Causes of the Frequent Executions at Tyburn* ([1725])

Manning, James and Archer Ryland, *Reports of Cases Argued and Determined in the Court of King's Bench* (1828)

Martin, Matthew, *An Appeal to Public Benevolence for the Relief of Beggars: With a View to a Plan for the Suppression of Beggary* (1812)

Massie, Joseph, *Farther Observations Concerning the Foundling-Hospital* (1759)

Memoirs of the Life and Times of Sir Thomas De Veil, Knight, One of His Majesty's Justices of the Peace, for the Counties of Middlesex, Essex, Surrey and Hertfordshire, The City and Liberty of Westminster, The Tower of London, and the Liberties thereof, &c. (1748)

Miles, William Augustus, *A Letter to Sir John Fielding* (1773)

The Miseries of Goals, and the Cruelty of Goalers. Being a Narrative of Several Persons now under Confinement (1729)

Misson, Henri, *M. Misson's Memoirs and Observations in his Travels over England*, trans. M. Ozell ([1719])

Morris, Corbyn, *Observations on the Past Growth and Present State of London* (2nd edn, 1758)

Munn, Thomas, *The Life of Thomas Munn ... who was Executed with John Hall* (1750)

A Narrative of All the Robberies, Escapes, etc. of John Sheppard... The whole Published at the particular Request of the Prisoner (1724)

A Narrative of the Barbarous and Unheard of Murder of Mr John Hayes (1726)

Nourse, Timothy, *Campania Foelix: Or, a Discourse of the Benefits and Improvements of Husbandry* (1706)

O'Neale, Dennis, *Memoirs of the Life and Remarkable Exploits of the Noted Dennis Neale* (1754)

The Only Authentic Life and Trial of William Cox ([1773?])

Paine, Thomas, *The Rights of Man, for the Use and Benefit of All Mankind*, Vol. II (1792, 1795 edn)

The Parliamentary History of England from the Earliest Period to 1803, Vol. XVI (1813)

Parsons, William, *A Genuine, Impartial and Authentick Account of the Life of William Parsons* (1751)

Memoirs of the Life and Adventures of William Parsons (1751)

Phipps, Joseph, *The Vestry Laid Open* (2nd edn, 1739)

Poulter, John, *The Discoveries of John Poulter, alias Baxter* (1754)

The Proceedings at the Assizes of the Peace, Oyer and Terminer, and General Gaol Delivery for the County of Surry [sic] (1745)

Proposals for a National Reformation of Manners (1694)

Proposals to the Legislature for Preventing the Frequent Executions and Exportations of Convicts (1754)

Ramsay, Allan, *A Letter to the Right Honourable the Earl of – Concerning the Affair of Elizabeth Canning* (1753)

Reasons Humbly Offered to this Honourable House why a Bill Pretended to Give Further Powers to the Corporation for Setting the Poor of the City of London... Should Not Pass (n.d., 1700)

A Report of all the Cases Determined by Sir John Holt, Knt. from 1688 to 1710 (1738)

The Report of the Committee Appointed by a General Vestry of the Inhabitants of the Parish of St Botolph without Aldersgate, London: February 22d 1732. With some methods proposed to prevent abuses for the future (1733)

Report of the Committee to whom the Petition of the Principal Inhabitants of ... Westminster... was referred (1742)

The Rev. William Winterbotham: A Sketch (1893)

Rowlandson, Thomas, *'More Miseries', Miseries of Human Life (1807–08)*, British Museum, 1869, 0213.100.

Rules and Orders to Be Observed by the Officers and Servants in St. Giles's Workhouse, and by the Poor Therein (1726)

Rules, Orders, and Regulations for the Management of the New House of Correction for the County of Middlesex (1795)

Saxby, Mary, *Memoirs of Mary Saxby, A Female Vagrant* (1806; repr. 1827)

Select Trials at the Sessions-House in the Old Bailey, 4 vols. (1742)

A Sixth Black List of Names or Reputed Names of Eight Hundred and Forty Three Leud and Scandalous 25 Persons, who, By the Endeavours of a Society for Promoting a Reformation of Manners in the City of London, and Suburbs thereof, have been Legally Prosecuted and Convicted (London, 1700)

[Smith, Alexander], *Memoirs of the Life and Times of the Famous Jonathan Wild* (London, 1726) (rprt, Garland Press, 1973)

Smith, William, *State of the Gaols in London, Westminster, and Borough of Southwark* (London, 1776)

Some Considerations of the Fatal Effects ... of the Present Excess of Publick Charities (London, 1763)

Steele, Richard, *The Englishman: Being the Sequel of the Guardian* (London, 1714)

Swift, Jonathan, 'Clever Tom Clinch Going to be Hanged', in *The Works of Jonathan Swift*, Vol. II: *Poetical Works* (Dublin, 1772)

A Trip from St James's to the Royal Exchange: The Manners, Customs and Amusements of the Inhabitants of London and Westminster (London, 1744)

A True, Genuine and Authentic Account of the Behaviour, Conduct and Transactions of John Rice, the Broker, and Paul Lewis, the Famous Highwayman, who were Executed at Tyburn May 4, 1763 (London, 1763)

T–t–m and V–d–t, A Collection of the Advertisements and Hand-Bills, Serious, Satyrical and Humorous, Published on Both Sides During the Election for the City and Liberty of Westminster (Dublin, 1749)

Tyburn's Worthies, or the Robberies and Enterprizes of John Hawkins and George Simpson (London, [1722])

Victor, Benjamin, *History of the Theatres of London and Dublin*, Vol. 1 (London, 1761)

Villette, John, *The Annals of Newgate; or Malefactors Register*, 4. Vols (London, 1776)

Welch, Saunders, *An Essay on the Office of Constable* (London, 1758)

Wesley, John, *A Sermon Preached before the Society for the Reformation of Manners* (London, 1763)

[Wesley, John], *Some Account of the Life and Death of Matthew Lee* (London, 2nd edn, 1752)

William, Charles, *et al.*, eds, *The Works and Correspondence of... Edmund Burke*, 8 Vols (London: J. Rivington, 1856)

Wilson, George, *Reports of Cases Argued and Adjudged in the King's Courts at Westminster* (London, 2nd edn, 1779)

Wilson, Ralph, *A Full and Impartial Account of all the Robberies Committed by John Hawkins, George Sympson (lately Executed for Robbing the Bristol Mails) and their Companions* (London, 4th edn, 1722)

Wood, Simon, *Remarks on the Fleet Prison: or, Lumber-House for Men and Women* (1733)

Woodward, Josiah, *An Account of the Rise and Progress of the Religious Societies in the City of London, etc. and of the Endeavours for Reformation of Manners* (2nd edn, 1698)

　The Duty of Compassion to the Souls of Others (1697)

　Sodom's Vices (1700)

　The Workhouse Cruelty; Being a Full and True Account of One Mrs. M. W., . . . in the Parish of St. Giles's in the Field (n.d., 1731)

　The Workhouse Cruelty: Workhouses Turn'd Goals; and Goalers [sic] Executioners . . . in the Parish of St. Giles's in the Fields (n.d., 1731)

　The Works of Benjamin Franklin: Containing Several Political and Historical Tracts not Included in any Former Edition, ed. Jared Sparks, 10 vols. (1840)

Wraxall, N. William, *Historical Memoirs of My Own Time* (Philadelphia, Penn., 1836)

MODERN PRINTED EDITIONS OF PRIMARY SOURCES

Aspinal, A., ed., *English Historical Documents 1783–1832* (London: Routledge, 1996)

Boswell, James, *Boswell's London Journal 1762–1763*, ed. Frederick A. Pottle (New York: McGraw-Hill, 1950)

Burn, James Dawson, *The Autobiography of a Beggar Boy*, ed. David Vincent (London: Europa, 1978)

Calendar of Home Office Papers of the Reign of George III: Preserved in the Public Record Office (London: HMSO, 1899)

Fielding, Henry, *The Covent-Garden Journal and A Plan of the Universal Register-Office*, ed. Bertrand A. Goldgar (Wesleyan edn, Oxford University Press, 1988)

　An Enquiry into the Causes of the Late Encrease in Robbers and Related Writings, ed. Malvin R. Zirker (Wesleyan edn, Oxford: Clarendon, 1988)

The Flying Highwayman (c. 1750), repr. in John Holloway and Joan Black, eds., *Later English Broadsides* (London: Routledge & Kegan Paul, 1975), pp. 103–4 and online at *Outlaws and Highwaymen* (www.outlawsandhighwaymen.com/flying.htm)

Gringer, John, ed., *Handel's Trumpeter: The Diary of John Grano* (Bucina: The Historic Brass Society Series, no. 3; Stuyvesant, NY: Pendragon Press, 1998)

Hitchcock, Tim and John Black, eds., *Chelsea Settlement and Bastardy Examinations, 1733–1766* (London Record Society, vol. 33, 1999)

Holloway, John and Joan Black, *Later English Broadside Ballads*, Vol. I (London: Routledge & Kegan Paul, 1975)

Lamoine, Georges, ed., *Charges to the Grand Jury 1689–1803*, Camden Fourth Series, vol. 43 (London: Royal Historical Society, 1992)

The Letters of William Shenstone, ed. Marjorie Williams (Oxford: Basil Blackwell, 1939)

Levene, Alysa (general ed.), *Narratives of the Poor in Eighteenth-Century Britain*, 4 vols. (London: Pickering & Chatto, 2006)

Port, M. H., ed., *The Commissions for Building Fifty New Churches: The Minute Books, 1711–1727: A Calendar* (London Record Society, vol. 22, 1986)

Savile, Alan, ed., *Secret Comment: The Diaries of Gertrude Savile 1721–1757* (Thoroton Society Record Series, vol. 41, 1995)

Smith, Greg T., ed., *Summary Justice in the City: A Selection of Cases Heard at the Guildhall Justice Room, 1753–1781* (London Record Society, vol. 48, 2013)

Sokoll, Thomas, ed., *Essex Pauper Letters, 1731–1837* (Oxford University Press, 2001)

Thale, Mary, ed., *Selections from the Papers of the London Corresponding Society, 1792–1799* (Cambridge University Press, 1983)

The Autobiography of Francis Place (1771–1854) (Cambridge University Press, 1972)

SECONDARY SOURCES

Amory, Henry, 'Henry Fielding and the criminal legislation of 1751–2', *Philological Quarterly*, 50 (1971), 175–92

Andrew, Donna T., *Philanthropy and Police: London Charity in the Eighteenth Century* (Princeton University Press, 1989)

'"To the charitable and humane": appeals for assistance in the eighteenth-century London press', in Hugh Cunningham and Joanna Innes, eds., *Charity, Philanthropy and Reform from the 1690s to 1850* (Basingstoke: Macmillan Press, 1998)

'Two medical charities in eighteenth-century London: The Lock Hospital and the Lying-In Charity for married women', in Jonathan Barry and Colin Jones, eds., *Medicine and Charity before the Welfare State* (London: Routledge, 1991)

Appleby, Joyce Oldham, *Economic Thought and Ideology in Seventeenth-Century England* (Princeton University Press, 1978; repr. 2004)

Babington, Anthony, *A House in Bow Street: Crime and the Magistracy: London 1740–1881* (Chichester: Barry Rose Law, 1999)

Military Intervention in Britain from the Gordon Riots to the Gibraltar Incident (London: Routledge, 1990)

Bahlman, Dudley W. R., *The Moral Revolution of 1688* (New Haven, Conn.: Yale University Press, 1957; repr. Archon Books, 1968)

Battestin, M.C. and Ruthe R., 'Fielding, Bedford and the Westminster election of 17 1749', *Eighteenth-Century Studies*, 11:2 (1977–8), 143–85

Henry Fielding: A Life (London: Routledge, 1989)

Beattie, John M., *Crime and the Courts in England, 1660–1800* (Princeton University Press, 1986)

The First English Detectives: The Bow Street Runners and the Policing of London, 1750–1840 (Oxford University Press, 2012)

'Garrow and the detectives: lawyers and policemen at the Old Bailey in the late eighteenth century', *Crime, History and Societies*, 11:2 (2007), 5–24 (chs. revues.org, 2 Jan. 2014)

'Garrow for the defence', *History Today*, February 1991, 49–53 (www.historytoday.com, 2 Jan. 2014)

'London crime and the making of the "Bloody Code", 1689–1718', in Lee Davison *et al.*, eds., *Stilling the Grumbling Hive: the Response to Social and Economic Problems in England 1689–1750* (Stroud: Alan Sutton, 1992)

'The pattern of crime in England 1660–1800', *Past & Present*, 62 (1974), 47–95

Policing and Punishment in London, 1660–1750: Urban Crime and the Limits of Terror (Oxford University Press, 2001).

'Scales of justice: defense counsel and the English criminal trial in the eighteenth and nineteenth centuries', *Law and History Review*, 9:2 (1991), 221–67

'Sir John Fielding and public justice: The Bow Street magistrates' court, 1754–1780', *Law and History Review*, 25:1 (2007), 93–100

Beier, A. L. and Roger Finlay, eds., *London 1500–1700: The Making of the Metropolis* (London: Longman, 1986)

Bertelsen, Lance, *Henry Fielding at Work: Magistrate, Businessman, Writer* (New York: Palgrave, 2000)

Black, John, 'Illegitimacy, sexual relations and location in metropolitan London, 1735–85', in Tim Hitchcock and Heather Shore, eds., *The Streets of London from the Great Fire to the Great Stink* (London: Rivers Oram Press, 2003)

Bohstedt, John, *The Politics of Provisions: Food Riots, Moral Economy, and Market Transition in England, c. 1550 – 1850* (Farnham, Surrey: Ashgate, 2010)

Böker, Uwe, '"The people that the maddest times were ever plagued with": English justice and fair trials after the Gordon Riots (1780)?', *Erfurt Electronic Studies in English*, 6 (2003), n.p. (webdoc.sub.gwdg.de/edoc/ia/eese/artic23/boeker/5_2003.html, 2 Jan. 2014)

Bondeson, Jan, *The London Monster: A Sanguinary Tale* (Philadelphia: University of Pennsylvania Press, 2001)

Borsay, Peter, ed., *The Eighteenth-Century Town: A Reader in English Urban History, 1688–1820* (London: Longman, 1990)

Boulton, Jeremy, 'Double deterrence: settlement and practice in London's West End, 1725–1824', in Anne Winter and Stephen King, eds., *Migration, Settlement and Belonging in Europe, 1500–1930s: Comparative Perspectives* (New York: Berghahn, 2013)

'Going on the parish: the parish pension and its meaning in the London suburbs, 1640–1724', in Tim Hitchcock, Peter King and Pamela Sharpe, eds., *Chronicling Poverty: The Voices and Strategies of the English Poor, 1640–1840* (Basingstoke: Macmillan, 1997)

'"It is extreme necessity that makes me do this": some "survival strategies" of pauper households in London's West End during the early eighteenth century', *International Review of Social History*, Supplement, 8 (2000), 47–70

'The most visible poor in England? Constructing pauper biographies in early-modern Westminster', *Westminster Historical Review*, 1 (1997), 13–21

'Welfare systems and the parish nurse in early modern London, 1650–1725', *Family & Community History*, 10:2 (2007), 127–51

Boulton, Jeremy and John Black, 'Paupers and their experience of a Georgian workhouse: St. Martin in the Fields, Westminster, 1725–1830', in J. Hamlett, L. Hoskins and R. Preston, eds., *Residential Institutions in Britain, 1725–1950: Inmates and Environments* (London: Pickering & Chatto, 2013)

Boulton, Jeremy and Leonard Schwarz, 'The parish workhouse, the parish and parochial medical provision in eighteenth-century London', in *Pauper Lives in Georgian London and Manchester* (research.ncl.ac.uk/pauperlives, 1 Jan. 2014)

Boulton, Jeremy, Romola Davenport and Leonard Schwarz, '"These ANTE-CHAMBERS OF THE GRAVE"? Mortality, medicine and the workhouse in Georgian London', in Jonathan Reinarz and Leonard Schwarz, eds., *Medicine and the Workhouse* (University of Rochester Press, 2013)

Branch-Johnson, William, *The English Prison Hulks* (London: Phillimore, 1970)

Brazell, J. H., *London Weather* (London: HMSO, 1968)

Brewer, John, *Party Ideology and Popular Politics at the Accession of George III* (Cambridge University Press, 1981)

   The Pleasures of the Imagination: English Culture in the Eighteenth Century (London: HarperCollins, 1997)

   'The Wilkites and the law, 1763–74: a study of radical notions of governance', in John Brewer and John Styles, eds., *An Ungovernable People: The English and their Law in the Seventeenth and Eighteenth Centuries* (London: Hutchinson, 1980)

Broad, John, 'Cattle plague in eighteenth-century England', *Agricultural History Review*, 31:2 (1983), 104–15

Brown, Roger Lee, *A History of the Fleet Prison, London*, Studies in British History, 42 (Lampeter: Edwin Mellen Press, 1996)

Byrne, Richard, *Prisons and Punishments of London* (London: Harrap, 1989)

Campbell, Charles, *Intolerable Hulks: British Shipboard Confinement 1776–1857* (London: Fenestra Books, 2001)

Cash, Arthur, *John Wilkes: The Scandalous Father of Civil Liberty* (London and New Haven, Conn.: Yale University Press, 2006)

Chalklin, C. W., 'The reconstruction of London's prisons 1770–99: an aspect of the growth of Georgian London', *London Journal*, 9:1 (1983), 21–34

Challis, Christopher Edgar, *A New History of the Royal Mint* (Cambridge University Press, 1992)

Charlesworth, Andrew, 'An agenda for historical studies of rural protest in Britain, 1750–1850', *Rural History*, 2 (1991), 231–40

Chartres, John, 'Food consumption and internal trade', in A. L. Beier and Roger Finlay, eds., *London 1500–1700: The Making of the Metropolis* (London: Longman, 1986)

Christopher, Emma, *A Merciless Place: The Lost Story of Britain's Convict Disaster in Africa* (Oxford University Press, 2011)

Clark, Peter, 'The "Mother Gin" controversy in the early eighteenth century', *Transactions of the Royal Historical Society*, 5th Series, 38 (1988), 63–84

Claydon, Tony, *William III and the Godly Revolution* (Cambridge University Press, 1996)

Clayton, Mary, 'The life and crimes of Charlotte Walker, prostitute and pickpocket', *London Journal*, 33:1 (2008), 3–19

Cockburn, J. S., 'Early-modern Assize records as historical evidence', *Journal of the Society of Archivists*, 5:4 (1975), 215–31

A History of English Assizes, 1558–1714 (Cambridge University Press, 1972)

Cody, Lisa Forman, *Birthing the Nation: Sex, Science and the Conception of Eighteenth-Century Britain* (Oxford University Press, 2005)

'Every lane teems with instruction, and every alley is big with erudition: graffiti in eighteenth-century London', in Tim Hitchcock and Heather Shore, eds., *The Streets of London from the Great Fire to the Great Stink* (London: Rivers Oram Press, 2003)

'Living and dying in Georgian London's lying-in hospitals', *Bulletin of the History of Medicine*, 78:2 (2004), 309–48

Coldham, Peter Wilson, *Emigrants in Chains: A Social History of Forced Emigration to the Americas of Felons, Destitute Children, Political and Religious Non-Conformists, Vagabonds, Beggars and Other Undesirables, 1607–1776* (Baltimore: Genealogical Pub. Co., 1992)

Connors, Richard, '"The grand inquest of the nation": parliamentary committees and social policy in mid-eighteenth-century England', *Parliamentary History*, 14:3 (1995), 285–313

Cowie, Leonard W., *Henry Newman: An American in London, 1708–1743* (London: SPCK, 1956)

Crawford, Patricia, *Parents of Poor Children in England, 1580–1800* (Oxford University Press, 2010)

Dabhoiwala, Faramerz, *The Origins of Sex: A History of the First Sexual Revolution* (London: Penguin, 2012)

'Sex and societies for moral reform, 1688–1800', *Journal of British Studies*, 46:2 (2007), 290–319

'Summary justice in early-modern London', *English Historical Review*, 121:492 (2006), 796–822

Daunton, Martin, *Progress and Poverty: An Economic and Social History of Britain, 1700–1850* (Oxford University Press, 1995)

Davison, Lee, 'Experiments in the social regulation of industry: gin legislation, 1729–1751', in Lee Davison *et al.*, eds., *Stilling the Grumbling Hive: The Response to Social and Economic Problems in England, 1689–1750* (Stroud: Alan Sutton, 1992)

Davison, Lee, Tim Hitchcock, Tim Keirn, and Robert B. Shoemaker, eds., *Stilling the Grumbling Hive: The Response to Social and Economic Problems in England, 1689–1750* (Stroud: Alan Sutton, 1992)

de Castro, J. Paul, *The Gordon Riots* (London: Oxford University Press, 1926)

de Certeau, Michel, *The Practice of Everyday Life* (Berkeley: University of California Press, 1988)

de Castro, J. Paul, *The Gordon Riots* (London: Oxford University Press, 1926)

de Certeau, Michel, *The Practice of Everyday Life* (Berkeley: University of California Press, 1988)

Devereaux, Simon, '"Death is more welcome to me than this pardon": execution, transportation, and convict resistance in London during the 1780s',

Proceedings of the University of Queensland History Research Group, 13 (2002), 53–65 (espace.library.uq.edu.au, 2 Jan. 2014)

'From sessions to newspaper? Criminal trial reporting, the nature of crime, and the London press, 1770–1800', *London Journal*, 32:1 (2007) 1–27

'Imposing the royal pardon: execution, transportation, and convict resistance in London, 1789', *Law and History Review*, 25:1 (2007), 101–38

'In place of death: transportation, penal practices, and the English State, 1770–1830', in Carolyn Strange, ed., *Qualities of Mercy: Justice, Punishment and Discretion* (Vancouver: UBC Press, 1996)

'The making of the Penitentiary Act, 1775–1779', *Historical Journal*, 42:2 (1999), 405–33

'Recasting the theatre of execution: the abolition of the Tyburn ritual', *Past & Present*, 202 (2009), 127–74

Dillon, Patrick, *The Much-Lamented Death of Madam Geneva: The Eighteenth-Century Gin Craze* (London: Headline Book Publishing, 2003)

Dobson, C. R., *Masters and Journeymen: A Prehistory of Industrial Relations, 1717–1800* (London: Croom Helm, 1980)

Durston, Gregory, 'Magwitch's forbears: returning from transportation in eighteenth-century London', *Australian Journal of Legal History*, 9:2 (2005), 137–58

Earle, Peter, *A City Full of People: Men and Women of London, 1650–1750* (London: Methuen, 1994)

Eccles, Audrey, *Vagrancy in Law and Practice under the Old Poor Law* (Farnham, Surrey: Ashgate, 2012)

Ekirch, A. Roger, *Bound for America: The Transportation of British Convicts to the Colonies, 1718–1775* (Oxford: Clarendon Press, 1987)

'Great Britain's secret convict trade to America, 1783–1784', *American Historical Review*, 89:5 (December 1984), 1285–91

Evans, Robin, *The Fabrication of Virtue: English Prison Architecture, 1750–1850* (Cambridge University Press, 1982; repr. 2011)

Farge, Arlette, *Fragile Lives: Violence, Power and Solidarity in Eighteenth-Century Paris* (Cambridge: Polity Press, 1993)

Farge, Arlette and Jacques Revel, *The Vanishing Children of Paris: Rumor and Politics before the French Revolution* (Cambridge, Mass.: Harvard University Press, 1993)

Field, Michelle and Tim Millett, *Convict Love Tokens: The Leaden Hearts the Convicts Left Behind* (Kent Town, South Australia: Wakefield Press, 1998).

Finlay, Roger and Beatrice Shearer, 'Population growth and suburban expansion', in A. L. Beier and Roger Finlay, eds., *London 1500–1700: the Making of the Metropolis* (London: Longman, 1986)

Fissell, Mary, *Patients, Power and the Poor in Eighteenth-Century Bristol* (Cambridge University Press, 1991)

Fitts, James L., 'Newcastle's mob', *Albion: A Quarterly Journal Concerned with British Studies*, 5:1 (1973), 41–9

Foucault, Michel, *Discipline and Punish: The Birth of the Prison* (Harmondsworth: Penguin Books, 1979)

French, Henry and Jonathan Barry, eds., *Identity and Agency in England, 1500–1800* (New York: Palgrave Macmillan, 2004)

Fumerton, Patricia, *Unsettled: The Culture of Mobility and the Working Poor in Early Modern England* (University of Chicago Press, 2006)

Gallanis, T. P., 'The mystery of Old Bailey counsel', *Cambridge Law Journal,* 65:1 (2006), 159–73

Ganev, Robin, *Songs of Protest, Songs of Love: Popular Ballads in Eighteenth-Century Britain* (Manchester University Press, 2009)

Gatrell, V. A. C., *The Hanging Tree: Execution and the English People, 1770–1868* (Oxford University Press, 1994)

George, M. Dorothy, *London Life in the Eighteenth Century* (London, 1925; Harmondsworth: Penguin Books, 2nd edn, 1966)

Gillen, Mollie, *The Founders of Australia: A Biographical Dictionary of the First Fleet* (Sydney: Library of Australian History, 1989)

Gillis, John, *For Better, For Worse: British Marriages, 1600 to the Present* (Oxford University Press, 1988)

Gladfelder, Hal, *Criminality and Narrative in Eighteenth-Century England: Beyond the Law* (Baltimore: Johns Hopkins University Press, 2001)

Gray, Drew, *Crime, Prosecution and Social Relations: The Summary Courts of the City of London in the Late Eighteenth Century* (Houndmills: Palgrave, 2009)

Green, David, *Pauper Capital: London and the Poor Law, 1790–1870* (Farnham, Surrey: Ashgate, 2010)

Groebner, Valentin, *Who Are You? Identification, Deception, and Surveillance in Early Modern Europe* (New York: Zone Books, 2007)

Haagen, Paul, 'Eighteenth-century English society and the debt law', in Stanley Cohen and Andrew Scull, eds., *Social Control and the State* (Oxford: Martin Robertson, 1983)

Hallett, Mark, *Spectacle of Difference: Graphic Satire in the Age of Hogarth* (London: Yale University Press, 1999)

Hallsworth, Simon, 'Gangland Britain? Realities, fantasies and industry', in Barry Goldson, ed., *Youth in Crisis? 'Gangs', Territoriality and Violence* (Abingdon: Routledge, 2011)

Harding, Vanessa, 'The population of London, 1550–1700: a review of the published evidence', *London Journal,* 15:2 (1990), 111–28

Harris, Andrew T., *Policing the City: Crime and Legal Authority in London, 1780–1840* (Columbus: Ohio State University Press, 2004)

Harris, Robert, *Politics and the Nation: Britain in the Mid-Eighteenth Century* (Oxford University Press, 2002)

Hay, Douglas, 'Dread of Crown Office: the English magistracy and King's Bench, 1740–1800', in Norma Landau, ed., *Law, Crime and Society* (Cambridge University Press, 2002)

'The laws of God and the laws of man: Lord George Gordon and the death penalty', in J. Rule and R. Malcolmson, eds., *Protest and Survival: The Historical Experience* (London: The Merlin Press, 1993)

'Legislation, magistrates and judges: high law and low law in England and the empire', in David Lemmings, ed., *The British and their Laws in the Eighteenth Century* (Woodbridge: Boydell Press, 2005)

'Prosecution and power: malicious prosecution in the English courts, 1750–1850', in Douglas Hay and Francis Snyder, eds., *Policing and Prosecution in Britain 1750–1850* (Oxford: Clarendon Press, 1989)

'War, dearth and theft in the eighteenth century: the record of the English courts', *Past & Present*, 95 (1982), 117–60

Hay, Douglas and Paul Craven, eds., *Masters, Servants and Magistrates in Britain and the Empire, 1562–1955* (Chapel Hill: University of North Carolina Press, 2004)

Hay, Douglas, Peter Linebaugh, John G. Rule, E. P. Thompson and Carl Winslow, *Albion's Fatal Tree: Crime and Society in Eighteenth-Century England* (London: Allen Lane, 1975)

Haydon, Colin, *Anti-Catholicism in England: A Political and Social Study* (Manchester University Press, 1993)

Hayter, Tony, *The Army and the Crowd in Mid-Georgian England* (London: Macmillan, 1978)

Hayton, David, 'Moral reform and country politics in the late seventeenth-century House of Commons', *Past & Present*, 128 (1990), 48–91

Haywood, Ian and John Seed, eds., *The Gordon Riots: Politics, Culture and Insurrection in Late Eighteenth-Century Britain* (*Cambridge University Press*, 2012)

Henderson, Tony, *Disorderly Women in Eighteenth-Century London: Prostitution and Control in the Metropolis, 1730–1830* (London: Longman, 1999)

Hibbert, Christopher, *King Mob: The Story of Lord George Gordon and the Riots of 1780* (London: Longman, 1959)

The Road to Tyburn: The Story of Jack Sheppard and the Eighteenth-Century London Underworld (London: World Pub. Co., 1957)

Hilton, Boyd, *A Mad, Bad, and Dangerous People? England 1783–1846* (Oxford University Press, 2006)

Hindle, Steve, 'Dependency, shame and belonging: Badging the deserving poor, c. 1550–1750', *Cultural & Social History*, 1:1 (2004), 6–35

On the Parish? The Micro-Politics of Poor Relief in Rural England, c.1550–1750 (Oxford University Press, 2004)

Hitchcock, Tim and Heather Shore, eds., *The Streets of London from the Great Fire to the Great Stink* (Rivers Oram Press: London, 2003)

Hitchcock, Tim and Robert Shoemaker, *Tales from the Hanging Court* (London: Hodder Arnold, 2006)

Hitchcock, Tim, 'You bitches ... die and be damned: Gender, authority and the mob in St Martin's roundhouse disaster of 1742', in *idem* and Heather Shore, eds, *The Streets of London from the Great Fire to the Great Stink* (London: Rivers Oram Press, 2003)

Hitchcock, Tim, 'Digital searching and the re-formulation of historical knowledge', in M. Greengrass and L. Hughes, eds., *The Virtual Representation of the Past* (Farnham, Surrey: Ashgate, 2008)

Down and Out in Eighteenth-Century London (London: Hambledon and London, 2004)

'Locating beggars on the streets of eighteenth-century London', in Kim Kippen and Lori Woods, eds., *Worth and Repute: Valuing Gender in Late Medieval and Early Modern Europe* (Toronto: Centre for Reformation and Renaissance Studies, 2011)

'The London vagrancy crisis of the 1780s', *Rural History*, 24, special issue 1 (2013), 59–72

'Renegotiating the bloody code: the Gordon riots and the transformation of popular attitudes to the criminal justice system', in Ian Haywood and John Seed, eds., *The Gordon Riots: Politics, Culture and Insurrection in Late Eighteenth-Century Britain* (Cambridge University Press, 2012)

'Unlawfully begotten on her body: illegitimacy and the parish poor in St Luke Chelsea', in Tim Hitchcock, Peter King and Pamela Sharpe, eds., *Chronicling Poverty: The Voices and Strategies of the English Poor, 1640–1840* (Basingstoke: Macmillan, 1997)

'You bitches ... die and be damned: gender, authority and the mob in St Martin's roundhouse disaster of 1742', in Tim Hitchcock and Heather Shore, eds., *The Streets of London from the Great Fire to the Great Stink* (London: Rivers Oram Press, 2003)

Hitchcock, Tim and Robert Shoemaker, *Tales from the Hanging Court* (London: Hodder Arnold, 2006)

Hitchcock, Tim and Heather Shore, eds., *The Streets of London from the Great Fire to the Great Stink* (London: Rivers Oram Press, 2003)

Hitchcock, Tim, Adam Crymble and Louise Falcini, 'Loose, idle and disorderly: vagrant removal in late eighteenth-century Middlesex', *Social History*, 39:4 (2014), 509–27

Hitchcock, Tim, Peter King and Pamela Sharpe, eds., *Chronicling Poverty: The Voices and Strategies of the English Poor, 1640–1840* (Houndsditch: Macmillan, 1997)

Holmes, Geoffrey, 'The Sacheverell riots: the crowd and the church in early eighteenth-century London', *Past & Present*, 72 (1976), 55–85

Honeyman, Katrina, *Child Workers in England, 1780–1820: Parish Apprentices and the Making of the Early Industrial Labour Force* (Aldershot: Ashgate, 2007)

Hoppit, Julian, *A Land of Liberty? England 1689–1727* (Oxford: Clarendon Press, 2000)

'The myths of the South Sea Bubble', *Transactions of the Royal Historical Society*, 6th Series, 12 (2002), 145–56

Hoskins, W. G., 'Harvest fluctuations and English economic history, 1620–1759', *Agricultural History Review*, 16:1 (1968), 15–31

The Making of the English Landscape (Harmondsworth: Penguin Books, 1970)

Hostettler, John and Richard Braby, *Sir William Garrow: His Life, Times, and Fight for Justice* (Hook, Hampshire: Waterside Press, 2010)

Howson, Gerald, *Thief-Taker General: The Rise and Fall of Jonathan Wild* (London: Hutchinson, 1970; repr. 1987)

Humble, J. G. and Peter Hansell, *Westminster Hospital 1716–1974* (London: Pitman Medical Publishing, 2nd edn, 1974)

Ignatieff, Michael, *A Just Measure of Pain: The Penitentiary in the Industrial Revolution, 1750–1850* (New York: Columbia University Press, 1978)

Innes, Joanna, *Inferior Politics: Social Problems and Social Policies in Eighteenth-Century Britain* (Oxford: OUP, 2009)

   'The "mixed economy of welfare" in early modern England: assessments of the options from Hale to Malthus (c. 1683–1803)', in Martin Daunton, ed., *Charity, Self-Interest and Welfare in the English Past* (London: UCL Press, 1996)

   'Origins of the factory acts: The Health and Morals of Apprentices Act, 1802', in Norma Landau, ed., *Law, Crime and Society, 1660–1830* (Cambridge University Press, 2002)

   'Politics and morals: the reformation of manners movement in later eighteenth-century England', in Eckhart Hellmuth, ed., *The Transformation of Political Culture: England and Germany in the Late Eighteenth Century* (Oxford and New York: German Historical Institute, 1990)

   'Prisons for the poor: English bridewells, 1555–1800', in Francis Snyder and Douglas Hay, eds., *Labour, Law and Crime: An Historical Perspective* (London: Tavistock,, 1987)

Isaacs, Tina, 'The Anglican hierarchy and the reformation of manners 1688–1738', *Journal of Ecclesiastical History*, 33 (1982), 391–411

Jones, D. W., *War and Economy in the Age of William III and Marlborough* (London: Basil Blackwell, 1988)

Jones, Gareth, *History of the Law of Charity, 1532–1827* (Cambridge University Press, 1969)

Jones, Peter D., '"I cannot keep my place without being deascent": pauper letters, parish clothing and pragmatism in the south of England, 1750–1830', *Rural History*, 20:1 (2009), 31–49

Kalman, Harold D., 'Newgate prison', *Architectural History*, 12 (1969), 50–61, 108–12

Ketelaar, Eric, 'Archival temples, archival prisons: modes of power and protection', *Archival Science*, 2 (2002), 221–38

King, Peter, *Crime and Law in England, 1750–1840: Remaking Justice from the Margins* (Cambridge, CUP, 2006)

   Crime, Justice and Discretion in England, 1740–1820 (Cambridge University Press, 2000)

   'The summary courts and social relations in eighteenth-century England', *Past & Present*, 183 (2004), 125–72

King, Steven and Alannah Tomkins, eds., *The Poor in England, 1700–1850: An Economy of Makeshifts* (Manchester University Press, 2003)

King, Steven, Thomas Nutt and Alannah Tomkins, eds., *Narratives of the Poor in Eighteenth-Century England*, Vol. I: *Voices of the Poor* (London: Pickering & Chatto, 2006)

Landau, Norma, *The Justices of the Peace, 1679–1760* (Berkeley: University of California Press, 1984)

'The trading justice's trade', in Norma Landau, ed., *Law, Crime and Society, 1660–1830* (Cambridge University Press, 2002)

Landers, John, *Death and the Metropolis: Studies in the Demographic History of London, 1670–1830* (Cambridge University Press, 1993)

Landsman, Stephan, 'The rise of the contentious spirit: advocacy procedure in eighteenth-century England', *Cornell Law Review*, 75 (1990), 498–609

Langbein, John H., 'The criminal trial before the lawyers', *University of Chicago Law Review*, 45:2 (1978), 311–12

The Origins of Adversary Criminal Trial (Oxford University Press, 2003)

Lees, Lynn Hollen, *The Solidarities of Strangers: The English Poor Laws and the People, 1700–1948* (Cambridge University Press, 2006)

Lemmings, David, *Law and Government in England during the Long Eighteenth Century: From Consent to Command* (Houndmills: Palgrave Macmillan, 2011)

Professors of the Law: Barristers and English Legal Culture in the Eighteenth Century (Oxford University Press, 2000)

Leslie-Melville, R., *The Life and Work of Sir John Fielding* (London: Lincoln Williams Ltd, 1935)

Levene, Alysa, *Childcare, Health and Mortality at the London Foundling Hospital, 1741–1800* (Manchester University Press, 2007)

The Childhood of the Poor: Welfare in Eighteenth-Century London (London: Palgrave Macmillan, 2012)

'Children, childhood and the workhouse: St Marylebone, 1769–1781', *London Journal*, 9:1 (2008), 41–60

'The mortality penalty of illegitimate children: foundlings and poor children in eighteenth-century England', in Alysa Levene, Samantha Williams and Thomas Nutt, eds., *Illegitimacy in Britain, 1700–1920* (Basingstoke: Palgrave Macmillan, 2005)

Linebaugh, Peter, *The London Hanged: Crime and Civil Society in the Eighteenth Century*, 2nd ed. (London: Verso, 2006)

'The Tyburn riot against the surgeons', in Douglas Hay *et al.*, eds., *Albion's Fatal Tree: Crime and Society in Eighteenth-Century England* (London: Allen Lane, 1975)

Lis, Catharina and Hugo Soly, *Disordered Lives: Eighteenth-Century Families and their Unruly Relatives* (Cambridge: Polity Press, 1996)

Lloyd, Sarah, *Charity and Poverty in England, c. 1680–1820: Wild and Visionary Schemes* (Manchester University Press, 2009)

Lockwood, Thomas, 'Cross-Channel dramatics in the Little Haymarket theatre riot of 1738', *Studies in Eighteenth-Century Culture*, 25 (1996), 63–74

Macfarlane, Stephen, 'Social policy and the poor in the later seventeenth century', in A. L. Beier and Roger Finlay, eds., *London 1500–1700: The Making of the Metropolis* (London: Longman, 1986)

MacKay, Lynn, 'Refusing the royal pardon: London capital convicts and the reactions of the courts and press, 1789', *London Journal*, 28 (2003), 21–40
  Respectability and the London Poor, 1780–1870: The Value of Virtue (London: Pickering & Chatto, 2013)
Mandler, Peter, ed., *The Uses of Charity: The Poor on Relief in the Nineteenth-Century Metropolis* (Philadelphia: University of Pennsylvania Press, 1990)
Maxwell-Stewart, Hamish, 'Convict transportation from Britain and Ireland 1615–1870', *History Compass*, 8 (2010), 1221–42
May, Allyson, 'Advocates and truth-seeking in the Old Bailey courtroom', *Journal of Legal History*, 26:1 (2005), 83–90
  The Bar and the Old Bailey, 1750–1850 (Chapel Hill: University of North Carolina Press, 2003)
McClure, Edmund, ed., *A Chapter in English Church History* (London: SPCK, 1888)
McClure, Ruth K., *Coram's Children: The London Foundling Hospital in the Eighteenth Century* (New Haven, Conn.: Yale University Press, 1981)
McGowen, Randall, 'The Bank of England and the policing of forgery 1797–1821', *Past & Present*, 186 (2005), 81–116
  '"Making examples" and the crisis of punishment in mid-eighteenth-century England', in David Lemmings, ed., *The British and their Laws in the Eighteenth Century* (Rochester, NY: Boydell Press, 2005)
McKenzie, Andrea, 'From true confessions to true reporting? The decline and fall of the Ordinary's *Account*', *London Journal*, 30:1 (2005), 55–70
  'God's tribunal: guilt, innocence and execution in England, 1675–1775', *Cultural and Social History*, 3:2 (2006), 121–44
  'Martyrs in low life? Dying "game" in Augustan England', *Journal of British Studies*, 42:2 (April 2003), 167–205
  'The real Macheath: social satire, appropriation, and eighteenth-century criminal biography', *Huntington Library Quarterly*, 69:4 (2006), 581–605
  '"This death some strong and stout hearted man doth choose": the practice of *peine forte et dure* in seventeenth- and eighteenth-century England', *Law and History Review*, 23:2 (2005), 279–313
  Tyburn's Martyrs: Execution in England, 1675–1775 (London: Hambledon Continuum, 2007)
Mitchell, Brian R., *British Historical Statistics* (Cambridge University Press, 1988)
Monod, Paul, *Jacobitism and the English People, 1688–1788* (Cambridge University Press, 1993)
Moore, Judith, *The Appearance of Truth: The Story of Elizabeth Canning and Eighteenth-Century Narrative* (Newark: University of Delaware Press, 1994)
Morgan, Gwenda and Peter Rushton, *Eighteenth-Century Criminal Transportation: The Formation of the Criminal Atlantic* (Basingstoke: Palgrave Macmillan, 2004)
Narayan, Deepa and Patti Petesch, *Voices of the Poor from Many Lands: A Compilation* (Oxford University Press, 2002)
Navickas, Katrina, *Loyalism and Radicalism in Lancashire, 1798–1815* (Oxford University Press, 2009)
Nicholson, John, *The Great Liberty Riot of 1780* (London: BM Bozo, 1985)

Norton, Rictor, *Mother Clap's Molly House: The Gay Subculture in England, 1700–1830* (London: GMP, 1992)

O'Donoghue, Edward G., *Bridewell Hospital: Palace, Prison, Schools*, 2 vols. (London: John Lane, The Bodley Head, 1929)

Paley, Ruth, 'Thief-takers in London in the age of the McDaniel Gang, c. 1745–1754', in Douglas Hay and Francis Snyder, eds., *Policing and Prosecution in Britain 1750–1850* (Oxford: Clarendon Press, 1989)

Parsons, Vivien, 'Robert Sideaway 1758–1809', in *Australian Dictionary of Biography*, Vol. II (Manchester University Press, 1967), (adb.anu.edu.au/biography, 2 Jan. 2014)

Paulson, Ronald, *The Life of Henry Fielding* (Wiley, 2000)

Payne, Dianne, 'Rhetoric, reality and the Marine Society', *London Journal*, 30:2 (2005), 66–84

Philips, David, '"A new engine of power and authority": the institutionalization of law-enforcement in England 1780–1830', in V. A. C. Gatrell, Bruce Lenman and Geoffrey Parker, eds., *Crime and the Law: The Social History of Crime in Western Europe since 1500* (London: Europa Publications, 1980)

Pincus, Steve, *1688: The First Modern Revolution* (New Haven, Conn.: Yale University Press, 2009)

Plummer, Alfred, *The London Weavers' Company* (London: Routledge, 1972)

Portus, G. V., *Caritas Anglicana: or, an Historical Inquiry into those Religious and Philanthropical Societies that Flourished in England between the Years 1678 and 1740* (Madison: University of Wisconsin Press, 1912)

Pounds, N. J. G., *A History of the English Parish: The Culture of Religion from Augustine to Victoria* (Cambridge University Press, 2000; paperback edn 2004)

Pringle, Patrick, *Hue and Cry: The Birth of the British Police* (London: Museum Press, 1955)

Rabin, Dana, 'Drunkenness and responsibility for crime in the eighteenth century', *Journal of British Studies*, 44:3 (2005), 457–77

Radzinowicz, Leon, *A History of English Criminal Law and its Administration from 1750*, Vol. I (London: Macmillan, 1948); Vol. II (London: Stevens and Sons, 1956); Vol. III (London: Stevens and Sons, 1957)

Radzinowicz, Leon and Roger G. Hood, *A History of English Criminal Law and its Administration from 1750*, Vol. IV (London: Stevens & Sons, 1968)

Randall, Adrian, *Riotous Assemblies: Popular Protest in Hanoverian England* (Oxford University Press, 2006)

Reay, Barry, *Microhistories: Demography, Society, and Culture in Rural England, 1800–1930* (Cambridge University Press, 2002)

Reynolds, Elaine A., *Before the Bobbies: The Night Watch and Police Reform in Metropolitan London, 1720–1830* (Basingstoke: Macmillan, 1998)

'Sir John Fielding, Sir Charles Whitworth, and the Westminster Night Watch Act, 1770–1775', in Louis A. Knafla, ed., *Policing and War in Europe*, Criminal Justice History, vol. 16 (Westport, Conn.: Greenwood Press, 2002)

Roberts, M. J. D., *Making English Morals: Voluntary Association and Moral Reform in England, 1787–1886* (Cambridge University Press, 2004)

Rockman, Seth, *Scraping By: Wage Labor, Slavery, and Survival in Early Baltimore* (Baltimore: Johns Hopkins University Press, 2009)

Rogers, H. C. B., *The British Army of the Eighteenth Century* (London: Allen and Unwin, 1977)

Rogers, Nicholas, 'Aristocratic clientage, trade and independency: Popular politics in pre-radical Westminster', *Past & Present*, 61 (1973), 70–106

'Confronting the crime wave: the debate over social reform and regulation, 1749–1753', in Lee Davison *et al.*, eds., *Stilling the Grumbling Hive: The Response to Social and Economic Problems in England, 1689–1750* (Stroud: Alan Sutton, 1992)

Crowds, Culture and Politics in Georgian Britain (Oxford: Clarendon Press, 1998)

Mayhem: Post-War Crime and Violence in Britain, 1748–1753 (New Haven, Conn., Yale University Press, 2012)

'Policing the poor in eighteenth-century London: the vagrancy laws and their administration', *Histoire sociale – Social History*, 29:47 (1991), 127–47

'Popular protest in early Hanoverian London', *Past & Present*, 79 (1978), 70–100

Rudé, George, 'The Gordon Riots: a study of the rioters and their victims', *Transactions of the Royal Historical Society*, 5th Series, 6 (1956), 93–114

Paris and London in the Eighteenth Century: Studies in Popular Protest (New York and London: Viking Press, 1971)

Wilkes and Liberty: A Social Study (Oxford: Clarendon Press, 1962)

Samuel, Raphael, 'Comers and goers', in H. J. Dyos and Michael Wolff, eds., *The Victorian City: Images and Reality*, Vol. I (London: Routledge & Kegan Paul, 1973)

Schwarz, Leonard, 'Income distribution and social structure in London in the late eighteenth century', *Economic History Revew*, 32:2 (1979), 250–9

London in the Age of Industrialisation: Entrepreneurs, Labour Force and Living Conditions, 1700–1850 (Cambridge University Press, 1992)

'The standard of living in the long run: London, 1700–1860', *Economic History Review*, 2nd Series, 38:1 (1985), 24–41

Scott, James C., *Domination and the Arts of Resistance: Hidden Transcripts* (New Haven, Conn.: Yale University Press, 2008)

Weapons of the Weak: Everyday Forms of Peasant Resistance (New Haven, Conn.: Yale University Press, 1985)

Scouten, A. H., ed., *The London Stage, 1660–1800: Part 3, 1729–1747* (Bloomington: Southern Illinois University Press, 1961)

Seleski, Patty, 'A mistress, a mother and a murderess too: Elizabeth Brownrigg and the social construction of the eighteenth-century mistress', in Katherine Kittredge, ed., *Lewd and Notorious: Female Transgression in the Eighteenth Century* (Ann Arbor: University of Michigan Press, 2003)

Sharpe, Pamela, '"The bowels of coampation": a labouring family and the law, c. 1790–1834', in Tim Hitchcock, Peter King and Pamela Sharpe, eds., *Chronicling Poverty: The Voices and Strategies of the English Poor, 1640–1840* (Basingstoke: Macmillan, 1997)

Shave, S. A., 'The dependent poor? (Re)constructing the lives of individuals "on the parish" in rural Dorset, 1800–1832', *Rural History*, 20:1 (2009), 67–97

Sheehan, W. H., 'Finding solace in eighteenth-century Newgate', in J. S. Cockburn, ed., *Crime in England 1550–1800* (London: Taylor & Francis, 1977)

Sheldon, Richard, 'The London sailors' strike of 1768', in Andrew Charlesworth
    et al., eds., *An Atlas of Industrial Protest in Britain 1750–1990* (Houndmills:
    Macmillan, 1996)
Shelton, Walter J., *English Hunger and Industrial Disorders: A Study of Social Conflict
    during the first Decade of George III's Reign* (University of Toronto Press, 1973)
Sherman, Sandra, *Imagining Poverty: Quantification and the Decline of Paternalism*
    (Columbus: Ohio State University Press, 2001)
Sherwood, Merika, 'Blacks in the Gordon Riots', *History Today*, 1 December
    1997, 24–8 (historytoday.com, 2 Jan. 2014)
Shoemaker, Robert, 'The London "mob" in the early eighteenth century',
    Journal of British Studies, 26:3 (1987), 273–304
    The London Mob: Violence and Disorder in Eighteenth-Century England (London:
    Hambledon and London, 2004)
    *Prosecution and Punishment : Petty Crime and the Law in London and Rural
    Middlesex, c. 1660–1725* (Cambridge: CUP, 1991)
    'Reforming the city: the reformation of manners campaign in London,
    1690–1738', in Lee Davison et al., eds., *Stilling the Grumbling Hive: The
    Response to Social and Economic Problems in England, 1689–1750* (Stroud:
    Alan Sutton, 1992)
    'Representing the adversary criminal trial: lawyers in the Old Bailey
    Proceedings, 1770–1800', in David Lemmings, ed., *Courtrooms and the
    Public Sphere in Britain, 1700–1850* (Farnham, Surrey: Ashgate, 2012)
    'The street robber and the gentleman highwayman: changing representations
    and perceptions of robbery in London, 1690–1800', *Cultural and Social
    History*, 3:4 (2006), 381–405
    'Streets of shame? The crowd and public punishments in London, 1700–1820',
    in Simon Devereaux and Paul Griffiths, eds., *Penal Practice and Culture,
    1500–1900: Punishing the English* (Basingstoke: Palgrave Macmillan, 2004)
Shore, Heather, *London's Criminal Underworlds, c. 1720 – c. 1930: A Cultural and
    Social History* (Basingstoke: Palgrave, 2015)
    '"The reckoning": disorderly women, informing constables and the
    Westminster justices, 1727–33', *Social History*, 34:4 (2009), 409–27
Siena, Kevin P., *Venereal Disease, Hospitals, and the Urban Poor: London's 'Foul
    Wards', 1600–1800* (Rochester, N.Y.: University of Rochester Press, 2004)
Slack, Paul, *The English Poor Law, 1531–1782* (Basingstoke: Macmillan, 1990)
    From Reformation to Improvement: Public Welfare in Early Modern England
    (Oxford: Clarendon Press, 1999)
    'Hospitals, workhouses and the relief of the poor in early-modern London', in
    Andrew Cunningham and Ole Peter Grell, eds., *Health Care and Poor Relief
    in Protestant Europe 1500–1700* (London: Routledge, 1997)
    Poverty and Policy in Tudor and Stuart England (London: Longman, 1988)
Smith, Bruce P., 'The presumption of guilt and the English law of theft,
    1750–1850', *Law and History Review*, 23:1 (2005), 133–71
Smith, Greg T., 'Civilised people don't want to see that kind of thing: the decline
    of public physical punishment in London, 1760–1840', in Carolyn Strange,
    ed., *Qualities of Mercy: Justice, Punishment and Discretion* (Vancouver: UBC
    Press, 1996)

'Violent crime and the public weal in England, 1700–1900', in R. McMahon, ed., *Crime, Law and Popular Culture in Europe 1500–1900* (Abingdon: Willan Publishing, 2008)

Snell, K. D. M., *Parish and Belonging: Community, Identity and Welfare in England and Wales, 1700–1950* (Cambridge University Press, 2006)

Sokoll, Thomas, ed., *Essex Pauper Letters, 1731–1837* (Oxford University Press, 2001)

Spence, Craig, *London in the 1690s: a Social Atlas* (London: Centre for Metropolitan History, 2000)

Spraggs, Gillian, *Outlaws and Highwaymen: The Cult of the Robber in England from the Middle Ages to the Nineteenth Century* (London: Pimlico, 2001)

Steedman, Carolyn, 'Lord Mansfield's women', *Past & Present*, 176 (2002), 105–43

Stern, Walter M., *The Porters of London* (London: Longman, 1960)

Stevenson, John, 'The London "Crimp" riots of 1794', *International Review of Social History*, 16:1 (1971), 40–58

Popular Disturbances in England: 1700–1832 (Harlow: Longman, 1992)

Straub, Kristina, 'The tortured apprentice: sexual monstrosity and the suffering of poor children in the Brownrigg murder case', in Laura J. Rosenthal and Mita Choudhury, eds., *Monstrous Dreams of Reason: Body, Self, and Other in the Enlightenment* (Lewisburg: Bucknell University Press, 2002)

Styles, John, 'Sir John Fielding and the problem of criminal investigation in eighteenth-century England', *Transactions of the Royal Historical Society*, 33 (1983), 127–49

Suarez, Michael F., 'Towards a bibliometric analysis of the surviving record, 1701–1800', in Michael F. Suarez and Michael L. Turner, eds., *The Cambridge History of the Book in Britain*, Vol. V: *1695–1830* (Cambridge University Press, 2009)

Survey of London, 47 vols. (London County Council, 1900-) (http://www.british-history.ac.uk/search/series/survey-london)

Taylor, James Stephen, 'The impact of pauper settlement, 1691–1834', *Past & Present*, 73 (1976), 42–74

Jonas Hanway, Founder of the Marine Society: Charity and Policy in Eighteenth-Century Britain (London: Scholar Press, 1985)

Poverty, Migration, and Settlement in the Industrial Revolution: Sojourners' Narratives (Palo Alto, Calif.: Society for the Promotion of Science and Scholarship, 1989)

Thomas, P. D. G., 'The St George's Fields "massacre" of 10 May 1768: an eye witness report', *London Journal*, 4:2 (1978), 221–6

Thompson, E. P., 'The crime of anonymity', in Douglas Hay *et al.*, eds., *Albion's Fatal Tree: Crime and Society in Eighteenth-Century England* (London: Allen Lane, 1975)

'Eighteenth-century English society: class struggle without class?', *Social History*, 3:2 (1978), 133–65

Whigs and Hunters: The Origin of the Black Act (London: Allen Lane, 1975)

Tomkins, Alannah, *The Experience of Urban Poverty, 1723–82: Parish, Charity and Credit* (Manchester University Press, 2006)

Turner, Janice, '"Ill-favoured sluts"? The disorderly women of Rosemary Lane and Rag Fair', *London Journal*, 38:2 (July, 2013), 95–109

Uglow, Jenny, *Hogarth: A Life and a World* (London: Faber and Faber, 1997)

Valenze, Deborah, *The Social Life of Money in the English Past* (Cambridge University Press, 2006)

Wales, Tim, 'Thief-takers and their clients in later Stuart London', in Paul
    Griffiths and Mark S. R. Jenner, eds., *Londinopolis: A Social and Cultural
    History of Early Modern London* (Manchester University Press, 2000)
Ward, Richard, *Print Culture, Crime and Justice in 18th-Century London* (London:
    Bloomsbury Academic, 2014)
    'Print culture, moral panic, and the administration of the law: The London
    crime wave of 1744', *Crime, History & Societies*, 16:1 (2012), 5–24
Ward, W. R., 'Power and piety: the origins of religious revival in the early
    eighteenth century', *Bulletin of the John Rylands Library of Manchester*, 63:1
    (1980), 231–52
    'The relation of enlightenment and religious revival in central Europe and in
    the English-speaking world' in Derek Baker, ed., *Reform and Reformation:
    England and the Continent c. 1500–1700* (Oxford: Blackwell, 1979)
Warner, Jessica, *Craze: Gin and Debauchery in an Age of Reason* (London: Profile,
    2003)
Warner, Jessica and Frank Ivis, '"Damn you, you informing bitch": *vox populi*
    and the unmaking of the Gin Act of 1736', *Journal of Social History*, 33:2
    (1999), 299–330
Warner, Jessica, Frank Ivis and Andreé Demers, 'A predatory social structure:
    informers in Westminster, 1737–41', *Journal of Interdisciplinary History*, 30:4
    (2000), 617–34
Webb, Sidney and Beatrice Webb, *English Local Government*, Vol. I: *The Parish
    and the County* (London: Frank Cass, 1906; repr. 1963)
    English Poor Law History, Part I: The Old Poor Law (London: Longmans, Green
    and Co., 1927; repr.1963)
    English Prisons under Local Government (London: Longmans, Green and Co.,
    1922; repr. 1963)
Weinreb, Ben *et al.*, *The London Encyclopedia* (1993; 3rd edn. London: Pan
    Macmillan, 2010)
Wheatley, Henry B., *London Past and Present*, 3 vols. (1891; repr. Cambridge
    University Press, 2011)
White, Jerry, *London in the Eighteenth Century: A Great and Monstrous Thing*
    (London: Bodley Head, 2012)
    'Pain and degradation in Georgian London: life in the Marshalsea prison',
    History Workshop Journal, 68 (2009), 69–98
White, Jonathan, 'The "slow but sure poyson": the representation of gin and its
    drinkers, 1736–1751', *Journal of British Studies*, 42:1 (2003), 35–64
White, Matthew, '"For the safety of the City": the geography and social politics of
    public execution – 1780 and the Gordon Rioters', in Ian Haywood and John
    Seed, eds., *The Gordon Riots: Politics, Culture and Insurrection in Late
    Eighteenth-Century Britain* (Cambridge University Press, 2012)
Whyman, Susan, *The Pen and the People: English Letter Writers, 1660–1800*
    (Oxford University Press, 2009)
Wilf, Steven, 'Imagining justice: aesthetics and public executions in late
    eighteenth-century England', *Yale Journal of Law & the Humanities*, 5
    (1993–4), 51–78 (digitalcommons.law.yale.edu/yjlh, 2 Jan. 2014)
Wilson, Adrian, 'Illegitimacy and its implications in mid-eighteenth-century
    London: the evidence of the Foundling Hospital', *Continuity and Change*, 4:1
    (1989), 103–64

The Making of Man-Midwifery: Childbirth in England, 1660–1770 (London: UCL Press, 1995)

Wrigley, E. A., *Poverty, Progress, and Population* (Cambridge University Press, 2004)

'A simple model of London's importance in changing English society and economy, 1650–1750', *Past & Present*, 37 (1967), 44–70

Wrigley, E. A. and R. S. Schofield, *The Population History of England, 1541–1871: A Reconstruction* (London: Edward Arnold, 1981)

INTERNET-ONLY SECONDARY SOURCES (LAST CONSULTED 14 JULY 2015)

Brown, Roly, 'Glimpses into the 19th century broadside ballad trade', number 20: 'Transports', *Musical Traditions*, 23 May 2006, n.p. (www.mustrad.org.uk/articles/bbals_01.htm)

Christopher, Emma, 'Steal a handkerchief, see the world: the trans-oceanic voyaging of Thomas Limpus', in Ann Curthoys and Marilyn Lake, eds., *Connected Worlds: History in Trans-National Perspective* (Canberra: ANU E Press, 2006) (http://press.anu.edu.au/titles/cw_citation/)

Convict Stockade: A Wiki for Australian Convict Researchers (www.historyaustralia.org.au/twconvic)

Fraas, Mitch, *The Records of the Asylum for Orphan Girls (Part II)*, 2 May 2012 (https://uniqueatpenn.wordpress.com//?s=Records+of+the+Asylum &search=Go)

Gregory, Mark, *Australian Folk Songs* (http;//folkstream.com/index.html)

'Historical weather events' (www.booty.org.uk/booty.weather/climate/wxevents.htm)

International Institute of Social History: 'Wheat and malt prices in Winchester, 1657–1817' (iisg.nl/hpw/data.php)

Joslin, Tim, '1740 and all that', 6 March 2010 (https://unchartedterritory.wordpress.com/2010/03/06/1740-and-all-that/)

London Lives. 1690–1800: Crime, Poverty and Social Policy in the Metropolis (http://www.londonlives.org/static/Lives.jsp):
   Clayton, Mary, 'Charlotte Walker, *c.* 1754–1806'
   Clayton, Mary, 'Edward Burnworth alias Frazier, d. 1726'
   Clayton, Mary, 'Quilt Arnold, 1687 – *c.*1726'
   Clayton, Mary, 'William Blewit, d. 1726'
   Duncan, Edward, 'Mary Nichols, alias Trolly Lolly, *c.* 1685–1715'
   Fisher, Molly, 'Roderick Awdry, *c.* 1698–1714'
   Gibbons, David, 'William Tidd, *c.* 1729–1750'
   Hitchcock, Tim, 'Paul Patrick Kearney, fl.1727–1771'
   Palk, Deirdre, 'Catherine Jones, *c.* 1757–1780'
   Palk, Deirdre, 'Charlotte Dionis, b. 1761'
   Palk, Deirdre, 'Timothy Dionis, 1704–1765'
   Payne, Diane, 'Daniel Vaughan, *c.* 1692–1716'
   Philpott, Victoria, 'Mary Knight, *c.* 1685–1716'
   Shore, Heather, 'Mary Harvey, fl. 1727–1733'
   Spencer, Emily, 'Nathaniel Hawes, *c.* 1701–1721'
   Wallace, Hannah, 'Elizabeth Yexley, d. 1769'

Oxford Dictionary of National Biography (2004) (www.oxforddnb.com):
Hanham, A. A., 'Bambridge, Thomas (d. 1741)'
Herrick, James A., 'Ilive, Jacob (bap. 1705, d. 1763)'
Innes, Joanna, 'Payne, William (1717/18–1782)'
McKenzie, Andrea, 'Wild, Jonathan (bap. 1683, d. 1725), thief-taker'
Rawlings, Philip, 'Dalton, James (bap. 1700?, d. 1730), street robber'
Rawlings, Philip, 'Fielding, Sir John (1721–1780)'
Sugden, Philip, 'Veil, Sir Thomas de (1684–1746)'
Wales, Tim, 'Rewse, Bodenham (d. 1725), thief-taker and prison warden'
Pauper Lives in Georgian London and Manchester (research.ncl.ac.uk/pauperlives/)
Pauper Lives in Georgian London and Manchester (research.ncl.ac.uk/pauperlives/)
'Purchasing power of British pounds from 1245 to present' (www.Present'
    measuringworth.com/ppoweruk)
The Workhouse: The Story of an Institution (www.workhouses.org.uk)

DISSERTATIONS AND UNPUBLISHED MANUSCRIPTS

Craig, A. G. 'The movement for the reformation of manners, 1688–1715'
    (PhD dissertation, Edinburgh University, 1980)
Cross, Pam, 'The operation of the workhouse in the parish of St Botolph Aldgate,
    c. 1734–1834' (BA dissertation, Fitzwilliam College, Cambridge, 1990)
Dabhoiwala, Faramerz, 'Prostitution and police in London, c. 1660–1760'
    (D.Phil., Oxford University, 1995)
Devereaux, Simon, 'Convicts and the state: the administration of criminal justice
    in Great Britain during the reign of George III' (PhD dissertation, University
    of Toronto, 1997)
Hitchcock, Timothy V., 'The English workhouse: a study of institutional poor relief
    in selected counties, 1696–1750' (D.Phil. thesis, Oxford University, 1985)
Innes, Joanna, 'Statute law and summary justice in early modern England'
    (unpublished paper, May 1986)
Isaacs, Tina Beth, 'Moral crime, moral reform, and the state in early eighteenth-
    century England: a study of piety and politics' (PhD dissertation, University
    of Rochester, 1979)
Paley, Ruth, 'The Middlesex Justices Act of 1792: Its origins and effects'
    (University of Reading, Ph.D., 1983)
Swindlehurst, Catherine, 'Trade expansion, social conflict and popular politics in
    the Spitalfields silkweaving community, c. 1670–1770' (University of
    Cambridge, Ph.D., 1999)
Tosney, Nicholas, 'Gaming in England, c. 1540–1760' (University of York,
    Ph.D., 2008)
Ward, Richard, 'Print culture and responses to crime in mid-eighteenth-century
    London' (University of Sheffield, Ph.D., 2010)
Williamson, Gillian, 'The nature of mid-eighteenth-century popular politics in
    the City of Westminster: the select vestry committee of 1742 and the parish
    of St George Hanover Square' (MA dissertation, Birkbeck College, London,
    2008)

Index

Named individuals with the following roles have been identified as: Bow Street Runners, constables, criminals (anyone accused of a crime), informers, justices of the peace ('JP'), lawyers, paupers (anyone in receipt of relief), prison keepers, prostitutes, thief-takers, vagrants.